MOON

CALIFORNIA

Road Trip

STUART THORNTON

Lake Tahoe
Carson City
SACRAMENTO
Walker Lake
Bodie State Historic Park
Mono Lake
San Francisco
Stockton
Yosemite
Yosemite National Park
Oakland
Manteca
Chinese Camp
Groveland
Tracy
Oakdale
Half Moon Bay
Modesto
Incline
Benton
Coaldale
San Jose
Turlock
Sugar Pine
NEVADA
CALIFORNIA
Mariposa
Gilroy
Merced
Bishop
Santa Cruz
Oakhurst
Salinas
MONTEREY
Carmel
Death Valley
Sequoia/ Kings Canyon National Park
Fresno
Lone Pine
BIG SUR
Pacific Coast Highway
Paso Robles
San Simeon
Cambria
Morro Bay
SAN LUIS OBISPO
Bakersfield
Arroyo Grande
PACIFIC OCEAN
Santa Maria
Mojave
SANTA BARBARA
Ventura
Channel Islands National Park
Los Angeles
Santa Catalina Island
0
50 mi
0
50 km
© MOON.COM

CALIFORNIA ROAD TRIP

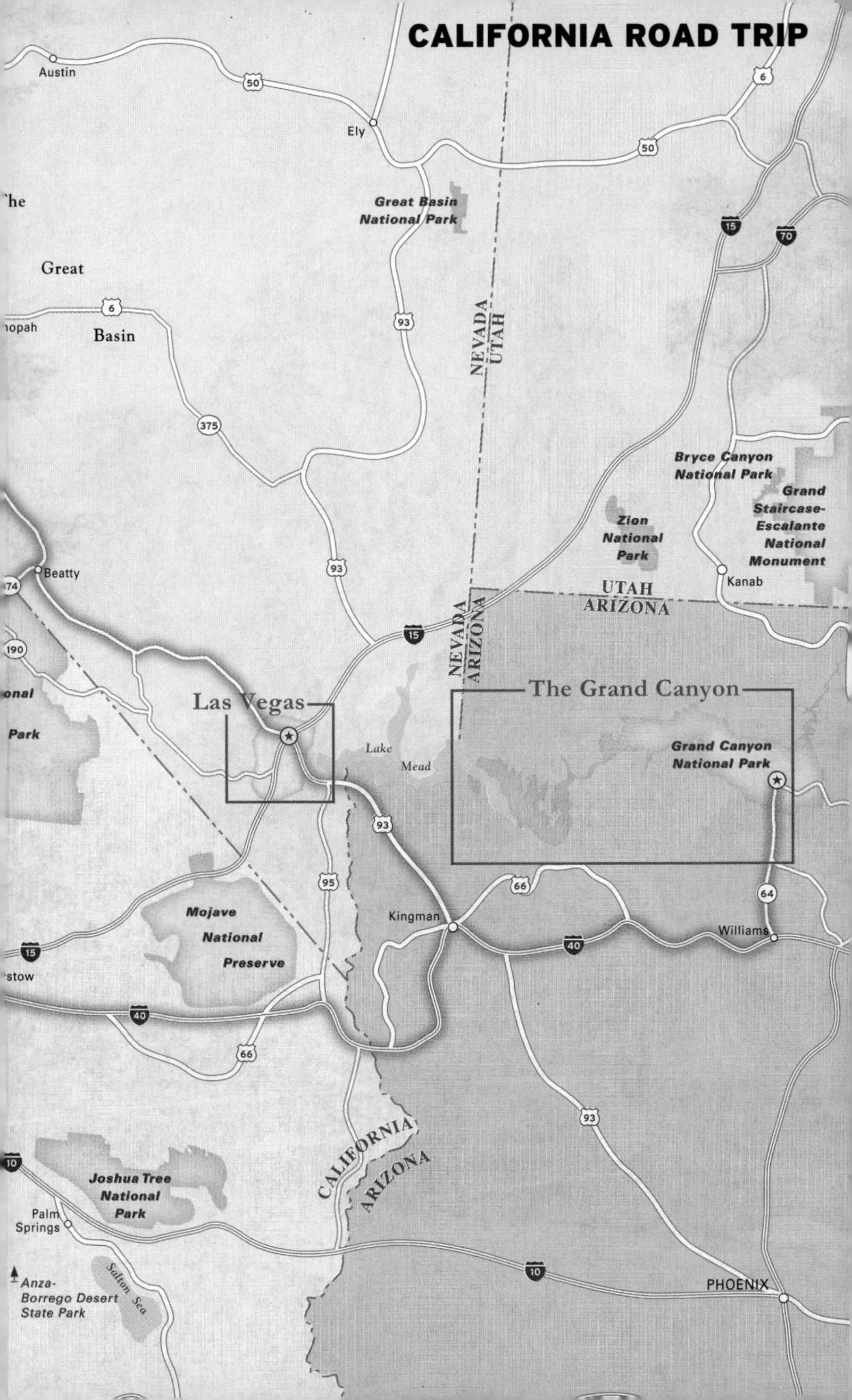

CONTENTS

Although every effort was made to make sure the information in this book was accurate when going to press, research was impacted by the COVID-19 pandemic and things may have changed since the time of writing. Be sure to confirm specific details, like opening hours, closures, and travel guidelines and restrictions, when making your travel plans. For more detailed information, *see p. 452.*

DISCOVER
the California Road Trip

San Francisco, Yosemite, Los Angeles, Las Vegas, and the Grand Canyon. Each is like no other place on earth. You can experience all of them in a 14-day road trip, with each stop roughly a day's drive from the next. You'll drive through a landscape that encompasses the best of the American West: modern skyscrapers and sandy beaches, granite peaks and towering trees, flat deserts and steep-sided canyons.

It's a landscape filled with overwhelming natural beauty and wide-open space. In Yosemite, waterfalls feather down faces of granite. At the Grand Canyon, layers of colorful geologic history travel back in time millions of years. Along the Pacific Coast, cliff sides tumble dramatically into the ocean.

This is nature at its most primal, but it's just a few hours away from the cosmopolitan pleasures of America's most distinctive cities. Whether it's the sunlight shimmering on the Golden Gate Bridge or the stripes of the rainbow flag, San Francisco is as proud of its colorful character as it is of its reputation as a culinary capital. Sprawling Los Angeles is a source of both world-class culture and amusement park fun. Las Vegas feels more like a mirage than a city, with its neon flashing against the otherwise dark desert sky.

Choose your own pace. Let your interests determine your routes and itineraries. Ride a cable car or hike to Half Dome. Stroll the Hollywood Walk of Fame or explore the Magic Kingdom. Descend deep into the Grand Canyon or dance until dawn in Sin City. Or just lie on the beach and soak up the sun. No matter who you are or what you're into, this road trip is for you.

10 TOP EXPERIENCES

1 **Wander and Wonder at San Francisco:** Experience this unique city by exploring its hilly streets, world-class museums, and iconic sights (page 38).

2 **Spend Time in the Surf and Sand:** No California road trip would be complete without a classic beach experience. You'll find some of the best stretches of sand in **Los Angeles** (page 319) and **Santa Barbara** (page 373).

3 **Hike in Yosemite National Park:** Follow trails to epic views of granite rock formations and waterfalls in **Yosemite Valley** (page 110) or wander amid alpine meadows and lakes in **Tuolumne Meadows** (page 134).

4 **Feast on California Cuisine:** With a range of flavors as varied as its landscape, the state abounds in culinary delights, especially in the cities of **San Francisco** (page 72) and **Los Angeles** (page 322).

5 Visit Larger-Than-Life Los Angeles: The biggest city on the West Coast is a world-class destination known for its Hollywood glamour, coastal enclaves, and hip downtown (page 294).

6 See the Grand Canyon from Above and Below: Views from the **Rim Trail** are stunning, while a hike down into the canyon on the **Bright Angel Trail** provides a deeper understanding of this natural wonder (page 244).

7 **Enjoy the High Life in Las Vegas:** Stroll the Strip and explore the city's **casinos** (page 156). Then take in views of the neon skyline from the top of the **High Roller** (page 174), the world's tallest observation wheel.

8 **Slow Down Along the Central Coast:** Relax in **Big Sur** (page 399), explore **Monterey** (page 419) and its famous aquarium, and stop in the hip surf town of **Santa Cruz** (page 428).

9 **Taste World-Class Wines:** California is known for its fine wines, so treat yourself to some samplings in **Napa** (page 59), **Santa Barbara** (page 370), and **Carmel** (page 415).

10 **Drive the Pacific Coast Highway:** The stretch of CA-1 between San Francisco and Los Angeles showcases some of the state's best scenery, including redwoods and vast ocean views, along with small towns and big attractions (page 360).

PLANNING YOUR TRIP

Where to Go

San Francisco

Located on a hilly peninsula between San Francisco Bay and the Pacific Ocean, San Francisco is one of the most beautiful cities in the world. Add in a renowned **food scene, world-class museums,** a healthy **arts culture,** and iconic attractions like the **Golden Gate Bridge** and **Alcatraz** for a mandatory stop on any serious road trip.

Yosemite

Wander amid **sequoia groves, granite peaks,** and **mountain lakes.** See national treasures like **Half Dome** and **El Capitan.** Yosemite National Park showcases the stunning Sierra Nevada at its rugged best.

Las Vegas

Rising out of the desert like a high-tech oasis, Las Vegas is an adult playground of **casinos, bars, over-the-top shows,** and **plush hotels.** Dig a little deeper to find fine food, a flourishing arts scene, and local hangouts in the shadows of **the Strip.**

The Grand Canyon

A mile-deep slice into the **Kaibab Plateau,** the Grand Canyon defies easy description. Stare in awe at the colorful layers from the canyon's edge—or descend deep into the canyon to meet its creator: the mighty **Colorado River.**

Los Angeles

Los Angeles is a massive mix of Southern California beach town, Hollywood dream factory, and 21st-century metropolis. Unmissable attractions include **world-class art,** a beach scene that begs for some time in the **sand and surf,** and an **amusement park** devoted to a cartoon mouse.

Pacific Coast Highway

Stunning coastal views will fill your windshield as you drive along the stretch of the **Pacific Coast Highway** that connects Los Angeles and San Francisco. The winding roadway hits its peak passing through the mountains of **Big Sur,** dramatically perched above the ocean. Seaside sights include **Hearst Castle,** the **Monterey Bay Aquarium,** and the **Santa Cruz Beach Boardwalk.**

Know Before You Go

High Season

The West's best feature is its all-season appeal. That said, this trip is best in the **summer** and **early fall,** when CA-120 through Yosemite will most likely be open, although Las Vegas and the Grand Canyon will be quite warm. It's possible to bypass CA-120 in the **winter** and **spring** by taking a different route, but it will add hours and miles to the trip. Be aware that summer brings the most visitors, which will not only add to the crowds at attractions along the way, but also add to the traffic on the highways. Plan a little extra time to get from place to place. Note that late summer-early fall is also **wildfire season,** during which access to affected areas can be impeded and air quality impacted.

The easiest places to **fly** into are **San Francisco, Los Angeles,** and **Las Vegas.** If you're flying into San Francisco, you can avoid some of the hassle of San Francisco International Airport (SFO) by flying into nearby **Oakland** or **San Jose.** Similarly, Los Angeles offers several suburban airports, including **Burbank, Long Beach,** and **Ontario,** which are typically less congested than Los Angeles International Airport (LAX). For more details, see page 442.

Advance Reservations

Book **hotels** and **rental cars** in advance for the best rates and availability, especially in the summer, which is high season for travel. If you plan to rent a car in one city and return it in another (for example, rent the car in San Francisco and return it in Los Angeles), you should expect to pay an additional fee, which can be quite high.

High-season travelers should also plan ahead for the **big-name attractions.** If you have your heart set on visiting **Alcatraz** in San Francisco or the **Hearst Castle** in San Simeon, purchase tickets at least two weeks in advance. You'll save money buying advance tickets for **Disneyland** online as well. Reservations are essential at **campgrounds** in Yosemite, the Grand Canyon, and along Big Sur. If you plan to stay at **The Ahwahnee** hotel in Yosemite or dine in its restaurant, make reservations as far in advance as possible.

What to Pack

Bring **layered clothing.** Expect desert heat in Las Vegas and the Grand Canyon in the summer, but also be prepared for cooler temperatures. Summer fog is likely along the California coast, and is pretty much guaranteed in San Francisco, making the air damp and chilly. No matter

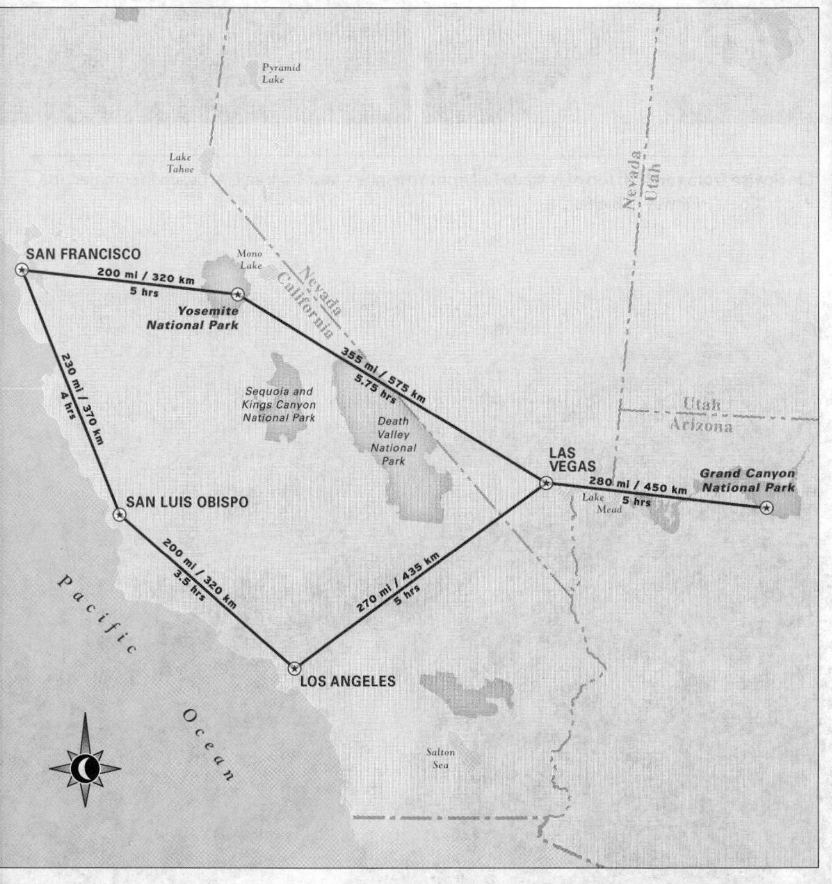

Clockwise from top left: top of Nevada Fall from Yosemite's Mist Trail; an L.A. beach in summer; the Pacific Coast Highway in Big Sur.

what, use **sunscreen;** that cold fog doesn't stop the rays from burning unwary beachcombers.

Coming to the United States from abroad? You'll need your **passport** and possibly a **visa.**

Driving Tips

Both **San Francisco** and especially **Los Angeles** suffer from serious **traffic congestion.** Avoid driving in or through San Francisco during rush hour traffic, typically weekdays 7am-9am and 4pm-6pm, though serious congestion can occur at other times. In Los Angeles, rush hour can stretch all the way from 5am-10am and 3pm-7pm. Of course, special events can create traffic jams in both cities on weekends. To view current traffic conditions in the San Francisco Bay Area, visit www.511.org. For Los Angeles, go to www.sigalert.com for a city map showing current traffic information. Though not as notorious as San Francisco or Los Angeles, **Las Vegas** has its own traffic problems, especially on Thursday and Friday evenings. The **Nevada Department of Transportation** (http://nvroads.com) has information on current road conditions.

Because it's located in the high-altitude Sierra Nevada, **access to Yosemite** is dependent on the weather and the seasons. Two of the most traveled roads in the park, **Tioga Road** and **Glacier Point Road,** are typically **closed November-early June.** In recent years, **forest fires** have occurred in the park and surrounding areas, limiting access in the summer and fall as well. Check for road conditions and closures online at www.nps.gov/yose.

Wildfires and landslides can also impede a drive along the **Pacific Coast Highway,** especially through **Big Sur.** Visit the **Caltrans website** (www.dot.ca.gov) for highway conditions throughout California.

Expect **high summer temperatures** on the drive between Yosemite and Las Vegas, especially if you take the route through Death Valley, where blazing hot temperatures of 120°F (49°C) or more can occur. Heat can also be a problem on the routes to and from the Grand Canyon. Make sure your car has sufficient **engine coolant** and working **air-conditioning,** and take along plenty of **drinking water.** You may also encounter **thunderstorms** in this area July-mid-September, which can lead to road flooding. Contact the **Nevada Department of Transportation** (http://nvroads.com) and **Arizona Department of Transportation** (www.az511.gov) for each state's road conditions.

Cell phone reception is limited or nonexistent in large sections of Yosemite, along the desert route to and from Las Vegas, and along the Pacific Coast Highway through Big Sur.

HIT THE ROAD

The 14-Day Best of the West

You can hit the top destinations in 14 days by driving in a rough loop. The day-by-day route below begins in San Francisco, but you can just as easily start in Los Angeles or Las Vegas if that works better for you. For detailed driving directions for each leg of this road trip, see ***Getting There*** at the beginning of each chapter. All mileage and driving times are approximate.

Days 1-2

SAN FRANCISCO

It's easy to fill two days with fun in San Francisco. On the first day, visit the foodie-friendly **Ferry Building,** then walk 1.5 miles (2.4 km) down the **Embarcadero** to the ferry that will take you out to **Alcatraz.** For dinner, indulge in Vietnamese fare at **The Slanted Door** or find old-school elegance at the **Tadich Grill.**

On your second day, head west to **Golden Gate Park,** where you can explore the art of the **de Young Museum** or the animals at the **California Academy of Sciences.** Visit the **Japanese Tea Garden** for tea and a snack before leaving the park. Spend the afternoon at the **San Francisco Museum of Modern Art** before dining at its touted on-site restaurant **In Situ.**

Rest your head at the tech-savvy **Hotel Zetta,** homey **Golden Gate Hotel,** or **Hotel G** with its three dining and drinking establishments. For more suggestions on how to spend your time in San Francisco, see page 38.

Day 3

DRIVING FROM SAN FRANCISCO TO YOSEMITE

200 mi / 320 km / 5 hrs

Grab a coffee from **Blue Bottle Café** to wake up for the drive to Yosemite. Leave San Francisco at 8am to reach Yosemite by noon. The drive to the **Big Oak Flat entrance** takes at least four hours; however, traffic, especially in summer and on weekends, can make it much longer.

Days 4-5

YOSEMITE

Explore **Yosemite Valley** and gawk at iconic attractions like **Half Dome** and **El Capitan.** Hit the **Mist Trail,** the park's most popular day hike. Make reservations ahead of time to spend the night in the comfort of **The Ahwahnee** hotel or in the mountain air at the park's **Tuolumne Meadows Campground,** which is only open in the summer. On the second day, plan a hike to **Tuolumne Meadows** or head to the more remote, less-visited **Hetch Hetchy** region, where worthwhile hikes include the **Wapama Falls Trail.**

Day 6

DRIVING FROM YOSEMITE TO LAS VEGAS

355 mi / 575 km / 5.75 hrs

You have a long drive ahead of you, so fuel up with a stop at the **Whoa Nellie Deli** just east of the park's Tioga Pass entrance or at the **Silver Lake Resort Café** on the June Lake Loop.

For most of the year, the best route is via **Tioga Pass** (if you're traveling in winter or spring, check to make sure that it's open before heading out). It's most direct to drive through **Nevada.** Follow **CA-120 East** to US-6 in Benton. Take **US-6 East** to Coaldale, where it shares the road with **US-95 South** to **Tonopah,** which makes a good stopover. It's then a 210-mile (340-km) straight shot on US-95 South to Vegas. In total, the 355-mile (575-km) drive to Las Vegas takes 5.75 hours.

Best Views

San Francisco

- **El Techo de Lolinda:** Located just above bustling Mission Street, this rooftop bar offers skyline views along with delicious cocktails and food (page 60).
- **Twin Peaks:** San Francisco's second-highest point offers fine views of the city's rows of residences, skyscrapers, and surrounding bay (page 70).

Yosemite

- **Glacier Point:** At 7,214 feet (2,199 m) high, Glacier Point has one of the best overall views of Yosemite Valley, including Half Dome and Yosemite Falls (page 119).
- **Olmsted Point:** Off Tioga Road, this easy-to-access viewpoint showcases lesser-known features in the park, including Tenaya Canyon and Clouds Rest (page 130).

Las Vegas

- **High Roller:** The world's highest observation wheel allows riders to see the candy-colored lights of the Strip from above (page 174).
- **The Strat SkyPod:** The **thrill rides** on the observation deck are hair-raising (page 190), and the **Top of the World restaurant** on the 106th floor gives revolving 360-degree views (page 199).

Grand Canyon

- **Mather Point:** Near the park entrance, the most-visited viewpoint in the Grand Canyon offers a classic panorama (page 239).
- **Yavapai Geology Museum and Observation Station:** Hanging off the South Rim, the station offers views and geological exhibits that put the canyon into context (page 239).

Los Angeles

- **The Getty Center:** On a clear day, the views from this state-of-the-art museum take in the entire Los Angeles skyline sprawling west to the Pacific (page 310).
- **Upstairs:** Feel like a star at this rooftop bar and deck located atop the hip downtown Ace Hotel (page 313).

Pacific Coast Highway

- **McWay Falls:** You can't get to the cove where this waterfall crashes into the sea, but you can catch views from Julia Pfeiffer Burns State Park or a nearby highway pullout (page 401).
- **Nepenthe:** Catch the sunset show over Big Sur's coastline on this bar-restaurant's expansive deck (page 407).

Clockwise from top left: the Grand Canyon from the South Rim; Yosemite National Park; San Francisco's Ghirardelli Square.

The **California route** is more scenic and only about 10 miles (16.1 km) longer, traversing Mammoth Lakes and Bishop. Take **CA-120 East** to **US-395 South.** East of Lone Pine, follow **CA-136,** which becomes **CA-190** and winds through Death Valley. A left turn onto Scotty's Castle Road and soon after a right onto Daylight Pass Road leads to the Nevada border and **NV-374** just before **Beatty,** which makes a good place to stop. From Beatty, **US-95** leads southeast to Las Vegas.

Day 7

LAS VEGAS

The glitz of the **Las Vegas Strip** makes it a surreal stopover between the natural wonders of Yosemite and the Grand Canyon. Stroll the Strip and explore the whole worlds inside casinos like **Caesars Palace** and the **Bellagio.** Watch the sun set from the 550-foot-tall (168-m) **High Roller** observation wheel and then get an upscale fried chicken dinner at **Yardbird** at **The Venetian.** Pick a hotel based on your taste and budget; **The Linq** and **Aria** are good bets. For more suggestions on how to spend your time in Las Vegas, see page 155.

Day 8

DRIVING FROM LAS VEGAS TO THE GRAND CANYON

280 mi / 450 km / 5 hrs

The 280-mile (450-km) drive to the Grand Canyon takes about five hours. Head south on **I-11** to **US-93,** then stop over in **Kingman, Arizona.** Then take **I-40 East** to **Williams** (115 mi/185 km) and overnight at the **Grand Canyon Railway Hotel.**

Day 9

THE GRAND CANYON

Enjoy a break from your car by taking the **Grand Canyon Railway** from **Williams** to **Grand Canyon National Park.** Enjoy the views from the **Rim Trail** or descend into the canyon on the **Bright Angel Trail.** Get an appetizer or a drink at the historic **El Tovar** hotel before taking the train back to **Williams.** For dinner, indulge in a prime cut of meat from **Rod's Steak House.**

Day 10

DRIVING FROM THE GRAND CANYON TO LOS ANGELES

500 mi / 805 km / 8 hrs

After a good night's sleep, head out for Los Angeles. The roughly 500-mile (805-km) drive to Los Angeles takes 7-8 hours. Take **I-40 West** to Barstow. From Barstow, take **I-15 South,** then take **I-10 West** into the heart of L.A. Be prepared to slow down when you hit the L.A. traffic, which may extend your driving time exponentially.

Days 11-12

LOS ANGELES

After appreciating the natural wonder of the Grand Canyon, it's time to appreciate the achievements of civilization in Los Angeles. On your first day, see the **Space Shuttle *Endeavour*** at the **California Science Center** or view the artistic masterpieces at **The Getty Center.** For a night in the heart of downtown, stay at the **Ace Hotel** and enjoy dinner at its downstairs restaurant, **Best Girl,** or head to nearby Koreatown and get some table-grilled Korean barbecue at **Quarters.**

On your second day, give your mind a rest and hit the beach. Choose the **Santa Monica Pier** for its beachside amusement park, **Venice Beach** for its lively boardwalk, or **Malibu** for its famous surf. For dinner, plan on fresh seafood at **Neptune's Net,** then sleep by the sea at the **Hotel Erwin** in Venice Beach. Kids (and kids at heart) might prefer a full day and night at the **Disneyland Resort.** For more suggestions on how to spend your time in Los Angeles, see page 294.

Days 13-14

DRIVING FROM LOS ANGELES TO SAN FRANCISCO

500 mi / 805 km / 8 hrs

This scenic route runs almost 500 miles (805 km) and can easily take 8 hours to

Clockwise from top left: view of the Colorado River; wild calla lilies in Big Sur; Monterey Bay Aquarium.

drive. While it's possible to make the drive in one long day, this is one stretch that you won't want to rush. Planning on two days allows you to take in some of the many fine attractions along the way. Alternate between **US-101 North** and **CA-1** (which are sometimes the same road) depending upon where you want to stop and linger. For a quicker drive, take the inland route **I-5,** which is just around 380 miles (610 km) and takes about six hours—but you'll miss the most scenic sections of the California coast.

PACIFIC COAST HIGHWAY

The most difficult part of this journey along PCH is deciding which of its many fine attractions deserve a stop. On the first day, soak up surf culture in **Ventura** or experience fine living in **Santa Barbara,** known for its beaches—it's been dubbed the American Riviera—and Spanish colonial revival architecture. **San Luis Obispo** is around the midway point and makes a good place to spend the night. On the second day, choose between **Hearst Castle** in San Simeon, the scenic coastal drive through **Big Sur, Monterey**—with its world-class **aquarium**—or bohemian surf town **Santa Cruz** on your way back to San Francisco. If you allow 3-4 days for this drive, you can see them all. Stay longer depending on where your interests lie. For specific suggestions on where to stop along the coast, see page 360.

San Francisco, Yosemite, and Los Angeles

In just **six days,** you can experience California's most famous cities and its biggest natural attraction. But you'll be doing a lot of driving. Make it a full **seven days** and you have enough time for the state's best coastal drive along Big Sur. If you have more time than that, it's well worth adding another day to each of the main stops. Mileage and driving times are approximate.

Day 1

SAN FRANCISCO

Spend your San Francisco day in **Golden Gate Park.** Indulge your artistic side at the **de Young Museum** or learn more about our world at the nearby **California Academy of Sciences.** Unwind with a walk through the park's **Japanese Tea Garden.** Then make your way to the **Golden Gate Bridge,** one of the world's most famous photo-ops. End your day with a meal at one of the city's culinary stars—or grab a **Mission burrito** at a local taqueria, which may be just as tasty. You won't have as many dining options once you make it to Yosemite. For more suggestions on how to spend your time in San Francisco, see page 38.

Day 2

DRIVING FROM SAN FRANCISCO TO YOSEMITE

200 mi / 320 km / 5 hrs

With a head full of art and science and a belly full of gourmet food, head to Yosemite. Leave San Francisco at 8am to reach Yosemite by noon. The drive to the **Big Oak Flat entrance** takes at least four hours; however, traffic, especially in summer and on weekends, can make it much longer.

Day 3

YOSEMITE

Spend a day touring around **Yosemite Valley,** seeing **Half Dome, El Capitan,** and **Yosemite Falls.** If you want to break a sweat, hike the **Mist Trail.** Spend a night under the stars at one of the park's campgrounds or enjoy a night indoors at **The Ahwahnee** (just be sure to make reservations well in advance), or head out of the park to splurge at the **Rush Creek Lodge,** located 1.5 miles (2.4 km) from Yosemite's Big Oak Flat entrance.

Best Hikes

San Francisco

- **Lands End Trail:** This trail in the Golden Gate National Recreation Area is rife with coastal views (page 69).
- **Twin Peaks:** The reward exceeds the work on this short hike up to the city's second-highest point, with its 360-degree views (page 70).

Yosemite

- **Columbia Rock Trail:** This 2-mile (3.2-km) round-trip trail out of Yosemite Valley gets you to a precariously perched rock that takes in the park's finest features (page 112).
- **Mist Trail:** This classic hike passes through refreshing waterfall spray from Vernal and Nevada Falls (page 112).

Nevada Fall in Yosemite

- **Wapama Falls Trail:** Explore the isolated grandeur of Yosemite's Hetch Hetchy region on this 5-mile (8-km) round-trip hike (page 123).

Grand Canyon

- **Rim Trail:** An easy all-day trail showcases the grandeur of the Grand Canyon's South Rim (page 244).
- **Bright Angel Trail:** Experience one of the country's finest adventures on this trail that descends into the immensity of the Grand Canyon (page 244).

Los Angeles

- **Hollyridge Trail:** This strenuous hike within Griffith Park leads to a unique view of the city from behind one of its best-known landmarks: the Hollywood sign (page 302).

Pacific Coast Highway

- **Bishop Peak:** This 4-mile (6.4-km) round-trip hike on 1,546-foot (471-m) volcanic Bishop Peak offers superb views of the Pacific Coast far below (page 383).
- **Ridge Trail and Panorama Trail Loop:** Big Sur's finest coastal trail is an 8-mile (12.9-km) loop that takes in bluffs, ridges, and a secluded beach (page 405).

Day 4

DRIVING FROM YOSEMITE TO LOS ANGELES

300 mi / 480 km / 6 hrs

Exit the park via its southern entrance and go south on **CA-41.** The majority of the trip will be spent on **CA-99 South** before using **I-5 South, CA-170 South,** and **US-101 South** as you get closer to the city.

Day 5

LOS ANGELES

You've been to the mountains; now it's time for the beach! Experience the best of Southern California beach culture at the chaotic but entertaining **Venice Boardwalk** or the **Santa Monica Pier.** If time allows, head inland a few miles to stroll the **Hollywood Walk of Fame** and snap a pic at **TCL Chinese Theatre.** Of course, some people would give all of that up for a day at **Disneyland** (you know who you are). For more suggestions on how to spend your time in Los Angeles, see page 294.

Days 6-7

DRIVING FROM LOS ANGELES TO SAN FRANCISCO

500 mi / 805 km / 8 hrs

You can make this drive in one long day if you make only a few stops (such as getting lunch midway in San Luis Obispo), but it's better to break it up over two days and enjoy the coast. On the first day, stop in **Santa Barbara** for lunch at one of the great restaurants off **State Street.** Continue on to **San Luis Obispo** to spend the night.

On the second day, plan on stopping for a tour of **Hearst Castle,** then driving up PCH through **Big Sur** on the way back to San Francisco. (If you really need to get from Los Angeles to San Francisco in one day, it's quicker to take **I-5,** which takes around six hours.)

Los Angeles, Las Vegas, and the Grand Canyon

In just **four days,** you can experience two major U.S. cities and the West's most famous natural attraction. But you'll be doing a lot of driving. With a full **seven days,** you can add a day to each place to experience them more fully.

Day 1

LOS ANGELES

If you have just one day in **Los Angeles,** don't try to do it all; you'll end up spending most of your time on the freeway. Instead, focus in on the part of town that interests you the most. Movie fanatics should go to **Hollywood** to wander the **Walk of Fame.** Outdoors lovers should target one of the beach towns (**Malibu, Santa Monica,** or **Venice Beach**) to enjoy the sun and sand. Families will most likely want to head to the house of the mouse (better known as **Disneyland**). For more suggestions on how to spend your time in Los Angeles, see page 294.

Day 2

DRIVING FROM LOS ANGELES TO LAS VEGAS

270 mi / 435 km / 5 hrs

Take **I-10 East** out of Los Angeles, and then use **I-15 North** for the majority of your drive.

LAS VEGAS

You've only got one night in **Las Vegas,** so spoil yourself. Stroll the Strip, popping into casinos like the **Cosmopolitan, Bellagio,** and **Caesars Palace** for food, drinks, a show, gambling—or all of the above. End your night with the **High Roller,** with its glittering views of the Strip. For more suggestions on how to spend your time in Las Vegas, see page 155.

Clockwise from top left: Universal Studios Hollywood; the Conservatory of Flowers in San Francisco's Golden Gate Park; on the Las Vegas Strip.

Stretch Your Legs

Quick roadside pullovers recharge your batteries and fight road weariness. The California Road Trip loop is flush with worthwhile roadside attractions, from stunning waterfalls to an alien-themed convenience store.

San Francisco to Yosemite

The **Knights Ferry Covered Bridge** (page 100) is the longest covered bridge west of the Mississippi.

Yosemite to Las Vegas

Ever wonder what it would be like to live upside down? Satisfy your curiosity at the **Upside-Down House** (page 153). Let your conspiracy theories run wild at the **Area 51 Alien Travel Center** (page 153). **Last Stop Arizona** (page 153) also celebrates life on other planets.

Los Angeles to Grand Canyon

Let the Los Angeles freeways thin out while spending an hour at the quirky **Watts Towers** (page 300). Arizona's **Historic Route 66 Museum** (page 219) tells the story of the celebrated roadway.

Grand Canyon to Los Angeles

You're not hallucinating: The giant golf ball teed up in the desert is called the **Golf Ball House,** and it's home to an alien-themed museum (page 291).

Los Angeles to San Francisco

The kitschy **Madonna Inn** (page 381) is the mother ship of roadside motels, while the appeal of **McWay Falls** (page 401), plunging 80 feet (24.4 m) down into the Pacific, is more sublime.

Day 3

DRIVING FROM LAS VEGAS TO THE GRAND CANYON

280 mi / 450 km / 5 hrs

This desert drive follows **I-11** to **US-93 South** and then **I-40 East** to the Arizona town of **Williams.** From there, take **AZ-64 North** to the **South Rim** of the **Grand Canyon.**

THE GRAND CANYON

Walk along the park's **Rim Trail** for outstanding, accessible views of the canyon. In **Grand Canyon Village,** stop into the **Hopi House** to see Native American art and the **Lookout Studio,** where you can use telescopes set up on the outdoor terrace to get better views of canyon features. Dip into the canyon on the **Bright Angel Trail.** Get a meal and spend the night at the **El Tovar** hotel, the national park's most elegant lodging option.

Day 4

DRIVING FROM THE GRAND CANYON TO LOS ANGELES

500 mi / 805 km / 8 hrs

The eight-hour trek from the Grand Canyon to Los Angeles is a grueling desert drive. Take **I-40 West** to Barstow. From Barstow, take **I-15 South,** then take **I-10 West** into the heart of L.A. Be prepared to slow down when you hit the L.A. traffic.

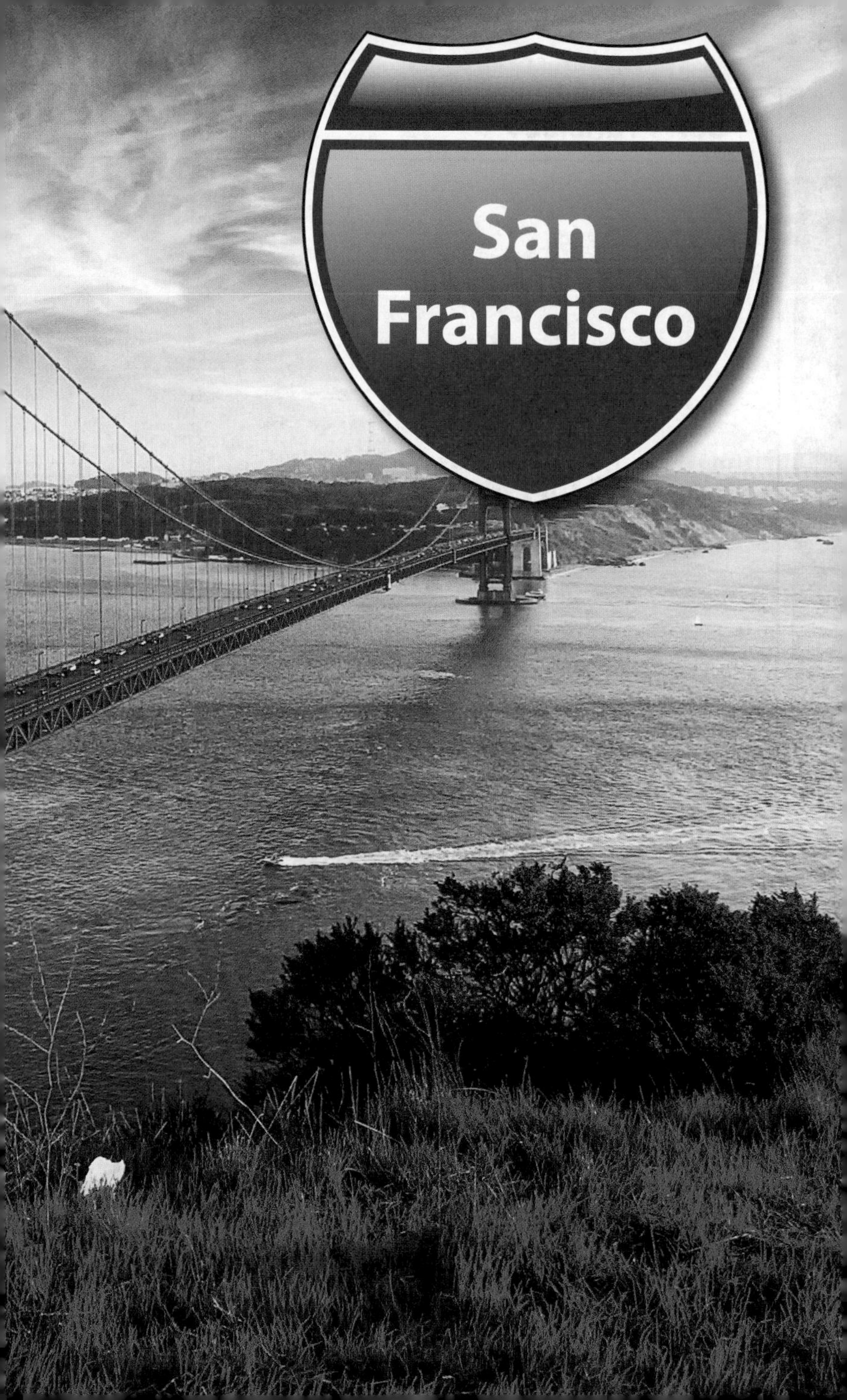
San Francisco

San Francisco

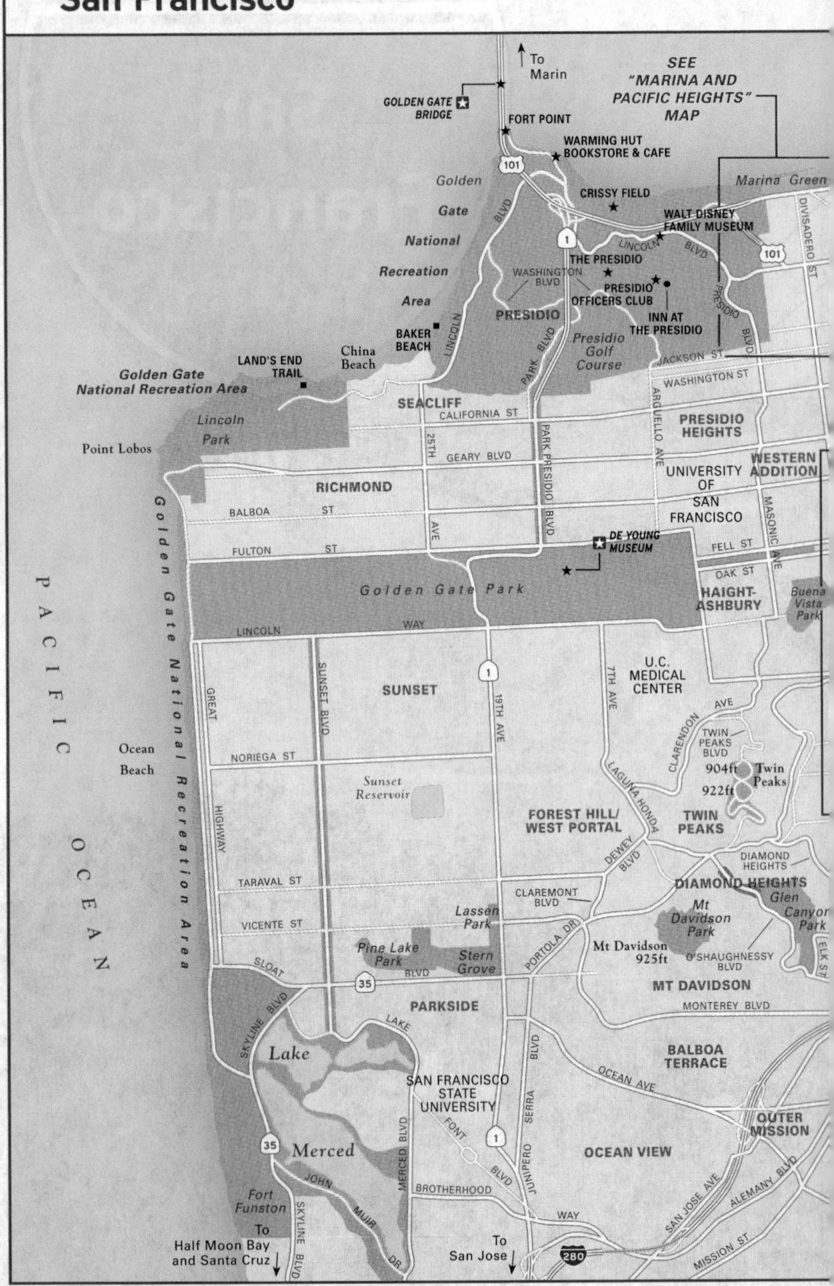

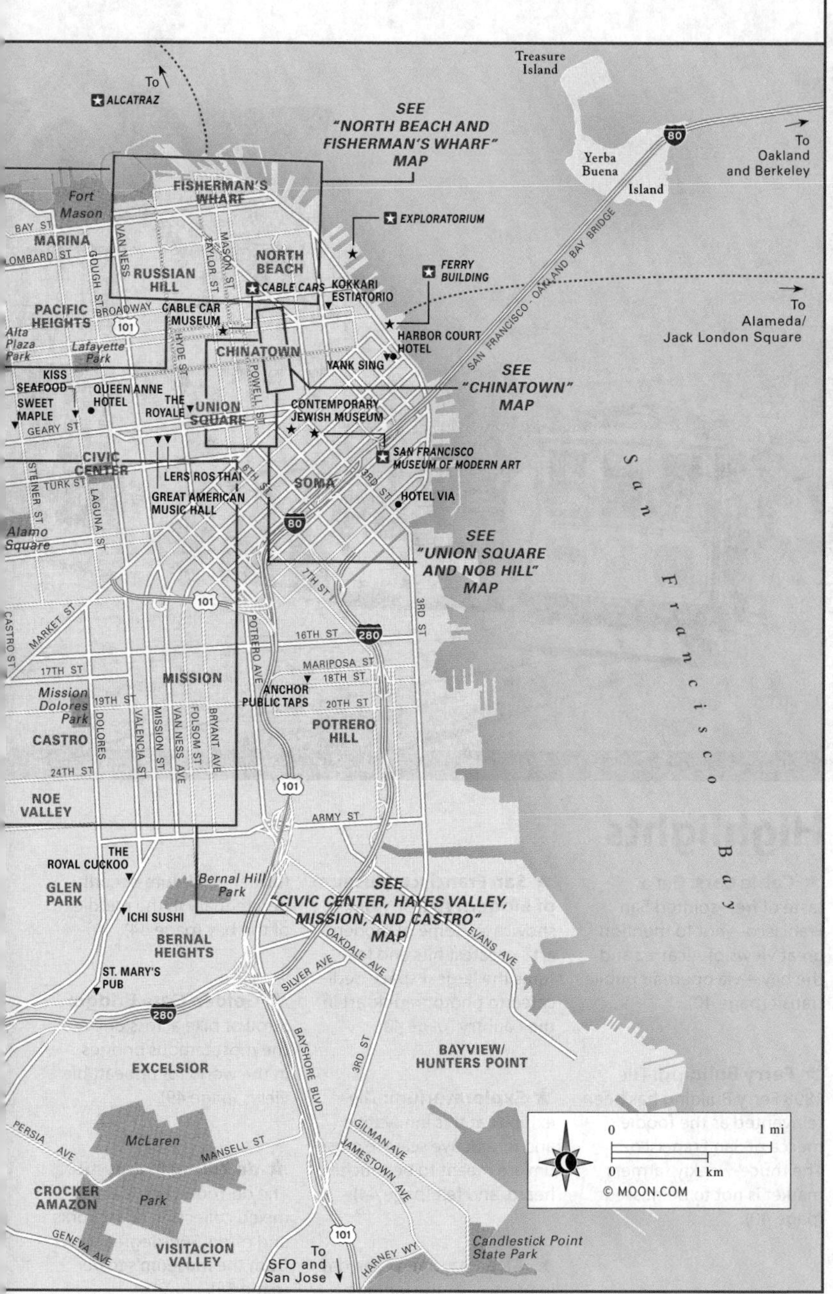

To
ALCATRAZ
SEE "NORTH BEACH AND FISHERMAN'S WHARF" MAP
Treasure Island
Yerba Buena Island
To Oakland and Berkeley
Fort Mason
FISHERMAN'S WHARF
EXPLORATORIUM
BAY ST
MARINA
LOMBARD ST
VAN NESS
GOUGH ST
TAYLOR ST
MASON ST
RUSSIAN HILL
NORTH BEACH
FERRY BUILDING
SAN FRANCISCO - OAKLAND BAY BRIDGE
CABLE CARS
KOKKARI ESTIATORIO
To Alameda/ Jack London Square
PACIFIC HEIGHTS
BROADWAY
CABLE CAR MUSEUM
Alta Plaza Park
Lafayette Park
HYDE ST
CHINATOWN
HARBOR COURT HOTEL
YANK SING
SEE "CHINATOWN" MAP
KISS SEAFOOD
QUEEN ANNE HOTEL
THE ROYALE
UNION SQUARE
POWELL ST
CONTEMPORARY JEWISH MUSEUM
SWEET MAPLE
GEARY ST
SAN FRANCISCO MUSEUM OF MODERN ART
CIVIC CENTER
TURK ST
LERS ROS THAI
6TH ST
SOMA
3RD ST
HOTEL VIA
STEINER ST
LAGUNA ST
GREAT AMERICAN MUSIC HALL
Alamo Square
SEE "UNION SQUARE AND NOB HILL" MAP
San Francisco Bay
7TH ST
101
80
280
CASTRO ST
MARKET ST
POTRERO AVE
16TH ST
3RD ST
17TH ST
MISSION
MARIPOSA ST
18TH ST
ANCHOR PUBLIC TAPS
20TH ST
Mission Dolores Park
19TH ST
CASTRO
DOLORES
VALENCIA ST
MISSION ST
VAN NESS AVE
FOLSOM ST
BRYANT AVE
POTRERO HILL
24TH ST
NOE VALLEY
ARMY ST
THE ROYAL CUCKOO
GLEN PARK
Bernal Hill Park
SEE "CIVIC CENTER, HAYES VALLEY, MISSION, AND CASTRO" MAP
ICHI SUSHI
BERNAL HEIGHTS
OAKDALE AVE
EVANS AVE
ST. MARY'S PUB
SILVER AVE
BAYSHORE BLVD
3RD ST
BAYVIEW/ HUNTERS POINT
EXCELSIOR
PERSIA AVE
McLaren Park
MANSELL ST
GILMAN AVE
JAMESTOWN AVE
CROCKER AMAZON
GENEVA AVE
VISITACION VALLEY
To SFO and San Jose
HARNEY WY
Candlestick Point State Park
0 1 mi
0 1 km
© MOON.COM

Highlights

★ **Cable Cars:** Get a taste of free-spirited San Francisco—not to mention great views of Alcatraz and the bay—via open-air public transit (page 40).

★ **Ferry Building:** The 1898 Ferry Building has been reinvented as the foodie mecca of San Francisco. The thrice-weekly farmers market is not to be missed (page 40).

★ **San Francisco Museum of Modern Art:** SFMOMA showcases some of modern art's greatest hits and features the largest space dedicated to photographic art in the country (page 42).

★ **Exploratorium:** The exhibits at this innovative and interactive science museum are meant to be touched, heard, and felt (page 44).

★ **Alcatraz:** Spend the day in prison—at the famous former maximum-security penitentiary in the middle of the bay (page 44).

★ **Golden Gate Bridge:** Stroll or bike across one of the most famous bridges in the world for unbeatable views (page 49).

★ **de Young Museum:** The de Young holds a vast mixed collection of artworks and offers 360-degree views from the museum's tower (page 54).

San Francisco perches restlessly on an uneven spit of land overlooking the bay on one side and the Pacific Ocean on the other.

Visitors come for its beauty, culinary innovation, great art, world-class music, and laid-back club scene. Famed for its diversity, liberalism, and dense fog, the city somehow manages to both embody and defy the stereotypes heaped upon it.

Street-corner protests and leather stores are certainly part of the landscape, but farmers markets and friendly communities also abound. English blends with languages from around the world in an often joyful cacophony. Those who have chosen to live here often refuse to live anyplace else, despite the infamous cost of housing and the occasional violent earthquake. Don't call it "San Fran" or, worse, "Frisco," or you'll be pegged as a tourist. To locals, this is The City, and that's that.

Getting to San Francisco

From Los Angeles

The Coastal Route

The **Pacific Coast Highway (CA-1)** from Los Angeles to San Francisco is one of the country's iconic drives. This coastal route has a lot to see and do, but it's not the fastest route between the two cities. It runs almost **500 miles (805 km)** and can easily take **eight hours** or longer, depending on traffic. It's worth the extra time to experience the gorgeous coastal scenery, which includes Santa Barbara, Big Sur, and Monterey. The highway is long, narrow, and winding; in winter rockslides and mudslides may close the road entirely. Always check **Caltrans** (www.dot.ca.gov) for highway traffic conditions before starting your journey.

From Los Angeles, take **US-101 North** (past Oxnard, US-101 also follows CA-1). At Gaviota, US-101 turns inland toward Buellton and Santa Maria before rejoining CA-1 again at Pismo Beach. At San Luis Obispo, US-101 and CA-1 split again: CA-1 continues west along the Big Sur coast; US-101 moves inland through Paso Robles up toward Salinas, Gilroy, and San Jose. Note that US-101 is a more direct route to San Francisco. CA-1, while scenic, is longer and often clogged with traffic in Santa Cruz, where it meets **CA-17.**

Stopping in San Luis Obispo

It's easier to enjoy the drive by dividing it up over two days and spending a night somewhere along the coast. Right off both CA-1 and US-101, the city of **San Luis Obispo** is close to halfway between the two cities, which makes it an ideal place to stop. It takes three hours to make the 200-mile (320-km) drive from Los Angeles if traffic isn't bad. The additional 230 miles (370 km) to San Francisco takes four hours or more. An affordable motel right off the highway is the **Peach Tree Inn** (2001 Monterey St., 800/227-6396, http://peachtreeinn.com, $89-299). For a wilder experience, stay at the popular tourist attraction **Madonna Inn** (10 Madonna Rd., 805/543-3000, www.madonnainn.com, $209-489), which offers the **Gold Rush Steak House** for dinner and the **Copper Café & Pastry Shop** for breakfast. **Novo** (726 Higuera St., 805/543-3986, www.novorestaurant.com, 11am-9pm Sun.-Thurs., 11am-1am Fri.-Sat., $18-37) has a truly international menu and outdoor dining on decks overlooking San Luis Obispo Creek. For something fast, the **Firestone Grill** (1001 Higuera St., 805/783-1001, www.firestonegrill.com, 11am-10pm Sun.-Wed., 11am-11pm Thurs.-Sat., $5-22) is known for its tasty tri-tip sandwich. For complete information on San Luis Obispo, see page 381.

Best Restaurants

★ **Yank Sing:** Sample dim sum from wheeled carts full of dumplings, pot stickers, spring rolls, and more (page 72).

★ **Brenda's French Soul Food:** Start the day with a hearty New Orleans-style breakfast at this Tenderloin eatery (page 73).

★ **Michael Mina:** A celebrity chef dishes out signature dishes at his Michelin-starred namesake restaurant (page 74).

★ **Tadich Grill:** Open since 1849, the city's oldest restaurant still serves an extensive menu of sensational seafood (page 74).

★ **The Cavalier:** Feast on upscale British pub food. The golden-fried lamb riblets alone are worth the trip (page 75).

★ **Tony's Pizza Napoletana:** This North Beach pizzeria employs seven different ovens to cook pies by World Pizza Champion award winner Tony Gemignani (page 77).

★ **Swan Oyster Depot:** Locals and visitors line up daily for a seafood lunch at this tiny restaurant (page 78).

★ **Lolinda:** Craving a big piece of perfectly cooked beef? Try this stylish Argentinean steak house in the foodie Mission District (page 80).

★ **Tartine Bakery:** Lines snake out the door all day long, but the fresh baked goods and sandwiches are worth the wait (page 81).

The Interior Route

A faster but much less interesting driving route is **I-5** from Los Angeles to San Francisco. It takes about **six hours** if the traffic is cooperating. On holiday weekends, the drive time can increase to 10 hours. From Los Angeles, most freeways lead or merge onto I-5 North and ascend to higher elevations before crossing the **Tejon Pass** over the Tehachapi Mountains. This section of the highway, nicknamed **the Grapevine,** can close in winter due to snow and ice (and sometimes in summer due to wildfires). November-March, tule fog (thick, ground-level fog) can also seriously impede driving conditions and reduce visibility to a crawl. After the Grapevine, the highway narrows to two lanes and is mostly straight and flat, not particularly scenic, and filled with trucks and highway patrol cars that can slow traffic considerably. Stay on I-5 for the first 310 miles (500 km), before diverting onto **I-580 West** (toward Tracy and San Francisco) for 62 miles (100 km). At that point, connect to **I-80 West.** Follow signs for San Francisco for the next 45-50 miles (72-81 km) to cross the **Bay Bridge** (toll $6) into the city. Always check **Caltrans** (www.dot.ca.gov) for highway traffic conditions before starting your journey.

From Yosemite

The drive from Yosemite to San Francisco involves lots of time on small highways that frequently pass orchards, farms, and sprawling valley towns. The drive of roughly **200 miles (320 km)** can take four

Best Hotels

★ **Golden Gate Hotel:** This bed-and-breakfast-like hotel has nice, moderately priced rooms near Union Square (page 82).

★ **Phoenix Hotel:** The Phoenix is popular with touring rock bands, but you don't have to be a rock star to enjoy this casual hotel's expansive pool deck (page 82).

★ **Hotel G:** This hotel comes on like an unassuming cool kid that impresses with understated style (page 82).

★ **Hotel VIA:** Modern and minimalist, this hotel has sleek rooms and a rooftop bar and lounge open only to overnight guests (page 83).

★ **Hotel Zetta:** This SoMa spot embraces the region's tech-savvy side; each room comes equipped with a gaggle of gadgets (page 83).

★ **Harbor Court Hotel:** You can't beat this location—a block from the Ferry Building, with views of the bay (page 85).

★ **Marina Motel:** Built in the 1930s but offering modern amenities, this moderately priced motel in the Marina District also has something most accommodations in the city don't: individual parking garages for guests (page 85).

★ **The Metro Hotel:** This family-owned hotel on bustling Divisadero Street near Haight-Ashbury is a gem, with a cool location, some of the better rates in the city, and comfy rooms (page 87).

hours if traffic is on your side, but plan on **five hours.** The trip may require navigating heavy traffic in and out of Yosemite National Park (especially on weekends), the annual closure of **Tioga Pass (CA-120)**, curvy mountain roads, and traffic in the Central Valley and greater Bay Area.

Summer Route

In summer, Yosemite's park roads and the surrounding freeways are open but are also heavily trafficked. From Yosemite, exit the park via the **Big Oak Flat Entrance** and drive 90 miles (145 km) west on CA-120 West toward Manteca. (Stay on CA-120 West when it merges with CA-49 and CA-108.) Near Manteca, CA-120 merges onto I-5. Take I-5 South for about 2 miles (3.2 km), then take I-205 West for 14 miles (22.5 km) to I-580 West. In about 45 miles (72 km), I-580 merges with I-80 West onto the **Bay Bridge** (toll $5-7) and into San Francisco.

Winter Route

If traveling from Yosemite September-May, your surest access is **CA-140** and the **Arch Rock Entrance.** From this entrance, follow **CA-140 West** for 80 miles (129 km) to Merced. In Merced, merge onto **CA-99 North** and drive 60 miles (97 km) toward Manteca. At Manteca, merge onto **CA-120 West** and continue the summer route to I-5, I-205, I-580, and I-80 into San Francisco.

Many Yosemite park roads are closed in winter. **Tioga Pass** and **CA-120**—the east-west access through the park—are closed from the end of September until May or June. In addition, CA-120 west

Two Days in San Francisco

TOP EXPERIENCE

Day 1

Start your day at the **Ferry Building.** Graze from the many vendors, including **Blue Bottle Café** and **Acme Bread Company,** then walk the handful of blocks to **Yank Sing** for a dim sum lunch. Catch the Muni F line (Steuart St. and Market St., $3) to Jefferson Street and take a stroll along **Fisherman's Wharf.** Stop into the **Musée Mécanique** to play a few coin-operated antique arcade games. Near Pier 39, catch the ferry to **Alcatraz**—be sure to buy your tickets well in advance.

After you escape from Alcatraz, take the N Judah line ($3) to 9th Avenue and Irving Street, then follow 9th Avenue north into **Golden Gate Park,** where you can delve into art at the fabulous **de Young Museum** or science at the **California Academy of Sciences.** Stroll the scenic **Japanese Tea Garden** and get a snack at the Tea House.

Catch a cab or ride share to the Financial District for dinner at San Francisco's oldest restaurant, **Tadich Grill,** still serving great seafood. Then catch some **live music** at one of the city's great venues.

Day 2

Fortify yourself for a day of sightseeing with a hearty breakfast at **Brenda's French Soul Food.** Although by this point you'll likely have caught glimpses of the **Golden Gate Bridge,** hop in a taxi or ride share to engage more closely with it this morning. For an active experience, head straight to the southern end of the bridge and walk across the famous span, or embark on the scenic **Lands End Trail** along the city's coastline, where you'll catch great views of the bridge. If it's just views sans walking you're after, head to **Crissy Field** in **The Presidio** or to **Baker Beach.**

Venture back toward downtown to wander the streets of **Chinatown** and adjacent

and north through the park and to San Francisco can also be closed due to snow. Chains can be required on park roads at any time.

From Big Sur

En route to San Francisco from the south, many visitors divert from **US-101** to **CA-1** to enjoy the narrow, twisting, two-lane, cliff-carved track to Big Sur. The drive is breathtaking both because of its beauty and because of its dangers. The **170-mile (275-km)** drive can be as little as **3-4 hours** long, continuing on CA-1 from Big Sur through Monterey and Santa Cruz and up to San Francisco. Compared to US-101, CA-1 adds a few miles to your trip along with another 20 to 30 minutes of driving.

If it's a busy summer weekend, consider heading inland to US-101 north of Big Sur to avoid traffic delays. This is also a good idea during October, when traffic backs up on CA-1 around Half Moon Bay due to its Art & Pumpkin Festival. Head out of the Big Sur Valley for 49 miles (79 km) on **CA-1 North,** then exit onto **CA-156 East,** which connects with US-101 North 6.5 miles (10.5 km) later. Continue for 97 miles (156 km) through San Jose and up into San Francisco.

Air, Train, or Bus

It's easy to fly into the San Francisco Bay Area. There are three major airports. Among them, you should be able to find a flight that fits your schedule. **San Francisco International Airport** (SFO, www.flysfo.com) is 13 miles (21 km) south. **Oakland Airport** (OAK, www.

Japanese Tea Garden in Golden Gate Park

North Beach. Have lunch at **Tony's Pizza Napoletana,** which has seven pizza ovens. Browse through **City Lights,** the legendary Beat Generation bookstore. Wind down with a cocktail at **Vesuvio,** a colorful bar and former Beat writer hangout located next door.

At night, head to the bustling **Mission** neighborhood, stopping first for a drink at the rooftop bar **El Techo de Lolinda** or **Trick Dog.** Then enjoy dinner at **Lolinda** or **Tartine Manufactory.**

oaklandairport.com) is 11 miles (17.5 km) east of the city but requires crossing the bay, via either the Bay Bridge or public transit. **San José International Airport** (SJC, www.flysanjose.com) is the farthest away, roughly 47 miles (76 km) to the south. These last two airports are less than an hour away by car, with car rentals available. Some San Francisco hotels offer complimentary airport shuttles as well.

Several public and private transportation options can get you into San Francisco. **Bay Area Rapid Transit** (BART, www.bart.gov, $2-15) connects directly with SFO's international terminal; an airport shuttle connects Oakland airport to the nearest station. **Caltrain** (www.caltrain.com, tickets $3.75-15) is a good option from San Jose; an airport shuttle connects to the train station. **Millbrae Station** is where the BART and Caltrain systems connect; it's designed to transfer from one line to the other.

Amtrak (800/872-7245, www.amtrak.com) does not run directly into San Francisco, but you can ride to the San Jose, Oakland, or Emeryville stations, then take a connecting bus to San Francisco. **Greyhound** (425 Mission St., 415/495-1569, www.greyhound.com, 5:15am-10:30pm daily) offers bus service to San Francisco from all over the country.

Sights

Union Square and Downtown

★ Cable Cars

Perhaps the most recognizable symbol of San Francisco is the **cable car** (www.sfcablecar.com), originally conceived by Andrew Smith Hallidie as a safer alternative for traveling the steep, often slick hills of San Francisco. The cable cars ran as regular mass transit from 1873 into the 1940s, when buses and electric streetcars began to dominate the landscape. Dedicated citizens, especially "Cable Car Lady" Friedel Klussmann, saved the cable car system from extinction, and the cable cars have become a rolling national landmark.

Today you can ride the cable cars from one tourist destination to another for $8 per ride. A full day "passport" **ticket** ($24, also grants access to streetcars and buses) is totally worth it if you want to run around the city all day. Cable car routes can take you up Nob Hill from the Financial District, or from Union Square along Powell Street, through Chinatown, and out to Fisherman's Wharf. Take a seat, or grab one of the exterior poles and hang on! Cable cars have open-air seating only, making for a chilly ride on foggy days.

The cars get stuffed to capacity with tourists on weekends and with local commuters at rush hours. Expect to wait an hour or more for a ride from any of the turnaround points on a weekend or holiday. But a ride on a cable car from Union Square down to the Wharf is more than worth the wait. The views from the hills down to the bay inspire wonder even in lifetime residents. To learn a bit more, make a stop at the **Cable Car Museum** (1201 Mason St., 415/474-1887, www.cablecarmuseum.org, 10am-6pm daily Apr.-Sept., 10am-5pm daily Oct.-Mar., free), the home and nerve center of the entire fleet. Here a sweet little museum depicts the life and times of the cable cars while an elevated platform overlooks the engines, winding wheels, and thick steel cable that keeps the cars humming. You can even glimpse the 1873 tunnels that snake beneath the city.

Grace Cathedral

Local icon **Grace Cathedral** (1100 California St., 415/749-6300, www.gracecathedral.org, 7am-6pm Thurs., 8am-6pm Fri.-Wed., 8am-4pm holidays) is many things to many people. The French Gothic-style edifice, completed in 1964, attracts architecture and Beaux-Arts lovers by the thousands with its facade, stained glass, and furnishings. The labyrinths—replicas of the Chartres Cathedral labyrinth in France—appeal to meditative walkers seeking spiritual solace. Concerts featuring world music, sacred music, and modern classical ensembles draw audiences from around the Bay Area and farther afield.

The 1.5-hour **Grace Cathedral Grand Tour** (415/749-6316, www.gracecathedral.org, $25) includes a walk up 94 steps to the top of the cathedral's South Tower. Download the GraceGuide app for information about the structure's architecture, history, and art.

★ Ferry Building

Restored to its former glory, the 1898 **San Francisco Ferry Building** (1 Ferry Bldg., 415/983-8030, www.ferrybuildingmarketplace.com, 10am-7pm Mon.-Fri., 8am-6pm Sat., 11am-5pm Sun., check with businesses for individual hours) stands at the edge of the bay, its 230-foot-tall (70.1-m) clock tower serving as a beacon to both land and water traffic. Photos and interpretive plaques just inside the main lobby describe its history. Free **walking tours** (www.sfcityguides.org) of the building are offered one day a week.

Inside, it's all about the food. Permanent shops provide top-tier artisanal food and drink, with local favorites like Cowgirl Creamery, Blue Bottle Café,

Union Square and Nob Hill

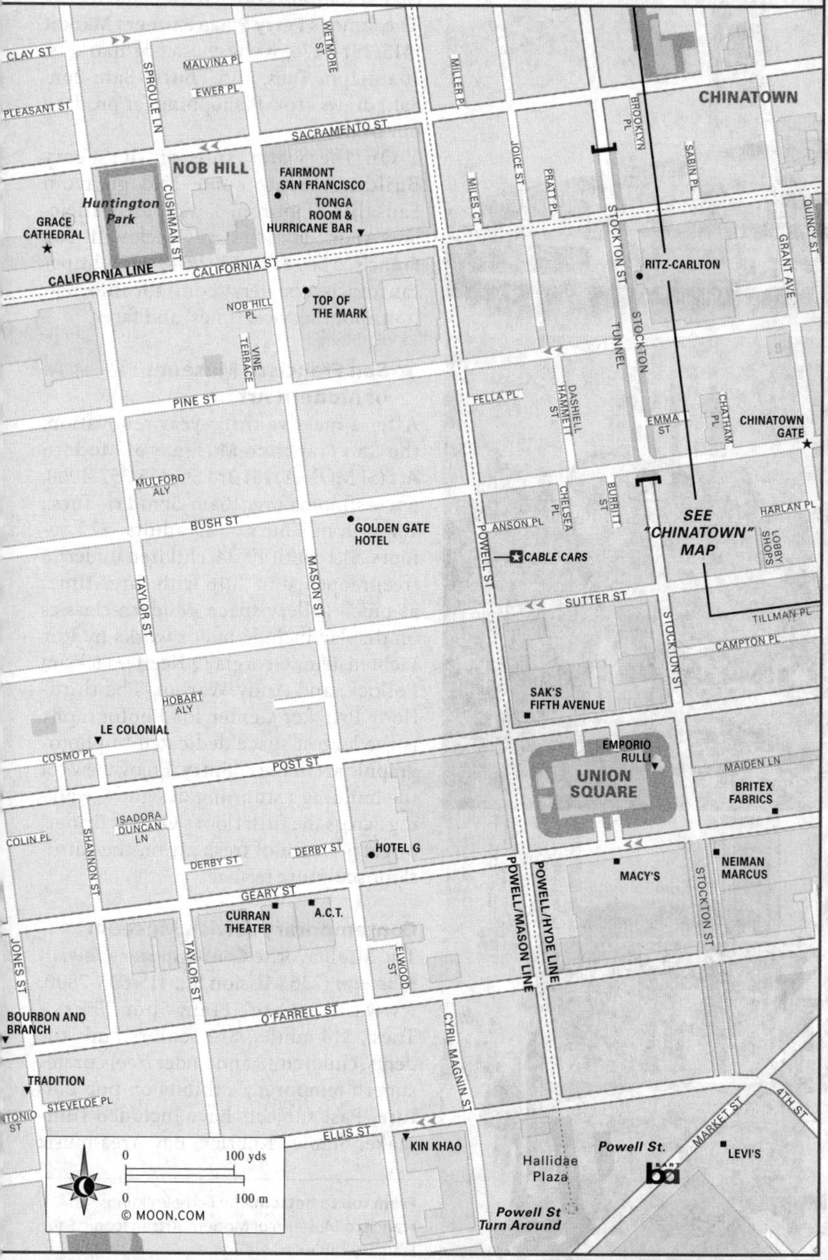

CLAY ST
MALVINA PL
WETMORE ST
EWER PL
SPROULE LN
PLEASANT ST
MILLER PL
CHINATOWN
BROOKLYN PL
SACRAMENTO ST
SABIN PL
NOB HILL
FAIRMONT SAN FRANCISCO
JOICE ST
MILES CT
PRATT PL
Huntington Park
CUSHMAN ST
TONGA ROOM & HURRICANE BAR
STOCKTON ST
QUINCY ST
GRACE CATHEDRAL
GRANT AVE
RITZ-CARLTON
CALIFORNIA LINE
CALIFORNIA ST
NOB HILL PL
TOP OF THE MARK
STOCKTON TUNNEL
VINE TERRACE
DASHIELL HAMMETT ST
PINE ST
FELLA PL
EMMA ST
CHATHAM PL
CHINATOWN GATE
MULFORD ALY
CHELSEA PL
BURRITT ST
BUSH ST
GOLDEN GATE HOTEL
ANSON PL
SEE "CHINATOWN" MAP
HARLAN PL
LOBBY SHOPS
CABLE CARS
TAYLOR ST
MASON ST
POWELL ST
SUTTER ST
TILLMAN PL
CAMPTON PL
STOCKTON ST
SAK'S FIFTH AVENUE
HOBART ALY
LE COLONIAL
EMPORIO RULLI
UNION SQUARE
COSMO PL
POST ST
MAIDEN LN
BRITEX FABRICS
ISADORA DUNCAN LN
COLIN PL
SHANNON ST
HOTEL G
DERBY ST
DERBY ST
MACY'S
NEIMAN MARCUS
POWELL/MASON LINE
POWELL/HYDE LINE
GEARY ST
CURRAN THEATER
A.C.T.
STOCKTON ST
JONES ST
TAYLOR ST
ELWOOD ST
CYRIL MAGNIN ST
BOURBON AND BRANCH
O'FARRELL ST
TRADITION
STEVELOE PL
ANTONIO ST
MARKET ST
4TH ST
ELLIS ST
KIN KHAO
Powell St.
LEVI'S
Hallidae Plaza
Powell St Turn Around
0 100 yds
0 100 m
© MOON.COM

Hog Island Oyster Company, and Acme Bread Company, while a few quick-and-easy restaurants offer reasonable meals. The famous **Ferry Plaza Farmers Market** (415/291-3276, www.cuesa.org/markets, 10am-2pm Tues. and Thurs., 8am-2pm Sat.) draws crowds shopping for produce out front.

On the water side of the Ferry Building, boats come and go from Sausalito, Tiburon, Larkspur, Vallejo, and Alameda each day. Check with **San Francisco Bay Ferry** (707/643-3779, http://sanfranciscobayferry.com) for information about service, times, and fares.

★ San Francisco Museum of Modern Art

After a massive three-year renovation, the **San Francisco Museum of Modern Art** (SFMOMA, 151 3rd St., 415/357-4000, www.sfmoma.org, 10am-5pm Fri.-Tues., 10am-9pm Thurs., $25 adults, $22 seniors, $19 youth 19-24, children under 18 free) reopened in 2016 with three times as much gallery space. Modern classics on display include major works by Roy Lichtenstein, Georgia O'Keeffe, Jackson Pollock, and Andy Warhol. The third-floor Pritzker Center for Photography is the largest space dedicated to photographic art in the country. Enjoy views of the building's stunning design by walking across the fifth floor's Oculus Bridge, or get a breath of fresh air on the third-floor sculpture terrace.

Contemporary Jewish Museum

The local favorite **Contemporary Jewish Museum** (736 Mission St., 415/655-7800, www.thecjm.org, 11am-5pm Thurs.-Tues., $14 adults, $12 seniors and students, children 18 and under free) curates superb temporary exhibits on pop culture. Past subjects have included filmmaker Stanley Kubrick, Bay Area music

From top to bottom: the Ferry Building; San Francisco Museum of Modern Art; an iconic San Franciso cable car.

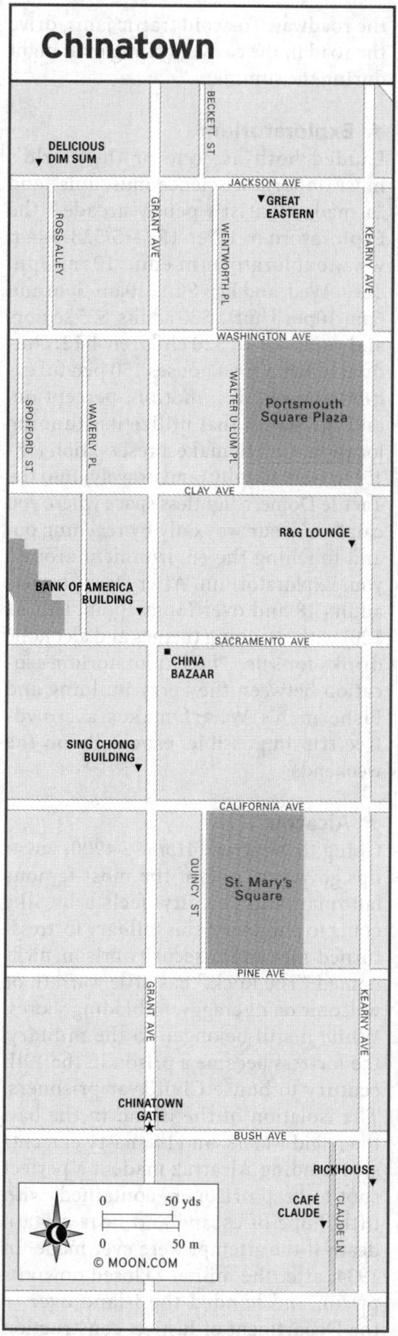

promoter Bill Graham, businessman Levi Strauss, and singer Amy Winehouse. The museum's sleek building is part historic power station and part blue steel structure that spells out the Hebrew word *chai*, meaning life.

Chinatown

Chinese migration to California began almost as soon as the news of easy gold in the mountain streams made it to East Asia. And despite rampant prejudice, Chinese people not only stayed, but persevered and eventually prospered. Many never made it to the gold fields, preferring instead to remain in bustling San Francisco to open shops and begin the business of commerce in their new home. They carved out a thriving community at the border of **Portsmouth Square,** then center of the young city, which became known as Chinatown. Along with much of San Francisco, the neighborhood was destroyed in the 1906 earthquake and fire.

Today visitors see the post-1906 visitor-friendly Chinatown that was built after the quake, particularly if they enter through the **Chinatown Gate** (Grant Ave. and Bush St.) at the edge of Union Square. In this historic neighborhood, beautiful Asian architecture mixes with more mundane blocky city buildings to create a unique skyline. Small alleyways wend between the touristy commercial corridors, creating an intimate atmosphere.

North Beach and Fisherman's Wharf

North Beach has long served as the Little Italy of San Francisco, a fact still reflected in the restaurants in the neighborhood. North Beach truly made its mark in the 1950s when it was, for a brief time, home to many writers in the Beat Generation, including Jack Kerouac, Gary Snyder, and Allen Ginsberg. You can learn about that vibrant period at **The Beat Museum** (540 Broadway Ave., 800/537-6822, www.kerouac.com, 10am-7pm daily, $8 adults, $5 students and seniors).

Coit Tower

Built in 1933 as a monument to benefactor Lillie Hitchcock Coit's beloved firefighters, **Coit Tower** (1 Telegraph Hill Blvd., 415/249-0995, http://sfrecpark.org, 10am-6pm daily Apr.-Oct., 10am-5pm daily Nov.-Mar., free) has beautified the city just as Coit intended. Inside the art deco tower, the walls are covered in the restored frescos painted in 1934 depicting city and California life during the Great Depression. For a fee ($9 adults, $6 seniors and youth, $3 children 5-11, children 4 and under free), you can ride the elevator to the top, where on a clear day, you can see the whole city and bay. Part of what makes Coit Tower special is the walk up to it. Rather than contributing to the acute congestion in the area, consider taking public transit to the area and walking up Telegraph Hill Boulevard through Pioneer Park to the tower, and descend down either the Filbert or Greenwich steps toward the Embarcadero. It's long and steep, but there's no other way to see the lovely little cottages and gardens of the beautiful and quaint Telegraph Hill.

Lombard Street

You've no doubt seen it in movies: **Lombard Street** (Lombard St., one-way from Hyde St. to Leavenworth St.), otherwise known as "the crookedest street in the world." The section of the street that visitors flock to spans only one block, from Hyde Street at the top to Leavenworth Street at the bottom. However, the line of cars waiting their turn to drive bumper-to-bumper can be just as legendary as its 27 percent grade. Bypass the car and take the hill by foot. The unobstructed vistas of San Francisco Bay, Alcatraz Island, Fisherman's Wharf, Coit Tower, and the city are reason enough to add this walk to your itinerary, as are the brick steps, manicured hydrangeas, and tony residences that line the roadway. To avoid traffic jams, drive the road in the early morning or at night during the summer.

★ Exploratorium

Lauded both as "one of the world's most important science museums" and "a mad scientist's penny arcade," the **Exploratorium** (Pier 15, 415/528-4444, www.exploratorium.edu, 10am-5pm Tues.-Wed. and Fri.-Sun., 10am-5pm and 6pm-10pm Thurs., $30 adults, $25 seniors and youth 13-17, $20 children 4-12, children under 3 free) houses 150 playful exhibits on physics, motion, perception, and the senses that utilize its stunning location. Call to make a reservation ($8-15) to walk blindly (and bravely) into the Tactile Dome, a lightless space where you can "see" your way only by reaching out and touching the environment around you. Exploratorium "After Dark" targets adults 18 and over (6pm-10pm Thurs., $20) with changing themes and alcoholic drinks for sale. The Exploratorium's location between the Ferry Building and Fisherman's Wharf makes a crowd-free trip impossible, especially on the weekends.

★ Alcatraz

Going to **Alcatraz** (415/561-4900, www.nps.gov/alca), one of the most famous landmarks in the city, feels a bit like going to purgatory; this military fortress-turned-maximum-security prison, nicknamed "The Rock," has little warmth or welcome on its craggy, forbidding shores. While it still belonged to the military, the fortress became a prison in the 19th century to house Civil War prisoners. The isolation of the island in the bay, the frigid waters, and the nasty currents surrounding Alcatraz made it a perfect spot to keep prisoners contained, with little hope of escape and near-certain death if the attempt were ever made. In 1934, after the military closed down its prison and handed the island over to the Department of Justice, construction

North Beach and Fisherman's Wharf

began to turn Alcatraz into a new style of prison ready to house a new style of prisoner: Depression-era gangsters. A few of the honored guests of this maximum-security penitentiary were Al Capone, George "Machine Gun" Kelly, and Robert Stroud, "the Birdman of Alcatraz." The prison closed in 1963.

Alcatraz is also significant as the site of protests that sparked the Native American civil rights movement. After a first attempt in 1964, in 1969 an intertribal group self-identified as the Indians of All Tribes occupied Alcatraz for 19 months in a rallying cry for Native American land rights. The reclamation efforts led to federal policy shifts allowing greater self-determination for North America's original inhabitants and laid the foundation for modern Indigenous activism such as the Standing Rock protests. Evidence of the occupation remains at Alcatraz and is explored as part of the island's compelling history.

Visit the island on tours offered by **Alcatraz Cruises** (Pier 33, 415/981-7625, www.alcatrazcruises.com), departing from Pier 33. Options include the **Day Tour** (daily, $40 adults and youth 12-17, $38 seniors, $25 children 5-11), **Night Tour** (Tues.-Sat., $47 adults and youth 12-17, $44 seniors, $28 children 5-11), **Behind the Scenes Tour** (Tues.-Sat., $92 adults, $88 youth 12-17, $86 seniors), and the **Alcatraz and Angel Island Tour** (days vary, $79 adults and youth 12-17, $77 seniors, $53 children 5-11). Tours typically sell out, especially on weekends, so reserve tickets at least two weeks in advance.

Fisherman's Wharf

Welcome to **Fisherman's Wharf** (Beach St. from Powell St. to Van Ness Ave., backs onto Bay St.,415/674-7503, http://fishermanswharf.org), the tourist mecca

From top to bottom: Lombard Street; the entrance to Ghirardelli Square; the Palace of Fine Arts.

of San Francisco! While warehouses, stacks of crab pots, and a fleet of fishing vessels let you know this is still a working wharf, it is also where visitors come and snap photos. Reachable by the Muni F line and the Hyde-Powell cable car, the Wharf sprawls along the waterfront and inland several blocks.

Be prepared to push through a sea of humanity to buy souvenirs, eat seafood, and enjoy fun pieces of San Francisco's heritage, like the **Musée Mécanique** (Pier 45, Fishermen's Wharf, 415/346-2000, www.museemechaniquesf.com, 10am-8pm daily, free), a strange collection of over 300 working coin-operated machines from the 1800s to today. Machines include a 3-D picture show of San Francisco after the catastrophic 1906 earthquake and fire, along with more modern favorites like Ms. Pac-Man.

Ghirardelli Square

Ghirardelli Square (900 North Point St., www.ghirardellisq.com, 11am-9pm daily), pronounced "GEAR-ah-DEL-ee," began its life as a chocolate factory in 1852 but has since reinvented itself as an upscale shopping, dining, and living compound. The **Ghirardelli Chocolate Manufactory** (900 North Point St., 415/474-3938, www.ghirardellisq.com, 9am-11pm Sun.-Thurs., 9am-midnight Fri.-Sat.) anchors the corner of the square. Here you can browse the rambling shop and pick up truffles, wafers, candies, and sauces for all your friends back home. Finally, get in line at the ice cream counter to order a hot fudge sundae. Once you've finished gorging on chocolate, wander out into the square to enjoy more shopping and an unbelievably swank condo complex overlooking the bay.

San Francisco Maritime National Historical Park

The real gem of the Wharf is the **San Francisco Maritime National Historical Park** (415/561-7000, www.nps.gov/safr), which spreads from the base of Van Ness to Pier 45. At the **visitors center** (499 Jefferson St., 415/447-5000, 9:30am-5pm daily), not only will rangers help you make the most of your visit, but you can also get lost in the labyrinthine museum that houses an immense Fresnel lighthouse lens and engaging displays that recount San Francisco's history. For $15, you can climb aboard the historic ships at the permanent dock across the street at the **Hyde Street Pier** (9:30am-5pm daily). The shiniest jewel of the collection is the 1886 square-rigged *Balclutha,* a three-masted schooner that recalls times gone by, complete with excellent historical exhibits below deck. There are also several steamboats, including the workhorse ferry paddle wheeler *Eureka* and a cool old steam tugboat called the *Eppleton Hall.* Farther down, at Pier 45, World War II buffs can feel the claustrophobia of the submarine **USS *Pampanito*** (415/775-1943, www.maritime.org, 9am-6pm Sun.-Thurs., 9am-8pm Fri.-Sat., $20 adults, $12 seniors, $10 children 6-12, children under 6 free) or the expansiveness of the Liberty ship **SS *Jeremiah O'Brien*** (415/544-0100, www.ssjeremiahobrien.org, 9am-4pm daily, $20 adults, $12 seniors, $10 children 5-12, children under 4 free).

The 1939 art deco **Aquatic Bathhouse Building** (900 Beach St., 415/561-7100, www.nps.gov/safr, 10am-4pm daily, $5 adults, children free), built in 1939, houses the Maritime Museum, where you can see rotating exhibits alongside its brilliant WPA murals.

Marina and Pacific Heights

The Marina and Pacific Heights are wealthy neighborhoods, with a couple of yacht harbors, plenty of open space, great dining, and shopping that only gets better as you go up the hill.

Palace of Fine Arts

The **Palace of Fine Arts** (3301 Lyon St.) was originally meant to be

Marina and Pacific Heights

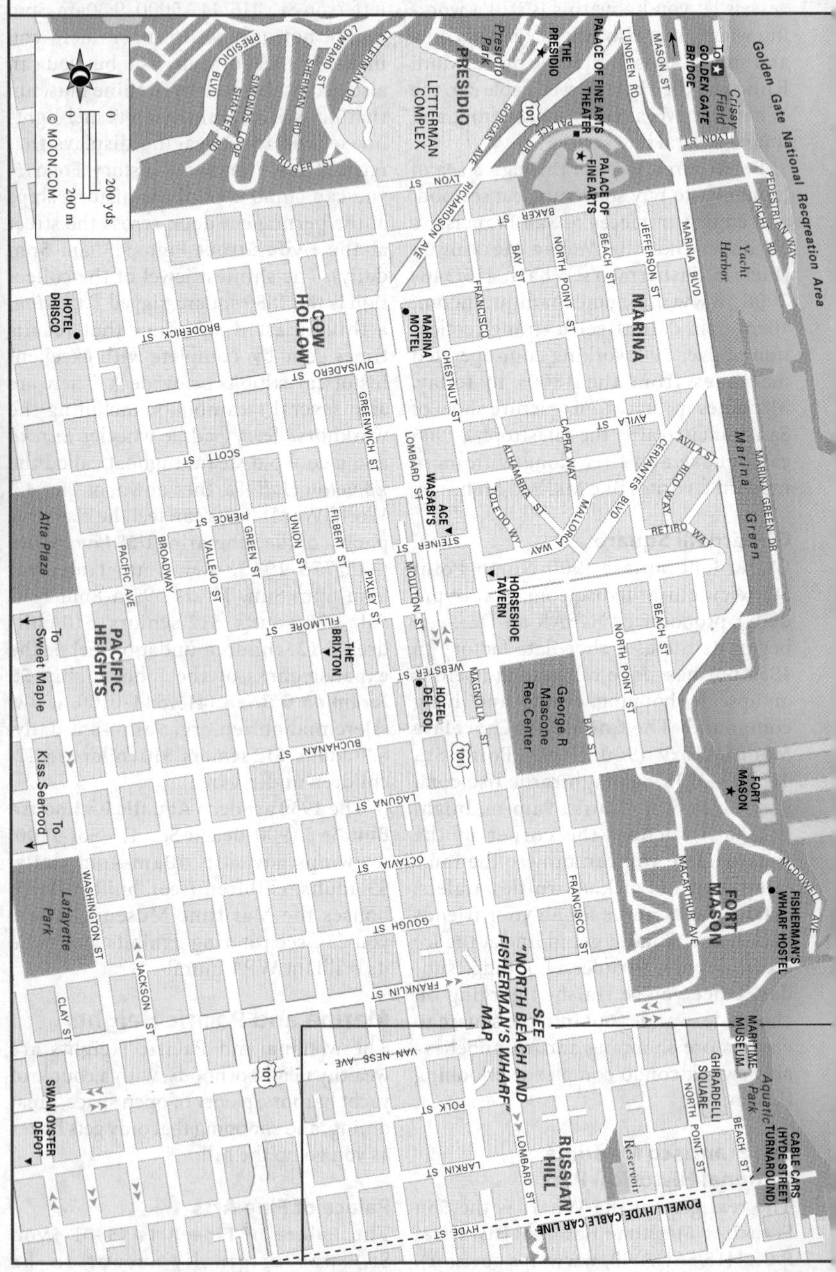

nothing but a temporary structure—part of the Panama-Pacific International Exposition in 1915. But the lovely building designed by Bernard Maybeck won the hearts of San Franciscans, and a fund was started to preserve the palace beyond the exposition. Through the first half of the 20th century, efforts could not keep it from crumbling, but in the 1960s and 1970s, serious rebuilding work took place, and today the Palace of Fine Arts stands proud, strong, and beautiful. It houses the **Palace of Fine Arts Theatre** (415/563-6504, www.palaceoffinearts.org), which hosts events nearly every day, from beauty pageants to conferences to children's musical theater performances.

The Presidio

It seems strange to think of progressive, peace-loving San Francisco as a town with a long military history, yet it is nowhere more evident than at **The Presidio** (Montgomery St. and Lincoln Blvd., 415/561-4323, www.nps.gov/prsf, visitors center 10am-5pm daily, trails dawn-dusk daily, free). This sweeping stretch of land running along the San Francisco Headlands down to the Golden Gate Bridge has been a military installation since 1776, when the Spanish created their El Presidio del San Francisco fort on the site. In 1846, the U.S. Army took over the site (peacefully), and in 1848 the Presidio military installation formally opened. The Presidio had a role in every Pacific-related war from the Civil War through Desert Storm. It was abandoned by the military and became a national park in 1994.

To orient yourself among the more than 800 buildings that make up the Presidio, start at the **William Penn Mott Jr. Presidio Visitor Center** (Bldg. 210, Lincoln Blvd., 415/561-4323, 10am-5pm daily), where exhibits include a model of the grounds. You can also explore the pioneering aviation area **Crissy Field** (www.parksconservancy.org), Civil War-era fortifications at **Fort Point National Historic Site** (end of Marine Dr., 415/504-2334, www.nps.gov/fopo, 10am-5pm Thurs.-Mon. summer, 10am-5pm Fri.-Sun. winter), and the **Walt Disney Family Museum** (104 Montgomery St., 415/345-6800, www.waltdisney.org, 10am-6pm Wed.-Mon., $25 adults, $20 seniors and students, $15 children 6-17), founded by Disney's daughter to examine the animator's life and work. Other highlights include art installations by Andy Goldsworthy, who works with natural materials. The most renowned is *Spire*, a sculpture that rises 90 feet (27.4 m) into the air, utilizing 35 cypress tree trunks.

★ Golden Gate Bridge

People come from the world over to gaze at the **Golden Gate Bridge** (US-101/CA-1 at Lincoln Blvd., 415/921-5858, www.goldengatebridge.org, southbound cars $8.35, pedestrians and bicyclists free). A marvel of human engineering constructed in 1936 and 1937, the suspension bridge spans the narrow "gate" from which the Pacific Ocean enters the San Francisco Bay. Walking or biking the 1.7-mile (2.7-km) bridge is a popular way to experience it. On a clear day, the whole bay, Marin Headlands, and city skyline are visible. Pedestrians and wheelchair users are allowed on the **east sidewalk** (5am-8pm daily early Mar.-early Nov., 5am-6:30pm daily early Nov.-early Mar.). You can do it yourself or join the nonprofit **City Guides** (415/557-4266, www.sfcityguides.org), which leads bridge walks twice a week (check the website for days and times). Cyclists are allowed on both sidewalks (check the website for the schedule). **Blazing Saddles** (www.blazingsaddles.com) has various locations around town and offers bike rentals and guided tours, including options that cross the bridge. Given how stunning the scenery is, stay aware of your surroundings as not everyone is always keeping

Side Trip to Muir Woods

Giant coast redwoods are located not far outside San Francisco's city limits. Some of the finest examples of these towering trees can be found at **Muir Woods National Monument** (1 Muir Woods Rd., 415/561-2850, www.nps.gov/muwo, 8am-sunset daily, admission $15 ages 16 and over, free under 16). More than 6 miles (9.7 km) of trails wind through the lush forest and cross verdant creeks. Note that given the large number of visitors and limited parking, Muir Woods has implemented a mandatory parking and shuttle reservation system. Reservations can be made up to 90 days in advance online or by phone (http://gomuirwoods.com, 800/410-2419). If you're arriving by foot, bicycle, or tour bus, reservations aren't necessary. Parking reservations start at $8.50 for a standard vehicle and go up to $45 for large vehicles, and shuttle reservations are $3.25 per person (free under 16).

Begin your exploration at the **Muir Woods Visitors Center** (1 Muir Woods Rd., 415/561-2580, from 8am daily, closing time varies). In addition to maps, information, and advice about hiking, you'll also find a few amenities. First-time visitors should follow the wheelchair- and stroller-accessible **Main Trail Loop** (1 mi/1.6 km), an easy and flat walk with an accompanying interpretive brochure that identifies and describes the flora and fauna. Serious hikers can continue the loop on the **Hillside Trail** for an elevated view of the valley.

After your hike, fill up on a hearty lunch of British comfort food at **The Pelican Inn** (10 Pacific Way, Muir Beach, 415/383-6000, www.pelicaninn.com, 11:30am-9pm Mon.-Fri., 8am-9pm Sat.-Sun., $15-30). Dark wood and a long trestle table give a proper Old English feel to the dimly lit dining room. It's just a short drive from the restaurant to lovely **Muir Beach** (www.nps.gov/goga, sunrise-sunset daily), perfect for wildlife-watching and beachcombing.

End the day with oysters and drinks at the Farley Bar at **Cavallo Point Lodge** (601 Murray Circle, Fort Baker, Sausalito, 415/339-4751, www.cavallopoint.com, 11am-11pm Sun.-Thurs., 11am-midnight Fri.-Sat., $12-56). Snag a blanket and a seat on the porch to watch the fog roll in over the Golden Gate Bridge.

Getting There

Take **US-101 North** out of the city and over the Golden Gate Bridge. Once on the north side of the bay, take the **Stinson Beach/CA-1 exit.** On CA-1, also named the **Shoreline Highway,** follow the road under the freeway and proceed until the road splits at a T junction at the light. Turn left, continuing on Shoreline Highway for 2.5 miles (4 km). At the intersection with **Panoramic Highway,** make a sharp right turn and continue climbing uphill. At the junction of Panoramic Highway and **Muir Woods Road,** turn left and follow the twisting road 1.5 miles (2.4 km) down to the Muir Woods parking lots on the right.

their eyes on where they're going. **Vista Point,** on the bridge's northern end, is a great perch for photos.

A vehicle **toll** (www.bayareafastrak.org) is charged by license plate recognition if you're crossing the bridge into San Francisco by car.

If you're looking for great views or photo ops of the Golden Gate Bridge in the city, head to **Baker Beach, Crissy Field,** or **Lands End.**

Civic Center and Hayes Valley

The Civic Center functions as the heart of San Francisco. Not only is the seat of government here, but so are venerable high-culture institutions: the War Memorial Opera House and Davies Symphony Hall, home of the world-famous San Francisco Symphony. As the Civic Center melts into Hayes Valley, you'll find fabulous hotels and restaurants serving both the city's politicos and the well-heeled.

City Hall

Look at San Francisco's **City Hall** (1 Dr. Carlton B. Goodlett Pl., 415/554-4000, www.sfgov.org, 8am-8pm Mon.-Fri., free) and you'll think you've somehow been transported to Europe. The stately Beaux-Arts building with the gilded dome is the pride of the city and houses the mayor's office and much of the city's government. Inside you'll find a combination of historical grandeur and modern accessibility and convenience as you tour the Arthur Brown Jr.-designed edifice. Docents offer guided hour-long tours (415/554-6139, 10am, noon, and 2pm Mon.-Fri., tour fee may be applicable). You can also just enjoy walking through the parklike square in front of City Hall. Do note that some of the city's unhoused population also often gathers around the park.

Asian Art Museum

Across from City Hall is the **Asian Art Museum** (200 Larkin St., 415/581-3500, www.asianart.org, 10am-5pm Tues.-Wed. and Fri.-Sun., 10am-9pm Thurs., $15 adults, $10 seniors, students, and children 13-17, children 12 and under free), with enormous Ionic columns. Inside you'll have an amazing window into the Asian cultures that have shaped and defined San Francisco and the Bay Area. The second and third floors of this intense museum are packed with great art from all across Asia, including a Chinese gilded Buddha dating from AD 338. The breadth and diversity of Asian culture may stagger you; the museum's displays come from Japan and Vietnam, Buddhist Tibet, and ancient China. Special exhibitions cost extra—check the website to see what will be displayed on the ground-floor galleries when you're in town. The curators regularly rotate items from the permanent

From top to bottom: brick buildings of the Presidio; Golden Gate Bridge in the fog; de Young Museum.

Civic Center, Hayes Valley, Mission, and Castro

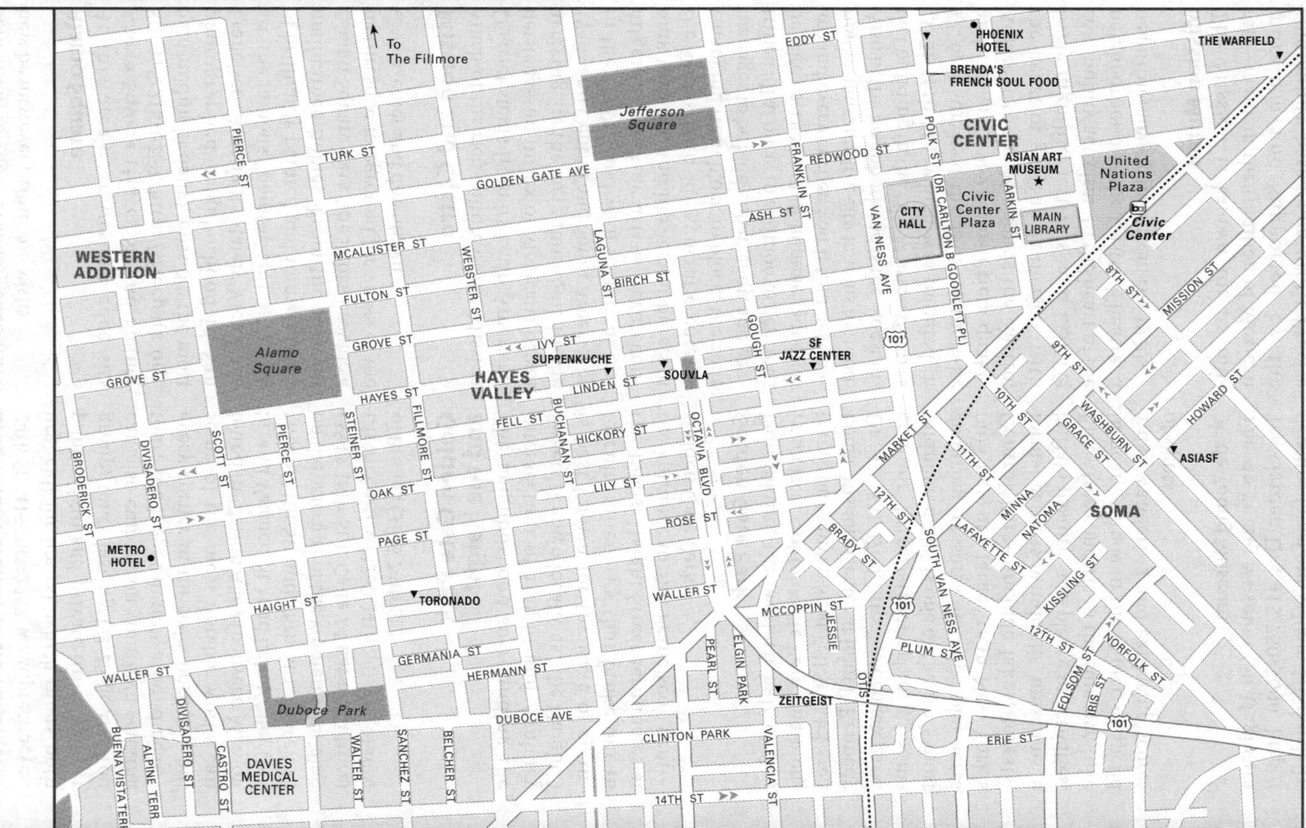
To The Fillmore
EDDY ST
PHOENIX HOTEL
BRENDA'S FRENCH SOUL FOOD
THE WARFIELD
Jefferson Square
CIVIC CENTER
ASIAN ART MUSEUM
United Nations Plaza
PIERCE ST
TURK ST
GOLDEN GATE AVE
REDWOOD ST
FRANKLIN ST
POLK ST (DR CARLTON B GOODLETT PL)
ASH ST
CITY HALL
Civic Center Plaza
LARKIN ST
MAIN LIBRARY
Civic Center
VAN NESS AVE
WESTERN ADDITION
MCALLISTER ST
WEBSTER ST
LAGUNA ST
BIRCH ST
FULTON ST
8TH ST
MISSION ST
Alamo Square
GROVE ST
IVY ST
SUPPENKUCHE
SOUVLA
GOUGH ST
SF JAZZ CENTER
101
9TH ST
GROVE ST
HAYES ST
HAYES VALLEY
LINDEN ST
10TH ST
HOWARD ST
WASHBURN ST
GRACE ST
STEINER ST
FILLMORE ST
FELL ST
BUCHANAN ST
HICKORY ST
OCTAVIA BLVD
MARKET ST
11TH ST
ASIASF
BRODERICK ST
DIVISADERO ST
SCOTT ST
PIERCE ST
OAK ST
LILY ST
MINNA
NATOMA
SOMA
12TH ST
ROSE ST
BRADY ST
LAFAYETTE ST
METRO HOTEL
PAGE ST
SOUTH VAN NESS AVE
KISSLING ST
WALLER ST
HAIGHT ST
TORONADO
MCCOPPIN ST
JESSIE
12TH ST
NORFOLK ST
PLUM ST
GERMANIA ST
HERMANN ST
PEARL ST
ELGIN PARK
OTIS
FOLSOM ST
IRIS ST
WALLER ST
ZEITGEIST
Duboce Park
DUBOCE AVE
CLINTON PARK
ERIE ST
BUENA VISTA TERR
ALPINE TERR
DIVISADERO ST
CASTRO ST
DAVIES MEDICAL CENTER
WALTER ST
SANCHEZ ST
BELCHER ST
14TH ST
VALENCIA ST

collection, so you'll probably encounter new beauty every time you visit.

Alamo Square

At this area's far western edge sits **Alamo Square** (Hayes St. and Steiner St., 415/218-0259, http://sfrecpark.org, 5am-midnight daily), possibly the most photographed neighborhood in San Francisco. Among its stately Victorians are the famous **"painted ladies,"** a row of brilliantly painted and immaculately maintained homes. From the adjacent Alamo Square Park, the ladies provide a picturesque foreground for views of the Civic Center and downtown.

Mission and Castro

Much of the rich culture of the Mission District stems from its Latin American heritage—an influx of Mexicans began arriving in the neighborhood in the 1940s and Central and South Americans in the 1980s—and with its mix of immigrants, working artists, tech economy workers, and hipsters, it bursts at the seams with idiosyncratic energy. Changing from block to block, the zone manages to be blue-collar, edgy, and gentrified all at once. In addition to delicious burritos served out of humble taquerias around every corner, you'll find destination restaurants in a city famous for food. Also in the neighborhood is the oldest intact building in the city, **Mission Dolores** (3321 16th St.), which was founded in 1776; it survived the 1906 earthquake and fire and 1989 Loma Prieta quake. Adjacent to the Mission is the Castro, the heart of gay San Francisco, with lively nightlife, festivals, and LGBTQ community activism. In the heart of the neighborhood is the Castro Theatre, a beautiful movie palace from the 1920s.

Mission Murals

The Mission is known for its murals—many in the tradition of Mexican muralism and supported by the community-based non-profit **Precita Eyes Mural Arts and Visitors Center** (2981 24th St., 415/285-2287, www.precitaeyes.org, call for hours), which offers both public ($20) and private (from $60 per group) tours lasting 1-2.25 hours. You can also embark on your own walking tour; you'll spot murals around nearly every corner in the neighborhood, but some of the most notable works can found in **Clarion Alley** (between Mission St. and Valencia St.) and **Balmy Alley** (between 24th St. and 25th St.), as well as on the exteriors of the **Women's Building** (3543 18th St.), **Calle 24 Latino Cultural District office** (3250 24th St.), and **House of Brakes** (3195 24th St.)

Golden Gate Park and the Haight

The neighborhood surrounding the intersection of Haight and Ashbury Streets (known locally as "the Haight") is best known for the wave of countercultural energy that broke out in the 1960s. Haight Street terminates at the entrance to San Francisco's gem—Golden Gate Park.

Golden Gate Park

Dominating the western half of San Francisco, **Golden Gate Park** (main entrance on Stanyan St. at Fell St., McLaren Lodge Visitors Center at John F. Kennedy Dr., 415/831-2700, http://goldengatepark.com or http://sfrecpark.org, 5am-midnight daily) is one of the city's most enduring treasures. Its 1,000-plus acres (405 ha)—it's larger than New York's Central Park—include lakes, forests, formal gardens, windmills, museums, a buffalo pasture, and plenty of activities. Enjoy free concerts in the summer, hike in near solitude in the winter, or spend a day wandering and exploring scores of sights.

★ de Young Museum

The **de Young Museum** (50 Hagiwara Tea Garden Dr., 415/750-3600, http://deyoung.famsf.org, 9:30am-5:15pm daily,

$15 adults, $12 seniors, $6 students, children 17 and under free) is staggering in its size and breadth: You'll see everything from pre-Columbian art to 17th-century ladies' gowns. View paintings, sculpture, textiles, ceramics, "contemporary crafts" from all over the world, and rotating exhibits that range from King Tut to the exquisite Jean Paul Gaultier collection. Competing with all of that is the building itself.

The museum's modern exterior is wrapped in perforated copper, while the interior incorporates pockets of manicured gardens. Poking out of the park's canopy is a twisted tower that offers spectacular 360-degree views of the city and the bay. Entrance to the museum's tower, as well as its lily pond and art garden, is free.

California Academy of Sciences

A triumph of the sustainable scientific principles it exhibits, the **California Academy of Sciences** (55 Music Concourse Dr., 415/379-8000, www.calacademy.org, 9:30am-5pm Mon.-Sat., 11am-5pm Sun., $40 adults, $35 seniors, students, and children 12-17, $30 children 4-11) drips with ecological perfection. From the grass-covered roof to the underground **aquarium,** visitors can explore every part of the universe. Wander through a steamy endangered **rainforest** contained inside a giant glass bubble, or travel through an all-digital outer space in the high-tech **planetarium.** More studious nature lovers can spend days examining every inch of the **Natural History Museum,** including favorite exhibits like the 87-foot-long (26.5-m) blue whale skeleton. The Academy of Sciences takes pains to make itself kid-friendly, with interactive exhibits, thousands of live animals, and endless opportunities for learning. On **Thursday nights** (6pm-10pm, $15), the academy is an adults-only zone, where DJs play music and the café serves cocktails by some of the city's most renowned mixologists.

Japanese Tea Garden

The **Japanese Tea Garden** (75 Hagiwara Tea Garden Dr., 415/752-4227, www.japaneseteagardensf.com, 9am-5:45pm daily summer, 9am-4:45pm daily winter, $10-12 adults, $7 seniors and children 12-17, $3 children 5-11, children under 5 free) is a haven of peace and tranquility that's a local favorite within the park, particularly in the spring. The planting and design of the garden began in 1894 for the California Exposition. Today the flourishing garden displays a wealth of beautiful flora, including stunning examples of rare Chinese and Japanese plants, some quite old. As you stroll along the paths, you'll come upon sculptures, bridges, ponds, and even traditional *tsukubai* (a tea ceremony sink). Take one of the docent-led tours and conclude your visit with tea and a fortune cookie at the Tea House.

San Francisco Botanical Garden

Take a bucolic walk in the middle of Golden Gate Park by visiting the **San Francisco Botanical Garden** (1199 9th Ave. at Lincoln Way, 415/661-1316, www.sfbg.org, opens 7:30am, closing times vary seasonally, $10-12 adults, $7 seniors and children 12-17, $3 children 5-11, children under 3 free). The 55-acre gardens (22-ha) are home to more than 8,000 species of plants from around the world and include a California Natives garden and a shady redwood forest. Fountains, ponds, meadows, and lawns are interwoven with the flowers and trees to create a peaceful, serene setting in the middle of the crowded city.

Conservatory of Flowers

For a trip to San Francisco's Victorian past, step inside the steamy **Conservatory of Flowers** (100 John F. Kennedy Dr., 415/831-2090, www.conservatoryofflowers.org, 10am-4:30pm Tues.-Sun., $9-11 adults, $6 students, children 12-17 and seniors, $3 children 5-11, children under 4 free). Built in 1878, the striking wood and glass greenhouse is home to more than 1,700 plant species that spill out of containers, twine around rainforest trees, climb trellises reaching the roof, and rim deep ponds where 8-foot (2.4-m) lily pads float serenely on still waters. Surrounded by the exotic flora illuminated only by natural light, it's easy to transport yourself to the heyday of colonialism when the study of botany was in its first bloom. Plus, it's one of the best places to explore on a rainy day. Strollers are not permitted inside; wheelchairs and power chairs are allowed.

Legion of Honor

A beautiful museum in a town filled with beauty, the **Legion of Honor** (100 34th Ave. at Clement St., 415/750-3600, http://legionofhonor.famsf.org, 9:30am-5:15pm Tues.-Sun., $15 adults, $12 seniors, $6 students, children 17 and under free) sits on its lonely promontory in Lincoln Park, overlooking the Golden Gate. A gift to the city from philanthropist Alma Spreckels in 1924, this French Beaux-Arts-style building was built to honor the memory of California soldiers who died in World War I. From its beginning, the Legion of Honor was a museum dedicated to bringing European art to the population of San Francisco. Today visitors can view gorgeous collections of European paintings, sculpture, decorative arts, ancient artifacts from around the Mediterranean, thousands of paper drawings by great artists, and much more. Special exhibitions come from the Legion's own collections and museums of the world.

Entertainment

San Francisco isn't a see-and-be-seen kind of town. You'll find gay clubs, vintage dance clubs, Goth clubs, and the occasional underground burner rave, mixed in with neighborhood watering holes.

Several bus services can ferry your party from club to club. Many of these

the Legion of Honor

offer VIP entrance to clubs and will stop wherever you want to go. **Think Escape** (800/823-7249, www.thinkescape.com) has buses and limos with drivers and guides to get you to the hottest spots with ease.

Nightlife

Union Square and Nob Hill

These ritzy areas are better known for their shopping than their nightlife, but a few bars hang in there, plying weary shoppers with good drinks. Most tend toward the upscale. Some inhabit upper floors of the major hotels, like the **Tonga Room & Hurricane Bar** (950 Mason St., 415/772-5278, www.tongaroom.com, 5pm-11:30pm Wed.-Thurs. and Sun., 5pm-12:30am Fri.-Sat.), where an over-the-top tiki theme adds a whimsical touch to the stately Fairmont Hotel on Nob Hill. Enjoy the tropical atmosphere with a fruity rum drink topped with a classic paper umbrella. Be prepared for the bar's virtual tropical storms that roll in every once in a while.

Part live music venue, part elegant bar, **Top of the Mark** (InterContinental Mark Hopkins, 999 California St., 415/392-3434, www.intercontinentalmarkhopkins.com, 2:30pm-11:30pm Sun.-Thurs., 2:30pm-12:30am Fri.-Sat.) has something for every discerning taste in nighttime entertainment. Since World War II, the views at the top of the InterContinental Mark Hopkins Hotel have drawn visitors to see the city lights. The dress code is business casual or better and is enforced, so leave the jeans in your room. Have a top-shelf martini, and let your toes tap along.

South of the Union Square area in the Tenderloin neighborhood resides a gem: **The Royale** (800 Post St., 415/441-4099, www.theroyalesf.com, 4pm-midnight Sun.-Wed., 4pm-2am Thurs.-Sat.) isn't a typical watering hole by any city's standards, but its intense focus on art fits perfectly with the endlessly eclectic ethos of San Francisco. It hosts free live music every night.

Financial District and SoMa

All those high-powered business suit-clad executive types working in the Financial District need places to drink too. One of these is the **Royal Exchange** (301 Sacramento St., 415/956-1710, http://royalexchange.com, 11am-11pm Mon.-Fri.). This classic pub-style bar has a green-painted exterior, big windows overlooking the street, and a long, narrow barroom. The Royal Exchange serves a full lunch and dinner menu, a small wine list, and a full complement of top-shelf spirits. But most of all, the Exchange serves beer. With 73 taps pouring out 32 different types of beer, the only problem will be choosing one. This watering hole is open to the public only on weekdays; on weekends, it hosts private parties.

In SoMa (South of Market), upscale wine bars have become an evening institution. Among the trendiest you'll find is **District** (216 Townsend St., 415/896-2120, www.districtsf.com, 4pm-close Mon.-Fri., 5pm-close Sat., 11am-2:30pm Sun.). A perfect example of its kind, District features bare brick walls, simple wooden furniture, and a big U-shaped bar at the center of the room with wine glasses hanging above it. While you can get a cocktail or even a beer, the point of coming to District is to sip the finest wines from California, Europe, and beyond. With more than 40 wines available by the glass each night, it's easy to find a favorite, or enjoy a flight of three similar wines to compare. While you can't quite get a full dinner at District, you will find a lovely lounge menu filled with small portions of delicacies to enhance your tasting experience (and perhaps soak up some of the alcohol).

Secret passwords, a hidden library, and an art deco vibe make **Bourbon & Branch** (501 Jones St., 415/346-1735, www.bourbonandbranch.com, 6pm-2am daily, reservations suggested) a must for lovers of the brown stuff. Tucked behind a nameless brown door, this resurrected 1920s-era speakeasy evokes its Prohibition-era past with passwords and secret passages. A business-class elite sips rare bourbon and scotch in dark secluded booths, while those without reservations step into the hidden library.

The **Rickhouse** (246 Kearney St., 415/398-2827, www.rickhousebar.com, 5pm-2am Mon., 3pm-2am Tues.-Fri., 6pm-2am Sat.) feels like a country shack plopped down in the midst of the Financial District. The artisanal cocktail bar draws in the city's plentiful hipsters. It's dimly lit, the walls and floors are wood, and stacks of barrels and old bottles line the mantle. There's also live music on Saturday and Monday nights.

Anchor Steam beer was first brewed in San Francisco back in 1896. **Anchor Public Taps** (495 De Haro St., 415/863-8350, www.anchorbrewing.com, noon-9pm Mon.-Wed., noon-10pm Thurs.-Sat., noon-8pm Sun.) is where you can sip that classic brew, as well as the unique beers of The Portero Project, which are brewed specifically for the public taps. The indoor beer garden hosts beer education events, game nights, and food trucks.

It's dark, it's dank, and it's very Goth. The **Cat Club** (1190 Folsom St., 415/703-8965, www.sfcatclub.com, 9pm-3am Tues.-Sun., cover charge) gets pretty energetic on 1980s dance nights, and it's still a great place to go for their Wednesday Bondage-A-Go-Go nights. Each of the two rooms has its own DJ, which somehow works perfectly even though they're only a wall apart from each other. Check the website to find the right party night for you, and expect the crowd to heat up after 11pm.

Monarch (101 6th St., 415/284-9774, www.monarchsf.com, 5:30pm-2am Tues. and Thurs., 5:30pm-midnight Wed., 5:30pm-2:30am Fri., 9pm-2:30am Sat., 9am-2am Sun.) aims to be a one-stop after-dark venue. Upstairs is a Victorian-inspired cocktail lounge, while the downstairs club hosts international and local DJs. You might also catch offbeat performers like acrobats twirling from the ceilings.

AsiaSF (201 9th St., 415/255-2742, www.asiasf.com, 7:15pm-11pm Sun. and Wed.-Thurs., 7:15pm-2am Fri., 5pm-2am Sat., cover charge) is famous for its transgender performers and servers, "The Ladies of AsiaSF." Weekend reservations for dinner and a show include free admission to the dance floor downstairs.

North Beach

Jack Kerouac loved **Vesuvio** (255 Columbus Ave., 415/362-3370, www.vesuvio.com, 8am-2am daily), which is why it's probably North Beach's most famous saloon. This cozy, bilevel hideout is an easy place to spend the afternoon with a pint of Anchor Steam. Its eclectic decor includes tables decorated with tarot cards.

To find **15 Romolo** (15 Romolo Pl.,

Side Trip to Napa

TOP EXPERIENCE

For oenophiles, no trip to California is complete without an excursion to the state's renowned wine country. Though the main draw is sampling wines at their source, Napa offers multiple ways to spoil yourself, including spas, fine hotels, revered restaurants, and understated natural beauty. It's less than 100 miles (161 km) north of San Francisco, about an hour's drive if traffic is light.

The city of Napa is located on the southern end of Napa Valley, with a scenic downtown perched on the Napa River. For an introduction to the area's vibrant food and wine scene, visit the **Oxbow Public Market** (610 and 644 1st St., 707/226-6529, www.oxbowpublicmarket.com, 9am-5pm Mon.-Thurs., 9am-8pm Fri.-Sun.), which has food vendors, produce markets, and cafés.

A multitude of vineyards are strung along the Silverado Trail and CA-29, two roads that head north out of the city of Napa and into serious wine country. Grape vines braid the scenic valley as you drive through the towns of Rutherford, St. Helena, and Calistoga. **Grgich Hills Estate** (1829 St. Helena Hwy., Rutherford, 707/963-2784, www.grgich.com, 9:30am-4:30pm daily, tasting $40) is the winery of Mike Grgich, who crafted the chardonnay for the Chateau Montelena that put Napa Valley on the map with a win at the Paris Wine Tasting of 1976. **Mumm** (8445 Silverado Trail, Rutherford, 866/783-5826 or 707/967-7700, www.mummnapa.com, 10am-6pm daily, tasting $20-35) produces sparkling wines worth a taste even for wine purists and has a patio, indoor salon, and terrace for sipping. **Clos Pegase** (1060 Dunaweal Ln., Calistoga, 707/942-4981 or 866/474-3021, www.clospegase.com, 10am-5pm daily, tasting $30-45) mixes in some culture with its wine, with over 100 artworks on the grounds, including sculptor Henry Moore's *Mother Earth* and a painting by Francis Bacon.

There is a range of options for staying overnight (and sleeping off an afternoon of wine tasting). One of the more luxurious is **Auberge du Soleil** (180 Rutherford Hill Rd., St. Helena, 707/963-1211, www.aubergedusoleil.com, $875-5,200). A less expensive option is St. Helena's **El Bonita Motel** (195 Main St./CA-29, 800/541-3284, www.elbonita.com, $160-345), which is within walking distance of the historic downtown and has a 1950s motel charm.

Getting There

To reach CA-29, the central conduit that runs north into the valley from the city of Napa, from San Francisco, take **US-101 North** across the Golden Gate Bridge to Novato. In Novato, take the exit for **CA-37 East** to Napa. CA-37 skirts the tip of the San Pablo Bay and runs all the way to Vallejo. From Vallejo, take **CA-29 (Sonoma Blvd.) North** for 7 miles (11.3 km) until you reach downtown Napa. CA-29 will take you as far north as Calistoga.

415/398-1359, www.15romolo.com, 5pm-2am daily), you'll have to hike up a steep little alley (Fresno St. crosses Romolo Pl., which can be hard to find). You'll love the creative cocktails, edgy jukebox music, and often mellow crowd. The bar is smallish and can get crowded on the weekend, so come on a weeknight if you prefer a quiet drink.

Known for its colorful clientele and cluttered decor, **Specs'** (12 William Saroyan Pl., 415/421-4112, 3pm-2am daily, cash only) is a dive bar located in a North Beach alley. Its full name is the Specs' Twelve Adler Museum Café due to the many oddities on display, including a mounted Alaskan king crab and a mummified walrus penis.

Marina

Marina and Pacific Heights denizens enjoy a good glass of vino. The **Bacchus Wine Bar** (1954 Hyde St., 415/928-2633, www.bacchussf.com, 5:30pm-11pm daily) is a tiny local watering hole that offers an array of wines, sake cocktails, and craft beers.

The Marina District's Chestnut Street is known for its high-end restaurants and swanky clientele. The **Horseshoe Tavern** (2024 Chestnut St., 415/346-1430, noon-2am Mon.-Wed., 7am-2am Thurs.-Sun.) is a place for people to let their hair down, shoot pool, and drink without pretension.

Get to really know your fellow beer drinkers at the tiny **Black Horse London Pub** (1514 Union St., 415/928-2414, www.blackhorselondon.com, 5pm-midnight Mon.-Thurs., 2pm-midnight Fri., 11am-2am Sat.-Sun., cash only), which can accommodate just nine people. Bottles of beer are served from a claw-foot bathtub located behind the bar.

Hayes Valley

Hayes Valley bleeds into Lower Haight (Haight St. between Divisadero St. and Octavia Blvd.) and supplies most of the neighborhood bars. For proof that the independent spirit of the Haight lives on despite encroaching commercialism, stop in and have a drink at the **Toronado** (547 Haight St., 415/863-2276, www.toronado.com, 11:30am-2am daily), a grimy cathedral to superb beer. This dimly lit haven with a metal- and punk rock-heavy jukebox maintains one of the finest beer selections in the nation, with a changing roster of several dozen microbrews on tap, including Russian River Brewing Company's Pliny the Elder, one of the most sought after beers in the state.

If you'd rather drink a cocktail than a beer, head over to **Smuggler's Cove** (650 Gough St., 415/869-1900, http://smugglerscovesf.com, 5pm-1:15am daily). The drink menu includes 70 cocktails and an impressive number of rare rums.

Mission

Trick Dog (3010 20th St., 415/471-2999, www.trickdogbar.com, 3pm-2am daily) is shaking up the city's cocktail scene. A new bar menu is unveiled every six months and features 12 creative cocktails. The menus are as playful as the drinks, presented as dog calendars, catalogs of paint swatch samples, and airline brochures. A small food menu includes thrice-cooked fries, a burger, and a standout kale salad.

Expect to hear some old-school vinyl from a lo-fi record player in the dimly lit **Royal Cuckoo** (3202 Mission St., 415/550-8667, http://royalcuckoo.com, 4pm-2am Mon.-Thurs., 3pm-2am Fri.-Sat., 3pm-midnight Sun.). There's also live music played on a vintage Hammond B3 organ Wednesday-Sunday. The cocktail list includes variations on the classics, including a sour old-fashioned.

Excellent draft beers, tasty barbecue plates, and a motorcycle-inclined crowd give **Zeitgeist** (199 Valencia St., 415/255-7505, www.zeitgeistsf.com, 9am-2am daily) a punk-rock edge. This Mission favorite, though, endears itself to all sorts, thanks to its spacious outdoor beer garden, 64 beers on tap, and popular Bloody Marys.

Get a sweeping view of the city with superb South American cocktails at **El Techo de Lolinda** (2516 Mission St., 415/654-5211, http://eltechosf.com, 4pm-10:30pm Mon.-Thurs., 4pm-12:30am Fri., 11am-12:30am Sat., 11am-10:30pm Sun.), a rooftop bar associated with the Argentinean steak house Lolinda, on the ground floor. The bar serves pitchers of margaritas and features agave- and rum-based drinks. The small food menu includes superb snacks like empanadas, ceviche, and a variety of skewers.

Just outside the Mission's southern edge, **St. Mary's Pub** (3845 Mission St., 415/529-1325, www.stmaryspub.com, 4pm-2am Mon.-Fri., noon-2am Sat.-Sun.) opened in 1933 right after Prohibition was repealed, and old tales swirl around the bar. A murder may have occurred here, and there might be a ghost that roams among the red banquettes. What is known is that St. Mary's Pub serves one of the best Bloody Marys in town, including a version made with masala sauce and another with sake and wasabi.

The Haight

Haight Street crowds head out in droves to the **Alembic** (1725 Haight St., 415/666-0822, http://alembicsf.com, 4pm-midnight Tues.-Wed., 4pm-2am Thurs.-Fri., 11am-2am Sat., 11am-midnight Sun.) for artisanal cocktails. On par with the whiskey and bourbon menu is the cuisine.

Hobson's Choice (1601 Haight St., 415/621-5859, www.hobsonschoice.com, noon-2am daily) claims the largest selection of rums in the country. Try your rum in everything from a Brazilian caipirinha to a Cuban mojito, or in one of Hobson's famous rum punches.

Featured in an episode of Anthony Bourdain's travel show *No Reservations,* **Aub Zam Zam** (1633 Haight St., 415/861-2545, 3pm-2am Mon.-Fri., 1pm-2am Sat.-Sun.) is an old-school bar with an Arabian feel. Zam Zam doesn't take credit cards, but it does have an Arabian mural behind the U-shaped bar, where an interesting mix of locals and visitors congregate for the cheap drinks.

Located at the west end of Golden Gate Park, the **Beach Chalet Brewery** (1000 Great Hwy., 415/386-8439, www.beachchalet.com, 9am-9:30pm daily) is an attractive brewpub and restaurant directly across the street from Ocean Beach. Sip a pale ale while watching the sunset, and check out the historical murals downstairs.

Gay and Lesbian

San Francisco's gay nightlife has earned a worldwide rep for both the quantity and quality of options, especially in its famed **Castro** neighborhood. In fact, the gay club scene totally outdoes the straight club scene for frolicsome, fabulous fun. While the city's queer nightlife caters more to gay men than to lesbians, there's plenty of space available for partiers of all persuasions. For a more comprehensive list of San Francisco's queer bars and clubs, visit http://sanfrancisco.gaycities.com/bars.

One of the best bars in the Castro is called simply **Q Bar** (456 Castro St., 415/864-2877, www.qbarsf.com, 4pm-2am Mon.-Fri., 2pm-2am Sat.-Sun.). Just look for the red neon Bar sign set in steel out front. Inside, expect to find the fabulous red decor known as "retro-glam," delicious top-shelf cocktails, and thrumming beats spun by popular DJs almost every night of the week. Unlike many Castro establishments, the Q Bar caters to pretty much everybody: gay men, gay women, and straight allies. You'll find a coat check and adequate restroom facilities, and the strength of the drinks will make you want to take off your jacket and stay awhile.

Looking for a stylin' gay bar turned club, Castro style? Head for **Badlands** (4121 18th St., 415/626-9320, www.sfbadlands.com, 3pm-2am Mon.-Thurs. and Sat., 2pm-2am Fri. and Sun.). This Castro icon was once an old-school bar with pool tables on the floor and license plates on the walls. Now you'll find an always-crowded dance floor, au courant peppy pop music, ever-changing video screens, gay men out for a good time, and straight women who count themselves as regulars at this friendly establishment, which attracts a youngish but mixed-age crowd. The dance floor gets packed and hot, especially on weekend nights. There's a coat check on the bottom level.

The Lookout (3600 16th St., 415/431-0306, www.lookoutsf.com, 3:30pm-2am Mon.-Fri., 12:30pm-2am Sat.-Sun., cover charge) gets its name and much of its rep from its balcony overlooking the iconic Castro neighborhood. Get up there for some primo people-watching as you sip your industrial-strength alcoholic concoctions and nibble on surprisingly edible bar snacks and pizza (kitchen hours 4pm-10pm Mon. and Wed.-Fri., 3pm-11pm Sat., 3pm-10pm Sun.). Special events come with a cover charge.

Yes, there's a Western-themed gay bar in San Francisco. **The Cinch Saloon** (1723 Polk St., 415/776-4162, 9am-2am Mon.-Fri., 8am-2am Sat.-Sun.) has a laid-back (no pun intended), friendly, male-oriented vibe that's all but lost in the once gay, now gentrified Polk Street hood. Expect fewer females and strong drinks to go with the unpretentious decor and atmosphere.

Live Music

In the late 1960s, **The Fillmore** (1805 Geary Blvd., tickets 800/745-3000, 415/346-3000, www.thefillmore.com, prices vary) became legendary for performances by rock acts like the Grateful Dead, Jefferson Airplane, and Carlos Santana. These days, all sorts of national touring acts stop by, sometimes for multiple nights. The Fillmore is also known for its distinctive poster art: Attendees to certain sold-out shows are given commemorative posters.

With its marble columns and ornate balconies, the **Great American Music Hall** (859 O'Farrell St., 415/885-0750, www.slimspresents.com, prices vary) has hosted live entertainment since 1907. It is also one of the nicest places to see a nationally touring act in the city, with bragging rights for shows by Arcade Fire and the legendary Patti Smith.

The beautiful **Warfield** (982 Market St., 415/345-0900, www.thewarfieldtheatre.com, prices vary) books all sorts of acts, from The Growlers to the Wu-Tang Clan. Choose from limited table seating on the lowest level (mostly by reservation), reserved seats in the balconies, or open standing in the orchestra below the stage.

The **Boom Boom Room** (1601 Fillmore St., 415/673-8000, www.boomboomroom.com, 4pm-2am Sun. and Tues.-Thurs., 4pm-3am Fri.-Sat., prices vary) has kept it real in the Fillmore for more than two decades. Today you'll find the latest in a legacy of live blues, boogie, groove, soul, and funk music in this fun, divey joint.

On the other side of town, **Biscuits & Blues** (401 Mason St., 415/292-2583, www.biscuitsandblues.com, 6pm-11pm Wed.-Thurs., 5:30pm-11:30pm Fri., 5pm-11pm Sat., 5:30pm-10:30pm Sun., prices vary) is a local musicians' favorite. Headliners have included Joe Louis Walker, Jimmy Thackery, and Jim Kimo. Dinner is served nightly and features a surprisingly varied and upscale menu.

Bringing jazz to the high culture of Hayes Valley is **SFJazz Center** (201 Franklin St., 866/920-5299, http://sfjazz.org, prices vary) a stunning 35,000-square-foot (3,251-sq-m) space with state-of-the-art acoustics. It's designed to feel like a small club, thanks to steep seating that brings the large audience close to the performers and has drawn major acts such as Herbie Hancock and the Afro-Cuban All Stars.

Comedy

Cobb's Comedy Club (915 Columbus Ave., 415/928-4320, www.cobbscomedy.com, shows 7:30pm, 8pm, 9:45pm, 10:15pm Thurs.-Sun., cover varies, two-drink minimum) has played host to star comedians, such as Sarah Silverman and Margaret Cho, since 1982. The 425-seat venue offers a full dinner menu and a bar to slake your thirst. Be sure to check your show's start time—some comics don't follow the usual Cobb's schedule.

The Arts

Theater

San Francisco may not be known as a big theater town, but it does boast a number of small and large theaters.

Just up from Union Square, the traditional San Francisco theater district continues to entertain crowds. The **American**

Conservatory Theater (A.C.T., 415 Geary St., 415/749-2228, www.act-sf.org, shows Tues.-Sun., prices vary) puts on a season filled with big-name, big-budget productions, such as high-production-value musicals, classics by the likes of Sam Shepard and Somerset Maugham, and intriguing new works. They perform plays in **The Geary Theater** (405 Geary St.), a venue near Union Square that was nearly destroyed by the 1989 Loma Prieta earthquake, and at the more intimate **The Strand Theater** (1127 Market St.).

The **Curran Theatre** (445 Geary St., 415/358-1220, http://sfcurran.com, prices vary), next door to A.C.T., has a state-of-the-art stage for high-budget productions, such as *Fun Home* and *Harry Potter and The Cursed Child*. Expect to pay a premium for tickets to these productions, which can sometimes run for months or even years. Check the schedule for current shows.

Classical Music and Opera

Right around the Civic Center, culture takes a turn for the upscale. This is the neighborhood where the ultra-rich and not-so-rich classics lovers come to enjoy a night out. Acoustically renovated in 1992, **Davies Symphony Hall** (201 Van Ness Ave., 415/864-6000, www.sfsymphony.org) is home to the world-renowned **San Francisco Symphony.** Loyal patrons flock to performances that range from the classic to the avant-garde. Whether you want to hear Mozart and Mahler or classic rock blended with major symphony orchestra, the San Francisco Symphony does it.

The **War Memorial Opera House** (401 Van Ness Ave., 415/621-6600, http://sfwarmemorial.org), a Beaux-Arts-style building designed by Coit Tower and City Hall architect Arthur Brown Jr., houses the **San Francisco Opera** (415/864-3330, http://sfopera.com) and **San Francisco Ballet** (415/865-2000, www.sfballet.org). Tours are available (415/552-8338, 10am-2pm Mon., $5-7).

Cinema

The **Castro Theatre** (429 Castro St., 415/621-6120, www.castrotheatre.com, $9-12) is a grand movie palace from the 1920s that has enchanted San Francisco audiences for almost a century. The Castro Theatre hosts everything from revival double features (from black-and-white through 1980s classics) to musical movie sing-alongs, live shows, and even the occasional book signing. The Castro also screens current releases and documentaries about queer life in San Francisco and beyond. Once inside, be sure to admire the lavish interior decor. If you get to your seat early, you're likely to be rewarded with a performance of the Mighty Wurlitzer pipe organ before the show.

Festivals and Events

San Francisco is host to numerous events year-round. Following are some of the biggest that are worth planning a trip around.

During the **Chinese New Year Parade** (Chinatown, 415/982-3000, http://chineseparade.com, Feb.), Chinatown celebrates the Lunar New Year with a parade of costumed dancers, floats, and firecrackers.

Join rowdy, costumed revelers for **Bay to Breakers** (Embarcadero to Great Highway, http://capstoneraces.com/bay-to-breakers.com, May), a 12K run/walk/stumble across the city through Golden Gate Park to a massive street party at Ocean Beach.

One of the year's biggest parties is the **San Francisco LGBT Pride Parade and Celebration** (Market St., 415/864-0831, www.sfpride.org, June). On the last weekend in June, the streets around City Hall close to traffic for a massive block party, with multiple stages and performers. For the main parade, which takes place on Sunday, hundreds of thousands of people of all orientations take to the streets for this quintessentially San Franciscan party-cum-social justice movement. Numerous other events and festivities take place around the city leading up to the main march, including the Trans March on the preceding Friday and the Dyke March and Rally—which typically begins at Dolores Park and ends in the Castro—the preceding Saturday.

Golden Gate Park is host to two wildly popular summer music festivals. **Outside Lands** (www.sfoutsidelands.com, Aug.) is a three-day music festival that floods the park with revelers, food trucks, and hundreds of bands. Headliners have included Paul Simon, Childish Gambino, Metallica, Neil Young, Janet Jackson, and Elton John. The park barely recovers in time for **Hardly Strictly Bluegrass** (www.hardlystrictlybluegrass.com, first weekend in Oct.), a free music festival celebrating a wide variety of sounds (not just bluegrass), from Lucinda Williams and Emmylou Harris to Robert Plant and Fantastic Negrito.

Shopping

Union Square

For the biggest variety of department stores and high-end international designers, plus a few select boutiques, locals and visitors alike flock to **Union Square** (bounded by Geary St., Stockton St., Post St., and Powell St.). The shopping area includes more than just the square proper: More designer and brand-name stores cluster for several blocks in all directions.

The big guys anchor Union Square. **Macy's** (170 O'Farrell St., 415/397-3333, www.macys.com, 10am-9pm Mon.-Sat., 11am-7pm Sun.) has two immense locations, one for women's clothing and another for the men's store and housewares. **Neiman Marcus** (150 Stockton St., 415/362-3900, www.neimanmarcus.com, 10am-7pm Mon.-Wed. and Fri.-Sat., 10am-8pm Thurs., noon-6pm Sun.) is a favorite among high-budget shoppers, and **Saks Fifth Avenue** (384 Post St., 415/986-4300, www.saksfifthavenue.com, 10am-7pm Mon.-Wed., 10am-8pm Thurs.-Sat., noon-7pm Sun.) adds a touch of New York style to funky-but-wealthy San Francisco.

Levi's (815 Market St., 415/501-0100, www.levi.com, 9am-9pm Mon.-Sat., 10am-8pm Sun.) may be a household name, but this three-floor fashion emporium offers incredible customization services while featuring new music and emerging art. Levi's got its start outfitting gold miners in 1849, so it's literally a San Francisco tradition.

The bones of fashion can be found at **Britex Fabrics** (117 Post St., 415/392-2910, www.britexfabrics.com, 10am-6pm Mon.-Sat.), which draws designers, quilters, DIYers, and costume geeks from all over the Bay Area to its legendary monument to fabric. If you're into any sort of textile crafting, a visit to Britex has the qualities of a religious experience. All

four floors are crammed floor to ceiling with bolts of fabric, swaths of lace, and rolls of ribbon. From $1-per-yard grosgrain ribbons to $95-per-yard French silk jacquard and $125-per-yard Italian wool coating, Britex has it all.

North Beach

One of the most famous independent bookshops in a city known for its literary bent is **City Lights** (261 Columbus Ave., 415/362-8193, www.citylights.com, 10am-midnight daily). It opened in 1953 as an all-paperback bookstore with a decidedly Beat aesthetic, focused on selling modern literary fiction and progressive political tomes. As the Beats flocked to San Francisco and to City Lights, the shop put on another hat—that of publisher. Allen Ginsberg's *Howl* was published by the erstwhile independent, which never looked back. Today City Lights continues to sell and publish the best of cutting-edge fiction and nonfiction.

Marina and Pacific Heights

The shopping is good in the tony Marina and its elegant neighbor Pacific Heights. **Chestnut and Union Streets** cater to the Marina's young and affluent residents with plenty of clothing boutiques and makeup outlets. Make a stop at **Books Inc.** (2251 Chestnut St., 415/931-3633, www.booksinc.net, 9am-10pm Mon.-Sat., 9am-9pm Sun.), one of the best bookstores in the city. You'll find everything from fiction to travel, as well as a great selection of magazines.

Fillmore Street is another major shopping corridor. It's funkier than its younger neighbors in the Marina, probably because of its proximity to Japantown and the Fillmore.

Hayes Valley

In Hayes Valley, adjacent to the Civic Center, shopping goes uptown, but the unique scent of counterculture creativity still permeates. This is a fun neighborhood to get your stroll on, checking

City Lights bookstore

out the art galleries and peeking into the boutiques for clothing and upscale housewares, and then stopping at one of the lovely cafés for a restorative bite to eat.

Paolo Iantorno's boutique **Paolo Shoes** (524 Hayes St., 415/552-4580, http://paoloshoes.com, 11am-7pm Mon.-Sat., 11am-6pm Sun.) showcases his collection of handcrafted shoes, for which all leather and textiles are conscientiously selected and then inspected to ensure top quality.

Miette (449 Octavia St., 415/626-6221, www.miette.com, 11am-7pm daily) is a cheery European-inspired candy shop, sister store to the Ferry Plaza bakery (Shop 10, 415/837-0300, 9am-7pm Mon.-Fri., 8am-7pm Sat., 10am-6pm Sun.). From macarons to double-salted licorice to handmade English toffee, the quality confections include imports from England, Italy, and France.

Mission

In a city known for its quirky style, the Mission was the last neighborhood with a funky, easy-on-the-wallet shopping district. Sadly, the days are gone when you could buy cool vintage clothes by the pound, but **Valencia Street** is still the most vibrant and diverse neighborhood for shoppers in the city.

Author Dave Eggers's tongue-in-cheek storefront at **826 Valencia** (826 Valencia St., 415/642-5905, www.826valencia.org, 9:30am-6pm Mon.-Fri.) doubles as a pirate supply shop and youth literacy center. While you'll find plenty of pirate booty, you'll also find a good stock of literary magazines and books. Almost next door, **Paxton Gate** (824 Valencia St., 415/824-1872, www.paxtongate.com, 11am-7pm Sun.-Wed., 11am-8pm Thurs.-Sat.) takes the typical gift shop to a new level with taxidermy. This quirky spot is

From top to bottom: the Castro Theatre; Haight-Ashbury neighborhood; biking along Ocean Beach.

surprisingly cheery, with garden supplies, books, and candles filling the cases in addition to the fossilized creatures.

Haight-Ashbury

The **Haight-Ashbury shopping district** isn't what it used to be, but if you're willing to poke around a bit, you can still find a few bargains in the remaining thrift shops. One relic of the 1960s counterculture still thrives on the Haight: head shops.

Music has always been a part of the Haight. To this day, you'll find homeless folks pounding out rhythms on *doumbeks* and congas on the sidewalks and on Hippy Hill in the park. Located in an old bowling alley, **Amoeba Music** (1855 Haight St., 415/831-1200, www.amoeba.com, 11am-8pm daily) is a larger-than-life record store that promotes every type of music imaginable. Amoeba's staff, many of whom are musicians themselves, are among the most knowledgeable in the business.

Award-winning **The Booksmith** (1644 Haight St., 415/863-8688, www.booksmith.com, 10am-10pm Mon.-Sat., 10am-8pm Sun.) boasts a helpful and informed staff, a fabulous magazine collection, and Northern California's preeminent calendar of readings by internationally renowned authors.

Originally a vaudeville theater, the capacious **Wasteland** (1660 Haight St., 415/863-3150, www.shopwasteland.com, 11am-8pm Mon.-Sat., 11am-7pm Sun.) has a traffic-stopping art nouveau facade, a distinctive assortment of vintage hippie and rock-star threads, and a glamour-punk staff.

Recreation

Beaches

Ocean Beach

San Francisco boasts of being a city that has everything, and it certainly comes close. This massive urban wonderland even claims several genuine sand beaches within its city limits. No doubt the biggest and most famous of these is **Ocean Beach** (Great Hwy., parking at Sloat Blvd., Golden Gate Park, and the Cliff House, 415/561-3003, www.parksconservancy.org). This 4-mile (6.4-km) stretch of sand forms the breakwater for the Pacific Ocean along the whole west side of the city. Because it's so large, you're likely to find a spot to sit down and maybe even a parking place along the beach, except perhaps on that rarest of occasions in San Francisco—a sunny, warm day. Don't go out for an ocean swim at Ocean Beach: Extremely dangerous rip currents cause fatalities every year.

It may be hard to believe that you can surf in San Francisco, but Ocean Beach has a series of beach breaks that are good in the fall and monstrous in the winter. It's not for beginners, and even accomplished surfers can find it difficult to paddle out. Five blocks from the beach, **Aqua Surf Shop** (3847 Judah St., 415/242-9283, www.aquasurfshop.com, 10am-5:30pm Sun.-Tues., 10am-7pm Wed.-Sat., surfboard rentals $25-35 per day, wetsuits $15 per day) rents shortboards, longboards, and the very necessary 4/3 wetsuit.

Aquatic Park

The beach at **Aquatic Park** (Beach St. and Hyde St., 415/298-8826, www.nps.gov/safr) sits at the west end of the Fisherman's Wharf tourist area. This makes Aquatic Park incredibly convenient for visitors who want to grab a picnic on the Wharf to enjoy down on the beach. It was built in the late 1930s as a bathhouse catering to wealthy San Franciscans, and today, swimming remains one of Aquatic Park's main attractions: Triathletes and hardcore swimmers brave the frigid waters to swim for miles in the protected cove. More sedate visitors can find a seat and enjoy a cup of coffee, a newspaper, and some people-watching.

Baker Beach

Baker Beach (Golden Gate Point and the Presidio, 415/561-4323, www.parksconservancy.org) is best known for its lovely views of the Golden Gate Bridge. It was also the birthplace of Burning Man in 1986. Currents get seriously strong and dangerous here, so this isn't a place to go swimming, but it's popular for sunbathing, flying kites, playing volleyball and Frisbee, and just strolling the stretch of sand. The northern end of the beach, closer to the Golden Gate Bridge, is clothing-optional. Baker is much smaller than Ocean Beach and often gets crowded in the summer; parking can be challenging, so consider catching a Muni 29 line bus, taxi, or ride-hailing service.

Parks

Golden Gate Park

The largest park in San Francisco is **Golden Gate Park** (main entrance at Stanyan St. and Fell St., McLaren Lodge Visitors Center at John F. Kennedy Dr., 415/831-2700, http://goldengatepark.com). In addition to housing popular sights like the **Academy of Sciences,** the **de Young,** and the **Japanese Tea Garden,** Golden Gate Park is San Francisco's unofficial playground. There are three botanical gardens, a **children's playground** (Martin Luther King Jr. Dr. and Bowling Green Dr.), tennis courts, and a golf course. **Stow Lake** (415/386-2531, http://stowlakeboathouse.com, 10am-5pm daily, $22-38 per hour) offers paddleboats for rent, and the park even has its own bison paddock. Weekends find the park filled with locals inline skating, biking, hiking, and even Lindy Hopping. John F. Kennedy Drive east of Transverse Drive is closed to motorists every Saturday April-September and Sunday year-round for pedestrian-friendly fun.

Crissy Field

Crissy Field (Marina Blvd. and Baker St., 415/561-3000, www.parksconservancy.org), with its beaches, restored wetlands,

view of Golden Gate Bridge from Baker Beach

wide promenade, and iconic views of the Golden Gate Bridge, is the playground of the **Presidio** (415/561-5300, www.presidio.gov, free). It's part of the Golden Gate National Recreation Area and is dedicated to environmental education. At the **Crissy Field Center** (1199 E. Beach, 415/561-7690, 8:30am-4:30pm daily) you'll find a list of classes, seminars, and fun hands-on activities for all ages. Many of these include walks out into the marsh and the Presidio.

Lands End

The **Lands End Trail** (Merrie Way, 415/561-4700, www.nps.gov/goga) is part of the Golden Gate National Recreation Area. Rising above rugged cliffs and beaches, Lands End (3 mi/4.8 km round-trip, 1.5 hours, easy) feels wild, but the trail from the **Lands End Lookout visitors center** (680 Point Lobos Ave., 415/426-5240, www.parksconservancy.org, 9am-5pm daily)—grab a cup of hot chocolate while you're there—to Eagle's Point near the Legion of Honor is perfect for any hiking enthusiast and on a clear day gives great views of the Golden Gate Bridge. For a longer adventure, there are plenty of auxiliary trails to explore that lead down to little beaches. You can also wander down to the ruins of the **Sutro Baths,** built in the 1890s by a self-made millionaire. Be sure to look out for the remains of three shipwrecks on the rocks of Point Lobos at low tide.

Dolores Park

If you're looking for a park where the most strenuous activity is people-watching, then head to **Mission Dolores Park** (Dolores St. and 19th St., 415/831-2700, http://sfrecpark.org, 6am-10pm daily). Usually called Dolores Park and situated in the Mission just adjacent to the Castro, it's a favorite of neighborhood locals and many others, with its gorgeous views of the city skyline. Bring a beach blanket to sprawl on the lawn and a picnic lunch supplied by one of the excellent nearby eateries. On weekends, festivals and cultural events often spring up at Dolores Park and, especially on sunny days, it has a party atmosphere.

Biking

In other places, bicycling is a sport or a mode of transportation. In San Francisco, bicycling is a religion. Some might say that the high church of this religion is the **San Francisco Bike Coalition** (415/431-2453, http://sfbike.org). In addition to providing workshops and hosting events, the Bike Coalition is an excellent resource for anyone who wants to cycle through the city. Check out its website for tips, maps, and rules of the road.

Newcomers to biking in the city may want to start off gently, with a guided tour that avoids areas with dangerous traffic. **Blazing Saddles** (2715 Hyde St., 415/202-8888, www.blazingsaddles.com, $8-9 per hour, $25-98 per day) rents bikes and offers tips on where to go. There are five locations, most in the Fisherman's

Twin Peaks

San Francisco from Twin Peaks

Twin Peaks rises up from the center of San Francisco and is the second-highest point in the city. Twin Peaks divides the city between north and south, catching the fog bank that rolls in from the Golden Gate and providing a habitat for lots of wild birds and insects, including the endangered Mission blue butterfly. Be sure to head to Twin Peaks on a sunny day; if the fog is in, as so often happens in the summertime, you won't see much.

While you'll barely need to get out of your car to enjoy the stunning 360-degree views of the city from the peaks, the best way to enjoy the views is to take a short hike. To scale the less-traveled **South Peak,** start at the pullout on the road below the parking lot. You'll climb a steep set of stairs up to the top of the South Peak in less than 0.2 mile (0.3 km). Stop and marvel at human industry: the communications tower that's the massive eyesore just over the peak. Carefully cross the road to access the red-rock stairway up to the **North Peak.** It's only 0.25 mile (0.4 km), but as with the South Peak, those stairs seem to go straight up! It's worth it when you look out across the Golden Gate to Mount Tamalpais in the north and Mount Diablo in the east.

Getting There

Drive west up **Market Street,** veering right onto **17th Street.** In a couple of hundred feet, turn left onto **Clayton Street,** which becomes **Twin Peaks Boulevard,** following it up to the top. Parking is free, and Twin Peaks is open year-round.

Wharf area. If you prefer the safety of a group, take the guided tour (10am, 1pm, and 4pm daily, 3 hours, $55 adults, $35 children, reservations required) through San Francisco and across the Golden Gate Bridge into Marin County. One of the most popular treks is the easy and flat 9-mile (14.5-km) ride across the **Golden Gate Bridge** and back. This is a great way to see the bridge and the bay for the first time, and it takes only an hour or two to complete. Another option is to ride across the bridge, stopping for a great photo op at **Vista Point,** and continuing into the town of Sausalito (8 mi/12.9 km) or Tiburon (16 mi/26 km); enjoy an afternoon and dinner, and then ride the ferry back into the city (bikes are allowed on board).

Other easy and low-stress options are the paved paths of **Golden Gate Park** (main entrance at Stanyan St. and Fell St., McLaren Lodge Visitors Center at John F. Kennedy Dr., 415/831-2700, http://goldengatepark.com) and the **Presidio** (Montgomery St. and Lincoln Blvd., 415/561-4323, www.nps.gov/prsf). A bike makes a perfect mode of transportation to explore the various museums and attractions of these two large parks, and you can spend all day and never have to worry about finding parking. At the entrance of Golden Gate Park, **Golden Gate Tours & Bike Rentals** (1816 Haight St., 415/922-4537, www.goldengateparkbikerental.com, Apr.-Oct. 9am-7pm daily, Nov.-Mar. 9am-5pm daily, $8-15 per hour, $40-80 per day) has a kiosk. **Golden Gate Park Bike and Skate** (3038 Fulton St., 415/668-1117, http://goldengateparkbikeandskate.com, summer 10am-6pm Mon.-Fri., 10am-7pm Sat.-Sun., winter 10am-5pm Mon.-Fri., 10am-6pm Sat.-Sun., $5-15 per hour, $25-75 per day) is just north of the park on Fulton near the de Young Museum.

Whale-Watching

With day-trip access to the marine sanctuary off the Farallon Islands, whale-watching is a year-round activity in San Francisco. **San Francisco Whale Tours** (Pier 39, Dock B, 415/706-7364, www.sanfranciscowhaletours.com, tours daily, $45-99) offers six-hour trips out to the Farallons almost every Saturday and Sunday, with almost-guaranteed whale sightings on each trip. Shorter whale-watching trips along the coastline run on weekdays, and 90-minute quickie trips out to see slightly smaller local wildlife, including elephant seals and sea lions, also go out daily. Children ages 3-15 are welcome on boat tours (for reduced rates), and kids often love the chance to spot whales, sea lions, and pelicans. Children under age three are not permitted for safety reasons.

Spectator Sports

Lovers of the big leagues will find fun in San Francisco. Major League Baseball's **San Francisco Giants** (www.mlb.com/giants), winners of the 2010, 2012, and 2014 World Series, play at **Oracle Park** (24 Willie Mays Plaza, 3rd St. and King St., 415/972-2000). Come out to enjoy the game, the food, and the views of the bay at San Francisco's ballpark. Giants games take place on weekdays and weekends, both day and night. It's not hard to snag last-minute tickets to a regular-season game. Check out the gourmet restaurants that ring the stadium; it wouldn't be San Francisco without top-tier cuisine.

The National Football League's **San Francisco 49ers** (www.49ers.com) left behind their longtime home at the city's Candlestick Park and now play at **Levi's Stadium** (4900 Marie P. DeBartolo Way, at Tasman Ave., 415/464-9377, www.levisstadium.com) in Santa Clara, 45 minutes south of the city.

In 2019, National Basketball Association favorite the **Golden State Warriors** (www.nba.com/warriors) moved from their longtime home base in Oakland to San Francisco. They now play at the **Chase Center** (1 Warriors Way, 888/479-4667, www.chasecenter.com).

Go Wild on the Farallon Islands

On one of those rare clear San Francisco days, you might catch a glimpse of something far offshore in the distance. It's not a pirate ship or an ocean-based optical illusion. It's the **Farallon Islands,** a series of jagged islets and rocks 28 miles (45 km) west of the Golden Gate Bridge.

At certain times, humans have attempted to make a living on these harsh rocky outcroppings. In the 1800s, Russians hunted the Farallons' marine mammals for their pelts and blubber. Following the gold rush, two rival companies harvested murre eggs on the Farallons to feed nearby San Francisco's growing population.

Now the islands have literally gone to the birds. The islands have been set aside as a national wildlife refuge, allowing the region's bird populations to flourish. The Farallons are home to the largest colony of western gulls in the world and have half the world's ashy storm petrels.

But this wild archipelago is also known for its robust population of great white sharks that circle the islands looking for seal and sea lion snacks. The exploits of a group of great white shark researchers on the island were detailed in Susan Carey's gripping book, *The Devil's Teeth*.

Nature lovers who want to see the Farallons' wildlife up close can book an all-day boat trip through **San Francisco Whale Tours** (415/706-7364, www.sanfranciscowhaletours.com) or **SF Bay Whale Watching** (415/331-6267, www.sfbaywhalewatching.com). Don't fall overboard.

Food

TOP EXPERIENCE

From near and far, people come to San Francisco to eat. Some of the greatest culinary innovations in the world come out of the kitchens in the city. The only problem is to narrow down the choices for dinner tonight.

Union Square and Nob Hill

Chinese

It may not be in Chinatown, but the dim sum at the James Beard Award-winning ★ **Yank Sing** (101 Spear St., 415/781-1111, www.yanksing.com, 11am-3pm Mon.-Fri., 10am-4pm Sat.-Sun., $4-11) is second to none. The family owns and operates both this restaurant and its sister location (49 Stevenson St., 415/541-4949), and now the third generation is training to take over. Expect traditional steamed pork buns, shrimp dumplings, and egg custard tarts. Note that it's open for lunch only.

Thai

Located in the Parc 55 Wyndham Hotel, **Kin Khao** (55 Cyril Magnin St., 415/362-7456, http://kinkhao.com, 11:30am-2pm and 5:30pm-10pm Sun.-Thurs., 11:30am-2pm and 5:30pm-11pm Fri.-Sat., $10-25) offers cuisine far beyond peanut sauces, with dishes like caramelized pork belly, vegetables in a sour curry broth, and green curry with rabbit meatballs. The curries are made from scratch, and the seafood is never frozen.

Just outside of the Union Square area, **Lers Ros Thai** (730 Larkin St., 415/931-6917, http://lersros.com, 11am-midnight daily, $9-18) is a great place to expand your knowledge of Thai cuisine. Daily specials might include stir-fried alligator or venison, while specialties include shredded green papaya salads, garlic quail, and stir-fried pork belly. Bring a handkerchief to mop up the sweat caused by these spicy dishes! Other locations are in Hayes Valley (307 Hayes St., 415/874-9661, 11am-11pm daily) and the Mission District (3189 16th St., 415/923-8978,

11:30am-10pm Sun.-Thurs., 11:30am-11pm Fri.-Sat.).

French

Tucked away in a tiny alley that looks like it might have been transported from Saint-Michel in Paris, **Café Claude** (7 Claude Ln., 415/392-3505, www.cafeclaude.com, 11:30am-10pm Mon.-Sat., 5:30pm-10pm Sun., $23-31) serves classic brasserie cuisine to French expatriates and locals alike. Much French is spoken here, but the simple food tastes fantastic in any language. Café Claude is open for lunch through dinner (dinner only on Sun.), serving an attractive post-lunch menu for weary shoppers looking for sustenance around 3pm. In the evening it can get crowded, but reservations aren't strictly necessary if you're willing to order a classic French cocktail or a glass of wine and enjoy the bustling atmosphere and live music (Thurs.-Sun.) for a few minutes.

Breakfast

Even on a weekday morning, there will be a line out the door of ★ **Brenda's French Soul Food** (652 Polk St., 415/346-8100, http://frenchsoulfood.com, 8am-3pm Mon.-Tues., 8am-10pm Wed.-Sat., 8am-8pm Sun., $12-17). People come in droves to this Tenderloin eatery for its delectable and filling New Orleans-style breakfasts. Unique offerings include crawfish beignets, an Andouille sausage omelet, and beef cutlet and grits. Entrées like chicken étouffée and red beans and rice top the dinner menu.

Bakeries and Cafés

Blue Bottle Café (66 Mint Plaza, 415/495-3394, www.bluebottlecoffee.net, 7am-7pm daily, $5-10), a popular local chain with multiple locations around

From top to bottom: a hearty breakfast at Brenda's French Soul Food; tasty lamb riblets at The Cavalier; creative food at State Bird Provisions.

the city, takes its equipment seriously. Whether you care about the big copper thing that made your mocha or not, you can get a good cup of joe and a small if somewhat pretentious meal at the Mint Plaza, which is Blue Bottle's only café with a full food program. It is in a building made famous by Dashiell Hammett's pulp fiction classic *The Maltese Falcon*. Expect a line.

Financial District and SoMa

California Cuisine

★ **Michael Mina** (252 California St., 415/722-2138, www.michaelmina.net, 11:30am-2pm and 6pm-9pm Mon.-Thurs., 11:30am-2pm and 5:30pm-10pm Fri., 5:30pm-10pm Sat., 5:30pm-9pm Sun., $195) finds the celebrity chef using Japanese ingredients and French influences to create bold California entrées. This sleek, Michelin-starred restaurant is where Mina showcases his signature dishes, including his ahi tuna tartare and Maine lobster pot pie. With the only dinner options available being the six-course menu, expect to spend some money. Service is attentive.

Seafood

It's easy to see why the ★ **Tadich Grill** (240 California St., 415/391-1849, www.tadichgrill.com, 11am-2pm and 5pm-9pm Mon.-Fri., 5pm-9pm Sat., $15-38), claiming to be the oldest restaurant in the city, has been around since 1849. Sit at the long wooden bar, which stretches from the front door back to the kitchen, and enjoy the attentive service by the white-jacketed waitstaff. The seafood-heavy menu has 75 entrées, including a dozen daily specials, and meals are classic and hearty. One of the standouts is the restaurant's delectable cioppino, which might just be the best version of this San Franciscan stew out there.

Italian

For fine Italian-influenced cuisine, make a reservation at **Quince** (470 Pacific Ave., 415/775-8500, www.quincerestaurant.com, 5:30pm-9pm Tues.-Thurs., 5pm-9:30pm Fri.-Sat., $195-298). Chef-owner Michael Tusk blends culinary aesthetics to create his own unique style of cuisine. There are two options: the single extended tasting menu with 8-10 courses and the 5-course salon menu.

Japanese

Forget your notions of the plain-Jane sushi bar; **Ozumo** (161 Steuart St., 415/882-1333, www.ozumosanfrancisco.com, 11am-2pm and 5:30pm-10pm Mon.-Fri., 5:30pm-11pm Sat., 5pm-9:30pm Sun., $28-46) takes Japanese cuisine upscale, San Francisco-style. Order some classic *nigiri*, tempura-battered dishes, or a big chunk of meat off the traditional *robata* grill. High-quality sake lines the shelves above the bar and along the walls. Non-imbibers can choose from a selection of premium teas. If you're a night owl, enjoy a late dinner on weekends and drinks in the lounge nightly.

Vietnamese

Probably the single most famous Asian restaurant in a city filled with eateries of all types is **The Slanted Door** (1 Ferry Plaza, Ste. 3, 415/861-8032, www.slanteddoor.com, 11am-10pm Mon.-Sat., 11:30am-10pm Sun., $11-45). Owner Charles Phan, more than 20 family members, and the rest of his staff pride themselves on welcoming service and top-quality food. Organic local ingredients get used in both traditional and innovative Vietnamese cuisine, creating a unique dining experience. Even experienced foodies remark that they've never had green papaya salad, glass noodles, or shaking beef like this before. The light afternoon-tea menu (2:30pm-4:30pm daily) can be the perfect pick-me-up for weary travelers who need some sustenance to get them through the long afternoon until dinner, and Vietnamese coffee is the ultimate Southeast Asian caffeine experience.

Greek

In the Greek fishing village of Kokkari, wild game and seafood hold a special place in the local mythology. At **Kokkari Estiatorio** (200 Jackson St., 415/981-0983, www.kokkari.com, 11:30am-2:30pm and 5:30pm-10pm Mon.-Thurs., 11:30am-2:30pm and 5:30pm-11pm Fri., 5pm-11pm Sat., 5pm-10pm Sun., $22-49), patrons enjoy Mediterranean delicacies made with fresh California ingredients amid rustic elegance, feasting on such classic dishes as crispy zucchini cakes, moussaka, and grilled lamb chops.

Steak

Alexander's Steakhouse (448 Brannan St., 415/495-1111, www.alexanderssteakhouse.com, noon-9pm daily, $21-148) describes itself as "where East meets beef." It's true: The presentation at Alexander's looks like something you'd see on *Iron Chef*, and the prices of the Wagyu beef look like the monthly payment on a small Japanese car. This white-tablecloth steak house is the antithesis of a bargain, but the food, including the steaks, is more imaginative than most, and the elegant dining experience will make you feel special as your wallet quietly bleeds out.

Gastropub

★ **The Cavalier** (360 Jessie St., 415/321-6000, http://thecavaliersf.com, 9am-9pm Tues.-Sat., $18-42) serves a California take on upscale British pub food. The restaurant is decorated like a British hunting lodge, with mounted game heads on the walls. A stuffed fox named Floyd reclines on a bookcase in the back. As for the food, it is inventive, tasty, sometimes rich, and surprisingly well priced. The lamb scrumpets (golden-fried riblets) are worth the trip, while other entrées include classics like fish-and-chips.

International

Located in the San Francisco Museum of Modern Art, the Michelin-starred **In Situ** (151 3rd St., 415/941-6050, http://insitu.sfmoma.org, 11am-3:30pm Mon., 11am-3:30pm and 5pm-9pm Thurs.-Sat., 11am-3:30pm and 5pm-8pm Sun., $12-28) is almost an art piece unto itself. The concept behind the dining room and lounge: Chef Corey Lee recreates popular dishes from fine restaurants around the world. The à la carte menu of mostly small plates features the stories of the chefs behind the creations, immersing diners in their creative process. Reservations for the dining room are recommended, but if you can't get in, opt for the 29-seat lounge.

Bakeries and Cafés

One of the Ferry Building mainstays, the **Acme Bread Company** (1 Ferry Plaza, Ste. 15, 415/288-2978, http://acmebread.com, 7am-7:30pm Mon.-Fri., 8am-7pm Sat.-Sun.) remains true to its name. You can buy bread here, but not sandwiches, croissants, or pastries. All the bread that Acme sells is made with fresh organic ingredients in traditional style; the baguettes are traditionally French, so they start to go stale after only 4-6 hours. Eat fast!

The motto of **Café Venue** (67 5th St., 415/546-1144, www.cafevenue.com, 7am-3pm Mon.-Fri., 7am-1pm Sat., $6-10) is "real food, fast and fresh." This simple strategy is clearly working: On weekdays, you can expect a long line of local workers grabbing a salad or a sandwich for lunch. The warm chicken pesto sandwich is a highlight.

Farmers Markets

While farmers markets litter the landscape in just about every California town, the **Ferry Plaza Farmers Market** (1 Ferry Plaza, 415/291-3276, www.ferrybuildingmarketplace.com, 10am-2pm Tues. and Thurs., 8am-2pm Sat.) is special. At the granddaddy of Bay Area farmers markets, you'll find a wonderful array of produce, cooked foods, and even locally raised meats and locally caught seafood. Expect to see the freshest fruits and veggies from local growers, grass-fed beef from Marin County, and seasonal seafood pulled from the Pacific beyond the Golden Gate. Granted, you'll pay for the privilege of purchasing from this market—if you're seeking bargain produce, you'll be better served at one of the weekly suburban farmers markets. Even locals flock downtown to the Ferry Building on Saturday mornings, especially in the summer, when the variety of California's agricultural bounty becomes staggering.

Chinatown

Chinese Banquets

Banquet restaurants offer tasty meat, seafood, and veggie dishes along with rice, soups, and appetizers, all served family-style. Tables are often round, with a lazy Susan in the middle to facilitate the passing of communal serving bowls around the table. In the city, most banquet Chinese restaurants have at least a few dishes that will feel familiar to the American palate, and menus often have English translations.

The **R&G Lounge** (631 Kearny St., 415/982-7877, www.rnglounge.com, 11am-9:30pm Sun.-Thurs., 11am-10pm Fri.-Sat., $12-40, reservations suggested) takes traditional Chinese American cuisine to the next level. The menu is divided by colors that represent the five elements, according to Chinese tradition and folklore. In addition to standards like moo shu pork, chow mein, and lemon chicken, you'll find spicy Szechuan and Mongolian dishes and an array of house specialties. Salt-and-pepper Dungeness crab, served whole on a plate, is the R&G signature dish, though many of the other seafood dishes are just as special. Expect your seafood to be fresh since it comes right out of the tank in the dining room. California-cuisine mores have made their way into the R&G Lounge in the form of some innovative dishes and haute cuisine presentations.

Dim Sum

One of the many great dim sum places in Chinatown is the **Great Eastern** (649 Jackson St., 415/986-2500, www.greateasternsf.com, 10am-11pm Mon.-Fri., 9am-11pm Sat.-Sun., $15-25), which serves its dim sum menu 10am-2:30pm daily. It's not a traditional dim sum place; instead of steam carts passing by with offerings, you'll receive a menu and a list. Check off everything you want on the list and hand it to your waiter, and your choices will be brought out to you. Make reservations or you may wait 30-60 minutes for a table. This restaurant jams up fast, right from the moment it opens, especially on weekends. The good news is that most of the folks crowding into Great Eastern are locals. You know what that means.

Ordering dim sum at **Delicious Dim Sum** (752 Jackson St., 415/781-0721, 7am-6pm Thurs.-Tues., $3) may pose challenges. The signs are not in English, and credit cards aren't accepted. Also, there's only one table inside so you'll probably be getting your dim sum to go. But the inexpensive dim sum, with popular pork buns and shrimp and cilantro dumplings, among other options, is worth rising to the challenge.

North Beach and Fisherman's Wharf

California Cuisine

San Francisco culinary celebrity Gary Danko has a number of restaurants, but the finest is the one that bears his name. **Gary Danko** (800 North Point St., 415/749-2060, www.garydanko.com, 5:30pm-10pm daily, prix fixe $97-143) offers the best of Danko's California cuisine, from the signature horseradish-crusted salmon medallions to the array of delectable fowl dishes. The herbs and veggies come from Danko's own farm in Napa. Choose 3-5 courses. Make reservations in advance to get a table, and dress up for your sojourn in the elegant white-tablecloth dining room.

Italian

North Beach is San Francisco's own version of Little Italy. Poke around and find one of the local favorite mom-and-pop pizza joints, or try a bigger, more upscale Italian eatery.

Want a genuine world-champion pizza while you're in town? Tony Gemignani, winner of 11 World Pizza Champion awards, can hook you up. ★ **Tony's Pizza Napoletana** (1570 Stockton St., 415/835-9888, www.tonyspizzanapoletana.com, noon-10pm Mon., noon-11pm Wed.-Sun., $15-30) has seven different pizza ovens that cook by wood, coal, gas, or electric power. You can get an American-style pie loaded with pepperoni, a California-style pie with quail eggs and chorizo, or a Sicilian pizza smothered in meat and garlic. The chef's special Neapolitan-style pizza margherita is a simple pizza made to perfection. The wood-fired atmosphere of this temple to the pie includes marble-topped tables, dark woods, and white linen napkins stuck into old tomato cans. The long bar dominates the front dining room, so grab a fancy bottle of wine or a cocktail to go with that champion pizza. For a slice or a whole pie to go, head next door to **Tony's Coal-Fired Pizza and Slice House** (1556 Stockton St., 415/835-9888, http://tonyscoalfired.com, 11:30am-8pm Tues., 11:30am-11pm Wed.-Sun., 11:30am-10pm Mon., $3-6).

Trattoria Contadina (1800 Mason St., 415/982-5728, www.trattoriacontadina.com, 5pm-9pm Mon.-Thurs., 5pm-9:30pm Fri., 4pm-9:30pm Sat.-Sun., $18-35) presents mouthwatering Italian fare in a fun, eclectic dining room. Dozens of framed photos line the walls, and fresh ingredients stock the kitchen in this San Francisco take on the classic Italian trattoria. Menu items include veal, spaghetti, and gnocchi. Kids are welcome, and vegetarians will find good meatless choices on the menu.

Breakfast

Smack-dab in the middle of North Beach, **Mama's on Washington Square** (1701 Stockton St., 415/362-6421, www.mamas-sf.com, 8am-3pm Tues.-Sun., $8-10) is perched right across from the green lawn of Washington Square. In business since 1951, this institution is the perfect place to fuel up on gourmet omelets, freshly baked breads that include a delectable cinnamon brioche, and daily specials like crab Benedict before a day of sightseeing. Arrive early, or be prepared to wait . . . and wait.

Bakeries and Cafés

Widely recognized as the first espresso coffeehouse on the West Coast, family-owned **Caffé Trieste** (601 Vallejo St., 415/392-6739, http://coffee.caffetrieste.com, 6:30am-11pm daily, cash only) first opened its doors in 1956. It became a hangout for Beat writers in the 1950s and 1960s and was where Francis Ford Coppola penned the screenplay for his classic film *The Godfather* in the 1970s. Sip a cappuccino, munch on Italian pastries, and enjoy frequent concerts at this treasured North Beach institution. There are now four locations, from Berkeley to Monterey.

Serving some of the most famous sourdough in the city, the **Boudin Bakery & Café** (Pier 39, Space 5-Q, 415/421-0185, www.boudinbakery.com, 9am-8pm daily, $6-8) is a Pier 39 institution. Grab a loaf of bread to take with you, or order in one of the Boudin classics. Nothing draws tourists like the fragrant clam chowder in a bread bowl, but if you prefer, you can try another soup, a signature sandwich, or even a fresh salad. For a more upscale dining experience with the same great breads, try **Bistro Boudin** (160 Jefferson St., 415/928-1849, 11am-8pm Mon.-Fri., 8am-8pm Sat.-Sun., $13-38).

Marina and Pacific Heights

Union Street and **Chestnut Street** are home to many restaurants in these neighborhoods.

Contemporary

The Brixton (2140 Union St., 415/409-1114, www.brixtonsf.com, 11:30am-10pm Mon.-Fri., 11am-10pm Sat.-Sun., $13-23) might have rock posters on the wall and loud music blaring overhead, but that doesn't mean you shouldn't try the food. The dinner menu goes late into the night and includes items like a tasty burger. The appetizer menu is worth grazing, and the "Tacos of the Day" can sate smaller appetites. The restaurant has done so well it opened another location (701 2nd St., 415/947-7955, 11:30am-10pm Tues.-Fri., 11am-10pm Sat., 11am-2:30pm Sun.).

Seafood

Anytime you come to the tiny ★ **Swan Oyster Depot** (1517 Polk St., 415/673-1101, 10:30am-5:30pm Mon.-Sat., $10-25, cash only), there will be a line out the door. With limited stools at a long marble bar, Swan, which opened in 1912, is an old-school seafood place that serves fresh seafood salads, seafood cocktails, and clam chowder, the only hot item on the menu. The seafood is so fresh that you pass it resting on ice while waiting for your barstool. The eatery is located on the lively Polk Street corridor, east of the Marina and Pacific Heights.

Japanese

With rolls named after rock acts U2 and Ozzy, it's no surprise that **Ace Wasabi's** (3339 Steiner St., 415/567-4903, www.acewasabisf.com, 5:30pm-10pm Mon.-Wed., 5:30pm-10:30pm Thurs., 5:30pm-11pm Fri.-Sat., 5pm-10pm Sun., $6-18 per item) advertises itself as a "rock 'n' roll sushi" joint. Some of the fish is flown in from Tokyo's Tsukiji Fish Market, and the menu includes unusual offerings like tuna tostadas.

If you're in Pacific Heights, give **Kiss Seafood** (1700 Laguna St., 415/474-2866, http://kissseafoodsf.com, 5:30pm-9:30pm Wed.-Sat., $38-78) a try. This tiny restaurant (12 seats total) boasts some of the freshest fish in town, which is no mean feat in San Francisco. The lone chef prepares all the fish himself, possibly due to the tiny size of the place. If you're up for sashimi, you'll be in raw-fish heaven. Round off your meal with a glass of chilled premium sake. Reservations are a good idea.

Steak

The Marina is a great place to find a big thick steak. One famed San Francisco steak house, **Boboquivari's** (1450 Lombard St., 415/441-8880, www.boboquivaris.com, 5pm-10pm Sun.-Thurs., 5pm-11pm Fri.-Sat., $33-190) prides itself on its dry-aged beef and fresh seafood. In season, enjoy whole Dungeness crab. But most of all, enjoy "The Steak," thickly cut and simply prepared to enhance the flavor of the beef. The 49-ounce porterhouse costs a pretty penny: $190!

A New York stage actress wanted a classic steak house in San Francisco, and so **Harris' Restaurant** (2100 Van Ness Ave., 415/673-1888, www.harrisrestaurant.com, 5:30pm-close Mon.-Fri., 5pm-close Sat.-Sun., $35-198), just east of the Marina and Pacific Heights, came to be. The fare runs to traditional steaks and prime rib as well as upscale features, with a Wagyu beef and surf-and-turf featuring a whole Maine lobster. Music lovers can catch live jazz in the lounge most evenings.

Breakfast

Sweet Maple (2101 Sutter St., 415/655-9169, www.sweetmaplesf.com, 8am-2:30pm Mon.-Fri., 8am-3pm Sat.-Sun., $11-22) takes breakfast to the next level. The varied menu takes eggs in new directions with morning pizzas, egg tacos, and creations including a Wagyu sliders Benedict. Wash it down with a morning cocktail. It's all served in an airy space with orchids and hanging lamps.

Civic Center and Hayes Valley

California Cuisine

State Bird Provisions (1529 Fillmore St., 415/795-1272, http://statebirdsf.com, 5:30pm-10pm Sun.-Thurs., 5:30pm-11pm Fri.-Sat., $14-22) burst onto the San Francisco dining scene in a big way, winning two James Beard Awards (Best New Restaurant in the Whole of the USA in 2013 and the Best Chef in the West in 2015). Part of the unique menu is devoted to "Pancakes and Toast," with items like a beef tongue and horseradish buckwheat pancake. Of course, they also serve the state bird (quail) with provisions.

French

Absinthe (398 Hayes St., 415/551-1590, www.absinthe.com, 11:30am-11pm Mon.-Wed., 11:30am-midnight Thurs.-Fri., 11am-midnight Sat., 11am-10pm Sun., $15-37) takes its name from the notorious "green fairy" drink made of liquor and wormwood. Absinthe indeed does serve absinthe, including locally made St. George Spirits Absinthe Verte. It also serves upscale French bistro fare, including what may be the best French fries in the city. The French theme carries on into the decor as well, so expect the look of a Parisian brasserie or perhaps a café in Nice, with retro-modern furniture and classic prints on the walls. The bar is open until 2am on Thursday, Friday, and Saturday, so if you want drinks or dessert after a show at the War Memorial Opera House or Davies Symphony Hall, just walk around the corner.

German

Suppenküche (525 Laguna St., 415/252-9289, www.suppenkuche.com, 4:30pm-8:30pm Tues.-Sat., $12.50-20) brings a taste of Bavaria to the Bay Area. The beer list is a great place to start, since you can enjoy a wealth of classic German brews on tap and in bottles, plus a few Belgians thrown in for variety. For dinner, expect German classics with a focus on Bavarian cuisine. Spaetzle, pork, sausage—you name it, they've got it, and it will harden your arteries right up. Suppenküche also has a **Biergarten** (424 Octavia St., 415/252-9289, http://biergartensf.com, 3pm-9pm Mon.-Fri., 2pm-9pm Sat., 1pm-7pm Sun.), two blocks away.

Greek

Souvla (517 Hayes St., 415/400-5458, www.souvla.com, 4pm-9pm Wed.-Fri., noon-8pm Sat.-Sun., $13-16) is inspired by Greece's casual souvlaki joints. Dine on spit-fired meats (pork shoulder, chicken, leg of lamb) or white sweet potato served in a sandwich or salad. Then treat yourself to some of the olive oil frozen yogurt. This popular Bay Area mini-chain also has locations in the Mission and Marina.

Mission and Castro

The Mission is known for its abundant taquerias, and specifically a local invention: the **Mission burrito**—essentially an incredibly large burrito (one can usually feed two people). Mission burritos come "regular" (a flour tortilla stuffed with a protein of your choosing, beans, rice) or "super" (which adds on avocado, cheese, and sour cream or *crema*). But the neighborhood is also a foodie destination for all manner of cuisine. **Mission Street** and **Valencia Street,** which run parallel to each other, are filled with restaurants, mostly concentrated between **16th and 24th Streets.**

Mexican

It seems that every local has a different go-to taqueria for Mission burritos, but two spots that often top lists are within a few blocks of each other: **El Farolito** (2779 Mission St., 415/824-7877, 10am-3am Mon.-Wed. and Sat., 10am-3:30am Thurs.-Fri., 10am-midnight Sun., $3-15) and James Beard-recognized **La Taqueria** (2889 Mission St., 415/285-7117, 11am-8:45pm Wed.-Mon., $4-13). El Farolito keeps later hours, and La Taqueria's burritos are notable for being rice-free. There are always lines snaking out the doors of both, but they move fairly quickly. Order at the counter and take your burritos (or tacos or quesadillas, which they also offer) to go and have a picnic at Dolores Park, or eat on-site at casual picnic-style tables.

For a spin on Mexican cuisine, try **Senor Sisig** (990 Valencia St., www.senorsisig.com, 11am-9pm daily, $5-13), which began as a popular food truck. It incorporates Filipino-style seasoned chopped meats into tacos, burritos, and quesadillas and on top of nachos. There isn't space to do much but put in your order at the small spot, but there's a parklet directly outside where you can eat.

Argentinean

Argentina is known for tango, wine, and beef. The latter is done superbly at ★ **Lolinda** (2518 Mission St., 415/550-6970, http://lolindasf.com, 5:30pm-midnight Fri.-Sat., 5:30pm-11pm Sun.-Thurs., $14-78). The six-ounce skirt steak has a big flavor for its modest size, while the "Gaucho," a 26-ounce bone-in rib eye, is the largest and priciest cut. All meat is cooked on a wood-fired *asador* (grill). The menu makes room for ceviche, empanadas, and grilled skewers. It's all served in a lively space featuring a bull mural and a trio of mounted bull heads above the open kitchen.

Seafood

For great seafood in a lower-key atmosphere, locals eschew the tourist traps on the Wharf and head for the **Anchor Oyster Bar** (579 Castro St., 415/431-3990, www.anchoroysterbar.com, 11:30am-10pm Mon.-Sat., 4pm-9:30pm Sun., $14-39) in the Castro. The raw bar features different ways to have oysters, including an oyster *soju* (Korean liquor) shot. The dining room serves seafood, including local favorite Dungeness crab. Service is friendly, as befits a neighborhood spot, and it sees fewer large crowds. This doesn't diminish its quality, and it makes for a great spot to get a delicious meal before heading out to the local clubs for a late night out.

Italian

Little Star Pizza (400 Valencia St., 415/551-7827, www.littlestarvalencia.com, noon-9pm daily, $12-23) is a jewel of the Mission District, a pizzeria specializing in Chicago-style deep-dish pies (though it also serves thin-crust pizzas for devotees of the New York style). Once you've found the all-black building and taken a seat inside the casual eatery, grab a beer or a cocktail from the bar if you have to wait for a table. Pick one of Little Star's specialty pizzas, or create your own variation from the toppings they offer. Can't get enough of Little Star? It's got a second location in the city (846 Divisadero St., 415/441-1118, 5pm-9pm Mon.-Thurs., 4pm-9pm Fri., 3pm-9pm Sat.-Sun.).

Delfina (3621 18th St., 415/552-4055, www.delfinasf.com, 5:30pm-9pm Mon.-Thurs., 5:30pm-10pm Fri.-Sat., 5pm-9pm Sun., $10-32) gives Italian cuisine a hearty California twist. From the antipasti to the entrées, the dishes speak of local farms and ranches and fresh seasonal produce. Dine in either the charming, warm indoor dining room or on the outdoor garden patio.

Thai

Farmhouse Thai (710 Florida St., 415/814-2920, www.farmhousethai.com, 11am-2:30pm and 5pm-10pm Mon.-Thurs., 11am-2:30pm and 5pm-10:30pm Fri., noon-10:30pm Sat., noon-10pm Sun., $15-29) bursts with color. Employees at this vibrant and hip Thai restaurant wear bright flower-print shirts as they deliver attractive dishes in bold colors, such as the blue jasmine rice. Thai staples fill the menu, including street food (fried rice, pad thai), curries, soups, and noodles. The atmosphere is fun, while the food is a creative take on classic Thai cuisine.

Bakeries and Cafés

A line snakes into the ★ **Tartine Bakery** (600 Guerrero St., 415/487-2600, www.tartinebakery.com, 8am-7pm Mon., 7:30am-7pm Tues.-Wed., 7:30am-8pm Thurs.-Fri., 8am-8pm Sat.-Sun.) almost all day long. You might think that there's an impromptu rock show or a book signing by a prominent author, but the eatery's baked goods, breads, and sandwiches are the stars. A slab of the transcendent quiche made with crème fraîche, Niman Ranch smoked ham, and organic produce is an inspired way to start the day, especially if you are planning on burning some serious calories. Meanwhile, there is nothing quite like a piece of Passion Fruit Lime Bavarian Rectangle, a cake that somehow manages to be both rich in flavor and light as air. **Tartine Manufactory** (595 Alabama St., 415/757-0007, 8am-10pm daily, $12-22), located in an industrial building with a bread-baking operation, is the bakery's restaurant and bar, serving breakfast, lunch, and dinner.

You can also satisfy your sweet tooth at **Bi-Rite Creamery & Bakeshop** (3692 18th St., 415/626-5600, http://biritecreamery.com, 11am-10pm daily). The ice cream is made by hand with organic milk, cream, and eggs; inventive flavors include honey lavender, salted caramel, and white chocolate raspberry swirl. Pick up a scoop to enjoy at nearby Dolores Park.

Golden Gate Park and the Haight

California Cuisine

One of the most famous restaurant locations on the San Francisco coast is the **Cliff House** (1090 Point Lobos Ave., 415/386-3330, www.cliffhouse.com). The high-end eatery inhabiting the famed facade is **Sutro's** (11:30am-9:30pm Mon.-Sat., 11am-9:30pm Sun., $25-39). The appetizers and entrées are mainly seafood in somewhat snooty preparations. Although the cuisine is expensive and fancy, in all honesty it's not the best in the city. What *is* amazing are the views from the floor-to-ceiling windows out over the vast expanse of the Pacific Ocean. These views make Sutro's a perfect spot to enjoy a romantic dinner while watching the sun set over the sea. The Cliff House also houses the more casual **Bistro** (9am-3:30pm and 4:15pm-9:30pm Mon.-Sat., 8:30am-3:30pm and 4:15pm-9:30pm Sun., $15-30).

Housed in a former bank, **Nopa** (560 Divisadero St., 415/864-8643, http://nopasf.com, 5:30pm-midnight Sun.-Thurs., 5:30pm-1am Fri.-Sat., $16-32) brings together the small neighborhood that the restaurant is named after (North of the Panhandle—the "panhandle" being the narrow park that stretches from Golden Gate Park's eastern end) with a whimsical mural by a local artist, a communal table, and a crowd as diverse as the surrounding area. A creative and inexpensive menu offers soul-satisfying dishes and keeps tables full into the wee hours. The cocktails are legendary.

Japanese

Sushi restaurants are immensely popular in these residential neighborhoods. **Koo** (408 Irving St., 415/731-7077, www.sushikoo.com, 5:30pm-10pm Tues.-Thurs., 5:30pm-10:30pm Fri.-Sat., 5pm-9:30pm Sun., $30-50) is a favorite in the Sunset. While sushi purists are happy with the selection of *nigiri* and sashimi, lovers of fusion and experimentation will enjoy the small plates and unusual rolls created to delight diners. Complementing the Japanese cuisine is a small but scrumptious list of premium sakes. Only the cheap stuff is served hot, as high-quality sake is always chilled.

Thai

Dining in the Haight? Check out the flavorful dishes at **Siam Lotus Thai Cuisine** (1705 Haight St., 415/933-8031, http://siamlotussf.com, noon-3:30pm and 5pm-9pm Mon., 5pm-9pm Wed.-Thurs., noon-3:30pm and 5pm-9:30pm Fri., noon-9:30pm Sat., noon-9pm Sun., $7-13). You'll find a rainbow of curries, pad thai, and all sorts of Thai meat, poultry, and vegetarian dishes. Look to the lunch specials for bargains, and to the Thai iced tea for a lunchtime pick-me-up. Locals enjoy the casually romantic ambiance, and visitors make special trips down to the Haight just to dine here.

Vietnamese

Thanh Long (4101 Judah St., 415/665-1146, http://thanhlongsf.com, 5pm-close Tues.-Sun., $30-50) was the first family-owned Vietnamese restaurant in San Francisco. Since the early 1970s, Thanh Long has been serving one of the best preparations of local Dungeness crab in the city: roasted crab with garlic noodles. This isn't a $5 pho joint, so expect white tablecloths and higher prices at this stately small restaurant in the outer Sunset neighborhood. Fans include actors Harrison Ford and Danny Glover.

Accommodations

Both the cheapest and the most expensive places tend to be in Union Square and downtown. Cheaper digs can be had in the neighborhoods surrounding Fisherman's Wharf. You'll find the most character in small boutique hotels, but plenty of big chain hotels have at least one location in town. Valet parking and overnight garage parking can be expensive. Check to see if your hotel has a "parking package" that includes this expense.

Union Square and Nob Hill

In and around Union Square and Nob Hill, you'll find approximately a zillion hotels. As a rule, those closest to the top of the Hill or to Union Square proper are the most expensive. For a one- or two-block walk away from the center, you get more personality and a genuine San Francisco experience for less money and less prestige. There are few inexpensive options in these areas. Hostels are located to the southwest, closer to the **Tenderloin;** note that this neighborhood is home to many of the city's social services, and you may encounter people struggling with homelessness and drug addiction on the streets.

$150-250

One of the best deals in town is at the ★ **Golden Gate Hotel** (775 Bush St., 415/392-3702, www.goldengatehotel.com, $180-280), centrally located between Union Square and the top of Nob Hill. This narrow yellow building has 25 rooms decorated with antiques, giving it a bed-and-breakfast feel. The cheapest option is a room with a shared bath down the hall, though there are rooms with their own baths. The Golden Gate serves a fine continental breakfast with fresh croissants.

The ★ **Phoenix Hotel** (601 Eddy St., 415/776-1380, www.phoenixsf.com, $190-409) has serious rock-and-roll cred. A former motor lodge in the rough Tenderloin neighborhood, the Phoenix has hosted a who's who of rock music, including the Red Hot Chili Peppers, Debbie Harry, and Sublime. When a Kurt Cobain letter was found mocking his wedding vows to Courtney Love, it was written on Phoenix letterhead. The main draw is the large deck with an inlaid, heated pool that has a mosaic on the bottom. Palm trees rising overhead make the Phoenix feel like a beachside oasis in the city. At night, the sounds of the surrounding Tenderloin remind you of the hotel's true location, but most guests don't come here to catch up on their sleep.

Over $250

★ **Hotel G** (386 Geary St., 415/986-2000, 877/828-4478, www.hotelgsanfrancisco.com, $239-529) comes on like an unassuming cool kid that impresses with understated style. The rooms in this boutique hotel are all simple and serene, with accoutrements like smart TVs, Nespresso coffee makers, Tivoli clock radios, and comfy beds with denim headboards (a nod to Levi's San Francisco roots). The lower-level rooms have bathrooms with subway-tiled floors and showers, while the upper-floor bathrooms have marble flooring and shower walls. Choose a room on the 8th floor if you enjoy rooms with high ceilings. There are three drinking and dining establishments within the building. Best of all, your room will feel like a homey apartment or studio even though the hotel is just a block from bustling Union Square.

Certain names just mean luxury in the hotel world. The **Fairmont San Francisco** (950 Mason St., 415/772-5000, www.fairmont.com, $300-600) is among the best of these. With a rich history, above-and-beyond service, and spectacular views, the Fairmont makes any stay in the city memorable. While on-site, head downstairs for a Mai Tai at the Tonga Room & Hurricane Bar.

Financial District and SoMa

Top business execs make it their, well, business to stay near the towering offices of the Financial District, down by the water on the Embarcadero, or in SoMa. Thus, most of the lodgings in these areas cater to the expense-account set. The big-name chain hotels run expensive; book one if you're traveling on an unlimited company credit card. Otherwise, look for smaller boutique and indie accommodations that won't tear your wallet to bits.

$150-250

The modern minimalism of ★ **Hotel VIA** (138 King St., 415/200-4977, www.hotelviasf.com, $195-400) is sleek yet functional and comfortable. Rooms come with elegantly tiled bathrooms featuring rain showerheads and electronic tablets that guests can use to request services, play music, or browse *The New York Times*. Enjoy views of the downtown skyline, the bay, and the Bay Bridge from the **Rooftop at VIA,** a rooftop bar and lounge open to overnight guests. It's across the street from Oracle Park, so you can soak up the excitement of a Giants game some nights.

Over $250

★ **Hotel Zetta** (55 5th St., 415/543-8555, 888/720-7004, www.viceroyhotelsandresorts.com, $300-400) embraces San Francisco's reputation as a technology hub. The ultra-modern rooms are equipped with a gaggle of gadgets, including a G-Link station for mobile devices and a device that streams content from your smartphone onto the large flat-screen TVs. There are also espresso machines and a large butcher-block desk for those who need to get work done. The hotel's common rooms are more playful, with shuffleboard, a pool table, and an oversize game of Jenga. Recycled art throughout the building includes chandeliers made of old eyeglasses, located in the lobby. The upscale on-site restaurant **The Cavalier** features superb British-meets-California cuisine.

For something small but upscale, check out **Hotel Griffon** (155 Steuart St., 415/495-2100, www.hotelgriffon.com, $250-500), a boutique business hotel with a prime vacation locale on the Embarcadero, just feet from the Ferry Building. The Griffon offers business and leisure packages to suit any traveler's needs. Although they're pricey, the best guest rooms have views of the Bay Bridge and Treasure Island.

The **Hotel Triton** (342 Grant Ave., 415/394-0500, www.hoteltriton.com, $299-349) reopened in 2019 after a $6 million renovation. The rooms are no longer decorated with text from Jack Kerouac's *On the Road;* instead, they now feature bold colors and lots of natural light. The Wi-Fi has been upgraded as well.

Hotel Vitale (8 Mission St., 888/890-8688 or 415/278-3700, www.jdvhotels.com, $300-450) professes to restore guests' vitality with its lovely guest rooms and exclusive spa, complete with rooftop hot soaking tubs and a yoga studio. Many of the good-size guest rooms also have private deep soaking tubs. The Vitale's **Americano Restaurant** serves Italian fare.

North Beach and Fisherman's Wharf

Perhaps it's odd, but the tourist mecca of San Francisco is not a district of a zillion hotels. Most of the major hostelries sit down nearer to Union Square. But you can stay near the Wharf or in North Beach if you choose; you'll find plenty of chain motels here, plus a few select boutique hotels in all price ranges.

Under $150

The unexpected **Fisherman's Wharf Hostel** (Fort Mason, Bldg. 240, 415/771-7277, www.hiusa.org, dorm beds $40-48, private rooms $105-130) sits in bucolic Fort Mason, seemingly remote yet within walking distance of downtown. The best amenities (aside from the free parking, free continental breakfast, and no curfews or chores) are the sweeping lawns, mature trees, and the views of Alcatraz and the bay.

The **San Remo Hotel** (2237 Mason St., 800/352-7366, www.sanremohotel.com, $124-264) is one of the best bargains in the city. The blocky old yellow building has been around since just after the 1906 earthquake, offering inexpensive guest rooms to budget-minded travelers. One of the reasons for the rock bottom pricing is the baths: You don't get your own. Four shared baths with shower facilities located in the hallways are available to guests day and night. The guest rooms boast the simplest of furnishings and decorations as well as clean, white-painted walls and ceilings. Some rooms have their own sinks, all have either double beds or two twin beds, and none have telephones or TVs, so this might not be the best choice of lodgings for large media-addicted families. Couples on a romantic vacation can rent the Penthouse, a lovely

the game room inside the high-tech Hotel Zetta

room for two with lots of windows and a rooftop terrace boasting views of North Beach and the bay.

$150-250

Hotel Bohème (444 Columbus Ave., 415/433-9111, www.hotelboheme.com, $194-320) offers comfort, history, and culture at a pleasantly low price for San Francisco. Guest rooms are small but comfortable, Wi-Fi is free, and the spirit of the 1950s bohemian Beats lives on. The warmly colored and gently lit guest rooms are particularly welcoming to solo travelers and couples, with their retro brass beds covered by postmodern geometric spreads. All guest rooms have private baths, and the double-queen room can sleep up to four people for an additional charge.

Over $250

Located on a quiet section of the Embarcadero, the ★ **Harbor Court Hotel** (165 Steuart St., 415/882-1300, www.harborcourthotel.com, $350-1,000) is housed in an attractive brick building a block from the Ferry Building. Spring for a harbor-view room to watch the ships pass by during the day and the pulsing lights of the Bay Bridge after dark. Modern touches include iPod docks and flat-screen TVs. Guests can get a day pass to the adjacent Embarcadero YMCA, which has a gym, a spa, and a swimming pool.

For a luxurious stay in the city, save up for a room at **The Argonaut** (495 Jefferson St., 415/563-0800 or 800/790-1415, www.argonauthotel.com, $364-849). With stunning bay views from its prime Fisherman's Wharf location and a yoga channel, The Argonaut is all San Francisco. The rooms feature exposed brick walls and nautical-inspired decor. Guest rooms range from cozy standards to upscale suites with separate bedrooms and whirlpool tubs. The San Francisco Maritime National Historical Park's visitors center and interactive museum is located in the same building as The Argonaut.

Marina and Pacific Heights

These areas are close enough to Fisherman's Wharf to walk there for dinner, and the lodgings are far more affordable than downtown digs.

$150-250

Staying at the ★ **Marina Motel** (2576 Lombard St., 415/921-9406 or 800/346-6118, www.marinamotel.com, $179-259) feels like you have your own apartment in the fancy Marina District. This European-style motor lodge features rooms above little garages where you can park your car. More than half the rooms have small kitchens with a stove, fridge, microwave, and dishes for taking a break from eating out. Though the Marina Motel was built in the 1930s, the rooms are updated with modern amenities, including sometimes-working Wi-Fi and TVs with cable. With attractions like the

Palace of Fine Arts and Presidio within walking distance, this reasonably priced motel is a great place to hunker down for a few days. Reserve a room away from Lombard Street if you are a light sleeper.

Pack the car and bring the kids to the **Hotel del Sol** (3100 Webster St., 415/921-5520, 877/433-5765, www.jdvhotels.com, $200-350). This unique hotel-motel embraces its origins as a 1950s motor lodge, with the guest rooms decorated in bright, bold colors with whimsical accents, a heated courtyard pool, palm trees, hammocks, and parking for $30 a night, which is a deal in this city. The Marina locale offers trendy cafés, restaurants, bars, and shopping within walking distance, as well as access to major attractions.

The stately **Queen Anne Hotel** (1590 Sutter St., 415/441-2828, www.queenanne.com, $150-700) brings the elegance of downtown San Francisco out to Pacific Heights. Sumptuous fabrics and rich colors in the guest rooms and common areas add to the feeling of decadence and luxury in this boutique hotel. Small, moderate guest rooms offer attractive accommodations on a budget, while superior rooms and suites are more upscale. Continental breakfast is included, as are high-end services such as courtesy car service in the morning and afternoon tea and sherry.

Over $250

Tucked in with the money-laden mansions of Pacific Heights, **Hotel Drisco** (2901 Pacific Ave., 415/346-2880, www.hoteldrisco.com, $400-500) offers elegance to discerning visitors. Away from the frenzied pace and noise of downtown, at the Drisco you get quiet, comfy guest rooms with overstuffed furniture, breakfast with a latte, and a glass of wine in the evening. Families and larger parties can

From top to bottom: guest room balcony at the Fairmont San Francisco; the colorful pool deck at the Phoenix Hotel; The Metro Hotel.

look into the hotel's suite with two bedrooms and two baths. They also have a daily morning car service to downtown.

The aptly named **Inn at the Presidio** (42 Moraga Ave., 415/800-7356, www.innatthepresidio.com, $320-525) is just minutes from the heart of the city, but its location in the Presidio's green space makes it feel a world away. The inn offers immediate access to the national park site's hiking trails and cultural attractions along with panoramic views of the bay and Alcatraz in the distance. Most of the rooms are within a former housing unit for bachelor officers. While the inn is modernized, it nods to its past with military decorations on the lobby's walls. Continental breakfast comes with your stay. Suites are spacious for the city, including a bedroom with an adjoining room, a pullout sofa, and a gas fireplace. The nearby four-bedroom **Funston House** is available for large groups.

Civic Center and Hayes Valley

You'll find a few reasonably priced accommodations and classic inns in the Civic Center and Hayes Valley areas.

$150-250

Take a step back into an older San Francisco at the **Chateau Tivoli** (1057 Steiner St., 800/228-1647, 415/776-5462, www.chateautivoli.com, $180-315). The over-the-top colorful exterior matches perfectly with the American Renaissance interior decor. Each unique guest room and suite showcases an exquisite style evocative of the Victorian era. Some furnishings come from the estates of the Vanderbilts and J. Paul Getty. Most guest rooms have private baths, although the two least expensive share a bath.

Golden Gate Park and the Haight

Accommodations around Golden Gate Park are surprisingly reasonable. Leaning toward Victorian and Edwardian inns, most lodgings are in the middle price range for well above average guest rooms and services. However, getting downtown from the quiet residential spots can be a trek; ask at your inn about car services, cabs, and the nearest bus lines.

Out on the ocean side of the park, motor inns of varying quality cluster on the Great Highway. They've got the advantages of more space, low rates, and free parking, but some can be drab or questionable; choose carefully.

Under $150

Just east of Haight-Ashbury in a lively neighborhood, ★ **The Metro Hotel** (319 Divisadero St., 415/861-5364, www.metrohotelsf.com, $118-244) is one of the best-priced lodging options in the city, and the rooms in this wonderful three-story building are also comfy. Some units have bay windows that bulge out over bustling Divisadero Street below, but don't worry; street noise is near nonexistent due to triple-paned windows. Enjoy the tranquil courtyard garden out back or pepper the friendly, 24-hour-staffed front desk with questions. The only real negative here for discerning budget travelers is the lack of designated parking.

$150-250

To say the **Seal Rock Inn** (545 Point Lobos Ave., 888/732-5762, www.sealrockinn.com, $174-214) is near Golden Gate Park pushes even the fluid San Francisco neighborhood boundaries. In fact, this pretty place perches near the tip of Lands End, only a short walk from the Pacific Ocean. All guest rooms at the Seal Rock Inn have ocean views, private baths, free parking, and free Wi-Fi. With longer stays in mind, the Seal Rock offers rooms with kitchenettes (two-day minimum stay to use the kitchen part of the room; weird but true). You can call and ask for a fireplace room that faces the Seal Rocks, so you can stay warm and toasty while training your binoculars on a popular mating spot for local sea lions. The restaurant downstairs serves breakfast and lunch; on Sunday, you'll be competing with brunch-loving locals for a table.

Transportation and Services

Air

San Francisco International Airport (SFO, 800/435-9736, www.flysfo.com) is actually about 12 miles (19.5 km) south of the city center, near the town of Millbrae. You can easily get a taxi, Lyft, Uber, or other ground transportation into the heart of the city from the airport. BART is available from SFO's international terminal, but Caltrain is only accessible via a BART connection from SFO. Some San Francisco hotels offer complimentary shuttles from the airport as well. You can also rent a car here.

As one of the 30 busiest airports in the world, SFO has long check-in and security lines much of the time and dreadful overcrowding on major travel holidays. Plan to arrive at the airport two hours prior to departure for domestic flights and three hours prior to an international flight.

All the major **car rental** agencies have a presence at the airport. In addition, most reputable hotels can offer or recommend a car rental. Rates tend to run $50-100 per day and $200-550 per week (including taxes and fees), with discounts for weekly and longer rentals.

Train and Bus

Amtrak does not run directly into San Francisco. You can ride the train into the San Jose, Oakland, or Emeryville station and then take a connecting bus into San Francisco.

Greyhound (425 Mission St., 415/495-1569, www.greyhound.com, 5:15am-10:30pm daily) offers bus service to San Francisco from all over the country.

Car

The **Bay Bridge** (toll $5-7) links I-80 to San Francisco from the east, and the **Golden Gate Bridge** (toll $8.35) connects CA-1 from the north. From the south, US-101 and I-280 snake up the peninsula and into the city. Be sure to get a detailed map and good directions to drive into San Francisco—the freeway interchanges, especially surrounding the east side of the Bay Bridge, can be confusing, and the traffic congestion is legendary. For traffic updates and route planning, visit **511.org** (www.511.org).

If you have your car with you, try to get a room at a hotel with a parking lot and either free parking or a parking package for the length of your stay.

Parking

Parking a car in San Francisco can easily cost $50 per day or more. Most downtown and Union Square hotels do not include free parking with your room.

Expect to pay $35-65 per night for parking, which may not include in-and-out privileges.

Street parking meters cost up to $7 per hour (especially during special events), often go late into the night, and charge during the weekends. At least many now take credit cards. Unmetered street parking spots are as rare as unicorns and often require residential permits for stays longer than two hours during the day. Lots and garages fill up quickly, especially during special events.

Public Transportation

Muni

The **Muni** transit system (www.sfmta.com, $3 adults, $1.50 youth and seniors, children under 4 free) can get you where you want to go as long as time isn't a concern. Bus and train tickets can be purchased from any Muni driver; underground trains have ticket machines at the entrance. Exact change is required, except on the cable cars, where drivers can make change for up to $20. See the website for a route map, tickets, and schedules.

BART

Bay Area Rapid Transit, or **BART** (www.bart.gov, $2-15), is the Bay Area's latecoming answer to major metropolitan underground railways like Chicago's L trains and New York's subway system. Sadly, there's only one arterial line through the city. However, service directly from San Francisco Airport into the city runs daily, as does service to Oakland Airport, the cities of Oakland and Berkeley, and many other East Bay destinations. BART connects to the Caltrain system and San Francisco Airport in Millbrae. See the website for route maps, schedules (BART usually runs on time), and fare information.

To buy tickets, use the vending machines found in every BART station. If

BART station

plan to ride more than once, you can ɹd money to a single ticket and then keep that ticket and reuse it for each ride.

Caltrain

This traditional commuter rail line runs along the peninsula into Silicon Valley, from San Francisco to San Jose, with limited continuing service to Gilroy. **Caltrain** (800/660-4287, www.caltrain.com, $3.75-15) Baby Bullet trains can get you from San Jose to San Francisco in an hour during commuting hours. Extra trains are often added for San Francisco Giants, San Francisco 49ers, and San Jose Sharks games.

You must purchase a ticket in advance at the vending machines found in all stations. The main Caltrain station in San Francisco is at the corner of 4th and King Streets, within walking distance of Oracle Park and Moscone Center.

Taxi and Ride Share

Ride-sharing drivers abound in the Bay Area. Download the apps for **Lyft** (www.lyft.com) and **Uber** (www.uber.com) on your smartphone and secure a ride. You'll find some taxis scooting around all the major tourist areas of the city. If you have trouble hailing a cab, try **City Wide Dispatch** (415/920-0700, www.citywidetransit.com).

Tours

San Francisco City Guides (415/557-4266, www.sfcityguides.org, free) is a team of enthusiastic San Francisco tour guides who want to show you more about their beloved city. Opt to learn about San Francisco sights like Fort Mason and Fisherman's Wharf, or choose a walk where you'll hear about the locales used by famed director Alfred Hitchcock in his films, including *Vertigo*. Visit the website for a complete schedule of the current month's offerings.

One of the most popular walking tour companies in the city is **Foot** (415/793-5378, www.foottours.com, prices vary). Foot was founded by stand-up comedian Robert Mac and hires comics to act as guides for its many different tours around San Francisco. The two-hour "San Francisco in a Nutshell" tour offers a funny look at the basics of city landmarks and history, and the three-hour "Whole Shebang" is a comprehensive if speedy look at Chinatown, Nob Hill, and North Beach. For visitors who are back for the second or third time, check out the more in-depth neighborhood tours that take in Chinatown, the Castro, or the Haight. You can even hit "Full Exposure," a look at the rise of 18-and-up entertainment in North Beach or "Take Me to the Castro," a history of gay culture in the Bay Area. Tour departure points vary, so check the website for more information about your specific tour and about packages of more than one tour in a day or two.

For an inside look at the culinary delights of Chinatown, sign up for a spot on **"I Can't Believe I Ate My Way Through Chinatown"** (415/795-8303, www.wokwiz.com, $95 adults, $50 children 8-10). This three-hour bonanza will take you first for a classic Chinese breakfast, then out into the streets of Chinatown for a narrated tour around Chinatown's food markets, apothecaries, and tea shops. You'll finish up with lunch at one of chef Shirley's favorite hole-in-the-wall dim sum places. For folks who just want the tour and lunch, or the tour alone, check out the standard "Wok Wiz Daily Tour" ($55 adults with lunch, $35 adults without lunch, $40 children with lunch, $25 children without lunch).

The **Chinatown Ghost Tour** (415/793-1183, www.sfchinatownghosttours.com, 7:30pm-9pm Fri.-Sat., $48) delves into the neighborhood's mysticism and rich history. The whole thing burned down more than a century ago, and it was rebuilt in exactly the same spot, complete with countless narrow alleyways. This tour will take you into these alleys after the sun sets, when the spirits are said to appear on the streets. You'll start out at Utopia Cafe (139 Waverly Pl.) and follow your loquacious guide along the avenues and side streets of Chinatown. As you stroll, your guide will tell you the stories of the neighborhood spirits, spooks, and ancestors. The curious get to learn about the deities worshipped by devout Chinese to this day, along with the folklore that permeates what was until recently a closed and secretive culture. Then you head into a former gambling den where a magician will attempt to conjure the soul of a long-dead gambler.

Information and Services

The high-tech, state-of-the-art **Moscone Visitor Information Center** (749 Howard St., 415/391-2000, www.sftravel.com, 9am-5pm Mon.-Fri., 9am-3pm Sat.-Sun.) can help with many travel needs including city tours, attraction tickets, and public transit passes. There are satellite locations in **Union Square** (170 O'Farrell St.), **Fisherman's Wharf** (Pier 39, Building B, Level 2), and **Chinatown** (625 Kearny St.).

The **San Francisco Police Department** (1251 3rd St., 415/553-0123, www.sanfranciscopolice.org) is headquartered on the bayside of downtown. For life-threatening emergencies or to report a crime in progress, dial 911.

San Francisco boasts a large number of full-service hospitals. The **UCSF Medical Center at Mount Zion** (1600 Divisadero St., 415/567-6600, www.ucsfhealth.org) is renowned for its research and advances in cancer treatments and other important medical breakthroughs. The main hospital is at the corner of Divisadero and Geary Streets. Right downtown, **St. Francis Memorial Hospital** (900 Hyde St., 415/353-6000, www.dignityhealth.org), at the corner of Hyde and Bush Streets, has an emergency department.

Yosemite

osemite National Park

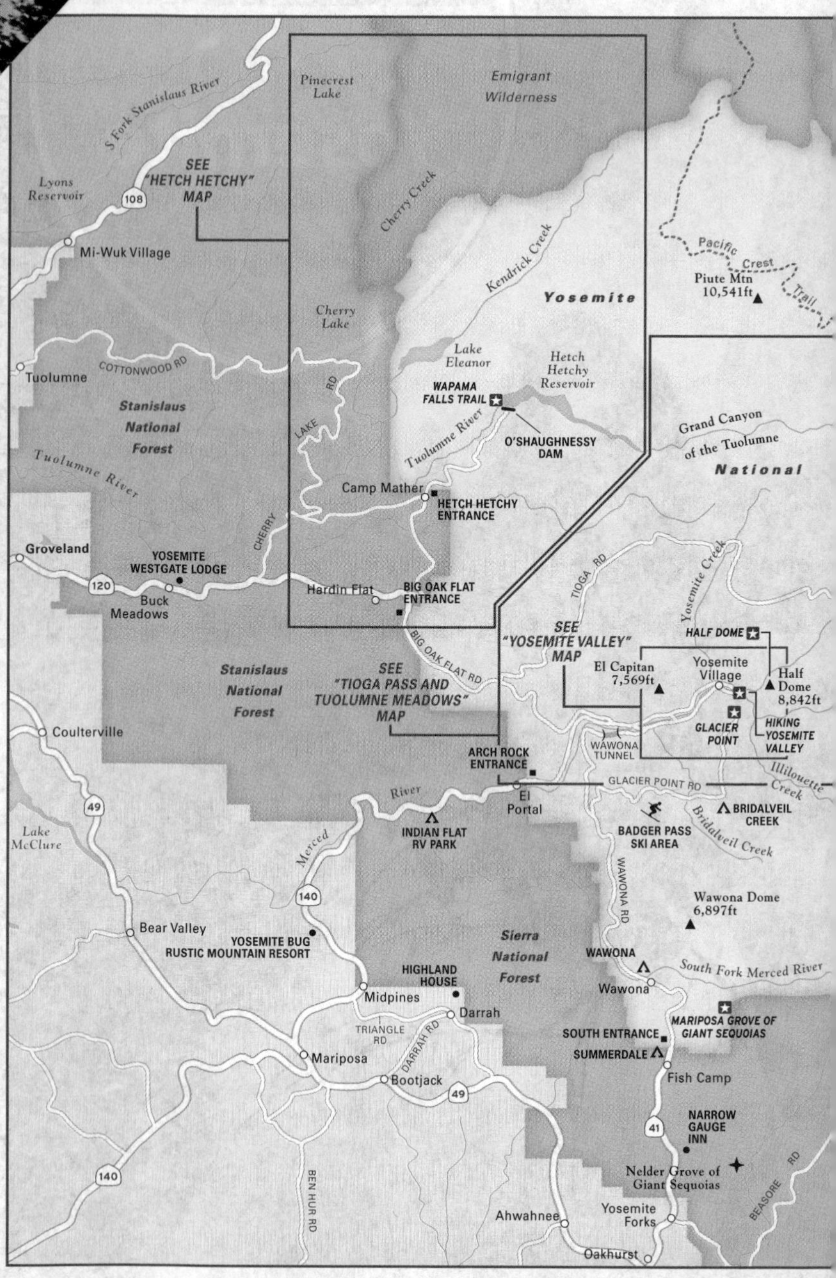

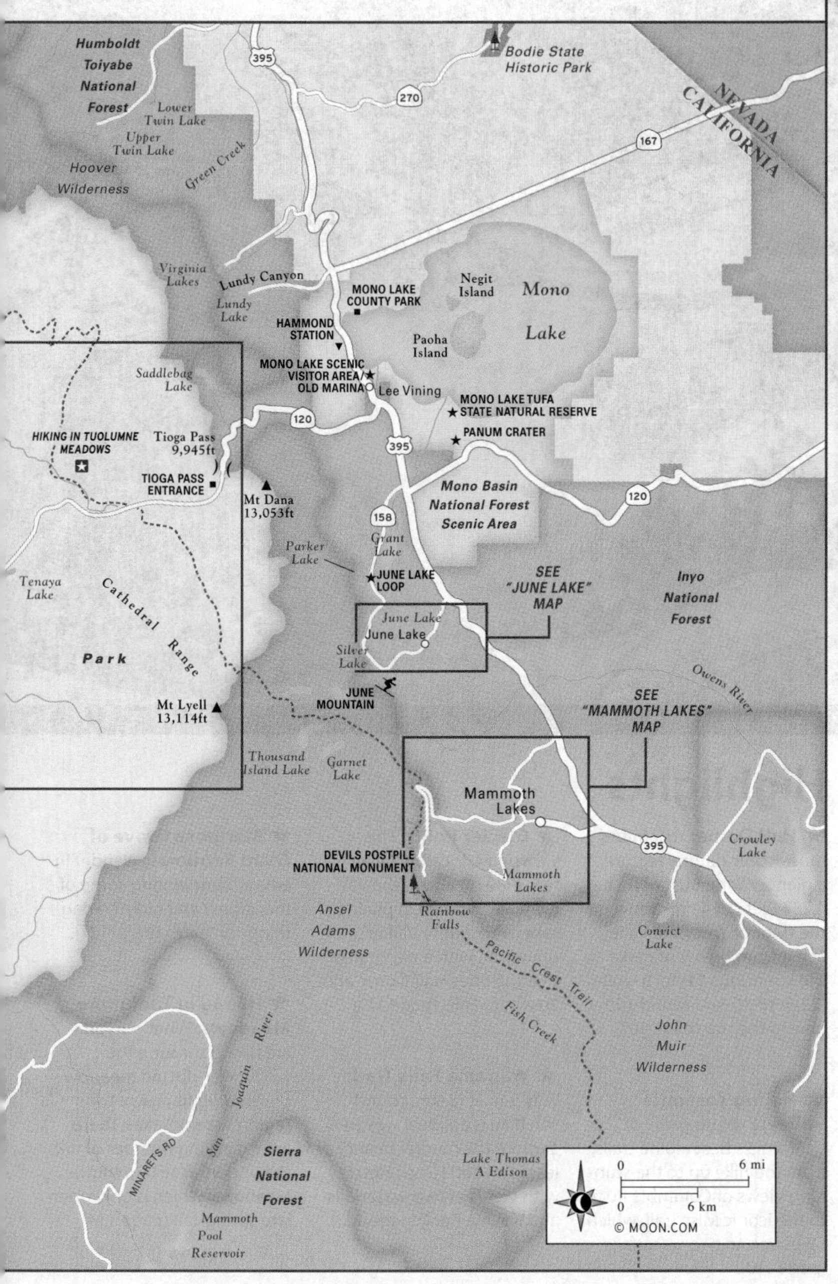

Humboldt Toiyabe National Forest
Bodie State Historic Park
395
270
167
NEVADA
CALIFORNIA
Lower Twin Lake
Upper Twin Lake
Green Creek
Hoover Wilderness
Virginia Lakes
Lundy Canyon
Lundy Lake
MONO LAKE COUNTY PARK
Negit Island
Mono Lake
HAMMOND STATION
Paoha Island
MONO LAKE SCENIC VISITOR AREA/ OLD MARINA
Lee Vining
MONO LAKE TUFA STATE NATURAL RESERVE
PANUM CRATER
Saddlebag Lake
120
HIKING IN TUOLUMNE MEADOWS
Tioga Pass 9,945ft
TIOGA PASS ENTRANCE
Mt Dana 13,053ft
Mono Basin National Forest Scenic Area
158
Grant Lake
Parker Lake
JUNE LAKE LOOP
Tenaya Lake
Cathedral Range
SEE "JUNE LAKE" MAP
Inyo National Forest
June Lake
Silver Lake
Park
JUNE MOUNTAIN
Owens River
Mt Lyell 13,114ft
SEE "MAMMOTH LAKES" MAP
Thousand Island Lake
Garnet Lake
Mammoth Lakes
DEVILS POSTPILE NATIONAL MONUMENT
Crowley Lake
Ansel Adams Wilderness
Rainbow Falls
Convict Lake
Pacific Crest Trail
Fish Creek
San Joaquin River
John Muir Wilderness
MINARETS RD
Sierra National Forest
Lake Thomas A Edison
Mammoth Pool Reservoir
0 6 mi
0 6 km
© MOON.COM

Highlights

★ **Half Dome:** Yosemite's most iconic natural feature is a giant granite bust of rock 4,737 feet (1,444 m) above the floor of Yosemite Valley. See it from below or make the strenuous 14- to 16-mile (22.5- to 26-km) round-trip hike to the top (page 107).

★ **Hiking Yosemite Valley:** Explore some of California's best alpine trails, from the hike up to the stunning views of Columbia Rock to the iconic Mist Trail, which takes you to two waterfalls (page 110).

★ **Glacier Point:** This viewpoint, located 3,214 feet (980 m) above the valley floor, is the best place to take in Yosemite Valley's full grandeur, with a panorama that includes Half Dome and Yosemite Falls (page 119).

★ **Wapama Falls Trail:** This 5-mile (8-km) round-trip hike is an ideal way to explore the natural beauty of less crowded Hetch Hetchy, with views of two waterfalls and Kolana Rock (page 123).

★ **Mariposa Grove of Giant Sequoias:** Wander in amazement among some of the largest and oldest living things on earth (page 127).

★ **Hiking in Tuolumne Meadows:** Whether you are hiking through the wildflower-dotted meadow or climbing to one of the region's scenic lakes, there are a dizzying number of hiking options from Tuolumne Meadows, which is only open late spring-fall (page 134).

With its giant granite rock faces, jagged peaks, and thundering waterfalls, Yosemite National Park inspires millions of road trippers.

Located in the Sierra Nevada, Yosemite is home to California's most iconic natural sights. It was the preservation of this landscape by President Abraham Lincoln in 1864 that paved the way for the country's national park system.

The park's best-known sights are located in Yosemite Valley: the giant rock wall of El Capitan, the granite bust of Half Dome, and North America's highest waterfall, Yosemite Falls. During the summer, the valley is crowded with visitors gawking at the stunning natural beauty. Even the most jaded individual will look past the crowds in amazement when wandering below the towering canyon walls.

Beyond the crowds, the park's more remote sections beckon those seeking (relative) solitude. In Glacier Point you can get the best view of Yosemite Valley, while in Mariposa Grove you can walk among the rust-colored spires of giant sequoias. Only accessible by car from spring to fall, Tuolumne Meadows is a large, high-elevation field dotted with mirrored lakes that reflect the scenery. The least-visited Hetch Hetchy region has granite outcroppings and waterfalls comparable to what you can see in the valley, but without the heavy crowds.

It's worth exploring the foothill and mountain towns surrounding the park for their own unique characters, from the gold rush vibe of Groveland to the peaceful high desert of Mono Lake. With plenty of restaurant and hotel options, these communities make ideal bases for visiting the park and stocking up on supplies.

Getting to Yosemite

Almost all the most popular sights, attractions, and trailheads are accessible by road. The **Arch Rock entrance** to the west of the park is accessed via **CA-140.** The **Big Oak Flat entrance** is accessed via **CA-120** from the north; it's about another 45 minutes to Yosemite Valley from there. Both entrances provide access to **Tioga Pass Road** via **Big Oak Flat Road.** Tioga Pass reconnects to CA-120 at the **Tioga Pass entrance** on the east side of the park. Tioga Pass closes in November or December each year and reopens in the spring, usually in May or June. Yosemite's **South entrance** is accessed via **CA-41** from Oakhurst. **Wawona Road** leads from the South entrance through Wawona and into Yosemite Valley. **Glacier Point Road** is reached from Wawona Road and allows access to Badger Pass. The more remote **Hetch Hetchy entrance** of the park is reached by taking CA-120 out of Groveland east for 23 miles (37 km) and then taking a left onto Evergreen Road for 8.2 miles (13.2 km). In the town of Camp Mather, take a right onto **Hetch Hetchy Road,** which heads to the park's Hetch Hetchy entrance. In winter, chains can be required on any road at any time, so check with the **National Park Service** (209/372-0200, www.nps.gov/yose) for **current road conditions.**

From San Francisco

Yosemite is approximately **200 miles (320 km)** east of San Francisco. The drive takes roughly **five hours** as motorists navigate urban traffic getting out of the city and its surrounding suburbs and continue along some two-lane highways on the way to the park.

The **Big Oak Flat entrance** is the closest to San Francisco, accessed via **CA-120 East.** Begin by taking **I-80 East** out of the city and over the Bay Bridge. Continue on **I-580 East** for 46 miles (74 km) before

Best Hotels & Campgrounds

★ **The Ahwahnee:** With its rock facade and superb Yosemite Valley views, this luxury hotel is a quintessential national parks property (page 116).

★ **Yosemite Bug Rustic Mountain Resort:** For those on a budget, this sprawling complex of hostel dorms, tent cabins, private bedrooms, and guest houses is just 26 miles (42 km) from Yosemite Valley (page 118).

★ **Rush Creek Lodge:** The newest resort in the Yosemite area is less than 2 miles (3.2 km) from the park's Big Oak Flat entrance and has a saltwater pool, game room for kids, and a tavern (page 126).

★ **Wawona Hotel:** Relax on a large veranda and take in the mountain air at this historic park hotel in Wawona near the Mariposa Grove of Big Trees (page 129).

★ **Far Meadow Base Camp Cabins:** Rent an off-the-grid A-frame, log cabin, or vintage trailer in a serene setting 45 minutes from the park's South entrance (page 129).

★ **Summerdale Campground:** This small U.S. Forest Service campground with roomy, idyllic campsites on a creek is a mere 1.5 miles (2.4 km) from the park's South entrance (page 130).

★ **Tuolumne Meadows Campground:** This sprawling campground provides access to Yosemite's stunning high country. Best of all, you can head out on a hike to Elizabeth Lake right from your campsite (page 141).

★ **High Sierra Camps:** Enjoy tent cabins in the park's backcountry without having to hike in supplies. A night's stay includes breakfast and dinner (page 142).

turning off on **I-205 East** toward Tracy and Stockton. Follow I-205 East for 14.5 miles (23.3 km) before hopping on **I-5 North** for 1 mile (1.6 km). Merge onto **CA-120 East** for 6 miles (9.7 km) and then take **CA-99 North** for less than 2 miles (3.2 km) before reconnecting with **CA-120 East.** The road will climb up into the Sierra Nevada and pass scenic towns, including **Groveland,** on the way to the park's **Big Oak Flat entrance.** Within the park, Big Oak Flat Road continues into Yosemite Valley. Time your drive for weekdays or early mornings to avoid traffic and crowds. From the Big Oak Flat entrance, it's about another 45 minutes to Yosemite Valley.

The **Arch Rock entrance** is another option. From San Francisco, take **I-580 East** to **I-205 East.** In Manteca, take **CA-99 South** for 56 miles (90 km) to Merced. In Merced, turn right onto **CA-140 East.** CA-140 will take you right to the Arch Rock entrance.

From Los Angeles

Getting from Los Angeles to Yosemite National Park involves driving roughly **300 miles (485 km),** about **six hours,** along two of the state's biggest highways. Take **US-101 North,** then **CA-170 North,** and finally **I-5 North,** following signs for Sacramento. Continue for 83 miles (134 km) on I-5, then get on **CA-99 North** for 132 miles (213 km), passing through Bakersfield and Fresno. Merge onto **CA-41 North** and continue for 62 miles (100 km), passing through the city of

Best Restaurants

★ **The Ahwahnee Dining Room:** Treat yourself to a meal at the historic hotel's fine restaurant, with its magnificent high-beamed ceiling and floor-to-ceiling windows (page 115).

★ **High Country Health Foods & Cafe:** This Mariposa health food store serves up smoothies and creative sandwiches. Eat in the nice dining area or take it to go for a picnic in the park (page 116).

★ **Wawona Hotel Dining Room:** Enjoy hearty meaty entrées or healthier fare surrounded by lots of windows and big tree-inspired hanging lamps (page 129).

★ **Whoa Nellie Deli:** Yes, this is a restaurant within a gas station mini-mart, but how many convenience stores serve lobster taquitos and sashimi (page 137)?

★ **Silver Lake Resort Café:** Located in June Lake, this tiny diner's hearty breakfasts make it an essential stop for those on Yosemite's eastern side (page 138).

Oakhurst, which is a good place to stock up on supplies. After the community of Fish Camp, CA-41 enters the park at its **South entrance.** In the park, the highway becomes Wawona Road. You can reach Yosemite Valley from the South entrance in about one hour.

From Las Vegas

If there's any chance **Tioga Pass** will be closed (and between October and May, that's likely), call the **National Park Service** at 209/372-0200 for the latest weather and road report. If the pass is open, you have your choice of two direct routes from Las Vegas to Yosemite. If that road is closed, you have no choice but to bypass Tioga Pass via a longer route through central California.

Via Tioga Pass: Nevada Route

Driving over Tioga Pass from Nevada into the park is only an option when Tioga Pass Road is open, usually June-October. To begin this roughly six-hour drive, head out of Las Vegas on **US-95 North** and stay on this highway through the desert for 250 miles (405 km). Then turn west on **US-6 West** in Tonopah. Continue for 40 miles (64 km) and then turn right on **CA-120 West.** The highway will merge into **US-395** just south of Mono Lake. Utilize US-395 North/CA-120 West for a couple of miles before turning left on **Tioga Pass Road,** which heads into the park via the **Tioga Pass entrance.** Be sure to fill up your car's tank at the Tioga Gas Mart (and fill your belly at Whoa Nellie Deli) before entering the park.

Stopping in Tonopah

Tonopah is a natural crossroads that rewards travelers with colorful mining history—it was known as the "Queen of the Silver Camps"—and one of the darkest starry skies in the country. Tequila, beer, and spice lovers will revel in the cheesy chile rellenos at **El Marques** (348 N. Main St., 775/482-3885, 11am-9pm Tues.-Sun., $10-15), and the salsa seals the deal. Or how about a beer and some barbecue? **Tonopah Brewing Co.** (315 S. Main St., 775/482-2000, www.tonopahbrewing.com, 11am-9pm daily, $12-20) is your stop. Taste its pilsners, hefeweizens, and IPAs in pint or pitcher form along with some delicious barbecued meats, including slow-simmered brisket, barbecue pork, and ribs cooked for at least seven hours.

Stretch Your Legs

Driving from San Francisco to Yosemite via CA-120, most people have no idea that there is a minor engineering marvel just a few miles off the highway. Just east of Oakdale is the **Knights Ferry Covered Bridge** (Knights Ferry Recreation Area, 17968 Covered Bridge Rd., Oakdale, 209/881-3517, 6am-sunset daily, $5), which is said to be the longest covered bridge west of the Mississippi. Built in 1864, this 330-foot bridge, spanning the Stanislaus River, was considered an example of state-of-the-art engineering at the time. Though you cannot drive across it, the bridge is open to pedestrians. To reach the bridge, head east out of Oakdale on CA-108/120 for 11 miles (17.7 km). Take a left on Kennedy Road and then, after 0.5 mile (0.8 km), take a left on Sonora Road. After 0.5 mile (0.8 km), take a right on Covered Bridge Road, and the attraction will appear soon.

The owners have faithfully restored the **Mizpah Hotel** (100 N. Main St., 775/482-3030, www.themizpahhotel.com, $100-165)—the "Grand Lady of Tonopah" was the epitome of luxury during the silver boom—with claw-foot tubs, wrought-iron bedsteads, and lots of carmine accents. You can dine on-site at the casual **Pittman Café** (6am-9pm daily, $12-20). Next door, the guest rooms at **Jim Butler Inn** (100 S. Main St., 800/635-9455, www.jimbutlerinn.com, $85-120) are bright and inviting, with wood furniture, cinnamon or emerald color schemes, and faux hearths. Some guest rooms have fridges and microwaves; all have free Wi-Fi.

Via Tioga Pass: California Route

When Tioga Pass is open, travelers can get to Yosemite from Las Vegas with some time on US-395, one of the most scenic highways in the state. Only a few miles farther, it is a far **more scenic route** that includes a drive through Death Valley National Park. If it is during the summer months, Death Valley can be extremely hot, so make sure your vehicle's fluids are topped off and your air conditioner is working. The route begins by taking **US-95 North** out of Las Vegas for 117 miles (188 km). At the town of Beatty, take a left, heading southwest on **NV-374.** In just 9 miles (14.5 km) you pass the Death Valley National Park boundary. After entering **Death Valley National Park,** the road becomes **Daylight Pass Road.** Turn left to head south on **Scotty's Castle Road** within the park; after 0.5 mile (0.8 km) take a right on **CA-190 West** and follow the road for 68 miles (109 km), at which point it becomes **CA-136.** After 17.5 miles (28 miles), take a right on scenic **US-395 North** for 123 miles (198 km) as it passes by the towns of Lone Pine, Big Pine, Bishop, and Mammoth Lakes. Just south of the town of Lee Vining, **US-395 North** connects with **CA-120 West,** also known as **Tioga Pass Road,** which heads into the park.

Stopping in Bishop

A 4.5-hour drive from Las Vegas, Bishop is a great place to spend the night on this route. From Bishop, it's a scenic 1.5-hour drive to the park's Tioga Pass entrance. The small town in the Owens Valley, between the Sierra Nevada and the White Mountains, is a world-class destination for climbing, bouldering, and hiking. Outdoor enthusiasts may want to linger here for a few days before heading onward to the park.

The volcanic tablelands north of town are known for the **Happy Boulders** and **Sad Boulders,** with over 2,000 opportunities for climbers. In the winter, you can camp for cheap at the nearby **Pleasant Valley Pit** (760/872-5000, www.blm.gov, $5), a primitive campground located in an old rock quarry. The Owens River provides opportunities for floating, and the landscape is dotted with many artesian wells that double as swimming holes during the summer. The helpful people at the **Bishop Chamber of Commerce** (760/873-8403, www.bishopvisitor.com) can give directions to these sites and provide other assistance.

The Hostel California (213 Academy Ave., 760/399-6316, www.thehostelcalifornia.com, dorm beds $25-35, private rooms $60-170) offers cheap accommodations and communal living. Amenities include a shared kitchen, outdoor hangout space, and free use of bikes to tool around town and crash pads for rock climbing. Showers are available for $5. Downtown, right on Bishop Creek, the **Creekside Inn** (725 Main St., 760/872-3044, www.bishopcreeksideinn.com, $149-329) offers free laundry, a pool, and a hot tub.

Across the street from Creekside Inn is **Holy Smoke BBQ** (772 N. Main St., 760/872-4227, www.holysmoketexasstylebbq.com, 11am-9pm Wed.-Mon., $7-17), where weary travelers chomp down on tasty barbecue sandwiches or "redneck tacos," a slab of cornbread topped with barbecued meat and coleslaw.

Bypassing Tioga Pass

If Tioga Pass is closed, the only way to reach Yosemite from Las Vegas is an ugly **8- to 10-hour, 500-mile (805-km)** ordeal. Take **I-15 South** from Las Vegas and continue for 160 miles (260 km) to Barstow. In Barstow, get on **CA-58 West** for 126 miles (203 km) to Bakersfield, where you'll merge onto **CA-99 North.** Stay on CA-99 North for 107 miles (172 km) before turning onto **CA-41 North.** Follow CA-41 North for 62 miles (100 km) to the park's **South entrance.**

Stopping in Bakersfield

While far from a tourist destination, Bakersfield is at least a diversion on the otherwise dreary winter Yosemite-Las Vegas route.

While there are plenty of chain hotels, travelers looking for more personality in their lodgings will have to look a little harder. The search pays off at the **Padre Hotel** (1702 18th St., 661/427-4900 or 888/443-3387, www.thepadrehotel.com, $129-299), rescued and restored to its 1930s grandeur with a Spanish colonial exterior and sleek rooms with modern furniture. Dine at the Belvedere Room or get a cup of coffee at the Farmacy Café. There are also two bars: Brimstone and Prairie Fire, a rooftop bar on the 2nd floor. Sound walls and thick insulation ensure a peaceful rest.

One well-regarded chain hotel off CA-99 is the **Hampton Inn & Suites Bakersfield North-Airport** (8818 Spectrum Park Way, 661/391-0600, www.hamptoninn.com, $89-144). Besides its convenient location, its pluses include an outdoor pool and a fitness room for getting some exercise after a day crammed in the car.

It's tough to decide among the Caribbean-style chicken, steak, and seafood at **Mama Roomba** (1814 Eye St., 661/322-6262, www.mamaroomba.com, 11am-10pm Mon.-Fri., 5pm-10pm Sat., $10-15). Both the calamari and the tri-tip are good bets. They also serve beer, wine, and cocktails to tamp down your road rage after hours in the car. A bit more highbrow, **Uricchio's Trattoria** (1400 17th St., 661/326-8870, www.uricchios.com, 11am-2pm and 5pm-9pm Mon.-Thurs., 11am-2pm and 5pm-10pm Fri., 5pm-10pm Sat., $15-30) serves the best lasagna in town. The lobster ravioli in clam sauce is no slouch either.

By Train or Bus

Train

Amtrak (324 W. 24th St., Merced, 209/722-6862, reservations 800/872-7245, www.amtrak.com) has a station in Merced, an hour away from the park. You can take the train there and then take the **Amtrak Thruway Service bus**

($15 one-way) to locations in Yosemite Valley, including Yosemite Valley Lodge, The Ahwahnee, Curry Village, Crane Flat, and the Yosemite Visitors Center. The bus schedule changes seasonally but runs all year. It is about a 2.5-hour bus ride from Merced to the park. The bus also goes to White Wolf and Tuolumne Meadows during the summer months (daily service July-Aug., weekends only June and Sept.).

Bus

The **Yosemite Area Regional Transit System** (YARTS, 877/989-2787, www.yarts.com, $19 one-way, $38 round-trip) operates daily buses from Merced to Yosemite. It also has seasonal buses that take passengers from towns along CA-120 (Sonora, Jamestown, and Groveland) to the park. In the summer months, an Eastern Sierra service connects Mammoth Lakes, June Lake, and Lee Vining to the park as well.

Visiting the Park

Entrances

Yosemite National Park is accessible via five park entrances: Big Oak Flat, Arch Rock, South, Tioga Pass, and Hetch Hetchy. The **Arch Rock entrance** (CA-140) and the **Big Oak Flat entrance** (CA-120 West) are usually open year-round. The **Tioga Pass entrance** (CA-120 East) is just a few miles from Tuolumne Meadows and is the eastern access to Yosemite from US-395. Tioga Road closes in November or December each year and reopens in the spring, usually in May or June. The **Hetch Hetchy entrance** in the northwest part of the park is only open during daylight hours. The **South entrance** is open year-round.

Park Passes and Fees

The **park entrance fee** includes entry and parking for up to seven days. The cost is

the road into Yosemite Valley

$35 per car and $30 per motorcycle. The entrance fee is $20 per person for those entering by bus, bike, or on foot, also good for seven days. A **one-year pass for an automobile** to Yosemite is available for $70.

The National Park Service offers several **annual passes** for frequent park visitors. The **America the Beautiful Pass** allows access to all the national parks for a year for $80, and the **Senior Pass** (age 62 or older) costs $20 for an annual pass or only $80 for lifetime access to the parks. To purchase passes, inquire at the entrance station or at one of the visitors centers in the park.

Visitors Centers

The **Yosemite Valley Visitors Center** (Yosemite Village, 209/372-0200, 9am-5pm daily year-round) is a great place to get information upon arriving in the park. At the staffed information desk, rangers can give you information about everything from trails to the upcoming weather. An exhibit hall offers insight into the park's natural and human history. The **Yosemite Museum** (west end of Yosemite Village, 209/372-0303, 9am-5pm daily year-round) is the place to learn about the area's native Miwok and Paiute people.

Stop in at the **Yosemite Valley Wilderness Center** (Yosemite Village, 209/372-0745, 9am-1pm daily May-Oct.) if you are planning a multiday backpacking hike. You can pick up your wilderness permit, bear canister, map, and backcountry information here. You can also secure wilderness permits at the **Tuolumne Meadows Wilderness Center** (off Tioga Rd., 8 mi/12.9 km west of Tioga Pass and 2 mi/3.2 km east of Tuolumne Meadows Visitors Center, 209/372-0309, 8am-4:30pm daily late May-Oct. 14).

Visitors entering the park's South entrance can get information while viewing the paintings of Thomas Hill at the **Wawona Visitors Center at Hill's Studio** (Wawona Hotel, 209/375-9531, 9am-1pm daily May-Oct.). The **Big Oak Flat Information Station** (209/379-1899, 9am-1pm daily May-Oct.) is to the right after passing through the Big Oak Flat entrance. It has information, wilderness permits, and a gift shop. The **Tuolumne Meadows Visitors Center** (Tioga Rd., west of the Tuolumne Meadows Campground, 209/372-0263, hours vary, late June-early Sept.) is housed in a small building where you can get info along with a great map and guide to Tuolumne Meadows for $4.

Reservations

Accommodations

All the lodges, hotels, and cabin-tent clusters in Yosemite are run by the same booking agency. Contact the **Yosemite Park concessionaire** (inside U.S. 888/413-8869, outside the U.S. 602/278-8888, www.travelyosemite.com) to make reservations. Coming to Yosemite in the summer high season?

Try to make reservations 6-9 months in advance, especially if you have a specific lodging preference. If you wait until the week before your trip, you may find the park sold out or end up in a tent cabin at Curry when you wanted a suite at The Ahwahnee.

For more accommodations options, try the communities outside Yosemite:

- **El Portal** (CA-140): 3 miles (4.8 km) from the Arch Rock entrance
- **Mariposa** (CA-140): 40 miles (64 km) from the South entrance
- **Groveland** (CA-120): 26 miles (42 km) from the Big Oak Flat entrance
- **Fish Camp** (CA-41): 2 miles (3.2 km) from the South entrance
- **Lee Vining** (US-395): 13 miles (20.9 km) from the Tioga Pass (eastern) entrance
- **Mammoth Lakes** (US-395): 40 miles (64 km) from the Tioga Pass (eastern) entrance

Campgrounds

Inside the park, you'll find 13 designated campgrounds and the High Sierra Camps. Seven of those designated campgrounds are on the reservation system. For any Yosemite National Park campground, make reservations early! All the major campgrounds fill up spring-fall, and reservations can be difficult to come by. Consider making your Yosemite campground reservation at least five months in advance to get the campsite you want. Make reservations through the **National Park Service** (inside U.S. 877/444-6777, outside the U.S. 606/515-6777, www.recreation.gov). Campgrounds outside the park boundaries are often less expensive and require less advance notice.

Information and Services

Published bi-weekly in summer and monthly in spring, fall, and winter, ***Yosemite Guide*** provides information about the park's places and services. Most important, it includes a detailed schedule of all classes, events, and programs in the park. You'll receive your copy when you enter the park at any of the entrance stations. Download a PDF version online at www.nps.gov/yose/planyourvisit/guide.htm.

Banking and Post Offices

ATMs are available throughout Yosemite Valley: in Yosemite Village at the Art and Education Center within the Village Store, in Yosemite Valley Lodge, and in Curry Village's gift and grocery store. Outside the valley, ATMs are located in the Wawona store and the Tuolumne Meadows grocery store.

Several post offices provide **mailing services** in Yosemite. Look for a **post office** in **Yosemite Village** (9017 Village Dr., 209/372-4475, www.usps.com, 8:30am-5pm Mon.-Fri., 10am-noon Sat.), inside **Yosemite Valley Lodge** (9015 Lodge Dr., 209/372-4853, www.usps.com, 12:30pm-2:45pm Mon.-Fri.), in **El Portal** (5508 Foresta Rd., 209/379-2311, www.usps.com, 8:30am-1pm and 1:30pm-3pm Mon.-Fri.), and in **Tuolumne Meadows** (14000 CA-120 E., 209/372-4475, 9am-5pm Mon.-Fri., 9am-noon Sat.).

Gas Stations and Car Repairs

Limited seasonal gas is available up at Tuolumne Meadows just past the visitors center on Tioga Pass. There's also gas within the park at the **Crane Flat Gas Station** (8028 Big Flat Rd., 209/379-2742, 8am-7pm daily), which is located at the junction of Tioga Pass Road and Big Oak Flat Road on CA-120, just 17 miles (27 km) from the valley. The Wawona area has a **Wawona Gas Station** (8310 Wawona Rd., 209/375-6567, 8am-6pm daily) near the park's South entrance. If your car breaks down, you can take it to the **Village Garage** (9002 Village Dr., 209/372-8320, 8am-5pm daily, towing 24 hours). Expect to pay a high premium for towing and repairs.

Groceries and Laundry

Laundry facilities are available at the **Housekeeping Camp** inside the Curry Village complex (8am-10pm daily). Within the Yosemite Village, the **Village Store** (9am-7pm daily) has a surprisingly large grocery section with fresh meat, produce, ice, wood, and unexpected specialty items including brown rice pasta and noodle bowls. Limited-stock, expensive grocery stores in Curry Village are the **Curry Village Gift and Grocery** (10am-6pm Fri.-Sun.) and the **Housekeeping Camp Grocery** (8am-8pm daily). In Wawona, the **Wawona Store** (10am-5pm daily) sells some groceries, wine, and souvenirs. For a better selection of goods and much lower prices, you're better off shopping outside the park. Stock up on healthy foodstuffs at Mariposa's **High Country Health Foods & Café** (5186 CA-49, Mariposa, 209/966-5111, www.highcountryhealthfoods.com, 8am-7pm Mon.-Fri., 8am-5pm Sat., 9am-5pm Sun.). Also in Mariposa, the **Pioneer Market** (5034 Coakley Cir., Mariposa, 209/742-6100, www.pioneersupermarket.com, 7am-9pm daily) has groceries along with a deli and meat counter.

Internet and Phone Service

Limited **Internet access** is available in a few spots in Yosemite Valley. The Ahwahnee and the Wawona Hotel provide Wi-Fi to guests only, while Yosemite Valley Lodge offers wireless access for a $6 fee. Degnan's Kitchen in Yosemite Village has free Wi-Fi. Guests who stay in Curry Village can access the Internet in the Curry Village Lounge. Meanwhile, the Mariposa County Library in the Valley Village also has free Wi-Fi (though donations are appreciated) along with three computers with Internet access that visitors can use.

Most **cell phones** will have no coverage in most areas of the park. Phones with AT&T and Verizon plans will work in some parts of Yosemite Valley.

Emergency Services

For any emergencies within the park, **dial 911.** In Yosemite Village, the **Yosemite Medical Clinic** (9000 Ahwahnee Cir., 209/372-4637, 9am-7pm daily summer, 9am-5pm Mon.-Fri. winter) has urgent and primary care along with emergency services through an ambulance that is available 24-7.

Getting Around

Parking

During busy days, it becomes wholly apparent that Yosemite Valley has more cars than parking spaces. It is recommended to come into the park before 10am and find a space in one of the three big parking lots (the **Yosemite Village Parking Lot,** the **Yosemite Falls Parking Area,** and the **Half Dome Parking Area**) and then utilize the free shuttle bus to travel to different attractions and trails.

Shuttle Services

Yosemite runs an extensive network of shuttles in different areas of the park. One of the most-used travels through the **Yosemite Valley** (7am-10pm daily year-round, free). The **El Capitan Shuttle** (9am-5pm daily mid-June-Oct., free) also runs around certain parts of Yosemite Valley during the summer season. There are also seasonal Mariposa Grove (hours vary mid-Mar.-Nov. depending on conditions, free) and Badger Pass Ski Area shuttles (hours vary mid-Dec.-Mar., free).

Bus Tours

Learn about Yosemite's natural and cultural history by taking a guided bus tour. The popular **Yosemite Valley Tour** (888/413-8869, www.travelyosemite.com, 10am, 11am, 1pm, 2pm, 3pm daily summer, 10am and 2pm daily fall-spring, $38 adults, $28 children) is a two-hour trip around the park's valley section. There's also the four-hour-long **Glacier Point**

One Day in Yosemite

The sights, waterfalls, and hikes here are enough to fill a lifetime, but try to squeeze as much as you can into one day.

Hikers climb up stairs on Yosemite's Mist Trail.

Morning

Arrive at Yosemite National Park through the Arch Rock entrance (CA-140), only 11 miles (17.7 km) from Yosemite Valley. Stop at **Bridalveil Fall** for a photo op, then continue on to the Valley Visitors Center, where you'll leave your car for the day. At the visitors center, check for any open campsites or tent cabins at Curry Village, and confirm your reservations for dinner later at The Ahwahnee. Explore **Yosemite Village,** stopping for picnic supplies and water, then board the Valley Shuttle Bus. The shuttle provides a great free tour of the park, with multiple points to hop on and off.

Afternoon

Choose one of the valley's stellar day hikes (tip: not Half Dome). Take the Valley Shuttle Bus to Happy Isles (shuttle stop 16) and the trailhead for the superb but strenuous **Mist Trail.** This hike is best done in spring when the waterfalls are at their peak, but it's still gorgeous at any time of year. Hike to the Vernal Fall Footbridge and gaze at the Merced River as it spills over Vernal Fall. Hardier souls can continue on the strenuous trail to the top of Vernal Fall, and then to the top of the even taller Nevada Fall. Return via the John Muir Trail back to the Happy Isles trailhead and the Valley Shuttle. A shorter option is the steep 2-mile (3.2-km) round-trip hike up the **Columbia Rock Trail** to stunning views of the valley and its granite rock formations.

Evening

With all that hiking, you probably built up an appetite. Fortunately, you have reservations at the **The Ahwahnee Dining Room.** Change out of your shorts and hiking shoes (and maybe grab a shower at Curry Village), and then catch the Valley Shuttle to The Ahwahnee (shuttle stop 3). Grab a drink in the bar and spend some time enjoying the verdant grounds and stellar views of this historic building. After dinner, take the shuttle back to Yosemite Village, where your car awaits, and immediately start planning your return.

Extending Your Stay

If you have more time to spend in the park, you can easily fill two or three days just exploring **Yosemite Valley,** with an excursion to **Glacier Point.** With a week, add the **Tuolumne Meadows** (summer only), **Hetch Hetchy,** and **Wawona** sections of the park.

Tour (888/413-8869, www.travelyosemite.com, 8:30am and 1:30pm daily late May-late Oct., round-trip $57 adults, $36 children 5-12, children under 5 free) and the eight-hour **Yosemite Valley to Tuolumne Meadows Hikers Bus** (888/413-8869, www.travelyosemite.com, 8:20am daily early summer-fall, pricing varies).

Yosemite Valley

The first place most people go when they reach the park is the floor of Yosemite Valley (CA-140, Arch Rock entrance). From the valley floor, you can check out the visitors center, the theater, galleries, museums, hotels, and outdoor historical exhibits. Numerous pullouts from the main road invite photographers to capture the beauty of the valley and its many easily visible natural wonders. It's the most visited place in Yosemite, and many hikes, ranging from easy to difficult, begin in the valley.

Sights

Valley Visitors Center

After the scenic turnouts through the park, your first stop in Yosemite Valley should be the **Yosemite Valley Visitors Center** (Yosemite Village, off Northside Dr., 209/372-0200, www.nps.gov/yose, 9am-5pm daily, hours vary by season). Here you'll find the ranger station as well as an intricate interpretive museum describing the geological and human history of Yosemite. The visitors center also shows two films on Yosemite every half hour 9:30am-4:30pm. Separate buildings house the **Yosemite History Museum** (9am-5pm daily) and the **Ansel Adams Gallery** (650/692-3495, www.anseladams.com, 9am-5pm daily). This is also where you'll find the all-important public restrooms.

A short, flat walk from the visitors center takes you down to the re-created Miwok Native American village. The village includes all different types of structures, including those of the later Miwoks who incorporated European architecture into their building techniques. You can walk right into the homes and public buildings of this nearly lost culture. One of the most fascinating parts of this reconstruction is the evolution of construction techniques—as nonnative settlers infiltrated the area, building cabins and larger structures, the Miwok took note. They examined these buildings and incorporated pieces that they saw as improvements.

El Capitan

The first natural stone monument you encounter as you enter the valley is **El Capitan** (Northside Rd., west of El Capitan Bridge). Formed of Cretaceous granite that's actually named for this formation, this granite monolith was created by millions of years of glacial action. The 3,000-foot (914-m) craggy rock face is accessible in two ways: You can take a long hike west from the Upper Yosemite Fall and up the back side of the formation, or you can grab your climbing gear and scale the face. El Cap boasts a reputation as one of the world's seminal big-face climbs.

★ Half Dome

At the far end of the valley, perhaps the most recognizable feature in Yosemite rests high above the valley floor. Ansel Adams's famed photographs of **Half Dome,** visible from most of the valley floor, made it known to hikers and photo-lovers the world round. Scientists believe that Half Dome was never a whole dome; in fact, it still towers 4,737 feet (1,444 m) above the valley floor in its original formation. This piece of a narrow granite ridge was polished to its smooth shape by glaciers tens of millions of years ago, giving it the fallacious appearance of half a dome. A Yosemite guidebook from 1868 (not a Moon guidebook!) proclaimed that "the summit of Half Dome will never be trodden by human feet." This statement

Yosemite Valley

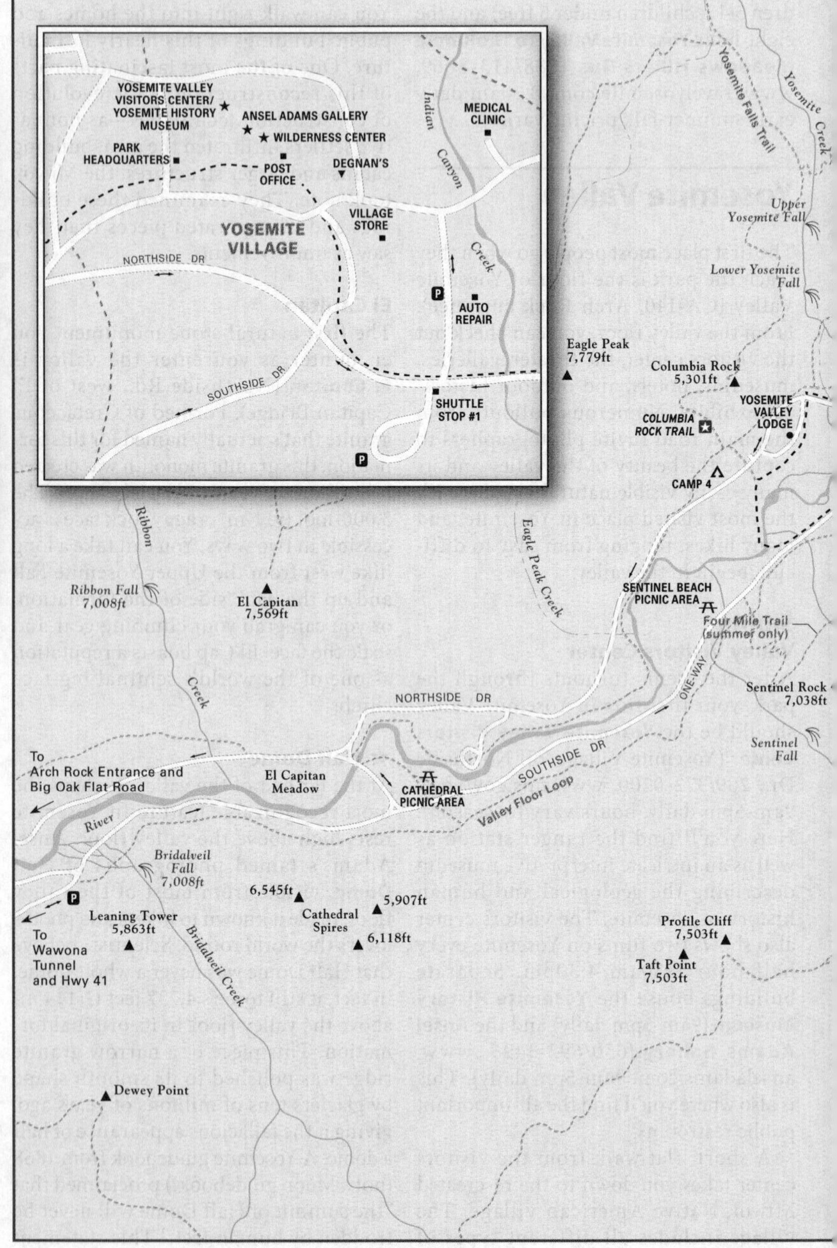

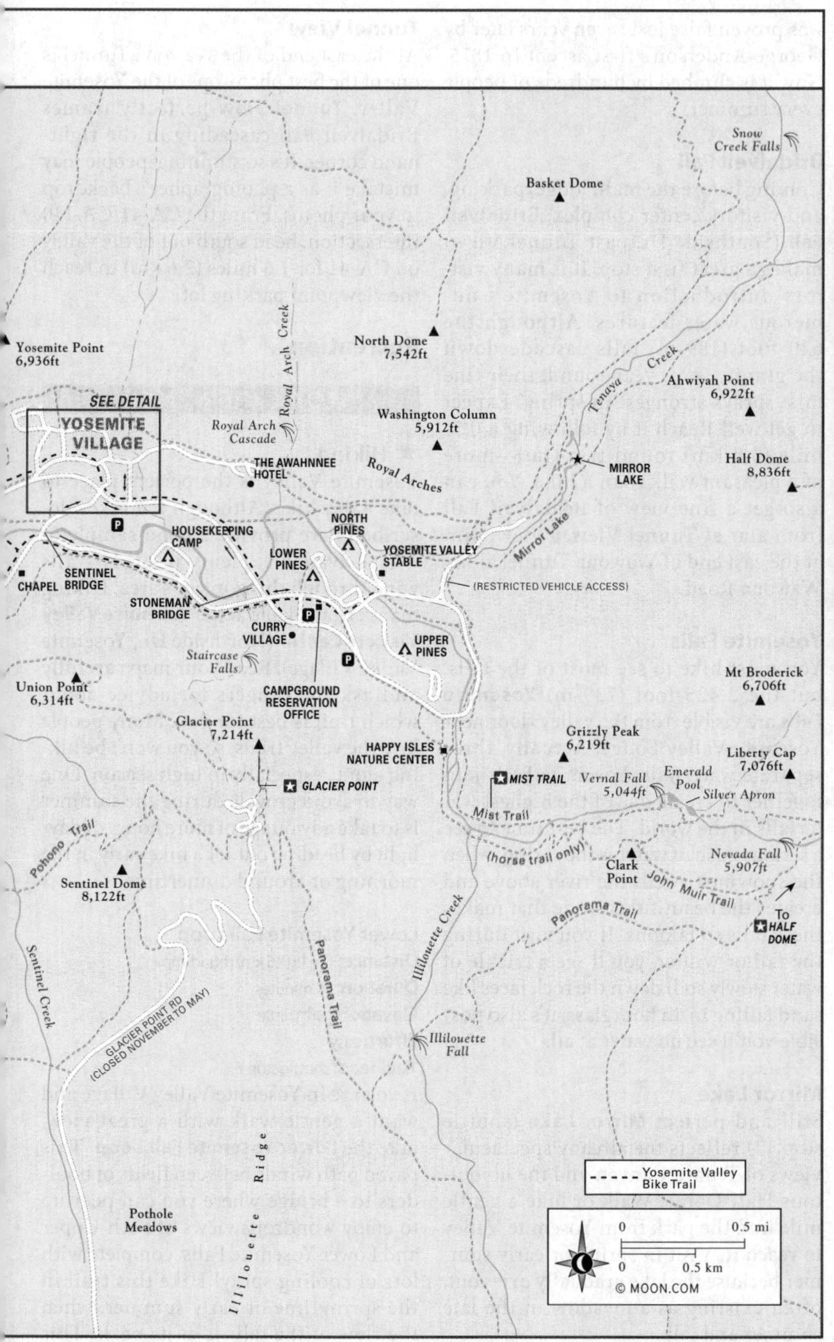
Snow Creek Falls
Basket Dome
North Dome 7,542ft
Royal Arch Creek
Tenaya Creek
Ahwiyah Point 6,922ft
Yosemite Point 6,936ft
SEE DETAIL
YOSEMITE VILLAGE
Royal Arch Cascade
Washington Column 5,912ft
THE AWAHNNEE HOTEL
Royal Arches
MIRROR LAKE
Half Dome 8,836ft
Mirror Lake
HOUSEKEEPING CAMP
NORTH PINES
LOWER PINES
YOSEMITE VALLEY STABLE
SENTINEL BRIDGE
CHAPEL
(RESTRICTED VEHICLE ACCESS)
STONEMAN BRIDGE
CURRY VILLAGE
UPPER PINES
Staircase Falls
Union Point 6,314ft
CAMPGROUND RESERVATION OFFICE
Mt Broderick 6,706ft
Glacier Point 7,214ft
HAPPY ISLES NATURE CENTER
Grizzly Peak 6,219ft
Liberty Cap 7,076ft
GLACIER POINT
MIST TRAIL
Vernal Fall 5,044ft
Emerald Pool
Silver Apron
Mist Trail
Pohono Trail
(horse trail only)
Clark Point
Nevada Fall 5,907ft
Sentinel Dome 8,122ft
John Muir Trail
Illilouette Creek
Panorama Trail
To HALF DOME
Sentinel Creek
Panorama Trail
GLACIER POINT RD (CLOSED NOVEMBER TO MAY)
Illilouette Fall
Illilouette Ridge
Yosemite Valley Bike Trail
Pothole Meadows
0 0.5 mi
0 0.5 km
© MOON.COM

was proven false just seven years later by George Anderson's first ascent in 1875. Now it is climbed by hundreds of people every summer.

Bridalveil Fall

Coming before the main lodge, parking, and visitors center complex, **Bridalveil Fall** (Southside Dr. past Tunnel View) makes a great first stop. It is many visitors' introduction to Yosemite's numerous water features. Although the 620-foot (189-m) falls cascade down the granite walls year-round, their fine mist sprays strongest in spring. Expect to get wet! Reach it by following a 0.5-mile (0.8-km) round-trip trail—more of a pleasant walk than a hike. You can also get a fine view of Bridalveil Fall from afar at Tunnel View, a viewpoint at the east end of Wawona Tunnel along Wawona Road.

Yosemite Falls

You must hike to see most of the falls, but the 2,425-foot (739-m) **Yosemite Falls** are visible from the valley floor near Yosemite Valley Lodge. Actually, three separate waterfalls, Yosemite Falls join together to create one of the highest waterfalls in the world. The best time to see a serious gush of water is the spring, when the snowmelt swells the river above and creates the beautiful cascade that makes these falls so famous. If you visit during the fall or winter, you'll see a trickle of water slowly spill down the rock faces like sand falling in an hourglass; it's also possible you'll see no water at all.

Mirror Lake

Still and perfect **Mirror Lake** (shuttle stop 17) reflects the already spectacular views of Tenaya Canyon and the ubiquitous Half Dome. Walk or bike a gentle mile into the park from Yosemite Valley to reach it. Visit in spring or early summer because the lake gradually dries out, often existing as a meadow in the late summer and fall.

Tunnel View

At the east end of the Wawona Tunnel is one of the best photo-ops of the Yosemite Valley. **Tunnel View** perfectly frames Bridalveil Fall cascading in the right-hand corner. It's so stunning, people may mistake it as a photographer's backdrop in your photos. From the CA-41/CA-140 intersection, head south out of the valley on CA-41 for 1.6 miles (2.6 km) to reach the viewpoint parking lot.

Recreation

TOP EXPERIENCE

★ Hiking

Yosemite Valley is the perfect place to take a day hike. Although the hikes described here provide a good sample of what's available, plenty of other trails wind through this gorgeous area. Hiking maps are available at the **Yosemite Valley Visitors Center** (Northside Dr., Yosemite Valley Village). Read your map carefully and ask the rangers for advice about which trail is best for you. Many people love the valley trails, so you won't be hiking alone, especially in high season. One way to avoid crowds during the summer is to take advantage of more hours of daylight by heading out for a hike early in the morning or around dinnertime.

Lower Yosemite Fall Loop

Distance: 1 mile (1.6 km) round-trip
Duration: 20 minutes
Elevation gain: little
Effort: easy
Trailhead: shuttle stop 6

If you are in Yosemite Valley Village and want a gentle walk with a great view, take the **Lower Yosemite Fall Loop.** This paved path winds between fields of boulders to a bridge where you can peer up to enjoy wondrous views of both Upper and Lower Yosemite Falls, complete with lots of cooling spray! Hike this trail in the springtime or early summer, when the flow of the falls is at its peak. This easy trail works well for families with kids who love the water.

Cook's Meadow Loop

Distance: 1 mile (1.6 km) round-trip
Duration: 30 minutes
Elevation gain: none
Effort: easy
Trailhead: Yosemite Valley Visitors Center (shuttle stops 5 and 9)

Quintessential Yosemite Valley views are visible along the **Cook's Meadow Loop,** a short walk through the heart of the valley. Perhaps the most famous is the view of Half Dome from the Sentinel Bridge, which was captured in the iconic photography of Ansel Adams. Farther on, you can gaze up at the Royal Arches and Glacier Point.

Mirror Lake Loop

Distance: 7 miles (11.3 km) round-trip
Duration: 2-3 hours
Elevation gain: 100 feet (30.5 m)
Effort: easy to moderate
Trailhead: Mirror Lake Junction (shuttle stop 17)

From the shuttle stop, a 1-mile (1.6-km), wheelchair-accessible paved road leads to **Mirror Lake,** the shallow body of water that gives this trail that follows its name. Exhibits around the lake discuss the ongoing natural process that is drying the lake out and will eventually transform it into a meadow. From this pool, the connected footpath make a 5-mile (8 km) loop around the lake, following Tenaya Creek, crossing two bridges, and offering great views of Half-Dome.

Valley Floor Loop

Distance: full loop 11.5 (18.5 km) miles round-trip; half loop 7.2 miles (11.6 km) round-trip
Duration: full loop 5-7 hours; half loop 2.5-3.5 hours
Elevation gain: little
Effort: moderate
Trailhead: Lower Yosemite Fall (shuttle stop 6), then head west on the bike path until you see the trail signs

From top to bottom: the bold rock face of El Capitan; flowering lupine in Yosemite National Park; Vernal Fall.

The **Valley Floor Loop** is a great way to see all the most beautiful parts of the Yosemite Valley while escaping the crowds on the roads. The full loop winds along the path of old wagon roads and historic trails through meadows and forests, and takes most of a day to hike. But it's worth it. Visitors who want a mid-length hike can just do the half-loop version. Cross the El Capitan Bridge to start back toward Yosemite Village. To complete the whole loop, hike past the bridge and continue west toward Bridalveil Fall. The route is not entirely clear on the trail map, so it's a good idea to talk to the rangers at the visitors center before your hike to avoid getting lost.

Upper Yosemite Fall

Distance: 7 miles (11.3 km) round-trip
Duration: 6-8 hours
Elevation gain: 2,700 feet (823 m)
Effort: strenuous
Trailhead: Camp 4 (shuttle stop 7 and El Capitan shuttle stop E2)

One of the more challenging hikes in Yosemite Valley, the trek up to **Upper Yosemite Fall** is also one of the most satisfying. Take the shuttle to the trailhead rather than walking up from Lower Yosemite Fall. The trail gets steep, climbing 2,700 vertical feet (823 m) in 3 miles (4.8 km) to reach the top of North America's tallest waterfall. Your efforts will be rewarded by some of the most astonishing aerial views to be found anywhere in the world. Look down over the fall and out over the valley, with its grassy meadows so far below. Plan on spending all day on this hike. Bring plenty of water and snacks to replenish your energy for the tricky climb down.

★ Columbia Rock Trail

Distance: 2 miles (3.2 km) round-trip
Duration: 2-3 hours
Elevation gain: 1,000 feet (305 m)
Effort: strenuous
Trailhead: Camp 4 (shuttle stop 7 and El Capitan shuttle stop E2)

To get a commanding view of the valley with a short but steep hike, opt for the **Columbia Rock Trail.** The trail climbs 1,000 feet (305 m) via many steep, stone stair switchbacks over the course of 1 mile (1.6 km). Its destination is Columbia Rock, a stone ledge with minimal handrails that offers stunning views of the valley below and Half Dome, which towers in the distance like a giant hooded figure. Continue on another 0.5 mile (0.8 km) to Upper Yosemite Fall for more amazing views.

★ Mist Trail

Distance: 2.4 miles (3.9 km) round-trip to Vernal Fall, 5.4 miles (8.7 km) round-trip to Nevada Fall, 7.3 miles (11.7 km) round-trip loop to Nevada Fall and return via Join Muir Trail
Duration: 3 hours round-trip to Vernal Fall, 5-6 hours round-trip to Nevada Fall
Elevation gain: 1,000 feet (305 m) to Vernal Fall, 2,000 feet (610 m) to Nevada Fall
Effort: strenuous
Trailhead: Happy Isles Nature Center (shuttle stop 16)

One of Yosemite's best day hikes, the **Mist Trail,** takes in some of the Yosemite Valley's most stunning scenery, from plunging waterfalls to rounded granite rock faces to sweeping canyon views. Starting at the Happy Isles Nature Center, the trail's first mile (1.6 km) is on a paved path to the Vernal Fall Footbridge. The trail then ascends much steep, slick granite and 600 stairs to the top of Vernal Fall, offering a unique perspective on the 317-foot (96.6-m) waterfall. It's possible to turn around at the top of Vernal Fall for a 2.4-mile (3.9-km) out-and-back hike.

If you have the stamina, continue on to the nearly twice-as-tall Nevada Fall. There's a fairly level section of trail between the top of Vernal Fall and the base of the second waterfall. Then the trail traverses some rocky switchbacks on its way to the top of the 594-foot (181-m) Nevada Fall. Handrails at the top of the falls allow you to take in the precipitous plunge of the Merced River over the sheer rock face. To make a loop back down to the bottom of the Mist Trail, take the scenic **John Muir Trail,** which will make your hike 7.3 miles (11.7 km) round-trip. You can also simply return via the Mist Trail for a shorter 5.4-mile (8.7-km) total hike.

Pack a lightweight parka, since this aptly named trail drenches intrepid visitors in the spring and early summer months.

Half Dome

Distance: 14-16 miles (22.5-26 km) round-trip
Duration: 10-12 hours
Elevation gain: 4,800 feet (1,463 m)
Effort: strenuous
Trailhead: Happy Isles Nature Center (shuttle stop 16)

Perhaps the most famous—and potentially dangerous—climb in Yosemite Valley takes you to the top of the monumental granite **Half Dome.** With a 4,800-foot (1,463-m) ascent, this arduous, all-day hike is not for children, the elderly, or the out-of-shape. Attempt this climb only late May-early October (weather permitting), when the cables

Mist Trail

are up to help climbers keep their balance and pull themselves the steep final 400 feet (122 m) to the top of the dome. Once you reach the top, you'll find a restful expanse of stone on which to sit and rest and enjoy the scenery. Only 300 people per day are allowed to take this hike. The first step is before you even go to the park: secure a permit ($20), distributed by lottery online at www.recreation.gov, or by calling 877/444-6777. For other questions, call 209/372-0826. There's also the chance of securing a last-minute permit by lottery two days prior to the hiking date. Bring along a pack with water, food, and essentials for safety.

Cycling

Cycling is a great way to get out of the car and off the crowded roads, but still explore Yosemite Valley at a quicker pace. The valley includes 12 miles (19.3 km) of paved, mostly flat trails. You can bring your own bikes, or rent from **bike stands** (209/372-0826, 8am-6pm mid-June-mid-Nov., $36 per day) at Yosemite Valley Lodge or Curry Village. Get a bike trail map while you're there.

Rock Climbing

The rock climbing at Yosemite is some of the best in the world. **El Capitan,** the face of **Half Dome,** and **Sentinel Dome** in the high country are challenges that draw climbers from all over. If you plan to climb one of these monuments, check with the Yosemite park rangers and the Mountaineering School well in advance of your planned climb for necessary information and permits.

Many of the spectacular ascents are not beginner climbs. If you try to scale El Capitan for your first climb ever, you'll fail, or worse. The right place to start is the **Yosemite Mountaineering School** (209/372-8344, www.travelyosemite.com, $172-215), where you can get one-on-one guided climbing experience. You'll find rock climbing lessons every morning at 8:30am as well as guided climbs out of Yosemite Valley and Tuolumne Meadows. In addition to guided hikes and backpacking trips, there are cross-country skiing lessons and treks in winter.

Entertainment

Theater

The **Valley Visitors Center Auditorium** (Yosemite Village Visitors Center, Northside Dr., www.yosemiteconservancy.org, live theater tickets $10 adults, children 12 and under free) in the heart of Yosemite Village acts as home to the Yosemite Theater. For an evening of indoor entertainment, check the copy of *Yosemite Guide* you received at the gate for a list of what shows are playing during your visit. You may see Ranger Shelton Johnson portray a buffalo soldier, or the extravagantly bearded actor Lee Stetson portray John Muir, as he has since 1983.

Photography and Art Classes

The unbelievable scenery of Yosemite inspires visitors young and old to create images to take home with them. Knowing this, Yosemite offers art and photography classes to help people catch hold of their inner Ansel Adams. In the summertime, art classes are offered for a nominal fee out of the **Yosemite Art Center** (Yosemite Village, next to the Yosemite Village Store, 209/372-4207, www.yosemiteconservancy.org, 9am-4pm daily Apr.-Oct.). Check the *Yosemite Guide* for a list of classes during your visit. You must bring your own art supplies, chair or cushion to sit on, and walking shoes (you'll take a brief walk out to a good location to see the scenery). If you don't have supplies, you can buy them at the Village Store just before class. Also check the *Guide* for guided tours of the **Ansel Adams Gallery** in the village.

Guided Tours

A wide variety of hikes and tours are available, led by various park staff. Some include ranger-led walks and evening programs, such as "Starry Skies over Yosemite." There are also group hikes, guided bus tours, and full-moon bike rides available for visitors. See the *Yosemite Guide* or www.travelyosemite.com for more information and a schedule of events.

Festivals and Events

A few annual events are designed to draw visitors back to the park during the less crowded winter months.

Vintners' Holidays (Nov.-early Dec., www.travelyosemite.com) puts the focus on wine, with celebrated winemakers highlighting rare releases, wine aficionados leading tasting seminars, and a five-course dinner paired with wines (the wines are chosen first, of course!).

Since 1927, The Ahwahnee Dining Room has been decorated like an 18th-century English manor for the holiday season. The accompanying seven-course **Bracebridge Dinner** (mid-Dec., www.travelyosemite.com) includes a program of Christmas carols and other entertainment. Famed photographer Ansel Adams was the first director of the Bracebridge Dinner.

For over 30 years, some of the state's most acclaimed chefs have descended on the historic Ahwahnee Hotel for **Chefs' Holidays** (mid-Jan.-late Jan., www.travelyosemite.com), a multiple-week foodie fest that includes culinary demonstrations, tastings, and five-course dinners.

Food

Inside the Park

The ★ **The Ahwahnee Dining Room** (The Ahwahnee, 209/372-1489, www.travelyosemite.com, 7am-10am, 11:30am-3pm, and 5:30pm-9pm daily, $12-21) enjoys a reputation for fine cuisine that stretches back to the 1920s. The grand dining room features high ceilings, wrought-iron chandeliers, and stellar valley views. The restaurant serves three meals daily, but dinner is a highlight, with California cuisine that mirrors top-tier San Francisco restaurants (with a price tag to match). Reservations are recommended for all meals, though it's possible to walk in for breakfast and lunch. Dinner requires "resort casual" attire.

At the other side of the valley, you can enjoy a spectacular view of Yosemite Falls at the **Mountain Room Restaurant** (Yosemite Valley Lodge, 209/372-1281, www.travelyosemite.com, 5pm-10pm Mon.-Sat., 9am-1pm and 5pm-10pm Sun., $17-38), part of Yosemite Valley Lodge. The glass atrium lets every guest at every table take in the view of the 2,424-foot (739-m) falls. The menu features steaks and seafood, and drinks are available from the full bar. They now do Sunday brunch as well. A casual bar menu is available at the **Mountain Room Lounge** (4:30pm-11pm Mon.-Fri., noon-11pm Sat.-Sun.) immediately across from the restaurant. Enjoy the patio in the summer and the fireplace in the winter. In the same building, the **Base Camp Eatery** (7am-9pm daily, $7-15) offers cafeteria food with less atmosphere but reasonable prices.

For more casual dining, head to Yosemite Village for **The Loft at Degnan's** (www.travelyosemite.com, 5pm-9pm daily May-Sept.) for barbecue from wings to ribs, and **Degnan's Kitchen** (7am-6pm daily) for an array of sandwiches, salads, and other take-away munchies. Behind the Village Store, the **Village Grill Deck** (11am-5pm daily) serves fast-food hamburgers, salads, and sandwiches.

In Curry Village, options include **Pizza Patio** (summer daily 11am-10pm, fall and winter hours vary), the **Pavilion** (7am-10am and 5:30pm-8:30pm daily late Mar.-late Oct.), and **Meadow Grill** (11am-8pm daily Apr.-mid Sept.), a coffee shop and bar.

Outside the Park

An hour west of the Yosemite Valley, there are some dining options in the gold rush town of Mariposa.

★ **High Country Health Foods & Café** (5186 CA-49, Mariposa, 209/966-5111, www.highcountryhealthfoods.com, store 8am-7pm Mon.-Fri., 8am-5pm Sat., 9am-5pm Sun., café 8am-3pm Mon.-Sat., 9am-3pm Sun., $6-10) is a great place to stock up on tasty sandwiches, revitalizing smoothies, and healthy produce. If you get the Midpines sandwich, a flavorful smoked chicken and feta cheese concoction, there is a chance you'll eat it all in the nice café setting before ever making it to the park.

With big windows looking out over Mariposa, **Savoury's Restaurant** (5034 CA-140, Mariposa, 209/966-7677, 5pm-9:30pm daily, $15-31) is a fine place for supper and a cocktail. The steak-heavy menu also includes seafood, pasta, and salad.

1850 Restaurant & Brewery (5114 CA-140, Mariposa, 209/966-2229, www.1850restaurant.com, 11am-9pm Tues.-Sun., $15-40) is a small craft brewery that serves up its own beers alongside a menu of pastas, steaks, and a lauded fried chicken. You can't go wrong with one of its burgers. Dine out front or inside in a booth constructed of reclaimed wood.

Accommodations

Inside the Park

Almost all of the lodging in Yosemite National Park is run by hospitality management company Aramark. There are a limited number of places to stay within the park's boundaries. If you would like to stay in the park during the summer high season, make **reservations** as early as possible—as much as **a year in advance**—by calling 888/413-8869 if in the United States or 602/278-8888 if outside the country. Another option is to do it all online at www.travelyosemite.com. Also book a year in advance for Christmas and holiday weekends. Spring reservations can be just as competitive during wet years that promise prime waterfall viewing.

If you're looking for luxury among the trees and rocks, check in to the ★ **The Ahwahnee** (inside U.S. 888/413-8869, outside the U.S. 602/278-8888, www.travelyosemite.com, $518-1,200). Built as a luxury hotel in the early 20th century, it lives up to its reputation with soaring ceilings in the common rooms, a gorgeous stone facade, and striking stone fireplaces. Guest rooms, whether in the hotel or in the individual cottages, drip sumptuous appointments. Influenced by Native American design, rooms feature intricate, multicolored geometric and zoomorphic patterns on linens, furniture, and pillows. Rooms with king beds invite romance for couples, while those with two doubles are perfect for families. Many have views of the valley, while a limited number include balconies and decks.

Yosemite Valley Lodge (inside U.S. 888/413-8869, outside the U.S. 602/278-8888, www.travelyosemite.com, $278-298), situated near Yosemite Village on the valley floor, has a location perfect for touring all over the park. The motel-style rooms are light and pretty, with polished wood furniture. Environmentally friendly features include energy-saving lighting and floors made from recycled products. Families should opt for the aptly named Family Rooms with one king bed and a bunk bed. Enjoy the heated pool in the summertime and the free shuttle transportation up to Badger Pass in winter. The amphitheater at the middle of the lodge runs nature programs and movies all year. The lodge has a post office, an ATM, and plenty of food options, and it is central to the Yosemite shuttle system.

Curry Village (inside U.S. 888/413-8869, outside the U.S. 602/278-8888, www.travelyosemite.com, $143-260) offers some of the oldest lodgings in the park. Locally called Camp Curry, this sprawling array of wood-sided and tent cabins was originally created in 1899 to provide affordable lodgings so that people of modest means could afford to visit and enjoy the wonders of Yosemite. At Curry Village, you can rent a hard-walled cabin or a tent cabin, with or without heat and with or without a private bath, depending on your budget and your needs. The tent cabins, the most affordable option, are small, fitting cot beds and a small dresser on the wood floor. Bear-proof lockers sit outside each tent cabin. Wood cabins have one or two double beds and electricity, but little else. The cabins with private baths are heated and boast daily maid service, but no TVs or phones. All cabins have an outdoor deck or patio for taking in the mountain air. Another option is a room in the Stoneman Cottage, a rustic motel with private bathrooms. With its perfect location on the valley floor, a swimming pool in the summer, and an ice skating rink in the winter, Camp Curry makes an inexpensive vacation at Yosemite a joyful reality.

Want to camp, but don't want to schlep all the gear into the park? Book a tent cabin at **Housekeeping Camp** (inside U.S. 888/413-8869, outside the U.S. 602/278-8888, www.travelyosemite.com, $108). Located on the banks of the Merced River, Housekeeping Camp has its own sandy river beach for playing and sunbathing. Cabins have cement walls, white canvas roofs, and a white canvas curtain that separates the bedroom from the covered patio that doubles as a dining room. Every cabin has a double bed plus a bunk bed (can also add two cots per unit), a bear-proof food container, and an outdoor fire ring. You can bring your own linens, or rent a "bed pack" (no towels) for $2.50 per night. No maid service is provided, but you won't miss it as you sit outside watching the sun set over Yosemite Valley.

From top to bottom: Yosemite Valley Lodge; sandwich at Mariposa's High Country Health Foods & Café; Yosemite Bug Rustic Mountain Resort.

Outside the Park: CA-140

You can't miss the **River Rock Inn** (4993 7th St., Mariposa, 209/966-5793, www.riverrockinncafe.com, $179-199) with its vivid orange-and-purple exterior in the heart of Mariposa. What was once a rundown 1940s motor lodge is now a quirky, fun motel with uniquely decorated rooms that make the most of the space with modern Pottery Barn-esque wrought-iron and wood styling. Have no fear: The colors become softer as you step through the door of your reasonably priced guest room. Four suites provide enough space for families, while the other five rooms sleep couples in comfort. Guests also enjoy a comprehensive continental breakfast before heading out. The River Rock is a 45-minute drive from the Arch Rock entrance to Yosemite, and at the southern end of the long chain of Gold Country towns, making it a great base of operations for an outdoorsy, Western-style California vacation.

If you prefer cozy seclusion to large lodge-style hotels, stay at the **Highland House** (3125 Wild Dove Ln., 559/250-0059, www.highlandhouseinn.com, $145-1'75), 11 miles (17.7 km) outside Mariposa to the west of Yosemite. The house is set deep in the forest far from town, providing endless peace and quiet. This tiny B&B has only three guest rooms, each uniquely decorated in soft colors and warm, inviting styles. All rooms have down comforters, sparkling clean bathtubs and showers, and TVs with hundreds of cable channels. There's also a game room with a pool table if you're feeling competitive. The morning breakfast leaves guests well fed.

On the western edge of Mariposa, the **Best Western Plus Yosemite Way Station** (4999 CA-140, 209/966-7545, www.bestwestern.com, $179-290) is a good bet for a chain motel, with everything you'll need for a night before venturing into the park. It's walking distance to Mariposa's restaurants, while the rooms have refrigerators and microwaves for leftovers. Adjacent to the swimming pool and hot tub is a small fitness room and, most important for those on long road trips, a coin-operated laundry.

Camping

Inside the Park

In Yosemite Valley, the campgrounds at **Upper Pines** (inside U.S. 877/444-6777, outside the U.S. 606/515-6777, www.recreation.gov, year-round, reservations required all year, $26), **Lower Pines** (inside U.S. 877/444-6777, outside the U.S. 606/515-6777, www.recreation.gov, Mar.-Oct., reservations required, $26), and **North Pines** (inside U.S. 877/444-6777, outside the U.S. 606/515-6777, www.recreation.gov, Apr.-Sept., reservations required, $26) allow trailers and RVs, and you can bring your dog with you. Camp Curry offers plenty of food options within walking distance, and showers are available nearby.

How many campgrounds are listed on the National Register of Historic Places? Not many, and **Camp 4** (near Yosemite Valley Lodge, 35 campsites, late May-early Sept., $6) has that distinction due to its importance to the sport of rock climbing. Patagonia founder Yvon Chouinard began his business career by selling climbing gear here. You'll find showers nearby and lots of food and groceries at Yosemite Valley Lodge. FYI: No RVs or trailers are allowed at these sites. Reservations (www.recreation.gov) are available via advance lottery the day before your desired date.

Outside the Park: CA-140

A hostel with a 10-person hot tub and a cedar sauna? The ★ **Yosemite Bug Rustic Mountain Resort** (6979 CA-140, Midpines, 209/966-6666 or 866/826-7108, www.yosemitebug.com) has that and more. Options begin at basic hostel-style dorm rooms ($39) and go up to uniquely decorated private bedrooms (shared bath $115-135, private bath

$159-199), including one with a steampunk theme and another with a psychedelic vibe. There are also tent cabins ($75-85) and two guesthouses: The **Barn Studio** ($159-199), with room for four people, and the **Starlite House** ($255), with room for 5-9. The hub of the property is the mountain lodge café, serving three meals a day and California beers on tap. The grilled rib-eye dinner is perfect after a long day of hiking.

RVers aiming for the Arch Rock entrance flock to the **Indian Flat RV Park** (9988 CA-140, 209/379-2339, www.indianflatrvpark.com, tent sites $30, RV sites $42-48, tent cabins $129-139, cottages $169-289, pet fee $5). This park is a full-service low-end resort, with everything from minimal-hookup RV sites through tent cabins and a couple of cabins with kitchenettes and cable TV. Showers are available here, even for passers-through who aren't staying at Indian Flat. The lodge next door has extended an invitation to all Indian Flat campers to make use of its outdoor pool. Because Indian Flat is relatively small (25 RV sites, 25 tent sites), reservations are strongly recommended. You can make your booking up to a year in advance, and this kind of planning is a really good idea for summertime Yosemite visitors.

Glacier Point

The best view of Yosemite Valley may not be from the valley floor. To get a different look at the familiar formations and falls, drive up Glacier Point Road to Glacier Point. The vista down into Yosemite Valley is anything but ordinary. Glacier Point Road stays open all year to allow access to Badger Pass.

Sights

★ Glacier Point

Located at the top of Yosemite Valley's south wall, **Glacier Point** offers what is arguably the best view within the whole park. At 7,214 feet (2,199 m) high, the spot looks down on the valley floor 3,214 feet (980 m) below, with stunning views of iconic features like Half Dome and Yosemite Falls. It also has a superb view of Vernal Fall and Nevada Fall, which flutter below like white ribbons. It's easy to get to the lookout area, which is wheelchair-accessible and includes a geology hut that explains how glaciers created the landscape. The road to Glacier Point is open late May-October or November, except when storms make it temporarily impassable. During winter, experienced cross-country skiers can ski 10.5 miles (16.9 km) in to the viewpoint.

Recreation

Hiking

If you love the thrill of heights, head up Glacier Point Road and take a hike up to or along one of the spectacular (and slightly scary) granite cliffs. Hikes in this area run from quite easy to rigorous; many of the cliff side trails aren't appro priate for children.

Sentinel Dome

Distance: 2 miles (3.2 km) round-trip
Duration: 2 hours
Elevation gain: 400 feet (122 m)
Effort: moderate
Trailhead: Sentinel Dome-Taft Point Trailhead

The round-trip hike up **Sentinel Dome** makes for a surprisingly easy walk; the only steep part runs right up the dome at the end of the trail. You can do this hike in two hours, and you'll find views at the top to make the effort and high elevation (more than 8,000 ft/2,438 m at the top) more than worthwhile. On a clear day, you can see from Yosemite Valley to the High Sierra and all the way out to Mount Diablo in the Bay Area to the west. Bring a camera! Be careful; there are no guardrails or walls to protect you from the long drop along the side of the trail and at the top of the dome.

Taft Point and the Fissures

Distance: 2 miles (3.2 km) round-trip
Duration: 2 hours
Elevation gain: 200 feet (61 m)
Effort: moderate
Trailhead: Sentinel Dome-Taft Point Trailhead

It doesn't take long to reach the magnificent vista point at **Taft Point and the Fissures.** The round-trip hike takes you along some of Yosemite's unusual rock formations, the Fissures, and continues through lovely woods to Taft Point. This precarious precipice boasts not a single stone wall, but only a rickety set of guardrails to keep visitors from plummeting 2,000 feet (610 km) down to the nearest patch of flat ground. Thrill seekers enjoy challenging themselves to get right up to the edge of the cliff and peer down. The elevation change from the trailhead to the point is only about 200 feet (61 m), even though you are hiking at an elevation of 3,500 feet (1,067 m) above the valley floor.

Four Mile Trail

Distance: 9.6 miles (15.4 km) round-trip; 4.8 miles (7.7 km) one-way
Duration: 6-8 hours round-trip; 3-4 hours one-way
Elevation gain: 3,200 feet (976 m)
Effort: round-trip strenuous; one-way moderate
Trailhead: Four Mile Trailhead (Southside Dr. in Yosemite Valley)

For the most spectacular view of *all* of Yosemite Falls anywhere in the park, take the **Four Mile Trail** that connects Glacier Point to Yosemite Valley. The easiest way to take this hike is to start at the top, from Glacier Point, and hike down to the valley. You can then catch a ride on the Glacier Point Tour Bus (buy tickets in advance!) back up to your car. The steep climb up the trail from the valley on the round-trip version can be much harder on your legs and lungs, but it affords an ascending series of views of Yosemite Falls and Yosemite Valley that grow more spectacular with each switchback.

Ostrander Lake

Distance: 11.4 miles (18.3 km) round-trip
Duration: 8-10 hours
Elevation gain: 1,600 feet (488 m)
Effort: strenuous
Trailhead: Ostrander Lake Trailhead (1.3 mi/2.1 km east of the Bridalveil Creek Campground turnoff)

For a longer high-elevation hike, take the walk to **Ostrander Lake** and back. (You can cross-country ski to the lake in the winter and stay overnight at the local ski hut.) This trek can take all day at a relaxed pace. In June and July, wildflowers bloom all along the trail. You can also still see the remnants of a 1987 fire and the regrowth in the decades since. The lake itself is a lovely patch of shining clear water surrounded by granite boulders and picturesque pine trees. Start up the trail in the morning, packing a picnic lunch to enjoy beside the serene water. Bring bug repellent; the still waters of the lake are mosquito heaven.

Skiing and Snowshoeing

Downhill skiing at **Badger Pass Ski Area** (Glacier Point Rd., 5 mi/8 km from Wawona, 209/372-1000, www.travelyosemite.com, 9am-4pm daily mid-Dec.-Apr., prices vary) is another favorite wintertime activity at Yosemite. This was the first downhill ski area created in California. Today, it's the perfect resort for families and groups who want a relaxed day or three of moderate skiing. With plenty of beginner runs and classes, Yosemite has helped thousands of kids (and adults!) learn to ski and snowboard as friends and family look on from the sundecks at the lodge. There are enough intermediate runs to make it interesting for mid-level skiers, and a terrain park for ripping boarders. Double-black-diamond skiers may find Badger Pass too tame for their tastes since there are just a few advanced runs. But everyone agrees that the prices are reasonable (it even has a one-ride ticket for $5.50!), and the focus is on friendliness and learning rather than showing off and extreme skiing.

Yosemite has 90 miles (145 km) of marked cross-country ski trails and 25 miles (40 km) of groomed track. In fact, many places in Yosemite are accessible in winter only by cross-country skis or snowshoes. Check out the **Badger Pass Ski Area School** (www.travelyosemite.com) for classes, rentals, and guided cross-country ski and snowshoeing tours. If you're looking for a fun day out in the snow, the groomed tracks from Badger Pass to Glacier Point run 21 miles (34 km) and are frequented by day skiers. You'll see fewer other skiers on the backcountry trails, which can also be traversed in a single day by a reasonably strong skier. For the hard-core XC skier who wants a serious skiing experience, check out the overnight and multiday tours; hiring a guide for these trips is recommended for most skiers.

Even if you're not up for hard-core skiing, you can get out and enjoy the snow-covered landscapes of wintertime Yosemite. Snowshoeing requires no experience and only minimal fitness to get started. "If you can walk, you can snowshoe," claims Yosemite's own website. You can rent snowshoes at several locations in Yosemite and acquire trail maps from the rental centers.

Food

During winter, Badger Pass has a fast-food grill and the **Snowflake Room** (11am-4pm winter weekends and holidays), which serve hot dogs, nachos, soda, and beer.

Accommodations

If you're planning an extended stay with friends or family, consider renting a condo or house with a full kitchen, privacy, and the comforts of home. You can find these at the **Yosemite West Condominiums** (559/642-2211, www.yosemitewestreservations.com, $195-800). The modular buildings can be divided into a number of separate units—or not—if you want enough space for a big crowd. The studio and loft condos sleep 2-6 people and have full kitchens and access to all complex amenities. Luxury suites are one-bedroom apartments with full kitchens, pool tables, and all sorts of other amenities. Two- and three-bedroom apartments sleep 6-10 people.

Camping

For a picturesque Yosemite camping experience, check out **Bridalveil Creek Campground** (Glacier Point Rd., 8 mi/12.9 km east of Wawona Rd., July-early Sept., 110 campsites, $18, $30 stock camp, $50 group). The campground sits at 7,200 feet (2,195 m) elevation and has a creek running around its perimeter. It's not possible to make reservations for the regular sites, which are all first-come, first-served. The campground fills up quickly, especially spring-fall. You can reserve one of three horse sites if you're traveling with your mount or two group camps by calling 877/444-6777; the group campsites also can be secured at www.recreation.gov. RVs are welcome.

Hetch Hetchy

Naturalist and wilderness activist John Muir noted that Hetch Hetchy Valley was once "a wonderfully exact counterpart of the great Yosemite." Perhaps the most disputed valley in all California, Hetch Hetchy today is a reservoir that supplies much of the San Francisco Bay Area with drinking water. Many environmental activists see the reservoir's existence as an affront and lobby continuously to have O'Shaughnessy Dam torn down and the valley returned to its former state of natural beauty. But there is plenty of beauty in this northwest corner of the park, including the Half Dome-like bump of Kolana Rock and two waterfalls that spill down 1,000-foot (305-m) cliff faces. Experience the grandeur of the Sierra Nevada without the crowds that clog up Yosemite Valley.

Sights

O'Shaughnessy Dam

Named for its chief engineer, **O'Shaughnessy Dam** is a 430-foot (131-m) concrete dam that diverts the Tuolumne River into the 117-billion-gallon Hetch Hetchy Reservoir. The spot had long been considered for a possible dam. The 1906 San Francisco earthquake established a need for a substantial water supply for San Francisco, leading to the Raker Act in 1913, which authorized construction of the dam. The first phase was completed 1923, with a second wave of building that raised the height of the structure lasting until 1938. Today, the reservoir's water flows 167 miles (265 km) to the Bay Area without any pumps; gravity does all the work.

The O'Shaughnessy Dam is easily accessible and has a small parking lot just feet away. Walk out onto the structure to see Kolana Rock and Wapama Falls in the distance and imagine what Hetch Hetchy Valley looked like before human engineering intervened.

Recreation

Hiking

The relatively low elevation of Hetch Hetchy means that snow thaws sooner, allowing for hiking year-round, though July and August can be very hot. The 287 miles (460 km) of hiking trails in the Hetch Hetchy watershed include a range of options, from the 2.8-mile (4.5-km) Lookout Point Trail to the 29-mile (47-km) Hetch Hetchy-Lake Vernon Loop.

Lookout Point Trail

Distance: 2.8 miles (4.5 km) round-trip
Duration: 1.5 hours
Elevation gain: 500 feet (152 m)
Effort: moderate
Trailhead: just past the Hetch Hetchy entrance station

The **Lookout Point Trail** climbs steadily up to a rock slab with a 260-degree view of the Hetch Hetchy Reservoir,

Hetch Hetchy

the O'Shaughnessy Dam, and Wapama Falls below. You can also see the Central Valley to the west if it's not too hazy. Expect plentiful wildflowers in early spring.

★ Wapama Falls Trail

Distance: 5 miles (8 km) round-trip
Duration: 2 hours
Elevation gain: 200 feet (61 m)
Effort: moderate
Trailhead: O'Shaughnessy Dam

The **Wapama Falls Trail** is an ideal introduction to the Hetch Hetchy area. The hike begins by crossing O'Shaughnessy Dam. After passing through a tunnel blasted into the rock, the trail hugs the rim of the reservoir, offering fine views of Kolana Rock. In spring, expect a profusion of wildflowers along the way. Eventually, the trail gets rockier, with some rock steps, before reaching wooden bridges over Falls Creek and the impressive view of Wapama Falls spilling over a giant rock face. Be careful crossing the four bridges, which can be slippery when the creek is rushing.

Backpacking

To head out into the backcountry from Hetch Hetchy, secure a free **wilderness permit** from the Hetch Hetchy entrance station, where you can also rent a **bear canister** ($5 per week with a credit card deposit) for backcountry food storage. One of the most popular multiday excursions is the **Hetch Hetchy-Lake Vernon Loop** (29 mi/47 km, strenuous), which goes northeast of the Hetch Hetchy Reservoir. The first 4 miles (6.4 km) head up and out of the valley on the old Lake Eleanor Road. The trail carries on to scenic Lake Vernon before heading to Rancheria Falls and then back along the north side of the reservoir. There is no access to the trails when Hetch Hetchy Road (typically 8am-5pm) is closed.

Swimming

On a hot day, a dip in the Hetch Hetchy Reservoir looks tempting, but resist the urge: entering the water is illegal. Instead, head to **Rainbow Pool** (CA-120 at South Fork Tuolumne River Bridge, east of the Rim of the World Viewpoint, www.fs.usda.gov), a U.S. Forest Service day-use area located between Groveland and the Big Oak Flat entrance to the park (11 mi/17.7 km west of the Big Oak Flat entrance). This was once a toll stop for stagecoaches, where a resort flourished before burning down in 1858. Today, all that remains from those days are some brackets and drill holes within the riverside rocks. The real attraction is a waterfall that spills into a deep, pooled section of the Tuolumne River. It's a favorite spot for locals. Watch in awe as kids jump off a 20-foot (6.1-m) ledge into the pool below—or try it yourself, but exercise caution.

Food

There are no dining options within the Hetch Hetchy region of the park; the

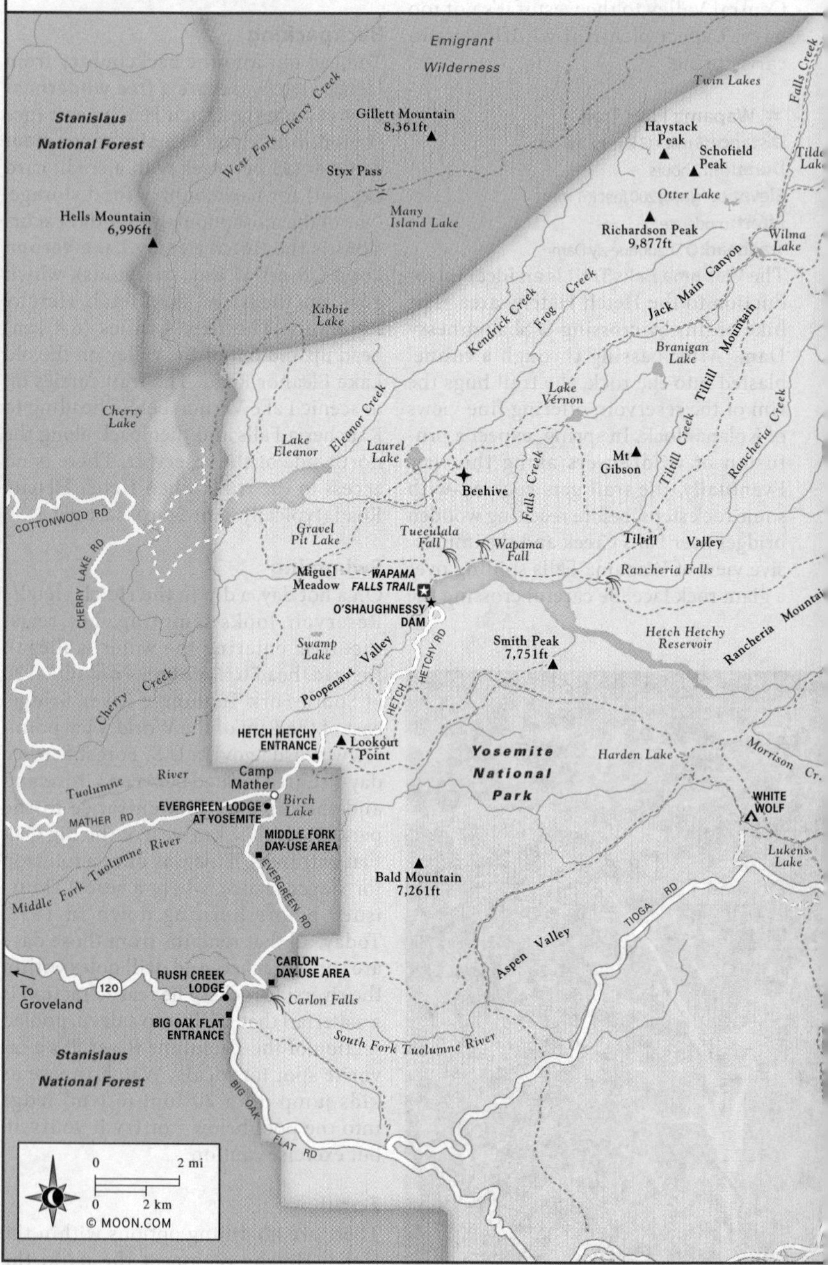
Hetch Hetchy
Emigrant
Wilderness
Twin Lakes
Falls Creek
Stanislaus
National Forest
West Fork Cherry Creek
Gillett Mountain
8,361ft
Haystack
Peak
Schofield
Peak
Styx Pass
Otter Lake
Hells Mountain
6,996ft
Many
Island Lake
Richardson Peak
9,877ft
Wilma
Lake
Jack Main Canyon
Kendrick Creek
Frog Creek
Kibbie
Lake
Branigan
Lake
Tiltill Mountain
Lake
Vernon
Cherry
Lake
Eleanor Creek
Lake
Eleanor
Laurel
Lake
Tiltill Creek
Rancheria Creek
Mt
Gibson
Falls Creek
Beehive
COTTONWOOD RD
CHERRY LAKE RD
Gravel
Pit Lake
Tueeulala
Fall
Wapama
Fall
Tiltill
Valley
Miguel
Meadow
WAPAMA
FALLS TRAIL
Rancheria Falls
O'SHAUGHNESSY
DAM
Hetch Hetchy
Reservoir
Smith Peak
7,751ft
Swamp
Lake
Poopenaut Valley
HETCH HETCHY RD
Cherry Creek
HETCH HETCHY
ENTRANCE
Lookout
Point
Yosemite
National
Park
Harden Lake
Morrison Cr.
Tuolumne River
Camp
Mather
Birch
Lake
EVERGREEN LODGE
AT YOSEMITE
MATHER RD
WHITE
WOLF
MIDDLE FORK
DAY-USE AREA
Middle Fork Tuolumne River
EVERGREEN RD
Lukens
Lake
Bald Mountain
7,261ft
TIOGA RD
Aspen Valley
CARLON
DAY-USE AREA
To
Groveland
120
RUSH CREEK
LODGE
Carlon Falls
BIG OAK FLAT
ENTRANCE
South Fork Tuolumne River
Stanislaus
National Forest
BIG OAK FLAT RD
0
2 mi
0
2 km
© MOON.COM

closest nearby options are in the mountain town of Groveland, on CA-120 just 26 miles (42 km) from the park entrance.

Outside the Park

Provisions Taproom & Bourbon Bar (Groveland Hotel, 18767 Main St., Groveland, 209/962-4000, www.groveland.com/provisions, $9-14) is the place for a cold beer and a snack outdoors on a warm summer night. Behind the Groveland Hotel, the taproom has a multitiered outdoor patio—set beneath trees and string lights—that frequently hosts live music. Sip on one of the 10 craft beers or 30 bourbons while grazing on a menu of small plates including a charcuterie board and a cheese board, as well as, on some nights, more substantial entrée-sized specials.

Craving authentic Mexican food? **Cocina Michoacana** (18730 Main St., Groveland, 209/962-6651, 11am-9pm Mon.-Sat., $10.50-14) is the place for tacos, burritos, and chimichangas. Try the chicken fajitas, which are served in a hot skillet. The dining room is narrow and the kitchen is small, so expect a wait on the weekend.

The **Iron Door Saloon** (18761 Main St., Groveland, 209/962-6244, 8am-9pm daily, $8-12) claims to be California's oldest bar; legend has it that it began as a store and constructed a bar out of a plank laid over flour barrels to serve thirsty miners. Whether or not that's true, it delivers serious gold rush-era ambience, from the bullet holes in its walls to the old pictures of Hetch Hetchy before the dam was constructed. Entertainment includes live bands most weekends and watching folks trying to get their dollar bills to stick to the high ceiling. As for the food, the menu includes burgers, onion rings, and fish-and-chips.

From top to bottom: the pool deck at Rush Creek Lodge; a bridge on the Wapama Falls Trail; Groveland's Iron Door Saloon.

Accommodations

Outside the Park

Just 1.5 miles (2.4 km) from Yosemite's Big Oak Flat entrance, the 20-acre (8.1-ha) ★ **Rush Creek Lodge** (34001 CA-120, 209/379-2373, www.rushcreeklodge.com, $430-625) is an ideal place to unwind after exploring the park. The superb deck beckons with a saltwater pool, two large soaking tubs, lounge chairs, fire pits, and a Ping-Pong table. Children will love the adjacent game room, while adults can imbibe in the lounge or tavern, which frequently hosts live music. The on-site restaurant has a wood-fired oven used for s'mores roasting in the evenings. The rooms in both the main lodge and the 16 hillside villas are rustic with a modern twist. All have a balcony or porch to take in the mountain air.

Just 1 mile (1.6 km) from Yosemite's Hetch Hetchy entrance, the **Evergreen Lodge** (33160 Evergreen Rd., 209/379-2606, www.evergreenlodge.com, camping $120-155, cabins and cottages $290-560) has different lodging options scattered across its 22 acres (8.9 ha) of pine-shaded land. For camping, don't even pack your gear, as you'll arrive to an already set-up mesh-topped tent outfitted with foam mattresses and toiletries. Even the cabins for budget-conscious visitors have Sirius satellite radios, Keurig coffeemakers, and mini fridges. Enjoy a dip in the pool or hot tub after a hike. Head out to the main lodge for a meal or walk to the tavern for a drink and live entertainment.

Most lodging options can be found in Groveland, a scenic mountain town right on CA-120 just 26 miles (42 km) from the park entrance. **Hotel Charlotte** (18736 Main St., Groveland, 209/962-6455, www.hotelcharlotte.com, $129-249) has been hosting visitors since way back in 1921. The starting rooms are cozy (small) but go up to deluxe suites and master suites. No matter what room you are in, you'll get to indulge in a complimentary breakfast buffet in the morning. For larger groups, the hotel also has vacation rentals ($259-299) available that can accommodate up to 11 people in a gated community located 10 minutes from Groveland.

Ten miles (16.1 km) east of the town of Groveland, in Buck Meadows, is the **Yosemite Westgate Lodge** (7633 CA-120, Groveland, 209/962-5281, www.yosemitewestgate.com, $120-300), a U-shaped family friendly complex with kitschy bear statues set up around the grounds. Rooms are nice and clean, and a stay also includes access to a heated pool, a spa, a small playground, and guest laundry facilities. The on-site Lucky Buck Café is a fine place to fuel up for a day of hiking in Yosemite.

Camping

Outside the Park: CA-120

To camp in Big Oak Flat along CA-120 near Groveland, try the Thousand Trails RV campground at **Yosemite Lakes RV Resort** (31191 Harden Flat Rd., 209/962-0103 or 800/388-7788, www.1000trails.com, tents $57, RVs $82, hostel beds $145-158, cabins $100-263, yurts $275-322) if you are in a pinch. This sprawling campground has more than 250 RV sites with full hookups, 130 tent sites, a few dozen cabins, tent cabins, yurts, and a 12-bed hostel. This is not a great campground, but there are frequent openings on summer weekends, which will put you close to the northern section of Yosemite.

Wawona

The small town-like area of Wawona (Wawona Rd./CA-41, 1.5 hours from Yosemite Valley) is only a few miles from the South entrance of Yosemite. The historic Wawona Hotel was built in 1917 and also houses a popular restaurant as well as a store.

Sights

Pioneer Yosemite History Center

The first thing you'll see at the **Pioneer Yosemite History Center** (trail from Wawona information station, open daily) is a big open barn housing an array of vehicles used for over a century in Yosemite. These conveyances range from big cushiony carriages for rich tourists to oil wagons once used in an ill-conceived attempt to control mosquitoes on the ponds. Continuing, walk under the Vermont-style covered bridge to the main museum area. This rambling, not-overcrowded stretch of land contains many of the original structures built in the park, most over 100 years ago. Most were moved from various remote locations. Informative placards describe the history of Yosemite National Park through its structures, from the military shacks used by soldiers who were the first park rangers to the homes of early settlers, presided over by stoic pioneer women. There's also a tiny rock building that was used as a jail and a morgue. Check your *Yosemite Guide* for living-history programs and live demonstrations held at the museum.

★ Mariposa Grove of Giant Sequoias

One of three groves of these rare, majestic trees in Yosemite, the **Mariposa Grove** (Wawona Rd./CA-41) offers the easiest access. This is the largest grove of sequoias in the park. Highlights include the Grizzly Giant with its impressive girth and the California Tunnel Tree, with a doorway through its trunk that you can walk through. Choose to hike through the grove on the easy **Big Trees Loop** (0.3 mi/0.5 km round-trip), moderate **Grizzly Giant Loop Trail** (2 mi/3.2 km round-trip), or strenuous **Guardians Loop Trail** (6.5 mi/10.5 km round-trip) or primary artery—the **Mariposa Grove Trail** (7 mi/11.3 km round-trip), which climbs up to 1,200-foot (366-m) Wawona Point and winds between the rust-colored spires of the giant sequoias and past rounds as big as dinner tables. For all hikes, park at the **Mariposa Grove Welcome Plaza,** where there are around 300 parking spaces—though note they can fill up by mid-morning—and then take the free shuttle to Mariposa Grove. Or opt for a longer hike by walking to the grove via the **Washburn Trail** (2 mi/3.2 km one-way), which begins at the Mariposa Grove Welcome Plaza.

Recreation

Hiking

It's not quite as popular or as crowded as Yosemite Valley, but the hikes near Wawona in southern Yosemite can be just as scenic and lovely.

Wawona Meadow Loop

Distance: 3.5-mile (5.6-km) loop or extended 5-mile (8-km) loop
Duration: 1.5-2.5 hours
Elevation gain: none for 3.5-mile (5.6-km) loop; 500 feet (152 m) for 5-mile (8-km) loop
Effort: easy
Trailhead: Wawona Hotel

Start with the **Wawona Meadow Loop,** a flat and shockingly uncrowded 3.5-mile (5.6-km) sweep around the lovely Wawona meadow and somewhat incongruous nine-hole golf course. Begin by taking the paved road across from the Wawona Golf Course and then turn left on the marked trail. This wide path was once fully paved, and is still bikeable, but the pavement has eroded over the years and now you'll find much dirt and tree detritus. Best in late spring when the wildflowers are blooming in profusion, this trail takes about two hours to navigate. If you'd like a longer trip, you can extend this walk to 5 miles (8 km) by taking the detour at the south end of the meadow.

Chilnualna Fall

Distance: 8.2 miles (13.2 km) round-trip
Duration: 5 hours
Elevation gain: 2,300 feet (701 m)
Effort: strenuous
Trailhead: Chilnualna Falls Parking Area

The hard-core hike along this trail to **Chilnualna Fall** offers tantalizing views of the cascades few visitors ever see. Sadly, there's no dedicated viewing area, so you'll need to peek through the trees. The trail runs all the way up to the top of the falls. Be careful to avoid the stream during spring and summer high flow—it can be dangerous. Plan 4-6 hours for the ascent, and bring water, snacks, and a trail map.

Horseback Riding

You'll find more horses than mules at **Wawona Stable** (Pioneer Yosemite History Center, Wawona Rd., 209/375-6502, www.travelyosemite.com), and more visitors, too; reservations are strongly encouraged. From Wawona, you can take a sedate two-hour ride (departure times 8am, 10am, noon, and 2pm daily May-Sept., $70) around the historic wagon trail running into the area. On Thursdays, the stables offer a challenging six-hour ride (9am-3pm Thurs. May.-Sept., $144).

Entertainment

It's worth making an evening trip out to Wawona to listen to the delightful piano music and singing of legendary Tom Bopp. He plays vintage camp music (and requests, and whatever else strikes his fancy) in the **Piano Lounge at the Wawona Hotel** (209/372-8243) Tuesday-Saturday 5:30pm-9:30pm. Older visitors especially love his old-style performance

The Mariposa Grove Trail goes through towering sequoias.

and familiar songs, but everyone enjoys the music and entertainment he provides. Even if you're just waiting for a table at the restaurant, stop in to say hello and make a request.

Food

The ★ **Wawona Hotel Dining Room** (Wawona Hotel, 209/375-1425, www.travelyosemite.com, 7am-10am, 11am-3pm, and 5pm-9pm daily, $20-32) serves upscale but homey California cuisine in an old-timey dining room with lots of windows. Check out the kitschy but cool redwood lamps hanging overhead. The menu offers options for both vegetarians (onion gratiné) and devout carnivores (pot roast, grilled filet). Reservations are recommended for groups of six or more. All other seating is first-come, first-served, but while you wait for your table you can enjoy drinks and live piano music by local legend Tom Bopp. There's a weekly outdoor barbecue on Saturday evenings during the summer.

Accommodations

Inside the Park

Near the South entrance of the park, the gleaming white ★ **Wawona Hotel** (inside U.S. 888/413-8867, outside the U.S. 602/278-8888, www.travelyosemite.com, $132-195), with its wide verandas, is reminiscent of a 19th-century riverboat. The interior matches the exterior, with furnishings in period style, private baths—and no TVs or telephones. Rooms with shared baths are also available for budget travelers. Dating back to 1879, this Yosemite institution has hosted Presidents Ulysses S. Grant and Theodore Roosevelt.

Outside the Park: CA-41

To soak in the tranquil beauty of the mountains, stay in one of the handsome ★ **Far Meadow Base Camp Cabins** (Beasore Rd., between Jone's Store and Globe Rock, 310/455-2425 or 866/687-9358, http://farmeadow.boutique-homes.com, $125-260 plus $100 cleaning fee, 3-night minimum). The two A-frames and one log cabin are perched on a 20-acre (8.1-ha) spread with woods and meadows, just a 45-minute drive from the park's South entrance. These structures are fully off the grid, equipped with solar power, well water, and satellite Internet access. Each cabin sleeps 2-4 people and is equipped with a kitchen and bath. Two vintage trailers that sleep two are also available at the lowest price point.

Just outside the South entrance, the **Tenaya Lodge** (1122 CA-41, 888/514-2167, www.tenayalodge.com, $359-950) offers plush lodge-style accommodations. Guest rooms are styled with rich fabrics in bold colors and modern wall art that evokes the woods and vistas of Yosemite. The beds are comfortable, the baths attractive, and the views forest-filled. Take advantage of the dining room, which offers three meals a day, a full-service spa, two indoor pools, and three outdoor pools.

Near the South entrance to Yosemite on CA-41, the **Narrow Gauge Inn** (48571

CA-41, Fish Camp, 559/683-7720, www.narrowgaugeinn.com, $209-419) recalls the large lodges inside the park, in miniature. This charming 26-room mountain inn offers one- and two-bed guest rooms done in wood paneling, light colors, and white linens or vintage-style quilts. Each room has its own outdoor table and chairs to encourage relaxing outside with a drink on gorgeous summer days and evenings. The restaurant and common rooms feature antique oil lamps, stonework, and crackling fireplaces. Step outside your door and you're in the magnificent High Sierra pine forest. A few more steps take you to the Yosemite Mountain Sugar Pine Railroad, the narrow-gauge steam train from which the inn takes its name.

Camping

Inside the Park

You can camp year-round at lovely forested **Wawona** (1 mi/1.6 km north of Wawona, 209/375-9535 or 877/444-6777, www.recreation.gov, reservations required Apr.-Sept., 93 sites, $26 family, $30 stock camp, $50 group). Several of the sites are perched right on the South Fork of the Merced River. RVs are welcome, though there are no hookups onsite. Two sites can accommodate horses. Most services (including showers) can't be found closer than Yosemite Valley.

Outside the Park: CA-41

Just 1.5 miles (2.4 km) from the park's South entrance, idyllic ★ **Summerdale Campground** (CA-41, Fish Camp, inside the U.S. 877/444-6777, outside the U.S. 606/515-6777, www.recreation.gov, May-Sept., $30) is alongside the refreshing waters of Big Creek. Each of the 30 roomy campsites has a campfire ring and a picnic table, while water spigots and vault toilets are nearby. Between the campsites and the highway, a trail leads to a small waterfall and pool.

Tioga Pass and Tuolumne Meadows

Tioga Pass, a.k.a. CA-120, is Yosemite's own "road less traveled." The pass (as locals call it) crosses Yosemite from west to east, leading from the populous west edge of the park out toward Mono Lake in the east. To get to Tioga Pass from Yosemite Valley, take Northside Road to Big Oak Flat Road to the CA-120 junction and turn east. Its elevation and location lead to annual winter closures, so don't expect to be able to get across the park November-May. Along the pass, you'll find a number of developed campgrounds, plus a few natural wonders that many visitors to Yosemite never see.

Sights

Olmsted Point

Olmsted Point (road marker T24, Tioga Rd., 30 mi/48 km east of the Crane Flat

turnoff) offers sweeping views of Tenaya Canyon, the mass of granite known as Clouds Rest, and the northern side of Half Dome, which, from this vantage point, looks like a giant helmet. Seeing them requires little effort. Turn your vehicle off Tioga Road into the parking area and then climb onto the large rock formation to the south. This spot is named after landscape architect Frederick Law Olmsted Jr., who worked as a planner in Yosemite National Park.

Tenaya Lake

Right off Tioga Road is **Tenaya Lake** (Tioga Rd., 2 mi/3.2 km east of Olmsted), a natural gem nearly a mile long and framed by granite peaks. The body of water was formed by the action of Tenaya Glacier. Both are named for a local Native American chief. It's a popular place for swimming, fishing, and boating. The northeastern side of the lake has a beach with picnic tables and restrooms.

Tuolumne Meadows

Once you're out of the valley and driving along Tioga Pass, you're ready to come upon **Tuolumne Meadows** (about 10 mi/16.1 km from the eastern edge of the park, accessible by road summer only). After miles of soaring rugged mountains, these serene alpine meadows almost come as a surprise. They are brilliant green and dotted with wildflowers in spring, gradually turning to golden orange as fall approaches. The waving grasses support a variety of wildlife, including yellow-bellied marmots. You may see moraines and boulders left behind by long-gone glaciers. Stop the car and get out for a quiet, contemplative walk through the meadows. Tuolumne Meadows is also a base camp for high-country backpacking.

Tenaya Lake

Tioga Pass and Tuolumne Meadows

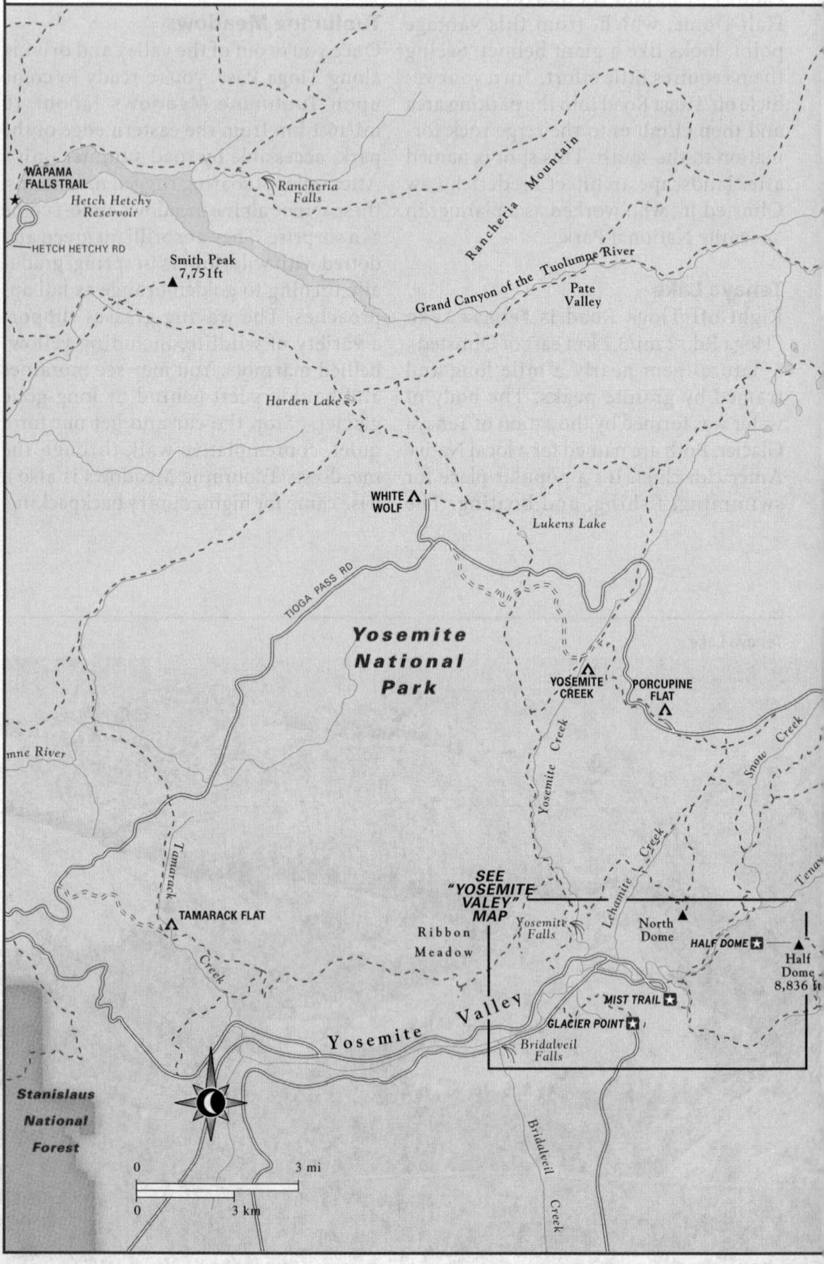

WAPAMA FALLS TRAIL
Hetch Hetchy Reservoir
HETCH HETCHY RD
Smith Peak 7,751ft
Rancheria Falls
Rancheria Mountain
Grand Canyon of the Tuolumne River
Pate Valley
Harden Lake
WHITE WOLF
Lukens Lake
TIOGA PASS RD
Yosemite National Park
YOSEMITE CREEK
PORCUPINE FLAT
Yosemite Creek
Snow Creek
mne River
Lehamite Creek
Tenaya
Tamarack Creek
TAMARACK FLAT
SEE "YOSEMITE VALLEY" MAP
Ribbon Meadow
Yosemite Falls
North Dome
HALF DOME
Half Dome 8,836 ft
MIST TRAIL
GLACIER POINT
Yosemite Valley
Bridalveil Falls
Bridalveil Creek
Stanislaus National Forest
0 3 mi
0 3 km

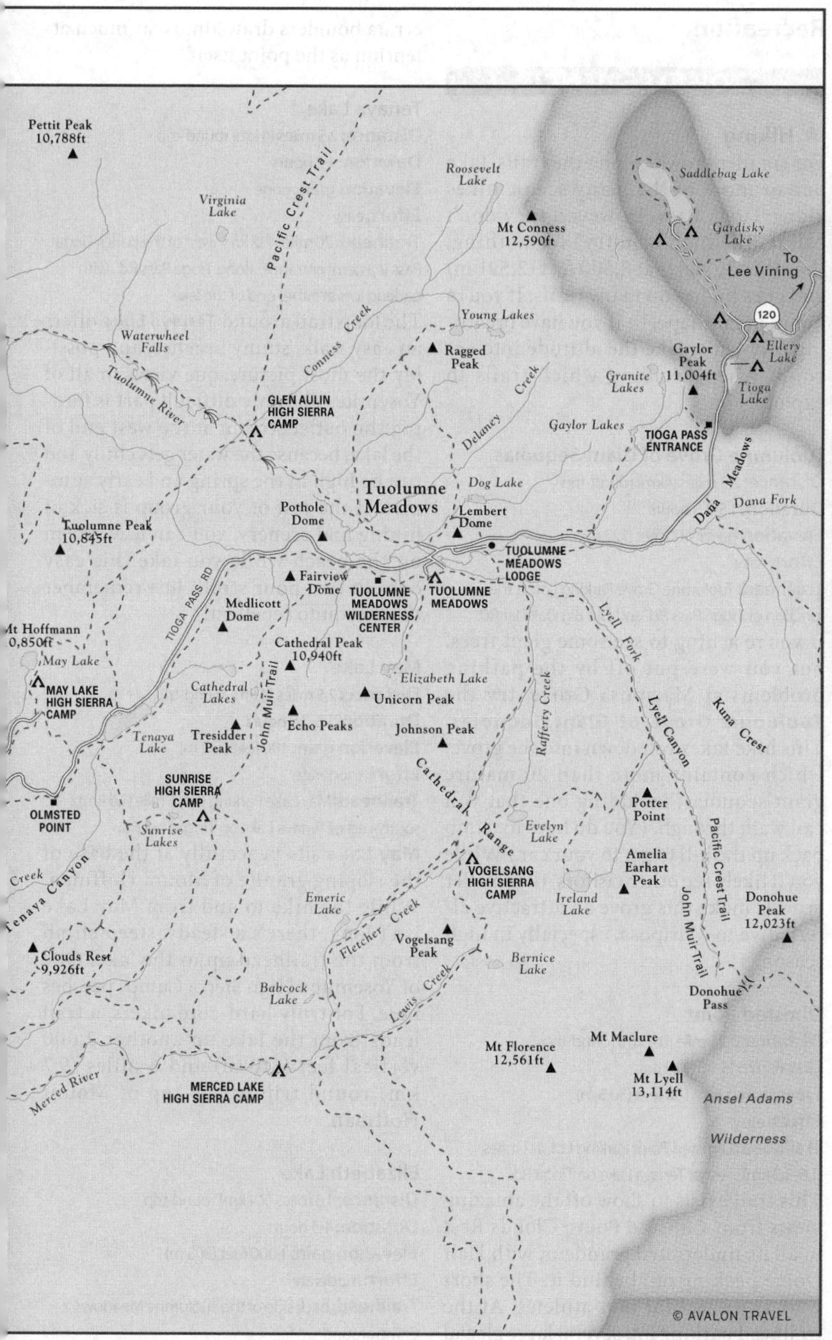
Pettit Peak
10,788ft
Virginia
Lake
Pacific Crest Trail
Roosevelt
Lake
Mt Conness
12,590ft
Saddlebag Lake
Gardisky
Lake
To
Lee Vining
120
Young Lakes
Conness Creek
Waterwheel
Falls
Tuolumne River
Ragged
Peak
Gaylor
Peak
11,004ft
Ellery
Lake
Tioga
Lake
Granite
Lakes
Delaney Creek
GLEN AULIN
HIGH SIERRA
CAMP
Gaylor Lakes
TIOGA PASS
ENTRANCE
Dana Meadows
Tuolumne
Meadows
Dog Lake
Dana Fork
Pothole
Dome
Lembert
Dome
Tuolumne Peak
10,845ft
TUOLUMNE
MEADOWS
LODGE
Fairview
Dome
TUOLUMNE
MEADOWS
WILDERNESS
CENTER
TUOLUMNE
MEADOWS
Medlicott
Dome
TIOGA PASS RD
Lyell Fork
Mt Hoffmann
10,850ft
Cathedral Peak
10,940ft
May Lake
MAY LAKE
HIGH SIERRA
CAMP
Cathedral
Lakes
Elizabeth Lake
Unicorn Peak
Echo Peaks
Tresidder
Peak
Tenaya
Lake
John Muir Trail
Johnson Peak
Rafferty Creek
Lyell Canyon
Kuna Crest
Cathedral Range
SUNRISE
HIGH SIERRA
CAMP
OLMSTED
POINT
Potter
Point
Sunrise
Lakes
Evelyn
Lake
Amelia
Earhart
Peak
Pacific Crest Trail
VOGELSANG
HIGH SIERRA
CAMP
Creek
Tenaya Canyon
Emeric
Lake
Fletcher Creek
Ireland
Lake
John Muir Trail
Donohue
Peak
12,023ft
Vogelsang
Peak
Clouds Rest
9,926ft
Bernice
Lake
Babcock
Lake
Lewis Creek
Donohue
Pass
Mt Maclure
Mt Florence
12,561ft
Mt Lyell
13,114ft
MERCED LAKE
HIGH SIERRA CAMP
Merced River
Ansel Adams
Wilderness
© AVALON TRAVEL

Recreation

TOP EXPERIENCE

★ Hiking

For smaller crowds along the trails, take one or more of the many scenic hikes along Tioga Pass. However, they don't call it "the high country" for nothing; the altitude *starts* at 8,500 feet (2,591 m) and goes higher on many trails. If you're not in great shape, or if you have breathing problems, take the altitude into account when deciding which trails to explore.

Tuolumne Grove of Giant Sequoias

Distance: 2.5 miles (4km) round-trip
Duration: 1.5-2.5 hours
Elevation gain: 400 feet (122 m)
Effort: easy
Trailhead: Tuolumne Grove Parking Lot, at the junction of Tioga Pass Rd. and Old Big Oak Flat Rd.

If you're aching to see some giant trees, but you were put off by the parking problems at Mariposa Grove, try the **Tuolumne Grove of Giant Sequoias.** This hike takes you down into the grove, which contains more than 20 mature giant sequoias, including one that you can walk through. (You do have to climb back up the hill to get to your car.) While you'll likely see other visitors, the smaller crowds make this grove an attractive alternative to Mariposa, especially in high season.

Olmsted Point

Distance: 0.25 mile (0.4 km) round-trip
Duration: 15-30 minutes
Elevation gain: 100 feet (30.5 m)
Effort: easy
Trailhead: Olmsted Point Parking Lot, 1-2 miles (1.6-3.2 km) west of Tenaya Lake on Tioga Rd.

This trail exists to show off the amazing views from **Olmsted Point:** Clouds Rest in all its underrated grandeur, with Half Dome peeking out behind it. The short walk is perfect for non-athletes. At the trailhead parking lot, several large glacial errata boulders draw almost as much attention as the point itself.

Tenaya Lake

Distance: 2.5 miles (4 km) round-trip
Duration: 1-2 hours
Elevation gain: none
Effort: easy
Trailhead: 20 miles (32 km) west of the park's Tioga Pass (eastern) entrance, along Tioga Pass Rd., with parking lots at either end of the lake

The loop trail around **Tenaya Lake** offers an easy walk, sunny beaches, and possibly the most picturesque views in all of Yosemite. The only difficult part is fording the outlet stream at the west end of the lake, because the water gets chilly and can be high in the spring and early summer. If the rest of your group is sick of hiking and scenery, you can leave them on the beach while you take this easy one- to two-hour stroll. Just remember the mosquito repellent!

May Lake

Distance: 2.5 miles (4 km) round-trip
Duration: 1.5-2.5 hours
Elevation gain: 400 feet (122 m)
Effort: moderate
Trailhead: May Lake Parking Lot, 1 mile (1.6 km) southwest of Tenaya Lake on Tioga Pass Rd.

May Lake sits peacefully at the base of the sloping granite of Mount Hoffman. While the hike to and from May Lake isn't long, there's a steady, steep climb from the trailhead up to the lake. One of Yosemite's High Sierra Camps perches here. For truly hard-core hikers, a trail leads from the lake up another 2,000 vertical feet (610 m) and 6 miles (9.7 km) round-trip to the top of Mount Hoffman.

Elizabeth Lake

Distance: 4.6 miles (7.4 km) round-trip
Duration: 4-5 hours
Elevation gain: 1,000 feet (305 m)
Effort: moderate
Trailhead: back side of the Tuolumne Meadows Campground

Side Trip to Sequoia and Kings Canyon

Kings Canyon

If you can't get enough of towering trees, majestic mountain peaks, and steep canyons, continue onward to **Sequoia and Kings Canyon National Park** (559/565-3341, www.nps.gov/seki, 7-day vehicle pass $35, foot or bicycle $20), two parks adjacent to one another in the southern section of the Sierra Nevada.

The oft-quoted John Muir called Kings Canyon, at 8,200 feet (2,499 m) deep, "a rival to Yosemite," but it also makes a good complement. The only accessible area of the canyon itself is **Cedar Grove,** which includes strolls like the 0.6-mile (1 km) walk to **Roaring River Falls** and longer hikes like the 8-mile (12.9-km) round-trip hike to **Mist Falls.** In **Grant Grove,** a 2-mile (3.2-km) round-trip walk leads to the **General Grant Tree,** one of the world's largest trees. Stay overnight at the **John Muir Lodge** (86728 Hwy. 180, Kings Canyon National Park, 866/807-3598, www.visitsequoia.com, $109).

South of Kings Canyon, Sequoia National Park has plenty of its namesake trees. Head to the **Giant Forest** to see the **General Sherman Tree,** which stands 275 feet (83.8 m) tall. Nearby **Moro Rock** offers a view of the national park from an impressive granite dome. It's accessible by a short but steep 0.3-mile (0.5-km) hike that ascends 300 vertical feet (91.4 m). Stay overnight at the **Wuksachi Lodge** (64740 Wuksachi Way, Sequoia National Park, 866/807-3598, www.visitsequoia.com, $238-299).

Getting There

Sequoia and Kings Canyon National Parks are just 2.5 hours' drive from Yosemite's South entrance. Head out of Yosemite's South entrance on **CA-41 South** toward Fresno for roughly 60 miles (97 km). In Fresno, turn on **CA-180 West** toward Mendota and Kings Canyon, and then merge onto **CA-180 East.** Follow the road for roughly 50 miles (80 km) until it enters Kings Canyon National Park at the **Big Stump entrance.**

Originating at the Tuolumne Meadows Campground's horse camp, the trail to **Elizabeth Lake** starts with a real climb through a boulder-strewn forest. Don't give up: The path levels out after 1,000 vertical feet (305 m), meandering along a little creek and through a meadow. The destination is a picturesque subalpine lake with an impressive mountain wall as a backdrop. The 10,823-foot (3,299-m) horn of Unicorn Peak tops the northernmost edge of the rocky ridge. Hop into the chilly water to cool off before returning down the same trail.

Gaylor Lakes and Granite Lakes

Distance: 3-6 miles (4.8-9.7 km) round-trip
Duration: 3-6 hours
Elevation gain: 700-1,000 feet (213-305 m)
Effort: moderate
Trailhead: parking lot just west of the Tioga Pass entrance station, on the north side of the road

If you're willing to tackle longer, steeper treks, you will find an amazing array of small scenic lakes within reach of Tioga Pass. **Gaylor Lakes** starts high (almost 10,000 ft/3,048 m elevation) and climbs a steep 600 vertical feet (183 m) up the pass to the Gaylor Lakes valley. Once you're in the valley, you can wander at will around the lovely Granite Lakes, stopping to admire the views out to the mountains surrounding Tuolumne Meadows. You can also visit the abandoned 1870s mine site above Upper Gaylor Lake. It's one of Yosemite's less crowded hikes.

North Dome

Distance: 8.8 miles (14.2 km) round-trip
Duration: 4-6 hours
Elevation loss: 560 feet (171 m)
Effort: moderate
Trailhead: Porcupine Creek Lot

For a different look at a classic Yosemite landmark, take the **North Dome** trail through the woods and out to the dome, which sits right across the valley from Half Dome. You'll hike almost 9 miles (14.5 km) round-trip, with a few hills thrown in. But getting to stare right into the face of Half Dome at eye level, and to see Clouds Rest beyond it, is worth the effort.

Cathedral Lakes

Distance: 8 miles (12.9 km) round-trip
Duration: 4-6 hours
Elevation gain: 1,000 feet (305 m)
Effort: moderate
Trailhead: Tuolumne Meadows Visitors Center, part of the John Muir Trail

If you can't get enough of Yosemite's

From top to bottom: looking up at a sequoia; Elizabeth Lake; John Muir Trail.

granite-framed alpine lakes, take the long walk out to one or both of the **Cathedral Lakes.** Starting at ever-popular Tuolumne Meadows, you'll climb about 800 vertical feet (244 m) over 3-4 miles (4.8-6.4 km), depending on which lake you choose. The picture-perfect lakes show off the dramatic rocky peaks above, surrounding evergreens, and crystalline waters of Yosemite at their best. Bring water, munchies, and a camera!

Glen Aulin Trail

Distance: 12 miles (19.3 km) round-trip
Duration: 6-8 hours
Elevation gain: 800 feet (244 m)
Effort: strenuous
Trailhead: Tuolumne Stables, Soda Springs

The **Glen Aulin Trail** to Tuolumne Fall and White Cascade is part of the John Muir Trail. Several of its forks branch off to pretty little lakes. There are some steep and rocky areas on the trail, but if you've got the lungs for it, you'll be rewarded by fabulous views of the Tuolumne River alternately pooling and cascading right beside the trail. This hike gets crowded in the high season. In the hot summertime, many hikers trade dusty jeans for swimsuits and cool off in the pools at the base of both White Cascade and Tuolumne Fall. If you want to spend the night, enter the High Sierra Camp lottery; if you win, you can arrange to stay at the Glen Aulin camp. If you do this, you can take your hike a few miles farther, downstream to California Fall, Le Conte Fall, and finally Waterwheel Fall.

Lembert Dome

Distance: 2.8 miles (4.5 km) round-trip
Duration: 2-3 hours
Elevation gain: 850 feet (259 m)
Effort: moderate
Trailhead: Dog Lake Trailhead

Lembert Dome rises like a giant shark's fin from Tuolumne Meadows. Seeing this granite dome, you may be inspired to climb it for views of the meadow. From the trailhead, follow the signs to Dog Lake before taking a left at a trail junction toward the dome. Follow the marked path to avoid exposed sections that are dangerous due to steep drops. The last section of the hike involves a steep ascent. This is a fine vantage point to take in the rising or setting sun.

Food

Inside the Park

Food options in this area of the park are limited.

The **Tuolumne Meadows Lodge Dining Room** (Tuolumne Meadows Lodge, 209/372-8413, www.travelyosemite.com, 7am-9am and 5:30pm-8pm daily mid-June-mid-Sept., $10-28), located along the Tuolumne River, is open for breakfast and dinner. Breakfast options are limited, while dinner is more varied and can include steak, trout, a burger, or beef stew. Reservations are necessary for dinner.

The **White Wolf Lodge Dining Room** (White Wolf Lodge, www.travelyosemite.com, 7:30am-9:30am and 6pm-8pm daily mid-June-mid-Sept., $29 adults, $26 seniors, $10 children) serves up one main item each night with a few sides in a wooden building on the grounds. Dinner reservations are required.

The **Tuolumne Meadows Grill** (8am-6pm mid-June-mid-Sept., $5-9) is located in the tent-like store and serves basic fare, including burgers, hot dogs, and breakfast items.

Outside the Park

Lee Vining

For a unique dining experience, stop in for a tank of gas and a meal at the ★ **Whoa Nellie Deli** (22 Vista Point Dr., CA-120 and US-395, 760/647-1088, www.whoanelliedeli.com, 6:30am-9pm daily Apr.-Nov., $8-12) at the Tioga Gas Mart. What other gas station deli counter serves tasty sashimi, wild buffalo meatloaf, and fish tacos with mango salsa and ginger coleslaw? The dinner menu also includes lighter fare like sandwiches. A hearty morning breakfast menu includes a grilled rib-eye steak and eggs. Grab-and-go pizza slices and sandwiches are also available. Expect to wait in line to order at the counter, then some more to pick up food. Seating, both indoor and out, is at a premium during high-traffic mealtimes. Heaven help you if you arrive at the same time as a tour bus.

If you're looking for Wild West atmosphere and good spicy sauce, have dinner at **Bodie Mike's Barbecue** (51357 US-395, 760/647-6432, 11:30am-10pm daily summer, $7-25). Use your fingers to dig into barbecued ribs, chicken, beef, brisket, and more. A rustic atmosphere with rough-looking wood, red-checked tablecloths, and local patrons in cowboy boots completes your dining experience. Just don't expect the fastest service in the world. At the back of the dining room you'll find a small, dark bar populated by local characters.

The **Mono Market** (51303 US-395, 760/647-1010, www.leeviningmarket.com, 7am-9pm daily summer, 7:30am-8pm daily winter) is a great place to pick up breakfast or lunch on the go. An array of breakfast sandwiches, pastries, and wraps are made fresh daily. Messier napkin-requisite entrées can be carried out for lunch or dinner.

June Lake

Locals love the hearty breakfasts at the ★ **Silver Lake Resort Café** (6957 CA-158, 760/648-7525, http://silverlakeresort.net, 7am-2pm daily, $6-12), a classic home-style restaurant. There are just six tables and six seats at the bar, and lots of folks waiting to get in on summer mornings. Wake up with three-egg omelets, scrambles, breakfast burritos, and specials including steak and eggs. Lunch includes a buffalo burger, some stacked sandwiches, and the Silver Lake Burger—the grilled beef patty on a fresh bun is the most popular item on the menu. Get ready to shop for a wider-waisted wardrobe!

Yet another reason to love June Lake is the **June Lake Brewery** (131 S. Crawford Ave., 760/616-4399, www.junelakebrewing.com, tasting room noon-8pm daily). The tasting room serves pale ales, brown ales, and a porter, among others. The beams, bar, tables, and benches are made from sections of a Jeffrey pine tree that once stood 120 feet (36.6 m) tall. Usually parked nearby, food truck **Ohanas 395** (http://ohanas395.com, noon-6pm daily) serves up Hawaiian tacos and plate lunches.

Mammoth Lakes

Plenty of dining options cluster in Mammoth Lakes. You can get your fast-food cheeseburger and your chain double-latte here, but why would you, with so many more interesting choices?

Petra's Bistro & Wine Bar (6080 Minaret Rd., 760/934-3500, www.petrabistro.com, 5pm-9pm Sun. and Tues.-Thurs., 5pm-9:30pm Fri.-Sat., $18-34) brings a bit of the California wine country all the way out to Mammoth Lakes. The menu changes seasonally, designed to please the palate and complement the wine list, an eclectic mix of vintages that highlight the best of California with a few European and South American options. The by-the-glass offerings change each night. Your server will happily cork your half-finished bottle to take home for tomorrow. Two dining rooms and a wine bar divide up the seating nicely. The atmosphere is romantic without being cave-dark. Reservations are a good idea during high season.

Roberto's Mexican Cafe (271 Old Mammoth Rd., 760/934-3667, http://robertoscafe.com, 11am-close Tues.-Sun., $11-30) serves classic California-Mexican food (chile rellenos, enchiladas, burritos, and so on) in large quantities perfect for skiers and boarders famished after a long day on the slopes (check out the huge three-combo platter). For a quiet meal, stay downstairs in the main dining room. To join in with a livelier crowd, head upstairs to the bar, which serves the full restaurant menu. Even the stoutest of drinkers should beware Roberto's lethal margaritas.

Accommodations

Inside the Park

In the high country, **Tuolumne Meadows Lodge** (inside U.S. 888/413-8869, outside the U.S. 602/278-8888, www.travelyosemite.com, mid-June-mid-Sept., $141) offers rustic lodgings and good food in a gorgeous subalpine meadow setting. Expect no electricity, no private baths, and no other plush amenities. What you will find are small, charming wood-frame tent cabins that sleep up to four, central bath and hot shower facilities, and a dining room. The tent cabins have beds and wood-burning stoves. The location is perfect for starting or finishing a backcountry trip through the high country.

The rustic **White Wolf Lodge** (inside U.S. 888/413-8869, outside the U.S. 602/278-8888, www.travelyosemite.com, mid-June-mid-Sept., $137) sits back in the trees off Tioga Pass. Amenities are few, but breathtaking scenery is everywhere. With only 28 cabins, it's a good place to get away from the crowds. You can rent either the standard wood-platform tent cabin with use of central bath and shower facilities, or a solid-wall cabin with a private bath, limited electricity, and daily maid service. All cabins and tent cabins include linens and towels.

Outside the Park

Lee Vining

Located a few miles outside Yosemite's eastern Tioga Pass entrance, Lee Vining offers no-frills motels and lodges on the shores of eerily still Mono Lake.

Rent clean, comfortable, affordable lodgings at **Murphey's Motel** (51493 US-395, 760/647-6316 or 800/334-6316, www.murpheysyosemite.com, $80-175). Open all year, this motel provides one or two queen beds with cozy comforters, TVs, tables and chairs, and everything you need for a pleasant stay. Its central location in downtown Lee Vining makes dining, shopping, and trips to the visitors center and chamber of commerce convenient.

At the intersection of CA-120 and US-395, stay at the comfortable and affordable **Lake View Lodge** (51285 US-395, 800/990-6614, 760/647-6543, www.lakeviewlodgeyosemite.com, rooms $149-179, cottages $164-299). This aptly named lodge offers both motel rooms and cottages. The cottages can be rented in the summer only, but the motel rooms are available all year. Whether you choose a basic room for only a night or two, or larger accommodations with a kitchen for more than three days, you'll enjoy the simple country-style decor, the outdoor porches, and the views of Mono Lake. All rooms have TVs with cable, and Internet access is available. Pick up supplies at the local market for a picnic on the lawns of the lodge, or enjoy one of the nearby restaurants in Lee Vining.

June Lake

June Lake is just 20 miles (32 km) from Yosemite's eastern gate and a 30-minute drive to Tuolumne Meadows. It's off the June Lake Loop, a roadway off US-395 that's open in the summer months. A sage-scented town with fantastic mountain views, June Lake makes a fine base of operations to explore Yosemite as well as Eastern Sierra treasures, including **Bodie State Historic Park** and **Mono Lake.** In the winter, **June Mountain** (888/586-3686, www.junemountain.com) has seven lifts that give skiers and riders access to the slopes. Summer means trout fishing, swimming, hiking, and backpacking. The mountain setting is so nice you may never want to leave.

Fern Creek Lodge (4628 CA-158, 760/648-7722 or 800/621-9146, www.ferncreeklodge.com, $150-425) is the oldest year-round resort in June Lake. Its cabins are strung along a U-shaped driveway and include an old 1930s

June Lake

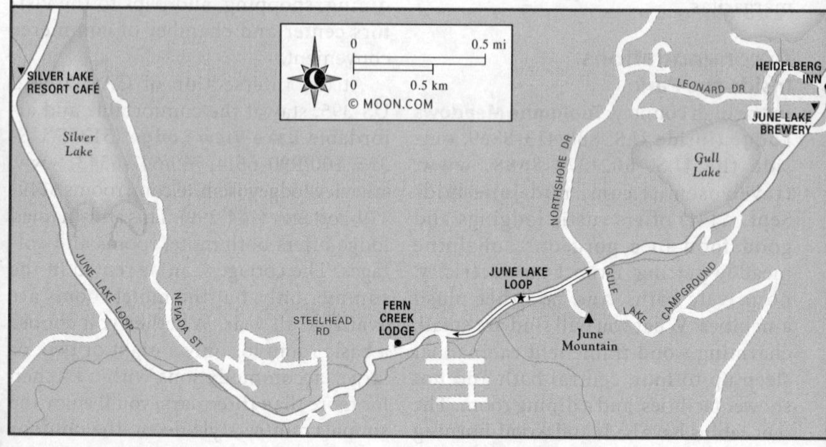

schoolhouse. Even the rustic cabins have modern conveniences like cable TV, Wi-Fi, and microwaves; all units have full kitchens. The rooms are decorated with playful fishing decor, which is no surprise since anglers flock to the area. The outdoor fireplace in the lodge's courtyard hosts barbecues, while the on-site store sells supplies.

Don't be surprised if you find yourself browsing homes for sale at June Lake's local real estate office. That was the effect it had on Hollywood celebrities like Buster Keaton, Charlie Chaplin, and Jimmy Durante. Frank Capra (director of 1946's *It's a Wonderful Life*) was so smitten with the area that he bought a cabin here. Remnants of this era can be seen at the **Heidelberg Inn** (2635 CA-158, 760/648-7781, www.heidelberginnresort.com, $179-289). Its lobby is decorated with photos of the Hollywood stars who used to hang out here. It also features a four-sided fireplace with a stuffed California grizzly bear on top. Every unit has a bedroom, a living room, and a kitchen. Even if you don't stay at the Heidelberg, visit its lobby, which is a monument to the resort's past glory.

Mammoth Lakes

Farther south, Mammoth Lakes offers a larger concentration of options if you are willing to drive 45 minutes from the park's eastern Tioga Pass entrance. Accommodations at Mammoth run from motels and inns to luxurious ski condos with full kitchens.

Economy rooms at the **Innsbruck Lodge** (913 Forest Trail, 760/934-3035, www.innsbrucklodge.com, $85-295) offer a queen bed, table and chairs, and access to the motel's whirlpool tub and lobby with stone fireplace at super-reasonable nightly rates. Other rooms can sleep 2-6, and some include kitchenettes. The quiet North Village location sits on the ski area shuttle route for easy access to the local slopes.

It's not cheap, but the **Juniper Springs Resort** (4000 Meridian Blvd., 800/626-6684, www.juniperspringsmammoth.com, $150-600) has absolutely every luxury amenity you could want to make your mountain getaway complete. Condos come in studio, one-bedroom, two-bedroom, three-bedroom, and townhouse sizes, sleeping up to eight people. The interiors boast stunning appointments, from snow-white down

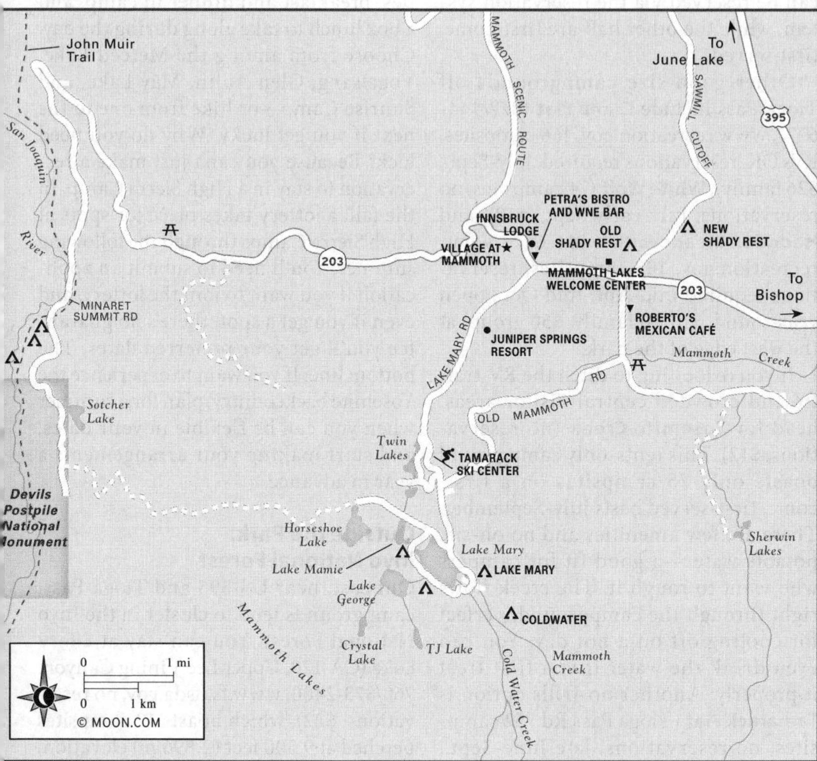

comforters to granite-topped kitchen counters to 60-inch flat-screen TVs. Baths include deep soaking tubs, perfect to relax aching muscles privately after a long day on the slopes. The resort also features heated pools year-round and three outdoor heated spas. Juniper Springs is close to local golfing and the Mammoth Mountain bike park.

Camping

Inside the Park

Yosemite visitors who favor the high country tend to prefer to camp rather than to stay in a lodge. Accordingly, most of Yosemite's campgrounds are north of the valley, away from the largest tourist crowds (excluding the High Sierra Camps, which are also up north).

★ **Tuolumne Meadows Campground** (Tioga Pass Rd. at Tuolumne Meadows, 877/444-6777, www.recreation.gov, reservations advised, July-late Sept., $26 family, $30 stock camp, $50 group) hosts the largest campground in the park, with over 300 individual campsites, plus four horse sites. The campground sprawls among trees and boulders. All the sites include fire rings and picnic tables along with food lockers to keep the bears at bay. You can hike to Elizabeth Lake from the campground. Expect Tuolumne to be crowded for the whole of its season. Tuolumne is RV-friendly and has most necessary services, including food and showers available at the Tuolumne Meadows Lodge. Half the campsites can be reserved via the reservation system, while the other half are first-come, first-served.

Other good-size campgrounds off Tioga Pass include **Crane Flat** (877/444-6777, www.recreation.gov, 166 campsites, RVs OK, reservations required, July-Sept., $26 family), **White Wolf** (74 campsites, no reservations, July-early Sept., $18), and **Hodgdon Meadow** (877/444-6777, www.recreation.gov, 105 campsites, reservations required mid-Apr.-mid Oct., open year-round, $18-26 family, $50 group) at the west edge of the park.

If you're looking to ditch the RV traffic and crowded central visitor areas, head for **Yosemite Creek** (no reservations, $12). This tents-only campground boasts only 75 campsites on a first-come, first-served basis July-September. There are few amenities and no on-site potable water—a good fit for campers who want to rough it. The creek flows right through the campground, perfect for cooling off on a hot day. You can even drink the water if you first treat it properly. Another no-frills option is **Tamarack Flat** (Tioga Pass Rd., 52 campsites, no reservations, late June-Sept., $12), located on Tamarack Creek, which is closer to Yosemite Valley.

The ★ **High Sierra Camps** (888/413-8869, www.travelyosemite.com; unguided trips $152-159 adults, $80-85 children; guided trips $706-1,048 adults, $372-553 children; saddle trips $1,320-2,056 adults, $1,068-1,643 children) at Yosemite offer far more than your average backcountry campground. Rather than carrying heavy packs filled with food, tents, and bedding, multiday hikers can plan to hit the High Sierra Camps, which provide tent cabins with amenities, breakfast and dinner in camp, and a box lunch to take along during the day. Choose from among the Merced Lake, Vogelsang, Glen Aulin, May Lake, and Sunrise Camp—or hike from one to the next if you get lucky. Why do you need luck? Because you can't just make a reservation to stay in a High Sierra Camp. In the fall, a lottery takes place for spots at High Sierra Camps through the following summer. You'll need to submit an application if you want to join the lottery, and even if you get a spot, there's no guarantee you'll get your preferred dates. The bottom line: If you want to experience the Yosemite backcountry, plan for a summer when you can be flexible in your dates, and start making your arrangements a year in advance.

Outside the Park: Inyo National Forest

Out east, near US-395 and Tioga Pass, campgrounds tend to cluster in the Inyo National Forest. You can stay at **Ellery Lake** (CA-120, Upper Lee Vining Canyon, 760/873-2400, www.fs.usda.gov, no reservations, $22), which boasts 12 campsites perched at 9,500 feet (2,896 m) elevation, with running water, pit toilets, and garbage cans available. Get there at dawn if you want a site on a weekend!

Another option is **Sawmill Walk-In** (Saddlebag Rd., 1.6 mi/2.6 km from CA-120, 760/873-2400, www.fs.usda.gov, June-Oct., $17). This primitive, no-reservations, hike-in campground has no water but an astonishing 9,800-foot (2,987-m) elevation that will, after a day or two, prepare you for any high-altitude activity you want to engage in.

Side Trip to Death Valley

a road in Death Valley

Death Valley National Park (760/786-3200, www.nps.gov/deva, 7-day vehicle pass $25) is a place of extremes. It's the lowest, driest, and hottest place in North America. But this park, located in the Mojave Desert, is also a place of rugged beauty, with colored badlands, impressive sand dunes, and otherworldly salt flats. It is amazing that such a place exists just four hours' drive from the waterfall-decorated granite cliffs of Yosemite.

Get the best views of the desert landscape at **Zabriskie Point,** which is breathtaking at sunrise or sunset. One of the park's most extreme places is **Badwater Basin,** the lowest point in North America at 282 feet (86 m) below sea level.

If you're staying overnight, **The Oasis at Death Valley** (CA-190, inside U.S. 800/236-7916, outside the U.S. 303/297-2757, www.oasisatdeathvalley.com) is a resort with two hotels: the upscale **Inn at Death Valley** ($369-639) and the family-friendly **Ranch at Death Valley** ($189-289). The rustic **Panamint Springs Resort** (40440 CA-190, 775/482-7680, www.panamintsprings.com, rooms and cabins $184-290, RV/tent sites and tent cabins $50-75) has cabins, motel rooms, and campsites.

Getting There

In the summer, when Tioga Pass is open, Death Valley is just a four-hour, 283-mile (460-km) drive from Yosemite. Head out of the park on **CA-120 East.** After 12 miles (19.3 km), take **US-395 South** and continue on the scenic highway for 123 miles (198 km). Turn left to follow **CA-136 East** for 17.5 miles (28 km). Continue straight onto **CA-190 East** into the park.

In winter, when Tioga Pass is closed, it's a grueling 8.5-hour drive around the Sierra Nevada. Take **CA-41 South** out of the park's South entrance. After 62 miles (100 km), get on **CA-99 South** for another 107 miles. Then take **CA-58 East** for 58 miles. Take **Exit 167** toward Bishop and Mojave. Make a left on **CA-14** and continue for 46 miles (74 km). Get on scenic **US-395 North** for 41.5 miles (67 km) before taking a right on **CA-190 Northeast,** which heads into Death Valley.

TO
LAS
NEVADA

Las Vegas

Las Vegas

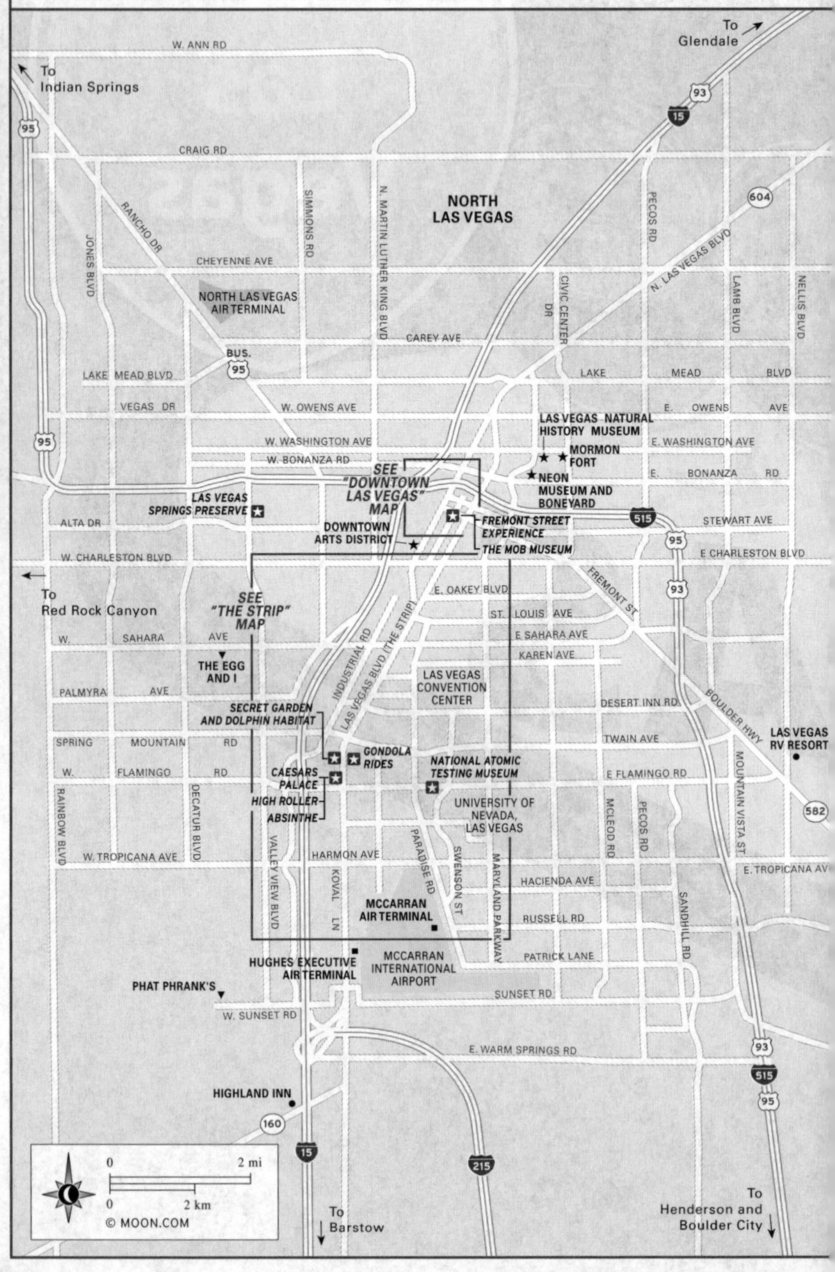

To Glendale
To Indian Springs
W. ANN RD
CRAIG RD
NORTH LAS VEGAS
RANCHO DR
JONES BLVD
SIMMONS RD
N. MARTIN LUTHER KING BLVD
PECOS RD
N. LAS VEGAS BLVD
CHEYENNE AVE
NORTH LAS VEGAS AIR TERMINAL
CIVIC CENTER DR
LAMB BLVD
NELLIS BLVD
CAREY AVE
BUS. 95
LAKE MEAD BLVD
VEGAS DR
W. OWENS AVE
E. OWENS AVE
LAS VEGAS NATURAL HISTORY MUSEUM
W. WASHINGTON AVE
E. WASHINGTON AVE
W. BONANZA RD
MORMON FORT
E. BONANZA RD
SEE "DOWNTOWN LAS VEGAS" MAP
NEON MUSEUM AND BONEYARD
LAS VEGAS SPRINGS PRESERVE
FREMONT STREET EXPERIENCE
STEWART AVE
ALTA DR
DOWNTOWN ARTS DISTRICT
THE MOB MUSEUM
W. CHARLESTON BLVD
E CHARLESTON BLVD
To Red Rock Canyon
SEE "THE STRIP" MAP
E. OAKEY BLVD
FREMONT ST
ST. LOUIS AVE
W. SAHARA AVE
E SAHARA AVE
KAREN AVE
THE EGG AND I
INDUSTRIAL RD
LAS VEGAS BLVD (THE STRIP)
LAS VEGAS CONVENTION CENTER
PALMYRA AVE
DESERT INN RD
BOULDER HWY
SECRET GARDEN AND DOLPHIN HABITAT
SPRING MOUNTAIN RD
TWAIN AVE
LAS VEGAS RV RESORT
GONDOLA RIDES
NATIONAL ATOMIC TESTING MUSEUM
W. FLAMINGO RD
E FLAMINGO RD
CAESARS PALACE
HIGH ROLLER
ABSINTHE
UNIVERSITY OF NEVADA, LAS VEGAS
MOUNTAIN VISTA ST
RAINBOW BLVD
DECATUR BLVD
VALLEY VIEW BLVD
PARADISE RD
SWENSON ST
MARYLAND PARKWAY
MCLEOD RD
PECOS RD
W. TROPICANA AVE
HARMON AVE
E. TROPICANA AV
KOVAL LN
HACIENDA AVE
SANDHILL RD
MCCARRAN AIR TERMINAL
RUSSELL RD
HUGHES EXECUTIVE AIR TERMINAL
MCCARRAN INTERNATIONAL AIRPORT
PATRICK LANE
PHAT PHRANK'S
SUNSET RD
W. SUNSET RD
E. WARM SPRINGS RD
HIGHLAND INN
0 2 mi
0 2 km
© MOON.COM
To Barstow
To Henderson and Boulder City

Highlights

★ **Caesars Palace:** This casino resort carries on the Roman Empire's regality and decadence with over-the-top excess (page 162).

★ **Gondola Rides:** Just like the real Grand Canal, The Venetian's waterway meanders along the Strip, with gondoliers providing the soundtrack (page 173).

★ **Secret Garden and Dolphin Habitat:** At The Mirage's twin habitats, the tigers, lions, and leopards can be seen playing impromptu games, while the bottlenose dolphins never shy from the spotlight (page 173).

★ **High Roller:** The world's largest observation wheel overwhelms the senses with driving music, videos, and unmatched views of the Strip (page 174).

★ **Fremont Street Experience:** Part music video, part history lesson, the six-minute shows are a four-block-long, 16-million-pixel burst of sensory overload (page 176).

★ **The Mob Museum:** Explore what some old-timers still refer to as "the good old days," when wiseguys ran the town, meting out their own brand of justice (page 178).

★ **Las Vegas Springs Preserve:** The city's birthplace, these natural springs now display the area's geological, anthropological, and cultural history along with what may be its future: water-conserving "green" initiatives (page 180).

★ **National Atomic Testing Museum:** Visit a fallout shelter and measure your body's radioactivity at this museum that traces the military, political, and cultural significance of the bomb (page 182).

★ ***Absinthe:*** Check your inhibitions and political correctness at the door and enjoy this heady cocktail of burlesque, vaudeville, and college toga party (page 183).

The chance at fortune has lured vacationers into the southern Nevada desert ever since the Silver State legalized gambling in 1931.

At first, the "sawdust joints"—named for the stuff spread on the floor to sop up spilled beer (and perhaps a few tears)—that popped up along downtown's Fremont Street were the center of the action, but they soon faced competition from a resort corridor blooming to the south on Highway 91. The burgeoning entertainment district reminded Los Angeles nightclub owner Billy Wilkerson of Sunset Boulevard in Hollywood, so he dubbed it "The Strip," and together with Bugsy Siegel built the Flamingo, the first upscale alternative to frontier gambling halls. Their vision left a legacy that came to define Las Vegas hotel-casinos. Las Vegas has gone through many reinventions in the decades since—from city of sleaze to Mafia haven, family destination, and upscale resort town. Today, Las Vegas is known for its fine restaurants, music festivals, and people-watching as much as its slot machines and craps tables.

So pack your stilettos, string bikini, money clip, and favorite hangover remedy and join the 35 million others who trek to Sin City every year to experience as many of the Seven Deadlies as they can cram into their vacation time. No one back home has to know you've succumbed to the city's siren song.

Getting to Las Vegas

From Los Angeles

Multilane highways ensure that the **270-mile (435-km), five-hour** drive from L.A. to Las Vegas is smooth, if not visually appealing. Even mild traffic can easily add an hour or more to your trip. Take **I-10 East** past Ontario to connect to **I-15 North.** Then continue 220 miles (355 km) through Victorville, Barstow, and Baker before reaching Las Vegas.

Stopping in Calico

About two hours outside the L.A. environs, the restored boomtown of Calico is tourist-trappy but can make for a fun stop. It's just 4 miles (6.4 km) off I-15 (take Exit 191 between Barstow and Yermo). The building exteriors at **Calico Ghost Town** (36600 Ghost Town Rd., Yermo, 760/254-1123, 9am-5pm daily, $8 adults, $5 children 4-11, children under 4 free) are restored to their 1880s appearance, and they now house shops, restaurants, and attractions. A small museum, located in an original adobe building, contains original furnishings and gives a thorough overview of the town and its mining history. Pretend you're back in the Wild West: Pan for gold, tour a mine, or trick your eyes at the Mystery Shack; each experience costs an additional fee ($3.50 adults, $2.50 children 5-10, children under 5 free). You can also take a ride on the Odessa Railroad ($5 adults, $2.50 children 5-10, children under 5 free).

The dining options stick to the ghost-town theme. At **Calico House Restaurant** (760/254-1970, 9am-5pm daily, $10-15), the meat is smoked, the chili simmers all day, and Western art adorns the walls. **Lil's Saloon** (760/254-2610, 9am-5pm daily, $8-15) is full of Western ephemera—roulette wheels, a manual cash register, and gun collections. Munchies, including pizza, hot dogs, and giant pretzels, dominate the menu.

There's really no reason to visit the ghost town for more than a couple of hours, but overnight guests can bed down in a 4-person **cabin** (800/862-2542, www.sbcountyparks.com, $65) or a **bunkhouse** ($160, 2-night minimum on weekends), which offers options for 6-20 people. There are 265 **camping sites** ($30-40,

$25-35 seniors) for tents and RVs with full and partial hookups.

Stopping in Goodsprings

About 45 minutes before you arrive in Las Vegas, you can make a stop at an Old West town just 7 miles (11.3 km) off of I-15; take Exit 12 for NV-161 to head west to Goodsprings, which used to be a mill town that supported several small local gold, silver, copper, and lead mines at the turn of the last century. You can poke around a couple decaying shacks and outbuildings and check out the town's old cemetery.

The star of Goodsprings is the **Pioneer Saloon** (310 W. Spring St., 702/874-9362, www.pioneersaloon.info, 9am-9pm Sun.-Thurs., 9am-11pm Fri.-Sat., $13-25). Built in 1913 from a kit ordered from the Sears, Roebuck and Co. catalog, the brass bar rail is the original issue, as are pressed-tin walls and the three bullet holes that mar them. The holes are courtesy of Joe Armstrong who, in 1915, caught Paul Coski cheating at poker and emptied his six-shooter; the three bullets that didn't hit the wall hit Coski, whose ghost is said to still roam the barroom, along with the specter of an old prospector.

That incident was not the Pioneer's last tragic event. Clark Gable sat at the bar for three nights straight in 1942, trying to calm his nerves with booze and cigarettes as he awaited news of his wife, actress Carole Lombard, whose plane had gone down at nearby Mount Potosi; he would learn that Lombard, her mother, and 20 others—everyone aboard—perished in the crash.

In modern times, the Pioneer Saloon serves burgers and sandwiches as well as hosts bachelor parties, weddings, and photo shoots. Country music stars Travis Tritt and Trace Adkins have done publicity shoots here. The bar also served as backdrop in scenes in movies including *Fear and Loathing in Las Vegas, The Mexican,* and *Miss Congeniality 2: Armed and Fabulous.*

From the Grand Canyon

From the West Rim

The good news is that the West Rim is the closest canyon point to Las Vegas—only about **120 miles (193 km),** or **2.5 hours,** even with the big detour south around the White Hills. The bad news is there's almost nothing to see along the way. From Meadview, take **Pierce Ferry Road** 40 miles (64 km) down past Dolan Springs. Turn right to pick up **US-93 North** and continue for 40 miles (64 km), until you cross into Nevada and US-93 becomes **I-11.** Follow I-11 for about 22 miles (35 km), then take **exit 23** for **I-215 West.** Continue on I-215 for about 10 miles (16.1 km), then take **exit 12A** for **I-15 North,** and the interstate will lead to the Strip.

From the South Rim

The South Rim is **280 miles (450 km)** from Las Vegas, a **five-hour** drive. Most summer weekends, you'll find this route crowded but manageable, unless there's an accident. From Grand Canyon Village, take **US-180/AZ 64 South** for 60 miles (97 km) to **Williams.** Turn right to join **I-40 West** and continue for 115 miles (185 km) to **Kingman,** a good **stopping point.**

From Kingman, jump on **US-93 North** for 70 miles (113 km), until you cross into Nevada and US-93 becomes **I-11.** Follow I-11 for about 22 miles (35 km), then take **exit 23** for **I-215 West.** Continue on I-215 for about 10 miles (16.1 km), then take **exit 12A** for **I-15 North,** and the interstate will lead to the Strip.

Stopping in Kingman

Kingman is located along the route from the South Rim of the Grand Canyon to Las Vegas. It has several well-curated museums that showcase its heritage, such as the **Historic Route 66 Museum** (Powerhouse Visitor Center, 120 W. Andy Devine Ave., 928/753-9889, www.mohavemuseum.org/az-route-66-museum.html, 9am-4pm Tues.-Sat., $4 adults, $3 seniors 60 and over, children

Best Restaurants

★ **The Egg & I:** You can order something other than eggs—but given the name, why would you (page 198)?

★ **Bazaar Meat:** José Andrés has created a carnivore's paradise, with an endless selection of beef, pork, fowl, and more exotic beasts prepared in every imaginable way (page 199).

★ **Yardbird:** A farm-fresh sit-down supper including fried chicken, biscuits, and dang tasty shrimp 'n' grits awaits you (page 200).

★ **Mon Ami Gabi:** Order the baked gruyère and a baguette and channel your inner Hemingway for a traditional French bistro experience (page 201).

★ **Le Thai:** The best of Las Vegas's impressive roster of Thai restaurants boasts playful interpretations of traditional cuisine in a trendy yet unpretentious atmosphere (page 202).

★ **VegeNation:** You'll find tasty plant-based chicken wings and meatball grinders here, but go for the portobello sliders or a tempura avocado taco (page 203).

under 12 free) and the **Mohave Museum of History and Arts** (400 W. Beale St., 928/753-3195, www.mohavemuseum.org, 9am-4pm Tues.-Fri., $4 adults, $3 seniors 60 and over, children under 12 free). Admission to either grants entry to the other.

The best restaurant for miles in any direction is **Mattina's Ristorante Italiano** (318 E. Oak St., 928/753-7504, 5pm-9pm Tues.-Sat., $13-25), where you can get perfectly prepared Italian food and fine wine. It's difficult to pass up the lobster ravioli or the creamy fettuccini alfredo. Don't leave without trying the tiramisu or the key lime pie. With a checkerboard floor, Formica tables, a long counter, and a comfort-food menu, **Rutherford's 66 Family Diner** (2011 E. Andy Devine Ave., 928/377-1660, 6am-8pm Mon.-Fri., 6am-3pm Sat.-Sun., $8-16) is a 1950s diner straight out of Central Casting. Skillet breakfasts and steak and meatloaf sandwiches will have you waxing nostalgic.

There are several affordable basic hotels on Andy Devine Avenue (Route 66) in Kingman's downtown area, some of them with retro road-trip neon signs and Route 66 themes. The Hollywood-themed **El Trovatore Motel** (1440 E. Andy Devine Ave., 928/692-6520, $66-76) boasts that Marilyn Monroe, James Dean, and Clark Gable all slept there. One of only a handful of prewar motels left in town, the motel retains its art deco sign and architecture. Rooms, which command views of the Hualapai Mountains, are utilitarian, with king or queen beds, a microwave, and a fridge. Pets are welcome.

From the North Rim

From the North Rim, it's a **5.5-hour, 280-mile (450-km)** drive to Vegas. This route may appeal to canyon lovers, as it takes drivers through Utah's Zion National Park for another opportunity to view nature's handiwork with stone, wind, and water. Only attempt this route during good weather; AZ-67 is subject to closure early November-late May, and all facilities at the North Rim are closed mid-October-mid-May. From the North Rim, take **AZ-67 North** for 44 miles (71 km) to **Jacob Lake** and head east on **US-89A** for 15 miles (24 km) to **Fredonia.** Then

Best Hotels

★ **Wynn:** No castles, no pyramids. Opting for class over kitsch, substance over splash, the Wynn is a worthy heir to "Old Vegas" joints (page 158).

★ **Harrah's:** It may seem middle-of-the-road, but its location puts it in the middle of the action (page 161).

★ **Bellagio:** All the romance of Italy manifests through dancing fountains, lazy gondola rides, and intimate bistros (page 164).

★ **Cosmopolitan:** Part Museum of Modern Art, part *Cabaret* Kit Kat Klub, this Strip resort blends visual overload with sensuous swank (page 166).

★ **Aria:** The centerpiece of City Center makes no concessions to old-school Sin City, choosing an urban feel accentuated by marble, steel, glass, and silk (page 167).

★ **Mandalay Bay:** Let the conscientious staff and serene elegance of this end-of-the-Strip hotel take you away from Vegas's pounding hip-hop and clanging slot machines (page 170).

★ **Golden Nugget:** A Strip-style resort in the otherwise staid downtown district, the Nugget features a waterslide surrounded by a shark-filled aquarium (page 171).

take **AZ-389 West,** which becomes **UT-59 North,** for 55 miles (89 km) to **Hurricane,** Utah. There pick up **UT-9 West** for 11 miles (17.7 km) to **I-15 South.** From there it's 125 miles (201 km) to Las Vegas.

Stopping in Overton

About 30 miles (48 km) after crossing into Nevada, look for the Overton exit as you approach Glendale. Twelve miles (19.3 km) off I-15, Overton is a compact agricultural community that makes a good pit stop on the way to Lake Mead. Overton's downtown is strung along several blocks of NV-169, also known as Moapa Valley Boulevard and Main Street. Overton offers two strong lunch options. **Sugars Home Plate** (309 S. Moapa Valley Blvd., 702/397-8084, 7am-9pm Tues.-Sun., $10-20) serves bacon and eggs, half-pound burgers—including the Sugar Burger, a cheeseburger with Polish sausage—and homemade pie. There's also a sports bar with bar-top video poker and sports memorabilia. Just a block away, **Inside Scoop** (395 S. Moapa Valley Blvd., 702/397-2055, 11am-8pm Mon.-Sat., 11am-7pm Sun., $7-15) has filling sandwiches, light salads, hearty soups, and 30-plus ice cream flavors. The baked potatoes come with whatever toppings you can imagine.

The **Plaza Motel** (207 Moapa Valley Blvd., 702/397-2414, $50-60) provides basic guest rooms and a jumping-off point for visits to Valley of Fire State Park. A few A great pool and hot tub are highlights of a stay at **Fun N Sun RV Park** (280 N. Cooper Ave., 702/397-8894, $30).

From Yosemite

If there's any chance that **Tioga Pass** might be closed, which generally happens October-May, check with the **National Park Service** (209/372-0200, www.nps.gov/yose) for the latest **road conditions.** If the pass is open, you have your choice of a few fairly direct routes to Las Vegas that start by heading on **CA-120 East** through the pass. If the pass is closed, prepare for a tedious **8- to 10-hour** trip through central California.

Via Tioga Pass: Nevada Route

If **Tioga Pass** is open, you have your choice of two fairly direct route options through Nevada to Las Vegas; both start out on **CA-120 East** from the Tioga Pass entrance to **Benton.**

The quickest route covers about **340 miles (545 km),** with a driving time of about **5.5 hours** from the Tioga Pass entrance. Follow **CA-120 East** for 45 miles (72 km) to Benton, where you'll turn left onto **US-6 East.** In 23 miles (37 km), turn right to head south on **NV-264**—which morphs into **CA-266** and **NV-266.** After 86 miles (138 km), turn right onto **US-95** and head south for 170 miles (275 km) to Vegas.

Instead of heading south on NV-264, you could also continue on **US-6** from Benton for 40 miles (64 km) to Coaldale, where the highway joins with **US-95,** and then simply follow it for another 40 miles (64 km) to **Tonopah.** From here it's a fairly straight shot south continuing on US-95 for 210 miles (340 km) to Vegas. This route is slightly longer at about **355 miles** (575 km), **5.75 hours.**

Stopping in Tonopah

Tonopah is a natural crossroads that rewards travelers with colorful mining history—it was known as the "Queen of the Silver Camps"—and one of the darkest starry skies in the country. Tequila, beer, and spice lovers will revel in the cheesy chile rellenos at **El Marques** (348 N. Main St., 775/482-3885, 11am-9pm Tues.-Sun., $10-15), and the salsa seals the deal. Or how about a beer and some barbecue? **Tonopah Brewing Co.** (315 S. Main St., 775/482-2000, www.tonopahbrewing.com, 11am-9pm daily, $12-20) is your stop. Taste its pilsners, hefeweizens, and IPAs in pint or pitcher form along with some delicious barbecued meats, including slow-simmered brisket, barbecue pork, and ribs cooked for at least seven hours.

The owners have faithfully restored the **Mizpah Hotel** (100 N. Main St., 775/482-3030, www.themizpahhotel.com, $100-165)—the "Grand Lady of Tonopah" was the epitome of luxury during the silver boom—with claw-foot tubs, wrought-iron bedsteads, and lots of carmine accents. You can dine on-site at the casual **Pittman Café** (6am-9pm daily, $12-20). Next door, the guest rooms at **Jim Butler Inn** (100 S. Main St., 800/635-9455, www.jimbutlerinn.com, $85-120) are bright and inviting, with wood furniture, cinnamon or emerald color schemes, and faux hearths. Some guest rooms have fridges and microwaves; all have free Wi-Fi.

Via Tioga Pass: California Route

Just a bit longer than the Nevada options at about **365 miles (590 km)** and **6 hours,** an arguably more scenic route traverses Mammoth Lakes, Bishop, and Big Pine, California, and includes views of Mount Whitney and the possibility of an overnight stay at Death Valley National Park. From the Tioga Pass entrance, follow **CA-120 East** to **US-395 South.** In 123 miles (198 km), at Lone Pine, take **CA-136 East,** which becomes **CA-190 East** and winds through Death Valley, for 85 miles (137 km). A left turn onto **Scotty's Castle Road** and soon after a right onto **Daylight Pass Road** leads to the Nevada border and **NV-374 North** in 14 miles (22.5 km). In another 13 miles (20.9 km), at **Beatty, US-95 South** leads 117 miles (188 km) to Las Vegas.

Stopping in Beatty

Once a center of Nevada mining, Beatty is a microcosm of Western history, serving at various times as a Shoshone settlement, a ranching center, and a railway hub.

Food options are scant here, but **Death Valley Nut & Candy Co.** (900 US-95, 775/553-2100, 6am-10pm daily) can tide you over until Las Vegas. The largest candy store in Nevada also sells

Stretch Your Legs

Ever wonder what it would be like to live upside down? Satisfy your curiosity at the **Upside-Down House** (Yosemite-Las Vegas Dr., corner of 1st Ave. and Matley Ave., Lee Vining, 760/647-6461, 10am-4pm Thurs.-Tues., Memorial Day-mid-Sept., $2), just a block off US-395 outside Yosemite National Park. Inspired by the children's stories "Upside Down Land" and "The Upsidedownians," the small wooden cabin features a bed, a rug, and furniture on the ceiling.

The infamous Area 51 is the focus of conspiracy theories about UFOs. Capitalizing on its location just south of the secret military installation, the **Area 51 Alien Travel Center** (Yosemite-Las Vegas Dr., 2711 E. US-95, Amargosa Valley, 775/372-5678) sells all sorts of extraterrestrial-influenced merchandise. Painted fluorescent yellow, it's hard to miss. (This being Nevada, there's also a brothel out back.)

Last Stop Arizona (Yosemite-Las Vegas Dr., 20606 N. US-93, White Hills, 928/767-4911, www.arizonalaststop.com, gift store 6:30am-8pm daily, restaurant 7am-6pm daily) also celebrates life on other planets. Pose for a photo in an alien cutout display and fill up your tank with "Uranus" gas. There's also a diner and a quirky gift shop, which doubles as a source of Powerball lottery tickets.

sandwiches, dried fruit, ice cream, and coffee. **Mel's Diner** (600 US-95 S., 775/553-9003, 6am-1pm daily, $8-12) serves breakfast and lunch.

The laundry room and small pool and spa at **Death Valley Inn** (651 US-95 S., 775/553-9400, $80-120) are welcome amenities greeting road-weary travelers. There's also a 39-space RV park—all pull-throughs with 50-amp hookups. Originally catering to defense contractor employees at the Nevada Test Site and Area 51, the **Atomic Inn** (350 S. 1st St., 775/553-2250, $70-80) has standard guest rooms, with lots of golds and honey-blond wood furniture and paneling.

Bypassing Tioga Pass

Tioga Pass is closed most years **October-May.** Check with the **National Park Service** (209/372-0200, www.nps.gov/yose) for the latest **road conditions.** If the pass is closed, your only option is a tedious **8- to 10-hour**, approximately **500-mile (805-km)** trip through central California. Take **CA-41 South** to **Fresno** (95 mi/153 km), then follow **CA-99 South** to **Bakersfield** (109 mi/175 km). Continue on **CA-58 East** to **Barstow** (131 mi/211 km) before catching **1-15 North** to Las Vegas (155 miles/250 km).

Stopping in Bakersfield

While far from a tourist destination, Bakersfield is at least a diversion on the otherwise dreary winter Yosemite-Las Vegas route.

Step back in time and treat yourself to a milkshake at the country's last working **Woolworth Luncheonette** (1400 19th St., 661/321-0061, 10:30am-4pm Mon.-Sat., noon-4pm Sun., $4-10). It's tucked away in a corner of downtown's Five & Dime Antique Mall, complete with two dozen counter seats, Formica tables, and checkerboard floor. More highbrow is **Uricchio's Trattoria** (1400 17th St., 661/326-8870, www.uricchios.com, 11am-2pm and 5pm-9pm Mon.-Thurs., 11am-2pm and 5pm-10pm Fri., 5pm-10pm Sat., $15-30), which serves the best chicken *piccata*. Seafood fans can't go wrong with the diver scallops or orange roughy almondine.

Skip the chains and treat yourself to lodgings with character. With eight stories of Spanish colonial revival architecture, the **Padre Hotel** (1702 18th St., 661/427-4900 or 888/443-3387, www.thepadrehotel.com, $149-199) has been faithfully restored to its 1930s grandeur. But the rooms are strictly 21st century, with sleek furniture and plush textiles.

Kick off your shoes, soak in a chromatherapy spa tub, then snuggle into a fine down comforter to guarantee a fine night's rest. Or bust a move in the hotel's 5th-floor Prospect Lounge.

A few blocks west, the guest rooms at **Hotel Rosedale** (2400 Camino Del Rio Ct., 661/327-0681, $79-140) lure guests with their springy umber, burnt orange, and green decor. The oversize pool is surrounded by plenty of shade and shrubbery. A small playground will keep little tykes busy.

By Air and Bus

Air

More than 50 million people arrive or depart **McCarran International Airport** (LAS, 5757 Wayne Newton Blvd., 702/261-5211, www.mccarran.com) every year, making it the ninth busiest in the country. Terminal 1 welcomes domestic flights, while Terminal 3 hosts domestic and international flights.

About 40 percent of the runway traffic at McCarran belongs to **Southwest Airlines,** by far the largest carrier serving Las Vegas. Other major players include **United, Delta, American,** and **Spirit.** The number of airlines keeps fares competitive. Given that Las Vegas is one of the world's top tourist destinations, it's best to make your reservations as early as possible. Last-minute deals are few and far between, and you'll pay through the nose to fly to Vegas on a whim or in advance of major events such as the Super Bowl, March Madness, New Year's Eve, and Cinco de Mayo.

Regular flights are available from **San Francisco** (1.5 hours) and **Los Angeles** (70 minutes).

Airport Transportation

McCarran International Airport is just 2 miles (3.2 km) east of the Lower Strip, and provides easy transfers to the Strip using **shuttle vans, buses, ride share** and **rental cars.** Limousines are available curbside for larger groups. A **taxi ride** from the airport to the Strip (15 minutes) or downtown (20 minutes) runs no more than $27. A $2 surcharge is assessed for pickups from the airport, and there is a $3 credit card processing fee. It's cheaper and often faster to take the surface streets from the airport to your destination rather than the freeway, which is several miles longer.

Citizen Area Transit (CAT, 702/228-7433, www.rtcsnv.com, 2 hours $6, 24 hours $8, children under age 5 free with a guardian) offers bus services from McCarran International Airport. Buy your single-ride tickets or passes as you board or through the terminal vending machines. The **Route 109 bus** departs from Level 0 at **Terminal 1** every 15 minutes. A six-minute ride deposits visitors at the South Strip Transit Terminal, where they can transfer to the **Deuce bus.** Typical travel times are 33 minutes to Mandalay Bay, 45 minutes to Harrah's, and 55 minutes to the Wynn. If you're headed downtown, stay on the bus to the end of the line. From McCarran's **Terminal 3,** catch CAT's **Centennial Express (CX)** at the departures curb on Level 2. Exit the terminal building and cross the pedestrian crosswalk. The bus stop is across from door 44. The bus takes you to the intersection of Sands Avenue and Spring Mountain Road on the Strip, near the Palazzo, in 30 minutes.

Bell Trans (702/739-7990, www.airportshuttlelasvegas.com), **ODS Chauffered Transportation** (702/688-7353, www.odslimo.com), and **AWG Ambassador** (702/740-3434, www.awgambassador.com) offer shuttle buses, vans, and chauffeured shuttle services that will ferry you to your Strip or downtown hotel for about $18 per person, round-trip. All have ticket kiosks inside the terminals, most near the baggage claim. These shuttles run continuously, leaving about every 15 minutes. You don't need reservations from the airport, but you will need reservations from your hotel to return to the airport.

Two Days in Las Vegas

Day 1

Rise bright and early and grab a ride share to Four Seasons, the hotel-within-the-hotel at **Mandalay Bay** on the Lower Strip. Dine al fresco for breakfast at its **Veranda** restaurant. Walk off a few calories with a 15-minute amble south to the famous **"Welcome to Fabulous Las Vegas" sign.**

Spend the day wandering the Strip. You can walk or catch the double-decker **Deuce bus,** which runs the length of Las Vegas Boulevard, stopping in front of nearly every resort on the Strip and ending in downtown. Explore the shops and restaurants of **Caesars Palace,** head to **The Mirage** to check out Siegfried and Roy's **Secret Garden**—where white tigers, leopards, and lions lurk—or hop on a **gondola ride** at **The Venetian.**

Spend the evening taking in the atmosphere and stocking up on Instagram fodder. Must-shoots include a Strip panorama from the **Eiffel Tower Viewing Deck,** an obligatory selfie in front of the **Fountains of Bellagio,** and snaps of and from the **High Roller.**

If you only have time for one show, make it vaudeville- and cabaret-inspired ***Absinthe.***

For a quiet night, book a room at the **Aria,** which has blackout curtains and touch-button climate control to create the perfect environment for drifting off. If you don't need no stinkin' sleep, **The Linq** may be more your speed, close to hip watering holes and rocking live music venues.

Day 2

Today, celebrate the kitsch and class of vintage Vegas. Channel a *Swingers* vibe by heading to the retro **Peppermill Restaurant & Fireside Lounge.** While it's daylight, make your way to the **Neon Museum and Boneyard,** the final resting place of some of Las Vegas's iconic signage. And while you're in the neighborhood, witness the rise and fall of the Mafia in Las Vegas at **The Mob Museum.**

Then spend some time wandering around **downtown Las Vegas.** Lunch on black bean and sweet potato quesadillas at **VegeNation,** catch a short sensory show at the **Fremont Street Experience,** check out watering holes and retro-chic boutiques in the **Downtown Container Park,** and browse galleries in the **arts district.**

At night, order up a neat bourbon and watch Sinatra try to ignore Sammy and Dino's distractions long enough to make it through a rendition of "Luck Be a Lady" in ***The Rat Pack Is Back.*** Then get out there and gamble into the wee hours.

Bus

The **Greyhound station** (200 S. Main St., 702/384-9561, www.greyhound.com) is on the south side of the Plaza Hotel. Buses arrive and depart frequently throughout the day and night to and from all points in North America, and they are a reasonable alternative to driving or flying.

Five or six buses originating at the **San Francisco station** (200 Folsom St., 415/495-1569) arrive in Las Vegas each day after 17- to 18-hour slogs through California and Nevada. Day-of-trip tickets can be had for as little as $60.

Eight to ten Greyhounds arrive from the **Los Angeles terminal** (1716 E. 7th St., 213/629-8401) each day. Travel time is about 5.5 hours, with a single stop in either San Bernardino or Barstow. Rates are a reasonable $15-30, with some as low as $6 when purchased well ahead of time.

Megabus (877/462-6342, http://us.megabus.com) runs two buses a day from Los Angeles for $50 per person. It delivers passengers to the Regional Transportation Center's South Strip Transfer Terminal. Those heading to the Strip or downtown can catch the

"Deuce" double-decker bus at Bay 14. It runs 24 hours a day, seven days a week, and the next one will be there in less than 15 minutes.

Orientation

Las Vegas Boulevard South—better known as the Strip—is the city's focal point, with 14 of the 29 largest hotels in the world welcoming gamblers and hedonists from around the world. Six of the world's 11 biggest hostelries line a 4-mile (6.4-km) north-south stretch between Tropicana and Sahara Avenues. Running parallel to I-15, this is what most folks think of when someone says "Vegas."

Major east-west thoroughfares include Tropicana Avenue, Harmon Avenue, Flamingo Road, Spring Mountain Road, Desert Inn Road, and Sahara Avenue. Koval Lane and Paradise Road parallel the Strip to the east, while Frank Sinatra Drive does likewise to the west, giving a tour of the loading docks and employee parking lots of some of the world's most famous resorts.

I-15 also mirrors the Strip to the east, as both continue north-northeast through **downtown** and its casino and arts districts. Main Street juts due south at Charleston Boulevard and joins Las Vegas Boulevard at The Strat. The Strip and I-15 continue parallel southeast and south out of town.

Casinos

TOP EXPERIENCE

Upper Strip

Ranging from Spring Mountain Road to The Strat, the **Upper Strip** is known for its throwback swagger, but has something for everyone. Visitors can opt for world-class art, celebrity chef creations, midway games, stand-up comedy—and friendly rates at old standby casinos.

The Strat

Restaurants: Top of the World, PT's Wings & Sports, Strat Café, McCall's Heartland Grill, 108 Eats, Crafted Buffet, Elation Pool Café & Bar, Nunzio's Pizzeria, Fat Tuesday, Starbucks, McDonald's
Entertainment: *MJ Live*, L.A. Comedy Club, *Celestia*
Attractions: SkyPod, SkyJump, observation deck, top-of-the-tower thrill rides, Elation Pool, Radius Pool and Wet Lounge, retail shops
Nightlife: McCall's Whiskey Bar, 107 Sky Lounge, 108 Drinks, View Lounge, Remix Lounge

It's altitude with attitude at this 1,149-foot-tall (350-m) exclamation point on the north end of the Strip. **The Strat** (2000 Las Vegas Blvd. S., 800/998-6937, www.thestrat.com, $65-146) is the brainchild of entrepreneur, politician, and professional poker player Bob Stupak. A $100 million renovation in 2019 led to a name change (the resort was formerly known as the Stratosphere), and imparted a more upscale vibe. The makeover upgraded the sportsbook, introduced several new restaurants, added natural lighting, modernized the guest rooms, and expanded the casino.

Daredevils will delight in the 40-mph (64.4-kmp) quasi-freefall at **SkyJump,** along with the other vertigo-inducing thrill rides on the tower's observation deck. The fainter of heart may want to steer clear not only of the rides but also the resort's double-decker elevators, which launch guests to the top of the tower at 1,400 feet (427 m) per minute. But even acrophobes should conquer their fears long enough to enjoy the views from the restaurant and bars more than 100 floors up at The Strat's **Top of the World** restaurant.

If the thrill rides on the observation deck aren't your style, get a rush of gambling action on the nearly 100,000-square-foot (9,290-sq-m) ground-floor casino. Or perhaps the two swimming pools (one is tops-optional) and the dozen bars and restaurants are more your speed.

Spot-on impersonators and elaborate choreography make The Strat's Michael

The Strip

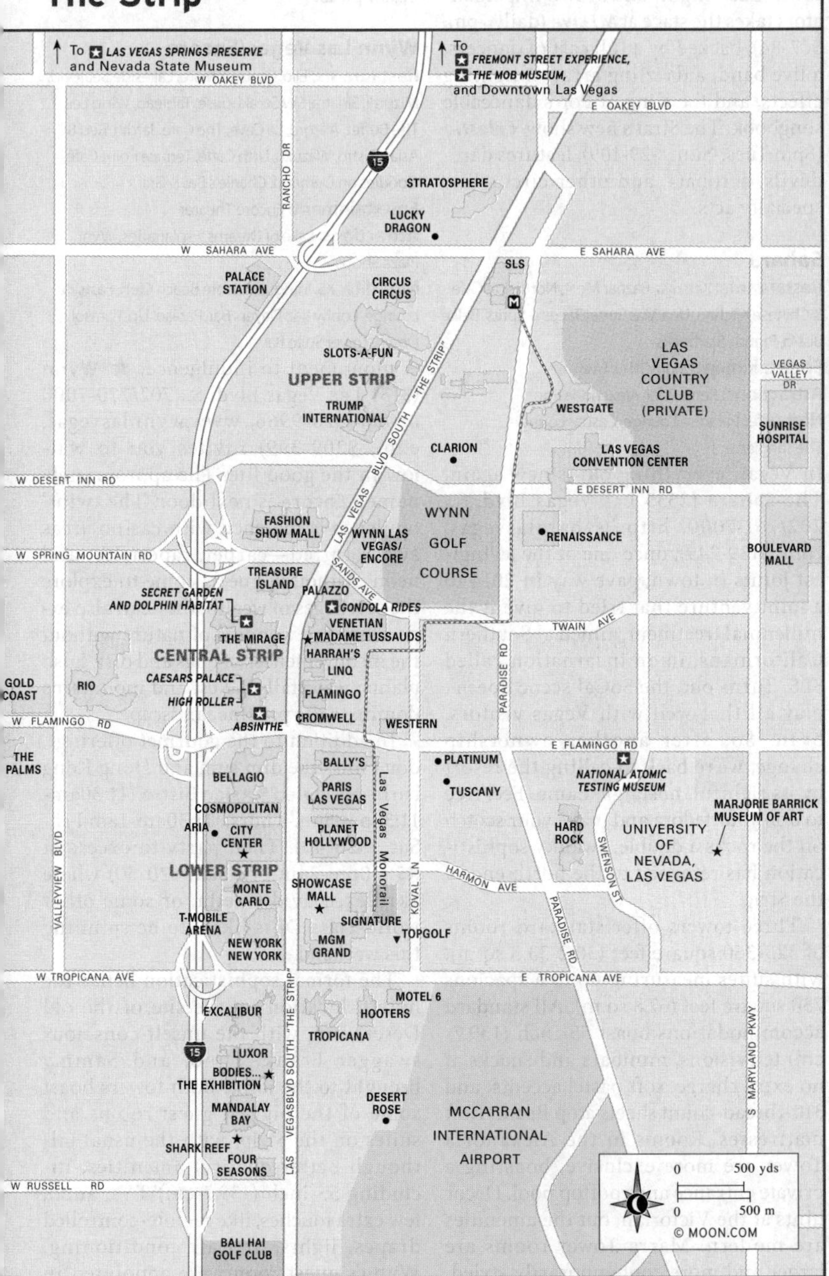

To LAS VEGAS SPRINGS PRESERVE and Nevada State Museum
To FREMONT STREET EXPERIENCE, THE MOB MUSEUM, and Downtown Las Vegas
W OAKEY BLVD
E OAKEY BLVD
RANCHO DR
15
STRATOSPHERE
LUCKY DRAGON
W SAHARA AVE
E SAHARA AVE
SLS
PALACE STATION
CIRCUS CIRCUS
SLOTS-A-FUN
UPPER STRIP
LAS VEGAS BLVD SOUTH "THE STRIP"
LAS VEGAS COUNTRY CLUB (PRIVATE)
VEGAS VALLEY DR
WESTGATE
SUNRISE HOSPITAL
TRUMP INTERNATIONAL
CLARION
LAS VEGAS CONVENTION CENTER
W DESERT INN RD
E DESERT INN RD
WYNN GOLF COURSE
RENAISSANCE
FASHION SHOW MALL
WYNN LAS VEGAS/ ENCORE
BOULEVARD MALL
W SPRING MOUNTAIN RD
SANDS AVE
TREASURE ISLAND
SECRET GARDEN AND DOLPHIN HABITAT
PALAZZO
GONDOLA RIDES
VENETIAN
TWAIN AVE
THE MIRAGE
MADAME TUSSAUDS
CENTRAL STRIP
HARRAH'S
PARADISE RD
LINQ
GOLD COAST
RIO
CAESARS PALACE
HIGH ROLLER
FLAMINGO
ABSINTHE
CROMWELL
WESTERN
W FLAMINGO RD
E FLAMINGO RD
THE PALMS
BALLY'S
PLATINUM
NATIONAL ATOMIC TESTING MUSEUM
BELLAGIO
PARIS LAS VEGAS
Las Vegas Monorail
TUSCANY
MARJORIE BARRICK MUSEUM OF ART
COSMOPOLITAN
ARIA
CITY CENTER
PLANET HOLLYWOOD
HARD ROCK
UNIVERSITY OF NEVADA, LAS VEGAS
SWENSON ST
VALLEYVIEW BLVD
LOWER STRIP
HARMON AVE
MONTE CARLO
SHOWCASE MALL
KOVAL LN
T-MOBILE ARENA
SIGNATURE
TOPGOLF
NEW YORK NEW YORK
MGM GRAND
W TROPICANA AVE
E TROPICANA AVE
EXCALIBUR
MOTEL 6
HOOTERS
TROPICANA
LUXOR
BODIES... THE EXHIBITION
S MARYLAND PKWY
MANDALAY BAY
DESERT ROSE
MCCARRAN INTERNATIONAL AIRPORT
SHARK REEF
FOUR SEASONS
W RUSSELL RD
BALI HAI GOLF CLUB
0 500 yds
0 500 m
© MOON.COM

Jackson tribute show among the best in town. Each night, one of two impersonators takes the stage at ***MJ Live*** (daily 7pm, $67-84), backed by a full cast of dancers, a live band, a dazzling array of lighting effects, and the King of Pop's danceable songbook. The Strat's new show, ***Celestia*** (8pm Tues.-Sun., $29-109), features daredevils, acrobats, and other circus-like specialty acts.

Sahara

Restaurants: Katsuya, Bazaar Meat, Northside Café & Chinese Kitchen, Una Mas Street Tacos + Sprits, Bella Bistro, Prendi, Starbucks

Entertainment: *Magic Mike Live*

Attractions: Retro Pool, Alexandria Pool

Nightlife: Paradise Lounge, Casbar Lounge, The Tangier

In Vegas, everything old is new again. The **Sahara** (2535 Las Vegas Blvd. S., 702/761-7000, http://saharalasvegas.com, $139-249), once one of the swingiest joints in town, gave way in 2014 to a joint venture that tried to give it the millennial treatment, aimed at Southern Californians, in an incarnation called SLS. Turns out, the SoCal scene doesn't play all that well with Vegas visitors, brah. So, after another ownership change, we're back to calling the resort by its rightful, nostalgic name. Feel free to don your fedora and make your scotch on the rocks a double; swanky sophistication has returned to the north end of the Strip.

Three towers offer standard rooms of 325-360 square feet (30.2-33.5 sq m), with suites measuring up to a spacious 730 square feet (67.8 sq m). All standard accommodations boast 55-inch (139.7-cm) televisions, minibars and snacks at no extra charge, soft pastel accents, and 310-thread-count sheets atop BeautyRest mattresses. Rooms in the Alexandria Tower are more exclusive, boasting a private entrance and rooftop pool. Decor hints at the Victorian, but the amenities are modern. Marra Tower rooms are larger and more contemporarily styled. Blanca Tower rooms are the most basic crash pads.

Wynn Las Vegas/Encore

Restaurants: Elio, Costa Di Mare, Lakeside Seafood, Mizumi, Sinatra, SW Steakhouse, Tableau, Wing Lei, The Buffet, Allegro, La Cave, The Café, Jardin, Red 8 Asian Bistro, Wazuzu, Urth Caffe, Terrace Point Café, Goodies on Demand, Charlie's Bar & Grill

Entertainment: Encore Theater

Attractions: Lake of Dreams, Esplanades, Wynn Plaza Shops

Nightlife: XS, Intrigue, Encore Beach Club, Eastside Lounge, Lobby Bar, Players Bar, Parasol Up, Parasol Down, Tower Suite Bar

A monument to indulgence, ★ **Wynn** (3131 Las Vegas Blvd. S., 702/770-7000 or 888/320-9966, www.wynnlasvegas.com, $209-399) invites you to wallow in the good life. The appropriately named **Encore** is next door. The twins' opulence is matched with casino areas awash in red—carpet, tapestries, and neon. Although guests come to explore the privileges of wealth, they can also experience the wonders of nature without the inconveniences of bugs and dirt. Lush plants, waterfalls, lakes, and mountains dominate the pristine landscape.

In addition to the gourmet offerings, don't miss the dim sum and Hong Kong barbecue at **Red 8 Asian Bistro** (11:30am-11:30pm Sun.-Thurs., 11:30am-1am Fri.-Sat., $20-40). Then party to excess at **XS** (10pm-2am Fri.-Sat., $20-50) where Skrillex, David Guetta, or some other world-class DJ is likely to be spinning this weekend.

The formal sophistication belies the hotels' location on the site of the old Desert Inn, with the unself-conscious swagger Frank, Dino, and Sammy brought to the joint. Both towers boast some of the biggest guest rooms and suites on the Strip, with the usual (although better-quality) amenities, including 55-inch (139.7-cm) TVs, and a few extra touches, like remote-controlled drapes, lights, and air-conditioning. Wynn's guest rooms are appointed in wheat, honey, and other creatively named shades of beige. Encore's all-suite accommodations are more colorful, with the color scheme running toward dark chocolate and cream.

Eponymous mogul Steve Wynn is no longer affiliated with the resort in the wake of numerous sexual misconduct allegations.

Center Strip

The **Center Strip** is between Flamingo Road and Spring Mountain Road. The casinos are packed tight, and though the sidewalks can become masses of humanity on weekend nights, all the temptations are within walking distance.

The Venetian

Restaurants: Factory Kitchen, Bouchon, Bouchon Bakery, Black Tap Burgers and Beer, CR Creat, Chica, Delmonico Steakhouse, Mercato della Pescheria, Grand Lux Café, Juice Farm, Noodle Asia, Public House, Sugarcane, Canyon Ranch Café, Yardbird, Zio Gelato, Buddy V's Ristorante, Canaletto, Canonita, Carlo's Bakery, Casanova, Cocolini, Lobster ME, Tao Asian Bistro, Coffee Bean and Tea Leaf, Trattoria Reggiano, Food Court
Entertainment: Venetian Theatre
Attractions: Madame Tussauds Las Vegas, gondola rides, Streetmosphere, Grand Canal Shoppes, The Void, Tao Beach
Nightlife: Tao Nightclub, Rosina, Bellini Bar, The Dorsey, Sin City Brewing Co., Rockhouse, Fat Tuesday, Gondola Bar

The Venetian (3355 Las Vegas Blvd. S., 702/414-1000 or 866/659-9643, www.venetian.com, $209-349) comes close to capturing the elegance of Venice. An elaborate faux-Renaissance ceiling fresco greets visitors in the hotel lobby, and the sensual treats just keep coming. A life-size streetscape—with replicas of the Bridge of Sighs, Doge's Palace, the Grand Canal, and other treasures—gives the impression that the best of the Queen of the Adriatic has been transplanted in toto.

From top to bottom: Harrah's; fountain at The Venetian; Caesars Palace.

Tranquil rides in authentic **gondolas** with serenading pilots are perfect for relaxing after a hectic session in the 120,000-square-foot (11,148-sq-m) casino. Canal-side, buskers entertain the guests in the **Streetmosphere** (St. Mark's Square, noon-6pm daily on the hour, free), and the **Grand Canal Shoppes** entice strollers, window-shoppers, and serious spenders.

World-class DJs, A-list celebrities, and wall-to-wall hardbodies pack **Tao Nightclub** (10:30pm-5am Thurs.-Sat.) at the end of each week to groove to thumping house and hip-hop. Reservations and advance tickets are recommended, as this is one of the hottest party spots in town, with a powerful light and sound system, two dance rooms, and open architecture. Scattered throughout, bathing beauties luxuriate, covered (more or less) only by rose petals.

After you've shopped till, you're ready to drop, **Madame Tussauds Las Vegas** invites stargazers for hands-on experiences with their favorite entertainers, superheroes, and athletes.

Dining options abound. Try the lobster ravioli or traditional pizza and pasta dishes in the bistro setting of **Trattoria Reggiano** (10am-midnight daily, $20-30). Or step away from the Italian theme. **Yardbird** pairs fried chicken with watermelon, lemon, honey, and other sweet and savory preparations. At Thomas Keller's **Bouchon** (702/414-6200, 7am-1pm and 5pm-10pm Mon.-Thurs., 7am-2pm and 5pm-10pm Sat.-Sun., $30-65), try the sensational croque madame sandwich with its rich Mornay sauce or climb a tower of French fries to recover from a night in Sin City. The luxe setting features high ceilings, wood columns, and tile floors.

The Venetian spares no expense in the hotel department. Its 4,027 suites are tastefully appointed with plum accents and Italian (of course) marble, and at 650 square feet (60.4 sq m), they're big. They include sunken living rooms and Roman tubs.

The Palazzo

Restaurants: Cut, Grand Lux Café, Once, Hong Kong Café, Espressamente Illy, Juice Farm, Lavo, Morels Steakhouse & Bistro, Grimaldi's Pizzeria, Sushisamba, Solaro, Canyon Ranch Grill, Coffee Bean and Tea Leaf

Attractions: Grand Canal Shoppes, Atrium Waterfall

Nightlife: Fusion Latin Mixology Bar, Laguna Champagne Bar, Lavo Lounge, Double Helix Wine and Whiskey Bar

An 80-foot (24.4-m) domed skylight illuminates a faux-ice sculpture, bronze columns, and lush landscaping surrounding the lobby at **The Palazzo** (3325 Las Vegas Blvd. S., 702/607-7777 or 866/263-3001, www.palazzo.com, $239-349). Motel 6 this ain't. A big chunk of the 100,000-square-foot (9,290-sq-m) casino is smoke-free, embodying the casino's efforts toward energy efficiency and environmentally friendly design.

The Palazzo is a gourmand's dream, with a handful of four-star establishments dominated, as you would expect, by Italian influences.

Accommodations are all suites, measuring even larger than The Venetian's, with Roman tubs, sunken living rooms, and sumptuous beds that would make it tough to leave the room if not for the lure of the Strip.

The Mirage

Restaurants: Tom Colicchio's Heritage Steak, Otoro, Cravings Buffet, Paradise Café, Pantry, LVB Burger, Osteria Costa, Stack, Paradise Café, California Pizza Kitchen, Blizz Frozen Yogurt, The Roasted Bean

Entertainment: Cirque du Soleil's *LOVE*, Aces of Comedy, Matt Goss

Attractions: Secret Garden and Dolphin Habitat, Aquarium, Mirage Volcano, Atrium

Nightlife: 1 Oak, Rhumbar, The Still, The Sports Bar, Lobby Bar, Center Bar, Parlor Cocktail Lounge, Heritage Steak Lounge, Stack Lounge, Otoro Lounge

The Mirage (3400 Las Vegas Blvd. S., 702/791-7111 or 800/627-6667, www.mirage.com, $140-300) was the first "understated" megaresort, starting a trend that brought Vegas full circle to the mature pursuits it was built on—gourmet dining, lavish production shows, hip music, and hard liquor. This Bali Hai-themed paradise lets guests bask in the wonders of nature alongside the sophistication and pampering of resort life. More an oasis than a mirage, the hotel greets visitors with exotic bamboo, orchids, banana trees, secluded grottoes, and peaceful lagoons. Dolphins, white tigers, stingrays, sharks, and a volcano provide livelier sights.

The Mirage's guest rooms have tasteful appointments and some of the most comfortable, down-comforter beds in town. The standard 396-square-foot (36.8-sq-m) rooms emit a modern and relaxing feel in golds, blacks, and splashes of tangerine, mauve, and ruby.

Bump and grind at **1 Oak** (10:30pm-4am Wed., Fri., Sat.), playing lots of hip-hop and showcasing socially aware artwork. Two separate rooms have bars, DJs, and crowded dance floors. With dark walls and sparse lighting, it's a sinful, sexy venue for the beautiful people to congregate.

The Mirage commands performances by the world's top headliners, but Cirque du Soleil's Beatles show ***LOVE*** packs them in every night for a celebration of the Fab Four's music.

Harrah's

Restaurants: Ruth's Chris Steak House, Flavors the Buffet, Oyster Bar, Pizza Cake, Ben & Jerry's, Toby Keith's I Love This Bar & Grill, Fulton Street Food Hall, Starbucks
Entertainment: *Menopause the Musical,* Mac King Comedy Magic, Tape Face, *X Country,* John Caparulo's Mad Cap Comedy, Big Elvis
Attractions: The Pool at Harrah's
Nightlife: Carnaval Court, Numb Bar, Piano Bar, Signature Bar

Adjacent to the happening Linq, ★ **Harrah's** (3475 Las Vegas Blvd. S., 800/214-9110, www.caesars.com/harrahs-las-vegas, $115-201) suddenly finds itself on the cutting edge of the Las Vegas party scene. The venerable property has taken a few baby steps toward hipsterism, booking the raunchy ***Menopause the Musical*** and topless ***X Country*** revue (10pm Thurs.-Mon.-Sat., $48-73). Still, conservative habits are hard to break, and **Mac King's** family-friendly comedy magic show remains one of the best afternoon offerings in town.

Carnaval Court, outside on the Strip's sidewalk, capitalizes on the street-party atmosphere with live bands and juggling bartenders. Just inside, Vegas icon **Big Elvis** (2pm, 3:30pm, and 5pm Mon., Wed., and Fri., free) performs in the **Piano Bar,** which invites aspiring singers to the karaoke stage Monday through Wednesday evenings, and dueling twin sister keyboardists take over each night at 9pm. The country superstar lends his name and unapologetic patriotism to **Toby Keith's I Love This Bar & Grill** (11:30am-2am Sun.-Thurs., 11:30am-3am Fri.-Sat., $20-30). Try the fried bologna sandwich.

Harrah's Mountain Tower (formerly the Mardi Gras Tower) and Valley Tower rooms are nearly identical: 300 square feet (27.9 sq m), featuring backlit mirrors and tinged in slate blue.

The Linq

Restaurants: Guy Fieri's Vegas Kitchen and Bar, Chayo Mexican Kitchen & Tequila Bar, Hash House a Go Go, Sticky Chicken, Corner Kitchen and Donuts, Nook Express, Off the Strip
Entertainment: Mat Franco: *Magic Reinvented Nightly,* Jimmy Kimmel's Comedy Club
Attractions: High Roller, Fly Linq Zipline, VR Adventures, Auto Collection, Kind Heaven, Club Tattoo, Regenerate Me, Influence pool, Brooklyn Bowl
Nightlife: 3535, Catalyst, O'Shea's, Purple Zebra, ICEBAR

Rooms at **The Linq** (3535 Las Vegas Blvd. S., 800/634-6441, www.caesars.com/linq, $99-249) are sleek, stylish, and smallish, at 250-350 square feet (23.2-32.5 sq m). Pewter and chrome are accented with eggplant, orange, or aqua murals inspired by vintage Vegas's neon glory days. Other amenities include marble countertops, 47-inch (119.4-cm) flat-screen TVs, and iPod docks. But the hotel is really just a way to stay close to all the Gen X-focused boutiques, bars, and restaurants in the adjacent outdoor promenade.

The high point of this pedestrian-friendly plaza is the **High Roller,** the highest observation wheel in the world, but there's plenty more to warrant a stop. **Brooklyn Bowl** has you covered on eat, drink, and be merry, combining tenpin excitement with dozens of beer taps, delectable finger foods, and live entertainment. The jalapeño coleslaw transforms the shrimp tacos at **Chayo Mexican Kitchen & Tequila Bar** (9am-10pm Sun.-Thurs., 9am-11pm Fri.-Sat., $16-28), but the menu takes a backseat to the tequila-fueled party. There's a mechanical bull in the middle of the dining room, for goodness' sake, and you can have a scorpion(!) tossed into your Patrón shot. Patio seating puts diners and drinkers in prime people-watching territory. Vegas icon and local favorite **O'Shea's** (24 hours daily) brings back the lowbrow frivolity of the St. Patrick's Day kegger party with cheap drafts, heated beer pong matches, and a rockin' jam band that keeps the festivities raging.

America's Got Talent winner **Mat Franco** combines jaw-dropping production illusions with how'd-he-do-that close-up tricks. His easygoing banter and anything-to-please attitude ensure it's never the same show twice.

Flamingo

Restaurants: Bugsy's and Meyer's Steakhouse, Paradise Garden Buffet, Jimmy Buffett's Margaritaville, Carlos N Charlie's, Beach Club Bar & Grill, Club Cappuccino, Café Express Food Court (Bonanno's New York Pizzeria, Johnny Rockets, L.A. Subs, Pan Asian Express)
Entertainment: Piff the Magic Dragon, *X Burlesque*, *RuPaul's Drag Race LIVE!*
Attractions: Wildlife Habitat
Nightlife: Bird Bar, Garden Bar, Bugsy's Bar

Named for long-legged Virginia Hill, the girlfriend of Benjamin "don't call me Bugsy" Siegel, the **Flamingo** (3555 Las Vegas Blvd. S., 702/733-3111, www.caesars.com/flamingo-las-vegas, $99-210) has at turns embraced and shunned its gangster ties, which stretch back to the 1960s. After Bugsy's (sorry, Mr. Siegel's) Flamingo business practices ran afoul of the Cosa Nostra and led to his untimely end, Meyer Lansky took over. Mob ties continued to dog the property until Hilton Hotels bought the Flamingo in 1970, giving the joint the legitimacy it needed. Today, its art deco architecture and pink-and-orange neon conjure images of aging mafiosi lounging by the pool in a Vegas where the mob era is remembered almost fondly. At the **Flamingo Wildlife Habitat** (8am-dusk daily, free), ibis, pelicans, turtles, koi fish, and, of course, Chilean flamingos luxuriate amid riparian plants and meandering streams.

Guests can search for their lost shaker of salt at **Jimmy Buffett's Margaritaville** (8am-1am Sun.-Thurs., 8am-2am Fri.-Sat., $20-30).

The Flamingo updated many of its Fab Rooms most recently, but the older Go Rooms are actually more modern, dressed in swanky mahogany and white. The rooms are only 350 square feet (32.5 sq m) but boast high-end entertainment systems and 42-inch (106.7-cm) TVs, vintage art prints, padded leather headboards, and all the other Vegas-sational accoutrements. Fab Rooms are more boldly decorated, incorporating swatches of hot pink.

★ Caesars Palace

Restaurants: Bacchanal Buffet, Gordon Ramsay Hell's Kitchen, Gordon Ramsay Pub & Grill, Restaurant Guy Savoy, Brioche by Guy Savoy, Pronto by Giada, Beijing Noodle No. 9, Amalfi, Old Homestead Steakhouse, Rao's, Mr. Chow, Searsucker, Nobu, Café Americano, Forum Food Court (Smashburger, The Halal Guys, Earl of Sandwich, Crepes and More, Difara Pizza, Tiger Wok and Ramen, TaCo), Starbucks
Entertainment: *Absinthe*

Attractions: *Fall of Atlantis*, aquarium, Appian Way Shops, Forum Shops
Nightlife: Omnia, Cleopatra's Barge, Spanish Steps, Numb Bar, Vanderpump Cocktail Garden, Alto Bar, Lobby Bar, Vista Lounge, Montecristo Cigar Bar

The Roman Empire probably would look a lot like Las Vegas had it survived this long. **Caesars Palace** (3570 Las Vegas Blvd. S., 866/227-5938, www.caesars.com, $175-300) has incorporated all of ancient Rome's decadence while adding a few thousand slot machines. Caesars opened with great fanfare in 1966 and has ruled the Strip ever since. Like the empire, it continues to expand and innovate, now boasting 3,348 guest rooms in six towers and 140,000 square feet (13,006 sq m) of gaming space accented with marble, fountains, gilding, and royal reds. Wander the grounds searching for reproductions of some of the world's most famous statuary, including Michelangelo's *David*.

Cleopatra's Barge (7pm-2am Tues.-Wed., 8pm-3am Thurs.-Sat.) is one of Vegas's more "Vegas-y" nightspots. A floating lounge, it hearkens back to the hedonistic 1970s and go-getter 1980s, attracting the full spectrum of the 21-and-over crowd for late-night bacchanalia. Local rockers and pop-choral fusionists often take the stage here, with occasional forays from touring groups taking the stage in for acoustic performances in the intimate, 170-seat venue.

Guests luxuriate in the **Garden of the Gods Pool Oasis** (9am-6pm Mon.-Thurs., noon-5pm Fri.-Sun.), with each of several distinct water-and-sun shrines catering to a different proclivity. Gamblers can play at a swim-up blackjack table at Fortuna; beach bunnies can flaunt it toplessly (Mon.-Thurs. only) at Venus; tanners can roast in peace at Apollo; kids can frolic at Temple; singles can mingle at Neptune; and the wealthy can splurge on cabanas at Bacchus. What, no aqueduct?

All roads lead to the **Forum Shops,** a collection of famous designer stores, specialty boutiques, and restaurants. An hour here can do some serious damage to your bankroll. You'll also find the ***Fall of Atlantis*** show (hourly 11am-7pm Sun.-Thurs., 11am-9pm Fri.-Sat., free), a multisensory, multimedia depiction of the gods' wrath.

Caesars is the center of the world for celebrity chefs, with culinary all-stars lending their names to multiple eateries. Epicureans enjoy beef Wellington or eggs in purgatory at **Gordon Ramsay Hell's Kitchen** (4pm-10:30pm daily, $40-70). More casual guests can get their British on at **Gordon Ramsay Pub & Grill** (11am-11pm Sun.-Thurs., 11am-midnight Fri.-Sat., $25-45). Try the steak and ale pie.

With so many guest rooms in six towers, it seems Caesars is always renovating somewhere. Most newer guest rooms are done in tan, wood, and marble, with streaks of bold yellow. Ask for a south-facing room in the Augustus or Octavius tower to get commanding vistas of both the Bellagio fountains and the Strip.

Lower Strip

The **Lower Strip**—roughly between the **"Welcome to Fabulous Las Vegas" sign** and Harmon Avenue—is a living city timeline. The Tropicana is here, providing a link to the mobbed-up city of the 1960s and 1970s. The Egyptian-inspired Luxor serves as prime example from the city's hesitant foray into becoming a "family" destination in the early 1990s. The emerald-tinted MGM Grand opened in 1993 as a salute to *The Wizard of Oz*. City Center puts the mega in megaresort—condos, boutique hotels, trendy shopping, a huge casino, and a sprawling dining and entertainment district—and cemented the city's biggest-is-best trend. The Lower Strip seems made for budget-conscious families. Rooms are often cheaper than mid-Strip, and there are plenty of arcades, animal attractions, candy shops, and other kid-friendly attractions.

The Palms

Restaurants: Scotch 80 Prime, Shark, Sara's, Vetri Cucina, Mabel's BBQ, Greene Street Kitchen, Tim Ho Wan, Send Noodles, Laguna Pool House & Kitchen
Entertainment: Pearl Theater, Brendan Theatres
Nightlife: Unknown Bar, Mr. Coco, Rojo Lounge, Tonic, Apex Social Club

Station Casinos spent nearly $1 billion to buy and renovate **The Palms** (4321 W. Flamingo Rd., 866/942-7777, www.palms.com, $110-175), where rock star excess was just another Tuesday night when it opened in 1999 to penthouse views, uninhibited pool parties, lavish theme suites, and several televised parties. Located just off the Strip, the resort is home to the 2,500-seat **Pearl Concert Theater,** which still regularly hosts rock concerts, and the Fantasy Tower still lets guest splurge on rooms with bowling lanes, basketball courts, curated art, and more. The original Ivory Tower offers large guest rooms. They're sleek, with geometric shapes and custom artwork, but their best features are the feathery beds and luxurious comforters. The rejuvenating shower and "spa-inspired" stone, glass, and chrome bathrooms help get the day started. The newest tower, Palms Place, has 599 studios and one-bedrooms with suite views, gourmet kitchens, and nearby restaurant, spa, and pool.

Bellagio

Restaurants: Lago, Yellowtail, Spago, Harvest by Roy Ellamar, Jasmine, Fix, Michael Mina, Picasso, Prime Steakhouse, Mayfair Supper Club, Le Cirque, Noodles, The Buffet, Bellagio Patisserie, Starbucks, Sadelle's Café, Pool Café, Juice Press
Entertainment: Cirque du Soleil's *O*
Attractions: Fountains of Bellagio, Bellagio Conservatory & Botanical Garden, Bellagio Gallery of Fine Art, public art
Nightlife: Hyde, Lily Bar & Lounge, Petrossian Bar, Baccarat Bar, Pool Bar, Sports Bar Lounge

With nearly 4,000 guest rooms and suites, ★ **Bellagio** (3600 Las Vegas Blvd. S., 702/693-7111 or 888/987-6667, http://bellagio.mgmresorts.com, $199-349) boasts a population larger than the village perched on Lake Como from which it borrows its name. To keep pace with its Italian namesake, Bellagio created an 8.5-acre (3.4-ha) lake between the hotel and Las Vegas Boulevard. The views of the lake and its **Fountains of Bellagio** (3pm-midnight Mon.-Fri., noon-midnight Sat., 11am-midnight Sun.) are free, as is the 80,000-flower aromatic fantasy at **Bellagio Conservatory & Botanical Garden** (24 hours daily). The **Bellagio Gallery of Fine Art** (10am-7pm daily, $18) would be a bargain at twice the price—you can spend an edifying day at one of the world's priciest resorts (including a cocktail and lunch) for less than $50. Even if you don't spring for gallery admission, art demands your attention throughout the hotel and casino. The 2,000 glass flower petals in Dale Chihuly's *Fiori di Como* sculpture bloom from the lobby ceiling, foreshadowing the opulent experiences to come. Masatoshi Izumi's *A Gift from the Earth,* comprising four massive basalt sculptures representing wind, fire, water, and land, dominates the hotel's main entrance.

The display of artistry continues but the bargains end at **Via Bellagio** (10am-midnight daily), the resort's shopping district, including heavyweight retailers Bvlgari, Prada, Chanel, Gucci, and their ilk.

Befitting Bellagio's world-class status, intriguing and expensive restaurants abound. **Michael Mina** (5:30pm-10pm Mon.-Sat., $70-100) is worth the price. Restrained decor adds to the simple elegance of the cuisine, which is mostly seafood with European and Asian influences. The weekend dim sum at **Noodles** (11am-3pm Fri.-Sun., $6-10 per plate) is a popular lunch option.

Bellagio's tower rooms are the epitome of luxury, with Italian marble, oversize bathtubs, remote-controlled drapes, Egyptian-cotton sheets, and 510 square feet (47.4 sq m) in which to spread out. The butterscotch, sage-plum and indigo-silver color schemes are refreshing changes from the goes-with-everything beige and the camouflages-all-stains paisley often found on the Strip.

Paris Las Vegas

Restaurants: Burger Brasserie, Brioche by Guy Savoy, Mon Ami Gabi, Hexx, Martoranos, Gordon Ramsay Steak, Eiffel Tower Restaurant, JJ's Boulangerie, Beer Park, Café Belle Madeleine, Sushi Street, La Creperie, Café Americano Paris, Le Village Buffet, 88 Noodles and Dim Sum
Entertainment: *Sex Tips for Straight Women from a Gay Man*, Anthony Cools, *Friends! The Musical Parody*
Attractions: Eiffel Tower, Le Boulevard
Nightlife: Napoleon's Lounge, Alexxa's Bar, Le Cabaret, Le Central, Le Bar du Sport, Gustav's, Chateau Nightclub & Rooftop

Designers used Gustav Eiffel's original drawings to ensure that the half-size tower that anchors **Paris Las Vegas** (3655 Las Vegas Blvd. S., 877/242-6753, www.caesars.com/paris-las-vegas, $149-245) conformed—down to the last cosmetic rivet—to the original. That attention to detail prevails throughout this property, which works hard to evoke the City of Light, from large-scale reproductions of the Arc de Triomphe, Champs-Élysées, and Louvre to more than half a dozen French restaurants and theme bars. The **Eiffel Tower Viewing Deck** (4pm-midnight daily, $22) is perhaps the most romantic spot in town to view the Strip; you'll catch your breath as the elevator whisks you to the observation deck 460 feet (140 m) up, then have it taken away again by the lights from one of the most famous skylines in the world. Back at street level, the cobblestone lanes and brass streetlights of **Le Boulevard** invite shoppers into quaint shops and patisseries. The casino offers its own attractions, not the least of which is the view of the Eiffel Tower's base jutting through the

From top to bottom: Bellagio Conservatory and Botanical Garden; MGM Grand; New York New York.

ceiling. Paris is one of the first casinos to test "skill-based" gaming, which bases payouts according to performance—think Wii free-throw shooting or putting—or pits players against each other in card, strategy, and quest-type games.

Entertainment veers toward the bawdy, with **Anthony Cools—The Uncensored Hypnotist** (9pm Tues. and Thurs.-Sun., $57-90) cajoling mesmerized subjects through very adult simulations. The same venue hosts the Broadway export ***Sex Tips for Straight Women from a Gay Man*** (9pm Mon., 7pm Tues. and Thurs.-Fri., 5pm and 7pm Sat., 7pm Sun., $52-92), in which the audience and flamboyant Dan help uptight Robyn shed her bedroom inhibitions. ***Friends! The Musical Parody*** is more teen-friendly. It's less satire and more tribute, and the six besties escort fans down memory lane, reliving and reimagining classic scenes from the show's 10 seasons.

You'll be wishing you had packed your beret when you order an éclair and cappuccino at **Café Belle Madeleine** (5am-noon daily, $10-20).

Standard guest rooms in the 33-story tower are decorated in a rich earth-tone palette and have marble baths. There's nothing Left Bank bohemian about them, however. The guest rooms exude little flair or personality, but the simple, quality furnishings make it a moderately priced option. Book a Red Room if modern decor in Moulin Rouge red is important to you.

Cosmopolitan

Restaurants: Scarpetta, Rose. Rabbit. Lie., E by Jose Andres, STK, Beauty & Exxex, Blue Ribbon, China Poblano, Zuma, Eggslut, The Henry, Holsteins, Jaleo, The Juice Standard, Milk Bar, Momofuku, Overlook Grill, Va Bene, Wicked Spoon, Secret Pizza, Starbucks, Block 16 Urban Food Hall (Ghost Donkey, Lardo, Pok Pok Wing, District: Donuts. Sliders. Brew, Tekka Bar: Handroll & Sake, Hattie B's Hot Chicken)
Entertainment: *Opium*
Attractions: dive-in movies
Nightlife: The Barbershop Cuts and Cocktails, Marquee, Clique, The Study, Vesper Bar, The Chandelier

Modern art, marble bath floors, and big soaking tubs in 460-square-foot (42.7 sq m) rooms evoke urban penthouse living at ★ **Cosmopolitan** (3708 Las Vegas Blvd. S., 702/698-7000, www.cosmopolitanlasvegas.com, $220-320). The hefty rates do nothing to harsh the NYC vibe. Because it's too cool to host production shows, the resort's entertainment schedule mixes the DJs of the moment with the most relevant headliners.

That nouveau riche attitude carries through to the dining and nightlife. **Rose. Rabbit. Lie.** (6pm-midnight Wed.-Sun., $60-100) is equal parts supper club, nightclub, and jazz club. Bluesy, jazzy torch singers, magicians, tap and hip-hop dancers, and a rocking sound system accompany dishes like a short rib stroganoff, glazed bone marrow, and sharable noshes.

The same depraved minds behind *Absinthe* present ***Opium***, a rousing variety show set aboard a spaceship. An eclectic array of talent delivers ribald (and sometimes downright dirty) jokes and banter, along with impressive displays of artistic and acrobatic talent.

Vesper Bar (24 hours daily), named for James Bond's favorite martini, prides itself on serving hipster versions of classic cocktails. Possibly the best day club in town, **Marquee** (11am-sunset daily Apr.-Oct.), on the roof, brings in the beautiful people with DJs and sweet bungalow lofts. When darkness falls, the day club becomes an extension of the pulsating Marquee nightclub (10:30pm-5am Mon. and Fri.-Sat.).

You can also enjoy **dive-in movies** (8pm Mon., $7 non-hotel guests) at the Cosmopolitan's Boulevard Pool, boasting a giant screen visible as you wade or lounge poolside.

Aria

Restaurants: Bardot, Catch, Blossom, Jean Georges Steakhouse, Carbone, Aria Patisserie Javier's, Lemongrass, The Buffet, Julian Serrano Tapas, The Pub, Burger Lounge, Din Tai Fung, Moneyline Pizza & Bar, Pressed Juicery, Starbucks

Entertainment: Cirque du Soleil's *Zarkana*

Attractions: public art, The Shops at Crystals

Nightlife: Jewel, Alibi, Baccarat Lounge, High Limit Lounge, Lift Bar, Liquid Lobby Lounge, Pool Bar, Gem Bar

All glass and steel, ultramodern ★ **Aria** (3730 Las Vegas Blvd. S., 702/590-7757, http://aria.mgmresorts.com, $159-299) would look more at home in Manhattan than Las Vegas. Touch pads control the drapes, the lighting, the music, and the climate in Aria's fern- or grape-paletted guest rooms. Program the "wake up scene" before bedtime, and the room will gradually summon you from peaceful slumber at the appointed time. A traditional hotel casino, Aria shares the City Center umbrella with **Vdara,** a Euro-chic boutique hotel with no gaming.

Guests are invited to browse an extensive public art collection, with works by Maya Lin, Jenny Holzer, and Richard Long, among others.

The Shops at Crystals, a 500,000-square-foot (46,452-sq-m) mall, lets you splurge among hanging gardens. At this mall, restaurants like Mastro's Ocean Club take the place of Sbarro and Cinnabon.

Park MGM

Restaurants: Primrose, Bavette's Steakhouse, Eataly, LaLa Noodle, Crack Shack, NoMad, Manso, Side Betty Grill, Best Friend, La Pizza e La Pasta, Starbucks

Entertainment: Park Theater

Nightlife: Mama Rabbit Mezcal & Tequila Bar, BetMGM Sportsbook & Bar, On the Record, Juniper Cocktail Lounge

The former Monte Carlo has gotten the MGM glam treatment and now, as **Park MGM** (3770 S Las Vegas Blvd., 702/ 730-7777, http://parkmgm.mgmresorts.com, $140-220), pulls the big names (Lady Gaga, Cher, Bruno Mars, Aerosmith) into its bustling **Park Theater.**

Rooms in the middle-of-the-action hotel weigh in at over 400 square feet (37.2 sq m). They feature curated original art and are decorated in hunter green. The alcove bed and blackout curtains screen guests, even when they choose the Strip-view accommodations. Curated art makes each room unique.

New York New York

Restaurants: Tom's Urban, Il Fornaio, Nine Fine Irishmen, Gallagher's Steakhouse, America, New York Pizzeria, Chin Chin Café & Sushi Bar, Broadway Burger Bar & Grill, Gonzalez y Gonzalez, Shake Shack, 48th and Crepe, Nathan's Famous, Starbucks, Village Street Eateries (Greenberg's Deli, Fulton's Fish Frye, Sirrico's Pizza, Greenwich Coffee)

Entertainment: Cirque du Soleil's *Zumanity,* Brooklyn Bridge buskers, dueling pianos, The Park

Attractions: Hershey's Chocolate World, Big Apple Coaster & Arcade, T-Mobile Arena

Nightlife: Coyote Ugly, The Bar at Times Square, Center Bar, Pour 24, Lobby Bar

One look at this loving tribute to the city that never sleeps, and you won't be able to fuhgedaboutit. From the city skyline outside (the skyscrapers contain the resort's hotel rooms) to laundry hanging between crowded faux brownstones indoors, **New York New York** (3790 Las Vegas Blvd. S., 702/740-6969 or 866/815-4365, http://newyorknewyork.mgmresorts.com, $130-255) will have even grizzled Gothamites feeling like they've come home again.

The **Big Apple Coaster** (11am-11pm Sun.-Thurs., 10:30am-midnight Fri.-Sat., $15, all-day pass $26) winds its way around the resort, an experience almost as hair-raising as a New York City cab ride, which the coaster cars are painted to resemble.

Dueling pianists keep **The Bar at Times Square** (1pm-2:30am Mon.-Thurs., 11am-2:30am Fri.-Sun.) rocking into the wee hours, and the sexy bar staff at **Coyote Ugly** (6pm-3am daily) defy its name.

Hang out at **The Park** before a Golden Knights home game for some of the best people-watching and pre-partying in town. The plaza surrounding T-Mobile Arena takes dining, drinking, and strolling to new heights. Even if you don't have tickets to the game, check out the sidewalk cafés, environmentally responsible landscaping, massive artwork, and artistic shade structures.

New York New York's 2,023 guest rooms are standard size, 350-450 square feet (32.5-37.2 sq m). The roller coaster zooms around the towers, so you might want to ask for a room out of earshot.

MGM Grand

Restaurants: Morimoto, Joël Robuchon, Tom Colicchio's Craftsteak, Michael Mina Pub 1842, Emeril's New Orleans Fish House, L'Atelier de Joël Robuchon, Wolfgang Puck Bar & Grill, Ambra, Hecho En Vegas, Crush, International Smoke, MGM Grand Buffet, Tap Sports Bar, Blizz, Avenue Café, Greek Sneek, Bonanno's New York Pizzeria, Pieology, Starbucks, Subway, Food Court (Pan Asian Express, Häagen-Dazs, Nathan's Famous, Original Chicken Tender, Tacos N 'Ritas, Johnny Rockets)
Entertainment: Cirque du Soleil's *Kà*, David Copperfield, Brad Garrett's Comedy Club, Jabbawockeez
Attractions: Topgolf, Hunger Games: The Exhibition, Level Up, CBS Television City Research Center
Nightlife: Wet Republic, Hakkasan, Whiskey Down, Losers Bar, Centrifuge, Lobby Bar

Gamblers enter **MGM Grand** (3799 Las Vegas Blvd. S., 888/646-1203, http://mgmgrand.mgmresorts.com, $110-200) through portals guarded by MGM's mascot, the 45-foot-tall (13.7-m) king of the jungle. The uninitiated may feel like a gazelle on the savanna, swallowed by the 171,000-square-foot (15,886-sq-m) casino floor, the largest in Las Vegas. But the watering hole, MGM's 6.5-acre (2.6-ha) pool complex, is relatively predator-free. MGM capitalizes on the movie studio's greatest hits. Even the hotel's emerald facade evokes the magical city in *The Wizard of Oz*.

Coming off a successful national tour, **The Hunger Games: The Exhibition** (10am-7pm Wed.-Sun., $45 adults, $35 children 4-11) allows fans to see if they have what it takes to become the Mockingjay. During your self-guided tour, you can visit the Hall of Justice and President Snow's office, acquiring knowledge and leadership experiences along the way. Relive Katniss's ascent to leader of the rebellion with interactive and immersive activities that help you hone your archery skills, demonstrate your knowledge of Panem trivia, and develop your communications ability through song mimicry.

MGM Grand houses enough top restaurants for a week of gourmet dinners. You can take your pick of celebrity chef establishments, but **L'Atelier de Joël Robuchon** (5pm-10pm daily, $75-200) offers the most bang for the buck. Counter service overlooks kitchen preparations, adding to the anticipation.

Standard guest rooms in the Grand

Tower are 450 square feet (41.8 sq m) and filled with the quality furnishings you'd expect. The West Tower guest rooms are smaller, at 350 square feet (32.5 sq m), but exude swinging style.

Luxor

Restaurants: Tender Steak & Seafood, Rice & Company, Public House, Diablos Cantina, The Buffet, Pyramid Café, Backstage Deli, Blizz, Food Court (Johnnie Rockets, Bonanno's New York Pizzeria, L.A. Subs, Nathan's Famous, Original Chicken Tender, Starbucks)

Entertainment: Carrot Top, Blue Man Group, *Fantasy*

Attractions: *Bodies . . . the Exhibition, Titanic* artifacts, HyperX Esports Arena

Nightlife: Centra, Aurora, Flight, High Bar, PlayBar

Other than its pyramid shape and name, not much remains of the Egyptian theme at the **Luxor** (3900 Las Vegas Blvd. S., 702/262-4000, http://luxor.mgmresorts.com, $99-220). In its place are upscale and decidedly post-pharaoh nightclubs, restaurants, and shops. Many are located in the **Shoppes at Mandalay Place** (10am-11pm daily), on the sky bridge between Luxor and Mandalay Bay. The huge base of the pyramid houses a cavernous 120,000-square-foot (11,148-sq-m) casino, while the slanted walls and twin 22-story towers contain 4,400 guest rooms. Luxor also has the largest atrium in the world, an intense light beam that is visible from space, and inclinators—elevators that move along the building's oblique angles.

Staying in the pyramid makes for interesting room features, such as a slanted exterior wall. Stay on higher floors for panoramic views of the atrium. Tower rooms are newer and more traditional in their shape, decor, and amenities.

Luxor is the first resort in Las Vegas to embrace major league video gaming. **HyperX Esports Arena** hosts casual play and international competitions. Players under 13 require a chaperone. Facilities include a 30,000-square-foot (2,787-sq-m) arena, 50-foot (15.2-m) LED video

Mandalay Bay

wall, arena seating, and a production studio for streaming live-audience events.

Mandalay Bay

Restaurants: Aureole, Fleur, RM Seafood, Kumi, Lupo, Charlie Palmer Steak, Strip Steak, Rivea, Citizens Kitchen and Bar, Mizuya, Della's Kitchen, Crossroads at House of Blues, Noodle Shop, Border Grill, Libertine Social, Raffles Café, Bayside Buffet, Press, Rx Boiler Room, Sports Bar and Grill, Veranda, Burger Bar, Ri Ra Irish Pub, Slice of Vegas, Hussong's Cantina
Entertainment: Cirque du Soleil's *Michael Jackson ONE,* Nashville Unplugged
Attractions: Shark Reef, Mandalay Place
Nightlife: House of Blues, Foundation Room, Hazel Coffee and Cocktails, Daylight Beach Club, Skyfall, Minus 5 Ice Bar, Rhythm & Riffs, Eyecandy Sound Lounge, Fat Tuesday, Bikini Bar, Verandah Lounge, 1923 Bourbon Bar, Big Chill

The South Pacific behemoth ★ **Mandalay Bay** (3950 Las Vegas Blvd. S., 877/632-7800, http://mandalaybay.mgmresorts.com, $150-300) has one of the largest casino floors in the world at 135,000 square feet (12,542 sq m). An 11-acre (4.5-ha) paradise comprises eight pools, including a lazy river, a 1.6-million-gallon (6-million-l) wave pool complete with a real beach made of five million pounds (2.3 million kg) of sand, an adults-only dipping pool, and tops-optional sunbathing deck. You could spend your entire vacation in the pool area, gambling at the beach's three-level casino, eating at its restaurant, and loading up on sandals and bikinis at the nearby Pearl Moon boutique. The beach hosts a concert series during summer.

Celebrity chefs converged on Las Vegas a decade ago, and a good many of them opened eateries at Mandalay Bay. The all-star lineup includes Michael Mina, Wolfgang Puck, Hubert Keller, Alain Ducasse, and more. You cannot go wrong with any of them. But to fill your belly without emptying your wallet, **Ri Ra Irish Pub** (8am-3am Mon.-Fri., 9am-3am Sat.-Sun., $15-25) serves traditional Irish fare: bangers and mash, fish-and-chips, and a savory shepherd's pie. Ri Ra began life as a restored pub in Ireland and lost none of its character during its trip across the Atlantic. The authentic 19th-century bar works its magic to turn strangers into friends faster than you can pour your first Guinness. Live music keeps the joint jumping into the night.

Even at 100,000 square feet (9,290 sq m), the **Shoppes at Mandalay Place** (10am-11pm daily), on the sky bridge between Mandalay Bay and the Luxor, is smaller and less hectic than other casino malls. It features unusual shops, such as **Karma and Luck,** offering products that celebrate Far East culture, and **Las Vegas Sock Market,** with colorful foot apparel depicting sports teams, pop icons, and other favorites so you can wear your heart on your shins. The shops share space with eateries and high-concept bars like **Minus 5 Ice Bar** (11am-3am daily), where barflies don parkas before entering the below-freezing (23°F/-5°C) establishment. The glasses aren't just frosted; they're fashioned completely out of ice.

A hip-hop worldview and the King of Pop's unmatched talent guide the vignettes in ***Michael Jackson ONE.*** Michael's musical innovation and the Cirque du Soleil trademark aerial and acrobatic acts pay homage to the human spirit.

Sheathed in Indian artifacts and crafts, the **Foundation Room** (5pm-3am daily, $20-50), the House of Blues' VIP club has private rooms piled with overstuffed furniture, fireplaces, and thick carpets; a dining room; and several bars catering to various musical tastes. The crowd and the music's volume increase as the night progresses.

Standard guest rooms are chic and roomy (550 square feet/51.1 sq m), with warm fabrics and plush bedding. Get a north-facing room and put the floor-to-ceiling windows to use gazing the full length of the Strip. Cool blue and green accents bolster the otherwise pedestrian (by Strip standards) decor. The baths, however, are fit for royalty, with huge tubs and mirrors, vanities, and glass-walled showers. To go upscale, check out the Delano boutique hotel or book at the Four Seasons—both are part of the same complex.

Downtown

Binion's

Restaurants: Top of Binion's Steakhouse, Binion's Deli, Binion's Café, Benny's Smokin' BBQ & Brews
Entertainment: Hypnosis Unleashed
Nightlife: Cowgirl Up Cantina, Whiskey Licker

Before Vegas became a resort city, it catered to inveterate gamblers, hard drinkers, and others on the fringes of society. Ah, the good old days! A gambler himself, Benny Binion put his place in the middle of downtown, a magnet for the serious player, offering high limits and few frills. **Binion's** (128 Fremont St., 702/382-1600, www.binions.com) now attracts players with occasional $1 blackjack tables and a poker room frequented by grizzled veterans. This is where the World Series of Poker began, and the quaint room still stages some wild action on its 10 tables. Players can earn $2 per hour in comps—about double what they can pull down in most rooms. A reasonable $4 maximum rake and big-screen TV add to the attraction. The little den on Fremont Street still retains the flavor of Old Vegas.

The **Apache Hotel** ($79-109), now part of Binion's, originally opened in 1932. Supposedly haunted (perhaps by Native American spirits offended by the name and stereotypical logo), the hotel was the stomping grounds for Clark Gable, Lucille Ball, and Humphrey Bogart, among others. It was the first in town to air condition its lobby and install an electric elevator.

Circa

Restaurants: Barry's Downtown Prime, Saginaw's Delicatessen, Victory Burger, 8 East, Project BBQ
Attractions: Sportsbook, Stadium Swim, Garage-Mahal

One of only a couple of resort-quality properties downtown, all of **Circa** (8 Fremont St., 702/247-2258 or 833/247-2258, www.circalasvegas.com, $179-299) is adults-only, including hotel rooms and the pool. Circa booked its first guests just before New Year's Eve in 2020. Its split-level casino has 55 table games and more than 1,300 slots. The **sportsbook** can accommodate 1,000 guests, and the viewing wall screen contains 78 million pixels for some of the biggest, clearest action in town. **Stadium Swim** (8am-11pm daily, free for hotel guests, fee for non-hotel guests), an aquatic amphitheater encompassing a six-pool complex covering three levels and a 40-foot-tall (12.2-m) hi-def screen, offers perfect vistas for people-watching or catching a big game. Even the parking lot is state-of-the-art; dubbed **Garage Mahal,** it incorporates two multimedia video walls and the latest creations by featured artists.

Rooms are 424 square feet (29.4 sq m) and decorated in dark wood and a rich royal blue. Walk-in showers and dual vanities make the bathrooms seem roomy.

Golden Nugget

Restaurants: Vic & Anthony's, Chart House, Grotto, Red Sushi, Cadillac Mexican Kitchen, Buffet, Saltgrass Steak House, The Grille, Claim Jumper, Chick-fil-A, Starbucks
Entertainment: 52 Fridays
Attractions: Hand of Faith, shark tank tours
Nightlife: Rush Lounge, Troy Liquor Bar, H2O Bar, Claude's Bar, Ice Bar, Bar 46, Cadillac Tequila Bar, Stage Bar, Sports Book Bar

The ★ **Golden Nugget** (129 E. Fremont St., 702/385-7111, www.goldennugget.com, $129-249) has been a fixture for 75 years, beckoning diners and gamblers with a 61-pound (27.7-kg) gold nugget in the lobby. Landry's, known for its chain restaurants, has been the Nugget owner since 2005; the company has maintained and restored the hotel's opulence, investing $300 million for casino expansion, more restaurants, and a 500-room hotel tower. Rooms are appointed in dark wood and warm autumn hues.

If you don't feel like swimming with the sharks in the poker room, you can get up close and personal with their finned namesakes at the **Golden Nugget Pool** (9am-6pm daily, free), an outdoor swimming hole with a three-story waterslide that takes riders through the hotel's huge aquarium, home to sharks, rays, and other exotic marinelife. Bathers can also swim up to the aquarium for a face-to-face with the aquatic predators. Waterfalls and lush landscaping help make this one of the world's best hotel pools. Book a **shark tank tour** (1:30pm Wed. and Sun., $50) and learn about various species and habitats. You even get to witness feeding time and go home with a real shark tooth.

Sights

Center Strip

Erotic Heritage Museum

The history and culture of sex is laid bare at the **Erotic Heritage Museum** (3275 S. Sammy Davis Jr Dr., 702/ 794-4000, www.eroticmuseumvegas.com, 11am-7pm daily, $38 adults, $10, students, seniors, and military), which examines eroticism's place in the world. Exhibits have included historic sexual aids and artifacts as well as erotic paintings, sculptures, and performance arts. Discussions have explored sexual practices in ancient Rome, pre-war Germany, and other cultures. The museum is largely focused on eroticism from an academic perspective, but the venue also hosts erotic scavenger hunts and strip shows. It also presents **Puppetry of the Penis** (8pm Fri.-Sat., $30-48), in which male performers create representations of everyday objects and art by bending, folding, and twisting . . . well, you get the idea.

Avengers S.T.A.T.I.O.N.

Immerse yourself in one of today's most enduring entertainment franchises at **Avengers S.T.A.T.I.O.N.** (Treasure Island, 3300 Las Vegas Blvd. S., 702/894-7722,

gondola rides at The Venetian

www.stationattraction.com, 11am-6pm Wed.-Sun., $42 adults, $32 children ages 4-11). Train to become a Marvel Avenger at this interactive Scientific Training and Tactical Intelligence Operative Network center, full of movie props like a life-size Iron Man suit and David Banner's laboratory. Guests will be tested on their knowledge of Marvel superhero history, science, engineering, genetics, and technology, and only the best will be invited to fight for justice alongside Captain America and Thor.

★ Gondola Rides

We dare you not to sigh at the grandeur of Venice in the desert as you pass beneath quaint bridges and idyllic sidewalk cafés, your gondolier serenading you with the accompaniment of the Grand Canal's gurgling wavelets. The **indoor gondolas** (Venetian, 3355 Las Vegas Blvd. S., 702/607-3982, www.venetian.com, 10am-11pm Sun.-Thurs., 10am-midnight Fri.-Sat., $29-36) skirt the Grand Canal Shoppes inside The Venetian under the mall's painted-sky ceiling fresco for 0.5 mile (0.8 km); **outdoor gondolas** (10am-midnight daily, weather permitting, $29-36) skim The Venetian's 31,000-square-foot (2,880-sq-m) lagoon for 12 minutes, giving riders a unique perspective on the Las Vegas Strip.

Madame Tussauds Las Vegas

Ever wanted to dunk over Shaq? Party with the Rock, Beyoncé, or Elvis? **Madame Tussauds Las Vegas** (Venetian, 3355 Las Vegas Blvd. S., 702/862-7800, www.madametussauds.com/lasvegas, 11am-6pm Mon.-Thurs., 11am-8pm Fri.-Sun., $25 adults, $20 children 4-12, children under 4 free) gives you the chance. Unlike most other museums, Madame Tussauds encourages guests to get up close and "personal" with its displays, including world leaders, sports heroes, and pop icons immortalized in wax. Photo ops and interactive activities abound. Club Tussauds puts you in the middle of the happening club scene, with A-listers all around. Share a cocktail with Angelina Jolie, ride a wrecking ball with Miley Cyrus, or discuss your screenplay with Will Smith.

★ Secret Garden and Dolphin Habitat

It's no mirage—those really are pure-white tigers lounging in their own plush resort on The Mirage casino floor. Legendary Las Vegas magicians Siegfried and Roy, who have dedicated much of their lives to preserving big cats, opened the **Secret Garden** (Mirage, 3400 Las Vegas Blvd. S., 702/791-7188, www.miragehabitat.com, 10am-6:30pm daily, $25 adults, $20 military and seniors over 65, $19 children 4-12, children under 4 free). In addition to the milky-furred tigers, the garden is home to blue-eyed, black-striped white tigers as well as black panthers, lions, and leopards. Although caretakers don't "perform" with the animals, if your visit is well-timed you could see the cats playing, wrestling, and even swimming in their pristine waterfall-fed pools. The cubs in the specially built nursery are sure to register high on the cuteness meter.

Visit the Atlantic bottlenoses at the **Dolphin Habitat** right next door, also in the middle of The Mirage's palm trees and jungle foliage. The aquatic mammals don't perform on cue either, but they're natural hams and often interact with their visitors, nodding their heads in response to trainer questions, turning aerial somersaults, and "walking" on their tails across the water. An underwater viewing area provides an unusual perspective into the dolphins' world. Feeding times are a hoot.

Budding naturalists (age 13 and over) won't want to miss the three-hour Dolphin Habitat's Trainer for a Day program ($400), which allows them to feed, swim with, and pose for photos with some of the aquatic stars while putting them through their daily regimen. Other interactive activities with the aquatic mammals include painting ($145) and yoga ($75).

TOP EXPERIENCE

★ High Roller

Taller than even the London Eye, the 550-foot (168-m) **High Roller** (Linq, 3545 Las Vegas Blvd. S., 702/777-2782 or 866/574-3851, www.caesars.com/linq/high-roller, 4pm-midnight Mon.-Thurs., noon-midnight Fri.-Sun., $23.50-37.75 adults, $8.50-17.50 youth, children 6 and under free) is the highest observation wheel in the world. Two thousand LED lights dance in intricate choreography among the ride's spokes and pods. The dazzling view from 50 stories up on one of the High Roller's 28 compartments is unparalleled. Ride at dusk for inspiring glimpses of the desert sun setting over the mountains. Ride at night for a perfect panorama of the famous Strip skyline. The ride takes about a half hour.

the High Roller

With **Happy Half Hour** tickets (age 21 and up, $52) passengers can board special bar cars and enjoy unlimited cocktails during the ride. Book online to save on tickets.

Lower Strip

Showcase Mall

With its 100-foot-tall (30.5-m) green Coke bottle and party-sized bag of M&M's on its facade, **Showcase Mall** (3785 Las Vegas Blvd. S., 702/597-3117, 9am-5pm daily) is conspicuous even among all that Strip neon. The mall's centerpiece, the original **M&M's World** (702/736-7611, www.mmsworld.com, 10am-5pm daily, free), includes a printing station where customers can customize their bite-size treats with words and pictures. The chocoholic's paradise is more than 30,000 square feet (2,787 sq m), offering souvenirs and the addicting treats in every color imaginable. Start with a viewing of the short 3-D film, *I Lost My M in Las Vegas.* On the third floor of the store, you can stock up on all things M: Swarovski crystal candy dishes, a guitar, T-shirts, and purses made from authentic M&M wrappers. A replica of Kyle Busch's M&M-sponsored No. 18 NASCAR stock car is on the fourth floor.

As you might expect, everything inside the **Everything Coca-Cola** store (702/270-5952, 10am-11pm daily, free) is related to the iconic soft drink. The small retail outlet has collectibles, free photo ops, and a soda fountain where you can taste 16 Coke products from around the world ($7). You also can buy Coke in bottles with customized logos; wedding dates, kids' names, and sports teams are popular choices.

Other mall tenants include a food court, a Hard Rock Café, and a half dozen other standalone restaurants; an eight-screen movie theater; and an Adidas. Target anchored a major expansion in 2020.

Bodies . . . the Exhibition and *Titanic* Artifacts

Although they are tastefully and respectfully presented, the dissected humans at ***Bodies . . . the Exhibition*** (Luxor, 3900 Las Vegas Blvd. S., 702/262-4400, http://luxor.mgmresorts.com, 10am-10pm daily, $32 adults, $30 military and seniors over 64, $24 children 4-12, children under 4 free) still have a creep factor. That uneasiness quickly gives way to wonder and interest as visitors examine 13 full-body specimens, carefully preserved to reveal bone structure and muscular, circulatory, respiratory, and other systems. Other system and organ displays drive home the importance of a healthy lifestyle, with structures showing the damage caused by overeating, alcohol consumption, and sedentary lifestyle. Perhaps the most sobering exhibit is the side-by-side comparisons of healthy and smoke-damaged lungs. A draped-off area contains fetal specimens, showing prenatal development and birth defects.

Luxor also hosts some 250 less surreal but just as poignant artifacts and reproductions commemorating the 1912 sinking of the ***Titanic*** (3900 Las Vegas Blvd. S., 702/262-4400, 10am-10pm daily, $32 adults, $30 military and seniors over 64, $24 children 4-12, children under 4 free). The 15-ton rusting hunk of the ship's hull is the biggest artifact on display; it not only drives home the *Titanic*'s scale but also helps transport visitors back to that frigid April morning a century ago. A replica of the *Titanic*'s grand staircase—featured prominently in the 1997 film—testifies to the ship's opulence, but it is the passengers' personal effects (a pipe, luggage, an unopened bottle of champagne) and recreated first-class and third-class cabins that provide some of the most heartbreaking discoveries. The individual stories come to life as each patron is given the identity of one of the ship's passengers. At the end of tour, they find out the passenger's fate.

Luxor offers combination admission to both attractions for $42.

Shark Reef

Just when you thought it was safe to visit Las Vegas. . . . This 1.6-million-gallon (6-million-l) habitat proves not all the sharks in town prowl the poker rooms. **Shark Reef** (Mandalay Bay, 3950 Las Vegas Blvd. S., 702/632-4555, www.sharkreef.com, 10am-8pm Sun.-Thurs., 10am-10pm Fri.-Sat., $22 adults, $18 military and seniors 65 and over, $15 children 4-12, children under 4 free) is home to 2,000 animals—almost all predators. Transparent walkthrough tubes and a sinking-ship observation deck allow terrific views, bringing visitors nearly face-to-face with some of the most fearsome creatures in the world. Among the 15 species of sharks on display is a sand tiger shark, whose mouth is so crammed with razor-sharp teeth that it doesn't fully close. Other species include golden crocodiles, moray eels, stingrays, giant octopuses, the venomous lionfish, jellyfish, water monitors, and the fresh-from-your-nightmares 8-foot-long (2.4-m) Komodo dragon. Guests can pay extra to feed the turtles, stingrays, or sharks.

Mandalay Bay guests with dive certification can dive in the 22-foot-deep (6.7-m) shipwreck exhibit at the reef. Commune with 8-foot (2.4-m) nurse sharks as well as reef sharks, zebra sharks, rays, sawfish, and other denizens of the deep. **Scuba excursions** (3pm daily, age 18 and over, $650 for 1 person, $1,000 for 2 people) include 3-4 hours underwater, a guided aquarium tour, a video, and admission for up to four guests. Wearing chain mail is required. One tour option will prove your love runs deep: Have a reef diver present a surprise proposal at the end of a guided one-hour tour ($100). The price includes a commemorative photo.

Downtown

★ Fremont Street Experience

With land at a premium and more and more tourists flocking to the opulence of the Strip, downtown Las Vegas in the last quarter of the 20th century found its lights beginning to flicker. Enter the **Fremont Street Experience** (702/678-5600, www.vegasexperience.com), an ambitious plan to transform downtown and its tacky "Glitter Gulch" reputation into a pedestrian-friendly enclave. Highlighted by a four-block-long canopy festooned with light-emitting diodes 90 feet (27.4 m) in the air, the Fremont Street Experience is downtown's answer to the Strip's erupting volcanoes and fantastic dancing fountains. The canopy, dubbed Viva Vision, runs atop Fremont Street between North Main Street and North 4th Street.

Once an hour, the promenade goes dark and all heads lift toward the 16-million-pixel canopy, supported by massive concrete pillars. For six minutes, visitors are enthralled by the multimedia shows that explore natural wonders, project dynamic art, and transport viewers to fantasy worlds, backed by tracks from the hottest rock bands of today and yesteryear. Viva Vision runs several different shows daily.

Downtown Las Vegas

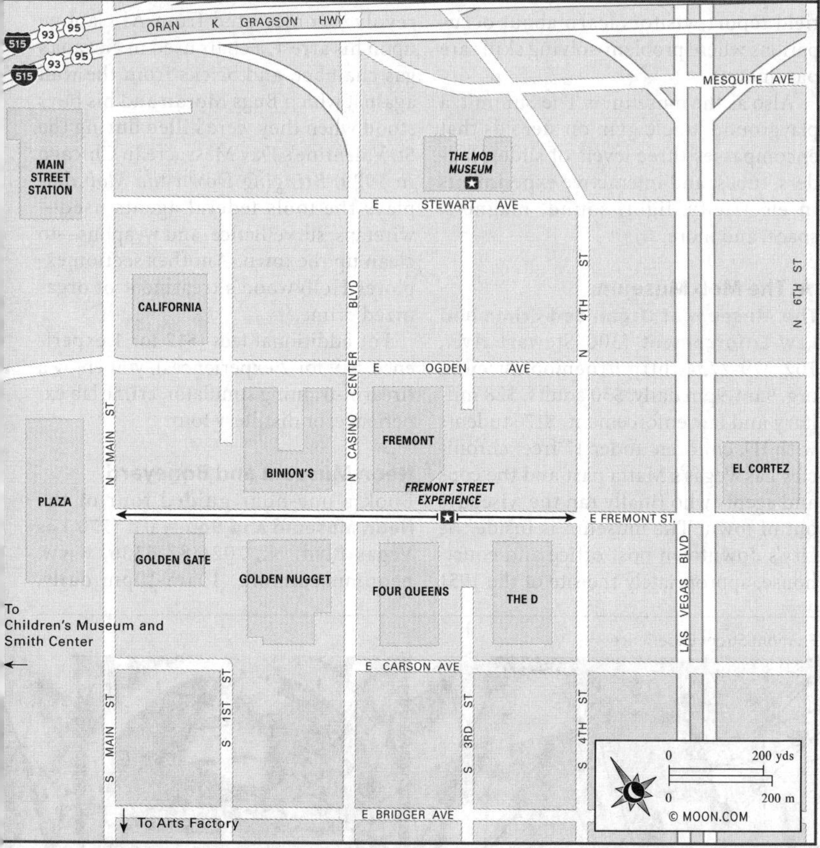

Before and after the light shows, strolling buskers sing for their supper, artists create five-minute masterpieces, caricaturists airbrush souvenir portraits, and (sometimes scantily) costumed characters pose for photos. Tipping is all but mandatory ($2-5 is fair). Fremont Street hosts top musical acts, including some A-listers during big Las Vegas weekends such as National Finals Rodeo, NASCAR races, and New Year's. The adjacent Fremont East Entertainment District houses quirky eateries, clubs, and art galleries.

Lied Discovery Children's Museum

Polls consistently rank the **Lied Discovery Children's Museum** (360 Promenade Pl., 702/382-3445, www.discoverykidslv.org, 10am-6pm Tues., 10am-5pm Wed.-Sat., noon-5pm Sun., $14.50) among the best museums in Las Vegas. Children enjoy themselves so much that they forget they're learning. In addition to rotating and traveling exhibits, the museum features more than 100 permanent, interactive scientific, artistic, and life-skill activities. *Solve It! Mystery Town* introduces children to the scientific method and challenges them to collect and analyze archaeological specimens. After filing their final field report, visitors learn about occupations where problem-solving skills are paramount.

Also as the museum is The Summit, a playground jungle gym on steroids that encompasses three levels of slides, ladders, tubes, and interactive experiments in electricity, light, sound, magnets, space, and more.

★ The Mob Museum

The Museum of Organized Crime and Law Enforcement (300 Stewart Ave., 702/229-2734, http://themobmuseum.org, 9am-9pm daily, $30 adults, $28 military and law enforcement, $17 students with ID, children under 11 free) chronicles Las Vegas's Mafia past and the cops and agents who finally ran the wiseguys out of town. The museum is inside the city's downtown post office and courthouse, appropriately the site of the 1951 Kefauver Hearing investigating organized crime.

Displays include the Smith & Wesson revolver confiscated from Al Capone upon his arrest, a chair used in Nevada's gas chamber, and bricks from the wall against which Bugs Moran and his boys stood when they were killed during the St. Valentine's Day Massacre in Chicago in 1929. *Bringing Down the Mob* displays the tools federal agents used—wiretaps, surveillance, and weapons—to clean up the town. Another section explores Hollywood's treatment of organized crime.

For additional fees ($12 for 1 experience, $19 for 2 experiences), you enjoy a firearm-training simulator, crime lab experience, or distillery tour.

Neon Museum and Boneyard

Book a one-hour guided tour of the **Neon Museum and Boneyard** (770 Las Vegas Blvd. N., 702/387-6366, www.neonmuseum.org, 10am-10pm daily,

Fremont Street Experience

$20-28) and take a trip to Las Vegas's more recent past. The boneyard displays 200 old neon signs that were used to advertise casinos, restaurants, bars, and even a flower shop and a dry cleaner. Several have been restored to their former glory and are illuminated for nighttime tours. The boneyard is not open for self-guided exploration, but the **visitors center,** housed in the scallop-shaped lobby of the historical La Concha Motel, offers a prime example of Googie architecture and can serve as a base for a do-it-yourself tour of restored neon displayed as public art. Note that the neighborhood surrounding the museum and public neon signs sees many of the city's unhoused population on its streets after dark.

Las Vegas Natural History Museum

Las Vegas boasts a volcano, a pyramid, and even a Roman coliseum, so it's little wonder that an animatronic *Tyrannosaurus rex* calls the valley home, too. Dedicated to "global life forms. . . from the desert to the ocean, from Nevada to Africa, from prehistoric times to the present," the **Las Vegas Natural History Museum** (900 Las Vegas Blvd. N., 702/384-3466, www.lvnhm.org, 9am-4pm daily, $12 adults, $10 students, seniors, and military, $6 children 3-11) is filled with rotating exhibits that belie the notion that Las Vegas culture begins and ends with neon casino signs.

Visitors to the Treasures of Egypt gallery can enter a realistic depiction of King Tut's tomb to study archaeological techniques and discover golden treasures of the pharaohs. The Wild Nevada gallery showcases the raw beauty and surprisingly varied life-forms of the Mojave Desert. Interactive exhibits also enlighten visitors on subjects such as marine life, geology, African ecosystems, and more.

The 35-foot-long (10.7-m) T. rex and his friends (rivals? entrées?)—a triceratops, a raptor, and an ichthyosaur—greet visitors in the Prehistoric Life gallery. And by "greet" we mean a bloodcurdling roar from the T. rex, so take precautions with the little ones and the faint of heart.

Mormon Fort

The tiny **Mormon Fort** (500 E. Washington Ave., 702/486-3511, http://parks.nv.gov, 8am-4:30pm Tues.-Sat., $3) is the oldest building in Las Vegas. The adobe remnant, constructed by Mormon missionaries in 1855, was part of their original town site, the first permanent nonnative settlement in the valley, which they abandoned in 1858. It then served as a store, a barracks, and a shed on the Gass-Stewart Ranch. After that, the railroad leased the old fort to various tenants, including the Bureau of Reclamation, which stabilized and rebuilt the shed to use as a concrete-testing laboratory for Hoover Dam. In 1955 the railroad sold the old fort to the Elks, who in 1963 bulldozed the whole wooden structure (except the little remnant) into the ranch swimming pool and torched it.

Now a state park, the museum includes a visitors center, a recreation of the original fort built around the remnant, and a recreation of the little spring-fed creek that enticed the Mormons to put down roots here in the first place. A tour guide presents the history orally while display boards provide it visually. Your visit will not go unrewarded—it's immensely refreshing to see some preservation of the past in this city of the ultimate now.

Downtown Arts District

Centered at South Main Street and East Charleston Boulevard, the district offers art lovers and fans of bohemian style a concentration of galleries, shops, restaurants, and bars. The **Arts Factory** (107 E. Charleston Blvd., 702/383-3133, www.theartsfactory.com, 9am-7pm daily) is the district's birthplace and epicenter. The two-story psychedelically painted industrial building is home to two dozen eclectic artists' studios and other creative tenants, including clothing designers and art instructors. Stop by Suite 210 and check out Deana Khoshaba's vibrant mixed-media creations.

Virtually all the galleries and other paeans to pop culture in the district participate in Las Vegas's **First Friday** (http://ffflv.org, 5pm-11pm 1st Fri. each month), which includes wine receptions, pub crawls, art lessons, and plenty of exhibits. Otherwise galleries keep limited hours, so if there's something you don't want to miss, call for an appointment.

Off the Strip

★ Las Vegas Springs Preserve

The **Las Vegas Springs Preserve** (333 S. Valley View Blvd., 702/822-7700, www.springspreserve.org, 10am-6pm daily, $19 adults, $17 students and seniors over 64, $11 ages 5-17, children under 5 free) is where Las Vegas began, at least from a Eurocentric viewpoint. More than 100 years ago, the first nonnatives in the Las Vegas Valley—Mormon missionaries from Salt Lake City—stumbled on this clear artesian spring. Of course, the native Paiute and Pueblo people knew about the springs, which were a source of water for them, millennia before the Mormons arrived. You can see examples of their tools, pottery, and houses at the site, now a 180-acre (72.8-ha) monument to environmental stewardship, historical preservation, and geographic discovery. The preserve is home to lizards, rabbits, foxes, scorpions, bats, and more. The nature-minded will love the cactus, rose, and sage gardens, and there's even an occasional cooking demonstration using the desert-friendly fruits, vegetables, and herbs grown here.

Las Vegas has become a leader in water conservation, alternative energy, and other environmentally friendly policies. The results of these efforts and tips on how everyone can reduce their carbon footprint are found in the Sustainability Gallery.

General admission tickets also include entry to the Nevada State Museum but do not include the preserve's **Butterfly Habitat** ($3). It's worth the extra fee to watch the monarchs, blue morphos, painted ladies, banded orange longwings, and more interact with their habitat. Installations offer fascinating lessons on what the flutterers eat, their coloration, and migratory habits.

Nevada State Museum

Visitors can spend hours studying Mojave and Spring Mountains ecology, southern Nevada wildlife (both contemporary and prehistoric), and local mining and railroad history at the **Nevada State Museum** (309 S. Valley View Blvd., 702/486-5205, http://nvculture.org, 9am-5pm Tues.-Sun., $19 adults, $17 students and seniors over 64, $11 ages 5-17, children under 5 free). Permanent exhibits on the 13,000-square-foot (1,208-sq-m) floor describe southern Nevada's role in warfare, mining, and westward expansion and include skeletons of a Columbian

Grand Canyon Tours from Vegas

Nearly a dozen tour companies relay visitors from Vegas to and through the Grand Canyon. Operators generally offer a basic package with several options you can bundle to extend your time or make it even more special. Start by choosing your preferred travel medium—ground, air, or water. Coupons and discounts for online reservations and off-season bookings are plentiful; it is not uncommon to book tours at less than half the per-person rack rates listed here.

Land Tours

The time-honored road trip is the most economical way to see this world wonder but driving yourself can be stressful and leave you too tired to fully experience the canyon's splendor. Many tour operators offer bus/van options. It's a four-hour drive one-way, including restroom and meal stops, so bus tours make for a long day, lasting about 13 hours total, with hotel pickup around 6am. **GC Tours** (3565 Las Vegas Blvd. S. #165, 702/997-2001, http://gc.tours, 8am-11pm daily) offers a South Rim bus tour ($78) that includes hotel pickup and drop-off; quick restroom/snack stops in Kingman, Arizona; a photo op on Route 66 in Seligman, Arizona; and three hours at the South Rim of the Grand Canyon. The West Rim bus tour ($102) includes three hours at Grand Canyon West, with an option to add on the Skywalk ($25). **Grand Canyon Destinations** (5125 W. Oquendo Rd. #16, 702/456-9200, www.grandcanyondestinations.com, 5am-10pm daily) offers similar itineraries. Its South Rim ($104) and West Rim ($124) trips include a guide-narrator for your entertainment and edification, a box lunch, and a stop at Grand Canyon Caverns.

Air Tours

Two companies dominate the helicopter-based tours from Las Vegas. **Papillon** (888/635-7272 or 702/736-7243, www.papillon.com) offers a basic flight, the Golden Eagle with Vegas Strip tour ($379), that includes West Rim aerial views and flyovers of the Strip, Hoover Dam, and Lake Mead. Flying time is about 1.5 hours and the total tour duration about 3-3.5 hours. This excursion doesn't allow for ground exploration of the canyon, but longer trips, with a landing on the canyon floor and a few hours to walk around, are also available. **Maverick** (702/261-0007, www.maverickhelicopter.com) offers a four-hour Wind Dancer tour (from $469), the highlight of which is a landing on a bluff 300 feet (91.4 m) above the Colorado River and 3,500 feet (1,067 m) below the canyon's rim. Alongside once-in-a-lifetime vistas, guests are served snacks and champagne.

Plane trips to the Grand Canyon are less common—and less costly—than helicopter flights. **Adrenaline** (888/992-3736, www.adrenaline.com) offers a South Rim Plane Tour with Landing ($349), flying over several scenic areas before landing and shuttling guests to lunch. The 7.5-hour trip leaves time for sightseeing and hiking.

River Tours

If you have time and money to spare on your Las Vegas visit, a multimodal, multi-activity, motorized rafting trip down the Colorado River is a great way to visit the Grand Canyon. **Advantage Grand Canyon** (928/351-7711 or 888/244-2224, www.advantagegrandcanyon.com, ages 8 and over) offers a three-day float to the West Rim ($1,489) via a 14-person raft. Guests first take a short flight to Bar 10 Ranch, where they can enjoy horseback riding, skeet shooting, country music entertainment, and more. The next day, a short helicopter hop puts guests at water's edge, where they board rafts for a day on the river, with frequent stops for hiking and exploring. After overnighting with tents and cots on the shore, a half-day's rafting and a sightseeing jetboat ride concludes the trip.

mammoth, which roamed the Nevada deserts 20,000 years ago, and the ichthyosaur, a whalelike remnant of the Triassic period. The *Nevada from Dusk to Dawn* exhibit explores the nocturnal lives of the area's animal species. Rotating and traveling exhibits detail the city's evolution into the resort capital of the world and topical artifacts from local, national, and global history.

Admission to the Nevada State Museum also includes admission to the Springs Preserve.

★ National Atomic Testing Museum

Members of the "duck and cover" generation will find plenty to spark Cold War memories at the **National Atomic Testing Museum** (755 E. Flamingo Rd., 702/794-5151, www.nationalatomictestingmuseum.org, 10am-5pm Mon.-Sat., noon-5pm Sun., $22 adults, $18 students, active military, and seniors 62 and over, $16 ages 7-14, children 6 and under free). Las Vegas embraced its role as ground zero in the development of the nation's atomic and nuclear deterrents after World War II. Business leaders welcomed defense contractors to town, and casinos hosted bomb-watching parties as nukes were detonated at the Nevada Test Site, a huge swath of desert 65 miles (105 km) away. One ingenious marketer promoted the Miss Atomic Bomb beauty pageant in an era when patriotism overcame concerns about radiation.

The museum presents atomic history without bias, walking a fine line between appreciation of the work of nuclear scientists, politicians, and the military and the catastrophic consequences their activities and decisions could have wrought. The museum's best permanent feature is a short video in the Ground Zero Theatre, a multimedia simulation of an actual atomic explosion. The theater, a replica of an observation bunker, is rigged for motion, sound, and rushing air.

One gallery helps visitors put atomic energy milestones in historical perspective, along with the age's impact on 1950s and 1960s pop culture. Another permanent exhibit explains the effects of radiation and how it is tracked and measured. Just as relevant today are the lectures and traveling exhibits that the museum hosts.

Computer simulators, high-speed photographs, Geiger counters, and other testing and safety equipment, along with first-person accounts, add to the museum's visit-worthiness.

Entertainment

Headliners and Production Shows

Las Vegas production show has evolved from distinct acts—a juggler, followed by a contortionist, magician, strongman, etc. Today, many shows incorporate these talented performers, but in the context of a connected story. The Cirque du Soleil franchise is a good example. More recently, Vegas has embraced a more traditional take on French burlesque; the Spiegelworld franchise's shows, like *Absinthe* and *Opium,* feature a bawdier brand of performance and politically incorrect humor. These shows, hosted in more intimate venues and supper clubs, are reminiscent of Vegas in the 1950s or Berlin in the 1930s.

As Las Vegas has grown more sophisticated, it has also attracted Broadway productions to compete with the superstar singers—many now signing miniresidency contracts—that helped launch the town's legendary status. In recent years, Lady Gaga, Bruno Mars, Aerosmith, Gwen Stefani and dozens more have performed extended engagements.

Since they're so expensive to produce, the big shows are fairly reliable. They do change on occasion; the smaller shows come and go with some frequency, but unless a show bombs and is gone in the first few weeks, it'll usually be around for at least a year.

★ *Absinthe*

As great as they are, the world-class singers and dancers and specialty acts featuring astounding acts of balance, athleticism, magic, striptease, and other vaudeville- and cabaret-inspired performances aren't even the main attraction in Spiegelworld's ***Absinthe*** (Caesars Palace, 3570 Las Vegas Blvd. S., 855/234-7469, http://spiegelworld.com/absinthe, 8pm and 10pm daily, $99-159). That distinction goes to the Gazillionaire, the show's foulmouthed, sleazeball ringmaster, and his female counterpart.

If you go, leave your inhibitions and prudishness at home, lest you find yourself the target of the Gazillionaire's barbs. In-the-round audience configuration assures there's not a bad seat in the house, but with VIP tickets, the performers are, sometimes literally, right in your lap.

Blue Man Group

Bald, blue, and silent (save for drums and homemade PVC musical instruments), **Blue Man Group** (Luxor, 3900 Las Vegas Blvd. S., 702/262-4400 or 877/386-4658, www.blueman.com, 7pm Thurs, 7pm and 9:30pm Fri.-Sat., 4pm Sun., $59-128) was one of the hottest things to hit the Strip when it debuted in 2000 after successful versions in New York, Boston, and Chicago. It continues to wow audiences with its thought-provoking, quirkily hilarious gags and percussion performances. It is part street performance, part slapstick, and all fun.

Carrot Top

His skater-dude appearance makes it hard to believe that **Carrot Top** (Luxor, 3900 Las Vegas Blvd. S., 702/262-4400 or 800/557-7428, http://carrottop.com, 8pm Mon.-Sat., $40-76) is the senior statesman among Vegas comedians. But with fresh observational humor, outrageous props, and flaming ginger locks, Scott Thompson stands alone as the only true full-time headlining stand-up comic in Las Vegas. His rapid-fire, stream-of-consciousness delivery ricochets from sex-aid props and poop jokes to current events, pop culture, and social injustice, making him the thinking person's class clown.

Chippendales

With all the jiggle-and-tease shows on the Strip, **Chippendales** (Rio, 3700 W. Flamingo Rd., 702/777-7776, www.chippendales.com, 8:30pm Sun.-Thurs., 8:30pm and 10:30pm Fri.-Sat., $55-83) delivers a little gender equity. Tight jeans and rippled abs bumping and grinding with their female admirers may be the main attraction, but the choreography is more tasteful than most similar shows, and the guys really can dance. The "firefighters," "cowboys," and other manly man fantasy fodder boys dance their way through sultry and playful renditions of "It's Raining Men" and other tunes with similar themes. They occasionally stroll through the crowd flirting and lap-sitting. However, there is a hands-off policy (wink, wink).

Kà

Cirque du Soleil's ***Kà*** (MGM Grand, 3799 Las Vegas Blvd. S., 702/531-3826, www.cirquedusoleil.com/ka, 7pm and 9:30pm Sat.-Wed., $79-94) explores the yin and yang of life through the story of separated twins journeying to meet their shared fate. Martial arts, acrobatics, puppetry, plenty of flashy pyrotechnics, and lavish sets and costumes bring cinematic drama to the variety-show acts. Battle scenes play out on two floating, rotating platforms. The show's title was inspired by the ancient Egyptian belief of *ka,* in which every human has a spiritual duplicate.

Legends in Concert

Elvis is still in the building every night at ***Legends in Concert*** (Tropicana, 3801

Las Vegas Blvd S., 702/253-1333, www.legendsinconcert.com, 7:30pm and 9:30pm Mon., 9:30pm Tues., 4pm and 9:30pm Wed.-Thurs. and Sat., 7:30pm Sun., $59-99), while other impersonators—Lady Gaga, Freddie Mercury, Pat Benatar, Tina Turner, and more—rotate. Each show features four acts.

LOVE

For Beatles fans visiting Las Vegas, all you need is ***LOVE*** (Mirage, 3400 Las Vegas Blvd. S., 866/983-4279, www.cirquedusoleil.com/love, 7pm and 9:30pm Tues.-Sat., $65-158). This Cirque du Soleil-produced stroll along Penny Lane features dancers, aerial acrobats, and other performers interpreting the Fab Four's lyrics and recordings. With the breathtaking visual artistry of Cirque du Soleil and a custom soundscape using the original master tapes from Abbey Road Studios, John, Paul, George, and Ringo have never looked or sounded so good.

Magic Mike Live

Is it hot in here, or is it just the 13 studs parading around the stage for ***Magic Mike Live*** (Sahara, 2535 Las Vegas Blvd. S., 702/761-7000, www.magicmikelivelasvegas.com, 7pm and 10pm Wed.-Sun., $49-159)? Based on the wildly popular movies, the show features baby oil-slathered hunks in tight jeans, tear-away T-shirts—and less—strutting around a facsimile of Club Domina.

Mat Franco: *Magic Reinvented Nightly*

Wine bottles, cell phones, and other everyday objects become enchanted in the hands of magician **Mat Franco** (Linq, 3535 Las Vegas Blvd. S., 855/234-7469 or 702/777-2782, www.caesars.com/linq, 7pm Sun.-Tues. and Thurs.-Fri., 7pm and 9:30pm Sat., $60-133), whose

From top to bottom: Cirque du Soleil's *LOVE;* Cirque du Soleil's *Kà;* Cirque du Soleil's *O.*

performance changes depending on the audience's composition and whims. Franco's humorous narration of each illusion adds to the intimate atmosphere.

Michael Jackson ONE

Cirque du Soleil acrobats and dancers augment the musical wizardry of the King of Pop in ***Michael Jackson ONE*** (Mandalay Bay, 3950 Las Vegas Blvd. S., 702/632-7777, www.cirquedusoleil.com/michael-jackson-one, 7pm and 9:30pm Thurs.-Mon., $69-170). A concert-quality sound system, multimedia visuals, and spot-on rock/R&B choreography that would have made Jackson proud round out the performance. This is a must-see for fans.

Mystère

Celebrating the human form in all its beauty, athleticism, and grace, ***Mystère*** (Treasure Island, 3300 Las Vegas Blvd. S., 702/894-7722 or 800/392-1999, www.cirquedusoleil.com/mystere, 7pm and 9:30pm Sat.-Wed., $115-155) is the Cirque du Soleil production that most resembles a traditional American circus. But among the trapeze artists, feats of strength, and clowning around, *Mystère* also plays on other performance archetypes, including classical Greek theater, Kabuki, and surrealism. The first Cirque show in Las Vegas, *Mystère* continues to dazzle audiences with its revelations of life's mysteries.

O

The Bellagio likes to do everything bigger, better, and more extravagant, and ***O*** (Bellagio, 3600 Las Vegas Blvd. S., 866/983-4279, www.cirquedusoleil.com/O, 7:30pm and 9:30pm Wed.-Sun., $110-165) is no exception. This Cirque du Soleil incarnation involves a $90 million set, 80 artists, and a 1.5-million-gallon (5.7-million-l) pool of water. The title comes from the French word for water, *eau,* pronounced like the letter O in English. The production involves both terrestrial and aquatic feats of human artistry, athleticism, and comedy.

Opium

From Spiegelworld, the producers of *Absinthe,* ***Opium*** (Cosmopolitan, 3708 Las Vegas Blvd. S., 702/698-7000, http://spiegelworld.com/opium, 8pm and 10pm Wed.-Sun., $69-129) invites you to stowaway on an interstellar burlesque show of R-rated joke, singers, and specialty acts that you will never see on *America's Got Talent.*

Penn & Teller

The oddball comedy magicians **Penn & Teller** (Rio, 3700 W. Flamingo Rd., 702/777-2782, www.pennandteller.com, 9pm Sat.-Wed., $99) have a way of making audiences feel special. Seemingly breaking the magicians' code, they reveal the preparation and sleight-of-hand involved in performing tricks. The hitch is that even when forewarned, observers still often can't catch on. And once they do, the verbose Penn and silent Teller add a wrinkle no one expects.

Raiding the Rock Vault

Join rock archaeologists as they unearth the treasures of the 1960s, '70s, and '80s in ***Raiding the Rock Vault*** (Rio, 3700 W. Flamingo Rd., 702/777-2782, www.raidingtherockvault.com, 7:30pm Sat.-Wed., $69-100). Each room of the vault brings a rock era to life, with members of music's hit-makers—Quiet Riot, Whitesnake, Guns N' Roses, Heart, and more—performing the best of hair band and headbanger anthems.

Thunder from Down Under

Say g'day to the buffest blokes this side of Brisbane. These six-packed Aussies dance up a storm in ***Thunder from Down Under*** (Excalibur, 3580 Las Vegas Blvd. S., 702/597-7600, http://excalibur.

mgmresorts.com, 9pm Sun.-Thurs. and 9pm and 11pm Fri.-Sat., $76) as they portray a variety of fantasy men in (and out of) uniform. Performers schmooze with guests, posing for photos and mingling with the audience.

Tournament of Kings

Pound on the table with your goblet and let loose a hearty "huzzah!" to cheer your king to victory over the other nations' regents at the ***Tournament of Kings*** (Excalibur, 3580 Las Vegas Blvd. S., 702/597-7600, http://excalibur.mgmresorts.com, 6pm and 8:30pm Sat.-Sun. and Wed.-Thurs., 6pm Fri. and Mon., $76). Each section of the equestrian theater rallies under separate banners as their hero participates in jousts, sword fights, riding contests, and lusty-maid flirting at this festival hosted by King Arthur and Merlin. A regal feast served medieval style (that is, without utensils), starts with a tureen of dragon's blood (tomato soup). But just as the frivolity hits its climax, an evil lord appears to wreak havoc. Can the kings and Merlin's magic save the day? Find out, as you dig into game hen, potatoes, and dessert. One of the best family shows in Las Vegas.

Zumanity

Cirque du Soleil seems to have succumbed to the titillation craze with the strange melding of sensuality, athleticism, and voyeurism that is ***Zumanity*** (New York New York, 3790 Las Vegas Blvd. S., www.cirquedusoleil.com/zumanity, 866/983-4279, 7pm and 9:30pm Fri.-Tues., $75-109). The cabaret-style show makes no pretense of story line, but instead takes audience members through a succession of sexual and topless fantasies ranging from teasing to torrid—cellmates, sexual awakening, bathing beauties, ménage à trois, and more for the uninhibited over-18 crowd.

Showroom and Lounge Acts

Showrooms are another Las Vegas institution, with most hotels providing live entertainment—usually magic, comedy, or tributes to the big stars who played or are playing the big rooms and theaters under the same roofs.

The Vegas lounge act is the butt of a few jokes and more than one satire, but they offer some of the best values in town—a night's entertainment for a fraction of the cost of seeing a Strip headliner. Every hotel in Las Vegas worth its salt has a lounge. These acts are listed in the free entertainment magazines and the *Las Vegas Review-Journal*'s helpful website, but unless you're familiar with the performers, it's the luck of the draw: They list only the entertainer's name, venue, and showtimes.

All Shook Up: A Tribute to the King

A swivel-hipped, curled-lip journey through his career, ***All Shook Up*** (Planet Hollywood, 3667 Las Vegas Blvd. S., 702/260-7200, www.vtheaterboxoffice.com, 6pm daily, $60-70) is the only all-Elvis impersonator show on the Strip. Both rotating impressionists bear a strong resemblance to the King, capturing not only his voice but also his mannerisms, as they recount Elvis's hits from rock-and-roll pioneer to movie idol. The intimate 300-seat showroom makes every seat a good one.

Friends! The Musical Parody

More of a tribute than a parody, ***Friends! The Musical Parody*** (Paris, 3655 Las Vegas Blvd. S., 855/234-7469 or 702/777-2782, www.caesars.com/paris-las-vegas, 7pm Fri.-Wed., $48-83) is the one that revives the catch phrases and enduring gags from the TV show and its six photogenic protagonists.

Gordie Brown

A terrific song stylist in his own right, **Gordie Brown** (Hooters, 115 E Tropicana

Ave., 702/739-9000, www.gordiebrown.com, 7pm Wed.-Thurs. and Sat.-Mon., $59-80) is the thinking person's singing impressionist. Using his targets' peccadilloes as fodder for his song parodies, Brown pokes serious fun with a surgeon's precision. Props, mannerisms, and absurd vignettes add to the madcap fun. But make no mistake—behind the gimmicks, Brown is not only a talented impressionist but a gifted singer in his own right, no matter whose voice he uses.

Mac King Comedy Magic Show

The quality of afternoon shows in Las Vegas is spotty at best, but **Mac King Comedy Magic Show** (Harrah's, 3475 Las Vegas Blvd. S., 866/983-4279, www.mackingshow.com, 1pm and 3pm Tues.-Sat., $36-47) fits the bill for talent and affordability. King's routine is clean both technically and content-wise. With a plaid suit, good manners, and a silly grin, he cuts a nerdy figure, but his tricks and banter are skewed enough to make even the most jaded teenager laugh.

Matt Goss

A worthy and dapper heir to Darin, Damone, and Sinatra, crooner **Matt Goss** (Mirage, 3400 Las Vegas Blvd. S., 702/791-7111, www.mirage.com, 7:30pm Tues. and Fri.-Sun., $18-88) is backed by a live band and the Dirty Virgins dance troupe. British-born Goss is a Vegas veteran, with previous residencies at the Palms and Caesars Palace.

Menopause the Musical

Four women of a certain age discuss "the change" via lyrics from popular songs from the 1960s, '70s, and '80s in ***Menopause the Musical*** (Harrah's, 3475 Las Vegas Blvd. S., 855/234-7469, www.menopausethemusical.com, 7:30pm Mon. and Wed.-Fri., 4pm and 7:30pm Tues. and Sat., $55-80). Hot flashes have never been so hilarious.

The Rat Pack Is Back

Relive the golden era when Frank, Dean, Sammy, and Joey ruled the Strip with ***The Rat Pack Is Back*** (Tuscany, 255 E. Flamingo Rd., 702/947-5981, www.ratpackisback.com, 7:30pm Mon.-Sat., $60-66). Watch Sinatra try to make it through "Luck Be a Lady" amid the others' sophomoric antics. Frank plays right along, pretending to rule his crew with an iron fist, as the crew treats him with the mock deference the Chairman of the Board deserves.

RuPaul's Drag Race LIVE!

Loosely based on the reality TV show, ***RuPaul's Drag Race LIVE!*** (Flamingo, 3555 Las Vegas Blvd. S., 702/733-3111, www.caesars.com/flamingo-las-vegas, 9:30pm Tues. and Thurs.-Sun., $49-75) puts contestants through their paces, challenging them to compete in dance-offs, lip-synch battles, and runway struts to see who will be crowned queen for the day. As you might expect, the music, lighting, and production values are fabulous.

Comedy

Nearly gone are the days of top-name comedians as resident headliners. However, A-listers like Ron White, George Lopez, Jerry Seinfeld, George Wallace, Kathleen Madigan, Jim Gaffigan, and others still make regular appearances as part of the **Aces of Comedy** (Mirage, 3400 Las Vegas Blvd. S., 702/791-7111, www.mirage.com, 7:30pm-10pm Fri.-Sat., $60-100). But most of the yuks nowadays come from the talented youngsters toiling in the comedy club trenches.

Jimmy Kimmel's Comedy Club (Linq, 3535 Las Vegas Blvd. S., 855/234-7469 or 702/777-2782, www.caesars.com/linq, 7pm Tues., 8pm and 10pm Thurs.-Fri. and Sun., 8pm, 10pm, and midnight Sat., $20-40), opened by the club's namesake—who grew up in Las Vegas—is the newest joint for touring comedians to test their mettle.

Comedy journeymen and women and next-big-things have half a dozen other places to land gigs when they're in town. Among the best are the **Comedy Cellar** (Rio, 3700 W. Flamingo Rd., 702/777-2782, www.comedycellar.com/las-vegas, 7pm and 9pm daily, $25-45), **Brad Garrett's Comedy Club** (MGM Grand, 3799 Las Vegas Blvd. S., 866/740-7711, www.bradgarrettcomedy.com, 8pm daily, $45-70, plus $25 when Garrett performs), **L.A. Comedy Club** (The Strat, 2000 Las Vegas Blvd. S., 702/275-3877 or 800/998-6937, www.thelacomedyclub.com, 8pm daily, 6pm and 10pm shows some nights, $47-64), **Laugh Factory** (Tropicana, 3801 Las Vegas Blvd. S., 702/739-2222, www.laughfactory.com, 8:30pm and 10:30pm daily, $38-55), **Las Vegas Live** (Planet Hollywood, 3667 Las Vegas Blvd. S., 702/260-7200, www.lasvegaslivecomedyclub.com, 9pm daily, $56-67), and **Jokesters** (OYO Casino & Hotel, 115 E. Tropicana Ave., 702/483-8056, www.jokesterslasvegas.com, 10pm daily, $30-40).

Magic

Magic shows are nearly as ubiquitous as comedy, with the more accomplished, such as Penn & Teller at Rio and **David Copperfield** (MGM Grand, 3799 Las Vegas Blvd. S., 866/740-7711, www.davidcopperfield.com, 7pm and 9:30pm Sun.-Fri., 4pm, 7pm, and 9:30pm Sat., $78-123, playing long-term gigs in their own showrooms.

In addition to Mac King at Harrah's, two other clean prestidigitators have taken up residency at Planet Hollywood. Both are *America's Got Talent* alumni. **Nathan Burton Comedy Magic** (Planet Hollywood, 3663 Las Vegas Blvd. S., 866/932-1818, www.nathanburton.com, 4pm daily, $50-60) serves up epic disappearing acts, while **Murray the Magician** (Tropicana, 3801 Las Vegas Blvd. S., 800/829-9034, www.murraymagic.com, 5pm Sun.-Tues., 7pm Thurs. and Sat., $40-60) boasts comedic timing as entertaining as his sleight of hand.

Variety Show

The traditional Las Vegas variety show format has been given new life at a few venues on the Strip and downtown. Tamer and more family-oriented than Spiegelworld shows like *Absinthe* or *Opium,* these productions are no less elaborate, and the performers no less talented.

Fittingly staged in the same theater that was home to *Jubilee!,* Vegas's last true showgirl show in town, ***Extravaganza*** (Bally's, 3645 Las Vegas Blvd. S., 702/777-2782, www.extravaganza-vegas.com, 7pm Sun.-Tues. and Thurs., Fri.-Sat. 7pm and 9pm, $48-108) brings back boa-wearing beauties in all their glory. The show includes innovative use of holograms and other technology to give a modern twist to traditional acts and feats of strength, balance, skill, comedy, and showmanship.

Rotating acts keep ***V – The Ultimate Variety Show*** (Planet Hollywood, 3663 Las Vegas Blvd. S., 866/932-1818, http://vtheshow.com, 7pm and 8:30pm daily, $54-91) fresh. Gymnasts, aerialists, comedians, and specialty acts of all kinds perform in rapid-fire succession behind emcee Wally Eastwood, "the world's fastest juggler." Other shows in this genre include ***Wow – The Vegas Spectacular*** (Rio, 3700 W. Flamingo Rd, 866/932-1818, www.caesars.com/rio-las-vegas, 7pm Tues.-Thurs., 7pm and 9pm Fri.-Sun., $65-126), which creates a watery world of wonder. Singers, dancers, and acrobats splash their way through innovative sequences, stirringly choreographed, in vibrant costumes. Specialty acts include plate spinners, acrobats, and an edge-of-your-seat William Tell performance. Taking a slightly different tack, ***Vegas! The Show*** (Planet Hollywood, 3663 Las Vegas Blvd. S., 866/932-1818, www.vegastheshow.com, $100-120) mixes in variety acts with tributes to classic Vegas performers. You might see the Rat Pack, Gladys Knight, Tina Turner, Tom Jones, or Elvis, along with statuesque showgirls in feathery headdresses.

Live Music

The best, hippest, and most convenient live music venue for visitors, **Brooklyn Bowl** (Linq, 3545 Las Vegas Blvd. S., Ste. 22, 702/862-2695, www.brooklynbowl.com, 5pm-late daily) replicates its successful New York City formula with 32 bowling lanes, comfortable couches, beer, food ($15-25)—a fried chicken platter will sate your whole crew—and big-name groups sprinkled among the party band lineup. Elvis Costello, Wu-Tang Clan, Jane's Addiction, and the Psychedelic Furs are among the notables that have played the Brooklyn. Several acts are slated throughout the day.

The best indie bands in Las Vegas, as well as touring jammers, electro-poppers, and garage bands, make it a point to play the **Bunkhouse Saloon** (124 S. 11th St., 702/982-1764, www.bunkhousedowntown.com, 6pm-midnight. Mon.-Thurs., 6pm-2am Fri.-Sat.). **Count's Vamp'd** (6750 W. Sahara Ave., 702/220-8849, www.vampdvegas.com, 11am-2am daily) books a mix of tribute bands and '80s metal icons appearing solo or with their newest project. Progressive metal and punk fans should check out **Backstage Bar & Billiards** (601 Fremont St., 702/382-2227, www.backstagebarlv.com, 8pm-3am Tues.-Sat.).

With more than 20,000 square feet (1,858 sq m) of space and a 2,500-square-foot (232-sq-m) dance floor, **Stoney's Rockin' Country** (6611 Las Vegas Blvd. S., Ste. 160, 702/435-2855, http://stoneysrockincountry.com, 5pm-11pm Sun.-Wed., 5pm-1am Thurs.-Sat.) in the Town Square mall could almost *be* its own country. It is honky-tonk on a grand scale, with a mechanical bull and line-dancing lessons. Muddy Waters, Etta James, B. B. King, and even Mick Jagger have graced the stage at the **Sand Dollar** (3355 Spring Mountain Rd., 702/485-5401, http://thesanddollarlv.com, 6pm-2am daily), where blue-collar blues and smoky jazz (but no cigarette smoke, thanks to a 2020 change) rule. The Boars on Parade pizza hits the spot after a few signature cocktails. Bands start around 10pm weekends. The people your mama warned you about hang out at the never-a-cover-charge **Double Down Saloon** (4640 Paradise Rd., 702/791-5775, www.doubledownsaloon.com, 24 hours daily), drinking to excess and thrashing to the punk, ska, and psychobilly bands on stage.

Festivals and Events

Several multiday musical parties have made Las Vegas their home over the last few years, taking over huge swaths of the city with eclectic displays of art, gourmet food, and flowing booze, in addition to musical stylings.

The three-day **Electric Daisy Carnival** (http://lasvegas.electricdaisycarnival.com, May, $300-650) turns the Las Vegas Motor Speedway into one big dance club, with house and trance from the best-known artists and jockeys in the genres. Much of the art at this festival is interactive, sparking conversations and shared experiences.

Over two days at the T-Mobile Arena, the **iHeartRadio Music Festival** (www.iheart.com/music-festival, Sept., $200-850) books a litany of A-listers from the rock-era spectrum. Acts include performers such as Camila Cabello, Def Leppard, Big Sean, and the Zac Brown Band.

Held just northeast of the Fremont Street Experience, downtown's **Life is Beautiful Music & Art Festival** (http://lifeisbeautiful.com, Sept., $400) is a celebration of music and art headlined by top names and filled out with rising and niche acts. Top-line performers have included The Killers, Outkast, Stevie Wonder, Weezer, and the Foo Fighters.

The Arts

With all the plastic and neon, it's easy to accuse Las Vegas of being a soulless, cultureless wasteland, and many have. But beyond the glitz, Las Vegas is a community. Why shouldn't the city enjoy and foster the arts?

The local theater scene thrives, thanks to the **Smith Center for the Performing Arts** (361 Symphony Park Ave., 702/749-2012, www.thesmithcenter.com), a major cog in the revitalization of downtown. It is home to the **Las Vegas Philharmonic** (702/258-5438, http://lvphil.org) and the **Nevada Ballet Theatre** (702/243-2623, www.nevadaballet.org) and also hosts local performances and theatrical touring companies performing last year's Broadway smashes.

Rides and Games

The Strat SkyPod

Daredevils will delight in the vertigo-inducing thrill rides on the observation deck at **The Strat SkyPod** (The Strat, 2000 Las Vegas Blvd. S., 702/383-5210, www.thestrat.com, 2pm-10pm Mon.-Thurs., noon-midnight Fri.-Sun., $34-130). The **SkyJump** invites the daring to plunge into space for a 15-second free fall. Angled guide wires keep jumpers on target and ease them to gentle landings. This skydive without a parachute costs $130.

The other rides are 100-story-high variations on traditional thrill rides: The **Big Shot** is a sort of 15-person reverse bungee jump; **X-Scream** sends riders on a gentle (at first) roll off the edge, leaving them suspended over Las Vegas Boulevard; **Insanity**'s giant arms swing over the edge, tilting to suspend riders nearly horizontally. Admission to the observation tower and one of these rides costs $34, or you can do all three rides for $44. All-day passes are also available but don't include the SkyJump.

Adventuredome

Behind Circus Circus, the **Adventuredome Theme Park** (2880 Las Vegas Blvd. S., 702/794-3939, www.circuscircus.com, 10am-9pm Sun.-Thurs., 10am-midnight Fri.-Sat., $40 over 48 inches /122 cm tall, $20 under 48 inches/122 cm) houses two roller coasters, a 4-D motion simulator, laser beam mazes, a climbing wall, miniature golf, and vertigo-inducing amusement machines—all inside a pink plastic shell. The main teen and adult attractions are the coasters—El Loco and Canyon Blaster, the only indoor double-loop, double-corkscrew coaster in the world, with speeds up to 55 mph (88.5 kph), which is pretty rough. The 5-acre (2-ha) fun park can host birthday parties and corporate outings. Carnival games, food vendors, and souvenir booths not included in the pass give parents extra chances to spend money. It's not the Magic Kingdom, but it has rides to satisfy all ages and bravery levels. Besides, Las Vegas is supposed to be the *adult* Disneyland.

Area 15

A combination entertainment complex, shopping mall, and modern art gallery, **Area 15** (3215 S. Rancho Dr., 702/846-1900, www.area15.com, 4pm-10pm daily, free entry) offers a new experience every time you visit. The massive "experience box" warehouse space hosts elaborate, immersive, and interactive—but temporary—art installations alongside traditional mall retailers and food vendors. Customizable spaces host pay-as-you-play video and augmented reality arcades, escape rooms, thrill rides, and more.

The Void

Join the Rebel Alliance, escape supernatural forces, and defend humankind from rampaging . . . kittens? **The Void** (Grand Canal Shoppes, Venetian, 3377 Las Vegas Blvd. S., 385/323-0090, www.

thevoid.com, 10am-11pm Sun.-Thurs., 10am-midnight Fri.-Sat., $40) is a virtual reality experience that incorporates all the senses. Interactive sets put visitors in contact with Star Wars Jedi, Wreck-It Ralph, aliens, and menacing demons. Priced separately, each 20-minute adventure challenges teams to solve puzzles, shoot down UFOs, and otherwise use their wits and physical abilities to survive. In the attraction's original "Secrets of the Empire" scenario, guests go undercover as Imperial Stormtroopers to solve puzzles, escape traps, and fight villains to steal plans vital to the rebel cause. "Nicodemus: Demon of Evanishment" transports teams back to the ruins of the haunted 1894 Chicago World's Fair. And "Ralph Breaks VR" traps players in a wild video game that takes a frightening twist. There's usually a limited-engagement scenario, as well, to keep things fresh.

HyperX Esports Arena

The Luxor has fired the first shot in what could become a huge eSports market in Las Vegas. Its 30,000-square-foot (2,787-sq-m) **HyperX Esports Arena** (Luxor, 3900 S. Las Vegas Blvd., 702/723-2355, http://luxor.mgmresorts.com, 4pm-11pm Mon.-Thurs., 4pm-midnight Fri., noon-midnight Sat., noon-11pm Sun., $15 first hour, multihour discounts) welcomes virtual athletes to show off their driving, shooting, and fighting skills on a huge LED display using either console or PC controls. Even the Donkey Kong generation can relive their glory days on retro-gaming consoles. There's plenty of viewing space for the professional gaming tournaments the Luxor hosts, and the space includes a 50-foot(15.2-m) video wall, private streaming booths, and a network-quality television production studio so the next big thing in sports can be broadcast to fans around the world.

SlotZilla

For an up close, high-speed view of the Fremont Street Experience canopy and the iconic casino signs, take a zoom on **SlotZilla** (425 Fremont St., 702/678-5780, www.vegasexperience.com, 4pm-1am Mon.-Thurs., noon-1am Fri.-Sun., $29-49), a 1,750-foot-long (533-m) zip line that takes off from a the world's largest slot machine (only in Vegas, right?). Riders are launched horizontally, Superman-style, for a 40-mph (64.4-kph) slide. For the less adventurous, SlotZilla also operates a lower, slower, half-as-long version.

Wet 'n' Wild

With rides conjuring Las Vegas, the desert, and the Southwest, **Wet 'n' Wild** (7055 Fort Apache Rd., 702/979-1600, www.wetnwildlasvegas.com, 10am-8pm Sun.-Thurs., 10am-10pm Fri.-Sat. June-Aug., hours vary Apr.-May and Sept., $35, discounts for seniors, guests under 42 inches/107 cm tall, and entrance after 4pm) provides a welcome respite from the dry heat of southern Nevada. Challenge the Royal Flush Extreme, which whisks riders through a steep pipe before swirling them around a simulated porcelain commode and down the tube. The water park boasts 12 rides of varying terror levels along with a lazy river, wave pool, and Kiddie Cove. Guests must be over 42 inches (107 cm) tall to enjoy all the rides.

Cowabunga Bay

Wet 'n' Wild's competitor on the east side of town, **Cowabunga Bay** (900 Galleria Dr., Henderson, 702/850-9000, www.cowabungabayvegas.com, 11am-7pm daily June-Aug., limited days and hours Apr., May, and Sept., $40, under 48 inches/122 cm $30) has 10 waterslides, five pools, and the longest lazy river in the state.

Driving Experiences

Calling all gearheads! Vegas has the driving experience you crave. Got a Brickyard fantasy or a Daytona dream? Check out the **Richard Petty Driving Experience** or the **Mario Andretti Driving Experience** (Las Vegas Motor Speedway, 7000 Las Vegas Blvd. N., 704/886-2400, www.drivepetty.com, days and times vary, $109-4,600). Ride along with an instructor or take the green flag yourself and try to set a new track record. After extensive in-car and on-track safety training, the Rookie Experience ($499) lets NASCAR and IndyCar wannabes put their stock or open-wheel car through its paces for five minutes around the 1.5-mile (2.4-km) tri-oval. Participants also receive a lap-by-lap breakdown of their run, transportation to and from the Strip, and a tour of the Driving Experience Race Shop. Even more intense—and more expensive—experiences, with more laps and more in-depth instruction, are available. To feel the thrill without the responsibility, opt for the three-lap ride-along ($109) in a two-seat stock car with a professional driver at the wheel.

Exotics Racing (7065 Speedway Blvd., 702/405-7223, www.exoticsracing.com, 9am-5pm Fri.-Tues., $300-450 for five laps), **Dream Racing** (7000 Las Vegas Blvd. N., 702/605-300, www.dreamracing.com, $99-600 for five laps), and **Speed Vegas** (14200 Las Vegas Blvd. S., 702/789-0568, www.speedvegas.com, $39-99 per lap) offer similar pedal-to-the-metal thrills in Porsches, Ferraris, Lamborghinis, McLarens, and more. All offer add-ons such as videos of your drive, passenger rates, and ride-alongs with professional drivers.

Sports

Vegas Golden Knights

The city went gaga over the **Vegas Golden Knights** (702/645-4259, www.nhl.com/goldenknights), Sin City's first major-league franchise. And why not? All the team did was advance to the Stanley Cup finals in its first season, making the Golden Knights the most successful expansion franchise in the history of forever. Raucous fans, a booming sound system, a perennial Cup contender, and only-in-Vegas promotions make for a wild game-day experience at T-Mobile Arena. Tickets are hard to come by, especially when West Coast rivals or Original Six teams come calling. Check the resale sites, if you're willing to pay a premium.

In 2020, the team bought and moved the San Antonio Rampage of the American Hockey League to Henderson, a bedroom community south of Las Vegas. Renamed the **Henderson Silver Knights,** the Golden Knights' top minor-league affiliate played the 2020-2021 season at the Orleans Arena in Las Vegas and is scheduled to move into its home rink next season.

Las Vegas Raiders

The **Las Vegas Raiders** (510/864-5000, www.raiders.com) moved from Oakland in time for the 2020 season, playing the $2 billion retractable-roof Allegiant Stadium across I-15 from Mandalay Bay. Virtually every ticket is in the hands of season ticket-holders and resell sites, so prepare to pay a premium if you want to go. The new state-of-the-art stadium also will host University of Nevada Las Vegas football, international soccer, and other events.

Las Vegas Aces

A'ja Wilson, the 2018 draft's No. 1 overall pick, leads the **Las Vegas Aces** (http://aces.wnba.com, $17-57) of the WNBA. Owned by MGM Resorts, the Aces play their home games at the gaming company's Mandalay Bay Events Center.

Las Vegas Aviators

Major League Baseball shows no sign of following the NHL and NFL's lead in rushing to Las Vegas. Instead, die-hard baseball fans must settle for the **Las Vegas Aviators** (702/943-7200, www.milb.com/las-vegas, $18-60) of the Pacific Coast League. Fans of and players for the AAA affiliate of the Oakland A's at least can enjoy major-league facilities and amenities at the organization's ballpark

Side Trip to Hoover Dam

aerial view of the Hoover Dam

The 1,400-mile (2,253-km) Colorado River has been carving and gouging great canyons and valleys with its red sediment-laden waters for 10 million years. For 10,000 years Native Americans, the Spanish, and Mormon settlers coexisted with the fitful river, rebuilding after spring floods and withstanding the droughts that often reduced the mighty waterway to a muddy trickle in fall. But the 1905 flood convinced the Bureau of Reclamation to "reclaim" the West, primarily by building dams and canals. The most ambitious of these was Hoover Dam: 40 million cubic yards (30.5 million cubic m) of reinforced concrete, turbines, and transmission lines.

Hoover Dam remains an engineering marvel, attracting millions of visitors each year. It makes an interesting half-day escape from the glitter of Las Vegas, only 30 miles (48 km) to the north. The one-hour **Dam Tour** (every 30 minutes, 9:30am-3:30pm daily, $30 ages 8 and over) offers a guided exploration of its power plant and walkways. The half-hour **Power Plant Tour** ($15 adults, $12 children, seniors, and military, children under 4 and uniformed military free) focuses on the dam's construction and engineering with multimedia presentations, exhibits, docent talks, and a walk through the original construction tunnels. Admission to the visitors center is included with either tour; it's $10 if purchased separately. It includes 360-degree views of the bridge and the dam and a 3-D model with narration.

Getting There

The bypass bridge diverts traffic away from Hoover Dam, saving time and headaches for both drivers and dam visitors. Still, the **35-mile (56-km) drive** from central Las Vegas to a parking lot at the dam will take **45 minutes** or more. From the Strip, **I-15 South** connects with I-215 southeast of the airport, and **I-215 East** takes drivers to **I-11 South.** Take the Hoover Dam approach on **NV-172** at the Gold Strike hotel. NV-172 goes all the way to the dam **parking garage** ($10), which is convenient to the visitors center and dam tours, but free parking is available at turnouts on both sides of the dam for those willing to walk.

Drivers continuing to the **Grand Canyon** must retrace **NV-172** to **I-11** and cross the bypass bridge. I-11 continues to the Arizona state line, where it connects with **US-93,** which leads toward the canyon.

in Summerlin, just south of the Golden Knights' training facility.

Las Vegas Lights FC

The neon-striped **Lights** attract rowdy, dedicated futbol fans to **Cashman Field** (850 N. Las Vegas Blvd., 702/728-4625, www.lasvegaslightsfc.com, $15-75) downtown for its United Soccer League games.

Golf

A world-class golfing destination and home to the PGA Tour's Shriners Hospitals for Children Open, Las Vegas is chock-full of picturesque courses. All are eminently playable and fair, although the dry heat makes the greens fast and the city's valley location can make for some havoc-wreaking winds in the spring. Many Las Vegas courses, especially in recent years, have removed extraneous water-loving landscaping, opting for xeriscape and desert landscape, irrigating the fairways and greens with reclaimed water. Still, lush landscaping and tricky water holes abound. Greens fees and amenities range from affordable municipal-type courses to some of the most exclusive country clubs anywhere. The following is a selective list in each budget category. There are bargains, if you're willing to brave the scorching afternoon temperatures. Fees are exponentially higher in the early morning and evening.

The only course open to the public on the Strip is **Bali Hai** (5160 Las Vegas Blvd. S., 888/427-6678, www.balihaigolfclub.com, $79-129), next to Mandalay Bay on the south end of casino row. The South Pacific theme includes lots of lush green tropical foliage, deep azure ponds, and black volcanic outcroppings. A handful of long par-4s are fully capable of making a disaster of your scorecard even before you reach the par-3 sphincter-clenching 16th. Not only does it play to an island green, it comes with a built-in gallery where others can enjoy your discomfort while dining on Bali Hai's restaurant patio.

There's plenty of water to contend with at **Siena Golf Club** (10575 Siena Monte Ave., 702/341-9200, www.sienagolfclub.com, $71-79). Six small lakes, deep fairway bunkers, and desert scrub provide significant challenges off the tee, but five sets of tee boxes even things out for shorter hitters. The large, flattish greens are fair and readable. The first Las Vegas course to adopt an eco-friendly xeriscape design, **Painted Desert** (5555 Painted Mirage Rd., 702/645-2570, www.painteddesertgc.com, $35-50) uses cacti, mesquite, and other desert plants to separate its links-style fairways. The 6,323-yard (5,782-m), par-72 course isn't particularly challenging, especially if you're straight off the tee, making it a good choice for getting back to the fundamentals. At the other end of the price spectrum, the signature **Wolf Course at Paiute Golf Resort** (10325 Nu-Wav Kaiv Blvd., 702/ 658-1400, www.clubcorp.com, $99-209) includes a pack of 18 predatory holes over an expansive 7,604 yards (6,953 m). The longest course in Las Vegas, Wolf can reduce even accomplished players to howls of anguish with its radical undulations and pucker-inducing island green on 15.

Las Vegas Motor Speedway

Home to two events (Feb. and Sept.) in the Monster Energy NASCAR Cup Series, the **Las Vegas Motor Speedway** (7000 Las Vegas Blvd. N., 702/644-4444, www.lvms.com) is a racing omniplex. In addition to the superspeedway, a 1.5-mile (2.4-km) tri-oval for NASCAR races, the site also brings in dragsters to its 0.25-mile (0.4-km) strip; modifieds, late models, bandoleros, legends, bombers, and more to its paved oval; and off-roaders to its 0.5-mile (0.8-km) clay oval. There's also a motocross track, go-kart track, and road course. The multimillion-dollar Neon Garage in the speedway's infield brings fans up close with their favorite drivers and their crews, providing an unprecedented interactive fan experience. Neon Garage has unique and gourmet concession stands, live entertainment, and the winner's circle.

Boxing and Mixed Martial Arts

Las Vegas also retains the title as heavyweight boxing champion of the world. Nevada's legalized sports betting, its history, and the facilities at the MGM Grand Garden, Mandalay Bay Events Center, T-Mobile Arena, and other locations make it a natural for the biggest matches. For the megafights, expect to dole out big bucks to get inside the premier venues. The "cheap" seats at MGM and Mandalay Bay often cost a car payment and require the Hubble telescope to see any action. Ringside seats require a mortgage payment. Check the venues' websites for tickets. Fight fans can find a card pretty much every month March-October at Sam's Town, Sunset Station, Palms, or another midsize arena or showroom. The fighters are hungry, the matches are entertaining, and the cost is low, with tickets priced $15-100.

Mixed martial arts also continues to grow in popularity, with MGM and Mandalay Bay hosting UFC title fights about every other month. With the Ultimate Fighting Championship headquartered in Las Vegas, the city hosts numerous MMA events at the **UFC Apex** (6650 El Camino Rd., 832/608-3238).

Shopping

Malls

The most Strip-accessible of the traditional, non-casino-affiliated, indoor shopping complexes, **Fashion Show** (3200 Las Vegas Blvd. S., 702/369-8382, www.thefashionshow.com, 10am-9pm Mon.-Sat., 11am-7pm Sun.), across from the Wynn, is anchored by Saks Fifth Avenue, Neiman Marcus, Macy's, and Nordstrom. Not all the stores are upscale; Dick's Sporting Goods and Crocs also have storefronts. The mall gets its name from the 80-foot (24.4-m) retractable runway in the Great Hall, where resident retailers put on fashion shows on weekend afternoons. Must-shop stores include Papyrus, specializing in stationery and gifts centering on paper arts and crafts, and The Lego Store, where blockheads can find specialty building sets tied to movies, video games, and television shows. Dine alfresco at a Strip-side café, shaded by "the cloud," a 128-foot-tall (39-m) canopy that doubles as a projection screen.

If your wallet contains dozens of Ben Franklins, **The Shops at Crystals** (Aria, 3720 Las Vegas Blvd. S., 702/590-9299, www.simon.com, 11am-7pm Mon.-Sat., 11am-6pm Sun.) is your destination for impulse buys like a hand-woven Olimpia handbag from Bottega Veneta or a pair of calf leather oxfords from Berluti.

Parents can reward their children's patience with rides on cartoon animals, spaceships, and other kiddie favorites in the carpeted, clean play area at **Meadows Mall** (4300 Meadows Ln., 702/878-3331, www.meadowsmall.com, 11am-7pm Mon.-Sat., 11am-6pm Sun.), and there's also a carousel in addition to 140 stores and restaurants—all the usual mall denizens along with some interesting specialty shops. It's across the street from the Las Vegas Springs Preserve, so families can make a day of it. The **Boulevard Mall** (3528 S. Maryland Pkwy., 702/735-8268, www.boulevard-mall.com, 11am-7pm daily) is similar. It's in an older and less trendy setting, but a new facade, family attractions, and better dining are driving a comeback. The mall's interactive **SeaQuest Aquarium** (702/906-1901, www.visitseaqauest.com, noon-6pm daily, $12 adults, $9 children 2-12, $12 students, military, and seniors 55 and over) is a big draw, with shark and stingray encounters and educational exhibits about fish, birds, and reptiles.

A visit to **Town Square** (6605 Las Vegas Blvd. S., 702/269-5001, www.mytownsquarelasvegas.com, 10am-9pm Mon.-Thurs., 10am-10pm Fri.-Sat., 11am-8pm Sun.) is like a stroll through a favorite suburb. "Streets" wind between stores in Spanish, Moorish, and Mediterranean-style buildings. Mall stalwarts like Victoria's Secret and Abercrombie & Fitch are here, along with some unusual treats—Tommy Bahama's includes a café. Just as in a real town, the retail outlets surround a central square, which holds 13,000 square feet (1,208 sq m) of mazes, tree houses, and performance stages. Around holiday time, machine-made snowflakes drift down through the trees. Nightlife ranges from laid-back wine and martini bars to rousing live entertainment and the 18-screen Rave movie theater.

Easterners and Westerners alike revel in the wares offered at **Chinatown Plaza** (4205 Spring Mountain Rd., 702/221-8448, http://lvchinatownplaza.com, hours vary by store), a pan-Asian clearinghouse. Tea sets, silk robes, Buddha statuettes, Eastern herbal tinctures, and jade carvings are of particular interest, as is the Diamond Bakery, with its elaborate wedding cakes and sublime mango mousse cake. You'll also find authentic Chinese, Thai, Vietnamese, and other Asian restaurants here.

Casino Plazas

Almost two-thirds of the Las Vegas Strip's $19 billion in annual casino revenue comes from nongaming activities. Restaurants and hotel rooms are the biggest contributors, but upscale shopping plazas—many with tenants that would feel right at home on Rodeo Drive, Ginza, or the Champs-Élysées—increasingly are doing their part to put brass in casino investors' pockets.

Caesars Palace initiated the concept of Las Vegas as a shopping destination

Forum Shops

in 1992 when it unveiled the **Forum Shops** (3570 Las Vegas Blvd. S., 702/893-3807, www.caesars.com, 10am-8pm Sun.-Thurs., 10am-10pm Fri.-Sat.). Top-brand luxury stores coexist with fashionable hipster boutiques amid some of the best people-watching on the Strip. A stained-glass-domed pedestrian plaza greets shoppers as they enter the 175,000-square-foot (16,258-sq-m) expansion from the Strip. You'll find one of only two spiral escalators in the United States. The gods come alive hourly to extract vengeance in the *Fall of Atlantis* show, and you can check out the feeding of the fish in the big saltwater aquarium twice daily.

Part shopping center, part theater in the round, the **Miracle Mile** (Planet Hollywood, 3663 Las Vegas Blvd. S., 702/866-0703, www.miraclemileshopslv.com, 10am-11pm Sun.-Thurs., 10am-midnight Fri.-Sat.) is a delightful (or vicious, depending on your point of view) circle of shops, eateries, bars, and theaters. If your budget doesn't quite stand up to the Forum Shops, Miracle Mile could be just your speed. Low-cost shows include Beatles and Elvis tributes, the campy *Zombie Burlesque,* two variety shows, and family-friendly animal acts and magicians.

Las Vegas comedy icon Rita Rudner loves the **Grand Canal Shoppes** (Venetian, 3377 Las Vegas Blvd. S., 702/414-4525, www.grandcanalshoppes.com, 10am-11pm Sun.-Thurs., 10am-midnight Fri.-Sat.) because "Where else but in Vegas can you take a gondola to the Gap?" There's not really a Gap here. It would stick out like a sore thumb among the shops that line the canal among streetlamps and cobblestones under a frescoed sky. Nature gets a digital assist in the photos for sale at Peter Lik gallery, and at Houdini's Magic Shop the salespeople demonstrate some of the tricks for sale. The "Streetmosphere" includes strolling minstrels and specialty acts, and many of these entertainers find their way to St. Mark's Square for seemingly impromptu performances.

Hermès, Prada, Rolex, and Loro Piana count themselves among the tenants at the **Esplanades** (Wynn/Encore, 3131 Las Vegas Blvd. S., 702/770-7000, www.wynnlasvegas.com, 10am-11pm Sun.-Thurs., 10am-midnight Fri.-Sat.). Wide, curved skylights, fragrant flowers, and delicate artwork create a pleasant window-shopping experience. The **Wynn Plaza Shops** extend your shopping opportunities with stores focusing on fashion, jewelry, fragrances, and wellness.

Perfectly situated in the flourishing arts district, the **Downtown Container Park** (707 E. Fremont St., 702/359-9982, www.downtowncontainerpark.com, 11am-9pm Mon.-Thurs., 11am-10pm Fri.-Sat., 11am-8pm Sun.) packs 40 boutiques, galleries, bars, and bistros into their own shipping containers. Visitors are greeted by a giant metal praying mantis spewing flames from its antennae. The Dome ($9-15), an IMAX-like theater with reclining chairs, shows immersive, surround-sound video rock band performances and nature documentaries. Container Park is the centerpiece of the Fremont East District, an ambitious development aimed at reclaiming a formerly dicey area with eateries, bars, and shops.

Unless you're looking for a specific item or brand, or you're attracted to the atmosphere, attractions, architecture, or vibe of a particular Strip destination, you can't go wrong browsing the shopping center in your hotel. You'll find shops just as nice at **Le Boulevard** (Paris, 3655 Las Vegas Blvd. S., 702/946-7000, www.boulevardmall.com, 8am-2am daily), **Grand Bazaar Shops** (Bally's, 3645 Las Vegas Blvd. S., 702/967-4366 or 888/266-5687, http://grandbazaarshops.com, 10am-10pm Sun.-Thurs., 10am-11pm Fri.-Sat.), **The Linq** (3545 Las Vegas Blvd. S., 702/694-8100 or 866/328-1888, www.caesars.com/linq, shop and restaurant hours vary), and **Mandalay Place** (Mandalay Bay, 3950 Las Vegas Blvd. S., 702/632-7777 or 877/632-7800, http://mandalaybay.mgmresorts.com, 10am-11pm daily).

Food

In Vegas, every hotel typically boasts a signature restaurant, typically a steakhouse. Themed resorts favor related cuisines at the top of their restaurant offerings. Most hotels also still have 24-hour coffee shops (often with a graveyard or gambler's special) and several other eateries offering food from around the world.

Non-casino restaurants around town are also proliferating quickly. In the "good old days," casinos would lure gamblers with loss-leading hotel room and meal prices. But today, non-gaming revenue contributes mightily to the resorts' bottom line. There are still bargains to be had in casino cafés and casual restaurants, but they are not as ubiquitous as they once were. Of course, you can expect to pay top dollar for prime rib in the high-brow and celebrity-chef spots.

Upper Strip

Breakfast

It's all about the hen fruit at ★ **The Egg & I** (4533 W. Sahara Ave., 702/364-9686, www.theeggworks.com, 6am-3pm daily, $10-15). The eatery serves other breakfast fare as well, of course—the banana muffins and stuffed French toast are notable—but if you don't order an omelet, you're just being stubborn. It has huge portions, fair prices, and on-top-of-it service. Go! You'll also find other locations—called EggWorks—around town.

The retro-deco gaudiness of the neon decor and bachelor pad-esque sunken fire pit may not do wonders for a Vegas-size headache, but the tostada omelet at the **Peppermill Restaurant & Fireside Lounge** (2985 Las Vegas Blvd. S., 702/735-7635, www.peppermilllasvegas.com, daily 24 hours, $12-20) will give it what-for. For more fruit and less fire, try the French toast ambrosia.

Bright, airy with a touch of South Beach, **Tableau** (Wynn, 3131 Las Vegas Blvd. S., 702/770-3330, www.wynnlasvegas.com, 7am-2:30pm daily, $20-25), overlooking the pools from the garden atrium, changes its menu to suit the season. Any meal is a treat here, but the pumpkin French toast with cinnamon and brown sugar pecan cream cheese makes breakfast the most important meal of the day.

French

The pink accents at **Pamplemousse** (400 E. Sahara Ave., 702/733-2066, www.pamplemousserestaurant.com, 5pm-10pm daily, $35-56) hint at the name's meaning (grapefruit) and set the stage for romance. The cuisine is so fresh that the menu changes daily. Specialties include leg and breast of duck in cranberry-raspberry sauce and a rosemary and pistachio rack of lamb. Save room for chocolate soufflé.

Italian

Long a hangout for the Rat Pack, athletes, presidents, and certain Sicilian "businessmen," **Piero's** (355 Convention Center Dr., 702/369-2305, http://pieroscuisine.com, 5:30pm-10pm daily, $40-60) still attracts the celebrity set with leather booths, stone fireplace, stellar service, and assurance they won't be bothered by autograph hounds. The menu hasn't changed much since the goodfellas started coming here in the early 1980s; it's heavy (and we do mean "heavy") on the veal, breading, cheese, and wine sauce.

Feel free to grab (the English translation of the café's name) and go or claim a table at **Prendi** (Sahara, 2535 Las Vegas Blvd. S., 702/761-7000, http://saharalasvegas.com, 7am-7pm daily, $10-15). Breakfast sweets like a homemade pop tart draw the crowd, but the restaurant also makes fine sandwiches of curried chicken salad or smoked salmon.

Steak

Chef José Andrés doesn't want guests at ★ **Bazaar Meat** (2535 Las Vegas Blvd. S., 702/761-7610, http://saharalasvegas.com Sun.-Thurs. 5:30pm-10pm, Fri.-Sat. 5:30pm-11pm, $65-140) ordering a huge bone-in rib eye, rack of lamb, or inch-thick tuna steak. He wants you to try them all. His Spanish-influenced meat-centric dishes are meant to be shared. The restaurant's decor reinforces that aim with long communal tables, open cooking stations, and a small gaming area.

The perfectly cooked steaks and attentive service that once attracted Frank Sinatra, Nat "King" Cole, Natalie Wood, and Elvis are still trademarks at **Golden Steer** (308 W. Sahara Ave., 702/384-4470, www.goldensteerlasvegas.com, 4:30pm-10:30pm Tues.-Sat., $45-65). A gold rush motif and 1960s swankiness still abide here, along with classics like crab cakes, big hunks of beef, and Caesar salad prepared tableside.

Vegas Views

The 360-seat, 360-degree **Top of the World** (The Strat, 2000 Las Vegas Blvd. S., 702/380-7711 or 800/998-6937, www.topoftheworldlv.com, 11am-11pm daily, $65-85), on the 106th floor of The Strat SkyPod more than 800 feet (244 m) above the Strip, makes a complete revolution once every 80 minutes, giving you the full city panorama during dinner. The views of Vegas defy description, and the food is a recommendable complement. Order the seabass and leeks or bone-in ribeye. It's even money that you will witness (or receive) an offer of marriage during your meal. If you're the one popping the question, ask about their proposal packages.

Center Strip

Asian

Sushi is the specialty at **Tao Asian Bistro** (Venetian, 3377 Las Vegas Blvd. S., 702/388-8338, www.taolasvegas.com, 5pm-midnight daily, $35-50), but we prefer the pan-Asian dishes—the roasted Thai Buddha chicken is our pick. Tear your eyes away from the decor that is a trip through Asian history, including imperial koi ponds and a floating Buddha to sample the extensive sake selection.

Italian

It's no surprise that a casino named after the most romantic of Italian cities would be home to one of the best Italian restaurants around. **Canaletto** (Venetian, 3377 Las Vegas Blvd. S., 702/733-0070, www.venetian.com, noon-9pm Sun.-Thurs., noon-midnight Fri.-Sat., $25-35), of course, focuses on Venetian cuisine and overlooks the Grand Canal. The kitchen staff perform around the grill and rotisserie—a demonstration kitchen—creating sumptuously authentic dishes under a high-vaulted ceiling. The spicy *salsiccia picante* thin-crust pizza gets our vote.

Just around the corner from the Strip

near the Flamingo, **Battista's Hole in the Wall** (4041 Linq Ln., 702/732-1424, www.battistaslasvegas.com, 4:30pm-10pm, $25-35) is a locals' favorite. As the name suggests, Battista's is tucked into an otherwise nondescript commercial center. A huge traditional Italian menu and even bigger portions invite diners to linger over wine (a bottle of house red is included at each table) and coffee while soaking up the old-school vibe.

Seafood

Shrimp, lobster, mussels, and more are served at **Oyster Bar** (Harrah's, 3475 Las Vegas Blvd. S., 702/369-5000, www.caesars.com/harrahs-las-vegas, 11:30am-11pm Sun.-Thurs., 11:30am-1am Fri.-Sat., $20-40). But stick with the eponymous bivalve in all its glorious forms—grilled, fried, Rockefeller, or Royale.

Southern

Southern hospitality reigns at ★ **Yardbird** (Venetian, 3355 Las Vegas Blvd. S., 702/297-6541, 11am-11pm Mon.-Fri, 9:30am-11pm Sat.-Sun., $38-50). The dinner menu is small, but when the fried chicken is this good, there's really no reason to look further. Sides are classic and hearty, including the likes of mac-and-cheese and grits that make the perfect accompaniment.

Vegas Views

The Bellagio's dancing fountains and the majestic Caesars Palace provide the eye candy at **Giada** (Cromwell, 3595 Las Vegas Blvd. S., 702/442-3271, www.giadadelaurentiis.com, 8am-2:30pm and 5pm-11pm daily, $35-65), opened by celebrity chef Giada De Laurentiis. The Italian entrées are specialties; order a spinach ricotta pizzette and split an antipasti platter for a nourishing brunch. Watch the chefs hard at work in the open kitchen.

Strip views await at **VooDoo Steakhouse** (Rio, 3700 W. Flamingo Rd., 702/777-7800, www.caesars.com/rio-las-vegas, 5pm-10:30pm daily, $55-80), along with steaks with a N'awlins Creole and Cajun touch. Getting to the restaurant and the lounge requires a minithrill ride to the top of the Rio tower in the glass elevator. The Rio contends that the restaurant is on the 51st floor and the lounge is on the 52nd floor, but they're really on the 41st and 42nd floors, respectively—Rio management dropped floors 40-49 as the number 4 has an ominous connotation in Chinese culture. Whatever floors they're on, the VooDoo double-decker provides a great view of the Strip. The food and drink are expensive and tame, but the fun is in the overlook, especially if you eat or drink outside on the decks. Diners get free entry into VooDoo nightclub.

Lower Strip

Asian

Lantern-like light fixtures, dark wood, and silvery illuminated strands evoke bamboo forests and silk at **Lemongrass** (Aria, 3730 Las Vegas Blvd. S., 702/590-8670, http://aria.mgmresorts.com, 6pm-11pm Sun.-Thurs., 6pm-2am Fri.-Sat, $15-25). The food is a nifty mix of authentic Thai and Asian fusion. Offerings from the satay bar make a satisfying dinner. You can choose your own spiciness level, but exercise caution: The scale runs hot.

Chinese art in a Hong Kong bistro setting with fountain and lake views makes **Jasmine** (Bellagio, 3600 Las Vegas Blvd. S., 702/693-8865, http://bellagio.mgmresorts.com, 5:30pm-10pm daily, $50-70) one of the most visually striking Chinese restaurants in town. The food is European-influenced Cantonese.

East meets West at **Red Lotus** (Tropicana, 3801 Las Vegas Blvd. S., 702/739-2222, www2.troplv.com, 11am-11pm, $15-25), whose chef earned his stripes at restaurants in Hong Kong and Italy before bringing his talents to Las

Vegas. Spice fans should try the green curry chicken; more sensitive palates could opt for the honey walnut shrimp.

Breakfast

The provocatively named **Eggslut** (Cosmopolitan, 3708 Las Vegas Blvd. S., 702/698-2344, www.cosmopolitanlasvegas.com, Sun.-Thurs. 7am-1pm, Fri.-Sat. 7am-3pm, $10-15) takes an innovative approach to breakfast sandwiches. Egg McMuffin this ain't, with brioche buns, scrambled or sunny side up eggs, and fresh ingredients like caramelized onions, chives, and arugula.

The **Veranda** (Four Seasons, 3960 Las Vegas Blvd. S., 702/632-5121, www.fourseasons.com, 6:30am-10pm Mon.-Fri., 7am-10pm Sat.-Sun., $30-45) transforms itself from a light, airy, indoor-outdoor breakfast and lunch nook into a late dinner spot oozing with Mediterranean ambience and a check total worthy of a Four Seasons restaurant. As you might expect from the name, dining on the terrace is a favorite among well-to-do locals, especially for brunch on spring and fall weekends. Tiramisu French toast? Yes, please! Dinner here, with wine, dessert, and tip, can easily run $100 per person.

French and Continental

The steaks and seafood at ★ **Mon Ami Gabi** (Paris, 3655 Las Vegas Blvd. S., 702/944-4224, www.monamigabi.com, 7am-11pm daily, $35-55) are comparable to those at any fine Strip establishment—at about half the price. It's a bistro, so you know the crepes and other lunch specials are terrific, but you're better off coming for dinner. Try the baked goat cheese appetizer.

When you name your restaurant after a maestro, you're setting some pretty high standards for your food. Fortunately, **Picasso** (Bellagio, 3600 Las Vegas Blvd. S., 702/693.8865, http://bellagio.mgmresorts.com, 5:30pm-9:30pm Wed.-Mon., $113-123) is up to the self-inflicted challenge. Because of limited seating in its cubist-inspired dining room and a small dining time window, the restaurant has a couple of prix fixe menus. It's seriously expensive, and if you include Kobe beef, lobster, wine pairings, and a cheese course, you and a mate could easily leave several pounds heavier and $500 lighter.

Gastropub

Book a table on the Brooklyn Bridge for some people-watching on the Strip at **Tom's Urban** (New York New York, 3790 Las Vegas Blvd. S., 702/740-6766, http://newyorknewyork.mgmresorts.com, Sun.-Thurs. 7pm-2am, Fri.-Sat.-7pm-3am, $15-25). Share some small plates or dig into traditional bar food like tacos, pizzas, and sliders.

Shed your culinary mores and enjoy as chef Shawn McClain blurs the lines between avant-garde and comfort food at **Libertine Social** (Mandalay Bay, 3950 Las Vegas Blvd. S., 702/632-7558, http://mandalaybay.mgmresorts.com, 5pm-10:30pm daily, $35-55).

Pizza

With lines snaking out its unmarked entrance, in a dark alleyway decorated with record covers, **Secret Pizza** (Cosmopolitan, 3708 Las Vegas Blvd. S., 3rd Fl., 702/698-7860, 11am-2am Wed.-Sun, slices $5-6) is not so secret anymore. Located next to Blue Ribbon Sushi on the Cosmopolitan's third floor, it's a great place to get a quick, greasy slice.

Seafood

Only the Atlantic's salt air is missing from the ultra-casual and family-friendly **Fulton Fish Frye** (New York, New York, 3790 S Las Vegas Blvd. S., 702/740-6969, 11am-11pm daily, $15-25), where the clam chowder in a bread bowl rules. The fried fish and seafood are great too, but, oh, that chowder!

Partially housed in what looks like a modern-art latticed hornet's nest, **Mastro's Ocean Club** (Shops at Crystals, 3720 Las Vegas Blvd. S., 702/798-7115, www.mastrosrestaurants.com, 5pm-11pm daily, $60-100) is dubbed "The Treehouse." The restaurant inside offers standard top-of-the-line dishes elevated through preparation and atmosphere. The sushi menu is limited but a perfectly viable option.

Steak

The care used by the small farms from which Tom Colicchio's **Craftsteak** (MGM Grand, 3799 Las Vegas Blvd. S., 702/891-7318, www.craftsteaklasvegas.com, 5pm-10pm Sun.-Thurs., 5pm-10:30pm Fri.-Sat., $40-70) buys its ingredients is evident in the full flavor of the excellently seasoned steaks and chops. Spacious with gold, umber, and light woodwork, Craftsteak's decor is conducive to good times with friends and family and isn't overbearing or intimidating.

Vegas Views

Paris's **Eiffel Tower Restaurant** (Paris, 3655 Las Vegas Blvd. S., 702/948-6937, http://eiffeltowerrestaurant.com, 11:30am-3pm and 5pm-11pm daily, $40-80) hovers 100 feet (30.5 m) above the Strip. Your first "show" greets you when the glass elevator opens onto the organized chaos of chef Jean Joho's kitchen. Order the soufflé, have a glass of wine, and bask in the romantic piano strains as the bilingual culinary staff perform delicate French culinary feats, with Bellagio's fountains as a backdrop.

Downtown

Asian

A perfect little eatery for the budding bohemia of East Fremont Street, ★ **Le Thai** (523 E. Fremont St., 702/778-0888, www.lethaivegas.com, 11am-11pm Mon.-Thurs., 11am-midnight Fri., noon-midnight Sat., 4pm-10pm Sun., $12-25) attracts a diverse clientele ranging from ex-yuppies to body-art lovers. Most come for the three-color curry, and you should too. There's nothing especially daring on the menu, but the *pad prik, ga pow,* and garlic fried rice are better than what's found at many Strip restaurants that charge twice as much. Choose your spice level wisely; Le Thai does not mess around.

French and Continental

Hugo's Cellar (Four Queens, 202 E. Fremont St., 702/385-4011, www.hugoscellar.com, 5pm-10pm daily, $55-75) is romance from the moment each woman in your party receives her red rose until the last complimentary chocolate-covered strawberry is devoured. Probably the best gourmet room for the money, dimly lit Hugo's is located below the casino floor, in a faux wine cellar, shutting it off from the hubbub above. It is pricey, but the inclusion of sides, fruits, a cheese lavosh, and salad—prepared tableside with your choice of ingredients—helps ease the sticker shock. Sorbet is served between courses. The house appetizer is the Hot Rock—four meats sizzling on a lava slab; mix and match the meats with the dipping sauces.

Italian

Decidedly uncave-like with bright lights, frescoes, and jade-colored chairs, **Grotto** (Golden Nugget, 129 E. Fremont St., 702/386-8341, www.goldennugget.com, 4pm-midnight daily, $16-28) offers top-quality northern Italian-influenced pastas and pizzas. Share a side of pepperoni mac-and-cheese.

Mexican

Some of the best tapas in town, burritos, and beer are on tap at **Cadillac Mexican Kitchen** (Golden Nugget, 129 East Fremont St., 702/386-8242, www.goldennugget.com, 4pm-11pm Mon.-Thurs., 11am-11pm Fri.-Sun., $15-25). A platter of wings, a couple of shrimp tacos, and a bucket of suds, and you and your buds are all set for kickoff. TVs ring the bar, and big screens are placed strategically around the dining area.

Seafood

The prime rib gets raves, but the seafood and the prices are the draw at **Second Street Grill** (Fremont, 200 Fremont St., 702/385-3232, www.fremontcasino.com, 5pm-10pm Wed.-Sun., $30-40). The grill bills itself as "American contemporary with Pacific Rim influence." The menu features steaks and chops, but do yourself a favor and order the crab legs with lemon ginger butter. If you can't shake your inner landlubber, the gorgonzola New York strip should do the trick.

Steaks and seafood get equal billing on the menu at **Triple George** (201 N. 3rd St., 702/384-2761, www.triplegeorgegrill.com, 11am-10pm Mon.-Fri., 4pm-10pm Sat.-Sun., $28-50), but again, the charbroiled salmon and the martinis are what brings the suave crowd back for more.

Steak

Fronted by ex-mob mouthpiece and former Las Vegas mayor Oscar Goodman, **Oscar's** (Plaza, 1 S. Main St., 702/386-7227, www.oscarslv.com, 5pm-10pm daily, $40-70) is dedicated to hizzoner's favorite things in life—beef, booze, and broads. With dishes named, apparently, for former wiseguy clients—Fat Herbie, Crazy Phil, No Nose, and Moose, you're in for an Old Vegas treat, full of the scents of leather, cigars, and broiling steaks.

Vegetarian

This is not your mother's beet loaf and tofurkey. While ★ **VegeNation** (616 E. Carson Ave #120, 702/366-8515, www.vegenationlv.com, 11am-8pm daily, $10-15) offers plant-based meat-mimicking substitutes, the best dishes don't try to hide their roots, with savory items likes of big, er, meaty, portobellos, avocado tacos, and eggplant with cashew ricotta cheese.

Off the Strip

You'll come for the $7.99 filet-cut sirloin dinner special at **Village Pub and Café** (Ellis Island, 4178 Koval Ln., 702/733-8901, www.ellisislandcasino.com, $10-20), but the fish-and-chips and apple pecan salad deserve equal billing. Most of the fare here is filling and cheap.

Thai Spice (4433 W. Flamingo Rd., 702/362-5308, www.thaispicelv.com, 11am-10pm Mon.-Thurs., 11am-10:30pm Fri., 11:30am-10:30pm Sat., $10-20) gives Le Thai a run for its baht as best Thai restaurant in town; the soups, noodle dishes, traditional curries, pad thai, and egg rolls are all well prepared. Tell your waiter how hot you want your food on a scale of 1 to 10. The big numbers peg the needle on the Scoville scale, so beware.

Accommodations

Casino accommodations offer the closest thing to a sure bet as you will find in Vegas: the most convenient setting for a vacation that includes gambling, dining, drinking, and show-going. See the *Casinos* section for information on these rooms. That being said, if you don't want to expose yourself or your kids to the smoke or vices on display at casinos, or need proximity to the airport, you will find plenty of choices. Even more affordable digs can be had at smaller motels in locations close to the Strip, downtown, the convention center, the university, and other high-traffic areas.

Even with more than 150,000 rooms, Vegas sells out completely on many three-day weekends, for major sports betting events like the Super Bowl and March Madness, big local events like music festivals, the National Finals Rodeo, and NASCAR week, and over U.S. and international holidays such as Chinese New

Year, Cinco de Mayo, New Year's Eve, and Valentine's Day. There are some relative quiet times, such as the three weeks before Christmas and July-August, when the mercury doesn't drop below 100°F (37.8°C). Finding the perfect room should not be a problem then.

If you're just coming for the weekend, keep in mind that many major hotels don't even let you check in on a Saturday night. You can stay Friday and Saturday, but not Saturday alone. It may be easier to find a room Sunday-Thursday, when there aren't as many large conventions, sporting events, or getaway visitors from Southern California. Almost all the room packages and deep discounts are only available on these days.

Most Strip hotels charge **resort fees** of $20-40 per night. These charges are not included in the quoted room rate. Many downtown hotel casinos, as well as the midlevel national chains, have not yet resorted to resort fees.

Hotels

Feel like royalty at City Center's **Waldorf Astoria** (City Center, 3752 Las Vegas Blvd. S., 800/925-3673 or 702/590-8888, www.waldorfastorialasvegas.com, $180-325). City View and Strip View rooms feature floor-to-ceiling windows and contemporary style. A master control panel in each of the modern rooms sets the atmosphere to your liking, controlling the lights, temperature, window curtains, music, and more. Valet closets allow hotel staff to deliver items to your room without entering your unit.

Rome meets Tokyo at **Nobu** (3570 Las Vegas Blvd. S., 800/727-4923, www.caesars.com, $199-319), Caesars Palace's venture into the boutique market. Reflecting the same style and attention to detail that highlight chef Nobu Matsuhisa's eponymous restaurants, the first Nobu hotel includes teak and cherry blossoms, as well as stylized dragon artwork and traditional Japanese prints. Guests are greeted with hot tea, and the nightly turndown service includes scented sleep oils and customizable bath and pillow menus. Nobu restaurant and lounge (5pm-11pm Sun.-Thurs., 5pm-midnight Fri.-Sat., $35-65) occupies the ground floor, so the indulgences can continue through the cocktail hour and mealtime.

Every guest room is a suite at the **Signature** (145 E. Harmon Ave., 702/797-6000 or 877/612-2121, www.signaturemgmgrand.com, $159-288) at MGM Grand. Even the standard Deluxe suite is a warm-toned and roomy 550 square feet (51.1 sq m) and includes a king bed, kitchenette, and spa tub. Most of the 1,728 smoke-free guest rooms in the gleaming 40-story tower include private balconies with Strip views, and guests have access to the complimentary 24-hour fitness center, three outdoor pools, a business center, and free wireless Internet throughout the hotel. A gourmet deli and acclaimed room service satisfy noshing needs.

Representing for many the definition of opulence, the **Four Seasons** (Mandalay Bay, 3960 Las Vegas Blvd. S., 702/632-5000, www.fourseasons.com, $199-319) entices guests with vibrant colors, lush landscaping, and an elaborate porte cochere that sets the art deco lemonade-on-the-veranda mood that induces a stress-shedding sigh at first sight. Floor-to-ceiling windows command Strip or mountain views from atop Mandalay Bay. The **Spa** (702/632-5302), which includes a nail bar, offers treatments that relax all the senses, from aromatherapy and eucalyptus steam to menthol wraps and citrus infusions.

Farther removed from the Strip, the panoramas from the top floors of the 18-story **Berkley** (8280 Dean Martin Dr., 702/224-7400, www.theberkleylasvegas.com, $179-249) rank among the best you will find. Studio units sleep two, but families can go up to two bedrooms to accommodate six comfortably. Fully equipped kitchens, laundry rooms, and living areas with 49-inch (124.5-cm) TVs provide a home-away-from-home experience. It's across the street from the Silverton Casino, so there is plenty of gaming action, plus dining options, and a shuttle can whisk you away to primo shopping venues. Still, you will want to rent a car to conveniently take in the whole Vegas experience.

Offering sophisticated accommodations and amenities without the hubbub of a rowdy casino, the **Renaissance** (3400 Paradise Rd., 702/784-5700, $132-219) has bright, airy standard guest rooms in slate-and-chrome decor that come complete with triple-sheeted 300-thread-count Egyptian cotton beds with down comforters and duvets, walk-in showers, full tubs, 42-inch (106.7-cm) flat-panel TVs, a business center, and high-speed Internet. Upper-floor guest rooms overlook the Wynn golf course. The pool and whirlpool are outside, and the concierge can score show tickets and tee times. Onyx- and burgundy-clad **Envy Steakhouse** (6:30am-11am and 5pm-10pm daily, $40-70) has a few poultry and seafood entrées, but the Angus beef is the draw.

Catering to families and vacationers seeking a more "residential" stay, **Platinum** (211 E. Flamingo Rd., 702/365-5000 or 877/211-9211, www.theplatinumhotel.com, $139-229) treats both guests and the environment with kid gloves. The resort uses the latest technology to reduce its carbon footprint through such measures as low-energy lighting throughout, ecofriendly room thermostats, and motion sensors to turn lights off when restrooms are unoccupied. Guests also can use PressReader to access thousands of digital publications. Standard suites are an expansive 910 square feet (84.5 sq m) of muted designer furnishings and accents, and they include all modern conveniences, such as high-speed Internet, high-fidelity sound systems, full kitchens, and oversize tubs. **Kil@wat** (6am-2pm daily, $12-20), with sleek silver decor accented with dark woods, is a feast for the eyes and the palate for breakfast and lunch.

The one- and two-bedroom condominium suites at **Desert Rose** (5051 Duke Ellington Way, 702/739-7000 or 888/732-8099, www.shellhospitality.com, $142-249) are loaded, with new appliances and granite countertops in the kitchen as well as private balconies or patios outside. One-bedrooms are quite large, at 650 square feet (60.4 sq m), and sleep four comfortably. Rates vary widely, but depending on your needs and travel dates, you might find a deal within walking distance of several casinos and the monorail.

No two rooms are the same at the **Artisan** (1501 W. Sahara Ave., 702/214-4000, $75-135), located 1 mile (1.6 km) northwest of the convention center. Most include playful, classic-style prints in baroque frames, dark wood, and bold colors; schemes range from burgundy to gold to emerald. The **Artisan Lounge** hosts one of the best early-night weekday parties in town. And you can nix the tan lines at the European-style (read: topless) pool.

Motels

Motels along the Lower Strip are well placed to visit all the new big-brand casino resorts. Prices here are much lower than at the resorts but higher than those to the north, reflecting premium real estate costs. Those costs also all but price out independent motels as well. An exception is **Hotel Galaxy** (5201 Dean Martin Dr., 702/778-7600, www.hotelgalaxyvegas.com, $69-129), off Flamingo and convenient to the Strip and the airport. The pool is clean, and the butterscotch-colored rooms come with a microwave and minifridge. You can also take your pick of established brands like **Travelodge Las Vegas Center Strip** (3735 Las Vegas Blvd. S., 702/736-3443, www.travelodgevegasstrip.com, $59-99) and a string of others lining nearby

Southwest Side Trip

Las Vegas is located just outside the "Grand Circle"—the largest concentration of national parks and monuments in the country—making it a great base for visiting colorful canyons, inspiring geological formations, and living history. The **Grand Canyon** should be the first Southwestern park on your list, but nine other national parks are within 500 miles (805 km) of Glitter Gulch.

Zion National Park is the most accessible (160 mi/260 km from Las Vegas), a straight shot up I-15 North for 128 miles (206 km) to UT-9 for the final 32-mile (52-km) stretch to the park. Zion's imposing monoliths, such as the Court of the Patriarchs, whose sandstone behemoths are named for Abraham, Isaac, and Jacob, contrast with the three serene Emerald Pools that reflect the region's features.

Continue on to **Bryce Canyon** (260 mi/420 km from Las Vegas; 72 mi/116 km from Zion), where it's easy to see why ancient Paiute people believed the narrow hoodoos were people turned to stone by angry gods. The haunting formations are the result of eons of the winds' and waters' masonry skills. From Zion, continue northeast on UT-9 for 13 miles (20.9 km) to US-89 North for 43 miles (69 km) to UT-12 East. Continue 14 miles (22.5 km) to UT-63 South for 2 miles (3.2 km) to the park gate.

Northeast of Bryce, **Capitol Reef National Park** (roughly 350 mi/565 km from Las Vegas; 112 mi/180 km from Bryce Canyon) is a vast network of natural bridges, domes, and cliffs created by the Waterpocket Fold, which was formed during an ancient geologic upheaval. From Bryce Canyon, take UT-63/Johns Valley Road/UT-22 North for 45 miles (72 km) to UT-62 North for another 26 miles (42 km). Turn right onto Browns Lane for 3 miles (4.8 km). Then turn right onto UT-24 East/East 300 Street South for the final 38 miles (61 km).

Farther afield from Las Vegas are **Arches National Park** (455 mi/735 km) and **Canyonlands National Park** (465 mi/750 km). The backdrop for any self-respecting Western, Arches is home to Delicate Arch, as well as more than 2,000 other natural arches, fins, towers, and crevasses. I-15 will get you most of the way to either of these eastern Utah parks. To get to Arches, take I-15 North for 425 miles (685 km) to US-191 and follow it for 27 miles (43 km) to Arches Entrance Road. Canyonlands was formed by the Colorado River system, which carved out its unique buttes, mesas, and sandstone spires. It's only 26 miles (42 km) from Arches: Take US-191 North for 7 miles (11.2 km) to UT-313; continue for 15 miles (24 km) to Grand View Point Road/Island in the Sky Road for 4 miles (6.4 km). To get to these two parks from Las Vegas, take I-15 for 245 miles (395 km) to I-70 toward Denver. Follow I-70 for 180 miles (290 km), then take US-191 for 21 miles (34 km). A right turn onto UT-313 West will take you the last 19 miles (31 km) to Canyonlands; it's just a little farther to Arches.

Nevada's only national park, **Great Basin** (295 mi/475 km from Las Vegas) is home to a glacier, the oldest living trees in the world (bristlecone pines), Nevada's second-highest peak (the majestic 13,000-ft/3,962-m Wheeler Peak), and the extensive Lehman Caves system, complete with stalagmites, stalactites, and rare shield formations. From Las Vegas, take US-93 North for 285 miles (460 km) to NV-487 West for 5 miles (8 km) then to NV-488 West for the final 5 miles (8 km).

Several Vegas-based tour companies offer full-day, round-trip excursions to Zion and Bryce Canyon National Parks. The professional guides at **Adventure Photo Tours** (702/889-8687 or 888/363-8687, 6am-8:30pm Tues. and Thurs. and by appointment, $319) take photographers and sightseers to both parks, serving a continental breakfast, lunch, bottled water, and snacks. **Viator** (6am-9pm Thurs., $277) offers a similar service.

Dean Martin Drive north and south of Allegiant Stadium.

There are several low-cost independent motels north of the Strip resorts and downtown, scattered along Las Vegas Boulevard and east of downtown along Boulder Highway. Few are recommendable, unless you merely want a place to crash. Just steps from the Fremont Street Experience, the **Downtowner** (129 N. 8th St., 702/384-1441, www.downtownerlv.com, $39-69) is a case in point. Its minimalist rooms are white with red, gray, and black accents. The pool and lounge areas are luxuries in this neighborhood and price range though you have to cross the street to get to the pool. A six-hole putting course is a neat touch. A reasonable choice east of the Strip, the three-story **Mardi Gras** (3500 Paradise Rd., 702/731-2020, www.mardigrasinn.com, $69-122) boasts largest-in-class 430-square-foot (40-sq-m) rooms, a free airport shuttle, and on-site slot casino. Similarly, **Fortune Hotel & Suites** (325 E. Flamingo Rd., 703/732-9100, www.fortunelasvegas.com, $55-90) offers a free ride to and from the airport and a clean pool. Rooms are 300 square feet (27.9 sq m).

Hostels

It's hard to beat these places for budget accommodations. They offer rock-bottom prices for no-frills "rack rooms," singles, and doubles. Closest to the Strip, **Hostel Cat** (1236 Las Vegas Blvd. S., 702/380-6902, http://hostelcat.com, $25-40) puts the focus on group activities, organizing pub crawls, beer pong and video game tournaments, movie nights, and more. There's even a 24-hour party table where there are always interesting fellow travelers to talk to. Book early if you want a private room. A bunk in a 6- or 10-person rack room is easier to come by.

Sin City Hostel (1208 Las Vegas Blvd. S., 702/868-0222, www.sincityhostel.com, $22-35) is reserved for international, student, and non-local travelers only (ID required). Perfect for the starving student's budget, rates include breakfast. The hostel features a barbecue pit, a basketball court, and Wi-Fi. Management organizes outings and on-site games and mixers.

Six blocks east of the downtown resorts, **Las Vegas Hostel** (1322 Fremont St., 702/385-1150 or 800/550-8958, http://lasvegashostel.net, $18-65) has a swimming pool and a hot tub. The rates include a make-your-own pancake breakfast, billiards and TV room, and wireless Internet connections. The hostel also arranges trips to the Strip and visits to the Grand Canyon and other outdoorsy attractions. Or you can borrow a bike and explore the area on your own.

RV Parking

A number of casinos have attached RV parks. Other casinos allow RVs to park overnight in their parking lots but have no facilities.

The best bet on the Strip, thanks almost exclusively to its location, the **RV Park at Circus Circus** (2880 Las Vegas Blvd. S., 702/794-3757 or 800/444-2472, www.circuscircus.com, $44-50) is big (170 spaces, all paved, including more than 70 pull-throughs), with a few grassy islands and shade trees. RVing families will appreciate the hotel/casino amenities and entertainment. The convenience store is open 24 hours daily. Ten minutes spent learning where the Industrial Road back entrance is will save hours of sitting in traffic on Las Vegas Boulevard. The free dog wash in the off-leash park is a nice touch.

Again, convenience and amenities, rather than lush surroundings, are the attraction at **Main Street Station RV Park** (200 N. Main St., 702/387-1896, $24-45). The showers and laundry have *hot* water, and the Fremont Street casinos are an easy walk away. Downtown has some struggles with street crime after dark, but Main Street's security patrol is diligent, and safety is not an issue. Highway noise and Vegas's famous flashing neon, however, may be, come bedtime.

Boulder Highway, which connects downtown with Lake Mead to the southeast, is RV park central. The cleanest and best-maintained along this road, the adults-only **Las Vegas RV Resort** (3890 S. Nellis Blvd., 866/846-5432 or 702/451-8005, www.lasvegasrvresort.com, $33-51) has level asphalt pads and palm tree landscaping. A guard is on-site 24 hours, and the laundry, restrooms, pool area, and fitness center are spotless. **Las Vegas KOA at Sam's Town** (5225 Boulder Hwy., 702/454-8055, http://koa.com, $41-50) has nearly 300 spaces for motor homes, all with full hookups and 20-, 30-, and 50-amp power. It's mostly a paved parking lot with spacious sites, a heated (if a bit dated) pool, and a spa; the rec hall has a pool table and a kitchen. And, of course, it's near the bowling, dining, and movie theater in the casino. **Arizona Charlie's Boulder** (4445 Boulder Hwy., 702/951-5911, www.arizonacharliesboulder.com, $38-40) has 239 spaces and weekly rates. The clubhouse contains a large-screen TV, fitness room, and pool tables. Spaces at the back are quieter and closer to the dog run but farther from the laundry room and pool area.

South of the airport, **Oasis RV Resort** (2711 W. Windmill Ln., 800/566-4707, www.oasislasvegasrvresort.com, $60-82) is directly across I-15 from the Silverton Casino. Oasis has more than 800 snug spaces with huge date palms and a cavernous 24,000-square-foot (2,230-sq-m) clubhouse. Each space is wide enough for a car and motor home but not much else and comes with a picnic table and patio. The foliage is plentiful and flanks an 18-hole putting course with real grass greens along with family and adult swimming pools. The resort features a full calendar of poker tournaments, movies, karaoke, and bar and restaurant specials. Wheelchair-accessible restrooms have

Las Vegas Monorail

flush toilets and hot showers; other amenities include a laundry, a grocery store, an exercise room, and an arcade.

Transportation and Services

Air

More than 500 planes arrive or depart **McCarran International Airport** (LAS, 5757 Wayne Newton Blvd., 702/261-5211, www.mccarran.com) every day, making it the sixth busiest in the country and 19th in the world. Terminal 1 hosts domestic flights, while Terminal 3 has domestic and international flights.

Bus

Citizen Area Transit (CAT, 702/228-7433, www.rtcsnv.com), the public bus system, is managed by the Regional Transportation Commission. CAT runs 39 routes all over the Las Vegas Valley.

Fares are $6 for 2 hours, $8 for 24 hours, free under age 5 when riding with a guardian. Call or access the ride guide online. Bus service is pretty comprehensive, but even the express routes with fewer stops take a long time to get anywhere. CAT's double-decker **Deuce bus** runs the length of Las Vegas Boulevard, stopping in front of nearly every hotel/casino on the Strip and ending downtown.

Car

Downtown Las Vegas crowds around the junction of I-15, US-95, and US-93. I-15 runs from Los Angeles (272 mi/435 km, 4-5 hours' drive) to Salt Lake City (419 mi/675 km, 6-8 hours). US-95 meanders from Yuma, Arizona, on the Mexican border, up the western side of Nevada, through Coeur D'Alene, Idaho, all the way up to British Columbia, Canada. US-93 starts in Phoenix and hits Las Vegas 285 miles (460 km) later, then merges with I-15 for a while only to fork off and shoot straight up the east side of Nevada and continue due north all the way to Alberta, Canada.

Car Rental

Most of the large car-rental companies have desks at the **McCarran Rent-A-Car Center** (702/261-6001). Dedicated McCarran shuttles leave the main terminal from outside exit doors 10 and 11 about every five minutes bound for the Rent-A-Car Center. International airlines and a few domestic flights arrive at Terminal 3. Here, the shuttle picks up outside doors 51 through 58. Taxicabs are also available at the center.

Monorail

The Sahara resort on the north end of the Strip and the MGM Grand near the south end are connected via the **Las Vegas Monorail** (702/699-8200, 7am-midnight Mon., 7am-2am Tues.-Thurs., 7am-3am Fri.-Sun., $5, 24-hour pass $13), with stops at the Sahara, Westgate,

Convention Center, Harrah's/The Linq, Flamingo/Caesars Palace, Bally's/Paris, and MGM Grand. More than 30 major resorts are now within easy reach along the Strip without a car or taxi. Reaching speeds up to 50 mph, the monorail glides above traffic to cover the 4-mile (6.4-km) route in about 14 minutes. Nine trains with four air-conditioned cars each carry up to 152 riders along the elevated track running on the east side of the strip, stopping every few minutes at the stations. Tickets are available at vending machines at each station as well as at station properties.

Taxi and Ride Share

Taxis and ride-hailing services are widely used in Las Vegas. Taxis form lines outside most Strip hotels, and **Uber** (www.uber.com) and **Lyft** (www.lyft.com) drivers respond in a few minutes.

Limo

Offering chauffeur-driven domestic and imported sedans, shuttle buses, and SUVs in addition to stretch and superstretch limos, **Earth Limos** (725/777-3333, www.earthlimos.com) can transport up to 24 people per vehicle to and from sporting events, corporate meetings, bachelor and bachelorette parties, sightseeing tours, and more. Rates are $60 per hour for a six-seat stretch limo, $80 and up for an eight-seat Lincoln Town Car stretch limo. The 14-person Hummer superstretch owns the road.

Presidential Limousine (702/438-5466, www.presidentiallimolv.com) charges $69 per hour for its six-seater stretch limo, $80 per hour for the superstretch eight-seater. All rates include bottled water and champagne; they don't include a mandatory fuel surcharge or driver gratuity. Splurge options include a hot pink stretch and 12-passenger ultrastretch Escalade. **Bell Limousine** (866/226-7206, www.belllimousine.com) has similar rates and a basic fleet.

Tours

Several companies offer the chance to see the sights of Las Vegas by bus, helicopter, airplane, or off-road vehicle. There are plenty of tour operators offering similar services. Refer to the *Grand Canyon Tours from Vegas* section; these operators also conduct tours of the Strip.

The ubiquitous **Gray Line** (702/739-7777 or 877/333-6556, www.graylinelasvegas.com, $50) takes riders on a double-decker bus tour of the entire length of the Strip and downtown. Tourists can explore at their own pace, hopping on and off at any of 20 stops. Visit the major Vegas free sights: the Fountains of Bellagio, the "Welcome to Fabulous Las Vegas" sign, the Fremont Street Experience, and some of the more opulent hotels.

Cruise Lake Mead on the *Desert Princess,* a 275-passenger paddle wheeler operated by **Lake Mead Cruises** (866/292-9191, www.lakemeadcruises.com; noon Nov.-Jan., noon and 2:30pm daily Feb.-Oct., $35 adults, $17 children 2-11; 10am Sun. champagne brunch cruise $59 adults, $29 children 2-11; dinner cruise 5:30pm Tues., Thurs., Sun. Mar.-Oct., $79 adults, $39 children 2-11). The boat gets you up close and personal with the Hoover Dam, an extinct volcano, and colorful rock formations.

Canyon Tours (866/218-3427 or 702/260-0796, www.canyoutours.com) has the full slate of canyon and national park bundles, as well as activities including an ATV ride to the Eldorado Canyon gold mine ($199) and white-water rafting the Colorado River below the Hoover Dam ($535-604).

Pink Jeep Tours (702/895-6778 or 888/900-4480, www.pinkjeeptourslasvegas.com) takes visitors in rugged but cute and comfortable 10-passenger ATVs to such sites as Red Rock Canyon, Valley of Fire, and Hoover Dam.

For history, nature, and entertainment

buffs looking for a more focused adventure, themed tours are on the rise in Las Vegas. **Haunted Vegas Tours** (866/218-4935, www.vegasspecialtytours.com, 8pm Mon.-Wed. and Fri.-Sat., $99) takes an interesting if macabre trip to the "Motel of Death," where many pseudo-celebrities have met their untimely ends. Guides dressed as undertakers equip guests with ghost-hunting gear and take you to the Redd Foxx haunted house, a creepy old bridge, and an eerie park. The same company offers the **Las Vegas Mob Tour** (3pm daily, $100), taking visitors to the sites of Mafia's greatest hits. Guides, dressed in black pin-striped suits and fedoras, tell tales of the 1970s, when Anthony "The Ant" Spilotro ran the city, and give the scoop on the fate of casino mogul Lefty Rosenthal. A pizza party is included in both tours.

Information and Services

The **Las Vegas Convention and Visitors Authority** (LVCVA, 3150 Paradise Rd., 702/892-0711 or 877/847-4858, www.lvcva.com, 8am-5pm daily) maintains a website of special hotel deals, show tickets, and other offers at www.lasvegas.com. One of LVCVA's priorities is filling hotel rooms. You can also call the same number for convention schedules and entertainment offerings. The **Las Vegas Chamber of Commerce** (575 Symphony Park Ave., Ste. 100, 702/641-5822, www.lvchamber.com) has a bunch of travel resources and fact sheets on its website. For-profit **Vegas.com** is a good resource for up-to-the-minute show schedules and reviews.

The **Las Vegas Metropolitan Police Department** (750 Sierra Vista Dr., 702/828-6430, www.lvmpd.com) operates several area command centers. The Convention Center Area Command patrols the Strip. If you need the police, the fire department, or an ambulance in an emergency, dial 911.

The centrally located **University Medical Center** (1800 W. Charleston Blvd., at Shadow Ln., 702/383-2000) has 24-hour emergency service, with outpatient and trauma-care facilities. Hospital emergency rooms throughout the valley are open 24 hours, as are many privately run urgent care centers.

Most hotels will have lists of dentists and doctors, and the **Clark County Medical Society** (2590 E. Russell Rd., 702/739-9989, www.clarkcountymedical.org) website lists members based on specialty. You can also get a physician referral from **Desert Springs Hospital** (702/733-8800).

The Grand Canyon

Grand Canyon National Park

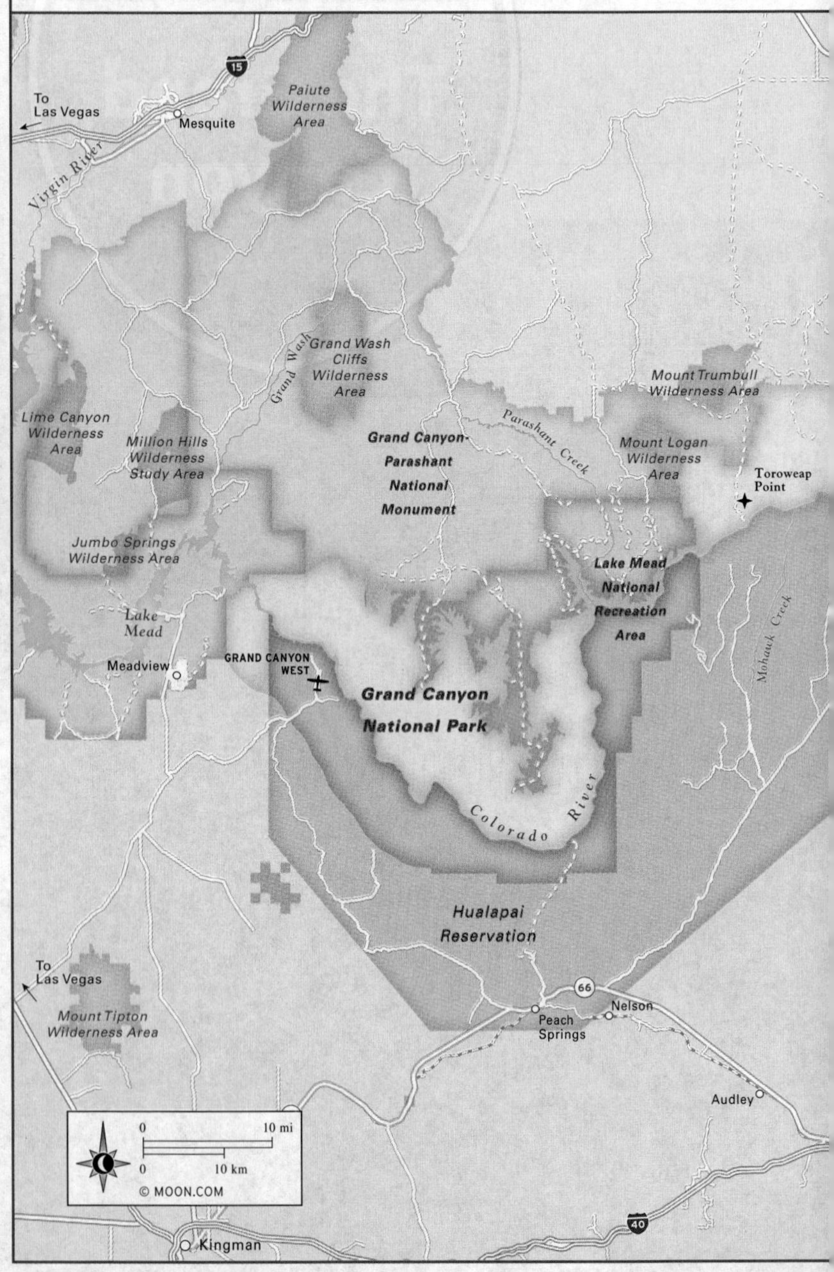

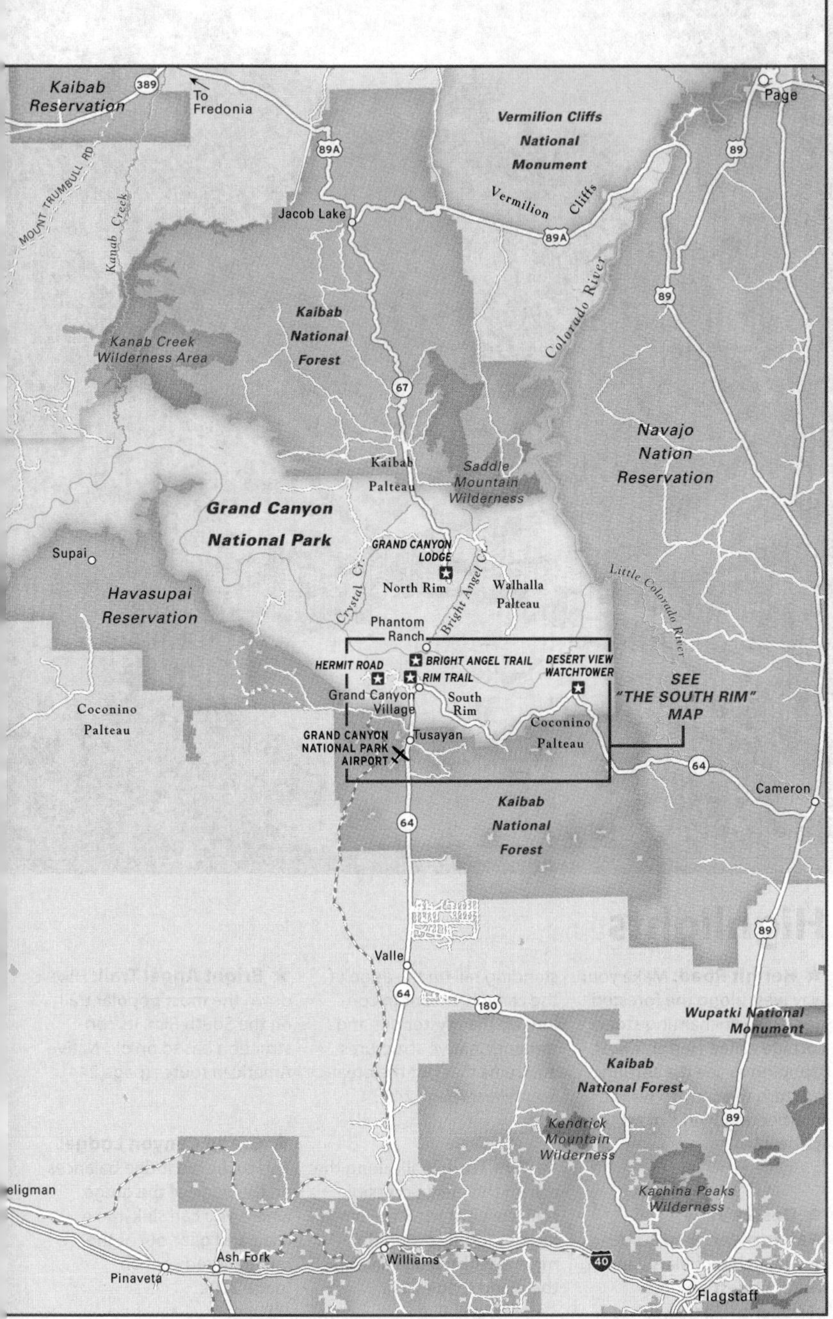

Kaibab Reservation
389
To Fredonia
Page
Vermilion Cliffs National Monument
89A
89
MOUNT TRUMBULL RD
Kanab Creek
Vermilion Cliffs
Jacob Lake
Colorado River
Kaibab National Forest
Kanab Creek Wilderness Area
67
Navajo Nation Reservation
Kaibab Palteau
Saddle Mountain Wilderness
Grand Canyon National Park
GRAND CANYON LODGE
Supai
North Rim
Walhalla Palteau
Little Colorado River
Havasupai Reservation
Crystal Cr.
Bright Angel Cr.
Phantom Ranch
BRIGHT ANGEL TRAIL
DESERT VIEW WATCHTOWER
HERMIT ROAD
RIM TRAIL
SEE "THE SOUTH RIM" MAP
Grand Canyon Village
South Rim
Coconino Palteau
Coconino Palteau
GRAND CANYON NATIONAL PARK AIRPORT
Tusayan
64
Cameron
Kaibab National Forest
Valle
180
Wupatki National Monument
Kaibab National Forest
Kendrick Mountain Wilderness
Kachina Peaks Wilderness
eligman
Ash Fork
Williams
40
Pinaveta
Flagstaff

Highlights

★ **Hermit Road:** Make your way west along the forested rim to the enchanting stone cottage called Hermit's Rest, stopping to see the setting sun turn the canyon walls into fleeting works of art (page 231).

★ **Desert View Watchtower:** Step inside one of architect Mary Jane Colter's finest accomplishments—a rock tower standing tall on the edge of the canyon, meant to conjure up the mysterious and romantic native structures and ruins that dot the great Southwest (page 243).

★ **Rim Trail:** Walk along the rim on this easy, accessible trail, past historical buildings, famous lodges—and the most breathtaking views in the world (page 244).

★ **Bright Angel Trail:** Hike down the most popular trail on the South Rim, its construction based on old Native American routes (page 244).

★ **Grand Canyon Lodge:** This rustic old lodge balances on the edge of the gorge, where you can sink into a chair and gaze out at the multicolored canyon (page 260).

There's a reason why Arizona's official nickname is "The Grand Canyon State." Any state with one of the wonders of the world would be keen to advertise its good luck.

The canyon must simply be seen to be believed. If you stand for the first time on one of the South Rim's easily accessible lookouts and don't have to catch your breath, you might need to check your pulse. Staring into the canyon brings up all kinds of existential questions; its brash vastness can't be taken in without conjuring some big ideas and questions about life and humanity. Take your time here—you'll need it.

If there are any sacred places in the natural world, this is surely one. The canyon is a water-wrought cathedral, and no matter what beliefs or preconceptions you approach the rim with, they are likely to be challenged, molded, cut away, and revealed—like the layers of primordial earth that compose this deep rock labyrinth and tell the history of the planet, a geology textbook for new gods. And it is a story in which humans appear only briefly, if at all.

Though impressive, the black-and-white statistics—repeated throughout the park on displays and interpretive signs along the rim and at the various visitors centers—do little to conjure an image that would do the canyon justice. It is some 277 river miles (450 km) long, beginning just below Lees Ferry on the north and ending somewhere around the Grand Wash Cliffs in northwestern Arizona. It is 18 miles (29 km) across at its widest point and an average of 10 miles (16.1 km) across from the South to the North Rim. It is a mile (1.6 km) deep on average; the highest point on the rim, the north's Point Imperial, rises nearly 9,000 feet (2,743 m) above the river. Its towers, buttes, and mesas, formed by the falling away of layers undercut by the river's incessant carving, are red and pink, dull brown, and green-tipped, though these basic hues are altered and enhanced by the setting and rising of the sun, changed by changes in the light, becoming throw-away works of art that astound and then disappear.

It is folly, though, to try too hard to describe and boost the Grand Canyon. The consensus, from the first person to see it to yesterday's gazer, has amounted to "You just have to see it for yourself." Perhaps the most poetic words ever spoken about the Grand Canyon, profound for their obvious simplicity, came from Teddy Roosevelt, speaking on the South Rim in 1903. "Leave it as it is," he said. "You cannot improve on it; not a bit."

Getting to the Grand Canyon

The majority of Grand Canyon visitors drive here, reaching the South Rim from either **Flagstaff** or **Williams** and entering the park through the south or east gates. The South entrance is usually the busiest, and during the summer traffic is likely to be backed up somewhat.

To get to the **South entrance** from Flagstaff, take **US-180** through the forest past the San Francisco Peaks. The road merges with **AZ-64** at Valle, for a total distance of about 80 miles (129 km) from Flagstaff to the park gate, which takes about 1.5 hours. The drive from Williams to the South entrance on AZ-64 is a more direct but less scenic route; it's about 60 miles (97 km) and takes about an hour. To reach the **East entrance,** take **US-89 North** from Flagstaff to Cameron, then take **AZ-64 West** to the entrance. The drive is about 80 miles (129 km) and takes about 1.5 hours. This route is recommended if you want to see portions of Navajo Country on your way to the

Best Hotels & Campgrounds

★ **El Tovar:** The South Rim's most stylish and storied lodge, built in arts-and-crafts style, overlooks the canyon (page 252).

★ **Bright Angel Lodge:** This historic, rustic lodge is on the edge of Grand Canyon's bustling South Rim (page 252).

★ **Historic Cameron Trading Post and Lodge:** This travelers' crossroads has sweeping views of the Navajo Nation (page 254).

★ **The Lodge on Route 66:** Along the Mother Road in nearby Williams you'll find this motor-court-style lodge with stylish rooms (page 254).

★ **Hotel Monte Vista:** Stay in a historic hotel in downtown Flagstaff and hear tales of the Hollywood greats who once stayed here (page 255).

★ **Mather Campground:** Sleep under starry skies at one of 300 campsites close to Grand Canyon Village (page 257).

★ **Grand Canyon Lodge:** This grand old hotel is perched high on the edge of the canyon's wild and forested North Rim (page 265).

★ **Phantom Ranch:** Few visit this small paradise deep in the canyon's bottomlands, but those who do never forget it (page 274).

canyon, and entering through the East entrance will put you right at Desert View, the Desert View Watchtower, and Tusayan Ruin & Museum—sights that otherwise you'll have to travel 25 miles (40 km) or so east from Grand Canyon Village to see.

From Las Vegas

South Rim

Las Vegas is **280 miles (450 km)** from the Grand Canyon's South Rim. The roughly **five-hour drive** to the South Rim—a very popular trip—is a relatively short one by Southwestern standards. Even if you get a late-morning start and make a few stops along the way, you're still likely to arrive at the park by dinnertime. Take **I-11/US-93 South** from Las Vegas to **Kingman,** then take **I-40 East** to reach **Williams or Flagstaff** and head north to the park. The speed limit on most sections of I-40 in Arizona is 75 mph, so all that highland forest scenery flashes by unless you stop a few times to take it in. Most summer weekends you'll find the route crowded but manageable. At all times of the year you'll be surrounded by 18-wheelers barreling across the land. If you feel like stopping overnight—and perhaps it is better to see the great canyon with fresh morning eyes—do so in Williams. It's just an hour or so from the park's **South entrance,** has a bit of Route 66 charm, and offers several distinctive and memorable hotels and restaurants, all of which you'll miss if you breeze through town in a hurry.

West Rim

Driving from Vegas, you may also want to stop at **Grand Canyon West** and the Hualapai Reservation's **Skywalk.** This area is only **125 miles (201 km) southwest** of Vegas (about a **2.5-hour drive**). However, this will add at least a full day to your trip, and the view from the South Rim is infinitely better and cheaper. Grand Canyon West charges a $39 entrance fee on top of $20 for the

Best Restaurants

★ **El Tovar Dining Room:** Enjoy locally sourced gourmet meals in a stylishly historical atmosphere on the canyon's edge (page 249).

★ **Harvey Burger:** This Fred Harvey-inspired eatery serves pre-hike American fare right next to the Bright Angel Trailhead (page 249).

★ **Rod's Steak House:** This institution in nearby Williams serves up Old West charm and juicy steaks (page 250).

★ **Criollo Latin Kitchen:** Dine on creative Latin-inspired dishes at this sleek restaurant in Flagstaff's historic downtown (page 250).

★ **Brix Restaurant & Wine Bar:** Find farm-to-table cuisine along with a fine selection of wine and cocktails at this Flagstaff restaurant (page 251).

Skywalk, and you'll probably have to ride a shuttle bus part of the way.

To reach Grand Canyon West from Las Vegas, take **I-11/US-93** out of the city, heading south for about 65 miles (105 km) to **mile marker 42,** where you'll see the Dolan Springs/Meadview City/Pearce Ferry exit. Turn north onto **Pearce Ferry Road.** About 30 miles (48 km) in, turn east on **Diamond Bar Road.** Then it's about 20 miles (32 km) to Grand Canyon West.

To continue on to the South Rim, about **225 miles (360 km) east,** head to Peach Springs along old **Route 66.** You can stop for the night at the Hualapai Lodge, or continue on for about an hour east on Route 66 to **Seligman.** Then head east on Route 66 to **Ash Fork,** where you can pick up **I-40 East** to **Williams,** the gateway to the South Rim. From there, head north along **AZ-64** to reach the park's **South entrance.**

From Los Angeles

It's **500 miles (805 km)** from Los Angeles to Grand Canyon's South Rim. Most of the **eight-hour** drive is along I-40, across an empty, hard landscape without much respite save the usual interstate fare. From Los Angeles, take **I-10 East** for 50 miles (81 km) to reach **I-15,** which heads **northwest** out of the region toward Barstow. The driving time from L.A. to Barstow is about two hours, but it takes considerably longer on weekends and during the morning and evening rush hours. Expect snarls and delays around Barstow as well. At **Barstow,** pick up **I-40** for the remainder of the trip to Williams, Arizona (about 5 hours). At **Williams,** take **AZ-64 North** for about an hour to the **South entrance.**

About 320 miles (515 km) from Los Angeles, but with 173 miles (280 km) still left to go until you reach the canyon, **Kingman,** Arizona, sits along I-40 and offers a few good restaurants and affordable places to sleep—unless you're willing to push on for the final three hours or so to reach the rim in one shot.

Stopping in Kingman

Kingman is located along the route to the South Rim of the Grand Canyon coming from either Las Vegas or Los Angeles. It has several well-curated museums that showcase its heritage, such as the **Historic Route 66 Museum** (Powerhouse Visitor Center, 120 W. Andy Devine Ave., 928/753-9889, www.mohavemuseum.org/az-route-66-museum.html, 9am-4pm Tues.-Sat., $4 adults, $3 seniors 60 and over, children under 12 free) and the **Mohave Museum of History and Arts** (400 W. Beale St., 928/753-3195,

www.mohavemuseum.org, 9am-4pm Tues.-Fri., $4 adults, $3 seniors 60 and over, children under 12 free). Admission to either grants entry to the other.

The best restaurant for miles in any direction is **Mattina's Ristorante Italiano** (318 E. Oak St., 928/753-7504, 5pm-9pm Tues.-Sat., $13-25), where you can get perfectly prepared Italian food and fine wine. It's difficult to pass up the lobster ravioli or the creamy fettuccini alfredo. Don't leave without trying the tiramisu or the key lime pie. With a checkerboard floor, Formica tables, a long counter, and a comfort-food menu, **Rutherford's 66 Family Diner** (2011 E. Andy Devine Ave., 928/377-1660, 6am-8pm Mon.-Fri., 6am-3pm Sat.-Sun., $8-16) is a 1950s diner straight out of Central Casting. Skillet breakfasts and steak and meatloaf sandwiches will have you waxing nostalgic.

There are several affordable basic hotels on Andy Devine Avenue (Route 66) in Kingman's downtown area, some of them with retro road-trip neon signs and Route 66 themes. The Hollywood-themed **El Trovatore Motel** (1440 E. Andy Devine Ave., 928/692-6520, $66-76) boasts that Marilyn Monroe, James Dean, and Clark Gable all slept there. One of only a handful of prewar motels left in town, the motel retains its art deco sign and architecture. Rooms, which command views of the Hualapai Mountains, are utilitarian, with king or queen beds, a microwave, and a fridge. Pets are welcome.

By Air, Train, or Bus

Air

Flagstaff, Tusayan, and Williams have small airports, but the closest major airport to Grand Canyon National Park is **Sky Harbor International Airport** (PHX) in Phoenix, a 3.5-hour drive south of the South Rim. The **Grand Canyon Airport** (GCN) at Tusayan, just outside the

From top to bottom: the Rim Trail along Grand Canyon's South Rim; morning on the Grand Canyon Lodge's veranda; Grand Canyon Railway.

Side Trip: Retro Fun on Route 66

Seligman, a tiny roadside settlement 87 miles (140 km) east of Kingman, holds on tightly to its Route 66 heritage. There are less than 500 full-time residents and often, especially on summer weekends, twice that number of travelers. Don't be surprised to see European visitors, classic car nuts, and 60-something bikers passing through town. John Lasseter, co-director of the 2006 Disney-Pixar film *Cars,* has said that he based the movie's fictional town of Radiator Springs partly on Seligman, which, like Radiator Springs, nearly died out when it was bypassed by I-40 in the late 1970s.

Stop at **Delgadillo's Snow Cap Drive-In** (301 E. Chino Ave., 928/422-3291, $5-10), off Route 66 on the east end of town, a famous food shack dedicated to feeding, entertaining, and teasing Route 66 travelers for generations. They serve a mean chili burger, a famous "cheeseburger with cheese," hot dogs, malts, soft ice cream, and much more. Expect a wait, especially on summer weekends, and you will be teased, especially if you have a question that requires a serious answer. The **Roadkill Café** (502 W. Route 66, 928/422-3554, 7am-9pm daily, $8-24) is more than just a funny name; it's a popular place for buffalo burgers, steaks, and sandwiches.

There are several small, affordable, locally owned motels in Seligman. The **Supai Motel** (134 W. Chino St., 928/422-4153, www.supaimotelseligman.com, $69-82), named for the nearby Grand Canyon village inhabited by the Havasupai people, has clean and comfortable guest rooms at a fair price. The **Historic Route 66 Motel** (928/422-3204, www.route66seligmanarizona.com, $69-82) offers free wireless Internet and refrigerators in clean, comfortable guest rooms, and the **Canyon Lodge** (114 E. Chino St., 928/422-3255, www.route66canyonlodge.com, $69-82) has free wireless Internet along with refrigerators and microwaves in its themed guest rooms. They also serve a free continental breakfast.

park's South entrance, has flights from Las Vegas daily. May-early September, the free **Tusayan Shuttle** runs between Tusayan and Grand Canyon Village every 20 minutes 8am-9:30pm daily. It departs from the IMAX Theater, making stops along the main drag (AZ-64) on its way into the park. You must purchase an entrance pass to the park before getting on the bus. These are available at any of the previously mentioned stops, and they cost the same as they would at the park entrance.

Flagstaff's small **Pulliam Airport** (FLG, 928/556-1234, www.flagstaff.az.gov), located about 5 miles (8 km) south of downtown, offers five flights daily to and from Sky Harbor in Phoenix through US Airways (800/428-4322 usairways.com). It's a roughly 50-minute flight, as opposed to a 2.5-hour drive from Phoenix, and costs $150-300. This is not the best option, as you must rent a car to explore the northland properly. If you are coming from Phoenix, it's best to rent a car there and make the scenic drive north.

Las Vegas to Grand Canyon

Grand Canyon Express (800/222-6966, reservation@airvegas.com) offers daily flights from Las Vegas to the Grand Canyon Airport in Tusayan. The flight time is about 1 hour and 10 minutes and costs about $210 one-way. Make sure to call ahead for flight times and reservations, as flights are scheduled based on demand and don't necessarily occur every day. Much more expensive but worth it if you're looking for a one-day tour of the canyon from Vegas, **Grand Canyon Airlines** offers the 9.5-hour **Grand Canyon Deluxe Tour** (866/735-9422, $344). The tour includes hotel-to-hotel service, access to the park, and a box lunch. For most people, driving from Las Vegas to the South Rim is the best option, in part because there's more to see from the ground than the air.

Los Angeles to Grand Canyon

You can fly to the Grand Canyon Airport from **Los Angeles International Airport** (LAX), but you'll likely layover at **Sky Harbor Airport** (PHX) in Phoenix for at least an hour. Another option is to fly into Sky Harbor and rent a car there to make the 3-4 hour drive from Phoenix to the South Rim. The route from Phoenix to the South Rim along **I-17** is quite scenic, moving from the cactus-choked desert to the high cool pines in a matter of hours.

US Airways (800/428-4322, www.usairways.com) and **United** (800/864-8331, www.united.com) both offer flights from LAX to Phoenix, then on to Grand Canyon Airport in Tusayan, which is about 7 miles (11.3 km) from the park's South Rim. These flights run $300-500 round-trip and can take up to five hours depending on your layover at Sky Harbor.

US Airways (800/428-4322, www.usairways.com) offers several daily flights from LAX to Flagstaff's small **Pulliam Airport** (FLG, 928/556-1234, www.flagstaff.az.gov), where you can rent a car or hire a shuttle to take you the remaining 1.5 hours to the park. These flights almost always have a layover of at least an hour at Phoenix's Sky Harbor Airport, so the flight from L.A. to Flagstaff and the subsequent drive to the South Rim can end up taking not too much longer than the drive straight from L.A. Expect to pay between $300 and $500 round-trip.

Renting a Car

Most of the major car-rental companies have a presence at Flagstaff's small **Pulliam Airport** (FLG, 928/556-1234, www.flagstaff.az.gov), about 5 miles (8 km) south of downtown. **Avis Downtown Flagstaff Car Rental** (175 W. Aspen Ave., 928/714-0713, www.avis.com, 7am-6pm Mon.-Fri., 8am-4pm Sat., 9am-1pm Sun.) is located right in the middle of all the action at the corner of Aspen Avenue and Humphreys Street. **Budget** (800/527-7000, www.budget.com) operates out of the same facility with the same hours and phone number. **Enterprise Rent-A-Car** (213 E. Route 66, 928/526-1377, www.enterprise.com, 8am-6pm Mon.-Fri., 9am-noon Sat.) is located on the eastern edges of town along I-40. If you're looking for a mythic Southwestern experience, stop by **EagleRider Flagstaff** (800 W. Route 66, 928/637-6575, www.route66rider.com, 8am-6pm daily, $159 per day, $931 per week) and rent a Harley-Davidson.

Train

If you're coming from L.A., a trip east on the train can be a fun and romantic way to see the interior West. **Amtrak's *Southwest Chief* route** (800/872-7245, www.amtrak.com) departs daily from **L.A.'s Union Station,** usually around 6pm. The 10-hour overnight trip ends at **Flagstaff's downtown depot** (1 E. Route 66) at around 5am, where you can book a shuttle straight to the South Rim or take a shuttle to Williams, about an hour west of Flagstaff, and pick up the Grand Canyon Railway there, arriving in the park about 2.5 hours later. A ticket on the *Southwest Chief* to Flagstaff costs $70-291 round-trip, depending on options.

A fun, retro, and environmentally conscious way to reach the park, the **Grand Canyon Railway** (800/843-8724, www.thetrain.com, $65-220 pp round-trip) re-creates what it was like to visit the great gorge in the early 20th century. It takes about 2.5 hours to get to the South Rim depot from the station in Williams, where the **Grand Canyon Railway Hotel** (235 N. Grand Canyon Blvd., 928/635-4010, www.thetrain.com, $205-370), just beyond the train station, makes a good base, attempting as it does to match the atmosphere of the old Santa Fe Railroad Harvey House that once stood on the same ground.

A trip to and from the Grand Canyon on the old train is recommended for anyone who is interested in the heyday

One Day at the Grand Canyon

The ideal South Rim-only trip lasts four days and three nights, with one day in each of the park's three major sections (Grand Canyon Village, Hermit Road, Desert View Drive), plus a day spent hiking into the canyon. Three days and two nights (with the first and last days including the trip to and from the rim) allow you to see all the sights on the rim, to take in a sunset and sunrise over the canyon, and even to do a day hike or mule trip below the rim. If you just have a day, about five hours or so will allow you to see all the sights in Grand Canyon Village plus take a ride out to Hermit's Rest, stopping at viewpoints.

Morning

If you have just one day to see the Grand Canyon, drive to the South Rim and park your car at one of the large, free parking lots inside the national park. Hop on one of the park's free shuttles or rent a bike or walk along the **Rim Trail** and head toward Grand Canyon Village. Spend a few hours looking at the buildings and, of course, the canyon from this central, busy part of the rim. Stop in at the **Yavapai Geology Museum and Observation Station,** check out the history of canyon tourism at the **Bright Angel Lodge,** watch a movie about the canyon at the visitors center, and have lunch at the **Arizona Steakhouse** or, better yet, **El Tovar Dining Room** (or save it for dinner).

Afternoon

After lunch, take the shuttle along the eastern **Desert View Drive,** stopping along the way at a few of the eastern viewpoints, especially at Mary Jane Colter's **Desert View Watchtower** on the far eastern edge of the park.

Evening

End your day by heading all the way to the western reaches of the park to see **Hermit's Rest.** If you time it right, you'll catch a gorgeous canyon sunset from one of the western viewpoints along the way. For dinner, try **El Tovar** or one of the cafeterias before turning in early.

If this is your only day at the canyon, visit Hermit's Rest first and leave the park via Desert View Drive, stopping at the watchtower and the **Tusayan Ruin & Museum** on your way out.

Extending Your Stay

If you're able to spend more time in the park, hit one of the **corridor trails** for a day hike below the rim. Rest up after rising out of the depths, then check the park newspaper to see what's happening at the **Shrine of the Ages,** where on most nights there's an entertaining and informative talk by a ranger.

If you include a North or West Rim excursion, add at least one or two more days and nights. It takes about 5 hours to reach the **North Rim** from the South, perhaps longer if you take the daily shuttle instead of your own vehicle, and the **West Rim** and the **Hualapai** and **Havasupai Indian Reservations** are about 4.5 hours away from the South Rim over slow roads—although it makes sense if you're coming from Vegas and on your way to the South Rim anyway. A visit to the **Hualapai Reservation's Skywalk** should not be substituted for the South Rim (and isn't recommended to those seeing the Grand Canyon for the first time; you have not truly seen the Grand Canyon unless you have seen the South or North Rim).

The most important thing to remember when considering a trip to the canyon is to plan far ahead, even if you're just, like the vast majority of visitors, going to spend time on the South Rim. Six months' advance planning is the norm, longer if you are going to ride a mule down or stay overnight at Phantom Ranch in the inner canyon.

of train travel or the Old West—or for anyone desiring a slower-paced journey across the northland. Besides, the fewer visitors who drive their vehicles to the rim, the better. Kids especially enjoy the train trip. Comedian-fiddlers often stroll through the cars, and on some trips there's even a mock train robbery complete with bandits on horseback with blazing six-shooters.

Bus

Flagstaff's **Greyhound bus station** (800 E. Butler Ave., 928/774-4573, www.greyhound.com) is located along industrial East Butler Avenue. The bus trip from Las Vegas to Flagstaff takes about six hours and costs $95 round-trip. From L.A., the bus trip takes about 12 hours and costs about $140.

Groome Transporation aka Arizona Shuttle (928/350-8466, http://groometransportation.com/arizona) offers comfortable rides from Flagstaff to the Grand Canyon three times daily (Mar.-Oct., $60 round-trip for adults). The company also goes between Phoenix's Sky Harbor International Airport and Flagstaff ($48 pp one-way) several times a day as well as from Flagstaff to Sedona, the Verde Valley, and Williams ($35-43 one-way).

Visiting the Park

Entrances

Unless you choose to ride the chugging train from Williams, there are only two ways, by road, in and out of the park's South Rim section. The vast majority of visitors to Grand Canyon National Park enter through the **South entrance** along AZ-64 from Williams. US-180 from Flagstaff meets up with AZ-64 near Valle, about 30 miles (48 km) south of the South entrance; it's about 55 miles (89 km) along scenic US-180 from Flagstaff to Valle. AZ-64 from Williams to the South entrance is 60 miles (97 km) of flat, dry grass and windswept plain, dotted with a few isolated trailers, manufactured homes, and gaudy For Sale signs offering cheap "ranchland." Entering through the busy South entrance will ensure that your first look at the Grand Canyon is from **Mather Point,** one of the most iconic views of the river-molded gorge. The entrance stations are open 24 hours daily, including all holidays.

A lesser-used but certainly no less worthy park entrance is the **East entrance,** in the park's **Desert View** section. About 25 miles (40 km) east of Grand Canyon Village and all the action, this route is a good choice for those who want a more leisurely and comprehensive look at the rim, as there are quite a few stops along the way to the village that you might not otherwise get to if you enter through the South entrance. To reach the East entrance station, take US-89 for 46 miles (74 km) north of Flagstaff, across a wide big-sky landscape covered in volcanic rock, pine forests, and yellow wildflowers, to Cameron, on the red-dirt Navajo Reservation. Then head west on AZ-64 for about 30 miles (48 km) to the entrance station.

The small, little-visited **North Rim entrance** is on AZ-67 about 30 miles (48 km) south of Jacob Lake and the US-89A junction. AZ-67 is the only road into and out of the park on this side and closes from December 1-May 15.

Park Passes and Fees

The **park entrance fee** is $35 per car and includes entry and parking for up to seven days. Payment of the entrance fee at the South Rim will be honored at the North Rim as long as you go within seven days. The entrance fee is $20 per person for those entering on foot or bicycle, and $30 per person for those entering on motorcycle, also good for seven days.

The National Park Service offers several **annual passes** for frequent park visitors, including one for $70 that allows unlimited access to Grand Canyon

National Park for a year. The **America the Beautiful Pass** allows access to all the national parks for a year for $80; a lifetime version of this pass is available to seniors (age 62 or older). To purchase passes, inquire at the entrance station or one of the visitors centers in the park.

Visitors Centers

South Rim

While Historic Grand Canyon Village is the heart of the South Rim, Mather Point and **Grand Canyon Visitor Center** (7am-6pm daily May-Sept., 9am-4pm daily Oct.-Apr.), about 2.2 miles (3.5 km) east of the village along the rim, provide easy and in-depth introductions to the canyon and the park. Entering from the main South entrance on AZ-64 from Williams or Flagstaff, keep to the South Entrance Road for 5.1 miles (8.2 km) to reach four large parking lots around the visitors center complex. After finding a spot, head directly to Mather Point, which is just a short walk from the visitors center parking lots. After seeing the canyon from this famous first vantage, head back to the visitors center, where you will find a water refill station, bathrooms, a bookstore with souvenirs and supplies, and a large, light-filled building with information about Grand Canyon and environs. Rangers staff the center all day to answer questions and help you plan your visit, and they offer ranger-led walks, hikes, and natural-history presentations around the park most days and evenings. A 20-minute film shown here on the hour and half hour, *Grand Canyon: A Journey of Wonder*, narrated by the great Peter Coyote, depicts the canyon's dawn-to-dusk cycle of mystery and beauty, and there are several maps and other exhibitions that explain and illuminate the somewhat confusing grandeur just outside.

In Grand Canyon Village, along the rim about 2.2 miles (3.5 km) west of Grand Canyon Visitor Center, is the smaller **Verkamp's Visitor Center** (8am-7pm daily early Mar.-mid-May and early Sept.-Nov., 8am-8pm daily mid-May-mid-Aug., 9am-8pm daily mid-Aug.-early Sept., 8am-6pm daily Dec.-early Mar.), near Hopi House and El Tovar. It began in a white-canvas tent when Grand Canyon National Park opened and was a famous curio and souvenir shop right on the rim for 100 years. Since 2015 the historic building has housed a visitors center run by the Grand Canyon Conservancy, which includes books, souvenirs, and displays about the history of Grand Canyon Village.

The farthest-flung of all the park's South Rim information and visitors centers is in the **Desert View Watchtower** (9am-5pm daily), about 25 miles (40 km) east of Grand Canyon Village. It is staffed with helpful rangers who have information about Desert View and the rest of the park.

North Rim

The **North Rim Visitor Center** (8am-6pm daily May 15-Oct. 16, 9am-3pm daily Oct. 17-30, free) is next to Grand Canyon Lodge and is staffed with several rangers and volunteers who can direct you to the best sights and trails. Here you'll find fascinating exhibits on canyon science and lore, as well as a bathroom and water station. Within the visitors center the nonprofit Grand Canyon Association operates an excellent bookstore with all the essential tomes and other media about Grand Canyon and the Great Southwest. This is where you go to find out the current ranger programs on offer and to bombard a hard-working ranger with all your questions about the canyon and the park.

Outside the Park

About 1 mile (1.6 km) south of the park's South entrance, the town of Tusayan is the home of the (non-NPS-affiliated) **Grand Canyon Visitor Center** (AZ-64, 928/638-2468, www.explorethecanyon.com, 8am-10pm daily Mar.-Oct.,

10am-8pm daily Nov.-Feb., IMAX tickets $13 over age 10, $10 children 6-10, children under 6 free), which has been a popular first stop for park visitors since the 1980s. You can purchase a park pass here, book tours, and check out some displays about the canyon, but the center wouldn't be worth the stop if not for its **IMAX Theater.** The colossal screen shows the 35-minute movie *Grand Canyon—The Hidden Secrets* every hour at half past. You can also leave your car here and hop on the **free shuttle bus (Tusayan Route/ Purple Line)** to the park.

Reservations

Accommodations

To obtain a room at one of the lodges inside Grand Canyon National Park, you must book far in advance, especially if you are hoping to visit during the busy summer season. Reservations for all of the lodges on the South Rim, including Phantom Ranch and Trailer Village, are handled by **Xanterra Parks and Resorts** (303/297-2757 or 888/297-2757, www.grandcanyonlodges.com). If at first it seems like you're not going to get the room you want, keep trying right up until you arrive. Call every day and check; if you are diligent, you can take advantage of cancellations. To reserve a room at Yavapai Lodge (which has the park's only pet-friendly rooms), contact **Delaware North** (877/404-4611, www.visitgrandcanyon.com).

Reservations for the North Rim's only in-park accommodations, **Grand Canyon Lodge** (928/638-2611 or 888/297-2757, www.grandcanyonlodgenorth.com), are handled separately.

Some of the towns outside the South Rim area of the park offer more accommodations options:

Tusayan (AZ-64): 1.5 miles (2.4 km, 5 minutes) from Grand Canyon National

From top to bottom: Verkamp's Visitor Center; a mule train along the North Kaibab Trail; Bright Angel Bicycles and Café.

Park South entrance; 7 miles (11.3 km) from Grand Canyon Village

Williams (I-40): 54 miles (87 km, 1 hour) from Grand Canyon National Park South entrance; 60 miles (97 km) from Grand Canyon Village

Flagstaff (I-40): 73.5 miles (118 km, 1.5 hours) from Grand Canyon National Park South entrance; 79 miles (127 km) from Grand Canyon Village

Campgrounds

All reservations for the South Rim's **Mather Campground** and the **North Rim Campground** go through **Recreation.gov** (877/444-6777, www.recreation.gov). To make reservations for the South Rim's **Trailer Village,** contact **Delaware North** (877/404-4611, www.visitgrandcanyon.com).

Mule Rides

Park concessionaire Xanterra's **Canyon Vistas Mule Ride** (303/297-2757 or 888/297-2757, www.grandcanyonlodges.com) along the South Rim goes year-round and includes one hour of orientation and a two-hour ride. Xanterra also offers overnight mule trips below the rim to Phantom Ranch.

On the North Rim, **Grand Canyon Trail Rides** (928/638-9875, www.canyonrides.com) offers three daily options during the high season: a one-hour trail ride through the forest and along the rim; a three-hour trail ride along the rim to Uncle Jim's Point; and a three-hour trail ride down the North Kaibab Trail to Supai Tunnel.

River Trips

A once-in-a-lifetime trip down the mighty Colorado River through the heart of the gorge takes a good deal of advance planning and booking. Book a tour or at least start the process at least 12-18 months in advance of your preferred departure date. The best place to start is the **Grand Canyon River Outfitters Association** (www.gcroa.org), a nonprofit group of about 16 licensed river outfitters, all of them monitored and approved by the National Park Service, each with a good safety record and similar rates. After you decide what kind of trip you want, the website links to the individual outfitters for booking. **O.A.R.S.** (800/346-6277, www.oars.com) is one highly recommended outfitter. Most of the companies offer trips between 3 and 18 days, and have a variety of boat styles. Choose two or three companies, call them up, and talk to someone live to make sure that you like the spirit of the tour. River trips are very social; you'll be spending a lot of time with your fellow boaters. Ask about previous trips so you can get a sense of the atmosphere and how many people are typically on a trip.

Seasons

At about 7,000 feet (2,134 m), the South Rim has a temperate climate: warm in the summer months, cool in spring and fall, and cold in the winter. It rains and snows in winter, and thunderstorms, sometimes quite violent, appear in the late afternoons of July, August, and early September. Summer brings the park's busiest season, and it is *very* busy. About three million visitors from all over the world visit the South Rim each summer, offering rare opportunities for people-watching and hobnobbing with fellow tourists from the far corners of the globe. Summer (May-Sept.) temperatures often exceed 110°F (43°C) in the inner canyon, which has a desert climate, but are cooler by 20-30°F (11-16°C) up on the forested rims. There's no reason for anybody to hike deep into the canyon in summer. It's not fun, and it is potentially deadly. Instead, plan your epic trek in the spring or fall, perfect times to visit the park: It's light-jacket cool on the South Rim and warm but not hot in the inner canyon.

Wintertime at Grand Canyon's South Rim lasts December-March, when the spring break traffic picks up. December is a festive and romantic time to be on the

South Rim, and there's always a chance that you'll wake up to a white Christmas. January and February are generally the park's slowest months, with just over 200,000 visitors per month (compared to, say, 750,000 visitors in July). These are the coldest months on the rim, with high temperatures in the 30s F (-1°C to 4°C) and 40s F (4-9°C) in January and the 40s F (4-9°C) and 50s F (10-15°C) in February. There is often snow and ice on the rim and on the upper stretches of the trails, and hiking may require crampons, which most of the shops in the park sell ($25). The best thing about visiting the canyon in winter is the relative solitude. It's much easier to secure reservations, and you encounter far fewer people on the roads, at the viewpoints, in the restaurants, stores, and visitors centers, and especially on the trails. There are, however, fewer services—there are no ranger programs at night during January and February, and the shuttle bus does not go to Hermit's Rest, though unlike during the summer months Hermit Road is open to private vehicles.

Information and Services

As you enter the South Rim, you'll get a copy of ***The Pocket Map,*** a newsprint publication that is indispensable. It's pretty comprehensive and will likely answer many of your questions. A **North Rim edition** is passed out at the North Rim entrance.

If you're driving to the park, note that the last place to fill up with gas is in **Tusayan,** 7 miles (11.3 km) from the park. The only in-park gas station is 26 miles (42 km) east of the central park at **Desert View.** The park operates a public garage near the rail depot (8am-noon and 1pm-5pm daily), where you can fix relatively minor car issues.

Most of the quotidian services are at the South Rim's **Market Plaza,** where there's a general store, **Chase Bank** and an ATM (foreign currency exchange for bank members only, 928/638-2437), a **post office** (928/638-2512), and **free Wi-Fi** in the **Canyon Village Market and Deli** (8am-8pm daily). There are also **ATMs** in the lobbies of the Bright Angel Lodge, El Tovar, and Maswik Lodge.

Free Wi-Fi can also be harnessed at **Park Headquarters** (8am-5pm Mon.-Fri., computers in research library available 8am-4:30pm) and the **Community Library** (10:30am-5pm Mon.-Sat., computers also available). If you are a guest at one of the in-park lodges, you will be able to access free Wi-Fi in the lobby, though probably not in the rooms.

At **Mather Campground** you'll find **coin-operated laundry machines and showers.**

For 24-hour medical services within the park, **dial 911.**

Take along an easy-to-carry receptacle to refill at the water fountains situated throughout the park. A **water bottle, CamelBak,** or **canteen** is simply required gear for a visit; you are going to get thirsty in the high, dry air along the rim. You might even bring along a cooler with cold water and other drinks, which you can leave in your car and revisit as the need arises.

Getting Around

Shuttles

The park operates excellent **free shuttle services** along the South Rim, with comfortable buses fueled by compressed natural gas. It's strongly encouraged you park your car for the duration of your visit and use the shuttle. It's nearly impossible to find parking at the various sights, and traffic through the park is not always easy to navigate—there are a lot of one-way routes and oblivious pedestrians that can lead to needless frustration. Make sure you pick up a free ***Pocket Map,*** which has a map of the various shuttle routes and stops, available at the entrance gate and at most visitors centers throughout the park.

March-September a route operates from the Grand Canyon Visitor Center and IMAX theater in Tusayan into the park, all day every day. You must have your park entrance pass before you board the shuttle. Entrance passes can be purchased at the IMAX theater as well as various other places around Tusayan, or online at www.recreation.gov. Just leave your car in the parking lot in Tusayan and take the free shuttles everywhere you want to go inside the park. Shuttles from the theater begin at 8am daily, and the last trip is at 9:45pm. The Tusayan shuttle drops you off at the Grand Canyon Visitor Center; the last shuttle out of the park leaves at 9:30pm. The shuttle runs every 20 minutes and takes about 20 minutes from Tusayan to the visitors center.

Pretty much anywhere you want to go in the park a shuttle will get you there, and you rarely have to wait more than 10 minutes at any stop. That being said, there is no shuttle that goes all the way to the Tusayan Ruin & Museum or the Desert View Watchtower near the East entrance.

Shuttle drivers are a good source of information about the park. They are generally very friendly and knowledgeable, and a few of them are genuinely entertaining. The shuttle conveniently runs from around sunup until about 9pm, and drivers always know the expected sunrise and sundown times and seem to be intent on getting people to the best overlooks to view these two popular daily park events.

The year-round **Kaibab/Rim Route (Orange)** will take you from Grand Canyon Visitor Center west to Yavapai Geology Museum and back, and east to the South Kaibab Trailhead, Yaki Point, and Pipe Creek Vista and back. Ride the year-round **Village Route (Blue)** west from the visitors center to Market Plaza, Shrine of the Ages, the Grand Canyon Railway Depot, Bright Angel Lodge, and the Hermit's Rest Route transfer area. Eastbound the Village Route goes from the transfer area to Maswik Lodge, the Backcountry Information Center, Shrine of the Ages, Mather Campground, Trailer Village, Market Plaza, and then back to the visitors center.

The **Hermit's Rest Route (Red)** runs March-November (Dec.-Feb. Hermit Road is open to private vehicles) and is the way most visitors reach the must-see western viewpoints along the South Rim. The route starts at the Village Route transfer area at the head of Hermit Road and heads west, stopping at Trailview Overlook, Maricopa Point, Powell Point, Mohave Point, The Abyss, Monument Creek Vista, Pima Point, and Hermit's Rest. Headed back east it makes stops only at Pima Point, Mohave Point, and Powell Point before returning to the Village Route transfer.

March-November, the **Tusayan Route (Purple)** runs south from the Grand Canyon Visitor Center outside the park to the IMAX theater in Tusayan, the Best Western Squire Inn, and the Grand Hotel, before returning back north to the visitors center.

Park shuttles have racks that fit 2-3 bikes. All shuttle buses are wheelchair accessible (up to 30 in/76 cm wide and 48 in/122 cm wide), with wheelchair ramps and low entrances and exits.

If you are in a hurry to get somewhere, the free shuttle bus is not what you need. Especially during the summer and on spring and early fall weekends, expect to stand in a line and watch several buses fill and depart before you get on.

Bicycle

Whether you're staying in the park or just visiting for the day, consider bringing your bike along. You can park your car at the **South Rim Backcountry Information Center parking lot** (across the train tracks from the village) and ride your bike all around the park from there using the paved **Tuyasan Greenway Trail.** Every hotel, restaurant, store, and sight has a bike rack; don't forget your bike lock. If you get tired, park shuttles have racks that fit 2-3 bikes. Remember, though, that the shuttles take a lot longer because

The Canyon and the Railroad

It wasn't until the **Santa Fe Railroad** reached the South Rim of the Grand Canyon in 1901 that the great chasm's now-famous tourist trade really got going. Prior to that, travelers faced an all-day stagecoach ride from Flagstaff at a cost of $20, a high price to pay for sore bones and cramped quarters. Thanks to the railroad, even travelers of a less seasoned variety could see the wonders of the West, including the Grand Canyon, with relative ease.

The railroad's main concessionaire, the **Fred Harvey Company,** in those years operated "Harvey House" hotels, restaurants, and lunch counters all along the Santa Fe line. Widely celebrated for their high-quality fare and service, these eateries often became the nicest place in town in places that were still little more than frontier outposts. Each Harvey Company restaurant was staffed by the famous **"Harvey Girls,"** young women often recruited in cities, intensively trained as waitresses, and then sent out to work at far-flung spots along the railway. Hard-working and efficient, they were expected to adhere to strict company rules and were held to high standards of service. Being a Harvey Girl provided the opportunity for women to be adventurous pioneers, living and working independently and helping to settle the West. There are today several women who worked as Harvey Girls buried in Grand Canyon's Pioneer Cemetery.

Along with bringing its special brand of service to the South Rim, the Harvey Company in the 1920s and 1930s enlisted the considerable talents of Arts and Crafts designer and architect **Mary Jane Colter** to build lodges, lookouts, galleries, and stores on the South Rim. These treasured buildings still stand today, and are now considered to be some of the finest architectural accomplishments in the entire national parks system. The Harvey Company's dedication to simple elegance, and Colter's interest in and understanding of Pueblo Indian architecture and lifeways, created an artful human stamp on the rim that nearly lives up to the breathtaking canyon it serves.

For half a century or more, the Santa Fe line from Williams took millions of tourists to the edge of the canyon. But finally the American love affair with the automobile, the rising mythology of the go-west road trip, and the interstate highway system killed train travel to Grand Canyon National Park by the late 1960s. In the 1990s, however, entrepreneurs revived the railroad as an excursion and tourist line. Today, the **Grand Canyon Railway** carries more than 250,000 passengers to the South Rim every year, which has significantly reduced polluting automobile traffic in the cramped park.

they make many stops. There's a good map of all the in-park bike routes in the free *Pocket Map* guide, and staff members at **Bright Angel Bicycles and Café** (928/814-8704, www.bikegrandcanyon.com, 6am-8pm daily Apr.-Nov., 7am-7pm daily Dec.-Mar.), right next to the Grand Canyon Visitor Center near the South entrance and Mather Point, can answer your questions and also offer bike rentals.

Tours

Bus Tours

Xanterra, the park's main concessionaire, offers in-park **motorcoach tours** (303/297-2757 or 888/297-2757, www.grandcanyonlodges.com, $70 pp adults, $30 pp kids 3-16). Options include sunrise and sunset tours, and longer drives to the eastern Desert View area and the western reaches of the park at Hermit's Rest. This is a comfortable, educational, and entertaining way to see the park, and odds are you will come away with a few new friends—possibly even a new email pal from abroad. Only pay for a tour if you like being around a lot of other people and listening to mildly entertaining banter from the tour guides for hours at a time. It's easy to see and learn about everything the park has to offer without spending extra money on a tour; as in most national parks, the highly informed and friendly rangers hanging around the

South Rim's sites offer the same information that you'll get on an expensive tour, but for free. Also, if you like being on your own and getting out away from the crowds, a tour is not for you. To book a tour through Xanterra, you can either plan ahead and book online, or when you arrive check at the activities desk at Maswik and Bright Angel Lodges, from which the tours begin.

Airplane and Helicopter Tours

Though not ideal from the back-to-nature point of view, a helicopter or plane flight over the canyon is an exciting, rare experience and can be well worth the rather expensive price—a chance to take some unique photos from a condor's perspective. Flights are only allowed in a few sections of the canyon, and most spend time over the plateau forests and the eastern canyon. Five companies offer air tours out of **Grand Canyon Airport** (www.grandcanyonairport.org), along AZ-64 in Tusayan, and most of them offer many more flights originating in Las Vegas. They all prefer reservations. While some companies offer you the choice of paying a little more for a quieter EcoStar helicopter, others use only EcoStars. Most of the companies offer narration in at least nine different languages.

One of the better operators is **Maverick Helicopters** (888/261-4414, www.maverickhelicopter.com), which offers the Canyon Spirit Tour that departs from Grand Canyon Airport in Tusayan and soars over the Kaibab National Forest, the confluence of the Colorado River and Little Colorado River, and Marble Canyon (45 minutes, $299 pp).

The South Rim

The South Rim is by far the most developed portion of Grand Canyon National Park and should be seen by every American, as Teddy Roosevelt once recommended. Here you'll stand side by side with people from all over the globe, each one breathless on their initial stare into the canyon and more often than not hit suddenly with an altered perception of time and human history. Don't let the rustic look of the buildings fool you into thinking you're roughing it. The food here is above average for a national park. The restaurant at El Tovar offers some of the finest, most romantic dining in the state, and all with one of the great wonders of the world just 25 feet (7.6 m) away.

The best way to explore the South Rim is to park your vehicle in one of the large parking lots near the main visitors center or at Market Plaza, and then take the free shuttle bus to the viewpoints and sights. It's also possible to explore on foot via the Rim Trail and greenways, or by bike on the roads and greenways.

Driving Tours

★ Hermit Road

7 miles (11.3 km)

- **Hermit Road** is open to **private vehicles** in **winter only** (Dec.-Feb.).
- In **spring, summer,** and **fall** (Mar.-Nov.), this makes a great **walking tour** or **shuttle tour.**

March-November, the park's free shuttle goes all the way to architect and Southwestern-design queen Mary Jane Colter's **Hermit's Rest,** about 7 miles (11.3 km) from Grand Canyon Village along the park's western scenic drive called the **Hermit Road.** It takes approximately two hours to complete the loop, stopping at eight viewpoints along the way. On the return route, buses stop only at Mohave and Hopi Points. The Hermit Road viewpoints are some of the best in the park for viewing the sunsets. To make it in time for these dramatic solar performances, catch the bus at least an hour before sunset. There is often a long wait at the **Hermit's Rest Transfer Stop,** just west of the Bright Angel Lodge. The bus drivers generally know the times of sunrise and sunset. The route is open to cars

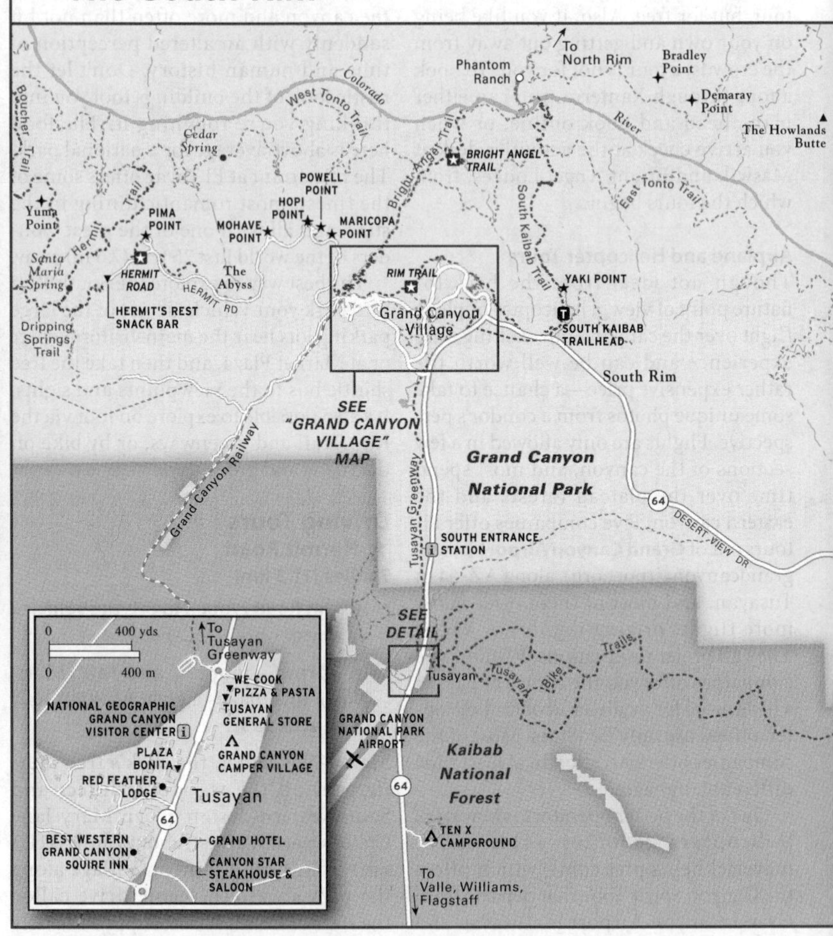

beginning in December, when you can drive to most of the viewpoints and stare at your leisure.

Each of the Hermit Road lookouts provides a slightly different perspective on the canyon, whether it be a strange, unnoticed outcropping or a brief view of the white-tipped river rapids far, far below.

The first stop along the route is the **Trailview Overlook** (1.5 mi/2.4 km from village), from which you can see the Bright Angel Trail twisting down into the canyon and across the plateau to overlook the Colorado River.

The next major stop along the route is **Maricopa Point** (2.7 mi/4.3 km from village), which provides a vast, mostly unobstructed view of the canyon all the way to the river. The point is on a promontory that juts out into the canyon over 100 feet (30 m). This is the former site of the Orphan Mine, first opened in 1893 as a source of copper and silver—and, for a

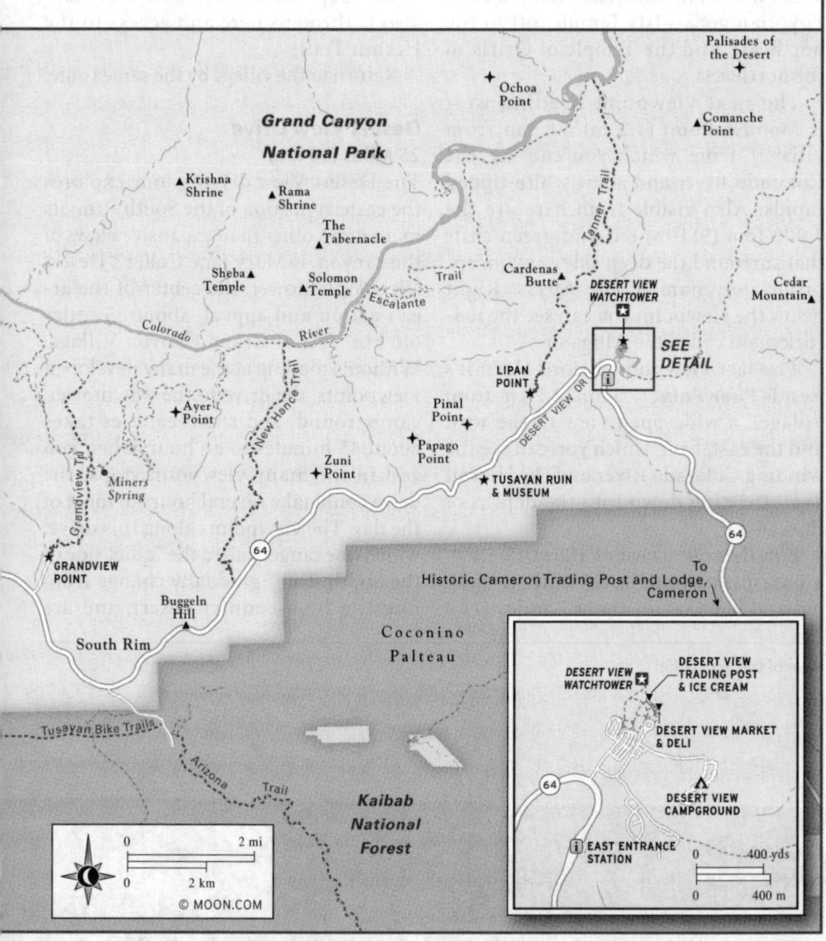

few busy years during the height of the Cold War, uranium.

Consider taking the 10- to 15-minute hike along the Rim Trail west through the piney rim world to the next viewing area, **Powell Point** (3.3 mi/5.3 km from village). Here stands a memorial to the one-armed explorer and writer John Wesley Powell, who led the first and second scientific river expeditions through the canyon in 1869 and 1871. The memorial is a flat-topped pyramid, which you can ascend to stand tall over the canyon. The views of the western reaches of the gorge are pretty good here, and this is a strong candidate for a sunset-viewing vantage point.

About 0.3 mile (0.5 km) along Hermit Road from Powell Point is **Hopi Point** (2.9 mi/4.7 km from village), which offers sweeping, open views of the western canyon. As a result, it is the most popular west-end point for viewing the sun dropping red and orange in the west.

North from here, across the canyon, look for the famous mesas named after Egyptian gods—Isis Temple, off to the northeast, and the Temple of Osiris to the northwest.

The next viewpoint heading west is **Mohave Point** (4.2 mi/6.8 km from village), from which you can see the Colorado River and a few white-tipped rapids. Also visible from here are the 3,000-foot (914-m) red-and-green cliffs that surround the deep side canyon, appropriately named The Abyss. Right below the viewpoint you can see the red-rock mesa called the Alligator.

The last viewpoint before Hermit's Rest is **Pima Point** (7.5 mi/12.1 km from village), a wide-open view to the west and the east, from which you can see the winding Colorado River and the Hermit Trail twisting down into the depths of the canyon.

Finally you arrive at **Hermit's Rest,** a charming stone hovel built to look old and haphazard, about 7 miles (11.3 km) from the village. Inside there's a gift shop and a snack bar. There are also bathrooms here and access to the Hermit Trail.

Return to the village by the same route.

Desert View Drive

25 Miles (40 km)

The Desert View driving tour explores the eastern portion of the South Rim; its main draw, other than expansive views of the canyon, is Mary Jane Colter's Desert View Watchtower, the center of the area's action and appeal, about 25 miles (40 km) east of Grand Canyon Village. Without stopping at the many developed viewpoints, the drive to the watchtower, campground, and small eateries takes about 45 minutes to an hour; when you add in the many viewpoint stops, the drive could take several hours to most of the day. The viewpoints along this drive, which one ranger called the "quiet side of the South Rim," gradually change from forest to high-country desert, and are

view of the South Rim

typically less crowded than those that can be reached by the shuttle.

The free shuttle goes only as far as **Yaki Point,** a great place to watch the sunrise and sunset, near the popular South Kaibab Trailhead. Yaki Point is at the end of a 1.5-mile (2.4-km) side road northeast of AZ-64. The area is closed to private vehicles, but all the other stops to the east can be reached only by private vehicle. If you want to make Yaki Point part of the Desert View driving tour, you can park your car at a small picnic area just east of the side road (about 2 mi/3.2 km from the village) and then cross the road and follow a path for about 0.5 mile (0.8 km) through the woods to the promontory and the South Kaibab Trailhead.

Along Desert View Drive, make sure not to miss the essential **Grandview Point,** where the original canyon lodge once stood long ago. From here the rough Grandview Trail leads below the rim. The viewpoint sits at 7,400 feet (2,256 m), about 12 miles (19.3 km) east of the village and then a mile (1.6 km) on a side road. It's considered one of the grandest views of them all, hence the name; the canyon spreads out willingly from here, and the sunrise in the east hits it strong and happy. To the east, look for the 7,844-foot (2,391-m) monument called the Sinking Ship, and to the north below look for Horseshoe Mesa.

Moran Point, east of Grandview, is just 8 miles (12.9 km) south of Cape Royal (as the condor flies) on the North Rim and offers some impressive views of the canyon and the river (18 mi/29 km from village).The point is named for the great painter of the canyon, Thomas Moran, whose brave attempts to capture the gorge on canvas helped create the buzz that led to the canyon's federal protection. Directly below the left side of the point you'll see Hance Rapid, one of the largest on the Colorado. It's 3 miles (4.8 km) away, but if you're quiet you might be able to hear the rushing and roaring.

Farther on Desert View Drive you'll come to **Tusayan Ruin & Museum** (22 mi/35 km from village). Stop here for a self-guided walking tour of the small Ancestral Puebloan ruin and a look around the small museum with exhibits about the rim's ancient inhabitants and the descendants who still call the region home.

As the drive winds down and the trees turn from pine to pinyon to scrub, **Lipan Point** (23.3 mi/37 km from village) offers wide-open vistas and the best view of the river from the South Rim. It's one of the most popular viewpoints on the South Rim for watching the sunrise and sunset.

Finally, at Desert View, there's a large parking lot, bathrooms, gift shops, a deli, a gas station, and a campground. From the patio of the amazing, can't-miss **Desert View Watchtower** (25 mi/40 km from village), you'll be able to catch a faraway glimpse of sacred Navajo Mountain near the Utah-Arizona border, the most distant point visible from within the park.

Turn around and head back to the village on the same road, stopping again at the viewpoints or just cruising along through the forest.

Sights

Though you wouldn't want to make a habit of it, you could spend a few happy hours at **Grand Canyon Village Historical District** with your back to the canyon. Then again, this small assemblage of hotels, restaurants, gift shops, and lookouts offers some of the best viewpoints from which to gaze comfortably at all that multicolored splendor. Here is a perfect vantage from which to spot the strip of greenery just below the rim called **Indian Garden,** and follow with your eyes—or even your feet—the famous **Bright Angel Trail** as it twists improbably down the rim's rock face. You can also see some of the most interesting and evocative buildings in the state, all of them registered National Historic Landmarks.

Bright Angel Lodge

The village's central hub of activity, rustic and charming **Bright Angel Lodge** was designed in 1935 by Mary Jane Colter to replace the old Bright Angel Hotel, which pioneer John Hance built in the 1890s, and the Bright Angel Camp tent-city near the trail of the same name. Originally meant to attract more middle-class tourists to the park, the lodge is still a romantic and comfortable place to stay, resembling a rough-hewn hunting lodge constructed of materials found nearby.

The **Bright Angel History Room,** just off the main lobby, has fascinating exhibits and artifacts telling the story of the Fred Harvey Company, architect Mary Jane Colter, the Santa Fe Railroad, and the early years of Southwestern tourism. Spend some time in here learning about the legendary Harvey Girls, who hosted a golden age of train travel from Chicago to Los Angeles. You'll also see Colter's "geologic fireplace," a 10-foot-high (3-m) re-creation of the canyon's varied strata.

Bright Angel Lodge in Grand Canyon Village

Geologists collected the stones from the inner canyon and loaded them on the backs of mules for the journey out. The fireplace's strata appear exactly like those stacked throughout the canyon walls, equaling a couple of billion years of earth-building from bottom to rim.

For a break from the outdoors, step into the **Bright Angel Cocktail Lounge,** a dark and cozy bar off the lobby where you can relax over a pint of Arizona-brewed beer. Don't miss the charming murals on the walls depicting Native American imagery and greenhorn tourists riding mules into the canyon. The Bright Angel lobby also has one of the best gift shops in the park.

El Tovar

Just east of the lodge is **El Tovar,** the South Rim's first great hotel and the picture of haute-wilderness style. Designed in 1905 by Charles Whittlesey for the Santa Fe Railroad, El Tovar has the look of a Swiss chalet and a log-house interior, watched over by the wall-hung heads of elk and buffalo; it is at once rustic, cozy, and elegant. This Harvey Company jewel has hosted dozens of rich and famous canyon visitors over the years, including George Bernard Shaw and presidents Teddy Roosevelt and William Howard Taft. On the rim side, a gazebo stands near the edge. While it is a wonderfully romantic building up close, El Tovar looks even more picturesque from a few of the viewpoints along the Hermit Road, and you can really get a good idea of just how close the lodge is to the rim by seeing it from far away. Inside you'll find two gift shops and a cozy lounge where you can have a drink or two while looking at the canyon. El Tovar's restaurant is the best in the park, and it's quite pleasant to sink into one of the arts-and-crafts leather chairs in the rustic, dark-wood lobby.

Hopi House

A few steps from the front porch of El Tovar is Mary Jane Colter's **Hopi House,** designed and built in 1905 as if it sat not at the edge of the Grand Canyon but on the edge of Hopi's Third Mesa. Hopi workers used local materials to build this unique gift shop and gallery for Native American art. The Fred Harvey Company even hired the famous Hopi-Tewa potter Nampeyo to live here with her family while demonstrating her artistic talents and Hopi lifeways to tourists. This is one of the best places in the region for viewing and buying Hopi, Navajo, and Pueblo art (though most of the art is quite expensive), and there are even items made by Nampeyo's descendants on view and for sale here.

Lookout Studio

Mary Jane Colter also designed the **Lookout Studio** west of the Bright Angel Lodge, a little stacked-stone watch house that seems to be a mysterious extension of the rim itself. The stone patio juts out over the canyon and is a popular place for picture taking. The Lookout was built in

1914 exactly for that purpose—to provide a comfortable but "indigenous" building and deck from which visitors could gaze at and photograph the canyon. It was fitted with high-powered telescopes and soon became one of the most popular snapshot scenes on the rim. It still is today, and on many days you'll be standing elbow to elbow with camera-carrying tourists clicking away. As she did with her other buildings on the rim, Colter designed the Lookout to be a kind of amalgam of Native American ruins and backcountry pioneer utilitarianism. Her formula of using found and indigenous materials, stacked haphazardly, works wonderfully here. When it was first built, the little stone hovel was so "authentic" that it even had weeds growing out of the roof. Inside, where you'll find books and canyon souvenirs, the studio looks much as it did when it first opened. The jutting stone patio is still one of the best places from which to view the canyon.

Kolb Studio

Built in 1904 right on the canyon's rim, **Kolb Studio** is significant not so much for its design but for the human story that went on inside. It was the home and studio of the famous Kolb Brothers, pioneer canyon photographers, moviemakers, river rafters, and entrepreneurs. Inside there's a gift shop, a gallery, and a display about the brothers, who, in 1912, rode the length of the Colorado in a boat with a movie camera rolling. The journey resulted in a classic book of exploration and river-running, Emery Kolb's 1914 *Through the Grand Canyon from Wyoming to Mexico.* The Kolb Brothers were some of the first entrepreneurs at the canyon. Around 1902 they set up a photography studio in a cave near the rim and later moved it to this house. After a falling-out between the brothers, the younger Emery Kolb stayed on at the

From top to bottom: El Tovar lodge; Lookout Studio; Hopi House.

canyon until his death in 1976, showing daily the film the brothers had made of their epic river trip to several generations of canyon visitors.

Viewpoints

While the canyon's unrelenting vastness tends to blur the eyes into forgetting the details, viewing the gorge from many different points seems to cure this; however, there are 19 named viewpoints along the South Rim Road, from the easternmost Desert View to the westernmost Hermit's Rest. Is it necessary, or even a good idea, to see them all? No, not really. For many it's difficult to pick out the various named buttes, mesas, side canyons, drainages, and other features that rise and fall and undulate throughout the gorge, and one viewpoint ends up looking not that different from the next.

The best way to see the canyon viewpoints is to park your car and walk along the **Rim Trail.** Attempts to visit each viewpoint tend to speed up your visit and make you miss the subtleties of the different views. Consider really getting to know a few select viewpoints rather than trying to quickly and superficially hit each one. Any of the viewpoints along the **Hermit Road** and **Desert View Drive** are candidates for a long love affair. The views from just outside **El Tovar** or the **Bright Angel Lodge,** right in the middle of all the bustling village action, are as gorgeous as any others, and it can be fun and illuminating to watch people's reactions to what they're seeing.

There isn't a bad view of the canyon, but if you have limited time, ask a ranger at the park's main Grand Canyon Visitor Center or Yavapai Geology Museum and Observation Station what their favorite viewpoint is and why. The shuttle bus drivers are also great sources of information and opinions. Try to see at least one sunset or sunrise at one of the developed viewpoints. The canyon's colors and details can seem monotonous after the initial thrill wears off (if it ever does), but the sun splashing and dancing at different strengths and angles against the multihued buttes and sheer, shadowy walls makes it all new again.

Mather Point

As most South Rim visitors enter through the park's South entrance, it's no surprise that the most visited viewpoint in the park is the first one along that route—**Mather Point,** named for the first National Park Service director, Stephen T. Mather. While crowded, Mather Point offers a typically astounding view of the canyon and is probably the mind's-eye view that most casual visitors take away. It can get busy, especially in the summer. Park at one of the four large lots near the visitors center complex and walk the short paved path from the **Grand Canyon Visitor Center.** At Mather Point you can walk out onto two railed-off jutting rocks to feel like you're hovering on the edge of an abyss, but you may have to stand in line to get right up to the edge.

Yavapai Geology Museum and Observation Station

Yavapai Geology Museum and Observation Station (928/638-7890, 8am-8pm daily summer, 8am-6pm daily winter, free) is the best place in the park to learn about the canyon's geology. This Kaibab limestone and ponderosa pine museum and bookstore is a must-visit for visitors interested in learning about what they're seeing.

Designed by architect Herbert Maier and first opened in 1928, the building itself is of interest. The stacked-stone structure, like Mary Jane Colter's buildings, merges with the rim itself to appear a foregone and inevitable part of the landscape. It's cool in here in the summer and warm in the winter. It's a place where time is easily lost, where you enter the gorge's deep time, and you may even forget that you are in a museum while staring through the large windows that face the canyon. That's because you're

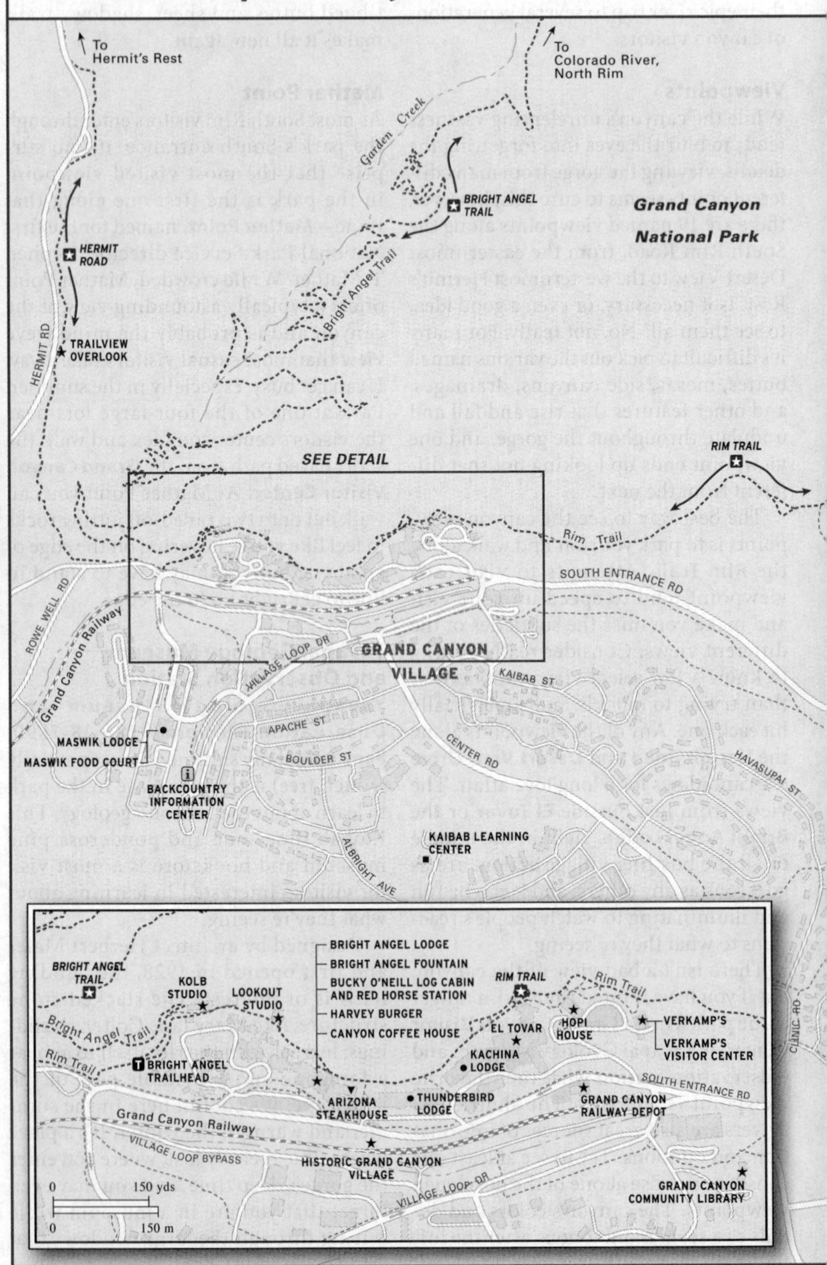
Grand Canyon Village
To Hermit's Rest
To Colorado River, North Rim
Garden Creek
BRIGHT ANGEL TRAIL
Grand Canyon National Park
HERMIT ROAD
Bright Angel Trail
HERMIT RD
TRAILVIEW OVERLOOK
SEE DETAIL
RIM TRAIL
Rim Trail
SOUTH ENTRANCE RD
ROWE WELL RD
Grand Canyon Railway
GRAND CANYON VILLAGE
VILLAGE LOOP DR
KAIBAB ST
APACHE ST
MASWIK LODGE
MASWIK FOOD COURT
BOULDER ST
CENTER RD
HAVASUPAI ST
BACKCOUNTRY INFORMATION CENTER
KAIBAB LEARNING CENTER
ALBRIGHT AVE
BRIGHT ANGEL LODGE
BRIGHT ANGEL FOUNTAIN
BUCKY O'NEILL LOG CABIN AND RED HORSE STATION
HARVEY BURGER
CANYON COFFEE HOUSE
BRIGHT ANGEL TRAIL
KOLB STUDIO
LOOKOUT STUDIO
Bright Angel Trail
Rim Trail
BRIGHT ANGEL TRAILHEAD
RIM TRAIL
Rim Trail
HOPI HOUSE
EL TOVAR
VERKAMP'S
VERKAMP'S VISITOR CENTER
KACHINA LODGE
CLINIC RD
SOUTH ENTRANCE RD
ARIZONA STEAKHOUSE
THUNDERBIRD LODGE
GRAND CANYON RAILWAY DEPOT
Grand Canyon Railway
VILLAGE LOOP BYPASS
HISTORIC GRAND CANYON VILLAGE
VILLAGE LOOP DR
GRAND CANYON COMMUNITY LIBRARY
0 150 yds
0 150 m

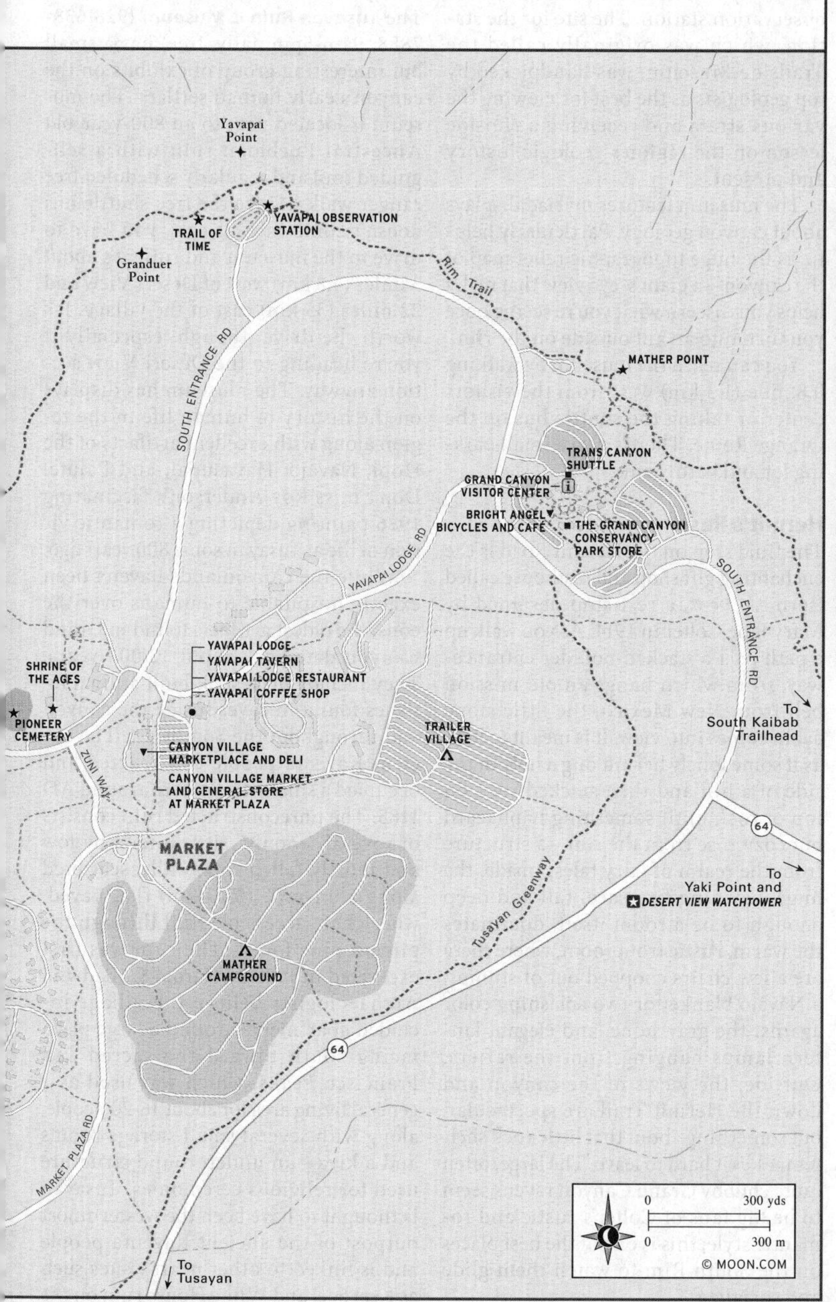
Yavapai Point
TRAIL OF TIME
YAVAPAI OBSERVATION STATION
Granduer Point
Rim Trail
SOUTH ENTRANCE RD
MATHER POINT
TRANS CANYON SHUTTLE
GRAND CANYON VISITOR CENTER
BRIGHT ANGEL BICYCLES AND CAFÉ
THE GRAND CANYON CONSERVANCY PARK STORE
YAVAPAI LODGE RD
SOUTH ENTRANCE RD
YAVAPAI LODGE
YAVAPAI TAVERN
YAVAPAI LODGE RESTAURANT
YAVAPAI COFFEE SHOP
SHRINE OF THE AGES
PIONEER CEMETERY
ZUNI WAY
CANYON VILLAGE MARKETPLACE AND DELI
CANYON VILLAGE MARKET AND GENERAL STORE AT MARKET PLAZA
TRAILER VILLAGE
To South Kaibab Trailhead
64
MARKET PLAZA
To Yaki Point and
DESERT VIEW WATCHTOWER
Tusayan Greenway
MATHER CAMPGROUND
64
MARKET PLAZA RD
0
300 yds
0
300 m
© MOON.COM
To Tusayan

not really in a museum, but rather an observation station. The site for the station, which was originally called the Trailside Museum, was handpicked by top geologists as the best for viewing the various strata and receiving a rimside lesson on the region's geologic history and present.

The museum features myriad displays about canyon geology. Particularly helpful is the huge topographic relief map of the canyon—a giant's-eye view that really helps you discern what you're seeing once you turn into an ant outside on the rim.

You can reach the museum by walking 0.8 mile (1.3 km) west from the visitors center or taking the shuttle bus on the Orange Route. There's also a small parking lot and bathrooms.

Hermit's Rest

The final stop on the Hermit Road is the enchanting gift shop and resthouse called **Hermit's Rest,** a rest-stop designed by Mary Jane Colter in 1914. As you walk up a path past a stacked-boulder entranceway, from which hangs an old mission bell from New Mexico, the little stone cabin comes into view. It is meant to look as if some lonely hermit dug a hole in the side of a hill and then stacked rock on top of rock until something haphazard but cozy rose from the rim—a structure from the realm of fairy tales. Inside, the huge, yawning fireplace, tall and deep enough to be a room itself, dominates the warm, rustic front room, where there are a few chairs chopped out of stumps, a Navajo blanket or two splashing color against the gray stone, and elegant lantern lamps hanging from the rafters. Outside, the views of the canyon and down the Hermit Trail are spectacular, but something about that little rock shelter makes it hard to leave. The large, often quite chubby Grand Canyon ravens seem to be big fans of Colter's rustic and romantic style; this is one of the best places on the South Rim to watch them glide and socialize.

Tusayan Ruin & Museum

The **Tusayan Ruin & Museum** (928/638-7888, 9am-5pm daily, free) has a small but interesting group of exhibits on the canyon's early human settlers. The museum is located next to an 800-year-old Ancestral Puebloan ruin with a self-guided trail and regularly scheduled free ranger walks. Since the free shuttle bus doesn't come this far east, you have to drive to the museum and ruin; it's about 3 miles (4.8 km) west of Desert View and 22 miles (35 km) east of the village. It's worth the drive, though, especially if you're heading to the Desert View section anyway. The museum has displays on the history of human life in the region along with excellent artifacts of the Hopi, Navajo, Havasupai, and Paiute. Don't miss Roy Anderson's fascinating 1986 painting depicting a romantic vision of life at Tusayan some 800 years ago.

While the canyonlands haven't been exactly hospitable to humans over the eons, the oldest artifacts found in Grand Canyon date back about 12,000 years. They include little stick-built animal fetishes found in caves inside the canyon and throughout the Southwest. The ancient Kayenta people constructed and occupied a small village here around AD 1185. The unreconstructed ruin consists of several "rooms" surrounded by low and mostly fallen rock walls, scattered along a 0.1-mile (0.16-km) flat, paved, wheelchair-accessible trail through the pinyon-pine forest. The ruin was first excavated in 1930 by Harold S. Gladwin. Archaeologists believe the village included apartments around a large plaza facing south toward the sacred San Francisco Peaks, which was used as a general living area for about 16-20 people, along with several small storage rooms and a kiva—an underground structure used for religious ceremonies. Tusayan is thought to have been the westernmost outpost of the ancient Kayenta people and is linked to other nearby sites such as Keet Seel and White House ruin on the

Navajo Reservation to the east. Follow the short entrance road off the Desert View Drive to the native-stone building and parking lot; you'll find bathrooms close by.

★ Desert View Watchtower

What is perhaps the most mysterious and thrilling of Mary Jane Colter's canyon creations, the **Desert View Watchtower** (built in 1932) is an artful homage to smaller Ancestral Puebloan-built towers found at Hovenweep National Monument and elsewhere in the Four Corners region, the exact purpose of which is still unknown.

You reach the tower's high, windy deck by climbing the twisting, steep steps winding around the open middle, past walls painted with visions of Hopi lore and religion by Hopi artist Fred Kabotie. From the deck of the watchtower, the South Rim's highest viewpoint, the whole arid expanse opens up, and you feel something like a lucky survivor at the very edge of existence, even among the crowds. Such is the evocative power, the rough-edged romanticism, of Colter's vision.

Recreation

Hiking

Something about a well-built trail twisting deep into an unknown territory can spur even the most habitually sedentary canyon visitor to begin an epic trudge. This phenomenon is responsible for both the best and worst of the South Rim's busy recreation life. It is not uncommon to see hikers a mile (1.6 km) or more below the rim picking along in high heels and sauntering blithely in flip-flops, not a drop of water between them. It's best to go to the canyon prepared to hike, with proper footwear and plenty of water and snacks. You'll probably want to hike

From top to bottom: Desert View Watchtower; Yavapai Geology Museum and Observation Station; hikers on the Bright Angel Trail.

a little, and since there's no such thing as an easy hike into the Grand Canyon, going in prepared, even if it's just for a few miles, will make your hike a pleasure rather than chore. Also, remember that there aren't any loop hikes here: If you hike in (down) a mile, you also must hike out (up) a mile.

TOP EXPERIENCE

★ Rim Trail

Distance: 12.8 miles (20.6 km) one-way
Duration: all day
Elevation gain: about 200 feet (61 m)
Effort: easy
Trailhead: Grand Canyon Village east to South Kaibab Trailhead or west to Hermit's Rest

If you can manage a nearly 13-mile (20.9 km), relatively easy walk at an altitude of around 7,000 feet (2,134 m), the **Rim Trail** provides the single best way to see all of the South Rim. The trail, paved for most of its length, runs from the South Kaibab Trailhead area on the east, through the village, and all the way west to Hermit's Rest, hitting every major point of interest and beauty along the way. The path gets a little tough as it rises a bit past the Bright Angel Trailhead just west of the village. Heading farther west, the trail becomes a thin, dirt single-track between Powell Point and Monument Creek Vista, but it never gets too difficult. (You can avoid these sections by walking on the road, which is paved.) It would be considered an easy, scenic walk by just about anybody, kids included. But perhaps the best thing about the Rim Trail is that you don't have to hike the whole 12.8 miles (20.6 km)—far from it. There are at least 16 shuttle stops along the way, and you can hop on and off the trail at your pleasure. Dogs are allowed on the Rim Trail with a leash, but you can't take them on the shuttle buses.

Few will want to hike the entire way, of course. Such an epic walk would in fact require twice the miles (or at least one long ride on the shuttle bus), as the trail is not a loop but a ribbon stretched out flat along the rim from west to east. It's better to pick out a relatively short stretch and take your time.

TOP EXPERIENCE

★ Bright Angel Trail

Distance: 3-9 miles (4.8-14.5 km) round-trip
Duration: 2-8 hours
Elevation gain: 3,040 feet (927 m) from trailhead to Indian Garden
Effort: moderate to difficult
Trailhead: Grand Canyon Village, just west of Bright Angel Lodge

Hiking down the **Bright Angel Trail,** you quickly leave behind the piney rim and enter a sharp and arid landscape, twisting down and around switchbacks on a path that is sometimes all rock underfoot. Step aside for the many mule trains that use this route, and watch for the droppings, which are everywhere. It doesn't take long for the rim to look very far away, and you soon feel like you are deep within a chasm and those rim-top people are mere ants scurrying about.

The Bright Angel Trail is the most popular trail in the canyon owing in part to its starting just to the west of the Bright Angel Lodge in the village center. It's considered by park staff to be the safest trail because it has two resthouses with water. The Bright Angel was once the only easily accessible corridor trail from the South Rim, and for years Grand Canyon pioneer Ralph Cameron charged $1 per person to use it. Many South Rim visitors choose to walk down the (now free) Bright Angel Trail a bit just to get a feeling of what it's like to be below the rim. If you want to do something a little more structured, the 3-mile (4.8-km) round-trip hike to the **Mile-and-a-Half Resthouse** is a good introduction to the steep, twisting trail. The going gets tougher on the way to **Three-Mile Resthouse,** a 6-mile (9.7 km) round-trip hike. Both resthouses have water available from mid-May to mid-October, but don't rely on it; breaks in the trans-canyon waterline sometimes shuts them down. One of the best day hikes from the South Rim is the 9-mile (14.5-km) round-trip to beautiful **Indian Garden,** a cool and green oasis in the arid inner canyon. This is a rather punishing day hike, not recommended in the summer.

South Kaibab Trail

Distance: 1.8-6 miles (2.9-9.7 km) round-trip
Duration: 1-6 hours
Elevation gain: 2,040 feet (622 m) from trailhead to Skeleton Point
Effort: moderate to difficult
Trailhead: near Yaki Point

Steep but relatively short, the 7-mile (11.3-km) **South Kaibab Trail** provides the quickest, most direct route from the South Rim to and from the river. It's popular with day hikers and those looking for the quickest way into the gorge, and many consider it superior to the often-crowded Bright Angel Trail. The trailhead is located a few miles east of the village near Yaki Point, which is closed to private vehicles; take the shuttle bus on the Kaibab/Rim Route (Orange).

The 1.8-mile (2.9-km) round-trip hike to **Ooh Aah Point** has great views of the canyon from steep switchbacks. A common turnaround point for day hikers, **Cedar Ridge** is a 3-mile (4.8-km) round-trip hike. If you are interested in a longer haul, the 6-mile (9.7-km) round-trip hike to **Skeleton Point,** from which you can see the Colorado River, is probably as far along this trail as you'll want to go in one day, though in summer you might want to reconsider descending that far.

There's no water anywhere along the trail, and there's no shade to speak of. Bighorn sheep have been known to haunt this trail, and you might feel akin to those dexterous beasts while hiking the rocky ridgeline, which seems unbearably steep in a few places, especially on the way back up. Deer and California condors are also regular residents of the South Kaibab Trail. This is the trail the mules use, so make sure to step aside and wait while the mule trains pass.

Hermit Trail to Dripping Spring

Distance: 6.2 miles (10 km) round-trip
Duration: 5-7 hours
Elevation gain: 1,600 feet (488 m)
Effort: difficult
Trailhead: just west of Hermit's Rest

Built by the Santa Fe Railroad as a challenge to the fee-charging keeper of the Bright Angel Trail, the **Hermit Trail** just past Hermit's Rest leads to some less visited areas of the canyon. This trail isn't maintained with the same energy as the well-traveled corridor trails, and it has no potable water. You could take the Hermit Trail 9 miles (14.5 km) deep into the canyon to the river, where Fred Harvey built the first below-rim camp for tourists, complete with a tramway from the rim, the ruins of which are still visible. But such a trudge should be left only to fully geared experts. Not so the 6.2-mile (10-km) round-trip hike to the secluded and green **Dripping Spring,** which is one of the best day hikes in the canyon for midlevel to expert hikers. Start out on the Hermit Trail's steep, rocky, almost stair-like switchbacks. You come to the Waldron Trail Junction after 1.3 miles (2.1 km). Look for the **Dripping Spring Trailhead** after about 0.2 mile (0.3 km) from the Waldron Trail Junction, once you reach a more level section dominated by pinyon pine and juniper. Veer left (west) on the trail, which begins to rise a bit and leads along a ridgeline across **Hermit Basin;** the views are so awe-inspiring that it's difficult to keep your eyes on the skinny trail. After about 1 mile (1.6 km), you'll come to the junction with the Boucher Trail. Continue heading west, hiking about 0.5 mile (0.8 km) up a side canyon to the cool and shady rock overhang known as Dripping Spring. And it really does drip: A shock of fernlike greenery creeps off the rock overhang, trickling cold spring water at a steady pace into a small collecting pool (don't drink without treating it). Get your head wet, have a picnic, and kick back in this out-of-the-way, hard-won oasis. But don't stay too long. The hike back up is nothing to take lightly: The switchbacks are punishing, and the end, as it always does when one is hiking up a trail in the Grand Canyon, seems to get farther away as your legs begin to gain fatigue-weight. There's no water on the trail, so make sure to bring enough along and conserve it.

Grandview Trail

Distance: 3.2 miles (5.1 km) one-way to Horseshoe Mesa
Duration: 1-2 days
Elevation gain: 2,500 feet (762 m)
Effort: difficult
Trailhead: Grandview Point, 12 miles (19.3 km) east of Grand Canyon Village

A steep, rocky, and largely unmaintained route built first to serve a copper mine at Horseshoe Mesa and then to entice tourists below the forested rim, the **Grandview Trail** should be left to hikers who are midlevel and above. The 6.4-mile (10.3-km) round-trip trek to Horseshoe Mesa and the mine's ruins makes a difficult but fun overnight backpacking trip. Hiking back up, you won't soon forget the steep slab-rock and cobblestone switchbacks, and hiking down will likely take longer than planned as the steepest parts of the route are quite technical and require heads-up attention. There are established primitive campsites at Horseshoe Mesa, including two group sites and pit toilets, but no potable water.

Biking

There are about 13 miles (20.9 km) of roads and greenways through the park that allow bikes, including a route from the Grand Canyon Visitor Center to Grand Canyon Village, and routes from the village to Mather Campground and Market Plaza—basically anywhere you need to go inside the park.

along the Hermit Trail

While the main park roads are open to bikes, they don't have wide shoulders or bike lanes. The exception is **Hermit Road,** which is closed to cars March-November. Seven miles (11.3 km) one-way between the village and the western end of the park at Hermit's Rest, the Hermit Road is the best and most popular bikeway on the South Rim. The only traffic you'll have to deal with on this rolling ride of tough ups and fun downs is the occasional shuttle bus. Just pull over and let them pass.

Only experienced road-bikers should attempt the 23-mile (37-km) ride along **Desert View Drive** to the park's eastern boundaries. It's a beautiful and only moderately difficult ride, but there isn't much of a shoulder and the traffic here is typically heavy during the high seasons.

Bikes are not allowed on the Rim Trail except for a 2.8-mile (4.5-km) section called the **Hermit Road Greenway Trail.** The paved trail begins at Monument Creek Vista along the Hermit Road and ends close to Hermit's Rest. This is about as close as you can get to the rim on a bike, and it's a fun and beautiful stretch of trail highly recommended to bicyclists. To get to the very edge of the rim, you have to park your bike and walk a bit, but never very far, and there are bike racks at each developed viewpoint.

You can also reach the rim by bike at Yaki Point and the South Kaibab Trailhead. Take the greenway near Grand Canyon Visitor Center to the Yaki Point Road, which is closed to private vehicles.

Bright Angel Bicycles and Café (10 S. Entrance Rd., 928/814-8704, www.bikegrandcanyon.com, 6am-8pm daily Apr.-Nov., 7am-7pm daily Dec.-Mar., adult rental $12.50 for 1 hour, $31.50 for 5 hours, $40 for full day, child rental $9.50 for 1 hour, $20 for 5 hours, $31.50 for full day) rents comfortable, easy-to-ride bikes as well as safety equipment and trailers for the tots. It also offers bike tours of varying length and difficulty. Bright Angel Bicycles is located next to the Grand Canyon Visitor Center, near the South entrance.

Mountain Biking on the Rim

The **Tusayan Bike Trails** are a series of single-track trails and old mining and logging roads organized into several easy to moderate loop trails for mountain bikers near the park's South entrance. The trails wind through a forest of pine, juniper, and pinyon. The longest loop is 16 miles (26 km), and the shortest is 3 miles (4.8 km) long. There's a map at the beginning of the trails that shows the various loops. Pick up the trails at Forest Road 605 on the west side of AZ-64 north of Tusayan. Coming south from the park, the trailhead is 0.4 mile (0.6 km) south of the Tusayan Ranger District (176 Lincoln Log Loop, 928/638-2443, www.fs.usda.gov) sign on the west side of AZ-64. Coming from Tusayan toward the park on AZ-64, go 0.3 mile (0.5 km) past town and turn west on Forest Road 605.

Lectures and Programs

Day Programs

Every day the park offers many free ranger-guided hikes and nature walks, as well as lectures and discussions on the animals, human history, and geology of the canyon, at various spots around the park. The programs are most numerous and varied in the high seasons of spring, summer, and fall. In January and February rangers typically offer only two programs per day—one on canyon critters and another on the geology of Grand Canyon. To make up for this, the park offers several special "Cultural Demonstrator" programs (though not daily) in winter featuring Native American artists at the Desert View Watchtower. During the high season the ranger programs can get crowded, so it's best to plan ahead by checking the schedule at the visitors center, the activity desks at Bright Angel and Maswik Lodges, or online (go.nps.gov/gc_programs).

Night Programs

Most nights during the summer there's a typically fascinating and free evening ranger program at the **McKee Amphitheater** if the weather's nice and the **Shrine of the Ages** if it isn't. Night programs are generally not offered during January and February, ending after Christmas and beginning again during spring break in March. This varied program of lectures and night walks, on subjects ranging from astronomy to the Colorado River to "Surviving the Apocalypse at the Grand Canyon," is usually very popular, so it's best to plan ahead. For some of the most popular programs you must get a ticket to secure a spot, starting at 7:30pm at the Shrine of the Ages venue near Park Headquarters for an 8:30pm program at either venue. The amphitheater is behind and east of the Shrine of the Ages and can be reached via a spur from the Rim Trail, about 1.4 miles (2.3 km) east of the village.

Shopping

There are more than a dozen places to buy gifts, books, souvenirs, supplies, and Native American arts and crafts at the South Rim. Nearly every lodge has a substantial gift shop in its lobby, as do Hermit's Rest, Kolb Studio, Lookout Studio, and the Desert View Watchtower.

The **Grand Canyon Conservancy** (www.grandcanyon.org), the park's nonprofit partner, publishes many excellent books about the history of Grand Canyon and the region, most of them deeply researched, finely written, and sumptuously illustrated. If you're a booklover, don't miss browsing these and other books—including a substantial selection of children's readers and picture books—at the **Grand Canyon Conservancy Park Store** (8am-6pm daily), right across the plaza from the main visitors center. Here you'll find books about how to hike the canyon, including detailed trail guides, nature guides, and maps, along with beautiful coffee table books, and volumes on the history of the human activity in the park from the rim's pioneer miners to the golden days of the 1930s.

Whether you forgot your water bottle, your crampons, your tent, or even your backpack itself, **Grand Canyon Outfitters** inside **Canyon Village Market and Deli** (1 Market Plaza Rd., 928/638-2262, 8am-8pm daily) likely has a last-minute top-shelf replacement. Here you'll find hiking boots, clothing, tents, hiking poles, sleeping bags, packs (to rent or buy), books, maps, and friendly and helpful staff members to recommend the best gear for your canyon hike.

Whether you're a semiserious collector or a first-time dabbler, the best place on the South Rim to find high-quality Native American arts and crafts is Mary Jane Colter's **Hopi House.** Shop here for baskets, overlay jewelry, sand paintings, kachina dolls, and other regional treasures. Don't expect to find too many great deals—most of the best pieces are priced accordingly.

Food

Inside the Park

★ **El Tovar Dining Room** (928/638-2631, ext. 6432, www.grandcanyonlodges.com, 6:30am-11am, 11:30am-2pm, and 5pm-10pm daily, $10-40, reservations highly recommended) truly carries on the Fred Harvey Company traditions on which it was founded in 1905. A serious, competent staff serves fresh, creative, locally inspired and sourced dishes in a cozy, mural-lined dining room that has not been significantly altered from the way it looked back when Teddy Roosevelt and Zane Grey ate here. The wine, entrées, and desserts are all top-notch and would be appreciated anywhere in the world—but they always seem to be that much tastier with the sun going down over the canyon. Pay attention to the specials, which usually feature some in-season local edible; they are always the best thing to eat within several hundred miles in any direction.

The **Arizona Steakhouse** (928/638-2631, www.grandcanyonlodges.com, 11:30am-3pm and 4:30pm-10pm daily Mar.-Oct., 4:30pm-10pm daily Nov.-Dec., $14-36), next to the Bright Angel Lodge, serves locally sourced, Southwestern-inspired steak, prime rib, fish, and chicken dishes in a stylish but still casual atmosphere. There's a full bar, and the steaks are excellent—hand-cut and cooked just right with unexpected sauces and marinades. The Arizona Steakhouse is closed for dinner in January and February and closes to the lunch crowd November-February.

★ **Harvey Burger** (928/638-2631, www.grandcanyonlodges.com, 6:30am-10pm daily, $9-22), just off the Bright Angel Lodge's lobby, is a perfect place for a big, hearty breakfast before a day hike below the rim. It serves all the standard, rib-sticking dishes amid decorations and ephemera recalling the Fred Harvey heyday. At lunch there's stew, chili, salads, sandwiches, and burgers, and for dinner there's steak, pasta, and fish dishes called "Bright Angel Traditions," along with a few offerings from the Arizona Steakhouse's menu. Nearby is the **Bright Angel Fountain** (11am-5pm daily in season), which serves hot dogs, ice cream, and other quick treats. **The Canyon Coffee House** (928/638-2631, www.grandcanyonlodges.com, 6am-10am daily, $1.60-4), just outside the Bright Angel Lodge main lobby, is open early and serves cinnamon rolls, croissants, bagels, yogurt and fruit, juice and coffee, but no espresso drinks.

Maswik Food Court (928/638-2631, www.grandcanyonlodges.com, 6am-10pm daily, $5-15), located inside Maswik Lodge, is a good place for a quick, filling, and delicious meal. You can find just about everything—burgers, salads, country-style mashed potatoes, french fries, sandwiches, prime rib, chili, and soft-serve ice cream, to name just a few of the dozens of offerings. Just grab a tray and pick your favorite dish, and you'll be eating in a matter of a few minutes.

If you're getting worn out from hiking the Rim Trail, look for multiple **Sustain Your Hike Carts** (11am-4pm daily, $2-7.50) near Bright Angel Lodge and other spots in the village for some jerky, trail mix, fruit, electrolyte drinks, sweets, and premade sandwiches.

Outside the Park

Tusayan

Tusayan makes for a decent stop if you're hungry. However, the food is just as good if not better inside the park, only about a mile (1.6 km) away. A lot of tour buses stop here, so you might find yourself crowded into waiting for a table at some places, especially during the summer high season.

If you're craving pizza after a long day exploring the canyon, try **We Cook Pizza & Pasta** (605 N. AZ-64, 928/638-2278, www.wecookpizzaandpasta.com, 11am-10pm daily Mar.-Oct., 11am-8pm daily Nov.-Feb., $10-30) for an excellent, high-piled pizza pie. It calls to you just as you enter Tusayan heading south from the park. The pizza, served in slices or whole pies, is pretty good considering the locale, and there's a big salad bar with all the fixings, plus beer and wine. It's a casual place, with picnic tables and an often harried staff. It gets really busy in here during the high summer season.

In the center of town, **Plaza Bonita** (352 AZ-64, 928/638-8900, www.myplazabonita.com, 7am-10pm Sun.-Thurs., 7am-11pm Fri.-Sat., $10-20) serves good Mexican food and great margaritas in a pleasant, family-style setting.

Inside the beautiful three-diamond Grand Hotel, on the southern side of town, the **Canyon Star Steakhouse & Saloon** (149 AZ-64, 928/638-3333, www.grandcanyongrandhotel.com, 7am-10pm daily, $11-30), with its high timber ceilings and elegant Old West aesthetic, is something of a mess hall for fancy cowboys, serving steaks, barbecue, fish, pasta, burgers, and more, and featuring a saloon that has stools topped with old mule saddles, 24 draft beers, and live music.

Williams

A northland institution with some of the best steaks in the region, ★ **Rod's Steak House** (301 E. Route 66, 928/635-2671, www.rods-steakhouse.com, 11am-9:30pm Mon.-Sat., $12-25) has been operating at the same site since 1946. The food is excellent, the staff is friendly and professional, and the menus are shaped like steers.

The **Pine Country Restaurant** (107 N. Grand Canyon Blvd., 928/635-9718, http://pinecountryrestaurant.com, 6:30am-9:30pm daily, $8-19) is a family-style place that serves good diner-style food and homemade pies. Check out the beautiful paintings of the Grand Canyon on the walls.

Cruiser's Route 66 Bar & Grill (233 W. Route 66, 928/635-2445, www.cruisers66.com, 11am-9pm daily, $7-18) offers a diverse menu, with superior barbecue ribs, burgers, fajitas, pulled-pork sandwiches, and homemade chili. It has a full bar and offers live music most nights. During the summer evenings the patio is lively and fun.

For something a bit more upscale and romantic, try the **Red Raven Restaurant** (135 W. Route 66, 928/635-4980, www.redravenrestaurant.com, 11:30am-2pm and 5pm-close daily, $11-25), a charming little place along Route 66 with big windows looking out on the bustling sidewalk and the tourists strolling by. It serves delicious and inventive dishes: steak wraps, Guinness stew, tasty lamb, sweet potato fries, and Southwest egg rolls, to name just a few. The restaurant also has a deep beer list with selections mainly from Arizona and Colorado, and a good wine selection heavy on Italy and California. Make a reservation for dinner.

The vegetarian's best bet this side of downtown Flagstaff is the **Dara Thai Café** (145 W. Route 66, 928/635-2201, 11am-2pm and 5pm-9pm Mon.-Sat., $7-15), an agreeable little spot in the Grand Canyon Hotel. The café serves a variety of fresh and flavorful Thai favorites and offer quite a few meat-free dishes.

Brewing and serving craft beers in a cavernous building near the railroad tracks, **The Grand Canyon Brewing + Distillery** (301 N. 7th St., 800/513-2072, www.grandcanyonbrewery.com, 2pm-close daily, $9-22) is a favorite with locals and tourists alike. It gets pretty busy here at times, especially around quitting time. Along with several excellent craft beers, it serves pub-style food and pizzas that do not disappoint.

Flagstaff

★ **Criollo Latin Kitchen** (16 N. San Francisco St., 928/774-0541, http://criollolatinkitchen.com, 11am-10pm Mon.-Fri., 9am-10pm Sat.-Sun., $10-30), in Flagstaff's historic downtown, creates an eclectic, ever-changing menu of gourmet, Latin-inspired dishes for brunch, lunch, and dinner from sustainable ingredients grown regionally on small farms and ranches. The sleek and refined interior, with eye-catching paintings and small tables that look out on downtown through a glass front, creates an urbane atmosphere that complements the creative food and somewhat belies the rural mountain setting.

★ **Brix Restaurant & Wine Bar** (413 N. San Francisco St., 928/213-1021, http://brixflagstaff.com, 5pm-close Tues.-Sun., $18-36) operates out of a historic building a few blocks north of downtown and serves creative and memorable food using local and sustainable ingredients. The menu here changes often based on what's new at Arizona's small farms, ranches, and dairies. The New American cuisine that results is typically spectacular. It also has fine selections of wine, a slew of creative cocktails, and desserts that should not be missed.

For the best burgers in the northland, head to **Diablo Burger** (20 N. Leroux St., #112, 928/774-3274, www.diabloburger.com, 11am-9pm Sun.-Wed., 11am-10pm Thurs.-Sat., $10-13), which serves a small but stellar menu of beef raised locally on the plains around Flagstaff. All the finely crafted creations, such as the "Cheech" (guacamole, jalapeños, and spicy cheese), or the "Vitamin B" (bleu cheese with bacon and a beet), come on Diablo's branded English muffin-style buns alongside a mess of Belgian fries. It also has a terrific veggie burger.

Brandy's Restaurant and Bakery (1500 E. Cedar Ave., #40, 928/779-2187, www.brandysrestaurant.com, 6:30am-3pm daily, $6-10) often wins the Best Breakfast honors from readers of the local newspaper, and those readers know what they're talking about. The homemade breads and bagels make everything else taste better. Try the Eggs Brandy, two poached eggs on a homemade bagel smothered in hollandaise sauce. For lunch there are crave-worthy sandwiches (Brandy's Reubens are some of the best in the business), burgers, and salads. Brandy's also serves beer, wine, and mimosas.

Josephine's Modern American Bistro (503 N. Humphreys St., 928/779-3400, www.josephinesrestaurant.com, 11:30am-2pm and 5pm-9pm Mon.-Fri., 10am-2pm and 5pm-9pm Sat., 9am-2pm Sun., $10-30) offers a creative fusion of tastes for lunch and dinner, such as the roasted pepper and hummus grilled-cheese sandwich and the chile relleno with sun-dried cranberry guacamole, from a cozy historic home near downtown. This is one of the best places in town for brunch.

Charly's Pub and Grill (23 N. Leroux St., 928/779-1919, www.weatherfordhotel.com, 8am-10pm daily, $11-26), inside the Weatherford Hotel, serves Navajo tacos, enchiladas, burritos, and a host of other regional favorites for breakfast, lunch, and dinner. Its Navajo taco, a regional delicacy featuring fry bread smothered in chili and beans, might be the best off the reservation. Try it for breakfast topped with a couple of fried eggs. Charly's also has more conventional but appetizing bar-and-grill food such as hot, high-piled sandwiches, juicy burgers, steaks, and prime rib.

Named Flagstaff's favorite pizza since 2002, **Fratelli Pizza** (119 W. Phoenix Ave., 928/774-9200, www.fratellipizza.net, 10:30am-9pm daily, $10-20) swears by its "stone deck oven" and eschews the "conveyer belt" mentality of the chains. The results are sublime. Try the popular Flagstaff, with basil pesto, sun-dried tomatoes, and artichoke hearts. You can also build your own pie from among dozens of fresh toppings or stop in for a huge slice ($3). Fratelli also serves salads, antipasti, and calzones and offers a decent selection of beer and wine. There's also a location on 4th Street (2120 N. 4th St., 928/714-9700, 10:30am-9pm daily).

For a big breakfast of eggs, bacon, and potatoes, or an omelet stuffed with cheese, a hot cup of coffee, and friendly service, head over to the **Downtown**

Diner (7 E. Aspen Ave., 928/774-3492, 6am-6pm daily, $5-15), right across from Heritage Square. This clean little greasy spoon also has good burgers, shakes, and hot dogs.

The **Morning Glory Café** (115 S. San Francisco St., 928/774-3705, http://morningglorycafeflagstaff.com, 10am-2:30pm Tues.-Fri., 9am-2:30pm Sat.-Sun., $8-11) serves natural, tasty vegetarian eats from a cozy little spot on San Francisco Street. Try the hemp burger for lunch, and don't miss the blue corn pancakes for breakfast. With local art on the walls, free wireless Internet, and friendly service, this is an ideal place to get to know the laid-back Flagstaff vibe. There are a lot of vegan and gluten-free options here. The café doesn't take credit cards, so bring some cash.

Macy's European Coffee House (14 S. Beaver St., 928/774-2243, www.macyscoffee.net, 6am-8pm daily, $5-10) south of the tracks is the best place to get coffee and a quick vegetarian bite to eat, or just hang out and watch the locals file in and out.

Accommodations

The park's lodging rates are audited annually and compare favorably to those offered outside the park, but you can sometimes find excellent deals at one of several gateway towns around canyon country. Using one of these places as a base for a visit to the canyon makes sense if you're planning on touring the whole of the canyonlands and not just the park. There are six lodges within Grand Canyon National Park at the South Rim—five operated by **Xanterra** (www.grandcanyonlodges.com) and one, Yavapai Lodge, operated by **Delaware North** (www.visitgrandcanyon.com). The hotels within the park are a green and sustainable choice: Xanterra and Delaware North both have robust sustainability programs aimed at conserving water and energy, reducing pollution, and increasing recycling while decreasing use of landfills. All the hotels within Grand Canyon National Park offer wheelchair-accessible rooms.

Inside the Park

A stay at ★ **El Tovar** (303/297-2757 or 888/297-2757, www.grandcanyonlodges.com, $217-263 standard room, $442-538 suite), one of the most distinctive and memorable hotels in the state, would be the secondary highlight—after the gorge itself—of any trip to the South Rim. Opened in 1905, the log-and-stone National Historic Landmark, standing about 20 feet (6.1 m) from the rim, has 78 rooms and suites. The hotel's restaurant serves some of the best food in Arizona for breakfast, lunch, and dinner, and there's a comfortable cocktail lounge off the lobby with a window on the canyon. A mezzanine sitting area overlooks the log-cabin lobby, and a gift shop sells Native American art and crafts as well as canyon souvenirs. If you're looking to splurge on something truly exceptional, there's a honeymoon suite overlooking the canyon.

When first built in the 1930s, the ★ **Bright Angel Lodge** (303/297-2757 or 888/297-2757, www.grandcanyonlodges.com, $95-210) was meant to serve the middle-class travelers then being lured by the Santa Fe Railroad, and it's still affordable and comfortable while retaining a rustic character that fits perfectly with the wild canyon just outside. Lodge rooms don't have TVs, and most have only one bed. The utilitarian "hikers" rooms have refrigerators and share several private showers, which have lockable doors and just enough room to dress. Bright Angel is the place to sleep before hiking into the canyon; you just roll out of bed onto the Bright Angel Trail. The lodge's cabins just west of the main building have private baths, TVs, and sitting rooms. Drinking and dining options include a small bar and coffeehouse, a Harvey House diner, and a restaurant with big windows framing the canyon.

Standing along the rim between El Tovar and Bright Angel, the **Kachina Lodge** (303/297-2757 or 888/297-2757, www.grandcanyonlodges.com, $225-243) offers basic, comfortable rooms with TVs, safes, private baths, and refrigerators. There's not a lot of character, but its location and modern comforts make the Kachina an ideal place for families to stay. The **Thunderbird Lodge** (303/297-2757 or 888/297-2757, www.grandcanyonlodges.com, $225-243) is in the same area and has similar offerings. Both properties have some rooms facing the canyon.

Maswik Lodge (303/297-2757 or 888/297-2757, www.grandcanyonlodges.com, $215) is located on the west side of the village about 0.25 mile (0.4 km) from the rim. The hotel has a cafeteria-style restaurant that serves just about everything you'd want and a sports bar with a large-screen TV. The rooms are motel-style basic but clean and comfortable, with TVs, private baths, and refrigerators, located in a series of two-story buildings around a parking lot north of the main lobby building. There are no elevators.

About 5 miles (8 km) from the park entrance at Market Plaza, **Yavapai Lodge** (11 Yavapai Lodge Rd., 928/638-4001 or 877/404-4611, www.visitgrandcanyon.com, $150-200) offers clean and comfortable rooms in a central forested setting. The East Section is a two-story building featuring air-conditioned rooms with refrigerators and TVs, and the King Family Room is a great option for families, with a king bed and twin bunk beds. The West Section, a retro motel-style structure, lacks air-conditioning but has pet rooms for an extra $25. Run by concessionaire Delaware North, Yavapai Lodge has a good casual restaurant and a pleasant lobby with a fireplace, a gift shop, and a tavern.

Outside the Park

Tusayan

Lining AZ-64, accommodations in Tusayan are about 1 mile (1.6 km) south of the park's South entrance. Most of Tusayan's accommodations are of the chain variety. Though they are generally clean and comfortable, few of them have any character to speak of, and most are rather overpriced for what you get. Staying in either Flagstaff or Williams is a better choice if you're looking for an independent hotel or motel with some local color, and you can definitely find better deals in those gateways.

You'll find one of the better deals in the whole canyon region in Valle, a tiny spot not far off AZ-64, about 30 miles (48 km) south of the South entrance. The **Red Lake Campground and Hostel** (8850 N. AZ-64, Valle, 928/635-4753, $20 pp per night), where you can rent a bed in a shared room, is a basic but reasonably comfortable place sitting lonely on the grasslands next to a gas station; it has shared bathrooms with showers, free Wi-Fi, a common room with a kitchen and a TV, and an RV park ($25) with partial hookups. If you're going super-budget, you can't beat this place, though it is about 45 minutes from the park's south gate.

Though more basic than some of the other places in Tusayan, the **Red Feather Lodge** (300 AZ-64, 928/638-2414, www.redfeatherlodge.com, $220-240) is a comfortable, affordable place to stay, with a welcoming lobby with Navajo rugs hanging on the walls, a pool, hot tub, and separate hotel and motel complexes.

Resembling a high-end hunting lodge, the **Grand Hotel** (149 AZ-64, 928/638-3333, www.grandcanyongrandhotel.com, $200-400) is one of the more luxurious places to stay in the region, with prices to match. The sprawling sandstone-and-log hotel with a shining, green metal roof pops up just as you enter Tusayan, and its beautiful lobby sets the Craftsman, wood-and-leather tone of the whole place with a fireplace lounge and large gift shop. A cowboy wilderness chic and elegant Old West hunting lodge aesthetic pervades, with heads of beasts on the walls, including a mountain lion, a bobcat, and a buffalo. The hotel has very clean and comfortable rooms; a pool, hot tub, and fitness center; as well as a large saloon and steak house.

Cameron

On the Navajo Nation about 50 miles (81 km) north of Flagstaff along US-89, near the junction with AZ-64 (the route to the park's east gate), sits the ★ **Historic Cameron Trading Post and Lodge** (800/338-7385, www.camerontradingpost.com, $79-199), established in 1916. It takes about one hour to drive there from the Desert View area of the park and is a good place to start your tour. Starting from the East entrance, you'll see the canyon gradually becoming grand. Before you reach the park, the Little Colorado drops some 2,000 feet (610 m) through the arid, scrubby land, cutting through gray rock on the way to its marriage with the big river and creating the **Little Colorado Gorge.** Stop here and get a barrier-free glimpse at this lesser chasm to prime yourself for what is to come. There are usually a few booths set up selling Navajo arts and crafts and a lot of touristy souvenirs at two developed pullouts along the road.

The Cameron Lodge is a charming and affordable place to stay and makes a perfect base for a visit to the Grand Canyon. It has a good **restaurant** (6am-9:30pm daily summer, 7am-9pm daily winter, $7-16) serving American and Navajo food, including excellent beef stew, heaping Navajo tacos, chili, and burgers. There's also an art gallery, a visitors center, a huge trading post/gift shop, and an RV park ($35 full hookup, no bathroom or showers). A small grocery store has packaged sandwiches, chips, and sodas. The rooms are decorated in a Southwestern Native American style and are clean and comfortable, some with views of the Little Colorado River and the old 1911 suspension bridge that spans the stream just outside the lodge. There are single-bed rooms, rooms with two beds, and a few suites that are perfect for families. The stone-and-wood buildings and the garden patio, laid out with stacked sandstone bricks with picnic tables and red-stone walkways below the open-corridor rooms, create a cozy, history-soaked setting and make the lodge a memorable place to stay. The vast, empty red plains of the Navajo Reservation spread out all around and create a lonely, isolated atmosphere, especially at night; but the rooms have cable TV and free Wi-Fi, so you can be connected and entertained even way out here.

If you're visiting in the winter, the lodge drops its prices significantly during this less crowded touring season.

Williams

Williams has some of the most affordable independent accommodations in the Grand Canyon region as well as several chain hotels.

★ **The Lodge on Route 66** (200 E. Route 66, 877/563-4366, http://thelodgeonroute66.com, $99-189) has stylish rooms with sleep-inducing pillow-top mattresses; it also has a few civilized two-room suites with kitchenettes, dining areas, and fireplaces—perfect for a family that's not necessarily on a budget. The motor court-style grounds, right along the Mother Road, feature a romantic cabana with comfortable seats and an outdoor fireplace. No pets.

It's difficult to find a better deal than the clean and basic **El Rancho Motel** (617 E. Route 66, 928/635-2552 or 800/228-2370, www.elranchomotelwilliams.us, $80-125), an independently owned, retro motel on Route 66 with few frills save comfort, friendliness, and a heated pool open in season.

The **Canyon Country Inn** (442 W. Route 66, 928/635-2349, www.thecanyoncountryinn.com, $89-115) is an enchanting little place right in the heart of Williams's charming historic district. Its country-Victorian decor is not for everyone, but it's a comfortable and friendly place to stay while exploring the canyon country.

The **Grand Canyon Railway Hotel** (235 N. Grand Canyon Blvd., 928/635-4010, www.thetrain.com, $169-189) stands now where Williams's old Harvey House once stood. It has a heated indoor pool, two restaurants, a lounge, a hot tub, a workout room, and a huge gift shop. The hotel serves riders on the Grand Canyon Railway and offers the highest-end accommodations in Williams.

The original **Grand Canyon Hotel** (145 W. Route 66, 928/635-1419, www.thegrandcanyonhotel.com, $79-195) opened in 1891, even before the railroad arrived and made Grand Canyon tourism something not just the rich could do. New owners refurbished and reopened the charming old redbrick hotel in Williams's historic downtown in 2005, and now it's an affordable, friendly place to stay with a lot of character and a bit of an international flavor. Spartan single-bed rooms go for $79 a night with a shared bathroom, and individually named and eclectically decorated double rooms with private baths are $93-105 a night—some of the most distinctive and affordable accommodations in the region. There are no televisions in the rooms. Several larger rooms with private baths and other amenities go for $150-195. There are also hostel rooms for $33-38.

The **Red Garter Bed & Bakery** (137 W. Railroad Ave., 928/635-1484, www.redgarter.com, $175-199) makes much of its original and longtime use as a brothel (which, like many similar places throughout Arizona's rural regions, didn't finally close until the 1940s), where the town's lonely, uncouth miners, lumberjacks, railway workers, and cowboys met with unlucky women, ever euphemized as "soiled doves," in rooms called "cribs." The 1897 frontier-Victorian stone building, with its wide, arching entranceway, has been beautifully restored with a lot of authentic charm, without skimping on the comforts—like big brass beds for the nighttime and delightful, homemade baked goods, juice, and coffee in the morning. Famously, this place is haunted by some poor unquiet, regretful soul, so you might want to bring your night-light along.

Flagstaff

Flagstaff, 79 miles (127 km) southeast of the park's main South entrance, was the park's first gateway town, and it's still in many ways the best. The home of Northern Arizona University is a fun, laid-back college town with a railroad and Route 66 history. To reach the Grand Canyon from Flagstaff, take US-180 northwest for about 1.5 hours, and there you are. The route is absolutely the most scenic of all the approaches to the canyon (with apologies to desert rats who prefer the eastern Desert View approach), passing through Coconino National Forest and beneath the San Francisco Peaks.

Historic hotels downtown offer both good value and a unique experience. East Flagstaff, as you enter along Route 66, has a large number of small hotels and motels, including chains and several old-school motor inns. It lacks the charm of downtown but is an acceptable place to stay if you're just passing through. If you're a budget traveler, try the hostels in the Historic Southside District.

The ★ **Hotel Monte Vista** (100 N. San Francisco St., 928/779-6971 or 800/545-3068, www.hotelmontevista.com, $85-125 Apr. 15-Nov. 5, $50-175 Nov. 6-Apr. 14), a historic downtown hotel, is a retro-swanky, redbrick high-rise, built in 1927, which once served high-class and famous travelers heading west on the Santa Fe Railroad. These days it offers comfortable and convenient rooms with historic charm, cable TV, and private bathrooms, as well as hostel-style rooms with a shared bathroom. There's a cocktail lounge and sleek coffee bar off the lobby. As with many of the grand old railroad hotels, there are lots of tales to be heard about the Hollywood greats who stayed here and the restless ghosts who stayed behind. Parking is not easy downtown, so if you have a big rig consider staying somewhere else. The **Weatherford Hotel** (23 N. Leroux St., 928/779-1919, www.weatherfordhotel.com, $80-190) is the other historic hotel downtown. It's basic but romantic, like stepping back in time when you head off to bed. There are no TVs or phones in most of the rooms, the cheapest of which share a bathroom. While the whole place is a little creaky, the location and the history make this a fun place to rest. With live music at the hotel's two pubs and the odd wedding or private party in the historic ballroom, the Weatherford can sometimes get a bit noisy. It's not for those looking for the tranquility of the surrounding pine forest.

The **Grand Canyon International Hostel** (19 S. San Francisco St., 888/442-2696, www.grandcanyonhostel.com, $26-78) is a clean and friendly place to stay on the cheap, located in an old 1930s building in the Southside neighborhood, in which you're likely to meet some lasting friends, many of them foreign tourists tramping around the Colorado Plateau. The hostel offers bunk-style sleeping arrangements and private rooms, mostly shared bathrooms, a self-serve kitchen, Wi-Fi, a free breakfast, and a chance to join in on tours of the region. It's a rustic but cozy and welcoming hippie-home-style place to stay. The same folks operate the **Motel DuBeau** (19 W. Phoenix St., 800/398-7112, www.modubeau.com, $26-75), a clean and charming hostel-inn with a small dorm and eight private rooms. They offer a free breakfast, Wi-Fi, and a friendly atmosphere in an old motor hotel built in 1929. Make sure to spend some time at the on-site **Nomad's Global Lounge** (4:30pm-10pm Mon.-Thurs., 4pm-11pm Fri.-Sat., 4pm-9pm Sun.), kicking back a few cold ones with your new friends.

The Inn at 410 Bed and Breakfast (410 N. Leroux St., 928/774-0088 or 800/774-2008, www.inn410.com, $195-325) has eight artfully decorated rooms in a classic old home on a quiet, tree-lined street just off downtown. This is a wonderful little place, with so much detail and stylishness. Breakfasts are interesting and filling, often with a Southwestern tinge, and tea is served every afternoon. You certainly can't go wrong here. Booking far in advance, especially for a weekend stay, is a must.

The stately **England House Bed and Breakfast** (614 W. Santa Fe Ave., 928/214-7350 or 877/214-7350, www.englandhousebandb.com, $149-219) is located in a quiet residential neighborhood near downtown at the base of Mars Hill, where sits the famous Lowell Observatory. This beautiful old Victorian has been sumptuously restored, and its rooms are booked most weekends. If you're just passing through, the innkeepers are happy to show you around, after which you will probably make a reservation for some far future date. They pay as much attention to their breakfasts here as they do to details of the decor. This is one of the best little inns in the region.

The hosts at **Elden Trails Bed & Breakfast** (6073 Snowflake Dr., 928/266-0203, www.eldentrailsbedandbreakfast.com, $149-169 d, $40 per night each additional adult) are committed to living a sustainable-as-possible lifestyle, including growing a lot of their own food in a large garden and greenhouse full of native plants and organic crops. Both ecotourists and foodies will feel at home in this comfortable and inspiring B&B at the base of Mount Elden, about 5 miles (8 km) east of downtown Flagstaff. It's a small place, just one detached studio suite that sleeps four adults. A healthy, organic (and if you prefer, vegan) breakfast is served in the studio's sunny nook, and your new home-away-from-home sits amid tall pines and hiking trails. Make reservations far in advance.

For a touch of wilderness adventure with all the comforts, try the

Arizona Mountain Inn (4200 Lake Mary Rd., 928/774-8959, www.arizonamountaininn.com, $137-247), offering 17 rustic but comfortable family-perfect cabins ($135-600) in the pines not far from town as well as four B&B-style rooms ($120-160). Dogs are welcome in most rooms and cabins.

Camping

Inside the Park

★ **Mather Campground** (877/444-6777, www.recreation.gov, $18 Mar.-Nov., $15 Dec.-Feb.) takes reservations up to six months ahead for the March-November 20 peak season and thereafter operates on a first-come, first-served basis. Located near the village and offering more than 300 basic campsites with grills and fire pits, the campground typically fills up by about noon during the summer busy season. It has restrooms with showers, and coin-operated laundry machines. The campground is open to tents and trailers but has no hookups and is closed to RVs longer than 30 feet (9.1 m). Even if you aren't an experienced camper, a stay at Mather is a fun and inexpensive alternative to sleeping indoors. Despite its large size and crowds, the campground gets pretty quiet at night. Even in summer, the night takes on a bit of chill, making a campfire not exactly necessary but not out of the question. Bring your own wood or buy it at the store nearby. A large, clean restroom and shower facility is within walking distance from most sites, and they even have blow-dryers. Everything is coin operated, and there's an office onsite that gives change. Consider bringing bikes along, especially for the kids. The village is about a 15-minute walk from the campground on forested, paved trails, or you can take the free shuttle from a stop nearby. Pets are allowed but must be kept on a leash, and they're not allowed on shuttle buses.

About 25 miles (40 km) east of the village, near the park's East entrance, is **Desert View Campground** (877/444-6777, www.recreation.gov, first-come, first-served, May-mid-Oct. depending on weather, $12), with 50 sites for tents and small trailers only, with no hookups. There's a restroom with no showers and only two faucets with running water. Each site has a grill but little else. Pets are allowed but must be kept on a leash.

If you're in a rolling mansion, try **Trailer Village** (888/297-2757, www.xanterra.com, $45) next to Mather Campground, near the village, where you'll find hookups for trailers up to 50 feet (15.2 m) long.

The North Rim

Standing at Bright Angel Point on the Grand Canyon's North Rim, crowded together with several other gazers as if stranded on a jetty over a wide, hazy sea, blurred evergreens growing atop great jagged rock spines banded with white and red, someone whispers, "It looks pretty much the same as the other rim."

It's not true—far from it—but the comment brings up the main point about the North Rim: Should you go? Only about 10 percent of canyon visitors make the trip to the North Rim, which is significantly less developed than the South; there aren't many activities other than gazing, unless you are a hiker and a backcountry wilderness lover. The coniferous mountain forests of the Kaibab Plateau are themselves worth the trip—broken by grassy meadows and painted with summer wildflowers, populated by often-seen elk and mule deer, and dappled with aspens that turn yellow and red in the fall and burst out of the otherwise uniform dark green like solitary flames. But it is a long trip, and you need to be prepared for a land of scant services—in return you'll find the simple, contemplative pleasures of nature in the raw.

Grand Canyon Lodge and the restaurants, shops, and visitors centers close from October 31-May 15. Between

October 31 and December 1, you can drive into the park and look around but you can't stay overnight. From December 1, when AZ-67 closes, until May 15, the North Rim Campground remains open as a primitive campground. To stay here, however, you need a backcountry permit and the energy to hike or ski 45 miles (72 km) from Jacob Lake.

Getting There

The nearly 300-mile (485 km), five-hour drive from the Grand Canyon National Park's South Rim section to the park's lesser-visited North Rim is a memorable journey through a true American outback: across the western edge of the Navajo Nation, over the Colorado River, through the lonely Arizona Strip, up onto the high Kaibab Plateau, and ending at the Grand Canyon Lodge hanging off the forest rim.

Leave the South Rim through the Desert View area along AZ-64, which meets US-89 North at Cameron. Head north across Navajo land to Bitter Springs, about an hour north of Cameron. Pick up US-89A going west, cross the Colorado River via the Navajo Bridge, and then head across the Arizona Strip to the Kaibab Plateau. US-89A meets AZ-67 to the North Rim on top of the plateau at Jacob Lake. From there it's about 45 miles (72 km), a drive of about an hour, to Grand Canyon National Park. Note AZ-67 from Jacob Lake to the North Rim typically closes to vehicles December to mid-May.

In case you forget anything before venturing into this relative wilderness, you can always stop at the well-stocked **North Rim Country Store** (AZ-67, mile marker 605, 928/638-2383, www.northrimcountrystore.com, 7am-7pm daily mid-May-late Oct.), about 43 miles (69 km) along AZ-67 from Jacob Lake. The store has just about anything you'll need, from snacks to gas to camping supplies. There's also a small auto shop here in case you're having car troubles or catch

viewpoint behind the Grand Canyon Lodge

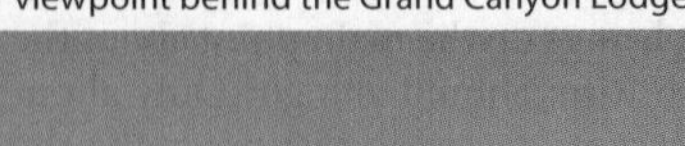

a flat that you can't fix yourself. The store closes for winter, as does the whole region, around the beginning of November.

The **Trans-Canyon Shuttle** (928/638-2820, www.trans-canyonshuttle.com, $90 one-way, reservations required) makes a daily round-trip excursion between the North and South Rims, departing the North Rim at 7am and arriving at the South Rim at 11:30am. The shuttle then leaves the South Rim at 1:30pm and arrives back at the North Rim at 6pm. During the spring and summer, shuttles run twice daily from the South Rim to the North Rim (8am-12:30pm and 1:30pm-6pm), and twice daily from the North Rim to the South Rim (7am-11:30am and 2pm-6:30pm).

The Grand Canyon Lodge offers a **hiker shuttle** (daily May 15-Oct. 15, first person $7, each additional person $4) to the North Kaibab Trailhead, which leaves every morning from the lodge at 5:30am and 6am. Tickets must be purchased 24 hours in advance at the lodge.

If you paid your park entrance fee at the South Rim, this will be honored at the North as long as you go within seven days. If not, you'll have to pay again. A North Rim edition of the park's helpful newspaper ***The Pocket Map*** is passed out at the North Rim entrance.

Driving Tours

Cape Royal Scenic Drive

23 miles (37 km) one-way, plus 3-mile (4.8-km) one-way side trip

This outrageously scenic drive along the rim to Cape Royal is an essential part of the North Rim experience. The paved two-lane road twists and undulates through the green, white, and fire-blackened highland forest of tall and skinny quaking aspen, thick and shaggy conifers, and black stumps and husks of all sizes. There are several developed viewpoints along the rimside with parking, picnic tables, interpretive signs, and a few rustic benches on which you can sit back and contemplate the views. Plan to spend at least two hours one-way (it's 23 mi/37 km from Grand Canyon Lodge to Cape Royal), and at least another 30-40 minutes at nearby Point Imperial (a 3-mi/4.8-km one-way side trip; the route branches off from Cape Royal Road at mile 5.4/km 8.7). You reach several of the viewpoints via short and easy trails, so plan on doing some walking. Bring water, food, and warm clothing, and make sure that your vehicle is road-ready (no rigs over 30 ft/9.1 m long); there are no services of any kind on this road, though there are small bathrooms at Point Imperial and Cape Royal. Keep a look out for wildlife along this road, especially wild turkeys.

Get an early start and take AZ-67 north from **Grand Canyon Lodge** for 3 miles (4.8 km) to **Cape Royal Road** and turn right. At mile 5.4 (km 8.7) you need to decide whether to veer left to **Point Imperial,** a southeast-facing view of the white-rock peak **Mount Hayden** and across the red-and-green canyon to the

Painted Desert on Navajoland, or continue on to the right and catch it on the way back. Either way, Point Imperial is a stop that should not be missed. Each viewpoint provides a different perspective on the canyon, so it's best to stop and spend some time at each one.

At mile 8 (km 12.9) is **Greenland Lake,** a beautiful lush meadow with a natural sink that traps rainwater and snowmelt, making this "lake" a highly variable prospect. There's also an old ranching cabin in this peaceful clearing about 200 yards (183 m) off the road, which you can reach by a short dirt trail.

At mile 10 (km 16.1) is **Vista Encantada** ("enchanting view"), which has a gorgeous view and is a great spot for a picnic. Stop here and contemplate another white-tipped, attention-grabbing peak—**Brady Peak,** just east of the picnic spot. The peak was named for Arizona pioneer Peter Brady (no relation to the Brady Bunch), who came to the territory in the impossibly early days of the 1850s and was a longtime elected official. Here you'll also see the often dry Nankoweap Creek etched beige against the red-and-green canyon landscape, and beyond that, if it's a clear day, you may see all the way to Navajoland and the Painted Desert.

Just up the road a bit at mile 11.7 (km 18.8) is **Roosevelt Point,** named for Teddy Roosevelt, the former U.S. president who loved Grand Canyon and spent time hunting game on the North Rim. A short loop trail (0.2 mi/0.3 km round-trip) provides the best views; take some time here strolling the trail and relaxing on the well-placed benches. Roosevelt Point, like Point Imperial and Vista Encantada, has awesome views of the eastern canyon off the **Walhalla Plateau,** a sliver plateau that sits alongside the Kaibab Plateau on its southeast side. **Tritle Peak,** topped white Kaibab limestone same as Brady and Hayden, rises 8,300 feet (2,530 m) to the east along a ridge that juts out into the canyon. It was named for F. A. Tritle, a territorial governor in 1881-1885 and early owner of the famous Jerome Copper Mine.

At mile 17.2 (km 27.7) you'll come to the **Cape Final Trailhead;** the trail is 4.2 miles (6.8 km) round-trip to a spectacular viewpoint with awesome looks at **Unkar Creek,** the **Painted Desert,** and **Freya Castle.**

Just ahead at mile 18 (km 29) are **Walhalla Overlook** and the ruin of **Walhalla Glades Pueblo,** which was occupied for about 100 years (about AD 1050-1150) by seasonal farmers from the **Unkar Delta** inside the canyon. A great red deposit at the confluence of Unkar Creek and the Colorado River, the Unkar Delta was populated and farmed from about AD 850 to AD 1200 and is visible from Walhalla Overlook. In the visitors center there's a pamphlet describing a self-guided tour of the ruin across the road.

To see where the farmers of Walhalla Glades likely obtained some of their water, stop at mile 19.1 (km 31) and take the approximately 1-mile (1.6-km) round-trip trail into the forest to **Cliff Spring.**

Finally, at mile 19.7 (km 32), you come to **Cape Royal,** a wonderful terminus with breathtaking views of the Colorado River and across the canyon to the South Rim, reached by an easy, paved trail (about 1 mi/1.6 km round-trip) lined with cliffrose, wind-sculpted pinyons and junipers, and random multicolored boulders. Along the trail you'll pass the rock arch **Angels Window,** which offers a perfectly framed view of the river.

Drive back to the lodge via the same road, and don't forget to stop at Point Imperial if you didn't already.

Sights

★ Grand Canyon Lodge

You don't need to have a reservation to enjoy the best parts of **Grand Canyon Lodge,** the very center of the North Rim universe and one of the most dramatic and enchanting railroad-built lodges in the West. Here's a plan for your first sight of Grand Canyon from this high forested rim: Park at the lodge, enter through the front doors, and proceed down a short flight of stairs to the sunroom. Through the large, south-facing picture windows you will catch your first glimpse of the awful, impossible labyrinth, accompanied by clear, streaming sunlight and the soft, sinking comfort of a couch facing the edge of world. After a while, if you can bring yourself to rise, head out to the lodge's amazing veranda, sit back down in one of the Adirondack chairs hanging over the canyon, and explore the forest-and-desert dichotomy with the added benefit of a cool, sap-scented breeze. Once you've taken in the view from both of these comfortable and contemplative vantages, descend the veranda stairs and walk the easy trail down to Bright Angel Point.

Working for the Union Pacific Railroad and North Rim concessionaire Utah Parks Co. in 1927, Gilbert Stanley Underwood, a master of the National Park Service Rustic style who also designed Bryce Canyon Lodge and Zion Lodge, created the original lodge building out of local plateau rock and wood. After a fire in 1932 destroyed all but the limestone foundation, a scaled-back lodge was built on the ruin using similar local materials; it reopened in 1937. This treasured National Historic Landmark is still a dreamed-of destination nearly a century on.

Don't miss the adorable sunroom statue of **Brighty,** a legendary North Rim mule and the subject of the 1953 children's book *Brighty of the Grand Canyon* by Marguerite Henry, for sale in the gift shop. The lodge is closed mid-October-mid-May.

Viewpoints

There are three developed viewpoints at the North Rim, each of them offering a slightly different look at the canyon. **Bright Angel Point,** about an 0.5-mile (0.8-km) round-trip walk outside the lodge's back door, looks over Bright Angel Canyon with a view of Roaring Springs, the source of Bright Angel Creek and fresh water for the North Rim and inner canyon; **Point Imperial,** at 8,803 feet (2,683 m) the highest point on the North Rim, probably has the best all-around view of the canyon; and **Cape Royal,** a 23-mile (37-km) one-way drive across the Walhalla Plateau, looks toward the South Rim.

Recreation

Hiking

It's significantly cooler on the high, forested North Rim than it is on the South, making hiking, especially summer hiking below the rim, much less of a chore. There are a few easy rim trails to choose from and several tough but unforgettable day hikes into the canyon along the North Kaibab Trail.

Easy trails lead to and from all the developed scenic overlooks on the rim, their trailheads accessible and well marked. *The Pocket Map* has a comprehensive listing of the area's trails and where to pick them up. The 4-mile (6.4-km) round-trip **Transept Trail** is an easy hike through the forest from the Grand Canyon Lodge to the campground. It has a few nice views and is a good introduction to the North Rim.

Uncle Jim Trail

Distance: 5 miles (8 km) round-trip
Duration: 2-3 hours
Elevation gain: about 200 feet (61 m)
Effort: easy to moderate
Trailhead: North Kaibab Trail parking lot, 3 miles (4.8 km) north of Grand Canyon Lodge on the main park entrance road

Take this easy, flat trail through the forest to watch backpackers winding their way down the North Kaibab Trail's twisting switchbacks and maybe be passed by a mule train or two along the way. The **Uncle Jim Trail,** named for an old game

warden who bragged of killing more than 500 Kaibab Plateau mountain lions, winds through old stands of spruce and fir, sprinkled with quaking aspen, to **Uncle Jim Point,** where you can let out your best roar into the tributary known as **Roaring Springs Canyon.**

Widforss Trail

Distance: 10 miles (16.1 km) round-trip
Duration: 4-6 hours
Elevation gain: 1,000 feet (305 m)
Effort: easy
Trailhead: From Grand Canyon Lodge, drive north on AZ-67 for 2.7 miles (4.3 km), turn left (west) onto a dirt road (Point Sublime Rd.), and follow signs to trailhead.

Named for the 1920s-1930s canyon painter Gunnar Widforss, the undulating, wildflower-lined **Widforss Trail** leads along the rim of Transept Canyon and through ponderosa pine, fir, and spruce forest, with a few stands of aspen and burned areas mixed in, for 5 miles (8 km) to **Widforss Point,** where you can stare across the great chasm and rest before heading back.

The trail starts out on the edge of **Harvey Meadow,** home to an early North Rim tourist camp. Across the meadow there's a cave with a doorway, which famed lion-killer Uncle Jim Owens used from time to time. Intermediate to expert hikers will have no problem hiking the entire 10-mile (16.1-km) round-trip route in less than four hours.

For a **shorter hike,** pick up the **free guide** to the Widforss Trail at the trailhead or the visitors center. It proposes a **5-mile (8-km) round-trip hike** on the first half of the trail (about 2-3 hours) and includes a map and information on the natural and human history of the North Rim.

There is no water available along this trail, so come prepared.

From top to bottom: along the Transept Trail; Widforss Trail; Point Imperial.

North Kaibab Trail

Distance: 1.5-9.4 miles (2.4-15.1 km) round-trip
Duration: 2-8 hours
Elevation gain: 3,050 feet (930 m)
Effort: moderate to difficult
Trailhead: 1.5 miles (2.4 km) north of Grand Canyon Lodge on east side of AZ-67

The **North Kaibab Trail** starts out among the coniferous heights of the North Rim. The forest surrounding the trail soon dries out and becomes a red-rock desert, the trail cut into the rock face of the cliffs and twisting down improbable routes hard against the cliffs, with nothing but your sanity keeping you away from the gorge. This is the only patrolled North Rim route down into the inner canyon and to the Colorado River. Sooner than you realize, the walls close in, and you are deep in the canyon, the trees on the rim just green blurs now.

A good introduction to this corridor trail and ancient native route is the short, 1.5-mile (2.4-km) round-trip jog down to the **Coconino Overlook,** from which, on a clear day, you can see the San Francisco Peaks and the South Rim. A 4-mile (6.4-km) round-trip hike down will get you to **Supai Tunnel,** opened up out of the red rock in the 1930s by the Civilian Conservation Corps. A little more than a mile (1.6 km) onward you'll reach **The Bridge in the Redwall** (5.2 miles round-trip), built in 1966 after a flood ruined this portion of the trail.

For a tough, all-day hike that will likely have you sore but smiling the next morning, take the North Kaibab roughly 5 miles (8 km) down to **Roaring Springs,** the source of life-giving Bright Angel Creek. The springs fall headlong out of the cliffside and spray mist and rainbows into the hot air. Just remember, you also have to go 5 miles (8 km) back up.

Start hiking as early as you can no matter what the season. In the summer it's not even debatable. You may be on the North Rim, but it's still dangerously hot inside the canyon. Try to be out and done by 10am during the hot months. Though not as important from a safety perspective in spring and early fall, an early start will then put you ahead of the crowds and more likely to see wildlife along the trail.

The trailhead has a decent-sized parking lot, though it fills up during the high season, so the earlier you get here the better. You can also arrange for a shuttle from Grand Canyon Lodge, or walk 1.5 miles (2.4 km) from the lodge to the trailhead via the Bridle Path.

Mule Rides

Sure-footed and indomitable mules work hard all season on the North Rim just as they do on the South, carrying tourists up and down the North Kaibab Trail and through the rimtop forest in one of the foundational experiences of Grand Canyon National Park. Look at the old photos and you'll see that everybody used to do it—presidents, celebrities, aristocrats, and the Brady kids. Of course, that was long ago in those leisurely days before rushing rim-to-rim in one day became the fashion. Mules are fascinating creatures, and if you don't mind being in a large group, a ride can be a memorable and anecdote-inspiring activity. **Grand Canyon Trail Rides** (desk inside Grand Canyon Lodge, 928/638-9875, www.canyonrides.com, 8:30am-1:30pm daily May 15-Oct. 15, $45-90), the same company that works the mules at nearby Zion and Bryce Canyon National Parks, offers three daily options during the high season: a one-hour trail ride through the forest and along the rim (must be at least 7 years old and 222 lbs. or less, $45); a three-hour trail ride along the rim to Uncle Jim's Point (at least 10 years old, 200 lbs. or less, $90); and a three-hour trail ride 2 miles (3.2 km) down the North Kaibab Trail (2,300 ft/701 m) to Supai Tunnel (at least 10 years old, 200 lbs. or less, $90), where there are pit toilets and drinking water. If you are trying to choose between the two three-hour tours, take the ride into the canyon to Supai Tunnel. It's a whole different world below the rim and you have a chance to see some of it on this ride, so take it. A shuttle bus picks you up at the lodge a half hour before your ride and takes you to the trailhead.

Food

With its native stone walls and picture windows framing the impossible vastness of the canyon, the **Grand Canyon Lodge Dining Room** must be seen even if you don't eat here. Its high ceilings, wrought-iron chandeliers, Native American symbols, and exposed wood rafters give this large, bright, and open space an unforgettable atmosphere and represent the height of the National Park Service Rustic style. Reservations for dinner are highly recommended (928/638-8560 or gnrfbmgr@gcnr.com, 9am-4pm Mon.-Fri.). All the dining options at Grand Canyon Lodge are closed from mid-October to mid-May. To make reservations for spring, summer, or fall while the lodge and restaurants are closed, call Forever Resorts (877/386-4383). The restaurant is a member of the Green Restaurant Association and serves dishes with a touch of regional and national park history made from fresh, organic, and sustainable produce, meat, chicken, and fish. Breakfast (6:30am-10am daily, $6.70-17.50; buffet $17.50 adults, $9.25 children) features all the hearty and healthy (yogurt, oatmeal, etc.) classics plus Arizona favorites like tamales and eggs and huevos rancheros. Vegetarians will like the grilled vegetable wrap and the braised portobello on offer at lunch (11:30am-2:30pm daily, $6.20-19.50), and everybody will love the fantastic soup, salad, and sandwich buffet ($17.50 adults, $9.25 children). For dinner (4:30pm-9:30pm daily, $11.35-33.95) choose between the Bright Angel Buffet with prime rib (4:30pm-6:30pm daily, $32.95 adults, $18.95 children) and a menu featuring fresh fish, grilled veggie kababs, pasta, steaks, and bison burgers.

To the left as you exit the Grand Canyon Lodge through the main doors, **Deli in the Pines** (10:30am-9pm daily) is an ultracasual eatery serving premade sandwiches, salads, pizza, chips, cookies, and more, primarily for takeout back to your cabin or to put in your backpack for a lunchtime picnic on the rim. This is really the only place within the park that you can get a quick and relatively inexpensive bite to eat (most items are under $10). There's often a line for dinner. Grab some plastic forks and paper plates before you leave, or sit down and relax at one of the few tables inside.

Next to the lodge, a **coffee shop** (5:30am-11am daily) serves espresso and lattes, baked goods, and breakfast burritos before 11am. After 11am and for the rest of the day into the night (11am-11pm) it becomes the **Roughrider Saloon,** named for Teddy Roosevelt's personal fighting crew in the Spanish-American War, several volunteers for which he found in Arizona's northland. The cozy wood interiors here are the perfect complement to a cold regional brew, of which

there is an excellent selection on tap ($6.50). They also serve canyon-themed cocktails ($9-10), a range of bottled beer ($5), and various bar snacks.

The only other option within 50 miles (81 km) of the park is the **Kaibab Lodge** (5 mi/8 km north of park entrance at AZ-67, mile marker 605, 928/638-2389), a charming knotty-pine space with picture windows, checkered tablecloths, and an old woodstove for atmosphere. The food is generally homemade, hearty, and delicious. About 18 miles (29 km) north of the rim along AZ-67, the lodge serves breakfast ($6-12) and dinner ($11-30)—burgers, pasta, ribs, steaks, etc.—daily during the high season (mid-May-mid-Oct.) and is closed in the winter (mid-Oct.-mid-May). It offers gluten-free options, and for vegetarians there's a garden burger and few pasta dishes.

Accommodations

The historic ★ **Grand Canyon Lodge** (877/386-4386, www.grandcanyonforever.com, mid-May-mid-Oct.) rises from the North Rim at the end of AZ-67, a rustic masterpiece of local sandstone and pine gloriously isolated at 8,000 feet (2,438 m) on what feels like the very edge of the known world. The main lodge building hangs rimside above Bright Angel Point, the bottom of a U-shaped complex connected by porticos, and it houses the reception desk, the bright and high-ceilinged dining room, and the enchanting sunroom with its huge picture windows overlooking the canyon. Even if you aren't staying here, spend some time in the sunroom and on the lodge's terrace, both of which are essential North Rim experiences. Cabins of various sizes dot the forest north, east, and west of the lodge, along with two large outbuildings with motel-style rooms. The motel rooms ($148 per night) are charming and comfortable, and some have connecting doors useful for families, but the cabins—including some with incredible views of the canyon—are the lodge's main draw.

the Grand Canyon Lodge

The stone-and-pine cabins all have private bathrooms and romantic stone fireplaces that have been converted to gas. Staying in one can make you feel like a wilderness wanderer bedded down in rare comfort. They come in three sizes: the small and basic Frontier Cabin ($163); the two-room Pioneer Cabin, which sleeps up to six ($188-191); and the larger Western Cabin ($262-301) with two queen beds and a front porch with rough-hewn rocking chairs. There are mini-fridges and coffeemakers in most of the rooms and cabins, and kids under 15 stay free (though it's an extra $15 per night if you want a rollaway bed, which are not allowed in the Frontier Cabins). If you want to stay here, and you should, start hunting for a reservation at least 13 months ahead of your trip. Because the lodge closes during the winter (mid-Oct.-mid-May), there's a relatively small window for a visit, so planning far ahead is the only strategy that works consistently. It is possible, however, to stumble onto a last-minute reservation if the dates of your trip are flexible, you inquire over the phone several times, and you get lucky with a cancellation. But this is not the norm. Four of the Western Cabins are ADA accessible, as are two of the Pioneer Cabins and two of the Frontier Cabins. Additionally, the lodge's main lobby, sunroom, veranda, and dining room are all accessible via three lifts. Outside the main building, the gift shop, the deli, and the coffee shop/saloon are accessible via wide, wheelchair-friendly walkways.

Tucked along the tree line on the edge of an expansive green meadow, 18 miles (29 km) from the rim and 16 miles (26 km) from the North Kaibab Trailhead, the **Kaibab Lodge** (5 mi/8 km north of park entrance at AZ-67, mile marker 605, 928/638-2389, mid-May-mid-Oct., $100-185) is a rustic wilderness haven that's been welcoming North Rim wanderers since the late 1920s. The charming main lodge building has a warm, inviting atmosphere with a fire crackling in the corner and hearty smells wafting from the restaurant. Guests and their pets stay in a variety of cabins and motel-style rooms hiding among the pines and aspens. While all the rooms and cabins are generally rustic but comfortable (and all have private bathrooms), some are more rustic than others, and there's a reason why the older cabins and rooms are less expensive. There are no TVs here, no Wi-Fi, and cell phones don't work. The Hiker's Special is one of the best deals on the plateau: $100 per night for a small, basic room with a double bed and a bathroom. Kaibab Lodge offers ADA-accessible rooms.

The **Jacob Lake Inn** (US-89A and AZ-67, 928/643-7232, www.jacoblake.com, open year-round, $128-165 rooms, $96-144 cabins) is the third-best hotel on a plateau that has only three. The biggest drawback of this historic waystation, owned by the same family since 1923, is that it's 41 miles (66 km) from the North Kaibab Trailhead and 45 miles (72 km), about an hour's drive, from the park and the rim. Jacob Lake, which also has a gas station and a campground but not a lake, is the center of the action on the Kaibab Plateau, and at the inn you'll find all the non-campers that couldn't get a reservation inside the park or at Kaibab Lodge. The forested complex includes a main lobby building with a lunch counter, dining room, bakery, and gift shop; a scattering of very rustic cabins that have seen a lot of hard wear and history; and a host of motel- and hotel-style rooms in various states of decline (all rooms and cabins have private bathrooms). The cabins and some of the motel rooms do not have TVs, phones, or Wi-Fi. That being said, Jacob Lake is a fine place to stay, clean and comfortable and bustling with fellow travelers and activity during the summer. The nicest rooms are in the newer hotel building behind the main lodge, and have up-to-date decor, air-conditioning, cable TV, and Wi-Fi. Jacob Lake Inn offers ADA-accessible rooms.

Camping

The North Rim's warm summer days and cool, star-filled nights are often ideal for camping out; the park's 90-site **North Rim Campground** (www.recreation.gov, mid-May-mid-Oct., $6 for walk-to sites, $18-25 standard nonelectric) typically fills up quickly during the summer and early fall. Keep in mind that, during a good year, you can expect regular late-afternoon rainstorms, often quite dramatic with thunder and lightning, from early July through September. All sites are non-electric with picnic tables, fire rings, and grills. The campground offers tent-only sites, ADA-accessible sites, and pull-through sites for rigs up to 27 feet (8.2 m) long. There's a dump station here but no hookups. A central complex has coin-op showers, laundry, and a drinking-water station, and there's a nearby general store with spotty Wi-Fi and a good selection of groceries and supplies. The campground spreads through an open, park-like forest of pine and aspen about 1.5 miles (2.4 km) north of the lodge, and some of the more expensive spots have rimside views. The easy Transept Trail runs along the rim from the campground to the lodge area, as does the Bridle Path (along AZ-67 rather than the rim), the only trail in the North Rim section of the park that allows bikes and dogs. From December 1-May 15, AZ-67 is closed to vehicles, but the North Rim Campground remains open as a primitive campground. Requiring a backcountry permit, which is also your reservation ($10 plus $8 pp per night), the campground offers no services and is primarily used by wintertime rim-to-rim hikers.

About 18 miles (29 km) north of the rim along AZ-67, the **Demotte Campground** (Forest Road 616, 877/444-6777, www.recreation.gov, mid-May-mid-Oct., $22) has 38 nonelectric campsites for tents, trailers, and small motorhomes. There are no hookups. Operated by the Kaibab National Forest, the sites have tables and fire grills, and there are drinking-water stations and vault toilets within the campground, which is woodsy and peaceful like the rest of the plateau. You may be able to get spotty cell coverage here, especially if you have T-Mobile.

At Jacob Lake, about 45 miles (72 km) north of the rim, **Kaibab Camper Village** (928/643-7804, www.kaibabcampervillage.com, mid-May-mid-Oct., $20-45) has the only sites on the plateau with full hookups. The village has pull-through and back-in spots for rigs up to 40 feet (12.2 m), as well as tent sites with tables and fire pits. The complex has chemical toilets, coin-op laundry and showers, and a store. Head south on AZ-67 from the US-89A junction for 0.25 mile (0.4 km) and turn right on Forest Road 461, then drive 1 mile (1.6 km). This campground is owned and operated by the folks from the nearby Kaibab Lodge.

The Inner Canyon

Inside the canyon is a strange desert, red and green, pink and rocky. It's those sheer rock walls, tight and claustrophobic in the interior's narrowest slots, that make this place a different world altogether. A large part of a canyon-crossing hike takes place in Bright Angel Canyon along Bright Angel Creek. As you hike along the trail beside the creek, greenery and the cool rushing water clash with the silent heat washing off the cliffs on your other side.

On any given night there are only a few hundred visitors sleeping below the rim—at either Phantom Ranch, a Mary Jane Colter-designed lodge near the mouth of Bright Angel Canyon, or at three campgrounds along the corridor trails. Until a few decades ago visiting the inner canyon was something of a free-for-all, but these days access to the interior is strictly controlled; you have to purchase a permit, and they're not always easy to get—each year the park receives

30,000 requests for backcountry permits and issues only 13,000.

No matter which trail you use, there's no avoiding an arduous, leg- and spirit-punishing hike there and back if you really want to see the inner canyon. It's not easy, no matter who you are, but it is worth it; it's a true accomplishment, a hard walk you'll never forget.

Exploring the Inner Canyon

If you want to be one of the small minority of canyon visitors to spend some quality time below the rim, stay at least one full day and night in the inner canyon. Even hikers in excellent shape find that they are sore after trekking down to the river, Phantom Ranch, and beyond. A rim-to-rim hike, either from the south or from the north, pretty much requires at least a day of rest below the rim. The ideal inner canyon trip lasts three days and two nights: one day hiking in, one day of rest, and one day to hike out.

River trips range from three days up to three weeks and often include a hike down one of the corridor trails to the river. Depending on how long you want to spend on the river, plan far, far in advance, and consider making the river trip your only major activity on that particular canyon visit. Combining too much strenuous, mind-blowing, and life-changing activity into one trip tends to water down the entire experience.

Backcountry Permits

To camp overnight below the rim, you have to purchase a **permit** ($10 plus $8 pp per night). The earliest you can apply for an inner-canyon permit is 10 days before the first of the month that is four months before your proposed trip date. The easiest way to get a permit is to go to the **park's website** (www.nps.gov/grca), print out a backcountry permit request form, fill it out, and then fax it first thing in the morning on the date in question—for example, if you want to hike in October, you would **fax** (928/638-2125)

The Colorado River rolls through the inner gorge.

your request May 20-June 1. On June 1 rangers will begin randomly processing all the requests for October, and they'll let you know in about three weeks. On the permit request form you'll indicate at which campgrounds you plan to stay. The permit is your reservation. For more information on obtaining a backcountry permit, call the **Backcountry Information Center** (928/638-7875, 8am-noon and 1pm-5pm daily year-round).

Guided Backpacking Trips

You certainly don't need a guide to take a classic backpacking trip into the Grand Canyon along one of the corridor trails. The National Park Service makes it a relatively simple process to plan and complete such a memorable expedition, and, while hikers die below the rim pretty much every year, the more popular regions of the inner canyon are as safe as can be expected in a vast wilderness. Then again, having some friendly, knowledgeable, and undoubtedly badass canyonlander plan and implement every detail of your trip sure couldn't hurt. Indeed, it would probably make the whole expedition infinitely more enjoyable. As long as you're willing to pay for it—and it is never cheap—hiring a guide is an especially good idea if you want to go places where few tourists and casual hikers dwell.

There are more than 20 companies authorized, through a **guide permit** issued by the National Park Service, to take trips below the rim. If your guide does not have such a permit, do not follow him or her into the Grand Canyon. For an up-to-date list, go to www.nps.gov/grca.

The **Grand Canyon Field Institute** (928/638-2481, www.grandcanyon.org, $690-815), which is operated by the nonprofit Grand Canyon Association, offers several three- to five-day guided backpacking trips to various points inside the canyon, including trips designed specifically for women, beginners, and those interested in the canyon's natural history. Operating out of Flagstaff, **Four Season Guides** (1051 S. Milton Rd., 928/779-6224, www.fsguides.com, $799-1,450) offers more than a dozen different backpacking trips below the rim, from a three-day frolic to Indian Garden to a nearly weeklong, 36-mile (58-km) expedition on some of the canyon's lesser-known trails. The experienced and friendly guides tend to inspire a level of strength and ambition that you might not reach otherwise. These are the guys to call if you want to experience the lonely, out-of-the-way depths of the canyon but don't want to needlessly risk your life doing it alone.

Hiking

Into the Inner Canyon

Although there are many lesser-known routes into and through the canyon, most hikers stick to the **corridor trails—Bright Angel, South Kaibab,** and **North Kaibab.**

A classic Grand Canyon backpacking journey begins at either the Bright Angel Trailhead or the South Kaibab Trailhead on the **South Rim.** Consider going up the one you don't use going down, mostly for variety's sake. Via the South Kaibab Trail, it's a 7-mile (11.3-km) hike to the **Bright Angel Campground,** which is just a short walk from the Colorado River and also from **Phantom Ranch.** Ideally, spend at least two days (the hike-in day and one full day after that) and two nights in the Phantom Ranch area, hiking up the North Kaibab a short way to see the narrow and close walls, talking to the rangers, sitting on the beach watching the river-trippers float by, and losing yourself to the calm, quiet soul of the wilderness.

When it's time to leave the oasis that is Bright Angel Campground and Phantom Ranch, a question arises: Should you rise headlong to the rim (7 mi/11.3 km up on the South Kaibab or 9.5 mi/15.3 km up on the Bright Angel) or move on leisurely to the next oasis? Those inclined to choose the latter should stay an **extra night** below the rim at the campground at **Indian Garden,** a green and lush spot 4.7 miles (7.6 km) up the Bright Angel Trail from the Bright Angel Campground. The small campground is primitive but charming, and the area around it is populated by deer and other creatures. After setting up camp and resting a bit, head out on the flat, 3-mile (4.8 km) round-trip hike to Plateau Point and a spectacular view of the canyon and river, especially at sunset. When you wake up beneath the shady trees at Indian Garden, you face a mere 4.8-mile (7.7-km) hike to the rim.

From the **North Rim,** the North Kaibab is the only major corridor trail to the river and Phantom Ranch.

Some people prefer to spend their time in the canyon recovering from the hard walk or mule ride that brought them here, and a day spent cooling your feet in Bright Angel Creek or drinking beer in the cantina is not a day wasted. However, if you want to do some exploring around Phantom Ranch, there are a few popular day hikes from which to choose. When you arrive, the friendly rangers will usually tell you, unsolicited, all about these hikes and provide detailed directions. If you want to get deeper out in the bush and far from other hikers, ask one of the rangers to recommend a lesser-known route.

Rim to Rim

For an epic, **23.9-mile (39-km)** rim-to-rim hike, you can choose, as long as the season permits, to start either on the north or south. Starting from the South Rim, you may want to go down the **Bright Angel Trail** to see beautiful Indian Garden; then again, the **South Kaibab Trail** provides a faster, more direct route to the river. If you start from the north, you may want to come out of the canyon via the South Kaibab; it is shorter and faster, and at that point you are probably going to want to take the path of least resistance. Remember though, while it's shorter, the South Kaibab is a good deal steeper than the Bright Angel, and there is no water available.

No matter who you are or what trail you prefer, the hike out of the Grand Canyon is, at several points, a brutal trudge. It's even worse with 30-40 pounds (13.6-18.1 kg) of stuff you don't really need on your back. Try to take only the essentials to keep your pack weight down. The best rim-to-rim hikes include at least one full day at Phantom Ranch or the Bright Angel Campground. You could do the hike without a permit with a bit of preplanning: Reserve a room on the North Rim and hike there from the South Rim in one day. Then after a day of rest and another night, hike back to the South Rim in one day.

No matter how you do it, when you finally gain the final rim after a cross-canyon hike, a profound sense of accomplishment washes away at least half of the fatigue. The other half typically hangs around for a week or so.

Day Hikes Around Phantom Ranch

Some people prefer to spend their time

Hiking Rim to Rim . . . the Easy Way

One of the first things you notice while journeying through the inner canyon is the advanced age of many of your fellow hikers. It is not uncommon to see men and women in their 70s and 80s hiking along at a good clip, packs on their backs and big smiles on their faces. At the same time, all over the South Rim you'll see warning signs about overexertion, each featuring a buff young man in incredible shape suffering from heatstroke or exhaustion, with the warning that most of the people who die in the canyon—and people die every year—are people like him. You need not be a wilderness expert or marathon runner to enjoy even the long rim-to-rim hike through the inner canyon. Don't let your fears hold you back from what is often a life-changing trip.

Several strategies can make a canyon hike much easier than a forced march with a pack of gear on your back:

- Don't go in the summer; wait until **October or even November,** when it's cooler, though still quite warm, in the inner canyon.
- Try your best to book a cabin or a dorm room at **Phantom Ranch** rather than camping. This way, you'll need less equipment, you'll have all or most of your food taken care of, and there will be a shower and a beer waiting for you upon your arrival.
- Consider that for $76 each way, you can **hire a mule** to carry up to 30 pounds (13.6 kg) of gear for you, so all you have to bring is a day pack, with water and snacks. So instead of suffering while you descend and ascend the trail, you'll be able to better enjoy the magnificence of this wonder of the world.

in the canyon recovering from the hard walk or mule ride that brought them here, and a day spent cooling your feet in Bright Angel Creek or drinking beer in the cantina is not a day wasted. However, if you want to do some exploring around Phantom Ranch, there are a few popular day hikes from which to choose. When you arrive, the friendly rangers will usually tell you, unsolicited, all about these hikes and provide detailed directions. If you want to get deeper out in the bush and far from the other hikers, ask one of the rangers to recommend a lesser-known route.

River Trail

Distance: 1.5 miles (2.4 km) round-trip
Duration: 1-2 hours
Elevation gain: negligible
Effort: easy
Trailhead: Start at Phantom Ranch on north side of river or at end of Bright Angel Trail on south side.

This short hike is along the precipitous **River Trail,** high above the Colorado just south of Phantom Ranch. The Civilian Conservation Corps (CCC) blasted this skinny cliffside trail out of the rock walls in the 1930s to provide a link between the Bright Angel and the South Kaibab Trails. Heading out from Phantom, it's about a 1.5-mile (2.4-km) loop that takes you across both suspension bridges and high above the river. It's an easy walk with fantastic views and is a good way to get your sore legs stretched and moving again. And you are likely to see a bighorn sheep's cute little face poking out from the rocks and shadows on the steep cliffs.

Clear Creek Loop

Distance: about 1.5 miles (2.4 km)
Duration: 1-2 hours
Elevation gain: 826 feet (252 m)
Effort: easy to moderate
Trailhead: about 0.3 mile (0.5 km) north of Phantom Ranch on the North Kaibab Trail

Another popular CCC-built trail near

Phantom, the 1.5-mile (2.4-km) **Clear Creek Loop** takes you high above the river to **Phantom Overlook,** where there's an old stone bench and excellent views of the canyon and Phantom Ranch below. The rangers seem to recommend this hike the most, but, while it's not tough, it can be a little steep and rugged, especially if you're exhausted and sore. The views are, ultimately, well worth the pain.

Phantom Ranch to Ribbon Falls

Distance: 11 miles (17.7 km) round-trip
Duration: 5-6 hours to all day
Elevation gain: 1,174 feet (358 m)
Effort: easy to moderate
Trailhead: North Kaibab Trail, on north side of Phantom Ranch

If you hiked in from the South Rim and you have a long, approximately 11-mile (17.7-km) round-trip day hike in you, head north on the **North Kaibab Trail** from Phantom Ranch to beautiful **Ribbon Falls,** a mossy, cool-water oasis just off the hot, dusty trail. The falls are indeed a ribbon of cold water falling hard off the rock cliffs, and you can scramble up the slickrock and through the green creekside jungle and stand beneath the shower. Look for the sign for Ribbon Falls on the left side of the trail 5.5 miles (8.9 km) from Phantom. A section of this hike will also give you a chance to see the eerie, claustrophobic **"Box,"** one of the strangest and most exhilarating stretches of the North Kaibab. This narrow stretch through the **inner gorge** is easy and flat but low and hot, boxed in by Vishnu schist about 1.7 billion years old. Don't hike in the inner canyon after 10am in the summer.

Mule Rides

For generations the famous Grand Canyon mules have been dexterously picking along the skinny trails, loaded with packs and people. Even the Brady Bunch rode them, so they come highly recommended. A descent into the canyon on the back of a friendly mule—with an often-taciturn cowboy-type leading the train—can be an unforgettable experience, but don't assume because you're riding and not walking that you won't be sore in the morning.

Park concessionaire **Xanterra** offers two mule trips to Phantom Ranch, a one-night excursion and a two-night expedition. The **one-night trip** is offered **year-round** and includes accommodations at Phantom Ranch (by booking a mule trip, you automatically reserve a spot at Phantom Ranch without having to enter the lottery), dinner and breakfast in the Phantom Ranch Canteen, and a sack lunch. The cost for the one-night trip is $692.59 per person, $1,204.51 for two people, and $533.31 for each additional person. The **two-night trip** is offered **November-March** and includes accommodations at Phantom Ranch, meals in the canteen, and sack lunches. The cost for the two-night trip is $1,009.42 per person, $1,657.50 for two people, and $690.86 for each additional person. For reservations call 888/297-2757 or visit www.grandcanyonlodges.com. You can make a reservation up to 13 months in advance, and you really should do it as soon as you know your plans. There's a 225-pound (102-kg) weight restriction.

The mule trips begin in the stone corral next to the Bright Angel Lodge and descend into the canyon via the Bright Angel Trail, stopping for a box lunch at Indian Garden. The trips ascend from the inner gorge via the South Kaibab Trail. Expect to be in the saddle for about 5.5 hours each way. You are provided with a small plastic bag about the size of a 10-pound (4.5-kg) bag of ice to carry your toiletries and other items. If you need more luggage than this, you can send a duffel bag ahead for $76 each way (30 lbs/13.6 kg maximum, 36 by 20 by 13 in/91 by 51 by 33 cm, www.grandcanyonlodges.com/lodging/phantom-ranch).

River Trips

People who have been inside the Grand Canyon often have one of two reactions—either they can't wait to return, or they swear never to return. This is even the case for those intrepid souls who ride the great river, braving white-water roller coasters while looking forward to a star-filled evening—dry, and full of gourmet camp food—camping on a white beach deep in the gorge. To boat the Colorado is one of the most exciting and potentially life-changing trips the American West has to offer.

Rafting season in the canyon runs **April-October,** and there are myriad trips to choose from—from a 3-day long-weekend ride to an 18-day full-canyon epic. An **upper-canyon trip** will take you from River Mile 0 at Lees Ferry through the canyon to Phantom Ranch, while a **lower-canyon trip** begins at Phantom, requiring a hike down the Bright Angel with your gear on your back. Furthermore, you can choose between a motorized pontoon boat (as some three-quarters of rafters do), a paddleboat, a kayak, or some other combination. It all depends on what you want and what you can afford.

Choosing a Trip

Expect to pay about $1,400 per person for a 3-day motor trip, $2,600 per person for a 6-day motor trip, $2,000 per person for a 6-day oar trip, and up to $5,000 per person for a 13-day oar trip. Many of the outfitters offer trips tailored to certain interests, such as trips with a naturalist or trips that make a lot of stops for hiking.

Choosing an Outfitter

If you are considering taking a river trip, the best place to start is the website of the **Grand Canyon River Outfitters Association** (www.gcroa.org), a nonprofit

From top to bottom: on the South Kaibab Trail; river-trippers; taking a break over the Colorado River.

Lees Ferry: River Mile 0

Lees Ferry (www.nps.gov/glca) is the only spot in hundreds of miles where you can drive down to the Colorado River. Located in the Glen Canyon National Recreation Area, Lees Ferry provides the dividing line between the upper and lower states of the Colorado River's watershed, making it "river mile 0," the gateway and crossroads to both the upper and lower Colorado, and the place where its annual flows are measured and recorded.

This lonely spot is named for a man who occupied the area rather briefly in the early 1870s, Mormon outlaw John D. Lee, who was exiled here after he and others attacked and murdered more than 100 westbound Arkansas emigrants moving through Utah Territory during a period when relations between the Utah Mormons and the U.S. government were strained, to say the least. He didn't stay long, escaping as a fugitive before his capture and execution. One of Lee's wives, Emma Lee, ended up running the ferry more than Lee ever did.

Today Lees Ferry is the starting block for thousands of brave river-trippers who venture into the Grand Canyon on the Colorado River every year. It's also a popular fishing spot, though the trout here have been introduced and were not native to the warm, muddy flow before the dam at Glen Canyon changed the Colorado's character. For guides, gear, and any other information about the area, try **Lees Ferry Anglers** (928/355-2261 or 800/962-9755, www.leesferry.com, 6am-9pm daily), located at the Cliff Dwellers Lodge. The guides at **Marble Canyon Outfitters** (800/533-7339, www.leesferryflyfishing.com) and **Kayak the Colorado** (928/856-0012, www.kayakthecolorado.com) will also take you out fishing or kayaking on the Colorado River beyond the dam, including trips to Horseshoe Bend.

Food and Accommodations

The small **Cliff Dwellers Lodge** (US-89A near Marble Canyon, 928/355-2261 or 800/962-9755, http://leesferry.com, $90) is nearly drowned by the scenery around it, tucked beneath the base of the red cliffs. This lodge offers charming, rustic-but-

group of 13 licensed river outfitters, all of them monitored and approved by the National Park Service, each with a good safety record and relatively similar rates. Your guide takes care of all the permits you need to spend nights below the rim. After you decide what kind of trip you want, the website links to the individual outfitters for booking. Most of the companies offer trips lasting 3-18 days and have a variety of boat styles. It's a good idea to choose two or three companies, call them up, and talk to someone live. You'll be putting your life in their hands, so you want to make sure that you like the spirit of the company. Also consider the size of the group. These river trips are very social; you'll be spending a lot of time with your fellow boaters. Talk to a company representative about previous trips so you can get a gauge of what kind of people, and how many, you'll be floating with.

If you are one of the majority of river explorers who can't wait to get back on the water once you've landed at the final port, remember that the National Park Service enforces a strict limit of one trip per year, per person.

Food and Accommodations

Designed by Mary Jane Colter for the Fred Harvey Company in 1922, ★ **Phantom Ranch** (888/297-2757, www.grandcanyonlodges.com, dormitory $51 pp, 2-person cabin $149, $13 each additional person), the only noncamping accommodations inside the canyon, is a shady, peaceful place that you're likely to miss and yearn for once you've visited and left it behind. Perhaps Phantom's strong draw is less comfortable rooms with satellite television, and the restaurant serves good breakfasts, lunches, and dinners ($10-30), with everything from fajitas and ribs to falafel and halibut. It also serves liquor, beer, and wine, which you can sip on the little patio here at what seems like the very end of the world.

The **Lees Ferry Lodge at Vermilion Cliffs** (US-89A near Marble Canyon, 928/355-2231 or 800/451-2231, www.vermilioncliffs.com, $65) has romantic little rooms in a retro-West, rock-built structure that blends into the tremendous background wonderfully. This lodge has undergone major renovations in recent years.

The trading post first established by Lorenzo Hubbell at **Marble Canyon Lodge** (US-89A near Marble Canyon, 800/726-1789, www.marblecanyoncompany.com, $82-185) has been open for business since 1920, serving wanderers under the ever-blue sky—which is the only thing bigger out here than the wide-open landscape. This is a friendly and comfortable place to stop. It offers rooms with kitchenettes and has an excellent restaurant serving tasty fry bread and other Southwestern staples ($10-20). The trading post here has a superior selection of books about the region. The lodge also operates a gas station and convenience store just up the road.

The **Lees Ferry Campground** ($20 per night) has 51 sites with grills, tables, and shade structures on a rise above the Colorado River. The sites have access to bathrooms and potable water. For more information, call Glen Canyon National Recreation Area (928/608-6200). To reach the campground, drive about 4.5 miles (7.2 km) from the junction of US-89A and Lees Ferry Road and turn left, following signs to the campground.

Getting There

Lees Ferry is located in the vast, empty regions along the road between the South and North Rims, about 60 miles (97 km) from the North Rim. Just after crossing over **Navajo Bridge** at Marble Canyon, along **US-89A,** turn on **Lees Ferry Road.** The river is about 7 miles (11.3 km) along the road from the Navajo Bridge Visitors Center.

about its intrinsic pleasures and more about it being the only sign of civilization in a deep wilderness that can feel like the end of the world, especially after the 14-mile (22.5-km) hike in from the North Rim.

Phantom Ranch has 11 rustic, air-conditioned **cabins** and four hiker-only **dormitories.** The cabins vary in size, sleeping 2-10 people. Each cabin has a sink with cold water, a toilet, bedding, and towels. Hot-water sinks and showers are available in a separate "showerhouse" building, where towels, soap, and shampoo are also provided. There are two dormitories for men and two for women (families with children five or under must stay in a cabin). Each dormitory has five bunk beds, a toilet, and a shower. Bedding, towels, soap, and shampoo are provided. The dorms and the cabins are all heated in the winter and air-conditioned in the summer.

The lodge's center point is the **Phantom Ranch Canteen,** a welcoming, air-conditioned, beer- and lemonade-selling sight for anyone who has just descended one of the trails. There is no central lodge building at Phantom Ranch, but the canteen is the closest thing to it, with its family-style tables often filling up during the heat of the day with beer-drinkers and tale-tellers. The canteen offers two meals per day—**breakfast,** made up of eggs, pancakes, and thick slices of bacon ($23.65), and **dinner,** with a choice of steak ($47.91), stew ($29.43), or vegetarian ($29.43). The cantina also offers a **box lunch** ($20.85) with a bagel, fruit, and salty snacks. Reservations for meals are also difficult to come by. You must make reservations at least a year ahead.

Most nights and afternoons, a ranger based at Phantom Ranch will give a talk on some aspect of canyon lore, history, or science. These events are always interesting and well attended, even in the 110°F (43°C) heat of summer.

Phantom is located near the mouth of Bright Angel Canyon, within a few yards of clear, babbling Bright Angel Creek, and shaded by large cottonwoods, some of them planted in the 1930s by the Civilian Conservation Corps. There are several day hikes within easy reach, and the Colorado River and the two awesome suspension bridges that link one bank to the other are only about 0.4 mile (0.6 km) from the lodge.

A **lottery system** governs Phantom Ranch **reservations.** You have to enter the lottery between the 1st and 25th of the month 15 months prior to your proposed trip. You'll be notified at least 14 months before your trip if you won a stay. Go to www.grandcanyonlodges.com/lodging/phantom-ranch/lottery for more details.

Camping

There are three developed campgrounds in the inner canyon: **Cottonwood Campground,** about 6.8 miles (10.9 km) from the North Rim along the North Kaibab Trail; **Bright Angel Campground,** along the creek of the same name near Phantom Ranch; and **Indian Garden Campground,** about 4.8 miles (7.7 km) from the South Rim along the Bright Angel Trail. To stay overnight at any of these campgrounds you must obtain a permit from the **South Rim Backcountry Information Center** (928/638-7875, $10 plus $8 pp per night). Your backcountry permit is your reservation. All three campgrounds offer toilets, a freshwater spigot (year-round at Bright Angel and Indian Garden only), picnic tables, food storage bins to keep the critters out, poles on which to hang your packs, and emergency phones. There are no showers or other amenities. It's a good idea to throw a roll of toilet paper into your pack just in case the campgrounds are out.

The best campground in the inner canyon is **Bright Angel Campground,** a shady, cottonwood-lined setting along cool Bright Angel Creek with 33 tent spots, each with pack poles, a picnic table, and ammo boxes to keep the raccoons out of your food. Because of its easy proximity to Phantom Ranch (about 0.4 mi/0.6 km), campers can make use of the Phantom Ranch Canteen, even eating meals there if they can get a reservation, and can attend the ranger talks offered at the lodge. There's nothing quite like sitting on the grassy banks beside your campsite and cooling your worn feet in the creek. Accessible from the Bright Angel Trail (9.9 mi/15.9 km one-way), South Kaibab Trail (7 mi/11.3 km one-way) and North Kaibab Trail (14 mi/22.5 km one-way), Bright Angel Campground has an emergency phone, a year-round potable water spigot, and bathrooms with sinks and toilets. There's also a ranger on-site who will greet you once you get settled in your spot.

The West Rim and Grand Canyon West

Since the Hualapai Tribe's Skywalk opened in 2007, the remote Grand Canyon West has become a fairly busy tourist attraction. The Skywalk is about a two-hour drive from the Hualapai Reservation's capital, Peach Springs, which is located along Route 66 west of Seligman. If you want to experience Grand Canyon West during your trip to the Grand Canyon National Park, remember that it is about 225 miles (360 km) from the South Rim and will take at least an extra two days. Along the way, you can drive on the longest remaining portion of Route 66 and, if you have a few days on top of that, hike down into Havasu Canyon and see its famous, fantastical waterfalls.

Getting There

The best way to get to **Grand Canyon West** from the **South Rim** is to take I-40 to the Ash Fork exit and then drive west on Route 66. Starting at Ash Fork and heading west to Peach Springs, the **longest remaining portion of Route 66** moves through **Seligman,** a small roadside town that's caught in the heyday of the Mother Road. The route through Seligman, which stands up to a stop and a walk around if you have the time, is popular with nostalgic motorcyclists, and there are a few eateries and tourist-style stores in town. Once you reach **Peach Springs** (about 140 mi/225 km from the South Rim, about a 2.5-hour drive), continue west on Route 66 for 29 miles (47 km), turn right on Antares Road and drive 32 miles (52 km), turn right onto Pearce Ferry Road and drive 3 miles (4.8 km), and then turn right on Diamond Bar Road and drive 21 miles (34 km). Diamond Bar Road ends at the only entrance to Grand Canyon West. The drive from Peach Springs to Grand Canyon West is 85 miles (137 km) and takes about 2 hours. The total drive from the South Rim to Grand Canyon West is about 225 miles (360 km) and takes about 4.5 hours.

To reach **Havasu Canyon** from the South Rim, take I-40 to the Ash Fork exit and then drive west on Route 66, passing through Seligman. About 30 miles (48 km) past Seligman, turn north on Indian Route 18 and drive 60 miles (97 km) north to a parking area at **Hualapai Hilltop,** where the **trailhead** is located. The drive from the South Rim to Hualapai Hilltop is 195 miles (315 km) total and takes about four hours. From there it's a moderate 8-mile (12.9 km) **hike** in to **Supai Village** and the lodge, and another 2 miles (3.2 km) to the campground. If you don't want to hike in, you can arrange to **rent a mule** (928/448-2121, 928/448-2174, or 928/448-2180, www.officialhavasupaitribe.com, $400 round-trip to campground) or even hire a **helicopter.**

Hualapai Reservation's Skywalk is only 125 miles (201 km) from **Las Vegas** (about a 2.5-hour drive), so it makes sense to include this remote side trip if you're headed to the South Rim from Vegas anyway. To reach Grand Canyon West from Las Vegas, take I-11/US-93 out of the city, heading south for about 65 miles (105 km) to mile marker 42, where you'll see the Dolan Springs/Meadview City/Pearce Ferry exit. Turn north onto Pearce Ferry Road. About 30 miles (48 km) in, turn east on Diamond Bar Road. Then it's about 20 miles (32 km) to Grand Canyon West.

Once you arrive at Grand Canyon West, you must park your vehicle and ride the free **hop-on/hop-off shuttle** between the viewpoints. There is a large parking area where you can leave your car and pick up the shuttle.

Havasupai Indian Reservation

Heavy with lime, the waters of Havasu Creek flow an almost tropical blue-green. The creek passes below the weathered red walls of the western Grand Canyon and cuts **Havasu Canyon,** home these many centuries to the Havasupai (Havasu 'Baaja), the "people of the blue-green water."

Thousands of tourists from all over the world flock to **Havasupai** (928/448-2121, http://theofficialhavasupaitribe.com, entry fee $50 plus $10 environmental fee) every year just to see the canyon's blue-green waterfalls, to swim in their pools, and to visit one of the most remote hometowns in North America.

The Havasupai (Pai means "people" in the Yuman language) have been living in Grand Canyon since at least the 12th century, tending small irrigated fields of corn, melons, beans, and squash, and small orchards of peach, apple, and apricot trees. For centuries the Havasupai farmed in Havasu Canyon and in other spring-fed areas of Grand Canyon—Indian Garden along the Bright Angel Trail and Santa Maria Spring along the Hermit Trail—in the summer and then hunted and gathered on the rim during the winter, ancient patterns that were disrupted by the settling of northern Arizona in the late 19th century.

Today the Havasupai rely primarily on tourism to their little hidden oasis in Grand Canyon, and their beautiful land is known the world over for its striking waterfalls. The ease with which the Internet allows images to spread inevitably brought what once was a kind of poorly hidden secret to the attention of the globe. Now it's harder than ever to obtain a reservation in the tribe's small lodge and campground, which can only be reached via a **hike into the canyon** (8 mi/12.9 km to lodge, 10 mi/16.1 km to campground) or a 10-minute **helicopter ride.**

Reservations

The tribe requires that you **stay overnight** and have a **reservation** to visit Supai and the falls; **no day trips** are allowed. To make a reservation to camp in Havasu Canyon, you have to reserve a space online at www.havasupaireservations.com beginning at 8am on February 1 of the year you want to go. Camping permits sell out fast! To make reservations at the Havasupai Lodge (which you should do far in advance), call 928/448-2111 or visit www.havasupaireservations.com.

Planning Tips

A visit to Havasupai takes some planning. It's unbearably hot in the deep summer, when you can't hike except in the very early morning; the **best months** to visit are **September-October** and **April-June.** If you aren't into **backpacking,** you can hire a **pack mule** ($400 round-trip) or take the **helicopter** ($85 one-way). A popular way to visit is to hike in and take the helicopter out. It's a 10-minute thrill ride through the canyon to the rim, and the helipad is only about 50 yards (46 m) from the trailhead parking lot.

Most visitors stay the night at one of the motels along **Historic Route 66** before hiking in. Get an early start, especially during the summer. It's a **60-mile (97-km) drive** to the **trailhead at Hualapai Hill** from the

Havasu Falls

junction of Route 66 and Indian Route 18, which leads to the trailhead. The closest hotels are the **Caverns Inn** and the **Hualapai Lodge** in **Peach Springs,** about 7 miles (11.3 km) west of the junction. You'll find cheaper accommodations in **Seligman,** about 30 miles (48 km) east of the junction.

Sights

Supai Village

Havasu Creek falls through the canyon on its way to join the Colorado River, passing briefly by the ramshackle, inner-canyon village of **Supai,** where it is not unusual to see horses running free in the dusty streets, where reggae plays all day through some community speaker, and where the supply helicopter alights and then hops out again every 10 minutes or so in a field across from the post office. The village has a small café, a general store, and a small lodge.

The Waterfalls

What used to be Navajo Falls, just down the trail from the village, was destroyed in a 2008 flash flood. Now there's a wider set of falls and a big pool that sits below a flood-eroded hill.

Perhaps the most famous of the canyon's blue-green falls, **Havasu Falls** comes on you all of a sudden as you get closer to the campground, which is about 2 miles (3.2 km) from the village. Few hikers refuse to toss their packs aside and strip to their swimsuits when they see Havasu Falls for the first time.

The other major waterfall, **Mooney Falls,** is another mile (1.6 km) down the trail, through the campground. It's not easy to reach the pool below; it requires a careful walk down a narrow, rock-hewn trail with chain handles, but most reasonably dexterous people can handle it.

Beaver Falls, somewhat underwhelming by comparison, is another 2 miles (3.2 km) toward the river, which is 7 miles (11.3 km) from the campground.

Hiking

Havasu Canyon Trail

Distance: 8 miles (12.9 km) one-way to Supai Village; 10 miles (16.1 km) one-way to campground
Duration: 3-5 hours one-way
Elevation gain: 2,000 feet (610 m)
Effort: moderate
Trailhead: Hualapai Hilltop

The 8-mile (12.9-km) one-way hike to the **village of Supai** from the trailhead at Hualapai Hilltop is one of the easier treks into the Grand Canyon. For the first 2 miles (3.2 km) or so, rocky, moderately technical switchbacks lead to the canyon floor, a sandy bottomland where you're surrounded by eroded humps of seemingly melted, pockmarked sandstone. This is not Grand Canyon National Park: You'll know that for sure when you see the trash along the trail. It doesn't ruin the hike, but it nearly breaks the spell.

When you reach the village, you'll see the twin rock spires, called **Wii'Gliva,** which tower over the little farms and homes of Supai. The trail continues 2 miles (3.2 km) to the campground, passing **Havasu Falls,** and then moves on to the Colorado River 7 miles (11.3 km) downcreek, passing

Mooney and Beaver Falls and through a gorgeous green riparian stretch. The Havasupai Reservation ends at Beaver Falls and Grand Canyon National Park begins.

It's difficult to the hike from the village or the campground to the Colorado River in one day—it's a long, wet route with many creek crossings and not always easy to follow; plus, there's no camping allowed at the river, so you must make it back by bedtime. Only experienced, strong hikers should attempt the trek to the Colorado River and back.

There are no water stations or toilets along the trail.

Food and Accommodations

The **Havasupai Lodge** (928/448-2111, $145 up to 4 people) is a small two-story wood building in a quiet corner of the village. The rooms are basic though relatively large, with two queen beds, air-conditioning, and private baths. The village also has a small **café** that serves decent breakfast, lunch, and dinner, and a **general store.**

Most visitors pack in and stay at the primitive **campground** (first-come, first-served, water and toilets available, $25) about 2 miles (3.2 km) from the village between Havasu and Mooney Falls—an area the tribe once used to cremate the dead. The campground holds about 300 people in sites along the creek beneath shady cottonwoods.

Hualapai Indian Reservation

Since the Hualapai Tribe's Skywalk opened in 2007, the remote **Grand Canyon West** has become a fairly busy tourist attraction. The Skywalk is about a two-hour drive from the Hualapai Reservation's capital, **Peach Springs,** which is located along Route 66 west of Seligman. If you want to experience Grand Canyon West during your trip to the Grand Canyon National Park, remember that it is about 225 miles (360 km) from the South Rim and will take at least an extra two days.

Although Peach Springs is the capital of the Hualapai (WALL-uh-pie) Reservation, there's not much there but a lodge and a few scattered houses. The real attractions are up on the West Rim about 85 miles (137 km) and two hours away. Peach Springs makes an obvious base for a visit to the West Rim, which has several lookout points, the famous Skywalk, and a kitschy Old West-style tourist attraction called Hualapai Ranch. The tribe's Hualapai River Runners will take you on a day trip on the river, and there are several all-inclusive package tours to choose from.

Grand Canyon West

Grand Canyon West (5001 Diamond Bar Rd., 928/769-2636 or 888/868-9378, www.grandcanyonwest.com, 9am-sundown daily, $39 general admission, $20 add-on for Skywalk, $19 add-on for meal) is the Hualapai Reservation's tourist area, comprising several viewpoints on the western rim of Grand Canyon and the Skywalk.

A general admission ticket gets you on the free hop-on/hop-off shuttle to **Eagle Point,** where the Skywalk juts out and there's a restaurant and a café, and on to **Guano Point,** with a wonderful view of the western canyon and a café on the edge of the rim. (Getting around by private vehicle is not permitted at Grand Canyon West; there is a large parking area where you can leave your car and pick up the shuttle.)

It's a good idea to book your general admission tickets and add-ons before you travel out to this remote sight. If you're coming from Las Vegas (as many Grand Canyon West visitors do), you can easily find an all-inclusive tour that includes admission. Expect to spend a long day out here, and the drive back to anywhere (Peach Springs or Las Vegas) takes at least two hours. Because of its remoteness and rather high cost, consider beforehand whether it is worth it to you. While the views of the Grand Canyon are indeed spectacular along the western rim, they are vastly less dramatic than those from

The Hualapai Nation

Before the 1850s, northwestern Arizona's small Hualapai Nation didn't really exist. It was the federal government's idea to group together 13 autonomous bands of Yuman-speaking Pai Indians, who had lived on the high dry plains near Grand Canyon's western reaches for eons, as the "People of the Tall Pines."

Before the colonial clampdown and the Hualapai Wars of the 1860s, the Pai bands were independent, though they "followed common rules for marriage and land use, spoke variations of one language, and shared social structures, kin networks, cultural practices, environmental niches, and so on," according to Jeffrey Shepherd's *We Are an Indian Nation: A History of the Hualapai People,* which the scholar spent 10 years researching and writing.

The U.S. Army nearly wiped out the bands during the land wars of the 1860s, and the internment of the survivors almost finished the job. But the bands persisted, and in 1883 the government established the million-acre (404,686-ha) Hualapai Reservation, with its capital at Peach Springs. Then it spent the next 100 years or so trying to take it away from them for the benefit of Anglo ranchers, the railroad, and the National Park Service.

These days the Hualapai Nation, though still impoverished, is a worldwide brand—Grand Canyon West. How did this happen?

The small, isolated tribe has always been willing to take economic risks, one of the many ways, as Shepherd argues, that the Hualapai have twisted colonial objectives for their own survival. A few years ago they partnered with Las Vegas entrepreneur David Jin and built the Hualapai Skywalk, a 70-foot-long (21.3-m) glass walkway hanging from the Grand Canyon's western rim. Now you can't walk two steps along the Vegas strip without a tour guide offering to drive you to one of the most isolated sections of Arizona.

Throughout their relatively short history as a nation, the Hualapai have consistently tried to make their windy and dry reservation economically viable, sometimes with the assistance of the government but often in direct contradiction to its goals. For generations they were cattle ranchers, but they could never get enough water to make it pay. They successfully sued the Santa Fe Railroad over an important reservation spring in a landmark case for Indigenous rights. For a time in the 1980s they even hesitantly explored allowing uranium mining on their reservation. Now, they have bet their future on tourism.

the South and North Rims—Grand Canyon West sits at around 4,000 feet (1,219 m) above sea level, so the views of the canyon are much shallower and more uniform than those in the park.

Grand Canyon Skywalk

The Skywalk (928/769-2636 or 888/868-9378, www.grandcanyonwest.com, $20 plus $39 admission fee to Grand Canyon West) is as much an art installation as it is a tourist attraction. A horseshoe-shaped glass and steel platform jutting out 70 feet (21 m) from the canyon rim, it appears futuristic surrounded by the rugged, remote western canyon. It's something to see for sure, but is it worth the long drive and the high price tag? Not really. If you have time for an off-the-beaten-path portion of your canyon trip, it's better to go to the North Rim and stand out on Bright Angel Point—you'll get a somewhat similar impression, and it's cheaper. There is something of the thrill ride to the Skywalk, however. Some people can't handle it: They walk out a few steps, look down through the glass at the canyon 4,000 feet (1,219 m) below, and head for (seemingly) more solid ground. It's all perfectly safe, but it doesn't feel that way if you are subject to vertigo. Another drawback of this site is that you are not allowed to take your camera out on the Skywalk. If you want a record of this adventure, you have to buy a "professional" photo taken by somebody else. You have to store all of your possessions, including your camera, in a locker before stepping out on the glass, with covers on your shoes.

Hualapai Ranch

At **Hualapai Ranch** (928/769-2636 or 888/868-9378, www.grandcanyonwest.com), you can take a zipline ride, go horseback riding, and stay overnight in a rustic cabin.

Diamond Creek Road

You can drive to the river's edge yourself along the 19-mile (31-km) **Diamond Creek Road** through a dry, scrubby landscape scattered with cacti. The road provides the only easy access to the river's edge between Lees Ferry, not far from the North Rim, and Pearce Ferry, near Lake Mead. You need a permit to drive the road; obtain one at the Hualapai Lodge in Peach Springs (the road is just across Route 66 from the lodge). A tribal police officer may check it at some point along the road.

At the end of the road, where Diamond Creek marries the Colorado, there's a sandy beach by an enchanting, lush oasis, and, of course, there's that big river rolling by.

The route is best negotiated in a high-clearance SUV; you have to cross Diamond Creek six times as the dirt road winds down through Peach Springs Canyon, dropping some 3,400 feet (1,036 m) from its beginning at Peach Springs on Route 66. The creek is susceptible to flash floods during the summer and winter rainy seasons, so call ahead to check **road conditions** (928/769-2230).

River Rafting

Though the Skywalk may not be worth the high price of admission and the long drive to reach it, the Hualapai offer one adventure that is worth the steep price tag: the canyon's only **one-day river**

The Skywalk

rafting experience, offered by **Hualapai River Runners** (928/769-2636 or 888/868-9378, www.grandcanyonwest.com, May-Oct., $450 pp). It generally takes up to a year of planning and several days of roughing it to ride the river and the rapids through the inner gorge, making a Colorado River adventure something that the average tourist isn't likely to try. Not so in Grand Canyon West. For about $450 per person, Hualapai river guides will pick you up in a van early in the morning at the Hualapai Lodge in Peach Springs and drive you to the Colorado via the rough Diamond Creek Road, where you'll float downstream in a motorboat over roiling white-water rapids and smooth and tranquil stretches. You'll stop for lunch on a beach and take a short hike through a watery side canyon to beautiful Travertine Falls. At the end of the trip, a helicopter picks you out of the canyon and drops you on the rim near the Skywalk. It's expensive, yes, but if you want to ride the river without a lot of preplanning and camping, this is the way to do it. Along the way the Hualapai guides tell stories about this end of the Grand Canyon, sprinkled with tribal history and lore.

Food and Accommodations

Bringing outside food and beverages to Grand Canyon West is not permitted. The dining scene at Grand Canyon West is not great, but there are three eateries with great views of the canyon. There's a restaurant and a café at Eagle Point and a café at Guano Point. To get a meal at one of the two viewpoints, you must add on a $19 meal ticket to your general admission price, which gives you the choice of a burger, veggie burger, or a chicken sandwich. As an alternative, consider eating at the excellent restaurant at the Hualapai Lodge in Peach Springs, **Diamond Creek** (900 Route 66, 928/769-2230 or 928/769-2636, www.grandcanyonwest.com, 6am-9pm daily, $10-15), which serves American and Native American dishes. The Hualapai taco (similar to the Navajo taco, with beans and meat piled high on a fluffy slab of fry bread) and the Hualapai stew (with luscious sirloin tips and vegetables swimming in a delicious, hearty broth) are both recommended. The restaurant also offers a heaping plate of delicious spaghetti—great if you're carbo-loading for a big hike to Havasupai. The menu also includes a few vegetarian choices, good chili, and pizza.

The **Hualapai Lodge** (900 Route 66, 928/769-2230 or 928/769-2636, www.grandcanyonwest.com, $150-170, wheelchair accessible) has a small heated saltwater pool, an exercise room, gift shop, 57 comfortable, newish rooms with soft beds, cable, free Wi-Fi, and train tracks right out the back door. This is a good place to stay the night before hiking into Havasupai, as it's only about 7 miles (11.3 km) west of the turnoff to Hualapai Hill and the trailhead.

More food and lodging options are available in **Kingman** and **Seligman** along Old Route 66.

Los
Angeles

Los Angeles and Orange County

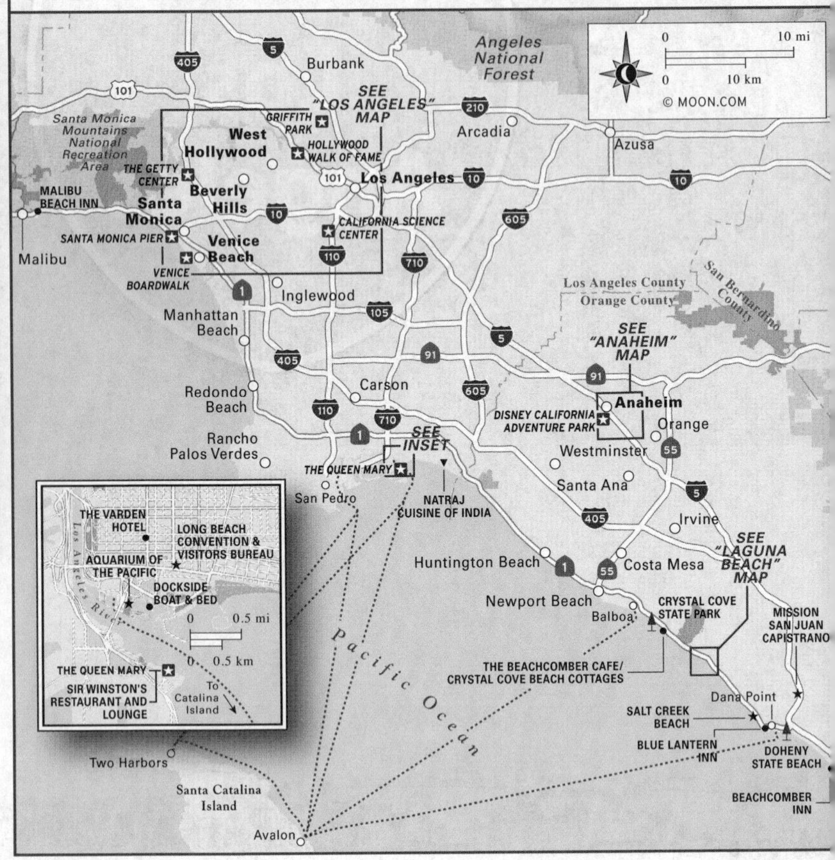

With palm trees lining sunny boulevards, surfers riding the deep-blue Pacific, and Hollywood glitz, Los Angeles is the California that lives in our imaginations.

It's true that the Pacific Ocean warms to a swimmable temperature here, there are palm trees, and stars are embedded in the sidewalks on Hollywood Boulevard. But celebrities don't crowd every sidewalk signing autographs, and movies aren't filming on every corner. Instead, L.A. combines the glamour, crowds, and speed of the big city with an easier, friendlier feel in its suburbs. Power shoppers pound the sparkling pavement lining the ultra-urban city streets. Visitors can catch a premiere at the Chinese Theatre, try their feet on a surfboard at Huntington Beach, and view prehistoric relics at the La Brea Tar Pits. For visitors who want a deeper look into the Los Angeles Basin,

Highlights

★ **California Science Center:** Come to see the retired Space Shuttle *Endeavour* and stay for displays on the world's ecosystems and humanity's amazing technological innovations (page 301).

★ **Griffith Park:** This large urban park in the Santa Monica Mountains is home to the iconic Hollywood sign and the Griffith Observatory (page 301).

★ **Hollywood Walk of Fame:** Walk all over your favorite stars—they're embedded in the ground beneath your feet (page 302).

★ **The Getty Center:** The art collections alone would make this sprawling museum complex worth a visit. The soaring architecture, beautiful grounds, and remarkable views of the skyline make it a must (page 310).

★ **Santa Monica Pier:** Ride the Scrambler, take in the view from the solar-powered Ferris wheel, or dine on a hot dog on a stick at this 100-year-old amusement park by the sea (page 310).

★ **Venice Boardwalk:** It's hard not to be amused when walking down this paved coastal path in L.A.'s most free-spirited beach community, crowded with street performers, bodybuilders, and self-identified freaks (page 311).

★ **Disney California Adventure Park:** Tour a Disneyfied version of the Golden State (page 338).

★ **The *Queen Mary:*** Take a tour, spend the evening, or stay the night on this huge art deco ocean liner docked in the Long Beach Harbor. Decide for yourself whether it's truly haunted (page 343).

Best Restaurants

★ **Philippe's:** This old-school L.A. spot is said to have invented the French dip sandwich (page 322).

★ **Quarters:** Head to this hip Korean barbecue joint and be sure to order the beef bulgogi (page 324).

★ **Cassell's Hamburgers:** This resurrected L.A. staple does a great hamburger and an even better potato salad (page 324).

★ **Taix French Restaurant:** This Echo Park institution serves elegant French cuisine in an Old World setting (page 325).

★ **Musso & Frank Grill:** Experience classic old Hollywood at this restaurant that dates to 1919 and features a fettucine alfredo based on the original recipe (page 325).

★ **The Griddle Café:** Industry insiders meet at this Hollywood restaurant for breakfast creations like red velvet pancakes (page 326).

★ **AOC:** Small plates of California cuisine pair perfectly with selections from an extensive wine list and creative cocktails at this Beverly Hills hot spot (page 327).

★ **Pann's:** Order the burger or the chicken and waffles at this diner that oozes old-school L.A. style (page 328).

★ **Neptune's Net:** The crispy shrimp tacos and pitchers of beer at this casual coast-side eatery hit the spot after a long day in the surf (page 328).

excellent museums dot the landscape, as do theaters, comedy clubs, and live music venues. L.A. boasts the best nightlife in California, with options that appeal to star-watchers, hard-core dancers, and cutting-edge music lovers alike.

In Orange County lies the single most recognizable tourist attraction in California: Disneyland. Even the most jaded local residents tend to soften at the bright colors, cheerful music, sweet smells, and sense of fun that permeate the House of Mouse.

Getting to Los Angeles

From San Francisco

The Coastal Route

The **Pacific Coast Highway (CA-1)** from Los Angeles to San Francisco is one of the nation's iconic drives. This coastal route has a lot to see and do, but it's not the fastest route between the two cities. It runs almost **500 miles (805 km)** and can easily take **eight hours** or longer, depending on traffic. It's worth the extra time to experience the gorgeous coastal scenery, which includes Monterey, Big Sur, and Santa Barbara. The highway is long, narrow, and winding; in winter, rockslides and mudslides may close the road entirely. Always check **Caltrans** (www.dot.ca.gov) for highway traffic conditions before starting your journey.

From San Francisco, take **CA-1 South** down the coast through the towns of Half Moon Bay, Santa Cruz, and Monterey. The section of **CA-1 South** that you don't want to miss is the 96-mile (155-km) winding drive along the coastline of **Big Sur,** which takes 2.5 hours or longer. (For

Best Hotels

★ **Freehand Los Angeles:** This hip complex is one part hostel, three parts boutique hotel (page 329)

★ **Ace Hotel:** This downtown hotel has a lot going for it, including a stunning on-site theater that hosts major entertainment events and a rooftop bar and pool that show off the L.A. skyline (page 329).

★ **Hotel Normandie:** This historic hotel in Koreatown gets extra points for having the city's best throwback burger joint and its most forward-looking bar in the same building (page 330).

★ **Magic Castle Hotel:** Next door to the acclaimed magic club, this hotel spoils its guests with great customer service, free snacks, and a pool open at all hours (page 331).

★ **Élan Hotel:** Here you'll find comfortable rooms at moderate prices, a rarity at the intersection of ritzy Beverly Hills and glitzy Hollywood (page 332).

★ **Hotel Erwin:** This eclectic hotel is feet from the raucous Venice Boardwalk. Take in the madness from the hotel's rooftop bar (page 332).

a quicker route, you can take **US-101 South** out of the city; you save roughly an hour, but miss the most scenic drives along the coast).

After Big Sur, in San Luis Obispo, **CA-1 South** merges with **US-101 South.** At Pismo Beach, **US-101 South** heads inland for 60 miles (97 km) before returning to the coast 35 miles (56 km) northwest of Santa Barbara. **US-101 South** follows the coast through Santa Barbara and Ventura for 72 miles (116 km) until Oxnard, where it heads inland to detour around the Santa Monica Mountains and dip into Los Angeles after 60 miles (97 km). **CA-1 South** splits off **US-101 South** in Oxnard for a more scenic drive of the coast, continuing 43 miles (69 km) through Malibu before hitting Santa Monica, where you can take a 13-mile (20.9-km) drive on **I-10 East** to downtown Los Angeles.

Stopping in San Luis Obispo

It's easier to enjoy the drive by dividing it up over two days and spending a night somewhere along the coast. Right off both CA-1 and US-101, the city of **San Luis Obispo** is close to halfway between the two cities, which makes it an ideal place to stop. It takes three hours to make the 200-mile (320-km) drive from Los Angeles if traffic isn't bad. The additional 230 miles (370 km) to San Francisco takes four hours or more. An affordable motel right off the highway is the **Peach Tree Inn** (2001 Monterey St., 800/227-6396, http://peachtreeinn.com, $89-299). For a wilder experience, stay at the popular tourist attraction **Madonna Inn** (10 Madonna Rd., 805/543-3000, www.madonnainn.com, $209-489), which offers the **Gold Rush Steak House** for dinner and the **Copper Café & Pastry Shop** for breakfast. **Novo** (726 Higuera St., 805/543-3986, www.novorestaurant.com, 11am-9pm Sun.-Thurs., 11am-1am Fri.-Sat., $18-37) has a truly international menu and outdoor dining on decks overlooking San Luis Obispo Creek. For something fast, the **Firestone Grill** (1001 Higuera St., 805/783-1001, www.firestonegrill.com, 11am-10pm Sun.-Wed., 11am-11pm Thurs.-Sat., $5-22) is known for its tasty tri-tip sandwich.

For complete information on San Luis Obispo, see page 381.

The Interior Route

A faster but much less interesting driving route is **I-5** from Los Angeles to San Francisco. It takes about **six hours** if the traffic is cooperating. On holiday weekends, the drive time can increase to 10 hours. Take **I-80 East** out of San Francisco, crossing the Bay Bridge into the East Bay suburbs. Then hop onto **I-580 East** for 63 miles (101 km). Not long after the outer suburb of Livermore, connect with **I-5 South,** which you will follow for the next 290 miles (465 km). I-5 crosses the **Tejon Pass** over the Tehachapi Mountains in the section of the highway nicknamed **the Grapevine,** which can close in winter due to snow and ice (and sometimes in summer due to wildfires). November-March, tule fog (thick, ground-level fog) can also seriously impede driving conditions and reduce visibility to a crawl. After crossing the Grapevine, you will enter the outer edge of the Los Angeles metro area. From I-5, take **CA-170 South** for 9.5 miles (15.3 km), then connect to **US-101 South** and continue into the city center. Always check **Caltrans** (www.dot.ca.gov) for highway traffic conditions before starting your journey.

From Yosemite

Getting from Yosemite National Park to Los Angeles involves driving about **300 miles (485 km)**, roughly **six hours**, along two of the state's biggest highways. It's best to head out of the park's **South entrance** and get on **CA-41 South** toward Fresno. After 62 miles (100 km), you'll reach Fresno, where you should get on **CA-99 South.** Stay on this major highway for 132 miles (213 km) until it becomes **I-5 South,** which you'll stay on for over 60 miles (97 km). From I-5, take **CA-170 South** for 9.5 miles (15.3 km), then connect to **US-101 South** and continue into the city center.

From Las Vegas

Multilane highways ensure that the **270-mile (435-km), five-hour** drive from Las Vegas to Los Angeles is smooth, if not especially visually appealing. From Las Vegas, take **I-15 South** for about 220 miles (355 km). In the San Bernardino area, turn off onto **I-210 West,** which you'll take for 27 miles (43 km) before continuing on **I-605 South.** Continue for 5.5 miles (8.9 km), then get on **I-10 West.** Take it for about 12 miles (19.3 km) to **US-101 North** and continue into the city center.

From the Grand Canyon

It's roughly **500 miles (805 km)** from the Grand Canyon's South Rim to Los Angeles, a grueling **eight-hour** drive through an empty, hard landscape without too much respite save the usual interstate fare. If you are at the popular South Rim of the Grand Canyon, head out of the park on **US-180 East** and then take **AZ-64 South** for about 50 miles (81 km) until it reaches the pleasant Southwest town of Williams. At Williams, catch **I-40 West,** which starts off as a scenic drive through a pine tree-dotted landscape before becoming more barren and crowded with trucks. The most exciting part of the drive is crossing the Colorado River at the California-Arizona border.

You'll have clocked about 320 miles (515 km) on I-40 West when it enters Barstow and becomes **I-15 South.** Beware the increasing traffic as you head toward Los Angeles on I-15 for about 66 miles (106 km). In the San Bernardino area, turn off onto **I-210 West,** which you'll take for 27 miles (43 km) before continuing on **I-605 South.** Continue for 5.5 miles (8.9 km), then get on **I-10 West.** Take it for about 12 miles (19.3 km) to **US-101 North** and continue into the city center.

Stopping in Needles

The Mojave Desert town of Needles is on the Colorado River, at the border of

Stretch Your Legs

Do you see a giant golf ball teed up in the desert off I-40? You're not hallucinating. It's called the **Golf Ball House** (Grand Canyon-Los Angeles Dr., east of the Alamo Rd. I-40 exit, Yucca, AZ). The orb, which has a 40-foot (12.2-m) diameter, was intended to be the Dinosphere, a nightclub and restaurant. But that development failed, and the orb now houses an alien-themed museum called **Area 66** (928/766-2877, 10am-5pm Thurs.-Sun., $5 ages 13 and over), which feels appropriate for the site. The museum includes a film about a purported 1953 UFO crash in nearby Kingman.

California, Arizona, and Nevada. It's three hours and 45 minutes from the Grand Canyon's South Rim and four hours and 15 minutes from Los Angeles. Translation: It's a good overnight spot for the long drive between the Grand Canyon and Los Angeles.

Relax after a long day of driving at the **Best Western Colorado River Inn** (2371 W. Broadway, 760/326-4552, www.bestwestern.com, $149-179). It has rooms equipped with a fridge and satellite TV. Even better, there's an outdoor pool, spa, and sauna. A complimentary hot breakfast at adjacent Juicy's River Café is included with your stay. The **Rio del Sol Inn** (1111 Pashard St., 760/326-5660, www.riodelsolinn.com, $95) has an outdoor swimming pool, hot tub, and steam room along with guest laundry.

Juicy's River Café (2411 W. Broadway, 760/326-2233, www.juicysrivercafe.com, 5:30am-10pm Sun.-Thurs., 5:30am-10:30pm Fri.-Sat. summer, 5:30am-9:30pm Sun.-Thurs., 5:30am-10:30pm Fri.-Sat. winter, $9-24) dishes out a diverse menu from very early until relatively late. This includes breakfast (eggs Benedict, omelets), lunch (wraps, salads, sandwiches), and dinner (steaks, ribs, pasta, seafood). They also have an acclaimed Bloody Mary made from a secret recipe. The awesomely and appropriately named **Munchy's** (829 Front St., 760/326-1000, 6:30am-6pm Mon.-Fri., 6:30am-3pm Sat., $5-10) satisfies Mexican food cravings with tacos and burritos.

By Air, Train, or Bus

L.A. is one of the most airport-dense metropolitan areas in the country. **Los Angeles International Airport** (LAX, 1 World Way, Los Angeles, 855/463-5252, www.flylax.com) has the most flights, which makes it the most crowded of the L.A. airports, with the longest security and check-in lines. If you can find a way around flying into LAX, do so. One option is to fly into other local airports, including **Hollywood Burbank Airport** (BUR, 2627 N. Hollywood Way, Burbank, 818/840-8840, http://hollywoodburbankairport.com) and **Long Beach Airport** (LGB, 4100 Donald Douglas Dr., Long Beach, 562/570-2600, www.longbeach.gov/lgb). It may be a slightly longer drive to your final destination, but it can be well worth it. If you use LAX, arrive a minimum of two hours ahead of your domestic flight time, three hours on busy holidays.

For train travel, **Amtrak** (800/872-7245, www.amtrak.com) has an active rail hub in Los Angeles. Most trains come in to **Union Station** (800 N. Alameda St., www.unionstationla.com, 4am-1am daily), which is owned by the Los Angeles Metropolitan Transportation Authority (MTA, 323/466-3876, www.metro.net). The ***Coast Starlight*** train connects the San Francisco Bay Area with Los Angeles. Union Station also acts as a hub for the **Metro** (www.metro.net, one ride $1.75, day pass $7), which includes both the subway system and a network of buses

Los Angeles

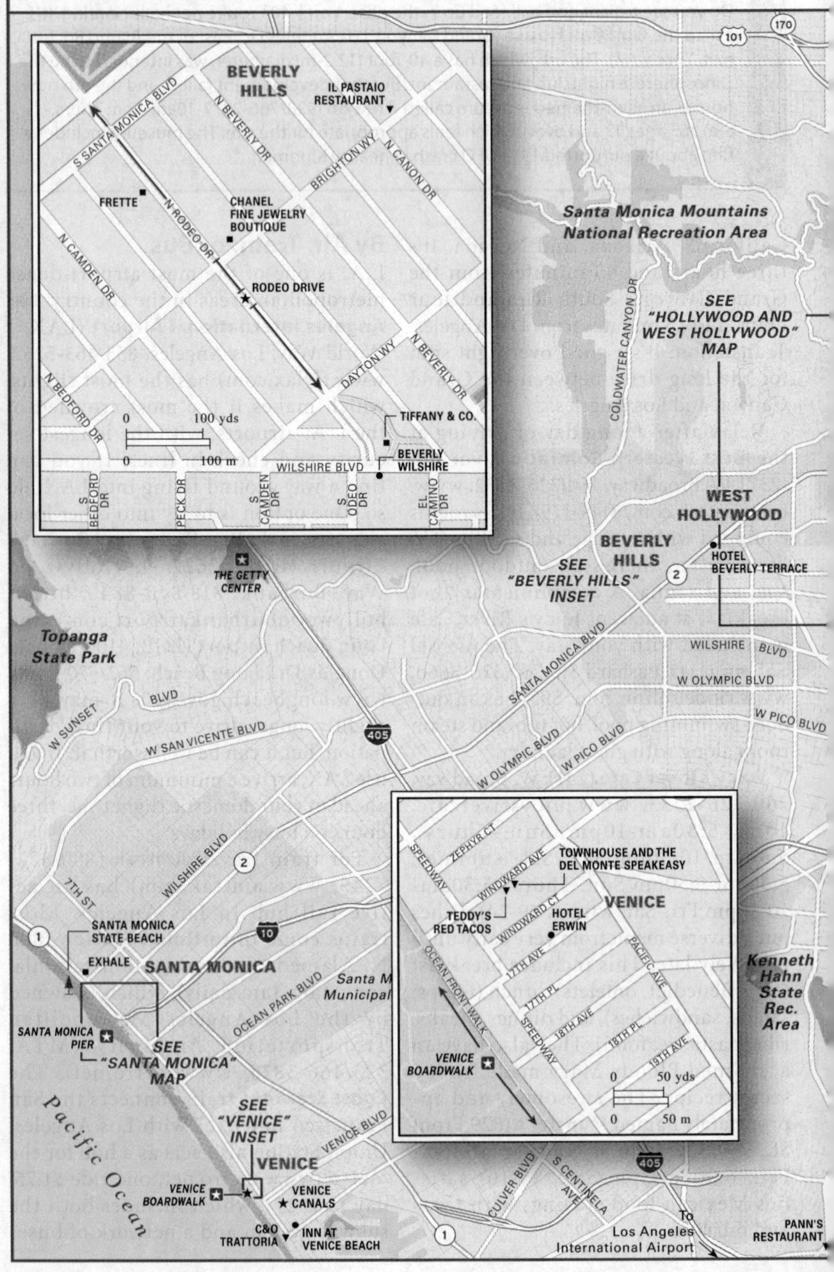

BEVERLY HILLS
IL PASTAIO RESTAURANT
S SANTA MONICA BLVD
N BEVERLY DR
BRIGHTON WY
N CANON DR
FRETTE
CHANEL FINE JEWELRY BOUTIQUE
N RODEO DR
N CAMDEN DR
RODEO DRIVE
DAYTON WY
N BEVERLY DR
N BEDFORD DR
0 100 yds
0 100 m
TIFFANY & CO.
BEVERLY WILSHIRE
WILSHIRE BLVD
S BEDFORD DR
PECK DR
S CAMDEN DR
S ODEO DR
EL CAMINO DR
101
170
Santa Monica Mountains National Recreation Area
COLDWATER CANYON DR
SEE "HOLLYWOOD AND WEST HOLLYWOOD" MAP
WEST HOLLYWOOD
BEVERLY HILLS
HOTEL BEVERLY TERRACE
SEE "BEVERLY HILLS" INSET
THE GETTY CENTER
Topanga State Park
SANTA MONICA BLVD
WILSHIRE BLVD
W OLYMPIC BLVD
W PICO BLVD
W SUNSET BLVD
W SAN VICENTE BLVD
405
W OLYMPIC BLVD
W PICO BLVD
WILSHIRE BLVD
7TH ST
SANTA MONICA STATE BEACH
EXHALE
SANTA MONICA
10
Santa M
Municipal
OCEAN PARK BLVD
SANTA MONICA PIER
SEE "SANTA MONICA" MAP
Pacific Ocean
SEE "VENICE" INSET
VENICE BLVD
VENICE
VENICE BOARDWALK
VENICE CANALS
C&O TRATTORIA
INN AT VENICE BEACH
SPEEDWAY
ZEPHYR CT
WINDWARD AVE
TOWNHOUSE AND THE DEL MONTE SPEAKEASY
VENICE
TEDDY'S RED TACOS
WINDWARD CT
HOTEL ERWIN
17TH AVE
PACIFIC AVE
OCEAN FRONT WALK
17TH PL
SPEEDWAY
18TH AVE
18TH PL
19TH AVE
VENICE BOARDWALK
0 50 yds
0 50 m
Kenneth Hahn State Rec. Area
CULVER BLVD
S CENTINELA AVE
405
To Los Angeles International Airport
PANN'S RESTAURANT

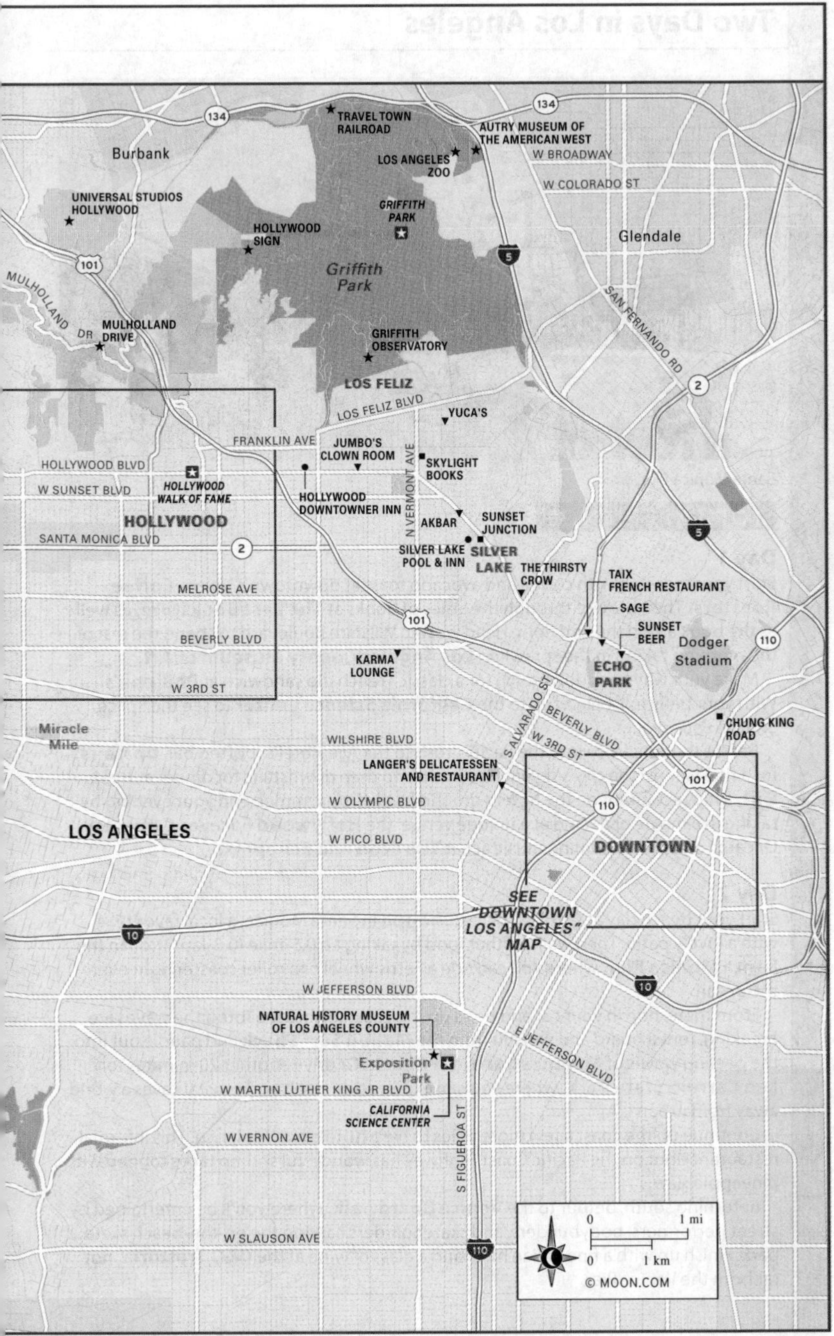
Burbank
TRAVEL TOWN RAILROAD
AUTRY MUSEUM OF THE AMERICAN WEST
LOS ANGELES ZOO
W BROADWAY
W COLORADO ST
UNIVERSAL STUDIOS HOLLYWOOD
GRIFFITH PARK
HOLLYWOOD SIGN
Griffith Park
Glendale
MULHOLLAND DR
MULHOLLAND DRIVE
GRIFFITH OBSERVATORY
SAN FERNANDO RD
LOS FELIZ
LOS FELIZ BLVD
YUCA'S
FRANKLIN AVE
JUMBO'S CLOWN ROOM
SKYLIGHT BOOKS
HOLLYWOOD BLVD
W SUNSET BLVD
HOLLYWOOD WALK OF FAME
HOLLYWOOD DOWNTOWNER INN
N VERMONT AVE
HOLLYWOOD
AKBAR
SUNSET JUNCTION
SANTA MONICA BLVD
SILVER LAKE POOL & INN
SILVER LAKE
THE THIRSTY CROW
TAIX FRENCH RESTAURANT
MELROSE AVE
SAGE
SUNSET BEER
Dodger Stadium
BEVERLY BLVD
KARMA LOUNGE
ECHO PARK
W 3RD ST
S ALVARADO ST
BEVERLY BLVD
CHUNG KING ROAD
Miracle Mile
WILSHIRE BLVD
W 3RD ST
LANGER'S DELICATESSEN AND RESTAURANT
W OLYMPIC BLVD
LOS ANGELES
W PICO BLVD
DOWNTOWN
SEE "DOWNTOWN LOS ANGELES" MAP
W JEFFERSON BLVD
NATURAL HISTORY MUSEUM OF LOS ANGELES COUNTY
E JEFFERSON BLVD
Exposition Park
W MARTIN LUTHER KING JR BLVD
CALIFORNIA SCIENCE CENTER
S FIGUEROA ST
W VERNON AVE
W SLAUSON AVE
0 1 mi
0 1 km
© MOON.COM

Two Days in Los Angeles

Santa Monica Pier

TOP EXPERIENCE

Day 1

Start your morning with coffee and avocado toast at downtown's **Verve Coffee Roasters.** Then browse through the aisles of books at **The Last Bookstore,** as well as the book art on the 2nd floor. Head west to Wilshire Boulevard to spend the rest of the morning taking in the sprawling **Los Angeles County Museum of Art.**

Make your way back downtown for a classic French dip sandwich at **Philippe's.** With your belly full, take a trip to the **California Science Center** to see the Space Shuttle *Endeavour.*

Before the sun drops into the Pacific, rush to the Ace Hotel's rooftop bar, **Upstairs,** for a fine view of the city's skyline at sunset, and then downstairs for dinner at **Best Girl,** a hip restaurant on the hotel's ground level. If it's summer, end your evening by taking in a movie or a band at a unique venue: the **Hollywood Forever Cemetery.** Or catch an up-and-coming music act at **The Echo and Echoplex.**

Day 2

Start your beach day at **Cora's Coffee Shoppe** in Santa Monica, a local favorite with a lovely patio. Then walk off that food by taking an 0.5-mile (0.8-km) stroll to the **Santa Monica Pier,** where you can ride a Ferris wheel or a roller coaster right over the ocean.

From there, hop in your car and head up the coast toward Malibu. If the waves are breaking, rent a board and wetsuit from the **Malibu Surf Shack** and paddle out into the peeling waves of **Malibu's Surfrider Beach.** Or drive another 20 minutes to **Leo Carrillo State Park,** where you can explore tide pools and coastal caves a world away from urban L.A.

Continue up the coast a few more miles to **Neptune's Net** for lunch. This informal restaurant right on the Pacific Coast Highway has wonderful shrimp tacos topped with pineapple slaw.

Returning south, detour to the **Venice Boardwalk,** where you'll be entertained by street performers, bodybuilders, and skateboarders carving the on-the-beach skate park. Finish up with a fine Italian meal and a glass of wine at the **C&O Trattoria,** not far from the Venice Pier.

throughout the L.A. metropolitan area. You can pay on board a bus if you have exact change. Otherwise, purchase a ticket or a day pass from the ticket vending machines at all Metro Rail Stations.

Some buses run 24 hours. The Metro Rail lines start running as early as 4:30am and don't stop until as late as 1:30am. See Metro's website (www.metro.net) for route maps, timetables, and fare details.

Sights

The only problem you'll have with the sights of Los Angeles and its surrounding towns is finding a way to see enough of them to satisfy you. You'll find museums, streets, ancient art, and modern production studios ready to welcome you throughout the sprawling cityscape.

Downtown and Vicinity

Downtown Los Angeles is experiencing serious renewal with streets of new restaurants, new bars, new hotels, and new attractions, including The Broad museum. The initials "DTLA" (which stands for downtown Los Angeles) can be found everywhere: from the sides of buildings to Internet hashtags.

El Pueblo de Los Angeles Historical Monument

For a city that is famously berated for lacking a sense of its own past, **El Pueblo de Los Angeles Historical Monument** (Olvera St. between Spring St. and Alameda St., 213/485-6855, tours 213/628-1274, http://elpueblo.lacity.org, visitors center 9am-4pm daily) is a veritable crash course in history. Just a short distance from where Spanish colonists first settled in 1781, the park's 44 acres (17.8 ha) contain 27 buildings dating 1818-1926.

Facing a central courtyard, the oldest church in the city, **Our Lady Queen of the Angels,** still hosts a steady stream of baptisms and other services. On the southern end of the courtyard stands a cluster of historic buildings, the most prominent being Pico House, a hotel built in 1869-1870. The restored **Old Plaza Firehouse** (10am-3pm Tues.-Sun.) dates to 1884 and exhibits firefighting memorabilia from the late 19th and early 20th centuries. On Main Street, **Sepulveda House** (10am-3pm Tues.-Sun.) serves as the Pueblo's visitors center and features period furniture dating to 1887.

Off the central square is **Olvera Street** (9am-6pm daily), an open-air market packed with mariachis, clothing shops, crafts stalls, and taquerias. Hidden in the midst of this tourist market is the **Avila Adobe** (9am-4pm daily), a squat adobe structure said to be the oldest standing house in Los Angeles. The home now functions as a museum detailing the lifestyle of the Mexican ranchero culture that thrived here before the Mexican-American War.

Free 50-minute docent-led **tours** (213/628-1274, www.lasangelitas.org, 10am, 11am, and noon Tues.-Sat.) start at the Las Angelitas del Pueblo office, next to the Old Plaza Firehouse on the southeast end of the plaza. Some of the best times to visit are during festive annual celebrations like the Blessing of the Animals, around Easter, and, of course, Cinco de Mayo.

Cathedral of Our Lady of the Angels

Standing on a hillside next to the Hollywood Freeway (U.S. 101), the colossal concrete **Cathedral of Our Lady of the Angels** (555 W. Temple St., 213/680-5200, www.olacathedral.org, 6:30am-6pm Mon.-Fri., 9am-6pm Sat., 7am-6pm Sun., free tours 1pm Mon.-Fri., $4-20 parking) is the third-largest cathedral in the world. Every aspect of Spanish architect Rafael Moneo's design is monumental: the 25-ton (22.7-m-ton) bronze doors, 27,000 square feet (2,508 sq m) of clerestory windows of translucent

Downtown Los Angeles

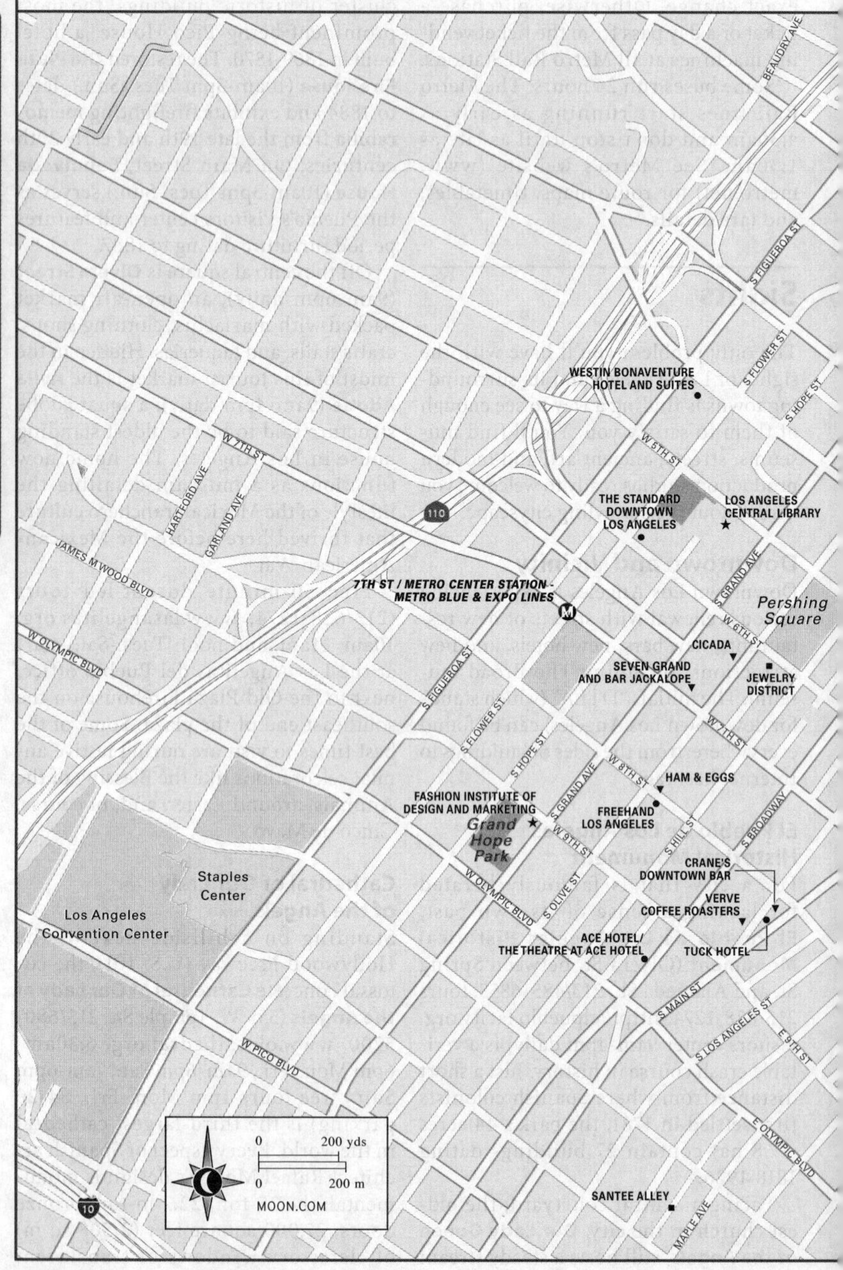

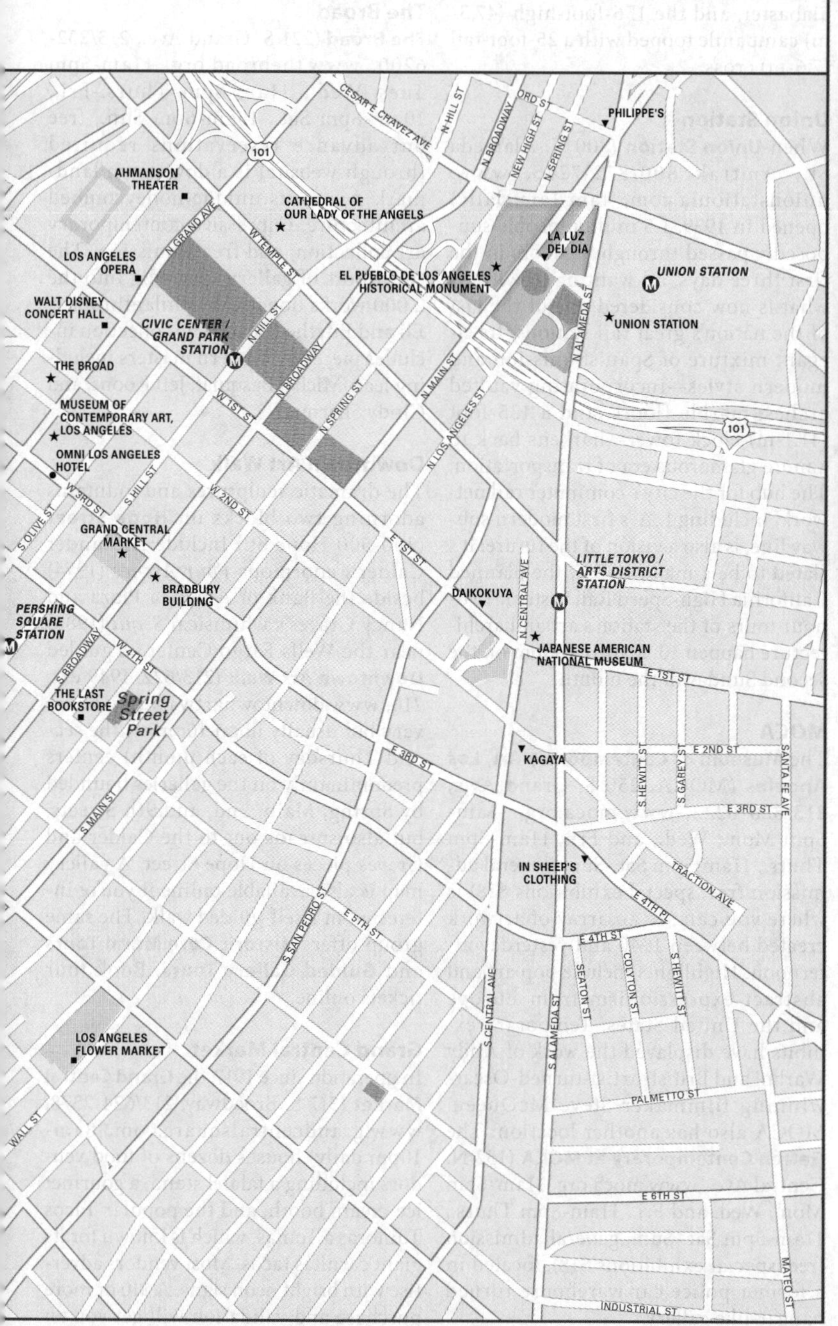

CESAR E CHAVEZ AVE
101
N HILL ST
N BROADWAY
ORD ST
NEW HIGH ST
N SPRING ST
PHILIPPE'S
AHMANSON THEATER
CATHEDRAL OF OUR LADY OF THE ANGELS
N GRAND AVE
W TEMPLE ST
LA LUZ DEL DIA
LOS ANGELES OPERA
EL PUEBLO DE LOS ANGELES HISTORICAL MONUMENT
UNION STATION
WALT DISNEY CONCERT HALL
CIVIC CENTER / GRAND PARK STATION
N HILL ST
N ALAMEDA ST
UNION STATION
N BROADWAY
N MAIN ST
THE BROAD
W 1ST ST
N SPRING ST
N LOS ANGELES ST
MUSEUM OF CONTEMPORARY ART, LOS ANGELES
101
OMNI LOS ANGELES HOTEL
S HILL ST
W 3RD ST
W 2ND ST
S OLIVE ST
GRAND CENTRAL MARKET
E 1ST ST
N CENTRAL AVE
LITTLE TOKYO / ARTS DISTRICT STATION
BRADBURY BUILDING
DAIKOKUYA
PERSHING SQUARE STATION
JAPANESE AMERICAN NATIONAL MUSEUM
S BROADWAY
W 4TH ST
E 1ST ST
THE LAST BOOKSTORE
Spring Street Park
KAGAYA
E 2ND ST
SANTA FE AVE
E 3RD ST
S HEWITT ST
S GAREY ST
S MAIN ST
E 3RD ST
IN SHEEP'S CLOTHING
TRACTION AVE
E 4TH PL
S SAN PEDRO ST
E 5TH ST
E 4TH ST
S CENTRAL AVE
S ALAMEDA ST
SEATON ST
COLYTON ST
S HEWITT ST
LOS ANGELES FLOWER MARKET
PALMETTO ST
WALL ST
E 6TH ST
MATEO ST
INDUSTRIAL ST

alabaster, and the 156-foot-high (47.5-m) campanile topped with a 25-foot-tall (7.6-m) cross.

Union Station

When **Union Station** (800 N. Alameda St., Amtrak 800/872-7245, www.unionstationla.com, 4am-1am daily) opened in 1939, 1.5 million people supposedly passed through its doors in the first three days, all wanting to witness what is now considered one of the last of the nation's great rail stations. Its elegant mixture of Spanish mission and modern styles—incorporating vaulted arches, marble floors, and a 135-foot (41.1-m) clock tower—harkens back to a more glamorous era of transportation. The hub for the city's commuter rail network, including L.A.'s first modern subway line, is also a vision of the future: It's slated to be a major hub of the planned California High-Speed Rail System. Two-hour tours of the station's art and architecture happen 10:30am-12:30pm on the second Sunday of the month.

MOCA

The **Museum of Contemporary Art, Los Angeles** (MOCA, 250 S. Grand Ave., 213/626-6222, www.moca.org, 11am-6pm Mon., Wed., and Fri., 11am-8pm Thurs., 11am-5pm Sat.-Sun., general admission free, special exhibitions $18) is where you can see an array of artwork created between 1940 and yesterday afternoon. Highlights include pop art and abstract expressionism from Europe and the United States. Temporary exhibits have displayed the work of Andy Warhol and British artist-turned-Oscar-winning filmmaker Steve McQueen. MOCA also has another location: The **Geffen Contemporary at MOCA** (152 N. Central Ave., www.moca.org, 11am-6pm Mon., Wed. and Fri., 11am-8pm Thurs., 11am-5pm Sat.-Sun., general admission free, special exhibitions $18), located in a former police car warehouse turned hangar-like gallery.

The Broad

The Broad (221 S. Grand Ave., 213/232-6200, www.thebroad.org, 11am-5pm Tues.-Wed., 11am-8pm Thurs.-Fri., 10am-8pm Sat., 10am-6pm Sun., free but advance reservations required through website) is a downtown landmark due to its unique honeycombed architecture, impressive contemporary art collection, and free admission. The two floors of gallery space dig into the 2,000 works donated by philanthropists Eli and Edythe Broad. The collection includes pieces by modern masters including Jean-Michel Basquiat, Jeff Koons, and Cindy Sherman.

Downtown Art Walk

The dramatic sculptures and fountains adorning two blocks on **Hope Street** (300-500 Hope St.) include Alexander Calder's enormous *Four Arches* (1974) beside the Bank of America Plaza and Nancy Graves's whimsical *Sequi* (1986) near the Wells Fargo Center. A guided **Downtown Art Walk** (213/622-4949 ext. 210, www.downtownartwalk.org, hours vary but usually noon-10pm on the second Thursday of each month) centers predominantly on the galleries bounded by Spring, Main, 2nd, and 9th Streets, but also spreads out to the Calder and Graves pieces on Hope Street. A gallery map is also available online if you're interested in a self-guided walk. The same group offers **Historic Core Mural Tours** and **Guided Gallery Tours.** Book tour tickets online.

Grand Central Market

In operation since 1917, the **Grand Central Market** (317 S. Broadway, 213/624-2378, www.grandcentralsquare.com, 8am-10pm daily) houses dozens of food vendors including a falafel stand, a gourmet ice cream booth, and the popular Tacos Tumbras a Tomas, which is known for its giant carnitas tacos. Most vendors advertise with bright neon signs. A $10 or more purchase and validation will get you an hour's free parking at the **garage** (308 S. Hill St.). The market also hosts events including live music and game nights. Right across the street is **Angel's Flight** (upper entrance 350 S. Grand Ave., lower entrance 351 S. Hill St., 213/626-1901, www.angelsflight.org, 6:45am-10pm daily, $1 one-way), the world's shortest railway, which was featured in the 2016 film *La La Land.*

Bradbury Building

One of several historic L.A. structures featured in the movies *Chinatown* (1974), *Blade Runner* (1982), and *The Artist* (2011), the 1893 **Bradbury Building** (304 S. Broadway, lobby 9am-5pm daily) is an office building that wows filmmakers with its light-filled Victorian court that includes wrought-iron staircases, marble stairs, and open-cage elevators. On Saturday mornings, the 2.5-hour, docent-led **Historic Downtown Walking Tour** (213/623-2489, www.laconservancy.org, 10am Sat. and 11am Weds., reservations required, $15 adults, $10 children 17 and under), run by the Los Angeles Conservancy, takes visitors through downtown to sights including the Bradbury Building.

Japanese American National Museum

The **Japanese American National Museum** (100 N. Central Ave., 213/625-0414, www.janm.org, 11am-5pm Tues.-Wed. and Fri.-Sun., noon-8pm Thurs., $16 adults, $7 students and seniors, children under 5 free) focuses on the experiences of Japanese people coming to and living in the United States, particularly California. This museum shows the Japanese American experience in vivid detail, with photos and artifacts telling much of the story.

From top to bottom: Union Station; vendor at Grand Central Market; California Science Center.

Watts Towers

Watts Towers

With almost 100-foot-tall (30.5-m) steel towers decorated with bottles, pottery, seashells, and tile, the **Watts Towers** (1727 E. 107th St., 213/847-4646, www.wattstowers.us, tours 11am-3pm Thurs.-Fri., 10:30am-3pm Sat., noon-3pm Sun., $7 adults, $3 children and seniors 13-17, children under 13 free) is outsider art on a grand scale. Italian immigrant Simon Rodia spent 33 years building the impressive landscape of spires, walls, birdbaths, and a gazebo without help. The whole structure is meant to resemble a ship stuffed with Rodia's memories. An informative half-hour guided tour is available. Because it's just feet from I-105 and minutes from I-405, a tour of Watts Towers makes a nice break from Los Angeles' crowded freeways.

Fashion Institute of Design and Marketing

The **Fashion Institute of Design and Marketing Museum and Galleries** (FIDM, 919 S. Grand Ave., Ste. 250, 213/623-5821, http://fidmmuseum.org, 10am-5pm Tues.-Sat., free) are open to the public, giving costume buffs and clotheshorses a window into high fashion and Hollywood costume design. FIDM pulls from its collection of more than 10,000 costumes and textiles to create exhibits based on style, era, movie genre, and whatever else the curators dream up. Parking is available in the underground garage for a fee. When you enter the building, tell the folks at the security desk that you're headed for the museum. A small but fun museum shop offers student work, unique accessories, and more.

Natural History Museum of Los Angeles County

If you'd like your kids to have some fun with an educational purpose, take them to the **Natural History Museum of Los Angeles County** (900 Exposition Blvd., 213/763-3466, www.nhm.org, 9:30am-5pm daily, $15 adults, $12 students and seniors, $7 children, $10 parking cash only). This huge museum features many amazing galleries; some are transformed into examples of mammal habitats, while others display artifacts of various peoples indigenous to the Western Hemisphere. The Discovery Center welcomes children with a wide array of live animals and insects, plus hands-on displays that let kids learn by touching as well as looking. Admission to the Butterfly Pavilion and special exhibits costs extra.

★ California Science Center

The **California Science Center** (700 Exposition Park Dr., 323/724-3623, www.californiasciencecenter.org, 10am-5pm daily, admission free, $10 parking) focuses on the notable achievements and gathered knowledge of humankind. There are many interactive exhibits here, including one that lets visitors "lift" a giant truck off the ground. The Ecosystems section showcases 11 different natural environments, such as a living kelp forest and a polar ice wall.

One major reason people come to the California Science Center is to view the last of NASA's space shuttles, the *Endeavour*. The 132-foot-long (40.2-m) shuttle hangs on display in a pavilion and eventually will be shown in its launch position. To see the shuttle exhibit, reserve a timed entry by calling (213/744-2019) or going online (www.californiasciencecenter.org).

Many people also come to the California Science Center for the **IMAX theater** (213/744-2019, $9 adults, $8 students and seniors, $7 children), which shows educational films on its tremendous seven-story screen. Your IMAX ticket also gets you onto the rideable attractions of the Science Court.

Los Feliz and Silver Lake

East of Hollywood and northwest of downtown, Los Feliz ("loss FEEL-is") is home to an eclectic mix of retired professionals, Armenian immigrants, and movie-industry hipsters lured by the bohemian vibe, midcentury modern architecture, and the neighborhood's proximity to Griffith Park.

★ Griffith Park

Griffith Park (Los Feliz Blvd., Zoo Dr., or Griffith Park Blvd., 323/644-2050, www.laparks.org, 5am-10:30pm daily, free) is the country's largest municipal park with an urban wilderness area. Griffith Park has also played host to many production companies over the years, with its land and buildings providing backdrops for many major films. Scenes from *Rebel Without a Cause* were filmed here, as were parts of the first two *Back to the Future* movies.

If you love the night skies, visit the **Griffith Observatory** (2800 E. Observatory Rd., 213/473-0800, www.griffithobservatory.org, noon-10pm Tues.-Fri., 10am-10pm Sat.-Sun., free), where free telescopes are available and experienced demonstrators help visitors gaze at the stars. Or take in a film about the earth or sky in the aluminum-domed **Samuel Oschin Planetarium** (www.griffithobservatory.org for showtimes, $7 adults, $5 students and seniors, $3 children).

If you prefer a more structured park experience, try the **L.A. Zoo and Botanical Gardens** (5333 Zoo Dr., 323/644-4200, www.lazoo.org, 10am-5pm daily, $22 adults, $19 seniors, $17 children, parking free), where you can view elephants, rhinos, and gorillas. If the weather is poor, step inside **The Autry National Center of the American West** (4700 Western Heritage Way, 323/667-2000, www.theautry.org, 10am-4pm Tues.-Fri., 10am-5pm Sat.-Sun., $14 adults, $10 students and seniors, $6 children), which showcases artifacts of the American West.

Kids love riding the trains of the operating miniature railroad at both the **Travel Town Railroad** (5200 Zoo Dr., 323/662-9678, www.griffithparktrainrides.com, 10am-3:30pm Mon.-Fri., 10am-5pm Sat.-Sun. summer, 10am-3:30pm Mon.-Fri., 10am-4:30pm Sat.-Sun. winter, $2.75), which runs the perimeter of the **Travel Town Museum** (5200 Zoo Dr., 323/662-5874, www.traveltown.org, 10am-5pm Mon.-Fri., 10am-6pm Sat.-Sun. summer, 10am-4pm Mon.-Fri., 10am-6pm Sat.-Sun. winter, free), and the **Griffith Park & Southern Railroad** (4730 Crystal Springs Rd., www.griffithparktrainrides.com, 10am-4:45pm Mon.-Fri., 10am-5pm Sat.-Sun. summer, 10am-4:15pm Mon.-Fri.,

10am-4:30pm Sat.-Sun. winter, $3.50 adults, $3 children, $2.75 seniors, which takes riders on a 1-mile (1.6-km) track.

The **Hollywood Sign** sits on Mount Lee, which is part of the park and indelibly part of the mystique of Hollywood. A strenuous 5-mile (8-km) hike will lead you to an overlook just above and behind the sign. To get there, drive to the top of Beachwood Drive, park, and follow the **Hollyridge Trail.**

Hollywood

You won't find blocks of movie studios in Hollywood, and few stars walk its streets except on premiere evenings. But still, if you've ever had a soft spot for Hollywood glitz, come and check out the crowds and bustle of downtown Tinseltown (and be aware that no local would *ever* call it that). Hollywood is also famous for its street corners. While the most stuff sits at Hollywood and Highland, the best-known corner is certainly Hollywood and Vine.

★ Hollywood Walk of Fame

One of the most recognizable facets of Hollywood is its star-studded **Walk of Fame** (Hollywood Blvd. from La Brea Ave. to Vine St., www.walkoffame.com). This area, portrayed in countless movies, contains more than 2,500 five-pointed stars honoring both real people and fictional characters that have contributed significantly to the entertainment industry and the Hollywood legend. Each pink star is set in a charcoal-colored square and has its honoree's name in bronze. Eight stars were laid in August 1958 to demonstrate what the walk would look like. Legal battles delayed the actual construction until February 1960, and the walk was dedicated in November 1960. At each of the four corners of Hollywood and Vine is a moon that honors the three Apollo 11 astronauts: Neil Armstrong, Michael Collins, and Edwin E. "Buzz" Aldrin Jr. At the edges of the Walk of Fame, you'll find blank stars waiting to

Griffith Observatory

be filled by up-and-comers making their mark on Tinseltown.

The complete walk is about 3.5 miles (5.6 km). You'll be looking down at the stars, so watch out for other pedestrians crowding the sidewalks in this visitor-dense area. Careful reading of the information on the Walk of Fame website (www.walkoffame.com) should help you find every star you need to see.

Hollywood Wax Museum

It immortalizes your favorite stars, all right. If you want to see the Hollywood heavyweights all dressed up in costume and completely unable to run away, visit the **Hollywood Wax Museum** (6767 Hollywood Blvd., 323/462-5991, www.hollywoodwaxmuseum.com, 9am-midnight Sun.-Thurs., 9am-1am Fri.-Sat., $26 adults, $16 children 4-11, children under 3 free). The exhibits are re-creations of the sets of all sorts of films, and as you pass through, you'll be right in the action (if staring at eerie, life-size wax likenesses of real people can be called action). You can even get a glimpse of stars on the red carpet at an awards show-style set. Save a dollar by purchasing a ticket online.

TCL Chinese Theatre

You can't miss the **TCL Chinese Theatre** (6925 Hollywood Blvd., 323/461-3331, www.tclchinesetheatres.com) on Hollywood Boulevard. With its elaborate 90-foot-tall (27.4-m) Chinese temple gateway and unending crowd of visitors, the Chinese Theatre may be the most visited and recognizable movie theater in the world. Along with the throngs of tourists out front, there are usually elaborately costumed movie characters, from Captain Jack Sparrow to Spider-Man, shaking hands with fans and posing for pictures (for a fee). Inside the courtyard, you'll find handprints and footprints of legendary Hollywood stars. Stop and admire the bells, dogs, and other artifacts in the courtyard; most are the genuine article, imported from China by special permit in the 1920s.

The studios hold premieres here all the time. Check the website for showtimes and ticket information. The Chinese Theatre has only one screen, but seats over 1,000 people per showing. Daily 20-minute **tours** (323/463-9576 or tours@chinesetheatres.com for tickets, $18 adults, $14 seniors, $6 children) featuring anecdotes about the fabled theater are available with a reservation. While you're welcome to crowd the sidewalk to try to catch a glimpse of the stars at a premiere, most of these are private events.

Egyptian Theater

Built under the auspices of the legendary Sid Grauman, the **Egyptian Theater** (6712 Hollywood Blvd., 323/466-3456, www.americancinemathequecalendar.com, $12 adults, $10 students and seniors) was the first of the grandiose movie houses in Hollywood proper and a follower of those in downtown Los Angeles. King

Hollywood and West Hollywood

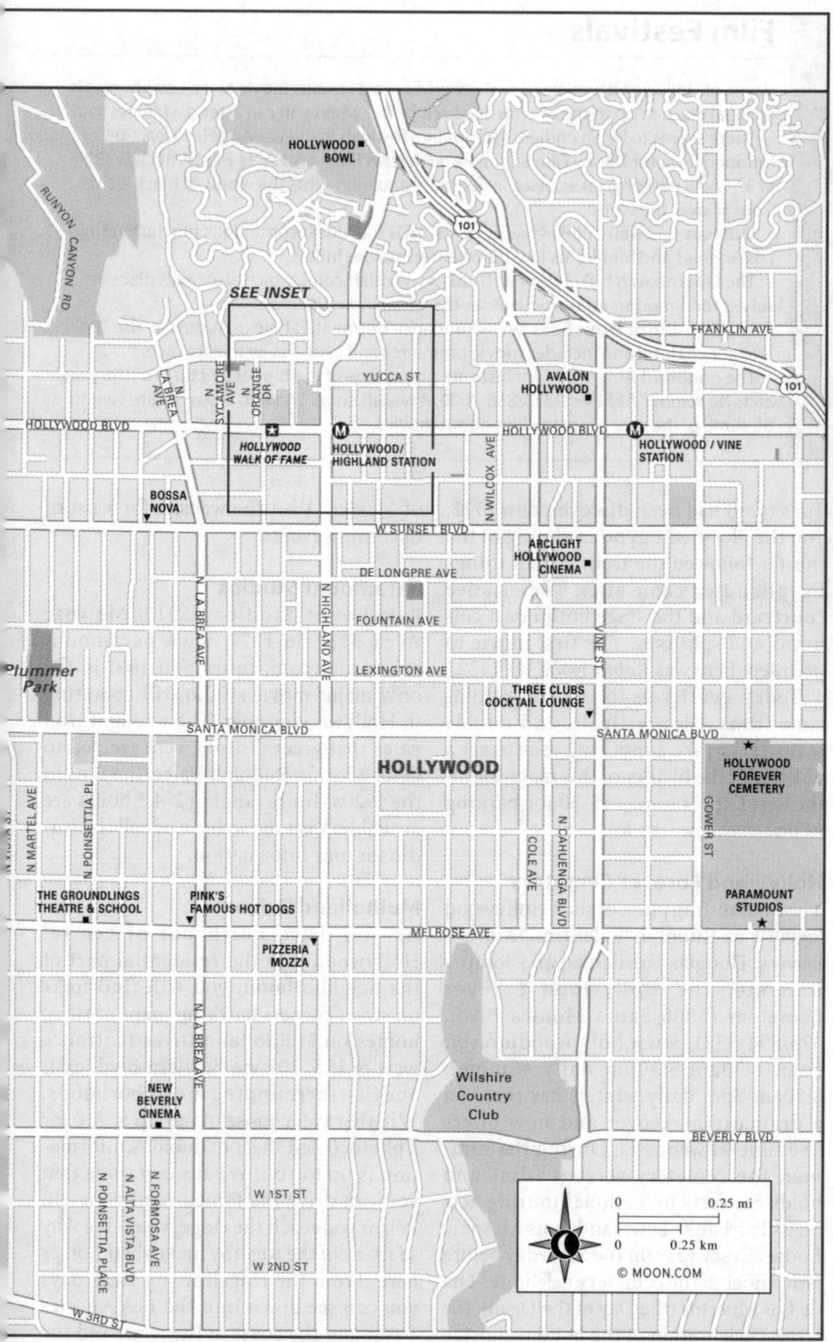
HOLLYWOOD BOWL
RUNYON CANYON RD
101
SEE INSET
FRANKLIN AVE
YUCCA ST
AVALON HOLLYWOOD
N LA BREA AVE
N SYCAMORE AVE
N ORANGE DR
HOLLYWOOD BLVD
HOLLYWOOD WALK OF FAME
HOLLYWOOD/ HIGHLAND STATION
N WILCOX AVE
HOLLYWOOD / VINE STATION
BOSSA NOVA
W SUNSET BLVD
ARCLIGHT HOLLYWOOD CINEMA
DE LONGPRE AVE
N HIGHLAND AVE
FOUNTAIN AVE
VINE ST
Plummer Park
LEXINGTON AVE
THREE CLUBS COCKTAIL LOUNGE
SANTA MONICA BLVD
HOLLYWOOD
HOLLYWOOD FOREVER CEMETERY
GOWER ST
N MARTEL AVE
N POINSETTIA PL
N CAHUENGA BLVD
COLE AVE
THE GROUNDLINGS THEATRE & SCHOOL
PINK'S FAMOUS HOT DOGS
PARAMOUNT STUDIOS
MELROSE AVE
PIZZERIA MOZZA
Wilshire Country Club
NEW BEVERLY CINEMA
BEVERLY BLVD
N POINSETTIA PLACE
N ALTA VISTA BLVD
N FORMOSA AVE
W 1ST ST
W 2ND ST
W 3RD ST
0
0.25 mi
0
0.25 km
© MOON.COM

Film Festivals

Home of Hollywood and many of the world's most famous movie stars, Los Angeles is an ideal place to go to the movies. It's even better when you can attend a film festival.

There seems to be an endless array of film festivals in the Los Angeles area. Co-founded by actor Danny Glover, the **Pan African Film and Arts Festival** (310/337-4737, www.paff.org) takes place in February and highlights the works of Black artists from all over the world.

Outfest (213/480-7088, www.outfest.org) is the oldest continuous film festival in Los Angeles and highlights LBGTQ-oriented movies in July.

The **Downtown L.A. Film Festival** (www.dtlaff.com), which also takes place in July, is for filmgoers who enjoy under-the-radar indie cinema.

The **Sundance Next Fest** (www.sundance.org/next) is held in August at The Theatre at Ace Hotel and includes movie premieres and concerts by musical acts.

The nonprofit American Film Institute plays some of the biggest pictures of the year at its November **AFI Fest** (323/856-7600, www.afi.com). Come to see what are sure to be some of the year's most talked-about movies.

Tut's tomb had been discovered in 1922, and the glorified Egyptian styling of the theater followed the trend for all things Egyptian that came after. The massive courtyard and the stage both boast columns and sphinxes. The first movie to premiere here was *Robin Hood,* in 1922.

Today, get tickets to an array of old-time films, film festivals, and double features, or take a morning tour to get a glimpse of the history of this magnificent theater. Expect to pay $5-20 for parking in one of the nearby lots.

Hollywood Forever Cemetery

The final resting place of such Hollywood legends as Rudolph Valentino, Marion Davies, Douglas Fairbanks, and Johnny Ramone, the **Hollywood Forever Cemetery** (6000 Santa Monica Blvd., 323/894-9571, www.hollywoodforever.com, 8:30am-5:30pm daily summer, 8:30am-5pm daily winter) has received a dramatic makeover and now offers live funeral webcasts. During the summer, the cemetery screens films and holds concerts by national touring acts on its Fairbanks Lawn and in its Masonic Lodge. Every year on the Saturday before November 2, the cemetery celebrates Día de Los Muertos (the Day of the Dead), the largest celebration of the holiday outside of Mexico. Visit the website for a list of upcoming events.

Paramount Studios

Paramount Studios (5515 Melrose Ave., 323/956-1777, www.paramountstudiotour.com, tours $60-189) is the only major movie studio still operating in Hollywood proper. The wrought-iron gates that greet visitors were erected to deter adoring Rudolph Valentino fans in the 1920s. Tours ranging 2-4.5 hours are available. Visit the website or call the studio for tour information.

Mulholland Drive

As you drive north out of central Hollywood into the residential part of the neighborhood, you will find folks on street corners hawking maps of stars' homes on **Mulholland Drive** (entrance west of U.S. 101 via Barham Blvd. exit) and its surrounding neighborhoods. Whether you choose to pay up to $10 for a photocopied sheet of dubious information is up to you. What's certain is that you can drive the famed road yourself. When you reach the ridge, you'll see why so many of the wealthy make their homes here. From the ridgeline, on clear days you can see down into the Los Angeles Basin and the coast to the west, and the fertile land of the San Fernando Valley to the east. Whether you care about movie-star homes or not, the view itself is worth the trip, especially if it has rained recently and the smog is down.

Universal Studios Hollywood

The longtime Hollywood-centric alternative to Disneyland is the **Universal Studios Hollywood** (100 Universal City Plaza, Los Angeles, 800/864-8377, www.universalstudioshollywood.com, hours vary, $99-259) theme park. (Save up to $10 by getting tickets online.) Kids adore this park, which puts them right into the action of their favorite movies. Flee the carnivorous dinosaurs of *Jurassic Park*, take a rafting adventure on the pseudo-set of *Waterworld*, quiver in terror of an ancient curse in *Revenge of the Mummy*, or explore the magic of Hogwarts Castle in the *Wizarding World of Harry Potter*. You can also experience the shape-shifting Transformers in a ride based on the movies and the Hasbro toy.

If you're more interested in how the movies are made than the rides made from them, take the Studio Tour with a recorded Jimmy Fallon as host. You'll get an extreme close-up of the sets of major blockbuster films like *War of the Worlds*. Better yet, get tickets at the Audiences Unlimited Ticket Booth and be part of the studio audience of TV shows currently taping. Serious movie buffs can get a VIP pass (from $345).

La Brea, Fairfax, and Miracle Mile

Lined with fabric emporiums, antiques dealers, and contemporary furniture design shops, Beverly Boulevard and La Brea Avenue north of Wilshire Boulevard are increasingly trendy haunts for interior decorators. Along bustling and pedestrian-friendly Fairfax Avenue,

From top to bottom: Universal Studios Hollywood; Hollywood Walk of Fame; TCL Chinese Theatre.

kosher bakeries and signs in Hebrew announce the presence of the neighborhood's sizable Jewish population. Around the corner on 3rd Street, The Original Farmers Market is one of L.A.'s historic gathering places. And farther south, Wilshire Boulevard is home to some of the city's many museums, including the Los Angeles County Museum of Art.

La Brea Tar Pits

Nothing can stop the smell of the **La Brea Tar Pits,** where untold thousands of animals became trapped in the sticky tar and met their ancient fate. Paved paths lead around the most accessible pits, while others (mostly those that are in active excavation) are accessible by guided tour only. If what interests you most are the fossilized contents, head for the beautiful **La Brea Tar Pits Museum** (5801 Wilshire Blvd., 213/763-3499, www.tarpits.org, 9:30am-5pm daily, $15 adults, $12 students and seniors, $7 children, $10 parking). The museum's reasonably small size and easy-to-understand interpretive signs make it great for kids. Genuine mammoths died and were fossilized in the tar pits, as were the tiniest of mice and about a zillion dire wolves. For a closer look at how the fossils were buried, get tickets to one of the **Excavator Tours** (noon, 1pm, 2pm, and 3pm daily, free with museum ticket), which are available online.

Los Angeles County Museum of Art

Travelers who desperately need a break from the endless, shiny, and mindless entertainments of L.A. can find respite and solace in the **Los Angeles County Museum of Art** (5905 Wilshire Blvd., 323/857-6000, www.lacma.org, 11am-5pm Mon.-Tues. and Thurs., 11am-8pm Fri., 10am-7pm Sat.-Sun., $15 adults, $10 students and seniors with ID, children under 17 free), the largest art museum in the western United States. Better known to its friends as LACMA, this museum complex prides itself on a diverse array of collections and exhibitions of art from

Día de los Muertos celebration at the Hollywood Forever Cemetery

around the world, from ancient to modern. With multiple buildings filled with galleries, don't expect to get through the whole thing in an hour, or even a full day. You'll see all forms of art, from classic painting and sculpture to all sorts of decorative arts (that is, ceramics, jewelry, metalwork, and more). All major cultural groups are represented, so you can check out Islamic, Southeast Asian, European, and Californian art, plus more.

The 120,000 objects at LACMA include pieces by Andy Warhol, David Hockney, and Roy Lichtenstein. Head outdoors for Chris Burden's *Urban Light,* a forest of street lamps, and Michael Heizer's *Levitated Mass,* a giant boulder displayed above a sunken walkway. Moving the rock to its current home was such a feat that it is documented in the 2013 film *Levitated Mass.*

LACMA is undergoing major renovations through 2024 as it builds the David Geffen Galleries, which will replace four of LACMA's buildings and house the museum's permanent collection. LACMA will still be open during construction and offering a full slate of exhibits and public programs.

Farmers Market

Begun in 1934 as a tailgate co-op for a handful of fruit farmers, **The Original Farmers Market** (6333 W. 3rd St., 323/933-9211 or 866/993-9211, www.farmersmarketla.com, 9am-9pm Mon.-Fri., 9am-8pm Sat., 10am-7pm Sun.) remains a favorite locale for shopping and people-watching. Along with the adjacent shopping center, The Grove, there are now more than 30 restaurants and 50 shops hawking everything from hot sauce to stickers. Annual events include free summer concerts every Friday.

Beverly Hills and West Hollywood

Although the truly wealthy live above Hollywood on Mulholland Drive, in Bel Air, or on the beach in Malibu, there's still plenty of money floating around Beverly Hills. Some of the world's best and most expensive shops line its streets. You'll also find plenty of high-end culture in this area, which bleeds into West L.A.

Sunset Strip

The **Sunset Strip** really is part of Sunset Boulevard—specifically the part that runs 1.5 miles (2.4 km) through West Hollywood from the edge of Hollywood to the Beverly Hills city limits. The Strip exemplifies all that's grandiose and tacky about the L.A. entertainment industry. You'll also find many of the Strip's legendary rock clubs, such as **The Roxy** and the **Whisky a Go Go** and the infamous after-hours hangout the **Rainbow Bar & Grill.** Over several decades, up-and-coming rock acts first made their names on the Strip and lived at the "Riot Hyatt."

Westwood

Designed around the campus of UCLA and the Westwood Village commercial district, this community situated between Santa Monica and Beverly Hills won national recognition in the 1930s as a model of innovative suburban planning.

University of California, Los Angeles

From its original quad of 10 buildings, the campus of the **University of California, Los Angeles** (UCLA, bounded by Hilgard Ave., Sunset Blvd., Le Conte Ave., and Gayley Ave., tours available at http://connect.admission.ucla.edu/portal/tours, www.ucla.edu) has become the largest in the University of California system, with more than 400 buildings set on and around 419 beautifully kept acres (170 ha). Today its facilities include one of the top medical centers in the country, a library of more than eight million volumes, and renowned performance venues, including **Royce Hall** and **Schoenberg Hall.**

★ The Getty Center

Located on a hilltop above the mansions of Brentwood and the 405 freeway, **The Getty Center** (1200 Sepulveda Blvd., 310/440-7300, www.getty.edu, 10am-5:30pm Sun. and Tues.-Thurs., 10am-9pm Fri.-Sat. summer, 10am-5:30pm Sun. and Tues.-Fri., 10am-9pm Sat. winter, admission free, $20 parking) is famous for art and culture in Los Angeles. Donated by the family of J. Paul Getty to the people of Los Angeles, this museum features European art, sculpture, manuscripts, and European and American photos. The magnificent works are set in fabulous modern buildings with soaring architecture, and you're guaranteed to find something beautiful to catch your eye and feed your imagination. The spacious galleries have comfy sofas to let you sit back and take in the paintings and drawings. There are frequent temporary exhibitions on diverse subjects. Take a stroll outdoors to admire the sculpture collections on the lawns as well as the exterior architecture.

On a clear day, the views from The Getty, which sweep from downtown L.A. clear west to the Pacific, are remarkable. But the museum pavilions themselves are also stunning. Richard Meier's striking design is multi-textured, with exterior grids of metal and unfinished Italian travertine marble. The blockish buildings have fountains, glass windows several stories high, and an open plan that permits intimate vistas of the city below. A stroll through the gardens is a must.

Pierce Brothers Westwood Village Memorial Park

The **Pierce Brothers Westwood Village Memorial Park** (1218 Glendon Ave., 310/474-1579, www.dignitymemorial.com, 8am-6pm daily) is the final resting place of some of the world's most popular entertainers and musicians. Under the shadows of the towering high-rises of Wilshire Boulevard, this small cemetery is the home of **Marilyn Monroe's crypt** (frequently decorated with lipstick marks), as well as Rat Packer **Dean Martin,** author **Truman Capote,** eclectic musician **Frank Zappa,** and the stars of *The Odd Couple,* **Walter Matthau** and **Jack Lemmon.**

Santa Monica, Venice, and Malibu

Some of the most famous and most expensive real estate in the world sits on this stretch of sand and earth. Of the communities that call the northern coast of L.A. County home, the focal points are Malibu to the north, Santa Monica, and Venice to the south.

★ Santa Monica Pier

For the ultimate in SoCal beach kitsch, you can't miss the **Santa Monica Pier** (Ocean Ave. at Colorado Ave., 310/458-8901, www.santamonicapier.org, hours vary). As you walk the rather long stretch of concrete out over the water, you'll see

Santa Monica Pier

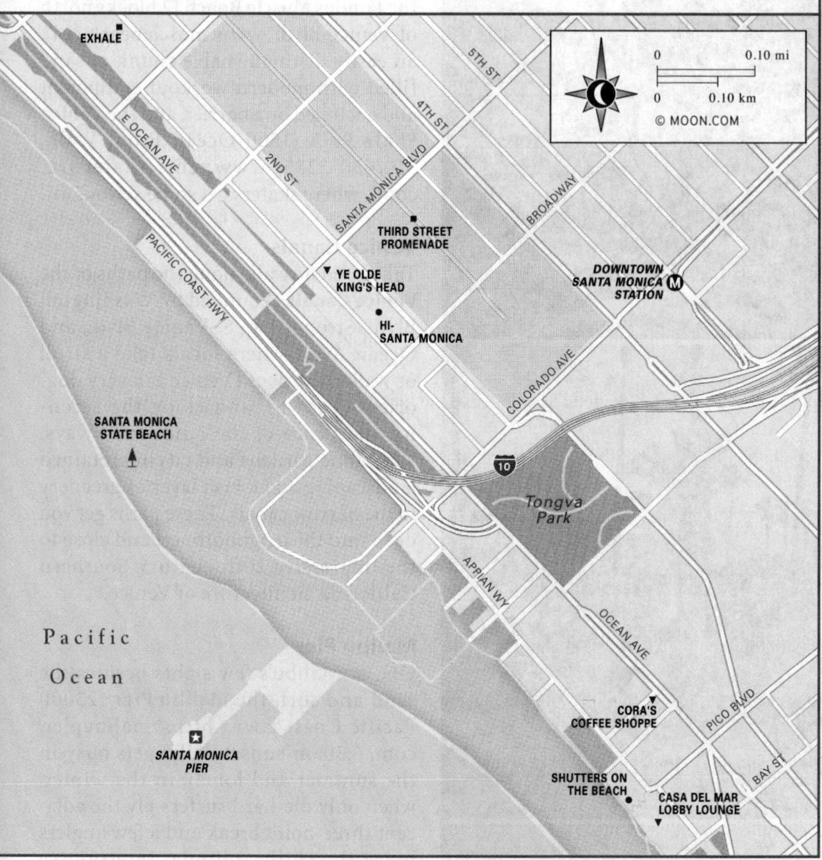

an amazing array of carnival-style food stands, an arcade, a small amusement park, a trapeze school, and restaurants leading out to the fishing area at the tip of the pier. There's even an aquarium under the pier. The main attraction is **Pacific Park** (310/260-8744, www.pacpark.com, hours vary, \$5-10 per ride, \$16-30 all-ride pass, \$6-15 parking). This park features a roller coaster, a Scrambler, and the world's first solar-powered Ferris wheel. Several rides are geared for the younger set, and a 20-game midway offers fun for all ages.

★ Venice Boardwalk

If the Santa Monica Pier doesn't provide you with enough chaos and kitsch, head on down to the **Venice Boardwalk** (Ocean Front Walk at Venice Blvd., www.laparks.org/venice) for a nearly unlimited supply of both year-round. As you shamble down the tourist-laden path, you'll pass an astonishing array of tacky souvenir stores, tattoo and piercing parlors, walk-up food stands, and more. On the beach side of the path, dozens of artists create sculptures and hawk their wares. This area has more than its share of L.A.'s

colorful characters, including some who perform for tips. The beach side includes the famous **Muscle Beach** (2 blocks north of Venice Blvd., www.musclebeach.net), an easily distinguishable chunk of sand filled with modern workout equipment and encircled by a barrier, and the **Venice Skate Park** (1500 Ocean Front Walk, 310/650-3255, www.veniceskatepark.com), where skaters get some serious air.

Venice Canals

Take a sedate walk along the paths of the **Venice Canals** (bounded by Washington Blvd., Strongs Dr., S. Venice Blvd., and Ocean Ave.), where locals take a stroll or walk their dogs (Venice is a very dog-oriented town), and enjoy the serenity and peace of the quiet waterways. The home gardens and city-maintained landscaping add a lush layer of greenery to the narrow canals. These paths get you deep into the neighborhood and close to the impressive 20th-century Southern California architecture of Venice.

Malibu Pier

One of Malibu's few sights besides the sand and surf, the **Malibu Pier** (23000 Pacific Coast Hwy., http://malibupier.com, 6:30am-sunset daily) gets busy in the summer and lonely in the winter, when only die-hard surfers ply the adjacent three-point break and a few anglers brave the chilly solitude. Interpretive signs describe the history of Malibu amid the food stands and sport-fishing and whale-watching charters. Check out the rotating display on surf and beach culture inside the **Malibu Farm Pier Café** (310/456-1112, www.malibu-farm.com/malibu-pier, 9am-3pm Mon.-Fri., 9am-4pm Sat.-Sun.) at the end of the pier. If you'd prefer to hit the waves yourself, you can rent boards and other beach toys.

From top to bottom: The Getty Center; Venice Boardwalk; a colorful tile fountain at The Getty Villa.

The Getty Villa

Even driving up to **The Getty Villa** (17985 Pacific Coast Hwy., Pacific Palisades, 310/440-7300, www.getty.edu, 10am-5pm Sun.-Mon. and Wed.-Fri., 10am-9pm Sat. summer, 10am-5pm Wed.-Mon. winter, reservations required, admission free, $15 parking) on its Roman-inspired stone driveway will send you back to ancient times. The two-floor villa is modeled after a Roman country house that was buried by the AD 79 eruption of Mount Vesuvius. The architecture and surrounding gardens are a fitting environment for the 1,200 works of art inside, including intact statues and jewelry. Tickets are free, but require advance reservations.

Entertainment

Nightlife

Bars

Whatever your taste in bars, whether it tends toward hipster dives, old-school watering holes, or beautiful lounges, L.A. can offer its version.

Downtown

For a money dive bar experience, head to **Crane's Downtown Bar** (810 S. Spring St., 323/787-7966, noon-2am daily) located inside a former bank vault. There's the occasional DJ spinning and comedy on the second Monday of the month. Next door inside the basement of the NCT Building is the Peking Tavern, if you get hungry for creative dumplings.

Upstairs (929 Broadway, 213/623-3233, www.acehotel.com/losangeles, noon-midnight Sun.-Thurs., noon-2am Fri.-Sat., by reservation only through www.opentable.com) is an only-in-L.A. spot on the roof of the Ace Hotel. Dress in upscale beachwear to lounge by the pool, or just come by for the fine views and cocktails. What makes Upstairs stand out is its impressive slate of events, including DJ sets and concerts.

At **Seven Grand** (515 W. 7th St., 213/614-0736, http://sevengrandbars.com/la, 3pm-2am daily), dapper bartenders steer you to the right fermented grain mash—commonly referred to as whiskey. Enjoy it while playing pool, watching live music, or sitting under deer heads mounted on the walls. Deep inside Seven Grand, the exclusive 18-seat **Bar Jackalope** (7pm-1am Sun.-Tues., 6pm-1am Wed.-Thurs., 8pm-1am Fri.-Sat.) zeroes in on Japanese whiskies.

Under a sign touting breakfast foods, the unassuming **Ham & Eggs Tavern** (433 W. 8th St., http://hamandeggstavern.com, 5pm-midnight Mon.-Thurs., 5pm-2am Fri.-Sat.) serves can beers and wine in one room and hosts music acts next door. The tiny stage has hosted larger-than-expected acts including Nick Waterhouse and The Gooch Palms.

In Sheep's Clothing (170 E. 4th Pl., 213/415-1937, www.insheepsclothinghifi.com, noon-10pm Sun.-Mon., noon-1am Tues.-Sat.) calls itself a "Hi-Fi Record Bar & Café"—and this is indeed a good place to listen to an album while enjoying a drink. The cocktail bar, which is hidden inside of Lupetti Pizzeria, is just as concerned with high-quality sound as its selection of Japanese whiskies. Its creative director is a music supervisor for film and television.

Koreatown

R Bar (3331 W. 8th St., 213/387-7227, 7pm-2am Mon.-Tues., 5pm-2am Wed.-Fri., 11am-2am Sat.-Sun.) doesn't look like much from the outside except a dingy corner building with a gold "R" affixed to it. But inside this speakeasy (the password can be found on the bar's Facebook page or on their Twitter page) oozes debauched gothic Victorian decor and a range of events including live music, DJs, storytellers, and karaoke on Wednesday, Thursday, and Sunday nights. There's good beer on tap, cocktails, and a weekly brunch touted by *L.A. Weekly* as well.

Silver Lake and Echo Park

In hip Silver Lake, **The Thirsty Crow** (2939 W. Sunset Blvd., 323/661-6007, www.thirstycrowbar.com, 5pm-2am Mon.-Sat., 2pm-2am Sun.) is a neighborhood bar with 100 different kinds of whiskey, including over 60 small-batch bourbons and a friendly happy hour (5pm-8pm Mon.-Fri., 2pm-8pm Sat.-Sun.).

Echo Park's beer lovers flock to the **Sunset Beer Company** (1498 W. Sunset Blvd., 213/481-2337, www.sunsetbeercompany.com, store hours noon-11pm Mon.-Thurs., noon-midnight Fri.-Sat., noon-10pm Sun.; bar hours 4pm-11pm Mon.-Thurs., 1pm-midnight Fri.-Sat., 1pm-10pm Sun.), an intimate space well-stocked with the latest craft brews from California and beyond. Sip your suds inside over board games or books or outside on a smoker's patio.

Beverly Hills and West Hollywood

Hit the **Rainbow Bar & Grill** (9015 W. Sunset Blvd., 310/278-4232, www.rainbowbarandgrill.com, 11am-2am daily, cover varies) to see an amazing myriad of rock-and-roll memorabilia and get a taste of music history. A group of musicians known as the "Hollywood Vampires," which included Alice Cooper, Keith Moon, John Lennon, Ringo Starr, Harry Nilsson, and Micky Dolenz, congregated here in the 1970s. Today, rockers still drop in after playing shows in the neighborhood. The crowds trickle in as the sun goes down; by the time the shows let out at the nearby Roxy and Whisky a Go Go, your chances of finding a booth diminish significantly. The back rooms also open up late, for dancing, drinking, and smoking (*sh!*). To the surprise of some diners, the hallowed haven also serves a tasty cheeseburger, available until 2am.

They say that Courtney Love used to dance at **Jumbo's Clown Room** (5153 Hollywood Blvd., 323/666-1187, http://jumbos.com, 4pm-2am daily, no cover). They also say David Lynch was inspired to write a section of his film, *Blue Velvet,* after a visit here. The one-of-a-kind dive bar with a blood-red interior and a circus theme features burlesque dancers doing their thing to an eclectic playlist.

Located in the Sunset Tower Hotel, **The Tower Bar** (8358 Sunset Blvd., 323/654-7100, www.sunsettowerhotel.com, 6pm-11pm Sun.-Thurs., 6pm-11:30pm Fri.-Sat.) offers a glimpse of old Hollywood. Mobster Bugsy Siegel once had an apartment here. Today, it has walnut-paneled walls, a fireplace, and dim lighting so that celebrities can keep their cool.

The Den on Sunset (8226 W. Sunset Blvd., 323/656-0336, www.thedenonsunset.com, 5pm-2am Mon.-Fri., 3pm-2am Sat., 10am-2am Sun.) has an outside fire pit, while inside there is a collection of board games including Rock 'Em, Sock 'Em Robots. Some nights have DJs and karaoke.

Nearby, in North Hollywood, **Idle Hour** (4824 Vineland Ave., 281/682-2280, www.idlehourbar.com, 5pm-close) serves up a shot of history with its cocktails. The wooden bar was built in 1941 to resemble a whisky barrel, part of a trend to lure passing motorists with eye-catching architecture that was particularly popular in California with the rise of car culture. Along these lines, Idle Hour also features a giant pipe-smoking bulldog, a replica of Bulldog Café, a kitschy eatery that opened in 1928 and closed in the mid-1960s and another example of this style. Americana is the theme, and cocktails served here today include drinks like an old-fashioned and a cosmopolitan.

Santa Monica, Venice, and Malibu

Ye Olde King's Head (116 Santa Monica Blvd., Santa Monica, 310/451-1402, www.yeoldekingshead.com, 10am-2am daily) is a British pub, restaurant, and gift shop that stretches down a long half block in Santa Monica. Crowds of imbibing patrons visit from far and near.

Upstairs at **Townhouse and the Del Monte Speakeasy** (52 Windward Ave., Venice Beach, 310/392-4040, www.townhousevenice.com, 5pm-2am Mon.-Fri., noon-2am Sat.-Sun.), you can enjoy the candlelit tables and pool table of the oldest bar in Venice. Downstairs, the speakeasy is a cellar space that hosts jazz bands, DJs, and comedians.

On the rooftop of Hotel Erwin, **High** (1697 Pacific Ave., Venice Beach, 424/214-1062, 4pm-10pm Wed.-Thurs., 3pm-10pm Fri., noon-close Sat.-Sun.) is the place to take in the hustle and bustle of Venice Beach with a fine cocktail in hand. Featuring 360-degree views including the Hollywood sign and Pacific Ocean, High is also an inspiring place to be during the golden glow of sunset. Reservations are available (http://resy.com).

Clubs

Which of the many dance and nightclubs in the L.A. area is the hottest, hippest, or most popular with the stars this week? Ask the locals or check the alternative weekly papers when you arrive. Clubs get crowded on weekend nights, and bouncers take joy in allowing only the chicest hipsters into the sacred spaces beyond the doors. Being young and beautiful helps, of course, as does being dressed in the latest designer fashions.

The **Three Clubs Cocktail Lounge** (1123 Vine St., Hollywood, 323/462-6441, www.threeclubs.com, 5pm-2am daily, no cover) acts both as a locals' watering hole and a reasonably priced nightclub catering mostly to the collegiate set. Expect to find the dance floor of the rear club crowded and sweaty, with modern dance mixes blaring out over the crush of writhing bodies. Two bars serve up drinks to the masses, and drinks are cheaper here than in the hotter spots. Three Clubs has no decent parking, so you may have to walk several blocks along Hollywood Boulevard long after dark. Bring friends along f or safety.

Gay and Lesbian

Sleek, glamorous, and candlelit, **The Abbey Food & Bar** (692 N. Robertson Blvd., West Hollywood, 310/289-8410, www.theabbeyweho.com, 11am-2am Mon.-Thurs., 10am-2am Fri., 9am-2am Sat.-Sun.) is a popular bar with a great outdoor patio and pillow-strewn private cabanas, all of which are usually jam-packed. Savvy bartenders mix 22 different specialty martinis in flavors that include chocolate banana and Creamsicle.

Every Thursday night, **Avalon Hollywood** (1735 Vine St., Hollywood, 323/462-8900, http://avalonhollywood.com, 10pm-3am Thurs., 9:30pm-4am Fri., 10pm-6am Sat.) hosts **TigerHeat,** which is said to be the West Coast's largest gay event. Lady GaGa, Britney Spears, and Elton John have made appearances in the club.

An alternative to glammed-up West Hollywood bars, Silver Lake's **Akbar** (4356 Sunset Blvd., 323/665-6810, www.akbarsilverlake.com, 4pm-2am daily) pulls in a gay-friendly crowd with its cozy Moroccan-themed decor, neighborhood vibe, and friendly, unpretentious bartenders.

Live Music

The clubs on the Sunset Strip incubated some of the biggest rock acts of all time. The **Whisky a Go Go** (8901 Sunset Blvd., West Hollywood, 310/652-4202, www.whiskyagogo.com, cover varies) helped launch The Doors, Mötley Crüe, and Guns N' Roses. Truth be told, these days you'll mostly catch greying hair metal bands, old punk acts, and cover groups here.

Almost next door, **The Roxy Theatre** (9009 Sunset Blvd., West Hollywood, 310/278-9457, www.theroxy.com, cover varies) opened in 1973 with a Neil Young performance. Bob Marley, Patti Smith, and Bruce Springsteen have all recorded live albums here since then. Today, it's still relevant, with acts like

Princess Nokia and Brendan Benson. The big black-box theater has an open dance floor, comfy-ish booths (if you can get one), and bare-bones food service. Street parking is nearly nonexistent, and nearby lots will cost $5-15 or more, so think about public transit or a cab. For one of the best after-hours parties on the Strip, try to get into **On the Rox,** located directly above The Roxy. Or stagger next door to the **Rainbow Bar & Grill** (9015 Sunset Blvd., West Hollywood, 310/278-4232, www.rainbowbarandgrill.com, 11am-2am daily).

It's not on the Strip, but **The Troubadour** (9081 Santa Monica Blvd., West Hollywood, 310/276-1158, www.troubadour.com, prices vary) is just as big and bad as its brethren. Over its more than 50 years, Bob Dylan jammed here, Tom Waits was discovered, and Billy Joel opened for somebody else. Countless A-listers have recorded songs in and even about The Troubadour. Buy tickets online; tickets are available at the on-site box office only on the day of the show—unless it's sold out.

With less history under its belt, **The Echo and Echoplex** (1822 W. Sunset Blvd., Echo Park, 213/413-8200, www.spacelandpresents.com, prices vary) hosts a lot of up-and-coming indie acts, along with the occasional big act (TV on the Radio) and some impressive coups, including a performance by the Rolling Stones in 2013.

The Theatre at Ace Hotel (929 Broadway, 213/325-9614, www.acehotel.com/losangeles/theatre, prices vary) has already hosted big acts like Coldplay. The restored 1,600-seat movie theater from the 1920s features more than just rock shows, including lectures, film festivals, and dance productions.

Proclaimed the city's best music venue by the *L.A. Weekly,* **The Fonda Theatre** (6126 Hollywood Blvd., 323/464-6269, www.fondatheatre.com, prices vary) can accommodate 1,200 people, which is pretty intimate if you're there for a concert by the Rolling Stones, Radiohead, or Lorde.

Comedy

L.A.'s live comedy scene is second only to Manhattan's. More than a dozen major live comedy clubs make their home in the smog belt. Pick your favorite, sit back, and laugh (or groan) the night away.

Located on the Strip, **The Comedy Store** (8433 Sunset Blvd., West Hollywood, 323/650-6268, www.thecomedystore.com, age 21 and older, $15-20) is where you'll find a show every night of the week; most start at 9pm or later (check the online calendar). In each of three rooms, you'll find a showcase with more than a dozen stand-ups all performing one after another, leaving space for possible celebrity drop-ins. Steve Martin, Whoopi Goldberg, and Yakov Smirnoff got their start here. Buy tickets online for bigger shows, or at the door for shows that don't sell out. Open mics are at 10pm on Sunday.

Will Ferrell, Kristen Wiig, Lisa Kudrow, and Will Forte are alumni of **The Groundlings Theatre and School** (7307 Melrose Ave., 323/934-4747, www.groundlings.com, prices vary). Get tickets to take in some sketch comedy by up-and-coming talents.

The Arts

Cinema

Crowds throng the streets to see stars tromp down the red carpets for premieres at the **Chinese Theatre** (6925 Hollywood Blvd., 323/461-3331, www.tclchinese theatres.com) and the **Egyptian Theater** (6712 Hollywood Blvd., 323/466-3456, www.americancinemathequecalendar.com, $12 adults, $10 students and seniors).

The current favorite movie house for star sightings is the **ArcLight Hollywood Cinema** (6360 W. Sunset Blvd., Hollywood, 323/615-2550, www.arclightcinemas.com), where 21-and-older-only screenings allow patrons to purchase beer and wine. Expect the best visual and sound technologies, all-reserved seating, and the updated geodesic Cinerama Dome theater. Make reservations in advance and ask for parking validation for a discount at the adjacent parking structure.

Acclaimed filmmaker and movie enthusiast Quentin Tarantino owns and programs the **New Beverly Cinema** (7165 Beverly Blvd., 323/938-4038, www.thenewbev.com). The slate of 35-millimeter films include spaghetti westerns, horror films, classics, and selections from the filmmaker's personal collection.

Theater

Even with all the hoopla over film in L.A., there's still plenty of room for live theatrical entertainment in and around Tinseltown.

In addition to the Academy Awards, the **Dolby Theatre** (6801 Hollywood Blvd., 323/308-6300, www.dolbytheatre.com, box office 10am-5pm Mon.-Sat., 10am-4pm Sun., prices vary) hosts various live performances, from ballet to shows from music legends like Bob Dylan. Of course, all shows utilize the theater's state-of-the-art Dolby sound system. Half-hour **tours** (on the half hour 10:30am-4pm daily, $25 adults, $19 children and seniors) that include a view of an Oscar statuette are available daily.

The **Ford Theater** (2580 Cahuenga Blvd. E., 323/850-2000, www.fordamphitheater.org, box office noon-5pm Tues.-Sun. and 2 hours before evening performances, prices vary) takes advantage of Hollywood's temperate climate to bring the shows outdoors in summer. Every sort of theatrical event imaginable can find a stage at the Ford, from jazz, folk, world music, hip-hop, and dance to spoken word.

The **Ahmanson Theater** (135 N. Grand Ave., 213/628-2772, www.centertheatregroup.org, box office noon-6pm Tues.-Sun. and 2 hours before performances, prices vary) specializes in big Broadway-style productions. You might see a grandiose musical, a heart-wrenching drama, or a gut-busting comedy. Expect to find the titles of classic shows alongside new hits on the schedule. With hundreds of seats (all of them expensive), there's usually enough room to provide entertainment, even for last-minute visitors.

The intimate **Kirk Douglas Theatre** (9820 Washington Blvd., Culver City, 213/628-2772, www.centertheatregroup.org, prices vary) hosts world premieres and edgy productions like David Mamet's *Race*.

Well-known television actors, including Jason Alexander and Neil Patrick Harris, frequently act in the productions at the **Geffen Playhouse** (10886 Le Conte Ave., 310/208-5454, www.geffenplayhouse.org, prices vary). Some shows developed here move on to Broadway.

Classical Music

Although L.A. is better known for its rock than its classical music offerings, you can still find plenty of high-culture concerts as well. The **Los Angeles Opera** (135 N. Grand Ave., 213/972-8001, www.laopera.org, box office 10am-6pm Tues.-Sat., prices vary) is one of the largest opera companies in the United States and has gained national recognition. The dazzling performances are held in the Dorothy Chandler Pavilion at the Music Center of Los Angeles County.

Better known to its friends as the L.A. Phil, the **Los Angeles Philharmonic** (111 S. Grand Ave., 323/850-2000 or 323/850-2000, www.laphil.com, prices vary) performs primarily at the **Walt Disney Concert Hall** (111 S. Grand Ave.). Concerts can range from classics by famed composers like Tchaikovsky, Bach, and Beethoven to the world music of Asha Bhosle or jazz by Bobby McFerrin. Guest performers are often the modern virtuosos of classical music.

With its art deco band shell set against canyon chaparral, the **Hollywood Bowl** (2301 N. Highland Ave., 323/850-2000, www.hollywoodbowl.com, box office noon-6pm Tues.-Sun.) has long been a romantic setting for outdoor summer concerts by the L.A. Philharmonic and other artists. It also hosts some rock and pop acts.

The **Los Angeles Doctors Symphony Orchestra** (310/259-9604, http://ladso.org, prices vary) has been performing regularly since its inception in 1953. Many, though not all, of the musicians are members of the medical profession. They play everything from Mozart to Schubert.

Shopping

Downtown and Vicinity

Lovers of the written word should not miss **The Last Bookstore** (453 S. Spring St., 213/488-0599, http://lastbookstorela.com, 10am-10pm Mon.-Thurs., 10am-11pm Fri.-Sat., 10am-9pm Sun.). The 22,000 square feet (2,044 sq m) of new and used books include several art pieces and a tunnel made of books, as well as a space devoted to L.A. writers. A full slate of events includes concerts and author readings.

Anyone can come and stroll the narrow aisles of the world-famous **L.A. Flower District** (700 block of Wall St., 213/622-1966, www.laflowerdistrict.com, 8am-noon Mon. and Wed., 6am-noon Tues. and Thurs., 8am-2pm Fri., 6am-2pm Sat., admission $1-2), where just about every kind of cut flower, potted plant, and exotic species can be purchased. One caution: While the flower market itself is safe for visitors, the area to the south is not. Don't wander the neighborhood on foot.

A mix of modern art galleries and fun, touristy gift shops line the 900 block of **Chung King Road** (http://chungkingroad.wordpress.com/galleries), a one-block stretch of Chinatown. Interior decorators often browse the eclectic selection. It can be quiet during the day, but it comes alive during art-opening evenings.

Located in the Fashion District, **Santee Alley** (between Santee St. and Maple Ave. from Olympic Blvd. to 12th St., http://fashiondistrict.org/santee-alley, 9:30am-6pm daily) is a bustling outdoor marketplace crammed in an alley. This is the place for deals on everything from dresses to bathing suits to suitcases to cellphone cases.

Los Feliz and Silver Lake

Artsy, hip boutiques, cafés, and restaurants line **Sunset Junction** (Sunset Blvd. from Santa Monica Blvd. to Maltman Ave.), a colorful stretch of Sunset Boulevard concentrated around where Sunset meets Santa Monica Boulevard (or, rather, where Santa Monica Boulevard ends). Weekend mornings bring floods of neighborhood locals down from the hills. This strip is also home to the **Silver Lake Certified Farmers Market** (323/661-7771, 2pm-7:30pm Tues., 9am-1pm Sat.).

The fiercely independent **Skylight Books** (1818 N. Vermont Ave., 323/660-1175, www.skylightbooks.com, 10am-10pm daily) in Los Feliz features alternative literature, literary fiction, Los Angeles-themed books, and an extensive film section. It hosts frequent author events and sells signed books.

Hollywood

The **Hollywood & Highland Center** (6801 Hollywood Blvd., 323/467-6412 or 323/817-0200, www.hollywoodandhighland.com, 10am-10pm Mon.-Sat., 10am-7pm Sun.) flaunts outlandish architecture that's modeled after the set of the 1916 film *Intolerance*. Stroll amid the more than 70 retail stores and 25 eateries that surround the open-air Babylon Court. Save yourself stress and park in the center's lot ($3 for up to 2 hours with validation).

La Brea, Fairfax, and Miracle Mile

The stretch of charming and eclectic shops on **West 3rd Street** (between Fairfax Ave. and La Cienega Blvd.) encompasses one-of-a-kind clothing boutiques, home stores, and bath-and-body shops. At one end, you'll find The Original Farmers Market and The Grove shopping center; at the other, the Beverly Center.

Beverly Hills and West Hollywood

Big spenders browse the three-block stretch of luxury stores on **Rodeo Drive** (www.rodeodrive-bh.com) in Beverly Hills. Among the upscale retailers are **Chanel** (400 N. Rodeo Dr., 310/278-5500, www.chanel.com, 10am-6pm Mon.-Sat., noon-5pm Sun.), **Tiffany's** (210 N. Rodeo Dr., 310/273-8880, www.tiffany.com, 10am-7pm Mon.-Sat., 11am-6pm Sun.), and **Frette** (445 N. Rodeo Dr., 310/273-8540, www.frette.com, 10am-6pm Mon.-Sat., noon-5pm Sun.). The Rodeo Drive Walk of Style salutes fashion and entertainment icons with sidewalk plaques.

Melrose Avenue (between San Vicente Blvd. and La Brea Ave.) is really two shopping districts. High-end fashion and design showrooms dominate the western end, near La Cienega Boulevard; head east past Fairfax Avenue for tattoo parlors and used clothing.

For vintage castoffs, check out **Decades** (8214 Melrose Ave., 323/655-1960, www.decadesinc.com, 11am-6pm Mon.-Sat., noon-5pm Sun.), while **Ron Robinson at Fred Segal** (8118 Melrose Ave., 323/651-1935, www.ronrobinson.com, 10am-7pm Mon.-Sat., noon-6pm Sun.) is a deluxe department store that has everything from the ridiculously trendy to the severely tasteful.

On the strip of Sunset Boulevard famous for nightlife, indie bookstore **Book Soup** (8818 Sunset Blvd., 310/659-3110, www.booksoup.com, 9am-10pm Mon.-Sat., 9am-7pm Sun.) crams every nook and cranny of its space, which includes a strong film section.

Recreation

You'll find an endless array of ways to get outside and have fun in the L.A. area. Among the most popular recreation options are those that get you out onto the beach or into the Pacific Ocean.

TOP EXPERIENCE

Beaches

Southern California has a seemingly endless stretch of public beaches with lots of visitor amenities, such as snack bars, boardwalks, showers, beach toy rental shacks, surf schools, and permanent sports courts. Note, however, that you won't always find clean water to swim in since pollution is a major issue on the L.A. coast, and water temperatures cool off significantly when you dive into the surf.

Leo Carrillo State Park

Just 28 miles (45 km) north of Santa Monica on the Pacific Coast Highway, **Leo Carrillo State Park** (35000 W. Pacific Coast Hwy., Malibu, 805/488-1827, www.parks.ca.gov, 8am-10pm daily, $12 per vehicle) feels like a Central Coast beach even though it's right outside the Los Angeles city limits. Explore the park's natural coastal features, including tide pools and caves. A point break offshore draws surfers when the right swell hits. Dogs are also allowed on a beach at the northern end of the park.

Zuma Beach

Zuma Beach (30000 Pacific Coast Hwy., Malibu, 19 miles (31 km) north of Santa Monica, surf report 310/457-9701, http://beaches.lacounty.gov, sunrise-sunset daily, parking $3-12.50) is a popular surf and boogie-boarding break, complete with a nice big stretch of clean white sand that fills up fast on summer weekends. Grab a spot on the west side of the Pacific Coast Highway (CA-1) for free parking, or pay for one of the more than 2,000 spots in the beach parking lot. Zuma has all the amenities you need for a full day out at the beach, from restrooms and showers to a kid-friendly snack bar and a beachside boardwalk.

Malibu Beach

Amid the sea of mansions fronting the beach, **Malibu Lagoon State Beach** (23200 Pacific Coast Hwy., 805/488-1827, www.parks.ca.gov, 8am-sunset daily, $12 per vehicle) and its ancillary **Malibu Surfrider Beach** offer public access to this great northern L.A. location. Running alongside the **Malibu Pier** (23000 Pacific Coast Hwy., www.malibupier.com), this pretty stretch of sugar-like sand offers a wealth of activities as well as pure California relaxation. It's likely to get crowded quickly in the summer, so get here early for a parking spot.

Santa Monica State Beach

Santa Monica State Beach (Pacific Coast Hwy., 310/458-8300, www.smgov.net, parking from $7) lines the water-side edge of town. For 3.5 miles (5.6 km), the fine sand gets raked daily beneath the sun that shines over the beach more than 300 days each year. Enjoy the warm sunshine, take a dip in the endless waves, stroll along the boardwalk, or look for dolphins frolicking in the surf. The best people-watching runs south of the pier area and on toward Venice Beach. For more elbow room, head north of the pier to the less populated end of the beach.

Manhattan Beach

Manhattan Beach (400-4500 The Strand, Manhattan Beach, http://beaches.lacounty.gov) is centered on a fishing pier that is an extension of Manhattan Beach Boulevard, a popular paved path. It's about 12 miles (19.3 km) south of Santa Monica.

Zuma Beach in Malibu

Hermosa Beach

Hermosa Beach (Hermosa Beach Blvd., Hermosa Beach, http://beaches.lacounty.gov) offers volleyball nets, pristine sand, and wave breaks that surfers love. A paved path is packed with bikers, runners, and in-line skaters. It's 2 miles (3.2 km) south of Manhattan Beach.

Redondo State Beach

The lack of surfers makes swimming a prime activity at **Redondo State Beach** (400-1700 Esplanade, Redondo, http://beaches.lacounty.gov), complete with lifeguards. You'll find the usual volleyball and beach games, a bike path (which is lit at night), and restaurants on the pier. There's restrooms and showers, and a large multilevel pay parking structure at the pier.

Surfing

The northern section of Los Angeles has some of the region's best surf breaks including County Line, which is on the L.A.-Ventura county line, and Zuma, a series of beach breaks along the beach of the same name. But L.A.'s premier surf spot is Malibu, one of the world's most famous waves. This is where the 1960s surf culture took hold, thanks to legends like Miki Dora, an iconic Malibu-based surfer. The southern section of L.A. County's coastline offers places to surf, but not with the same quality as the breaks around Malibu.

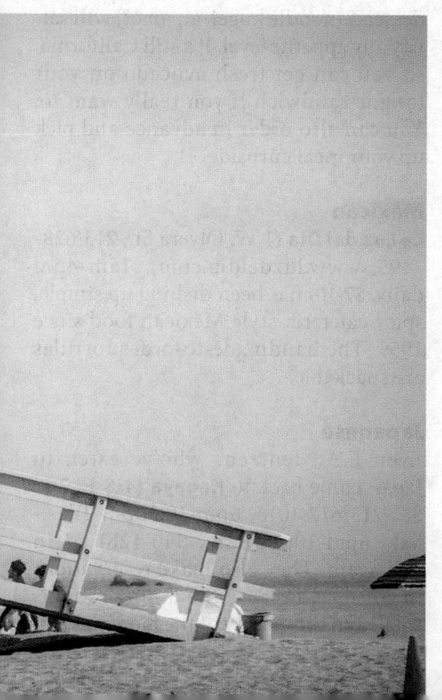

If you've left your board at home, run to the **Malibu Surf Shack** (22935 Pacific Coast Hwy., 310/456-8508, www.malibusurfshack.com, 10am-6pm daily, surfboards $25 per hour, $30-40 per day, wetsuits $10-15) to rent a board. It's walking distance to the break.

Learn to Surf LA (641 Westminster Ave., Ste. 5, Venice, 310/663-2479, www.learntosurfla.com, $130-380) has lessons on the beach near the Santa Monica Pier (near lifeguard tower no. 18), Manhattan Beach's 45th Street lifeguard tower, and Venice Beach's Navy Street lifeguard tower. Each lesson lasts almost two hours and includes all equipment (you'll get a full wetsuit in addition to a board), shore instruction and practice, and plenty of time in the water. Intermediate and advanced surfers can also find great fun with this school, which has advanced instructors capable of helping you improve your skills.

Spectator Sports

NFL teams the **Los Angeles Rams** (www.therams.com) and the **Los Angeles Chargers** (www.chargers.com) play in the **SoFi Stadium** (1000 S. Prairie Ave., Inglewood, 877/242-7437, www.sofistadium.com) at Hollywood Park.

The **L.A. Kings** (www.nhl/kings) play lightning-fast NHL ice hockey in downtown L.A. at the **Staples Center** (1111 S. Figueroa St., 888/929-7849, www.staplescenter.com).

The **Los Angeles Lakers** (www.nba.com/lakers) play at the **Staples Center** (1111 S. Figueroa St., 888/929-7849, www.staplescenter.com), along with the often-overlooked **L.A. Clippers** (www.nba.com/clippers), who are now rising in stature.

The **Los Angeles Dodgers** (www.mlb.com/dodgers) play often and well at **Dodger Stadium** (1000 Elysian Park Ave).

Food

TOP EXPERIENCE

Whatever kind of food you prefer, from fresh sushi to Armenian, you can probably find it in a cool little hole-in-the-wall somewhere in L.A. Local recommendations often make for the best dining experiences, but even just walking down the right street can yield a tasty meal.

Downtown and Vicinity

Sure, you can find plenty of bland tourist-friendly restaurants serving standard fare in the downtown area, but why would you, when one of downtown L.A.'s greatest strengths is its ethnic diversity and the great range of cuisine that goes along with it? An endless array of fabulous holes-in-the-wall awaits you. Getting local recommendations is the best way to find the current hot spots. The food stalls at the **Grand Central Market** (317 S. Broadway, 213/624-2378, www.grandcentralsquare.com, 8am-10pm daily) are also fun options.

Contemporary

Helmed by James Beard Award-winning chef Michael Cimarusti, **Best Girl** (929 Broadway, 213/235-9660, www.bestgirldtla.com, 7am-3pm and 5pm-10pm Mon.-Thurs., 7am-11pm Fri., 8am-11pm Sat., 8am-10pm Sun., $16-33), is a hip neighborhood bistro serving brunch, dinner, and drinks on the ground floor of the Ace Hotel. There's clearly an Italian influence on the menu, though classic American and Asian flavors also make strong showings.

Classic American

Who invented the French dip sandwich? This is one of the big food debates going around Los Angeles. Two eateries claim the distinction of being the originators: Cole's French Dip and ★ **Philippe's** (1001 N. Alameda St., 213/628-3781, www.philippes.com, 6am-10pm daily, $9-10). I'm not here to settle the feud, but Philippe's has a great origin story—the original owner accidentally dropped a sandwich he was making into a roasting pan with juices, inadvertently creating the French dip sandwich—an old-school feel (sawdust on the floors!), and a tasty sandwich served with some supremely spicy hot mustard.

The house specialty at **Langer's Delicatessen and Restaurant** (704 S. Alvarado St., 213/483-8050, www.langersdeli.com, 8am-4pm Mon.-Sat., $12-25), operating continuously since 1947, is a hot pastrami sandwich that some say is the best in the world (yes, that includes New York City). The hot and cold dishes in the traditional Jewish deli style, a vast breakfast menu, and plenty of desserts (noodle kugel, anyone?) will satisfy any appetite level. It's still California, so you can get fresh avocado on your tongue sandwich if you really want to. You can also order in advance and pick up your meal curbside.

Mexican

La Luz del Dia (1 W. Olvera St., 213/628-7495, www.luzdeldia.com, 11am-4pm daily, $7-10) has been dishing up simple, spicy cafeteria-style Mexican food since 1959. The handmade-to-order tortillas are snackable.

Japanese

Even L.A. denizens who've eaten in Japan come back to **Kagaya** (418 E. 2nd St., 213/617-1016, 6pm-10:30pm Tues.-Sat., 6pm-10pm Sun., $40-128) again and again. They also make reservations in advance, because the dining room is small and the quality of the food makes it popular even on weeknights. The *shabu-shabu* (paper-thin slices of beef and vegetables) is but one course in a meal that includes several appetizers, *udon* noodles, and dessert. You can pay a premium for Wagyu beef if you choose, but the king crab legs in season are part of the regular price of dinner. Sit at the counter to watch your food prepared before your eyes.

Busy, noisy **Daikokuya** (327 E. 1st St., 213/626-1680, www.daikoku-ten.com, 11am-9pm daily, under $10) is among the best ramen places in Little Tokyo, hailed by Pulitzer Prize-winning food writer Jonathan Gold. The steaming bowls of hearty pork broth and noodles satisfy even the brawniest appetite.

Italian

It seems odd to name a high-end restaurant after a decidedly low-end bug, but that's what the owners of **Cicada Restaurant** (617 S. Olive St., 213/488-9488, www.cicadarestaurant.com, 5:30pm-9pm Tues.-Sat., $24-42) did. Set in the 1920s Oviatt building, decorated in high French art deco style, the beautiful restaurant glitters with original Lalique glass panels—check out the elevator doors. There's a palatial dining room for large parties and balcony seating for intimate duos. The cuisine fuses Italian concepts with California ingredients, techniques, and presentations. Save room for dessert.

Coffee and Tea

Santa Cruz chain **Verve Coffee Roasters** (883 Spring St., 213/455-5991, www.vervecoffee.com, 7am-7pm Mon.-Fri., 7am-8pm Sat.-Sun.) feels right at home in DTLA, with a high-tech industrial setting and a small deck shaded with a canopy of tangled vines.

From top to bottom: a dish at La Luz del Dia; a burger at Cassell's Hamburgers; a meal at Taix French Restaurant.

Follow That Food Truck!

Some of the city's best culinary creations are being served out of food trucks. Gourmet chefs can follow their dreams with little overhead, and the result is some of the L.A. food scene's most blogged-about bites.

Websites including **Find LA Food Trucks** (www.findlafoodtrucks.com) and **Roaming Hunger** (http://roaminghunger.com) have sprung up to help you find some of your roving favorites.

Nashville-style hot chicken sandwiches are a crowd favorite these days. **Bad Chkn** (twitter @badchkn, www.badchkn.com) is known for its version with slaw and sauce on brioche buns. Sides include cheddar-and-chive grits with beer-battered shrimp.

For East Coast meets West Coast fare, search for **Cousins Maine Lobster** (twitter @CMLobster, http://cousinsmainelobster.com), serving lobster rolls and crustacean-stuffed quesadillas.

Food truck favorite **Kogi BBQ** (twitter @kogibbq, http://kogibbq.com) is still going strong, serving a Mexican-Korean hybrid menu that includes kimchi quesadillas and short-rib tacos.

Happy hunting!

Koreatown

Three miles (4.8 km) west of downtown, densely populated Koreatown has scores of great restaurants.

Korean

With loud music playing on the speakers, an industrial-chic interior, and an outdoor patio, ★ **Quarters** (3465 W. 6th St., C-130, 213/365-8111, http://quarterskbbq.com, 11am-2am daily, $9-24) is not your traditional Korean barbecue joint. The restaurant's name refers to the fact that you can order different quarter-pounds of meat to grill at your table; don't miss the very flavorful beef bulgogi. The popular spot has a youthful energy possibly fueled by the specialty cocktails and craft beers available on draft.

Classic American

Old-school gem ★ **Cassell's Hamburgers** (3600 W. 6th St., 213/387-5502, www.cassellshamburgers.com, 8am-11pm Sun.-Thurs., 8am-midnight Fri.-Sat., $6-12) has served its famous burgers since 1948. While the original location closed in 2012, it's reopened and modernized inside the Hotel Normandie. The burger is a thing of greasy beauty, still cooked up on the original crossfire broiler, while the can't-miss potato salad has a slight horseradish kick. Just feet from a rotating pie case, a bar serves up craft beers and cocktails. Cassell's also has a location **downtown** (421 W. 8th St., 213/372-5601, 8am-11pm Mon.-Thurs., 8am-midnight Fri.-Sat., 8am-11pm Sun.).

Greek

Originally a Greek import company in the 1960s, **Papa Cristos Taverna** (2771 W. Pico Blvd., 323/737-2970, www.papacristos.com, 9:30am-6pm Wed.-Sun., $7-20) still supplies the local Greek community with hard-to-come-by delicacies, which also become ingredients in the cuisine at the Taverna, from the salads to the kebabs to the baba ghanoush.

Los Feliz, Silver Lake, and Echo Park

Mexican

Not every taco stand wins awards from the James Beard Foundation. **Yuca's** (2056 Hillhurst Ave., 323/662-1214, www.yucasla.com, 11am-6pm Mon.-Sat., $5) received the honor in 2005, confirming what Los Feliz locals have known for decades: This shack serves truly memorable (and cheap) tacos and burritos.

Vegetarians beware: Even the beans are made with pork fat.

French

The ★ **Taix French Restaurant** (1911 W. Sunset Blvd., 213/484-1265, http://taixfrench.com, 11:30am-10pm Mon.-Thurs., 11:30am-11pm Fri., noon-11pm Sat., noon-10pm Sun., $13-34) has been serving superb French cuisine in a dimly lit Old World setting in Echo Park since 1927. The menu includes nightly dishes like roast chicken and frog legs Provençal as well as recurring weekly soups and entrées. Enjoy live music or comedy during your dinner at the on-site **321 Lounge.**

Vegetarian

Run by a true Renaissance woman (a spoken word poet, filmmaker, and chef), **Sage** (1700 W. Sunset Blvd., 213/989-1718, www.sageveganbistro.com, 8am-11pm daily, $12-15) keeps Echo Park's hipsters healthy with organic, plant-based cuisine. Order tempura-battered avocado tacos, house-made veggie burgers, flavorful veggie bowls, or butternut squash ravioli at the counter and then wait for your order at a table. (Dining this healthy means you can justify a scoop of gelato after your meal.) There are locations in Culver City (4130 Sepulveda Blvd., 424/228-5835, 11am-11pm Mon.-Thurs., 9am-11pm Sat.-Sun.) and Pasadena (41 Hugus Alley, 626/564-8111, 8am-11pm daily).

Hollywood

Hollywood has just as many tasty treats tucked away in strip malls as other areas of Los Angeles. If you want to rub elbows with rock stars, you're likely to find yourself at a big, slightly raunchy bar and grill. For a chance at glimpsing stars of the silver screen, look for upscale California cuisine or perhaps a high-end sushi bar. If all you need is tasty sustenance, you can choose from a range of restaurants.

Classic American

Experience classic old Hollywood at the ★ **Musso & Frank Grill** (6667 Hollywood Blvd., 323/7788, http://mussoandfrank.com, 11am-11pm Tues.-Sat., 4pm-9pm Sun., $19-55), which dates back to 1919. Slide into a leather booth or sit at the mahogany bar for cocktails along with a throwback menu that includes steaks, chops, seafood, and pastas. One menu entrée of note is the fettucine alfredo, made from the original recipe—it was brought to the restaurant by silent film stars Douglas Fairbanks and Mary Pickford after a visit to Italy. More recently, the restaurant had a role in Quentin Tarantino's *Once Upon a Time in Hollywood.*

Lit up like a Las Vegas show club into the wee hours of the morning, **Pink's Famous Hot Dogs** (709 N. La Brea Ave., 323/931-4223, www.pinkshollywood.com, 9:30am-2am Sun.-Thurs., 9:30am-3am Fri.-Sat., $3.50-7) is hot dog heaven. Frankophiles have been lining up at this roadside stand for variations on a sausage in a bun that range from the basic chili dog to the more elaborate Lord of the Rings Dog, topped with barbecue sauce and onion rings.

British

The Pikey (7617 Sunset Blvd., 323/850-5400, www.thepikeyla.com, 11:45am-2am Mon.-Fri., 10:30am-2am Sat.-Sun., $15-32) is an upscale British pub in the midst of Hollywood. The menu features a range of small plates and entrées with British flair, from Welsh rarebit to fish-and-chips. The buttery burger with cheddar and Worcestershire aioli is a highlight. Meanwhile, the cocktail menu includes playful offerings like the "Kate Moss," a glass of prosecco and a shot of tequila. Note it can get loud and crowded here at dinnertime.

Italian

The warm but clamorous dining room at **Pizzeria Mozza** (641 N. Highland Ave., 323/297-0101, www.

pizzeriamozza.com, noon-11pm Sun.-Thurs., noon-midnight Fri.-Sat., $15-29) has been packed since chef Nancy Silverton opened the doors. The wood-fired oven turns out rustic, blistered pizzas with luxurious toppings. Reservations are tough to get, but bar seats are available for walk-ins. They also have an outpost in Newport Beach and farther away in Singapore.

Brazilian

Need food really, really, *really* late? **Bossa Nova** (7181 W. Sunset Blvd., 323/436-7999, www.bossanovafood.com, 11am-3:30am Sun.-Wed., 11am-4am Thurs.-Sat., $10-20) can hook you up. A big menu of inexpensive entrées can satisfy any appetite from lunch to way past dinnertime. Some of the dishes bear the spicy flavors of the owners' home country of Brazil, but you'll also find pasta, salads, and pizzas. There are two other locations: one at 685 N. Robertson Blvd. (310/657-5070, 11am-11:30pm Mon.-Thurs., 11am-3:30am Fri.-Sat., 11am-midnight Sun.) and one in West L.A. at 10982 W. Pico Blvd. (310/441-0404, 11am-1am daily). Bossa also delivers.

Breakfast

If you're a flapjack fan, plan on breakfast at ★ **The Griddle Café** (7916 Sunset Blvd., 323/874-0377, www.thegriddlecafe.com, 7am-4pm Mon.-Fri., 8am-4pm Sat.-Sun., $11-30). This hectic, loud breakfast joint serves up creations like a Red Velvet pancake and a pancake with brown sugar-baked bananas. Those who prefer savory to sweet can opt for delicious breakfast tacos or a cobb omelet. The Director's Guild of America is next door, so you may spot a celebrity *auteur*.

From top to bottom: iconic Pann's diner sign; shrimp tacos at Neptune's Net; a healthy meal from Sage.

La Brea, Fairfax, and Miracle Mile

California Cuisine

Pairing meat and potatoes with a retro-clubby dining room, **Jar** (8225 Beverly Blvd., 323/655-6566, www.thejar.com, 5:30pm-close Tues.-Sun., $21-49) puts a Southern California spin on the traditional steak house. Meats and grilled fishes are served à la carte with your choice of sauce, and the side orders serve two. On Sunday, you can order a fried chicken plate.

Deli

Midnight snackers unhinge their jaws on the hulking corned beef sandwiches at **Canter's Deli** (419 N. Fairfax Ave., 323/651-2030, www.cantersdeli.com, 24 hours daily, $12-18), in the heart of the Jewish Fairfax district. This venerable 24-hour deli also boasts its share of star sightings, so watch for noshing rock stars in the wee hours of the morning.

Beverly Hills and West Hollywood

Between Beverly Hills and West L.A., you'll find an eclectic choice of restaurants. Unsurprisingly, Beverly Hills tends toward high-end eateries serving European and haute California cuisine. On the other hand, West L.A. boasts a wide array of international restaurants. You'll have to try a few to pick your favorites, since every local has their own take on the area's best eats.

California Cuisine

★ **AOC** (8700 W. 3rd St., 310/859-9859, www.aocwinebar.com, 11:30am-10pm Mon.-Wed., 11:30am-11pm Thurs.-Fri., 10am-11pm Sat., 10am-10pm Sun., $14-88) is wildly popular for three reasons: breakfast, lunch, and dinner. Breakfast is served until 3pm and includes fried chicken and cornmeal waffles along with house-made corned beef hash. Lunch features focaccia sandwiches, salads, and plate lunches. At dinner, you can go small (foccacias or salads) or big (roasted fish or meats). Sample from an acclaimed wine list and creative cocktails.

Italian

If you're looking for upscale Italian cuisine in a classy environment, enjoy lunch or dinner at **Il Pastaio Restaurant** (400 N. Canon Dr., Beverly Hills, 310/205-5444, www.ilpastaiobeverlyhills.com, 11:30am-11pm Mon.-Thurs., 11:30am-midnight Fri.-Sat., 11:30am-10pm Sun., $13-45). The bright dining room offers a sunny luncheon experience, and the white tablecloths and shiny glassware lend an elegance to dinner, served late even on weeknights. Il Pastaio offers a wide variety of salads, risotto, and pasta dishes. The blue-painted bar offers a tasteful selection of California and Italian vintages.

Seafood

With a roof that resembles a giant ray gliding through the sea, **Connie and Ted's** (8171 Santa Monica Blvd., 323/848-2722, www.connieandteds.com, 4pm-10pm Mon.-Tues., 11:30am-10pm Wed.-Thurs., 11:30am-11pm Fri., 10am-11pm Sat., 10am-10pm Sun., $12-44) brings the fruit of the sea to West Hollywood. The menu is inspired by New England clam shacks, oyster bars, and fish houses and includes a raw bar of oysters and clams. A West Coast influence creeps in on items like the smoked albacore starter, lobster rolls, and a Mexican shrimp dish.

Santa Monica, Venice, and Malibu

Yes, there's lots of junky beach food to be found in Santa Monica and Venice Beach, but there is also an amazing number of gems hiding in these towns.

Contemporary

Don't be fooled by the unpretentious exterior of **Cora's Coffee Shoppe** (1802 Ocean Ave., Santa Monica, 310/451-9562, www.corascoffee.com, 7am-3pm Sun.-Mon., 7am-5pm Tues.-Sat., $7-18). The small, exquisite restaurant is a locals' secret hiding in plain sight, serving breakfast and lunch to diners who are more than willing to pack into the tiny spaces, including the two tiny marble-topped tables and miniature marble counter inside, and a small patio area screened by venerable bougainvillea. The chefs use high-end and sometimes organic ingredients to create typical breakfast and lunch dishes with a touch of the unexpected, including a hamburger salad and rotisserie carnitas tacos.

Classic American

★ **Pann's** (6710 La Tijera Blvd., Westchester, 310/670-1441 or 323/776-3770, http://panns.com, 8am-3pm daily, $9-17) is a classic diner and coffee shop that's been around since 1958. It exudes classic Los Angeles style with its iconic sign and Googie architecture, distinguished by bold angles and big windows. The menu is full of hearty breakfast and lunch fare. Favorites include the Dreamburger and the chicken and waffles, which many say is the best version of that Southern dish in the city. Pann's is inland, about 7 miles (11.3 km) east of Venice.

Mexican

Teddy's Red Tacos (46 Windward Ave., Venice, 310/452-7910, 10am-10pm Sun.-Thurs., 10am-11pm Fri.-Sat., $3-14) has quickly evolved from pop-up to food truck to four and counting brick-and-mortar locations. Teddy's is known for its red broth, which infuses its tacos, tostadas, and *mulitas* (crispy tortillas filled with meat and cheese), as well as "vampiro" tacos, a kind of indulgently cheesy taco. Make sure you've got your phone ready to snap some pics of this very photogenic Mexican fare.

Italian

The **C&O Trattoria** (31 Washington Blvd., Marina del Rey, 310/823-9491, www.candorestaurants.com, 11:30am-10pm Sun.-Thurs., 11:30am-11pm Fri.-Sat., $13-23) manages to live up to its hype and then some. Sit outside in the big outdoor dining room, enjoying the mild weather and the soft pastel frescoes on the exterior walls surrounding the courtyard. C&O is known for its self-described gargantuan portions, which are best shared family-style. Start off with the addictive little garlic rolls. Your attentive but not overzealous server can help you choose from the creative pasta list; the rigatoni al forno is a standout. While C&O has a nice wine list, it's worth trying out the house chianti, where you get to serve yourself on an honor system.

Seafood

Situated on the Malibu coastline adjacent to the County Line surf break, ★ **Neptune's Net** (42505 Pacific Coast Hwy., Malibu, 310/457-3095, http://neptunesnet.com, 10:30am-8:30pm Mon.-Thurs., 10:30am-9pm Fri., 10am-8:30pm Sat.-Sun. summer, 10:30am-7pm Mon.-Thurs., 10:30am-8pm Fri., 10am-7pm Sat.-Sun. winter, $11-30) catches all kinds of seafood to serve to hungry diners. You'll often find sandy and salt-encrusted local surfers satisfying their enormous appetites after hours out on the waves, or bikers downing a beer after a ride on the twisting highway. One of the Net's most satisfying options is the shrimp tacos: crispy fried shrimp on tortillas topped with a pineapple salsa. The large menu includes a seemingly endless variety of other combinations, à la carte options, and side dishes.

Accommodations

From the cheapest roach-ridden shack motels to the most chichi Beverly Hills hotel, Los Angeles has an endless variety of lodgings to suit every taste and budget.

Downtown and Vicinity

If you want to stay overnight in downtown L.A., plan to pay for the privilege. Most hostelries are high-rise towers catering more to businesspeople than the leisure set. Still, if you need a room near the heart of L.A. for less than a month's mortgage, you can find one if you look hard enough. Like any big city, Los Angeles struggles with some street crime, especially notable in the Jewelry District and farther south toward the Flower Market and Fashion District. If you need a truly cheap room, avoid these areas and head instead to the San Fernando Valley.

Under $150

A testament to the DTLA renaissance, ★ **Freehand Los Angeles** (416 W. 8th St., 213/612-0021, www.freehandhotels.com/los-angeles, dorm beds $54-70, private rooms $152-819) has taken up shop in the old Commercial Exchange Building. The hip 226-room complex splits the difference between hotel and hostel with 167 private rooms and 59 shared rooms with bunk beds. There's much on-site including a communal lobby with bar, a coffee counter, a home goods store, the Israeli American restaurant **The Exchange,** and the rooftop bar **Broken Shaker** with an adjacent pool.

$150-250

The ★ **Ace Hotel** (929 Broadway, 213/623-3233, www.acehotel.com/losangeles, $199-650) is one of the hippest places to stay in downtown. You can enjoy an evening's entertainment without venturing off the hotel's grounds. The property's 1,600-seat theater hosts the Sundance Next Fest and music performances by big indie acts like Slowdive and Belle and Sebastian. DJs spin poolside at the rooftop bar on the 14th floor, called **Upstairs,** with the downtown skyline as a backdrop. On the ground floor, dine at neighborhood bistro **Best Girl.** The guest rooms, converted from the former offices of the United Artists film studio, feel like arty studio apartments, with concrete ceilings and exposed concrete floors. Some rooms have private terraces; all have Internet radios.

If you're yearning to stay someplace with a movie history, book a room at the **Westin Bonaventure Hotel and Suites** (404 S. Figueroa St., 213/624-1000, www.marriott.com, $199-2,500). The climactic scene of the Clint Eastwood thriller *In the Line of Fire* was filmed in one of the unusual elevators in the glass-enclosed, four leaf clover-shaped high-rise building. This hotel complex has every single thing you'd ever need: shops, restaurants, a day spa, and a concierge. Views range from innocuous street scenes to panoramic cityscapes. The **Bona Vista Lounge** slowly rotates through 360 degrees at the top of the building.

The **Tuck Hotel** (820 S. Spring St., 213/947-3815, www.tuckhotel.com, $150-250) is located in a sliver of a building between South Spring Street and South Main Street. It used to house a brothel, but now is home to a small boutique hotel with a lobby bar and restaurant below the rooms. The black walls in the units make it easy to sleep in, while smart TVs and Bluetooth speakers provide entertainment and a soundtrack during your stay.

Over $250

For a taste of true L.A. style, get a room at the **Omni Los Angeles at California Plaza** (251 S. Olive St., 213/617-3300, www.omnihotels.com, $276-542). From the grand exterior to the elegant lobby and on up to your guest room, the stylish decor, lovely accents, and plush amenities will make you feel rich, if only for one night. Business travelers can request a room complete with a fax machine and copier, while families can enjoy suites with adjoining rooms specially decorated for children. On-site meals are available at the **Noé Restaurant** and the **Grand Café.** Take a swim in the lap pool, work out in the fitness room, or relax at the spa.

The Standard (550 S. Flower St., 213/892-8080, www.standardhotels.com, $260-1,500) is a mecca for the see-and-be-seen crowd. From its upside-down sign to the minimal aesthetic in the guest rooms, the hotel gives off an ironic-chic vibe. If you're sharing a room, be aware that the shower is only separated from the rest of the room by clear glass. On-site amenities include a gym, a barbershop, and a restaurant open 24-7. The rooftop bar, seen in the 2005 film *Kiss Kiss, Bang Bang,* features spectacular views of the L.A. cityscape.

Koreatown

$150-250

★ **Hotel Normandie** (605 S. Normandie Ave., 800/617-4071, www.hotelnormandiela.com, $199-399) has been welcoming guests to Koreatown since opening in 1926, including British author Malcom Lowry, who completed his novel *Under the Volcano* here in the 1930s. Today the building has anything you'd want, including clean rooms, showers with superb water pressure and complimentary wine in the afternoon. The high-ceilinged lobby leads to the bar at the **Normandie Club** as well as the classic **Cassell's Hamburgers,** gussied-up for modern diners.

Over $250

A block away from the Hotel Normandie, **The Line** (3515 Wilshire Blvd., 213/381-7411, www.thelinehotel.com/los-angeles, $229-950) is a 1960s hotel spruced up for the modern age. The rooms have floor-to-ceiling windows, and the restaurants are run by famed chef Roy Choi. There's also a 1980s-throwback bar on-site called Break Room 86.

Silver Lake

$150-250

A great place to spend the night in one of L.A.'s hippest neighborhoods is the **Silver Lake Pool & Inn** (4141 Santa Monica Blvd., 323/486-7225, www.palisociety.com/hotel/silverlake, $225-500). The 54 guestrooms are designed to let in lots of natural sunlight, and each is decorated with live plants and antique rugs. The focal point of the property is the elevated pool deck, and there's also an on-site restaurant, **Marco Polo,** specializing in Italian fare.

Hollywood

If you're star-struck, a serious partier, or a rock music aficionado, you'll want to stay the night within staggering distance of the hottest clubs or the hippest music venues. You might find yourself sleeping in the same room where Axl Rose once vomited or David Lee Roth broke all the furniture.

Under $150

Hollywood motel rooms for around $100? They exist at the **Hollywood Downtowner Inn** (5601 Hollywood Blvd., 323/464-7191, www.hollywooddowntowner.com, $99-199). Just 1.5 miles (2.4 km) from sights such as the Chinese Theatre and Griffith Observatory, this 33-room motel offers basic amenities, including a courtyard pool, and, maybe most important, free parking.

The **Hollywood Celebrity Hotel** (1775 Orchid Ave., 323/850-6464 or 800/222-7017, www.hotelcelebrity.com, $119-159) is a nice budget motel that aspires to Hollywood luxury. Guest rooms have mini fridges for leftovers; some have kitchens as well. Leave your car in the gated, off-street parking lot for just $16 per night, a deal.

$150-250

Named for the world-renowned magic club next door, the ★ **Magic Castle Hotel** (7025 Franklin Ave., 323/851-0800, www.magiccastlehotel.com, $191-350) boasts the best customer service of any L.A.-area hostelry. Sparkling light guest rooms with cushy white comforters and spare decor offer a haven of tranquility. A courtyard pool invites lounging day and night. All suites have their own kitchens, and all guests can enjoy unlimited free snacks (sodas, candy, salted goodies). Enjoy the little luxurious touches, such as high-end coffee, plushy robes, and nightly turndown service. But the most notable perk is tickets to the exclusive **Magic Castle** (7001 Franklin Ave., 323/851-3313, www.magiccastle.com)—usually only accessible to those invited by a member—although there is a door charge.

Beverly Hills and West Hollywood

If you want to dive headfirst into the lap of luxury, stay in Beverly Hills. Choose wisely and save your pennies to see how the 1 percent lives. West Hollywood,

the sunny pool deck at the Silver Lake Pool & Inn

which serves as L.A.'s gay mecca, offers a wider range of accommodations, including budget options, chain motels, and unique upscale hotels.

$150-250

Comfortable and quiet, the ★ **Élan Hotel** (8435 Beverly Blvd., 323/658-6663, www.elanhotel.com, $169-249) has a great location where Beverly Hills and West Hollywood meet. With its friendly staff, this unassuming hotel makes a fine base for exploring Hollywood attractions and the Sunset Strip. The understated rooms are decorated with soothing abstract art. All have mini fridges, coffeemakers, flat-screen TVs; many rooms have small balconies or porches for a breath of fresh air. A complimentary continental breakfast is served every morning.

The affordable **Hotel Beverly Terrace** (469 N. Doheny Dr., Beverly Hills, 310/274-8141 or 800/842-6401, www.hotelbeverlyterrace.com, $220-260) is a spruced-up, retro-cool motor hotel that enjoys a great spot on the border of Beverly Hills and West Hollywood. Lounge in the sun in the garden courtyard or on the rooftop sundeck. In the morning, enjoy a complimentary continental breakfast. The on-site **Cafe Amici** can satisfy your Italian food cravings.

Over $250

The **Beverly Wilshire** (9500 Wilshire Blvd., Beverly Hills, 310/275-5200, www.fourseasons.com, rooms from $595, specialty suites from $3,500) is the most famous of all the neighborhood's grand hotels. Even the plainest guest rooms feature exquisite appointments such as 55-inch plasma TVs, elegant linens, and attractive artwork. The presidential suite resembles a European palace, complete with Corinthian columns, while the Veranda Suite includes a tent on a patio overlooking Rodeo Drive and the Hollywood Hills. Enjoy the in-house spa, a dining room, room service, and every other service you could imagine, and you might consider a stay here worth the expense.

In West Hollywood, the **Sunset Tower Hotel** (8358 Sunset Blvd., West Hollywood, 323/654-7100, www.sunsettowerhotel.com, $325-2,500) has a gorgeous art deco exterior and a fully renovated modern interior. Guest accommodations range from smallish guest rooms with smooth linens and attractive appointments up to luxurious suites with panoramic views and limestone baths. All guest rooms include flat-screen TVs, 24-hour room service, and free Wi-Fi.

Santa Monica, Venice, and Malibu

The best place to stay in Los Angeles is down by the beach. It's ironic that you can camp in a park for $25 in exclusive Malibu or pay over $1,000 for a resort room in "working-class" Santa Monica. Whichever you choose, you'll get some of the best atmosphere in town.

Under $150

The huge **HI-Santa Monica** (1436 2nd St., Santa Monica, 310/393-9913, www.hiusa.org, dorm beds $44-60, private rooms $145-240) offers 260 beds right in the thick of downtown Santa Monica, within walking distance of the pier, the Third Street Promenade, and good restaurants. This ritzy hostel offers tons of amenities for the price, including a computer room, a TV room, a movie room, excursions, wheelchair access, sheets with the bed price, and even a complimentary continental breakfast every morning. The local public transit system runs right outside the door.

Over $250

There's probably no hotel that is a better reflection of Venice's edgy attitude than ★ **Hotel Erwin** (1697 Pacific Ave., 800/786-7789, www.hotelerwin.com, $320-500), just feet from the boardwalk. Graffiti art adorns the outside wall and some of its rooms; all have balconies and playful decor, including lamps resembling the barbells used by the weightlifters at nearby Muscle Beach. Sitting atop the hotel is **High,** a rooftop bar that allows you to take in all the action of the bustling boardwalk while sipping a cocktail. The staff is laid-back, genial, and accommodating.

For a charming hotel experience only a block from the ever-energetic Venice Boardwalk, stay at the **Inn at Venice Beach** (327 Washington Blvd., 310/821-2557 or 800/828-0688, www.innatvenicebeach.com, $250-450). The charming orange-and-brown exterior, complete with a lovely bricked interior courtyard-cum-café, makes all guests feel welcome. Common spaces are decorated in a postmodern blocky style, while the guest rooms pop with brilliant yellows and vibrant accents. The two-story boutique hotel offers 45 guest rooms, and its location on Washington Boulevard makes it a perfect base from which to enjoy the best restaurants of Venice. Start each day with a complimentary continental breakfast, either in the dining room or outside in the Courtyard Café. There's complimentary Wi-Fi throughout.

One of this area's best-known resort hotels is **Shutters on the Beach** (1 Pico Blvd., Santa Monica, 310/458-0030, www.shuttersonthebeach.com, $795-1,165). You'll pay handsomely for the privilege of laying your head on one of Shutters' hallowed pillows. On the other hand, the gorgeous airy guest rooms will make you feel like you're home, or at least staying at the home you'd have if you could hire a famous designer to decorate for you. Even the most modest guest rooms have comfortable beds, white linens, plasma TVs, and oversize bathtubs. Head down to the famed lobby for a drink and people-watching. Get a reservation for the elegant **One Pico** or grab a more casual meal at beachside **Coast.**

If you've got silly amounts of cash to spare, stay at the **Malibu Beach Inn** (22878 Pacific Coast Hwy., Malibu, 310/456-6444 or 800/462-5428, www.malibubeachinn.com, $749-1,600), an ocean-side villa on an exclusive stretch of sand known as "Billionaire's Beach." Expect all the best furnishings and amenities. Your guest room will be done in rare woods, gleaming stone, and the most stylish modern linens and accents. A high-definition TV, plush robes, and comfy beds tempt some visitors to stay inside, but equally tempting are the balconies with their own entertainment in the form of endless surf, glorious sunsets, and balmy breezes (every room has an ocean view). Enjoy delicious cuisine at the airy, elegant, on-site **Carbon Beach Club.**

Transportation and Services

Air

L.A. is one of the most commercial airport-dense metropolitan areas in the country. Wherever you're coming from and whichever part of L.A. you're headed for, you can get there by air. **Los Angeles International Airport** (1 World Way, Los Angeles, 855/463-5252, www.flylax.com), known as LAX, has the most flights to and from the most destinations of any area airport. LAX is also the most crowded of the L.A. airports, with the longest security and check-in lines. If you can find a way around flying into LAX, do so.

One option is to fly into other airports in the area, including **Hollywood Burbank Airport** (BUR, 2627 N. Hollywood Way, Burbank, 818/840-8840, http://hollywoodburbankairport.com) and the **Long Beach Airport** (LGB, 4100 Donald Douglas Dr., Long Beach, 562/570-2600, www.longbeach.gov/lgb). It may be a slightly longer drive to your final destination, but it can be well worth it. If you must use LAX, arrive a minimum of two hours ahead of your domestic flight time for your flight out, and consider three hours on busy holidays.

Train

Amtrak (800/872-7245, www.amtrak.com) has an active rail hub in Los Angeles. Most trains come in to **Union Station** (800 N. Alameda St., 213/683-6875, www.unionstationla.com, 4am-1am daily), which is owned by the Los Angeles Metropolitan Transportation Authority (MTA, 323/466-3876, www.metro.net).

Union Station also acts as a Metro hub, with Metro Rail lines to various parts of Los Angeles. Against fairly significant odds in the region that invented car culture, Los Angeles has created a functional and useful public transit system.

Car

Los Angeles is crisscrossed with freeways, providing numerous yet congested access points into the city. From the north and south, I-5 provides the most direct access to downtown L.A. From I-5, U.S. 101 south leads directly into Hollywood; from here, Santa Monica Boulevard can take you west to Beverly Hills. Connecting from I-5 to I-210 will take you east to Pasadena. The best way to reach Santa Monica, Venice, and Malibu is via CA-1, also known as the Pacific Coast Highway. I-10 can get you there from the east, but it will be a long, tedious, and trafficked drive. I-710, which runs north-south, is known as the Long Beach Freeway. Along the coast, the Pacific Coast Highway (CA-1) can get you from one beach town to the next.

Parking

Parking in Los Angeles can be as much of a bear as driving. And it can cost you quite a lot of money. You will find parking lots and structures included with many hotel rooms, but parking on the street can be difficult or impossible, parking lots in certain areas (like the Flower and Jewelry Districts) can be unsafe, and parking structures at popular attractions can be expensive. Beach parking on summer weekends is the worst, but on weekdays and in the off-season, you can occasionally find a decent space down near the beach for a reasonable rate.

Metro

The **Metro** (323/466-3876, www.metro.net, cash fare $1.75, day pass $7) runs both the subway Metro Rail system and a network of buses throughout the L.A. metropolitan area. Pay on board a bus if you have exact change. Otherwise, purchase a ticket or a day pass from the ticket vending machines at all Metro Rail stations. Some buses run 24 hours. The Metro Rail lines start running as early as 4:30am and don't stop until as late as 1:30am.

Note that the Metro's Expo Line (E) extends to Santa Monica near the pier, saving you a long, congested drive. See the website (www.metro.net) for route maps, timetables, and fare details.

Taxi and Ride Share

Taxis aren't cheap, but they're quick, easy, and numerous. And in some cases, when you add up gas and parking fees, you'll find that the cab ride isn't that much more expensive than driving yourself.

To call a cab, try **Yellow Cab** (424/222-2222, www.layellowcab.com, L.A., LAX, Beverly Hills, Hollywood) or **City Cab** (888/248-9222, www.lacitycab.com, San Fernando Valley, Hollywood, and LAX), which now has a small fleet of green, environmentally friendly vehicles. Or check out www.taxicabsla.org for a complete list of providers and phone numbers.

Another option is to download a ride-sharing app on your smartphone. Both **Lyft** (www.lyft.com) and **Uber** (www.uber.com) are available all over the city.

Information and Services

The **Hollywood Los Angeles Visitor Information Center** (6801 Hollywood

Blvd., 323/467-6412, www.discoverlosangeles.com, 9am-10pm Mon.-Sat., 10am-7pm Sun.) is adjacent to a Metro station and includes a self-serve kiosk where you can purchase discount tickets to area attractions. There are additional self-serve centers at the Los Angeles Convention Center, the Port of Los Angeles (Berth 93), and the California Science Center.

For medical assistance, **LAC & USC Medical Center** (1200 N. State St., 323/266-2622, http://dhs.lacounty.gov/wps/portal/dhs/lacusc) can fix you up no matter what's wrong with you, or visit the emergency room at the **Long Beach Memorial Medical Center** (2801 Atlantic Ave., Long Beach, 562/933-5437, www.memorialcare.org).

Disneyland Resort

The "Happiest Place on Earth" lures millions of visitors of all ages each year with promises of fun and fantasy. During high seasons, waves of humanity flow through **Disneyland** (1313 N. Harbor Blvd., Anaheim, 714/781-4565 or 714/781-7290, http://disneyland.disney.go.com, 9am-midnight daily, $97-124, Hopper Ticket $166-185), moving slowly from land to land and ride to ride. The park is well set up to handle the often-immense crowds. Despite the undeniable cheese factor, even the most cynical and jaded resident Californians can't quite keep their cantankerous scowls once they're ensconced inside Uncle Walt's dream. It really *is* a happy place.

Getting There

The nearest airport to Disneyland, serving all of Orange County, is **John Wayne Airport** (SNA, 18601 Airport Way, Santa Ana, 949/252-5200, www.ocair.com). It's much easier to fly into and out of John Wayne than LAX, though it can be more expensive. John Wayne's terminal has plenty of rental car agencies, as well as many shuttle services that can get you where you need to go—especially to the House of Mouse.

If you have to fly into LAX for scheduling or budget reasons, catch a shuttle straight from the airport to your Disneyland hotel. Among the many companies offering and arranging such transportation, the one with the best name is **MouseSavers** (www.mousesavers.com). Working with various shuttle and van companies, MouseSavers can get you a ride in a van or a bus from LAX ($45 one-way) or John Wayne ($20 one-way) to your destination at or near Disneyland.

Disneyland is on Disneyland Drive in Anaheim and is most accessible from I-5 South where it crosses Ball Road (stay in the left three lanes for parking). The parking lot (1313 S. Disneyland Dr.) costs $20.

If you're coming to the park from elsewhere in Southern California, consider leaving the car (avoiding the parking fees) and taking public transit instead. **Anaheim Resort Transit** (ART, 1280 Anaheim Blvd., Anaheim, 888/364-2787, http://rideart.org, $6 adults, $2.50 children) can take you to and from the Amtrak station and all around central Anaheim. Buy passes via the website or at conveniently located kiosks.

Orientation

The Disneyland Resort is a massive kingdom that stretches from **Harbor Boulevard** on the east to **Walnut Street** on the west and from **Ball Road** to the north to **Katella Avenue** to the south. It includes two amusement parks, three hotels, and an outdoor shopping and entertainment complex. The Disneyland-affiliated hotels (Disneyland Hotel, Paradise Pier Hotel, and Disney's Grand Californian) all cluster on the western side of the complex, between Walnut Street and **Disneyland Drive (West Street).** The area between Disneyland Drive and Harbor Boulevard is shared by **Disneyland** in the northern

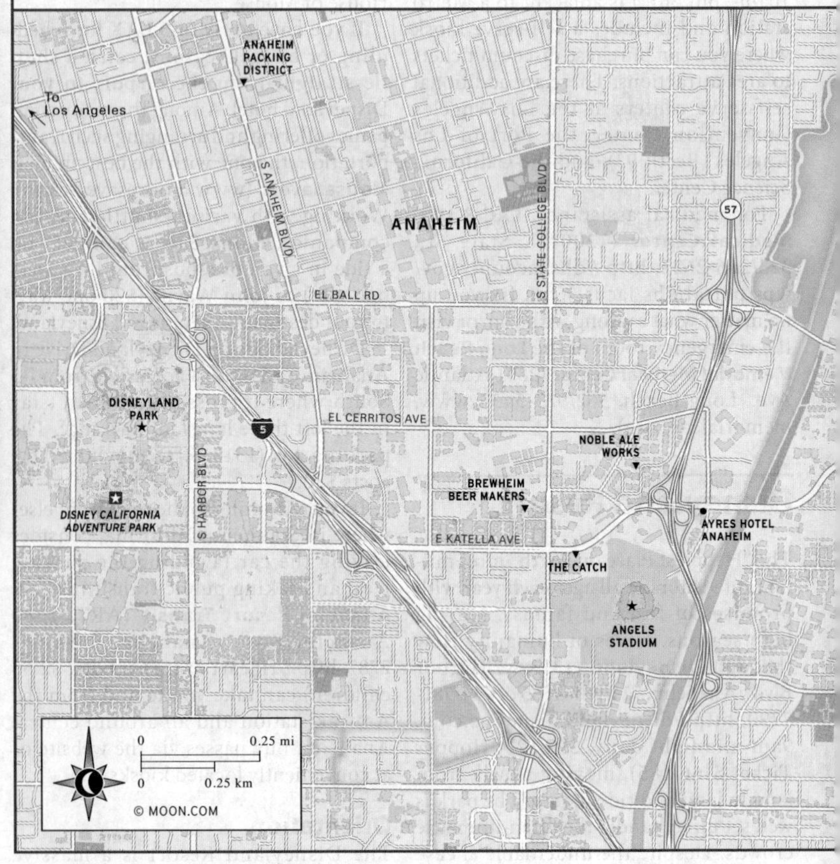

section and **Disney California Adventure Park** in the southern section, with **Downtown Disney** between them in the central-west section. There is no admission fee for Downtown Disney. You can reach the amusement park entrances via Downtown Disney (although visitors going to Disneyland or Disney California Adventure Park should park in the paid lots, rather than the Downtown Disney self-park lot, which is only free for the first three hours) or from the walk-in entrance (for those taking public transportation or being dropped off) on Harbor Boulevard. There are also trams from the parking lot to the entrance.

Your first stop inside the park should be one of the information kiosks near the front entrance gates. Get a map, a schedule of the day's events, and the inside scoop on what's going on in the park during your visit.

Tickets

There are as many varied ticket prices and plans as there are themes in the park. A single-day theme park ticket will run from $97 to $124. A variety of other combinations and passes are available online (http://disneyland.disney.go.com).

To buy tickets, go to one of the many kiosks in the central gathering spot that serves as the main entrance to both Disneyland and Disney California Adventure Park. Bring your credit card, since a day at Disney is not cheap. After you've got tickets in hand (or if you've bought them online ahead of time), proceed to the turnstiles for the main park. You'll see the Disneyland Railroad terminal and the large grassy hill with the flowers planted to resemble Mickey's famous face. Pass through the turnstiles and head under the railroad trestle to get to Main Street and the park center. You can exit and reenter the park on the days for which your tickets are valid.

The already expensive regular one-day Disneyland ticket doesn't include Disney California Adventure Park. If you're interested in checking out Disney California Adventure Park as well as Disneyland, your best bet is to buy a **Park Hopper pass** ($172-185 adults, $166-178 children 3-9), which lets you move back and forth between the two parks at will for a slight discount. If you're planning to spend several days touring the Houses of Mouse, buy multiday passes in advance online to save a few more bucks per day. It'll help you feel better about the cash you'll spend on junk food, giant silly hats, stuffed animals, and an endless array of Disney apparel.

Fastpasses are free with park admission and might seem like magic after a while. The newest and most popular rides offer Fastpass kiosks near the entrances. Feed your ticket into one of the machines and it will spit out both your ticket and a Fastpass with your specified time to take the ride. Come back during your window and enter the always-much-shorter Fastpass line, designated by a sign at the entrance. If you're with a crowd, be sure you all get your Fastpasses at the same time, so you all get the same time window to ride. It's possible to claim three Fastpasses at a time. Once you've used up your initial allotment, you can visit a Fastpass kiosk to reload.

Rides

In **New Orleans Square,** the favorite ride is the **Pirates of the Caribbean.** Beginning in the dim swamp, which can be seen from the Blue Bayou Restaurant, the ride's classic scenes inside have been revamped to tie in more closely to the movies. Lines for Pirates can get long, so grab a Fastpass if you don't want to wait. Pirates is suitable for younger children as well as teens and adults.

For a taste of truly classic Disney, line up in the graveyard for a tour of the **Haunted Mansion.** The sedate motion makes the Haunted Mansion suitable for younger children, but the ghosts and ghoulies that amuse adults can be intense for kids.

Adventureland sits next to the New Orleans Square area. **Indiana Jones Adventure** is arguably one of the best rides in all of Disneyland, and the details make it stunning. This one isn't the best for tiny tots, but the big kids love it. Everyone might want a Fastpass for the endlessly popular attraction.

In **Frontierland,** take a ride on a Wild West train on the **Big Thunder Mountain Railroad,** an older roller coaster that whisks passengers on a brief but fun thrill ride through a "dangerous, decrepit" mountain's mineshafts.

Fantasyland rides tend to cater to the younger set. For many Disneyphiles, **"it's a small world"** is the ultimate expression of Uncle Walt's dream, and toddlers adore this ride. Older kids might prefer **Mr. Toad's Wild Ride.** The wacky scenery ranges from a sedate library to the gates of hell. If it's a faster thrill you're seeking, head for the **Matterhorn Bobsleds.** You'll board a sled-style coaster car to plunge down a Swiss mountain on a twisted track that takes you past rivers, glaciers, and the Abominable Snowman.

Here at Disney, We Have a Few Rules

Think that anything goes at the Happiest Place on Earth? Think again. Uncle Walt had distinct ideas about what his dream theme park would look like, and that vision extended to the dress and manners of his guests. When the park opened in 1955, among the many other restrictions, no man sporting facial hair was allowed into Disneyland. The rules on dress and coiffure have relaxed since the opening, but you still need to mind your manners when you enter the Magic Kingdom.

- Adults may not wear costumes of any kind except on Halloween.
- No shirt, no shoes, no Disneyland.
- If you must use the F word, do it quietly. If staff members catch you cussing or cursing in a way that disturbs others, you can be asked to desist or leave.
- The happiest of happiness is strictly prohibited inside the Magic Kingdom. If you're caught having sex on park grounds, not only will you be thrown out, you'll also be banned from Disneyland for life (at least that's the rumor).
- Ditto for any illicit substances.

The best thrill ride of the main park sits inside **Tomorrowland. Space Mountain** is a fast roller coaster that whizzes through the dark. Despite its age, Space Mountain remains one of the more popular rides in the park. Get a Fastpass to avoid long lines.

Star Wars: Galaxy's Edge opened in 2019 and brings the popular sci-fi franchise to earth. In this land, which is supposed to be the Black Spire Outpost on the planet of Batuu, you have the opportunity to make a droid or light saber, and you might walk past a classic *Star Wars* character, like Chewbacca or a Stormtrooper. Star Wars: Galaxy's Edge has two state-of-the-art rides: **Millennium Falcon: Smugglers Run,** an interactive ride where you get to pilot Han Solo's spacecraft, and **Star Wars: Rise of the Resistance,** a can't-miss attraction that's a combination motion simulator and trackless ride.

★ Disney California Adventure Park

Disney California Adventure Park (http://disneyland.disney.go.com, 8am-10pm daily, ticket prices vary, one-day $99 adults, $93 children 3-9, one-day Park Hopper ticket to both parks $172-185 adults, $166-178 children 3-9) celebrates much of what makes California special. If Disney is your only stop on this trip, but you'd like to get a sense of the state as a whole, this park can give you a little taste.

Disney California Adventure Park is divided into themed areas. You'll find two information booths just inside the main park entrance, one off to the left as you walk through the turnstile and one at the opening to Sunshine Plaza.

Rides

Monsters, Inc. Mike & Sully to the Rescue! invites guests into the action of the movie of the same name. You'll help the heroes as they chase the intrepid Boo. This ride jostles you around but is suitable for smaller kids as well as bigger ones.

Get a sample of the world of tiny insects on **It's Tough to Be a Bug!** This big-group, 3-D, multisensory ride offers fun for little kids and adults alike. You'll fly through the air, scuttle through the grass, and get a good idea of what life is like on six little legs.

For the littlest adventurers, **Flik's Fun Fair** offers almost half a dozen rides geared toward toddlers and little children. They can ride pint-size hot-air balloons known as Flik's Flyers, climb aboard a bug-themed train, or run around under a gigantic faucet to cool down after hours of hot fun.

Paradise Pier mimics the Santa Monica Pier, with thrill rides and an old-fashioned midway. **California Screamin'** is a high-tech roller coaster designed after the classic wooden coasters of carnivals past. This extra-long ride includes drops, twists, a full loop, and plenty of time and screaming fun. California Screamin' has a 4-foot (1.2-m) height requirement and is just as popular with nostalgic adults as with kids. **Toy Story Midway Mania!** magnifies the midway mayhem as passengers of all ages take aim at targets in a 4-D ride inspired by Disney-Pixar's *Toy Story.*

In **Condor Flats, Soarin' Over California** is a combination ride and show that puts you and dozens of other guests on the world's biggest "glider" and sets you off over the hills and valleys of California. Get Disney's version of a wilderness experience at **Grizzly Peak.** Enjoy a white-water raft ride through a landscape inspired by the Sierra Nevada foothills on the **Grizzly River Run.**

Cars Land was inspired by the hit 2006 film *Cars.* Float on larger-than-life tires on the **Luigi's Flying Tires** ride or be serenaded by Mater as you ride in a tractor on **Mater's Junkyard Jamboree.** The **Radiator Springs Racers** finds six-person vehicles passing locations and characters from *Cars* before culminating in a real-life race with a car of other park visitors.

Parades and Shows

Watch your favorite Pixar characters come to life in the **Pixar Play Parade.** Other regular shows are **Disney Junior—Live on Stage!** and **Disney's Aladdin—A Musical Spectacular.** Both of these shows hark back to favorite children's activities and movies. Check your park guide and *Time Guide* for more information about live shows.

Food

Disneyland

One of the few things the Mouse doesn't do too well is haute cuisine. For a truly good or healthy meal, get a hand stamp and go outside the park. But if you're stuck inside and you absolutely need sustenance, you can get it. The best areas of the park to grab a bite are Main Street, New Orleans, and Frontierland, but you can find at least a snack almost anywhere in the park.

For a sit-down restaurant meal inside the park, make reservations in advance for a table at the **Blue Bayou Restaurant** (New Orleans Square, 714/781-3463, $35-60). The best part about this restaurant is its setting in the dimly lit swamp overlooking the Pirates of the Caribbean ride. Appropriately, the Bayou has Cajun-ish cuisine and a reputation for being haunted. You will get large portions, and tasty desserts make a fine finish to your meal. Watch your silverware, though; the alleged ghosts in this restaurant like to mess around with diners' tableware.

Ever wanted to drink in the intergalactic bar featured in *Star Wars: A New Hope*? **Oga's Cantina** in Star Wars: Galaxy's Edge is the place to drink a very exotic cocktail among alien friends. There are also concoctions for kids. This is the first public establishment in Disneyland to sell alcohol. Be aware that most of the day the only food served here is a snack mix. Reservations can be made up to 60 days in advance.

Disney California Adventure Park

If you need a snack break in Disney California Adventure Park, you'll find most of the food clustered in the Golden State area. For a Mexican feast, try **Cocina**

Alternatives to the Mouse

Universal Studios Hollywood

The longtime Hollywood-centric alternative to Disneyland is the **Universal Studios Hollywood** (100 Universal City Plaza, Los Angeles, 800/864-8377, www.universalstudioshollywood.com, hours vary, $99-259) theme park. Kids adore this park, which puts them right into the action of their favorite movies. Flee the carnivorous dinosaurs of *Jurassic Park,* take a rafting adventure on the pseudo-set of *Waterworld,* or quiver in terror of an ancient curse in *Revenge of the Mummy.* A new favorite is to soar above Hogwarts in *The Wizarding World of Harry Potter.* If you're more interested in how the movies are made than the rides made from them, take the **Studio Tour.** You'll get an extreme close-up of the sets of major blockbuster films like *War of the Worlds.* Better yet, be part of the studio audience of TV shows currently taping by getting tickets at the Audiences Unlimited Ticket Booth. If you're a serious movie buff, consider buying a **VIP pass**—you'll get a six-hour tour that takes you onto working sound stages, into the current prop warehouse, and through a variety of working build shops that service movies and programs currently filming.

Six Flags Magic Mountain

Six Flags Magic Mountain (Magic Mountain Parkway, Valencia, 661/255-4100, www.sixflags.com, hours vary, $93 adults, $60 children, $25 parking) provides good fun for the whole family. Magic Mountain has long been the extreme alternative to the Mouse, offering a wide array of thrill rides. You'll need a strong stomach to deal with the g-forces of the major-league roller coasters and the death-defying drops, including the Lex Luthor: Drop of Doom, where you plummet 400 feet (122 m) at speeds up to 85 mph. For the younger set, plenty of rides offer a less intense but equally fun amusement-park experience. Both littler and bigger kids enjoy interacting with the classic Warner Bros. characters, especially in Bugs Bunny World, and a kids' show features Bugs Bunny, Donald Duck, and more. Other than that, Magic Mountain has little in the way of staged entertainment—this park is all about the rides. The park is divided into areas, just like most other major theme parks; get a map at the entrance to help you maneuver around and pick your favorite rides.

Knott's Berry Farm

For a taste of history along with some ultramodern thrill rides and plenty of cooling waterslides, head for **Knott's Berry Farm** (8039 Beach Blvd., Buena Park, 714/220-5200, www.knotts.com, hours vary, on-site ticket $89 adults and $59 children and seniors, online ticket $55 adults and $49 children and seniors, $15 parking). From the tall landmark GhostRider wooden coaster to the 30-story vertical-drop ride to the screaming Silver Bullet suspended coaster, Knott's supplies excitement to even the most hard-core ride lover. For the younger crowd, Camp Snoopy offers an array of pint-size rides and attractions, plus Snoopy and all the characters they love from the *Peanuts* comics and TV shows.

In the heat of the summer, many park visitors adjourn from the coasters to **Knott's Soak City** (www.soakcityoc.com, hours vary daily Memorial Day-Labor Day, on-site ticket $55 adults and $45 children and seniors, online ticket $46 adults, $39 children and seniors, $15-20 parking), a full-size water park with 22 rides, a kid pool and water playground, and plenty of space to enjoy the O.C. sunshine.

Cucamonga Mexican Grill ($10-15), which also serves margaritas and beers. For standards like sandwiches, salads, and burgers, go to the **Pacific Wharf Cafe** ($10-12) or **Smokejumpers Grill** ($10-14).

Unlike in Disneyland proper, in Disney California Adventure Park, responsible adults can quash their thirst with a variety of alcoholic beverages. If you're just dying for a cold beer, get one at **Bayside Brews.** Or, if you love the endless array of high-quality wines produced in the Golden State, head for **Mendocino Terrace,** where you can learn the basics of wine creation and production. Have a glass and a pseudo-Italian meal at the sit-down **Wine Country Trattoria at the Golden Vine Winery** (714/781-3463, $15-35).

Downtown Disney

Downtown Disney is outside the amusement parks and offers additional dining options, with some chains (Starbucks, Jamba Juice) and some unique restaurants. The most distinctive of them, **Ralph Brennan's Jazz Kitchen** (1590 S. Disneyland Dr., Anaheim, 714/776-5200, www.rbjazzkitchen.com, 11am-11pm Mon.-Sat., 10am-3pm and 4pm-11pm Sun., $15-35), is meant to replicate the experience of eating in New Orleans's French Quarter. The Cajun menu hits all the staples, including jambalaya, beignets, and various blackened meats and seafood.

For a SoCal craft beer experience, try **Ballast Point Brewing Company** (1540 Disneyland Dr., 714/687-9813, http://ballastpoint.com, 11am-8pm daily, $14-23), where you'll find the San Diego-based brewery's beers on tap. Pub fare, like fish tacos and burgers, is also served.

The Patina Restaurant Group runs **Catal Restaurant** (1580 Disneyland Dr., Anaheim, 714/774-4442, www.patinagroup.com, 8am-11am and 5pm-9pm daily, $15-35), with Mediterranean fare; **Naples Ristorante** (1550 Disneyland Dr., Anaheim, 714/776-6200, www.patinagroup.com, 8am-10pm daily, $15-35) for Italian food; and **Tortilla Jo's** (1510 Disneyland Dr., Anaheim, 714/535-5000, www.patinagroup.com, 11am-10pm Sun.-Thurs., 11am-11pm Fri.-Sat., $15-35) for Mexican food.

La Brea Bakery (1556 Disneyland Dr., Anaheim, 714/490-0233, www.labreabakery.com, 11am-11pm Mon.-Fri., 9am-11pm Sat.-Sun., $15-35) is the Disney outpost of an L.A. favorite. This bakery, founded by Nancy Silverton, supplies numerous markets and restaurants with crusty European-style loaves. The morning scones, sandwiches, and fancy cookies are superb.

Accommodations

The best way to get fully Disney-fied is to stay at one of the park's hotels.

Disney Hotels

For the most iconic Disney resort experience, you must stay at the **Disneyland Hotel** (1150 Magic Way, Anaheim, 714/778-6600, http://disneyland.disney.go.com, $460-1,016). This nearly 1,000-room high-rise monument to brand-specific family entertainment has everything a vacationing Brady-esque bunch could want: themed swimming pools, themed play areas, and even character-themed rooms that allow the kids to fully immerse themselves in the Mouse experience. Adults and families on a budget can also get rooms with either a king or two queen beds and more traditional motel fabrics and appointments. The monorail stops inside the hotel, offering guests the easiest way into the park proper without having to deal with parking or even walking.

It's easy to find the **Paradise Pier Hotel** (1717 S. Disneyland Dr., Anaheim, 714/999-0990, http://disneyland.disney.go.com, $344-952); it's that high-rise thing just outside Disney California Adventure Park. This hotel boasts what passes for affordable lodgings within walking distance of the parks. Rooms are cute, colorful, and clean; many have two doubles or queens to accommodate families or couples traveling together on a tighter budget. You'll find a (possibly refreshing) lack of Mickeys in the standard guest accommodations at the Paradise, which has the feel of a beach resort motel. After a day of wandering the park, relax by the rooftop pool.

Disney's Grand Californian Hotel and Spa (1600 S. Disneyland Dr., Anaheim, 714/635-2300, http://disneyland.disney.go.com, $417-1,477) is inside Disney California Adventure Park, attempting to mimic the famous Ahwahnee Lodge in Yosemite. While it doesn't quite succeed (much of what makes the Ahwahnee so great is its views), the big-beam construction and soaring common spaces do feel reminiscent of a great luxury lodge. The hotel is surrounded by gardens and has restaurants, a day spa, and shops attached on the ground floor; it can also get you right out into Downtown Disney and thence to the parks proper. Rooms here offer more luxury than the other Disney resorts, with dark woods and faux-craftsman details creating an attractive atmosphere. Get anything from a standard room that sleeps two up to spacious family suites with bunk beds that can easily handle six people. As with all Disney resorts, you can purchase tickets and a meal plan along with your hotel room (in fact, if you book via the website, they'll try to force you to do it that way).

Outside the Parks

Away from the Disneyland complex and surrounding area, the accommodations in Orange County run to chain motels with little character or distinctiveness, but the good news is that you can find a decent room for a reasonable price.

The **Hyatt Regency Orange County** (11999 Harbor Blvd., Garden Grove, 714/750-1234, http://orangecounty.hyatt.com, $129-289) in Garden Grove is about 1.5 miles (2.4 km), a 10 minutes' drive on Harbor Boulevard, south of the park. The family-friendly suites have separate bedrooms with bunk beds and fun decor geared toward younger guests. Enjoy a cocktail in the sun-drenched atrium, or grab a chaise lounge by the pool or take a refreshing dip.

Information and Services

Each park has information booths near the park entrance. On the website for **Visit Anaheim** (714/765-2800, http://visitanaheim.org), you can plan a trip to the area in advance by looking at the upcoming events and suggested itineraries or by downloading the travel guide.

If you need to stow your bags or hit the restroom before plunging into the fray, banks of lockers and restrooms sit in the main entrance area. If mobility is a problem, consider renting a **stroller, wheelchair,** or **scooter.** Ask for directions to the rental counter when you enter the park.

Disneyland offers its own minor medical facilities, which can dispense first aid for scrapes, cuts, and mild heat exhaustion. They can also call an ambulance if something nastier has occurred. The **West Anaheim Medical Center** (3033 W. Orange Ave., Anaheim, 714/827-3000, www.westanaheimmedctr.com) is a full-service hospital with an emergency room.

Long Beach and Orange County Beaches

The Los Angeles coastline continues beyond the city limits, passing the Palos Verdes Peninsula and stretching farther south to Long Beach, where haunted ships and sunny coasts await.

The Orange County coast begins at Huntington Beach and stretches south across a collection of sunny, scenic beach towns (Newport Beach, Laguna Beach, and Dana Point) until ending at San Juan Capistrano. The surf here is world-renowned. If you've ever seen a surf magazine or surf movie, you've seen surfers ripping Orange County breaks like Salt Creek and Trestles.

Long Beach

Long Beach has several worthy attractions befitting its size, including the historic and possibly haunted *Queen Mary* ocean liner and the Aquarium of the Pacific. Long Beach Harbor is also one of the best places to catch a boat ride out to Catalina Island, about 22 miles (35 km) from shore.

Getting There

Long Beach is about 25 miles (40 km) directly south of downtown Los Angeles. Head down **I-5 South** for 2 miles (3.2 km) and then merge onto **I-710 South** toward Long Beach. Stay on the roadway for 17 miles (27 km), then turn off on Exit 1C for the downtown area and the aquarium.

Long Beach is just 20 miles (32 km) from Disneyland Resort. Take **CA-22 West** from Disneyland for 12 miles (19.3 km). The roadway turns into Long Beach's East 7th Street, with will take you to the Long Beach city center.

While you can get to the coast easily enough from LAX, the **Long Beach Airport** (LGB, 4100 Donald Douglas Dr., 562/570-2600, www.longbeach.gov/lgb) is both closer to Long Beach and less crowded than LAX.

Sights

★ The *Queen Mary*

The major visitor attraction of Long Beach is **The *Queen Mary*** (1126 Queens Hwy., 877/342-0738, www.queenmary.com, call for hours, $18-35 admission, parking with validation $10 day use, $25 overnight), one of the most famous ships ever to ply the high seas. This great ship, once a magnificent pleasure-cruise liner, now sits at permanent anchor in Long Beach Harbor. The *Queen Mary* acts as a museum—describing the history of the ship, which took its maiden voyage in 1936, with special emphasis on its tour of duty as a troop transport during World War II—and an entertainment center featuring several restaurants and bars. Other features include a *Queen Mary* model made out of 250,000 LEGO bricks and a film showing in a 4-D theater. The *Queen Mary* is also a **hotel** (877/342-0742, $120-499). Book a stateroom and stay aboard, come for dinner, or just buy a regular ticket and take a self-guided tour.

It's not just the extensive museum and the attractive hotel that make the *Queen Mary* well known today. The ship is also one of the most famously haunted places in California. Over its decades of service, a number of people lost their lives aboard the *Queen Mary*. Rumors say several of these unfortunate souls have remained on the ship since their tragic deaths.

Various tours (for additional fees) focusing on the ship's history as well as its paranormal activity are available; check the website for the most up-to-date offerings.

The *Queen Mary* offers a large paid parking lot near the ship's berth. You'll walk from the parking area up to a square with a ticket booth and several shops and a snack bar. Purchase your general-admission ticket to get on board the ship. It's also a good idea to buy any

Side Trip to Catalina Island

Catalina Island

You can see Catalina from the shore of Long Beach on a clear day, but for a better view, you've got to get onto the island. The port town of Avalon welcomes visitors with Mediterranean-inspired hotels, restaurants, and shops. But the main draw of Catalina lies outside the walls of its buildings. Catalina beckons hikers, horseback riders, ecotourists, and, most of all, water lovers.

The **Catalina Casino** (1 Casino Way, www.visitcatalinaisland.com) is a round, white art deco building, opened in 1929 not for gambling but as a community gathering place. Today, it hosts diverse activities, including the Catalina Island Jazz Festival. You

guided tour tickets at this point. Night tours can fill up in advance, so call ahead to reserve a spot.

Aquarium of the Pacific

The **Aquarium of the Pacific** (100 Aquarium Way, 562/590-3100, www.aquariumofpacific.org, 9am-6pm daily, $35 adults, $32 seniors, $25 children) hosts animals and plant life native to the Pacific Ocean, from the local residents of SoCal's sea up to the northern Pacific and down to the tropics. The large modern building includes a new bright-blue Pacific Visions wing. You'll find sea stars, urchins, and rays in touch-friendly tanks, and a Shark Lagoon where you can pet a few of the more than 150 sharks that live here. Go deeper with the aquarium's **Behind the Scenes Tour** (reservations 562/590-3100 ext. 0, $19 pp).

Food

Combining elegance, fine continental-California cuisine, and great ghost stories, **Sir Winston's Restaurant and Lounge** (1126 Queens Hwy., 562/499-1657, www.queenmary.com, 5pm-9pm Tues.-Thurs., 5pm-10pm Fri.-Sat., $30-78) floats gently on board the *Queen Mary*. For the most beautiful dining experience, request a window table and make reservations for sunset. Dress in your finest; Sir Winston's requests that diners adhere to their semiformal dress code.

A locals' favorite down where the shops and cafés cluster, **Natraj Cuisine of India** (5262 E. 2nd St., 562/930-0930, www.natrajlongbeach.com, 10:30am-10pm Tues.-Thurs. and Sun., 10:30am-11pm Fri.-Sat., $12-20) offers good food for reasonable prices. Come by for the can also take a tour of the casino, which includes a movie theater, and hear tales of Hollywood stars here on a 90-minute **tour** (310/510-0179, $30 adults, $28 children and seniors).

Stroll through the serene **Wrigley Memorial and Botanical Garden** (Avalon Canyon Rd., 1.5 mi/2.4 km west of town, 310/510-2897, www.catalinaconservancy.org, 8am-5pm daily, $8 adults, $6 seniors, $4 students and children, children under 5 and active military free) in the hills above Avalon.

Outdoor recreation is the main draw. Swim or snorkel at the **Avalon Underwater Park** (Casino Point). A protected section at the north end of town offers access to a reef with plentiful sea life, including bright orange garibaldi fish. Out at the deeper edge of the park, nearly half a dozen wrecked ships await exploration. For a guided snorkel or scuba tour, visit **Diving Catalina** (310/510-8558, http://divingcatalina.com). If you need snorkeling gear, hit up **Wet Spot Rentals** (120 Pebbly Beach Rd., 310/510-2229, www.wetspotrentals.com, snorkel gear $10 per hour, $20 per day).

Jeep Eco-Tours (310/510-2595, www.catalinaconservancy.org, chartered half-day $79-119) will take you out into the wilderness to see bison, wild horses, and plant species unique to the island.

The best dining option is **The Lobster Trap** (128 Catalina St., 310/510-8585, www.catalinalobstertrap.com, 11am-late daily, $14-44), which serves up its namesake crustacean in various forms, along with other seafood.

Getting There

The **Catalina Express** (310/519-1212, www.catalinaexpress.com, round-trip: $74.50-76.50 adults, $68-70 seniors, $59-61 children 2-11, $6 children under 2, $7 bikes and surfboards) offers multiple ferry trips every day, even in the off-season. During the summer, you can depart from Long Beach, San Pedro, or Dana Point. Bring your bike, your luggage, and your camping gear aboard for the hour-long ride.

all-you-can-eat lunch buffet Monday-Saturday to sample a variety of properly spiced meat and vegetarian dishes created in classic Indian tradition.

Accommodations

The Varden (335 Pacific Ave., 562/432-8950, www.thevardenhotel.com, $149-199) offers the type of tiny, clean, and modern rooms you'd expect to find in Europe. If you don't mind your bath being a foot or two from your bed, the sleek little rooms in this hotel, which dates back to 1929, are a great deal. The oldest operating hotel in Long Beach, it is named after an eccentric circus performer named Dolly Varden, who is rumored to have hoarded jewels on the premises. The staff is friendly and helpful, and coffee, ice, and fresh fruit are available to guests 24 hours a day. It's also one block from Pine Street, which is lined with restaurants and bars.

Looking for something completely different? At **Dockside Boat and Bed** (Dock 5A, Rainbow Harbor, 562/436-3111, www.boatandbed.com, $220-350, overnight parking $10-24, unless you get the $10 discount parking pass from Dockside), you won't get a regular old hotel room, you'll get one of five yachts. The yachts run 38-54 feet (11.6-16.5 m) and can sleep four or more people each ($25 pp after the first 2). Amenities include TVs with DVD players, stereos, kitchen facilities, wet bars, and ample seating. The boats are in walking distance from the harbor's restaurants and the aquarium. Don't expect to take your floating accommodations out for a spin; these yachts are permanent residents of Rainbow Harbor.

Information and Services

For information, maps, brochures, and advice about Long Beach and the surrounding areas, visit the **Long Beach Convention and Visitors Bureau** (301 E. Ocean Blvd., Ste. 1900, 562/436-3645, www.visitlongbeach.com, 8am-5pm Mon.-Fri.).

Huntington Beach

This Orange County beach town is known for its longtime association with surfing and surf culture, beginning when Hawaiian legend Duke Kahanamoku first rode waves here back in 1922. Surfers still ride the surf on either side of the **Huntington Beach Pier,** a large concrete pier that offers fine views of the beach scene on both sides. Across the Pacific Coast Highway, Huntington Beach's Main Street is full of restaurants, bars, and shops, including lots of surf shops.

Getting There

It can take just 45 minutes to get to Huntington Beach from central Los Angeles. Take **I-5 South** out of downtown for 9 miles (14.5 km). Then get on **I-605 South** for 11 miles (17.7 km) before merging onto **I-405 South.** Take the Seal Beach Boulevard exit from I-405 and turn left on Seal Beach Boulevard. After 2.5 miles (4 km), turn left on the **Pacific Coast Highway,** which you'll take for 8 miles (12.9 km) to Huntington Beach.

Huntington Beach is one of the closest beaches to Disneyland, just 16 miles (26 km) away. From Disneyland, get on **CA-22 West** for 4 miles (6.4 km) and then turn on the Beach Boulevard exit. Take Beach Boulevard (CA-39) for 8 miles (12.9 km) to Huntington Beach.

The beach route between Long Beach and Huntington Beach is the **Pacific Coast Highway (CA-1).** Take it south out of Long Beach for 9.6 miles (15.4 km) to reach Huntington Beach. If it's a crowded beach weekend, hop on **CA-22 East** to reach **I-405 South.** Continue for 6.8 miles (10.9 km) to the CA-39/Beach Boulevard exit and follow the road to the beach.

Beaches

Huntington City Beach (Pacific Coast Hwy. from Beach Blvd. to Seapoint St., beach headquarters 103 Pacific Coast Hwy., 714/536-5281, www.huntingtonbeachca.gov, beach 5am-10pm daily, office 8am-5pm Mon.-Fri.) runs the length of the south end of town, petering out toward the oil industry facilities at the north end. This famous beach hosts major sporting events such as the U.S. Open of Surfing and the X Games. But even the average beachgoer can enjoy all sorts of activities on a daily basis, from sunbathing to beach volleyball, skim-boarding to surfing; a free recorded surf report is also available for the beach (714/536-9303). There's a cement walkway for biking, in-line skating, jogging, and walking. Plus, you'll find a dog-friendly section at the north end of the beach where dogs can be let off-leash.

Food

The Black Trumpet Bistro (18344 Beach Blvd., 714/842-1122, www.theblacktrumpetbistro.com, 11:30am-10pm Tues.-Fri., 4pm-10pm Sat., 4pm-9pm Sun., $12-23) has paintings of jazz legends adorning the walls. The owner wants to represent Mediterranean cuisine from tapas to more substantial entrées. His endeavor has caused The Black Trumpet to be proclaimed one of Huntington Beach's best restaurants by the *OC Weekly.*

For a quick bite to eat, stop off at the **Bodhi Tree Vegetarian Cafe** (501 Main St., Ste. E, 714/969-9500, 11am-10pm Mon. and Wed.-Sun., $6-10) for vegetarian soups, salads, and sandwiches. **Sugar Shack Café** (213 Main St., 714/536-0355, www.hbsugarshack.com, 6am-2pm Mon.-Fri., 6am-3pm Sat.-Sun., $7-10) is a great place for breakfast, serving omelets and breakfast burritos.

Accommodations

The 17-room **Sun 'n Sands Motel** (1102 Pacific Coast Hwy., 714/536-2543, www.sunnsands.com, $249-399) is a tiny place where you can expect the standard motel room, but the main attraction is across the treacherous Pacific Coast Highway: long, sweet Huntington Beach. Be careful crossing the highway to get to the sand. Find a traffic light and a crosswalk rather than risking life and limb for the minor convenience of jaywalking.

For something more upscale, book a room at the **Shorebreak Hotel** (500 Pacific Coast Hwy., 714/861-4470, www.shorebreakhotel.com, $329-749). Some rooms have private balconies looking out over the beach and pier. Everyone can enjoy the hotel's on-site restaurant, fitness center, and courtyard with fire pits.

Information and Services

Get assistance at the **Huntington Beach Marketing and Visitors Bureau** (155 Fifth St., Ste. 111, 714/969-3492, www.surfcityusa.com), which also has a visitor information kiosk in front of the Huntington Beach Pier (325 Pacific Coast Hwy., 10:30am-7pm Mon.-Fri., 10am-7pm Sat.-Sun. summer, noon-5pm Mon.-Fri., 11am-5pm Sat.-Sun. winter). Huntington Beach has a **post office** (316 Olive Ave., 714/536-4973, www.usps.com, 9am-5pm Mon.-Fri.) and the **Huntington Beach Hospital** (17772 Beach Blvd., 714/843-5000, www.hbhospital.org).

Newport Beach

Affluent Newport Beach is known for its beaches, harbor, and The Wedge, a notorious bodysurfing and bodyboarding wave.

Getting There

It takes less than an hour to drive the 40 miles (64 km) between the L.A. city center and Newport Beach. Disneyland is even closer, just 26 miles (42 km). From either starting point, take **I-5 South** and then merge onto **CA-55 South,** which leads the remaining 10 miles (16.1 km) into town. From Huntington Beach, Newport Beach is just a 5-mile (8-km) drive on the **Pacific Coast Highway (CA-1).**

Beaches

Most of the activity in **Newport Beach** (www.visitnewportbeach.com) centers around Newport Pier (McFadden Pl.) and Main Street on the Balboa Peninsula. This 10-mile (16.1-km) stretch of sand is popular for fishing, swimming, surfing, and other ocean activities. On the east end of Balboa Peninsula, **The Wedge** is the world's most famous bodysurfing spot. On south swells, the wave jacks up off the adjacent rock jetty and creates monsters up to 30 feet (9.1 m) high that break almost right on the beach. Beginners should stay out of the water and enjoy the spectacle from the sand.

Food

For something French, colorful **Pescadou Bistro** (3325 Newport Blvd., 949/675-6990, www.pescadoubistro.com, 5:30pm-9pm Tues.-Sun., $21-36) fills the bill. Meanwhile, **Eat Chow** (211 62nd St., 949/423-7080, www.eatchownow.com, 9am-8pm Mon.-Fri., 8am-8pm Sat.-Sun., $9-18) is a local favorite, with items like breakfast *carnitas* tacos and braised short rib burritos.

Expect a line outside **Cappy's Café & Cantina** (5930 W. Coast Hwy., 949/646-4202, 7am-2pm Thurs.-Tues., 8am-8pm Wed., $10-20), a low-slung building that has served breakfast and lunch since 1957. Cappy's serves expand-your-waistband items including a 20-ounce porterhouse steak and eggs and a knockwurst and eggs dish. Enjoy the fare while mellowing out in a beachy atmosphere with plenty of colorful murals.

Accommodations

South of downtown Newport Beach, the **Crystal Cove Beach Cottages** (35 Crystal Cove, 949/376-6200, http://crystalcove.

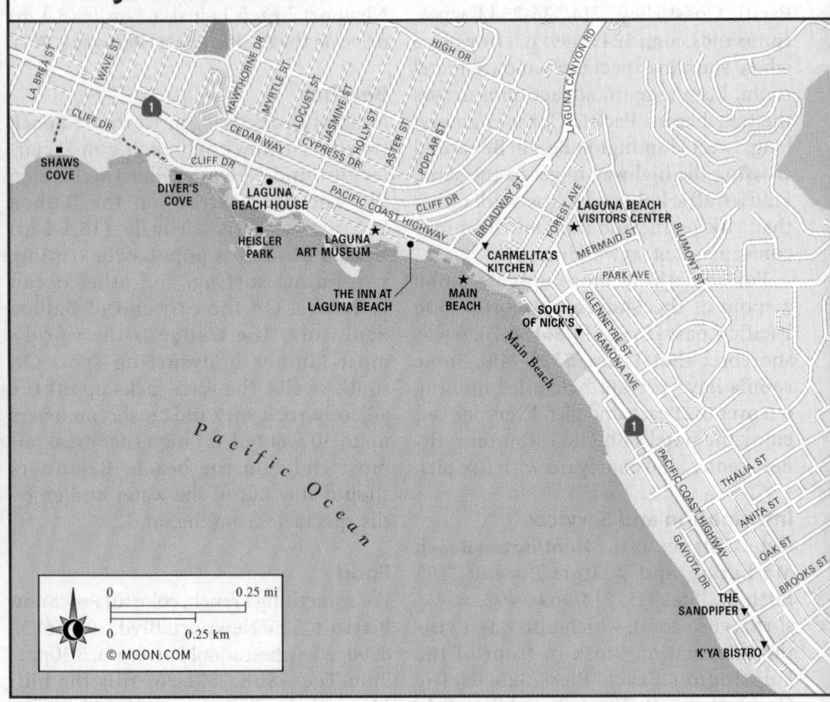

org, reservations 800/444-7275 or www.reservecalifornia.com, dorms $37-122, cottages $185-261) give anyone the opportunity to experience life right on the Southern California sand. Some of the cabins are individual rentals that you can have all to yourself. The dorm cottages offer by-the-room accommodations for solo travelers (linens included; room doors lock). None of the cottages have TVs or any type of digital entertainment. And all the cottages include a common refrigerator and microwave, but no full kitchen, so plan to eat out, perhaps at the adjacent **Beachcomber Cafe** (15 Crystal Cove, 949/376-6900, www.thebeachcombercafe.com, 7am-9pm Sun.-Thurs., 7am-10pm Fri.-Sat., $18-37), where items like breakfast chilaquiles and crab-stuffed salmon are served.

Laguna Beach Area

Laguna Beach stands apart from other Orange County beach communities with its long-running arts scene, touted fine-dining restaurants, tide-pool-pocked coastline jammed between sandy beaches, and clear ocean water that beckons snorkelers and divers underwater.

Getting There

Laguna Beach is just 50 miles (81 km) from central Los Angeles, although the highway traffic may make the drive feel a lot longer. Take **I-5 South** for 37 miles (60 km) and then get on **CA-133 South** for 9.5 miles (15.3 km) into town.

If I-5 is jammed up, there's an **alternate route,** but it involves a **toll road,** CA-73, that requires electronic payment. You can register an account or pay a one-time fee online at www.thetollroads.com. From

I-5 South, merge onto **I-605 South,** following it for 11 miles (17.7 km). Then take **I-405 South** for 14 miles (22.5 km). From there, take **CA-73 South** for 11 miles (17.7 km). Exit on **CA-133** (Laguna Canyon Rd.) and take a right to drive a few miles into Laguna Beach.

The drive from Disneyland to Laguna Beach is only 30 minutes without traffic. Just take **I-5 South** for 13 miles (21 km) and then get on **CA-133 South** for 10 miles (16.1 km). Laguna Beach is an 11-mile (17.7-km) drive south of Newport Beach on the **Pacific Coast Highway (CA-1).**

Beaches

Heisler Park and **Main Beach Park** (Pacific Coast Hwy., Laguna Beach, www.lagunabeachinfo.com) offer protected waterways, with tide pools and plenty of water-based playground equipment. The two parks are connected, so you can walk from one to the other. If you're into scuba diving, there are several reefs right off the beach. You'll find all the facilities and amenities you need at Heisler and Main Beach Parks, including picnic tables, lawns, and restrooms. Park on the street if you find a spot, but the meters get checked all the time, so feed them well.

Laguna Beach has a lot more undeveloped space than other Orange County communities, and **Crystal Cove State Park** (8471 N. Coast Hwy., 949/494-3539, www.crystalcovestatepark.org, 6am-sunset daily, $15 per vehicle) just north of town has 3.2 miles (5.1 km) of lightly developed coastline with sandy coves and tide pools. Offshore is the Crystal Cove Underwater Park, which has several snorkeling and diving sites. The park also includes a 2,400-acre (971-ha) inland section with unpaved roads and trails that are open to hikers, bikers, and horseback riders.

At the southern tip of the O.C., Dana Point has a **harbor** (24800 Dana Point Harbor Dr., 949/248-3555, www.danapoint.org) that has become a recreation marina that draws locals and visitors from all around. It also has several beaches nearby.

Also in Dana Point, **Doheny State Beach** (25300 Dana Point Harbor Dr., 949/496-6171, www.parks.ca.gov, 6am-10pm daily, $15) is popular with surfers and anglers. The northern end of Doheny has a lawn along with volleyball courts, while the southern side has a popular campground with 121 campsites.

Visit **Salt Creek Beach** (33333 S. Pacific Coast Hwy., 949/923-2280, www.ocparks.com, 5am-midnight daily, parking $1 per hour) for a renowned surf break and a great place to spend a day in the sun.

Entertainment

The Sandpiper (1183 S. Coast Hwy., 949/494-4694, 1pm-2am daily), known locally as "The Dirty Bird," has been Laguna Beach's favorite dive bar since the 1940s. Boasting live music nightly and open every day of the year until 2am, this unassuming spot used to be a favorite watering hole of Dennis Rodman, although these days you'll probably just encounter one of the reality TV stars of *The Real Housewives of Orange County.*

Food

Carmelita's Kitchen De Mexico (217 Broadway, 949/715-7829, www.carmelitaskdm.com, 11am-10pm Mon.-Fri., 9am-10pm Sat., 9am-9pm Sun., $14-28) is a popular local favorite serving upscale Mexican cuisine. The open kitchen puts out terrific entrées including *tampiqueña* (marinated skirt steak) and a seafood trio platter with a lobster enchilada, shrimp taco, and crab relleno. Carmelita's also does some twists on the classic margarita, with cilantro-cucumber and strawberry-jalapeño versions.

Ideal for a shareable meal and a drink, **K'ya Bistro** (1287 S. Coast Hwy., 949/376-9718, www.kayabistro.com, 5pm-9pm daily, $10-15) serves tapas, seafood, and meats with a Mediterranean slant. Its popular happy hour (5pm-6pm daily)

allows for half-off a menu item with every alcoholic beverage purchase. May we recommend the fruit mojitos?

South of Nick's (540 S. Coast Hwy., 949/715-3717, www.nicksrestaurants.com, 11am-10pm Mon.-Thurs., 11am-11pm Fri.-Sat., 10am-10pm Sun., $10-38) offers a menu with an upscale Mexican twist. The bar keeps up with the kitchen's creativity by serving up regular margaritas as well as coconut and cucumber versions.

Accommodations

Perched on a bluff over Laguna Beach's Main Beach, **The Inn at Laguna Beach** (211 N. Pacific Coast Hwy., 800/544-4479, $219-1,199) is the ideal place to stay for an upscale beach vacation. Half of its rooms face the ocean, and a majority of those have balconies to take in the salt air and sound of the sea. Hit up the inn's beach valet for complimentary beach umbrellas, chairs, and towels. After time on Main Beach, retire to the inn's brick pool deck with its pool and hot tub, or head up to the rooftop terrace and warm up by the fire pit.

The **Laguna Beach House** (475 N. Pacific Coast Hwy., 800/297-0007, www.thelagunabeachhouse.com, $165-399) is a casual, surfing-obsessed motel geared toward wave riders and surf-culture aficionados, with killer decor (including a surfboard shaped by the owner) in each of its 36 rooms and a daily surf report written up on a chalkboard in the lobby. The U-shaped structure surrounds a pool deck with pool, hot tub, and fire pit. Before hitting the waves, enjoy a complimentary breakfast parfait and coffee put out in the lobby.

The **Blue Lantern Inn** (34343 Street of the Blue Lantern, Dana Point, 800/950-1236, www.bluelanterninn.com, $300-799) crowns the bluffs over the Dana

From top to bottom: the *Queen Mary* in Long Beach; The Inn at Laguna Beach's pool deck; view from Blue Lantern Inn.

Point Harbor. This attractive contemporary inn offers beachfront elegance in 29 rooms boasting soothing colors, charming appointments, and lush amenities, including a spa tub in every bath, gas fireplaces, and honest-to-goodness free drinks in the mini fridge; some feature patios or balconies with impressive views of the harbor and the Pacific. The inn also offers complimentary bike usage and breakfast.

Stay in a historic and stunning Spanish colonial villa at the **Beachcomber Inn** (533 Avenida Victoria, San Clemente, 949/492-5457, http://thebeachcomberinn.com, $255-450). The 13 standard villas and two deluxe villas all come with porches, full kitchens, and full views of the ocean, the beach, and the pier.

Getting Around

The **Orange County Transportation Authority** (OCTA, 714/636-7433, www.octa.net, one trip $2, day pass $5) runs buses along the O.C. coast. The appropriately numbered **Route 1** bus runs right along the Pacific Coast Highway (CA-1) from Long Beach down to San Clemente and back. Other routes can get you to and from inland O.C. destinations, including Anaheim. Regular bus fares are payable in cash on the bus with exact change. You can also buy a day pass from the bus driver.

The one true highway on the O.C. coast is the **Pacific Coast Highway,** often called "PCH" for short and officially designated **CA-1.** You can get to PCH from **I-405** near Seal Beach, or catch **I-710** to Long Beach and then drive south from there. From Disneyland, take **I-5** to **CA-55,** which takes you into Newport Beach. If you stay on I-5 going south, you'll eventually find yourself in San Juan Capistrano.

Parking along the beaches of the O.C. on a sunny summer day has been compared to one of Dante's circles of hell. You're far better off staying near the beach and walking out to your perfect spot in the sand. Other options include public transit and paid parking.

The **Laguna Beach Trolley** (949/497-0766, www.lagunatrolley.com, daily summer, Fri.-Sun. fall-spring, free) offers free transportation in Laguna Beach's downtown and coastal areas.

Pacific
Coast
Highway

Pacific Coast Highway

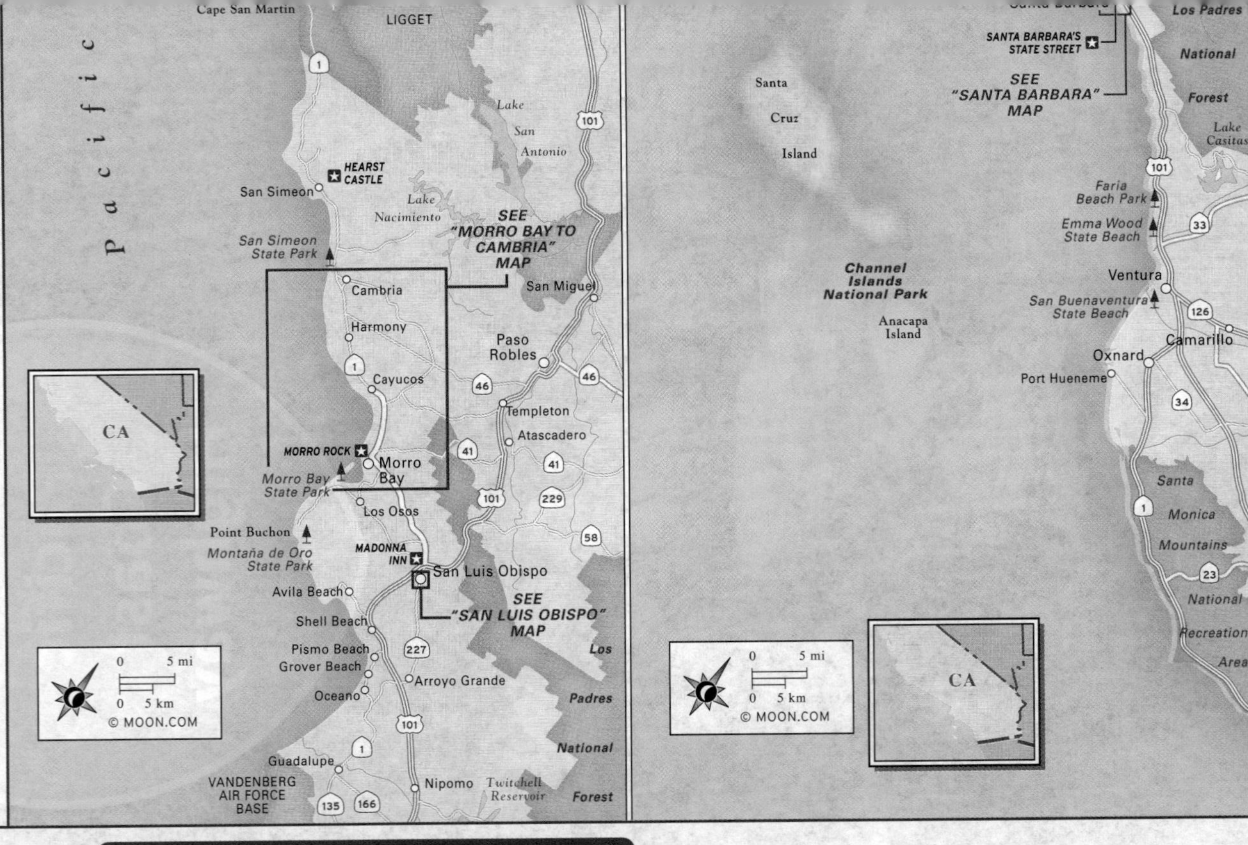

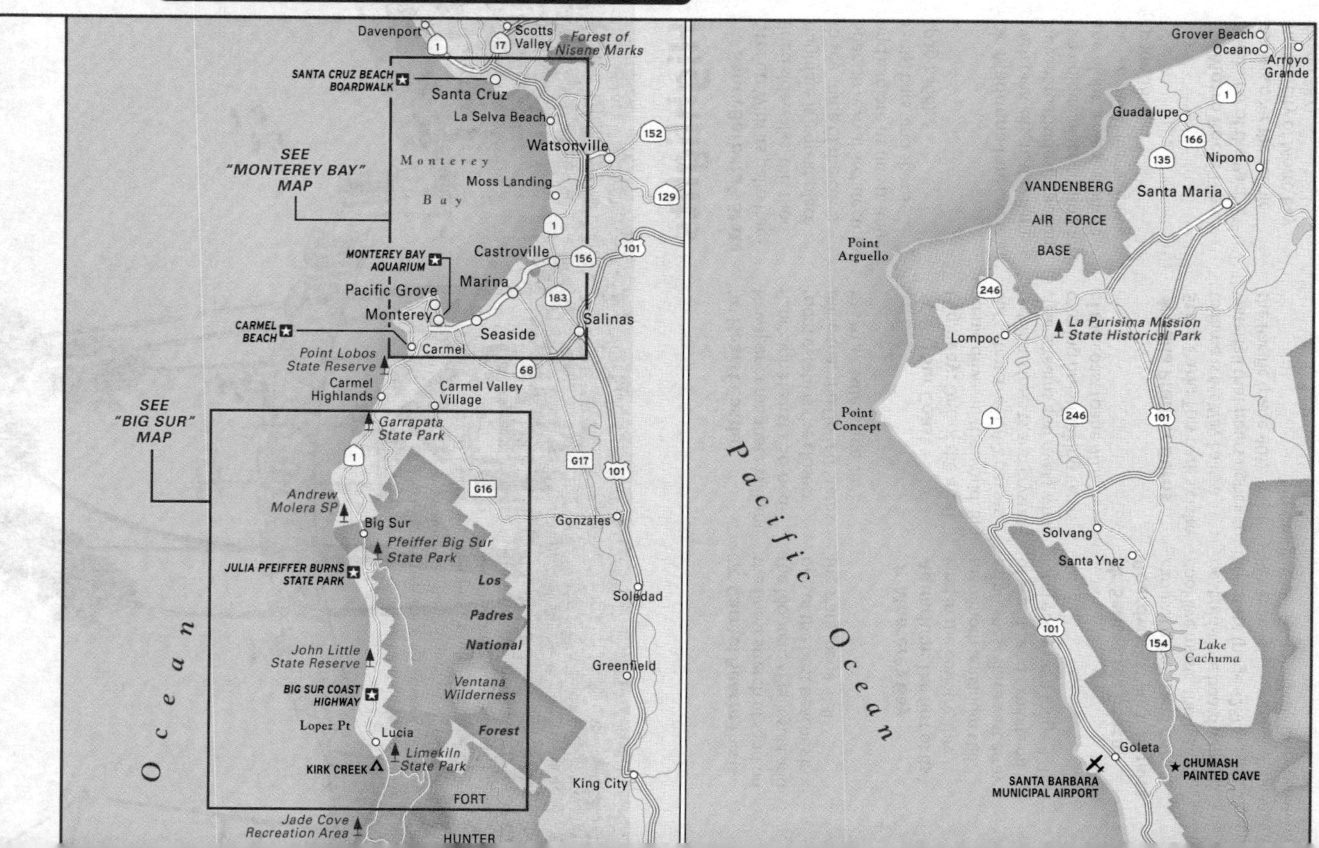
Davenport
Scotts Valley
Forest of Nisene Marks
SANTA CRUZ BEACH BOARDWALK
Santa Cruz
La Selva Beach
Watsonville
SEE "MONTEREY BAY" MAP
Monterey Bay
Moss Landing
MONTEREY BAY AQUARIUM
Castroville
Marina
Pacific Grove
Monterey
Salinas
CARMEL BEACH
Carmel
Seaside
Point Lobos State Reserve
Carmel Highlands
Carmel Valley Village
SEE "BIG SUR" MAP
Garrapata State Park
Andrew Molera SP
Big Sur
Pfeiffer Big Sur State Park
Gonzales
JULIA PFEIFFER BURNS STATE PARK
Los Padres National Forest
Soledad
John Little State Reserve
Ventana Wilderness
Greenfield
BIG SUR COAST HIGHWAY
Lopez Pt
Lucia
Limekiln State Park
KIRK CREEK
King City
FORT HUNTER
Jade Cove Recreation Area
Ocean
1
17
152
129
156
101
183
68
G17
G16
Grover Beach
Oceano
Arroyo Grande
Guadalupe
166
135
Nipomo
VANDENBERG AIR FORCE BASE
Santa Maria
Point Arguello
246
Lompoc
La Purisima Mission State Historical Park
Point Concept
Pacific Ocean
Solvang
Santa Ynez
154
Lake Cachuma
Goleta
SANTA BARBARA MUNICIPAL AIRPORT
CHUMASH PAINTED CAVE

Highlights

★ **Santa Barbara's State Street:** With its palm tree-lined sidewalks, this thoroughfare is a great place to see some of the city's Spanish revival architecture and explore its fine restaurants, bars, and shops (page 368).

★ **Madonna Inn:** Overrun with pink kitsch, this flamboyant roadside attraction is a unique place to stop for the night, a meal, a photo-op—or even just to gawk (page 381).

★ **Morro Rock:** The "Gibraltar of the Pacific" towers over the scenic harbor city of Morro Bay (page 387).

★ **Hearst Castle:** Newspaper magnate William Randolph Hearst's 56-bedroom estate is the closest thing that the United States has to a castle (page 397).

★ **Big Sur Coast Highway:** One of the most scenic drives in the world, Big Sur's stretch of CA-1 passes redwood forests and crystal-clear streams and rivers while offering breathtaking views of the coast (page 401).

★ **Julia Pfeiffer Burns State Park:** This park's claim to fame is McWay Falls, a waterfall that pours right into the Pacific (page 401).

★ **Carmel Beach:** This is the finest stretch of sand on the Monterey Peninsula and one of the best beaches in the state (page 413).

★ **Monterey Bay Aquarium:** The first of its kind in the country, this mammoth aquarium still astonishes with a vast array of sea life and exhibits on the local ecosystem (page 421).

★ **Santa Cruz Beach Boardwalk:** With thrill rides, carnival games, and retro-cool live music, this is the best old-time boardwalk in the state (page 428).

Never far from the ocean, PCH twists and turns through coastal cities and surf towns. This is the edge of the continent—where it dramatically meets the sea.

The Pacific Coast Highway is one of the world's best drives. The route itself is sometimes a highway, sometimes a city street, and often a slow, winding roadway. It all begins with Ventura and Santa Barbara, two coastal cities that enjoy the near-perfect Southern California climate without the sprawl of nearby Los Angeles. Following the coastline's contours up past Point Conception, the roadway is dotted with the communities of San Luis Obispo, Morro Bay, and Cambria. These unassuming towns make ideal stops for road-trippers, especially those who want to explore some of the state's best beaches. Head out on a kayak or try your hand at surfing. And nearby is one of California's most popular attractions: opulent Hearst Castle.

Big Sur is the standout section of the drive along PCH. The roadway perches between steep coastal mountains and the Pacific and snakes through groves of redwood trees, passing by beaches, waterfalls, and state parks along the way. North of Big Sur, the highway straightens, heading into the Monterey Peninsula. There you'll find Carmel, with its stunning white-sand beach, and the cannery town turned tourist magnet Monterey. The north end of the Monterey Bay is the location of the quirky surf town Santa Cruz. Enjoy the mild but worthwhile thrills of the Santa Cruz Beach Boardwalk, a seaside amusement park that has been operating since 1907.

The final leg up the coast from Santa Cruz to San Francisco has plenty of wide-open space. Its coastal terraces are punctuated by surprisingly undeveloped towns like Half Moon Bay. These are ideal places to indulge in some hiking, surfing, or kayaking before returning to the urban atmosphere of San Francisco.

Driving PCH

The drive from **Los Angeles** to **San Francisco** on the **Pacific Coast Highway (CA-1)** is **roughly 500 miles (805 km).** This can take eight hours or longer depending on traffic (and you should expect traffic, especially as you enter or leave the Los Angeles and San Francisco metropolitan areas). While you can drive straight through in one day, it's worth planning on spending two days so that you can slow down and make some stops along the way. Some of California's best attractions (**Hearst Castle, Monterey Bay Aquarium**) are along this route, not to mention its best beaches and scenery. Of course, the route can also be driven in the opposite direction, from San Francisco to Los Angeles, if that works better for your road trip.

The pleasant city of **San Luis Obispo,** halfway between the two cities, is right on CA-1 and US-101, making it a good place to stop for the night. It is a little closer to Los Angeles; expect the 201-mile (320-km) drive from the city to take three hours if traffic isn't bad. The drive up to San Francisco is 232 miles (370 km) and will take about four hours or more. The coastal towns of **Morro Bay** (15 mi/24 km north of San Luis Obispo) and **Cambria** (30 mi/48 km north of San Luis Obispo) on CA-1 are also fine places to lay your head.

Best Restaurants

★ **Spencer Makenzie's Fish Company:** Fans of fish tacos should flock to Ventura for a stellar sushi-grade, Baja-style version (page 364).

★ **La Super-Rica Taqueria:** There are many authentic Mexican taquerias in California, but this one in Santa Barbara—touted by Julia Childs and the *New York Times*—is destination-worthy (page 378).

★ **Firestone Grill:** The tri-tip steak cut is a glorious Central Coast invention and no one does it better (in sandwich form) than this San Luis Obispo staple (page 385).

★ **Sea Chest Oyster Bar:** Feet away from Cambria's Moonstone Beach, this homey spot serves up oysters, clams, and other delicious seafood (page 395).

★ **Nepenthe:** This restaurant is also one of Big Sur's biggest attractions; come for a sunset dinner and drink on its large outdoor deck and you'll learn why. If there's a line, head below to the restaurant's more casual **Café Kevah,** which also has an outdoor terrace (page 407).

★ **Hula's Island Grill:** A lively atmosphere and menu with South Pacific flair, including potent tropical cocktails, make this one of Monterey's best restaurants for a good time (page 426).

★ **Passionfish:** This longtime Monterey Peninsula fine dining restaurant serves up seafood with a side of sustainability (page 426).

★ **Sam's Chowder House:** This classic seafood restaurant in Half Moon Bay offers oceanfront dining indoors and outdoors and serves everything from clam chowder to lobster rolls (page 438).

Ventura

Ventura is short for San Buenaventura, which means "city of good fortune." There is much that is good about Ventura, including its weather (daytime temperatures average 70°F/21°C), consistent waves for surfers, and a historic downtown. Downtown Ventura is compact and easy to walk around; it is three blocks from the beach and still feels somehow unfettered by "progress," with buildings that date to the 1800s (a long time by California standards).

In recent years, the city has encouraged the growth of an impressive arts community and a thriving restaurant scene. A few blocks from Main Street is Surfer's Point, a coastal area also known as C Street. A ribbon of pavement by the ocean, the Omer Rains Bike Trail almost always hosts a collection of walkers, runners, and cyclists. Farther away, Ventura Harbor has a cluster of restaurants, bars, and hotels located around the harbor, which is the gateway to the nearby Channel Islands National Park.

Getting There

There are several ways to get from Los Angeles up to Ventura. The drive should take just 1-1.5 hours unless you get ensnared in L.A.'s notorious freeway traffic. Check the Los Angeles Department of Transportation's live traffic information website (http://trafficinfo.lacity.org) before heading out of the city.

The most direct route is **US-101 North**

Best Hotels

★ **Hotel Indigo Santa Barbara:** This artfully stylish boutique hotel also boasts a prime location smack dab in Santa Barbara's hip Funk Zone, halfway between the beach and downtown (page 379).

★ **Madonna Inn:** At this legendary inn and roadside attraction, you might stay in a cavern-like room with rock walls or one resembling a Swiss chalet; each of its 110 guest rooms is unique (page 385).

★ **Hotel Cerro:** Located in downtown San Luis Obispo, this boutique hotel boasts spacious rooms and a sun-soaked rooftop pool deck, not to mention on-site amenities like a distillery, a pie shop, and a 2nd-floor garden (page 386).

★ **Pfeiffer Big Sur State Park:** Camp in the redwood forest along the river at Big Sur's most popular campground (page 411).

★ **La Playa Carmel:** Carmel-by-the-Sea is a place to indulge yourself, and this historic hotel—originally built for a Ghirardelli—fits the bill (page 418).

★ **Spindrift Inn:** With canopy beds, wood-burning fireplaces, and views of Monterey Bay, this Cannery Row hotel is ideal for a romantic retreat (page 427).

★ **Santa Cruz Dream Inn:** Perched over a lively, scenic stretch of sand in Santa Cruz, this inn has retro-chic rooms offering adjoining balcony or patio spaces and striking ocean views (page 435).

from central Los Angeles. After 60 miles (97 km), a 1.25-hour drive without traffic, you'll reach the exits for Ventura. The more scenic route is **CA-1 North** from Santa Monica. You'll pass Malibu and some surprisingly undeveloped coastal areas before merging onto US-101 North at Oxnard. It is about 10 miles (16.1 km) longer than the **US-101 North** route, but adds 20-30 minutes to your drive, depending on traffic.

To get to Ventura from **Los Angeles International Airport** (LAX, 1 World Way, Los Angeles, 855/463-5252, www.lawa.org), contact the **Ventura County Airporter** (805/650-6600, www.venturashuttle.com, $45 adults, $30 children). The small and efficient **Oxnard Airport** (2889 W. 5th St., 805/947-6804, www.iflyoxnard.com) has no scheduled flights but welcomes private aircraft and hosts rental car agencies.

The nearest **Greyhound bus station** is in Oxnard, but the *Pacific Surfliner* by **Amtrak** (800/872-7245, www.amtrak.com) still stops in Ventura (Harbor Blvd. and Figueroa St.) several times each day in both directions on its runs between San Diego and San Luis Obispo.

Sights

Main Street

The seven-block section of Ventura's **Main Street** (Main St. between Ventura Ave. and Fir St.) combines the best of the city's past and present. Cultural and historic sites include Mission San Buenaventura (211 E. Main St.), the missionary Junípero Serra's ninth California mission; and the Ortega Adobe (215 W. Main St.), where the Ortega Chile Packing Company originated. But Main Street is not stuck in the past; it's also home to a range of restaurants and boutiques.

C Street

The **California Street** area (on the coast from the end of Figueroa St. to the end

Two Days Along the Pacific Coast

TOP EXPERIENCE

A handful of the California coast's best attractions can be enjoyed on a two-day trip up the **Pacific Coast Highway** from Los Angeles to San Francisco.

Day 1

Take US-101 out of Los Angeles 1.5 hours north to the scenic coastal city of **Santa Barbara.** Stroll down the city's palm-fringed main thoroughfare, **State Street,** and have a pizza, salad, or sandwich at local favorite **Opal.** At the end of the street, you can head to either **East Beach** or **Leadbetter Beach** for some time on the sand.

Continue up US-101 for two hours to the Central Coast towns of **San Luis Obispo, Morro Bay,** and **Cambria.** If you are into quirky attractions, stop at the **Madonna Inn,** a kitschy hotel complex dating to 1958. If natural landmarks are more your thing, take the brief detour off the highway at Morro Bay to see **Morro Rock** towering over a scenic fishing harbor. Or if you want to see California's version of a castle, continue 45 minutes north of San Luis Obispo to **Hearst Castle.** Just make sure you secure a reservation for one of the tours.

San Luis Obispo, Morro Bay, and Cambria are also ideal places to spend the evening. Budget travelers can choose San Luis Obispo's **Peach Tree Inn.** For something completely different, book the rock-walled "Caveman Room" at San Luis Obispo's **Madonna Inn.**

Day 2

Wherever you stay, head to **Frankie & Lola's** in Morro Bay for a fine breakfast and coffee. You're now fortified for the morning drive up through **Big Sur,** a highlight of any Pacific Coast drive. After 2.5 hours driving north on **CA-1,** you'll reach **Julia Pfeiffer Burns State Park,** a worthwhile stop for its view of **McWay Falls** spilling into the ocean. The overlook is accessible by a short walk. Stop for lunch at **Nepenthe,** a restaurant with tasty burgers and stellar views of the coast, or **Big Sur Taphouse** for a taco and beer with the locals.

Continue north on **CA-1,** stopping for the breathtaking views and photo-ops like **Bixby Bridge.** It's an hour and 15 minutes' drive to your next stop in Monterey. At the **Monterey Bay Aquarium,** you'll see everything from jellyfish to sharks behind glass. Or take an hour-long **kayaking or paddling tour** of Monterey Bay, where you can get fairly close to harbor seals, sea lions, and sea otters.

From Monterey, continue along **CA-1** for another two hours to **Half Moon Bay** for a sunset seafood dinner at **Sam's Chowder House.** From Half Moon Bay, it's just a 45 minutes' drive to **San Francisco.**

of California St.), or **C Street,** hosted the world's first pro surfing event: 1965's Noseriding International. Today, extending 0.75 mile (1.2 km) from Surfer's Point Park to the cove beside Ventura Pier, it's Ventura's recreation hub. Lines of white water streaming off the point entice surfers and stand-up paddleboarders, while old long-boarders relive their glory days catching waves that can continue for 0.75 mile (1.2 km). You might see pro surfers like Ventura local Dane Reynolds out ripping apart the waves or practicing aerials. It's worth a visit even if you don't surf. The vibrant coastal scene includes the Promenade walkway, which bustles with joggers and power walkers, and the popular Omer Rains Bike Trail. Facilities include an outdoor shower, restrooms, and a picnic area. Parking can be challenging: There's a free lot that fills up quickly as well as a paid lot ($2 per day).

El Camino Real: The King's Highway

As you drive US-101 from Ventura up through Paso Robles and beyond, you'll begin to notice signs along the road that look like a shepherd's crook with a bell on it and the words "El Camino Real." The signs are peppered along a nearly 600-mile (970-km) route in California. At the same time that the American colonies were rebelling against England, a handful of Spaniards and Mexicans were establishing outposts up the California coast. In 1769, a fortress and the first mission were established in San Diego. A footpath called El Camino Real, meaning "the king's highway," was created to connect each of the subsequent missions as they were constructed. The missions were situated in areas where large populations of Indigenous people lived and where the soil was fertile enough to sustain a settlement. The establishment of this series of religious colonies in some cases led to the displacement or enslavement of local Indigenous people. Each mission was designed to be a day's travel from the next, all linked by El Camino Real. As time progressed and more missions were built, the path became a roadway wide enough to accommodate horses and wagons. It was not, however, until the last mission was completed in Sonoma in 1823 that the little pathway became a major road. Ultimately, El Camino Real linked all 21 of California's missions, pueblos, and four presidios, from San Diego to Sonoma. In 1904 the El Camino Real Association was formed to preserve and maintain California's historic road. The first commemorative bell was placed in 1906 in front of the Old Plaza Church in downtown Los Angeles, and by 1915 approximately 158 bells had been installed along El Camino Real. The bells were made of cast iron, which encouraged theft, and the number of original bells plummeted to about 75. New bells made of concrete were installed in 1974. US-101 loosely follows this original footpath.

Entertainment

Bars and Clubs

Filling multiple rooms in a house dating back to 1912, **The Tavern** (211 E. Santa Clara St., 805/643-3264, http://tavernordie.com, 5pm-2am Mon.-Sat., 11:30am-2am Sun.) is quite a bar. If you're interested in conversation, head for the room to the left upon entering, which has a fireplace and a couch, or opt for the large outdoor deck out back. It serves handcrafted cocktails and rotating craft beers. While sipping your spirits, be on the lookout for a spirit: They say The Tavern is haunted by the ghost of a young girl who died here in the late 1800s.

Located in an industrial park southeast of downtown Ventura, **Surf Brewery** (4561 Market St., Ste. A, 805/644-2739, www.surfbrewery.com, 4pm-9pm Tues.-Thurs., 1pm-9pm Fri., noon-9pm Sat., noon-7pm Sun.) is the place to go for a pint of Mondo's Blonde Ale, County Line Rye Pale Ale, or Oil Piers Porter.

By the end of the evening, a lot of people end up at dive bar **Sans Souci Cocktail Lounge** (21 S. Chestnut St., 805/643-4539, 2pm-2am daily), which stays open late. The small interior, with red-couch seating, can get a bit claustrophobic on crowded nights; escape to the semi-covered courtyard out front before it fills up with drinkers and smokers.

Live Music

The Majestic Ventura Theater (26 S. Chestnut St., 805/653-0721, www.venturatheater.net, box office 11am-6pm Tues.-Fri.) gets a variety of pretty big national acts, including music icons Alice Cooper and more recent acts like Durand Jones & The Indications. The 1,200-seat Mission-style theater opened in 1928 as a movie house; decades later it was converted into a concert venue. The old chandeliers still hang in the auditorium, and other remnants of the 1920s decor remain.

Performing Arts

The **Rubicon Theatre Company** (1006 E. Main St., 805/667-2900, www.rubicontheatre.org) stages plays in a 186-seat venue that was once a church. Expect classics like Thornton Wilder's *Our Town* as well as new works; there is usually one wholly original show each season. One of Rubicon's original plays, *Daddy Long Legs,* landed on the London stage. Rubicon has also begun performing some plays in Spanish with English subtitles.

Owned by comedian Andres Fernandez, the **Ventura Harbor Comedy Club** (1559 Spinnaker Dr., Ste. 205, 805/644-1500, http://venturaharborcomedyclub.com, shows 7pm Thurs.-Sat., noon, 3pm, and 7pm Sun., $15) hosts heavy hitters like Ron White and Bobcat Goldthwaite. It also hosts open-mic nights.

Festivals and Events

The **Ventura County Fair** (10 W. Harbor Blvd., 805/648-3376, www.venturacountyfair.org) goes down every summer on the Ventura County Fairgrounds, next to the city's main coastal recreation area. Expect the usual attractions: a Ferris wheel, cotton candy, and livestock exhibits.

While it began as a chamber music festival, the **Ventura Music Festival** (805/648-3146, www.venturamusicfestival.org) has expanded to include jazz and crossover artists such as Sérgio Mendes. It takes place at the end of April and early May.

Shopping

Main Street in downtown Ventura is home to a surprising number of unique local and specialty stores and has managed to retain a sense of individuality.

Downtown Ventura County's Farmers Market (Santa Clara St. and Palm St., www.vccfarmersmarkets.com, 8:30am-noon Sat.) has produce stands along with vendors selling tamales and pot stickers. If you miss that one, there's still the **Midtown Ventura Market** (Pacific View Mall, West Parking Lot, 3301 N. Main St., www.vccfarmersmarkets.com, 9am-1pm Wed.) on Wednesday.

The **Pacific View Mall** (3301 E. Main St., 805/642-5530, www.shoppacificview.com, 10am-9pm Mon.-Sat., 11am-7pm Sun.) features 140 brand-name stores and restaurants. Farther south are the **Camarillo Premium Outlets** (740 E. Ventura Blvd., off Los Posas Ave., Camarillo, 805/445-8520, www.premiumoutlets.com, 10am-9pm Mon.-Sat., 10am-8pm Sun., holiday hours vary), with 160 stores peddling reduced-price merchandise.

Beaches

San Buenaventura State Beach

San Buenaventura State Beach (San Pedro St., off US-101, 805/968-1033, www.parks.ca.gov, dawn-dusk daily, day use $10) has an impressive 2 miles (3.2 km) of beach, dunes, and ocean. It also includes the 1,600-foot (488-m) Ventura Pier, home to Eric Ericsson's Seafood Restaurant and Beach House Tacos. The historic pier was built way back in 1872. This is a safer place to swim than some area beaches because it doesn't get the breakers that roll into the nearby point. Cyclists can take advantage of trails connecting with other nearby beaches, and sports enthusiasts converge on the beach for occasional triathlons and volleyball tournaments. Facilities include a snack bar, an equipment rental shop, and an essential for the 21st-century beach bum: Wi-Fi, although to pick up the signal, you need to be within about 200 feet (61 m) of the lifeguard tower.

Emma Wood State Beach

Emma Wood State Beach (W. Main St. and Park Access Rd., 805/968-1033, www.parks.ca.gov, dawn-dusk daily, day use $10) borders the estuary north of the Ventura River, and it includes the remnants of a World War II artillery site. There are no facilities, but a few minutes' walk leads to the campgrounds (reservations required mid-May-Labor Day, first-come, first-served winter), one for RVs and one group camp. At the far eastern side of the parking lot is a small path leading out to the beach that goes under the train tracks. To the right are views up the coast to the Rincon. It's a great spot for windsurfing, as the winds come off Rincon Point just up from the mouth of the Ventura River to create ideal windy conditions. There's a 0.5-mile (0.8-km) trail leading through the reeds and underbrush at the far end of the parking lot; although you can hear the surf and the highway, you can't see anything, and you'll feel like you're on safari until you reach the beach where the Ventura River ends.

Harbor Cove Beach

Families flock to **Harbor Cove Beach** (1900 Spinnaker Dr., dawn-dusk daily, free), located directly across from the Channel Islands Visitors Center at the end of Spinnaker Drive. The harbor's breakwaters provide children and less confident swimmers with relative safety from the ocean currents. In addition, it's a great place to try your hand at stand-up paddleboarding. There's plenty of free parking, lifeguards during peak seasons, restrooms, and foot showers.

Recreation

Surfing

Ventura is definitely a surf town. The series of point breaks referred to as California Street, **C Street** for short, is the best place for consistent right breaks. There are three distinct zones along this mile-long (1.6-km) stretch of beach. At the point is the Pipe, with some pretty fast short breaks. Moving down the beach is Stables, which continues with the right breaks with an even low shoulder, and then C Street, breaking both right and left. The waves get mushier and easier for beginners the closer you get to Ventura Pier. There is a paid parking lot right in front of the break across the street from the Ventura County Fairgrounds (10 W. Harbor Blvd.).

Long-boarders and beginners should head to **Mondos Beach** (6 mi/9.7 km north of town) for soft peeling waves. It's a little north of town toward Santa Barbara; take US-101 north to the State Beaches exit. Then head 3.5 miles (5.6 km) north on the Pacific Coast Highway. Park in the dirt lot on the right side of PCH.

If you just need gear, swing by **Seaward Surf and Sport** (1082 S. Seaward Ave., 805/648-4742, www.seawardsurf.com, 9am-7pm daily, surfboard rental $30-50 per day), which is the place to buy or rent almost anything for the water, including body boards and wetsuits. It's half a block from the beach, so you can head straight to the water. **Ventura Surf Shop** (88 E. Thompson Blvd., 805/643-1062, www.venturasurfshop.com, 9am-6pm Mon.-Sat., 9am-5pm Sun., board rental $30 per day, wetsuit $20 per day) rents out surfboards, wetsuits, body boards, and a couple of stand-up paddleboards.

Ventura Surf School (461 W. Channel Islands Blvd., 805/218-1484, www.venturasurfschool.com, private lesson $145, group lesson $95) can also teach you to surf. Beginner lessons are at Mondos Beach (6 mi/9.7 km north of town) and last two hours. It also runs a weeklong surf camp and kids-only classes.

Whale-Watching

December-March is the ideal time to see Pacific gray whales pass through the channel off the coast of Ventura. Late June-late August has the narrow window for both blue and humpback whales as they feed offshore near the islands. **Island Packers Cruises** (1691 Spinnaker Dr., Ste. 105B, 805/642-1393, www.islandpackers.com, $38-68 adults, $34-62 seniors, $28-55 children) has operated whale-watching cruises for years and is the most experienced. It also runs harbor cruises with a variety of options, including dinner cruises and group charters. Summer outings last 5-6 hours, while winter excursions run about 3 hours. Remember that whale watching is weather-dependent, so cancellations can occur.

Cycling

The paved **Omer Rains Bike Trail** runs 8 miles (12.9 km) along Ventura's beachfront from San Buenaventura State Beach past the Ventura Pier and Surfer's Point to Emma Wood State Beach. The **Ventura River Trail** (Main St. and Peking St., www.cityofventura.net) follows the Ventura River inland from Main Street just over 6 miles (9.7 km) one-way, ending at Foster Park. From here it joins the **Ojai Trail,** a two-lane bike path that follows CA-33 into Ojai (16 mi/26 km one-way).

If you want to pedal it, **Wheel Fun Rentals** (850 Harbor Blvd., 805/765-5795, www.wheelfunrentals.com, 9am-sunset daily summer, 9am-sunset Fri.-Sun. and holidays winter, bike rentals $12-27 per hour) rents out beach cruisers, surreys, mountain bikes, and low-riding chopper bikes. The **Ventura Bike Depot** (239 W. Main St., 805/652-1114, http://venturabikedepot.com, 9:30am-5:30pm Mon.-Wed. and Fri., 11am-5:30pm Thurs., 9am-6pm Sat.-Sun., bike rentals $15-30 per hour) rents out mountain bikes, road bikes, hybrid bikes, beach cruisers, and surreys for two-hour, four-hour, and all-day stints.

Food

Seafood

Housed in a building that resembles a boat, ★ **Spencer Makenzie's Fish Company** (806 E. Thompson Blvd., 805/643-8226, www.spencermakenzies.com, 11am-8:30pm Sun.-Thurs., 10:30am-9pm Fri-Sat., $5-12.50) is known for its giant fish tacos, a tasty fusion of Japanese and Mexican flavors. The sushi-grade fish is hand-dipped in tempura batter and then fried, while the white sauce, cabbage, and cilantro are traditional Baja ingredients. Choose from the array of homegrown sauces along the counter to add splashes of sweet and heat.

Mexican

In a prime spot on the Ventura Pier, ★ **Beach House Tacos** (668 Harbor Blvd., 805/648-3177, 11am-8pm Mon.-Fri., 8:30am-8:30pm Sat.-Sun., $2.25-7.25) doesn't coast on its enviable location. Creative ingredients include soy ginger lime cream sauce-soaked ahi and fish tacos with fruit salsa. Weekend breakfasts include chilaquiles and churro French toast. Order at the counter and dine in an enclosed seating section on the pier. Expect long lines on summer weekends.

Italian

Bolstered by a popular wood bar, **Café Fiore** (66 California St., 805/653-1266, www.cafefiore.net, 11:30am-10pm Mon.-Thurs., 11:30am-11pm Fri.-Sat., 11:30am-9pm Sun., $16-32) is a hot spot for Ventura professionals grabbing a cocktail or meal after work. The food includes Italian favorites like cioppino and osso buco, served in a sleek, high-ceilinged room decorated with furnishings that recall the interior of a Cost Plus World Market. Expect to wait a while for service on crowded nights and during happy hour.

Breakfast

Most mornings you'll have to wait to get inside the popular **Pete's Breakfast House** (2055 E. Main St., 805/648-1130, www.petesbreakfasthouse.com, 7am-2pm daily, $5-12). Pete's fresh-squeezed orange juice, biscuits made daily, strawberry jam made in-house, pancakes, and omelets make it worth the wait. But the homemade corned beef hash and eggs are the real stars, inspiring breakfast lovers to drive all the way up from Los Angeles to spend the morning at Pete's.

Side Trip to the Channel Islands

Inspiration Point on Anacapa Island

Channel Islands National Park (805/658-5720, www.nps.gov/chis) sweeps visitors back to a time when the California coastline was undeveloped and virtually pristine. Due to its remote location, Channel Islands National Park is only accessible by boat or plane, placing it in the top 20 least crowded national parks. It's worth a detour even if just for a day.

The best islands to visit are also the two closest to the mainland: Santa Cruz Island and Anacapa Island. The largest and most hospitable of the islands, **Santa Cruz** is also by far the most popular island to visit. It has more buildings and a campground near Scorpion Bay where you can pitch a tent and store your food in metal lockers. Its main draws are amazing sea caves that can be explored by kayak. Other activities include hiking and snorkeling opportunities.

Anacapa is wilder and more barren than nearby Santa Cruz. Anacapa actually comprises three islets, together 5 miles (8 km) long and 0.25 mile (0.4 km) wide, with a land area totaling just 1 square mile (2.6 sq km). There's a 2-mile (3.2-km) trail system, a small visitors center, and a campground. Hiking trails offer stunning views. If you have seen a photo of the Channel Islands on a calendar or a postcard, it's most likely the spectacular view from Inspiration Point. From this high vantage point on the west end of the island, Middle Anacapa Island and West Anacapa Island rise out of the ocean like a giant sea serpent's spine. Another iconic sight is Arch Rock, a 40-foot-high (12.2-m) rock window off the islet's eastern tip.

Getting There

Get to Santa Cruz Island or Anacapa Island by hopping aboard a boat run by **Island Packers Cruises** (1691 Spinnaker Dr., Ste. 105B, Ventura Harbor, 805/642-1393, www.islandpackers.com). Even the boat ride out to the islands is an adventure, with porpoises frequently racing beside the boats. In addition to trips to the islands, Island Packers hosts wildlife cruises, whale-watching tours, and Ventura Harbor dinner cruises. Trips to Anacapa and Santa Cruz are offered 5-7 days a week year-round. The most common landing at **Santa Cruz** (daily Apr.-Oct., Tues. and Fri.-Sun. Nov.-Mar., $59 adults, $54 seniors, $41 children 3-12) is Scorpion Cove, with a crossing time of 1.5 hours. Trips to **Anacapa** (daily June-Aug., 3-4 days per week Sept.-May, $59 adults, $54 seniors, $41 children 3-12) take an average of 45 minutes. Keep a close eye on the weather as your trip approaches, as weather and ocean conditions can change quickly. In case of inclement weather, call Island Packers the morning of your journey to confirm your trip.

Accommodations

Under $150

The **Bella Maggiore Inn** (67 S. California St., 805/652-0277, www.bellamaggioreinn.com, $75-180) has not changed its prices since 2001, making it a great place to stay for budget travelers. The inn has a great location a few blocks from the beach and just a block off Ventura's Main Street. Some of the guest rooms are no larger than a college dorm room, but there is a lobby with couches, Italian chandeliers, a piano, and a fireplace. Even better is the courtyard with a fountain and a dining area surrounded by vines. There's free overnight parking behind the building.

$150-250

If you are traveling to Channel Islands National Park out of Ventura Harbor, the ★ **Four Points by Sheraton Ventura Harbor Resort** (1050 Schooner Dr., 805/658-1212, www.fourpoints.com, $150-230) is a great place to lay your head before an early-morning boat ride or to relax after a few days of camping on the islands. The guest rooms are clean and comfortable, with balconies and patios. With a gym, a tennis court, a pool, and a basketball court, there is a wide array of recreational opportunities available at the resort. For folks who have hiked all over the Channel Islands, Four Points has a hot tub in a glass dome to ease your aching muscles.

Information and Services

The **Ventura Visitors Center** (101 California St., 805/648-2075, http://visitventuraca.com, 9am-5pm Mon.-Sat., 10am-4pm Sun. summer, 9am-4pm Mon.-Sat., 10am-4pm Sun. winter) occupies a big space in downtown Ventura and offers a lot of information, including a historical walking tour guide of the city.

Community Memorial Hospital (147 N. Brent St., 805/652-5011, www.cmhshealth.org) has the only emergency room in the area. Police services are the **City of Ventura Police Department** (1425 Dowell Dr., 805/339-4400); in case of emergency, call 911 immediately.

Getting Around

Travel Ventura in a cab by calling **Gold Coast Cab** (805/444-6969, www.goldcoastcab.com). Both Uber (www.uber.com) and Lyft (www.lyft.com) operate in Ventura, so download one of the apps on your smartphone if interested.

Santa Barbara

It's been called the American Riviera, with sun-drenched beaches reminiscent of the Mediterranean coast. In truth, Santa Barbara is all California. It's one of the state's most picturesque cities, with a plethora of palm trees and chic residents.

It's famous for its Spanish colonial revival architecture. After a 1925 earthquake, the city rebuilt itself in the style of the Santa Barbara Mission, arguably the most beautiful of the California missions, with white stucco surfaces, red-tiled roofs, arches, and courtyards.

Nestled between the Pacific Ocean and the mountains, its wide roads, warm sandy beaches, and challenging mountain trails inspire physical activity and healthy living. Along the waterfront, a paved path allows anyone on two feet, two wheels, or anything else that moves to enjoy the coastline alongside grassy areas with palm trees gently swaying in the breeze. Several weekly area farmers markets make healthy produce abundant and accessible.

Getting There

From Ventura, drive 28 miles (45 km) on **US-101 North** to Santa Barbara. It's a quick drive unless there is a traffic jam, which is often the case on Friday afternoons and evenings as L.A. locals head north to escape the city. Check the Ventura County Transportation

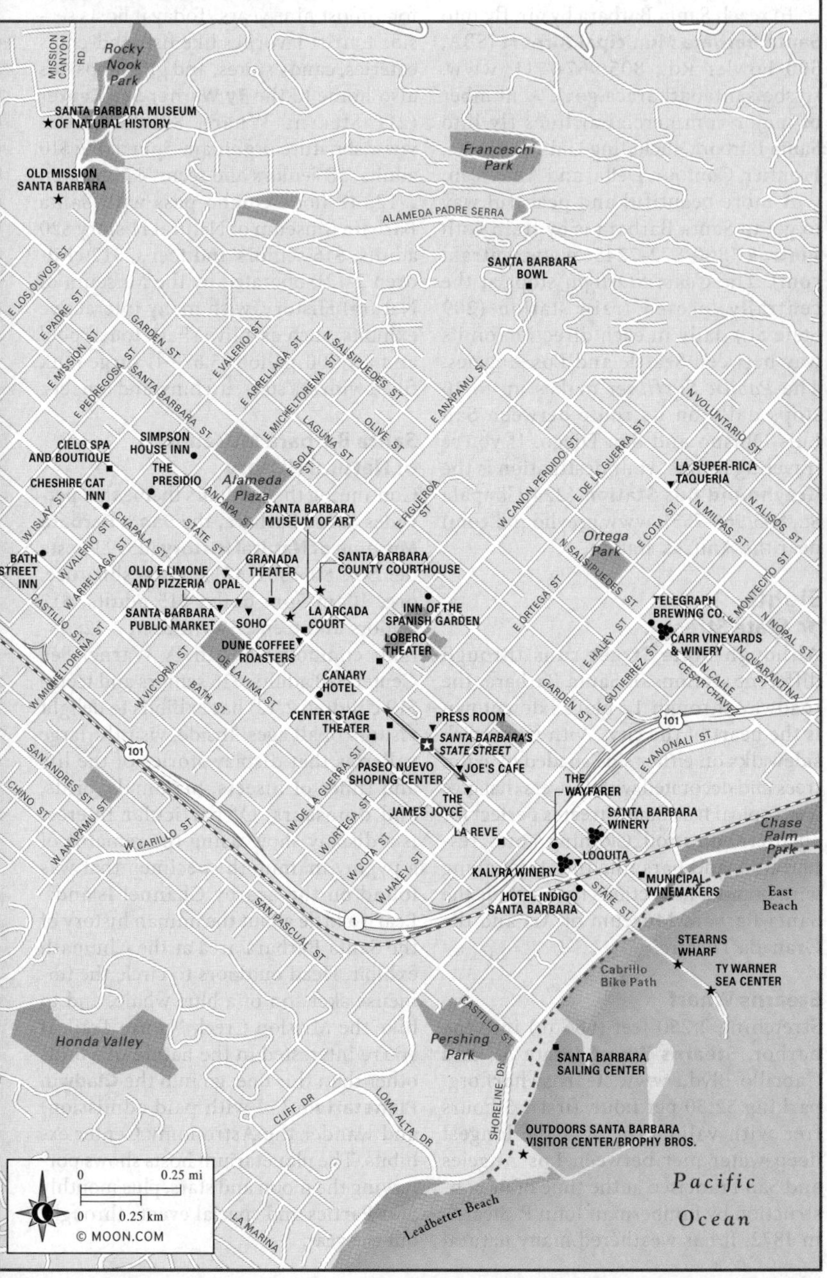

Santa Barbara
Rocky Nook Park
SANTA BARBARA MUSEUM OF NATURAL HISTORY
OLD MISSION SANTA BARBARA
Franceschi Park
ALAMEDA PADRE SERRA
SANTA BARBARA BOWL
CIELO SPA AND BOUTIQUE
SIMPSON HOUSE INN
THE PRESIDIO
CHESHIRE CAT INN
Alameda Plaza
SANTA BARBARA MUSEUM OF ART
BATH STREET INN
OLIO E LIMONE AND PIZZERIA
OPAL
GRANADA THEATER
SANTA BARBARA COUNTY COURTHOUSE
SANTA BARBARA PUBLIC MARKET
SOHO
LA ARCADA COURT
INN OF THE SPANISH GARDEN
DUNE COFFEE ROASTERS
LOBERO THEATER
CANARY HOTEL
CENTER STAGE THEATER
PRESS ROOM
SANTA BARBARA'S STATE STREET
JOE'S CAFE
PASEO NUEVO SHOPING CENTER
THE JAMES JOYCE
LA REVE
LA SUPER-RICA TAQUERIA
Ortega Park
TELEGRAPH BREWING CO.
CARR VINEYARDS & WINERY
THE WAYFARER
SANTA BARBARA WINERY
LOQUITA
KALYRA WINERY
HOTEL INDIGO SANTA BARBARA
MUNICIPAL WINEMAKERS
Chase Palm Park
East Beach
STEARNS WHARF
TY WARNER SEA CENTER
Cabrillo Bike Path
Honda Valley
Pershing Park
SANTA BARBARA SAILING CENTER
OUTDOORS SANTA BARBARA VISITOR CENTER/BROPHY BROS.
Pacific Ocean
Leadbetter Beach
101
1
0 0.25 mi
0 0.25 km
© MOON.COM

Commission website (www.goventura.org) for current highway conditions.

To reach Santa Barbara by air, fly into **Santa Barbara Municipal Airport** (SBA, 500 Fowler Rd., 805/967-7111, www.flysba.santabarbaraca.gov). A number of major commercial airlines fly into Santa Barbara, including United, Alaska, Frontier, Contour, Delta, and American.

A more beautiful and peaceful way to get to Santa Barbara is by train with **Amtrak** (800/872-7245, www.amtrak.com). The *Coast Starlight* stops at the centrally located train station (209 State St.) daily in each direction on its way between Seattle and Los Angeles. The *Pacific Surfliner* makes up to 10 stops daily on its route between San Luis Obispo and San Diego. If you're traveling by bus, your destination is the **Greyhound Bus Station** (224 Chapala St., 805/965-7551, www.greyhound.com) near the Amtrak station.

Sights

★ State Street

Although **State Street** runs through different sections of Santa Barbara, the roadway through 12 blocks downtown is the heart of the city. With wide brick sidewalks on either side shaded by palm trees and decorated with flowers that give it a tropical feel, State Street is perfect for an afternoon stroll. Clothing stores, restaurants, and bars line the street along with popular attractions that include the Santa Barbara Museum of Art and the Granada Theatre.

Stearns Wharf

Stretching 2,250 feet (686 m) into the harbor, **Stearns Wharf** (State St. and Cabrillo Blvd., www.stearnswharf.org, parking $2.50 per hour, first 1.5 hours free with validation) was the longest deep-water pier between Los Angeles and San Francisco at the time of its construction by lumberman John P. Stearns in 1872. It has weathered many natural disasters, including storms and fires; a restaurant fire in 1973 caused its closure for almost nine years. Today it hosts seaside tourist favorites like fish-and-chips eateries, candy stores, and gift shops. It's also home to the **Ty Warner Sea Center** (211 Stearns Wharf, 805/962-2526, www.sbnature.org, 10am-5pm daily; $10 adults, $8 seniors and teens, $7 children 2-12; 48-hour combo pass with Santa Barbara Museum of Natural History $20 adults, $16 seniors and teens, $12 children 2-12), operated by the Museum of Natural History, with many interactive exhibits, such as a live shark touch pool and a 1,500-gallon (5,678-l) surge tank filled with sea stars, urchins, and limpets.

Santa Barbara Museum of Natural History

Continuing the outdoors theme that pervades Santa Barbara, the **Santa Barbara Museum of Natural History** (2559 Puesta del Sol, 805/682-4711, www.sbnature.org, 10am-5pm daily; $15 adults, $12 seniors and teens, $9 children 2-12; 48-hour combo pass with Ty Warner Sea Center $20 adults, $16 seniors and teens, $12 children 2-12) has exhibits to delight visitors of all ages. Inside, visit the large galleries that display stories of the life and times of insects, mammals, birds, and dinosaurs. Of particular interest is a display showcasing the remains of a pygmy mammoth specimen that was found on the nearby Channel Islands. Learn a little about the human history of the Santa Barbara area at the Chumash exhibit. Head outdoors to circle the immense skeleton of a blue whale, and to hike the Mission Creek Nature Trail. If you're interested in the nature of worlds other than this one, go into the **Gladwin Planetarium** ($4 with paid admission) and wander the Astronomy Center exhibits. The planetarium hosts shows portraying the moon and stars, plus monthly Star Parties and special events throughout the year.

Santa Barbara Mission

It's easy to see why the **Santa Barbara Mission** (2201 Laguna St., 805/682-4713, www.santabarbaramission.org, 9am-4:30pm daily, self-guided tours 9am-4:15pm day after Labor Day-early July, 9am-5:15pm early July-Labor Day, $15 adults, $13 seniors, $10 children 5-17) is referred to as the "Queen of the Missions." Larger, more beautiful, and more impressive than many of the 20 other missions, it's second to none for its art displays and graceful architecture, all of which are complemented by the serene local climate and scenery. Unlike many of the California missions, the church at Santa Barbara remained in use after the secularization of the mission chain in the 19th century. When you visit, you'll find the collection of buildings, artwork, and even the ruins of the water system in better shape than at the other missions.

The self-guided tour includes a walk through the mission's striking courtyard, with its blooming flowers and towering palm trees. You also have access to the mission museum, which has, among other displays, a collection of Chumash artifacts. Chumash people were the area's Indigenous inhabitants, and the original purpose of the mission was to convert them to Christianity. Many of the mission's artful features were made by Chumash people, including the fountain and the tabernacle—the only mission tabernacle built by Native Americans. A Chumash village at the mission, which had 252 houses at one point, was located in what's now the parking lot. Due to crowded living quarters and a lack of adequate sanitation facilities, many Chumash people died from European diseases such as smallpox, measles, and the flu. The mission's cemetery is the final resting place of more than 4,000 Chumash people.

From top to bottom: State Street; the Santa Barbara County Courthouse; the Simpson House Inn.

The mission offers hour-long guided docent tours ($16 adults, $14 seniors, $11 children 5-17), during which knowledgeable and highly trained staff will tell you more about this California landmark.

Santa Barbara Museum of Art

The two-floor **Santa Barbara Museum of Art** (1130 State St., 805/963-4364, www.sbma.net, 11am-5pm Tues.-Wed. and Fri-Sun., 11am-8pm Thurs., $5 adults, $3 seniors and children) has an impressive art collection that would make some larger cities envious. Wander the spacious, well-curated museum and take in some paintings from the museum's collection of Monets, the largest collection of the French impressionist's paintings in the West. The museum also has ancient works like a bronze head of Alexander from Roman times and a collection of Asian artifacts, including a 17th- or 18th-century Tibetan prayer wheel. There are interesting temporary exhibitions on display as well.

Santa Barbara County Courthouse

If only all government buildings could be as striking as the **Santa Barbara County Courthouse** (1100 Anacapa St., 805/962-6464, http://sbcourthouse.org, info booth 8:30am-4:30pm Mon.-Fri., 10am-4:30pm Sat.-Sun., docent-led tours 10:30am and 2pm Mon.-Fri., 2pm Sat.-Sun., free). Constructed in 1929 after the devastating 1925 earthquake, the courthouse, which comprises four buildings covering a full city block, is one of the city's finest examples of Mediterranean architecture. The interior features high ceilings, tile floors, ornate chandeliers, and art-adorned walls. The old Board of Supervisors room is impressive, with 6,700 square feet (623 sq m) of murals depicting the county's history and its resources. Also visit El Mirador, the clock tower, an 85-foot-high (26-m) open deck that provides great views of the towering Santa Ynez Mountains and the Pacific Ocean, with the city's red-tiled roofs in the foreground.

TOP EXPERIENCE

Wineries

The wines of Santa Barbara County have been receiving favorable reviews in the national media. The area is known predominantly for wines made from pinot noir and chardonnay grapes, but with the diversity of microclimates, there are over 50 grape varietals grown here.

Not all wine tasting happens in vineyards. On the **Urban Wine Trail** (http://urbanwinetrailsb.com), you can sample some of the county's best wines without even seeing a vine.

The oldest winery in the county, **Santa Barbara Winery** (202 Anacapa St., 805/963-3633, www.sbwinery.com, 10am-6pm Sun.-Thurs., 10am-7pm Fri.-Sat.) started in 1962. The chardonnay is delightful and truly expresses a Santa Barbara character with its bright citrus notes. Other varieties include pinot noir, sangiovese, and sauvignon blanc.

Municipal Winemakers (22 Anacapa St., 805/931-6864, www.municipalwinemakers.com, 11am-8pm Sun.-Wed., 11am-11pm Thurs.-Sat., tasting $12) is in an unpretentious small space with an even smaller deck. Inside are rough wood ceilings and plain walls, with a four-top table and standing room at the bar. The offerings are Rhône-style wines, including grenache, syrah, and a sparkling shiraz.

Carr Winery (414 N. Salsipuedes St., 805/965-7985, www.carrwinery.com, 11am-9pm Mon.-Sat., 11am-6pm Sun., tasting $12-15) focuses on small lots of syrah, grenache, cabernet franc, and pinot noir. The tasting room is in a World War II Quonset hut, with a bar up front and tables in the back. The wine bar hosts live music 6pm-8pm every Friday night.

Nothing improves a great glass of wine like a great view. The **Deep Sea Wine Tasting Room** (217 Stearns Wharf, 805/618-1185, www.conwayfamilywines.com, 11am-7pm Sun.-Thurs., 11am-9pm Fri.-Sat., tasting $8-20) takes advantage of this fact with a location right on Stearns Wharf, offering views of the harbor, the shoreline, and the distant Channel Islands. Sample Conway Family Wines, including the popular signature Deep Sea Red, a blend of five grapes that are mostly syrah.

Entertainment

A wealthy town with close ties to cosmopolitan Los Angeles, Santa Barbara offers visitors a wealth of live cultural displays, from a symphony and opera to a near-endless parade of festivals. The students of UCSB add zest to the town's after-dark scene.

Bars and Clubs

The proximity of the University of California to downtown Santa Barbara guarantees a livelier nighttime scene than you'll find elsewhere on the Central Coast. Bars cluster on State Street and beyond, and plenty of hip clubs dot the landscape.

The best place to start an evening out on the town is at **Joe's Café** (536 State St., 805/966-4638, www.joescafesb.com, 7:30am-1am daily), a steak house and bar with a throwback feel known for the stiffest drinks in town. Don't expect a fancy cocktail menu; just go with the classics at this historic establishment, which dates to 1928 and has checkered tablecloths, a tin-paneled ceiling, and framed black-and-white photos of mostly old men adorning the walls.

A half block off State Street, **The Press Room** (15 E. Ortega St., 805/963-8121, 11am-2am daily) calls itself both an "untraditional English pub" and the "unofficial British Consulate since 1995." The long, narrow room with red walls distinguishes itself from nearby State Street bars by being a place where you can actually have a conversation while enjoying a pint of Bass, Boddingtons, or the lesser-known Bombardier. It has a great jukebox playing punk and indie music.

For a traditional Irish bar experience in downtown Santa Barbara, head to **The James Joyce** (513 State St., 805/962-2688, www.sbjamesjoyce.com, 11am-2am daily). Peanut shells litter the floor as locals sip Guinness at the bar or play competitive games of darts in the backroom. The James Joyce has live entertainment six days a week.

Telegraph Brewing Company (418 N. Salsipuedes St., 805/963-5018, www.telegraphbrewing.com, tasting room 3pm-9pm Mon., 2pm-10pm Tues.-Fri., noon-10pm Sat., noon-7pm Sun.) is located in a renovated World War II-era Quonset hut. Up to 10 taps pour tastes of small-batch beers, including the flagship California Ale, Stock Porter, and Cerveza de Fiesta, a pilsner-style lager, and the experimental Telegraph Obscura beers.

Live Music

A great place to take in a concert during the warm summer and fall months is the **Santa Barbara Bowl** (1122 N. Milpas St., 805/962-7411, www.sbbowl.com, box office hours 11am-6pm Mon.-Fri.), which has hosted concerts by artists such as Bob Dylan, Arcade Fire, Lorde, Lana Del Rey, and local girl Katy Perry. Built in 1936, it's the largest outdoor amphitheater in the county. The seats on the left side have the best views of the city below.

Founded in 1873, the **Lobero Theater** (33 E. Canon Perdido St., 805/963-0761, www.lobero.org) is the oldest continuously operating theater in the state. While it used to host entertainers like Tallulah Bankhead and Bela Lugosi, it now welcomes jazz acts like Charles Lloyd and Dianne Reeves along with indie rock darlings like Jenny Lewis and salsa-funk outfit Ozomatli. The medium-size theater has only one level, and it's filled with cushy red velvet seats, perfect for a music-filled night out on the town.

Located in an upstairs suite, **Soho** (1221 State St., Ste. 205, 805/962-7776, www.sohosb.com, from 5pm daily) has hosted big-time touring acts that include Jimmy Cliff, Real Estate, and Built

to Spill. It has live music seven nights a week. With its brick walls, Soho is going for a sophisticated New York City-type atmosphere.

Classical Music

The **Santa Barbara Symphony** (Granada Theatre, 1214 State St., 805/898-9386, tickets 805/899-2222, www.thesymphony.org) aspires to compete with its brethren in Los Angeles and San Francisco. The symphony orchestra puts on seasons that pay homage to the great composers, plus the works of lesser-known talented artists. Whether you prefer Mozart or Mahler, you can listen to it at the concert hall at the Granada Theatre. Every seat has a great view of the stage, and the acoustics were designed with music in mind, making for an overall great symphony experience.

Opera Santa Barbara (805/898-3890, www.operasb.org) focuses on the classics and little-known works of the Italian masters, staging operas such as *Aida, Don Pasquale*, and *Madame Butterfly* at the Granada Theatre.

Dance

The **Center Stage Theater** (751 Paseo Nuevo, 805/963-0408, www.centerstagetheater.org) focuses on dance, including ballet and modern performances. A handful of local groups, including the Lit Moon Theatre and Out of the Box Theater Company, have also made the Center Stage their home, staging everything from plays with a formerly incarcerated cast to improv comedy.

Festivals and Events

Painters use Mission Plaza as their canvas at the **I Madonnari Italian Street Painting Festival** (805/964-4710, www.imadonnarifestival.com, late May, free), inspired by a similar event in Grazie di

From top to bottom: blue whale skeleton at the Santa Barbara Museum of Natural History; Santa Barbara Winery; paella at Loquita.

Curtatone, Italy. Participants and their sponsors buy sections of the street, with proceeds benefiting the nonprofit Children's Creative Project.

Fiesta (various venues in Santa Barbara, 805/962-8101, www.sbfiesta.org, Aug., some events free), or Old Spanish Days, is Santa Barbara's biggest annual festival. Since 1924, it has paid tribute to the city's Spanish and Mexican heritage with parades, live music, horse shows, bull riding, and the erection of public marketplaces known as *mercados*. During Fiesta, hotel rooms become near impossible to find, with rare vacancies filled at premium rates.

The longest day of the year gets its due at the annual **Solstice Parade** (805/965-3396, www.solsticeparade.com, late June, free). A line of extravagantly dressed participants and colorful floats proceeds nine blocks down State Street and three blocks down West Micheltorena Street before ending in Alameda Park.

The 11-day **Santa Barbara International Film Festival** (various venues, 805/963-0023, http://sbiff.org, Jan.-Feb.) showcases over 200 films and includes 20 world premieres, drawing big Hollywood players like Quentin Tarantino, Jennifer Lawrence, Daniel Day-Lewis, Amy Adams, and Ben Affleck.

Shopping

In Santa Barbara, even the malls and shopping districts are visually interesting. They are all outdoor malls, fun for hanging out. From end to end, the busy main drag **State Street** hosts an unbelievable array of chain stores, plus a few independent boutiques for variety. You'll find lots of lovely women's apparel and plenty of housewares.

Explore the **Paseo Nuevo Shopping Center** (651 Paseo Nuevo, 805/963-7147, www.paseonuevoshopping.com, 10am-9pm Mon.-Fri., 10am-8pm Sat., 11am-6pm Sun.), a series of pathways off State Street that have clothing stores, including Nordstrom and PacSun, along with chain eateries like California Pizza Kitchen. Also right off State Street is **La Arcada Court** (1114 State St., 805/966-6634, www.laarcadasantabarbara.com), a collection of shops, restaurants, specialty stores, and art galleries. Along the tile-lined walkways, playful humanlike sculptures appear in front of some of the shops.

TOP EXPERIENCE

Beaches

There's nothing easier than finding a beach in Santa Barbara. Just follow State Street to its end, and you'll be at the coast.

East Beach

Named because it is east of Stearns Wharf, **East Beach** (1400 Cabrillo Blvd., 805/564-5418, www.santabarbaraca.gov, sunrise-10pm daily) is all soft sand and wide beach, with a dozen volleyball nets in the sand close to the zoo. If you look closely you can see the giraffes and lions. It has all the amenities a sun worshipper could need: a full beach house, a snack bar, a play area for children, and a path for cycling and in-line skating. The beachfront has picnic facilities and a full-service restaurant at the East Beach Grill. The **Cabrillo Pavilion Bathhouse** (1118 E. Cabrillo Blvd.), built in 1927 and renovated in 2020, offers a fitness room, lockers, an event space, and on-site restaurant La Sirena.

West Beach

On the west side of Stearns Wharf, **West Beach** (Cabrillo Blvd. and Chapala St., between Stearns Wharf and the harbor, 805/897-1982, www.santabarbaraca.gov, sunrise-10pm daily) has 11 acres (4.5 ha) of picturesque sand for sunbathing, swimming, kayaking, windsurfing, and beach volleyball. There are also large palm trees, a wide walkway, and a bike path, making it a popular spot. Outrigger canoes also launch from this beach.

Leadbetter Beach

Considered by many to be the best beach in Santa Barbara, **Leadbetter Beach** (Shoreline Dr. and Loma Alta Dr., 805/564-5418, www.santabarbaraca.gov, sunrise-10pm daily) divides the area's south-facing beaches from the west-facing ones. It's a long, flat beach with a large grassy area. Sheer cliffs rise from the sand, and trees dot the point. The beach, which is also bounded by the harbor and the breakwater, is ideal for swimming because it's fairly well protected, unlike the other flat beaches.

Many catamaran sailors and windsurfers launch from this beach, and you'll occasionally see surfers riding the waves. The grassy picnic areas have barbecue sites that can be reserved for more privacy, but otherwise there is a lot of room. There are restrooms, a small restaurant, and outdoor showers.

Arroyo Burro Beach

To the north of town, **Arroyo Burro Beach** (Cliff Dr., 805/568-2461, www.sbparks.org, 8am-sunset daily), also known as Hendry's, is a favorite for locals and dog owners. To the right as you face the water, past Arroyo Burro Slough, dogs are allowed off-leash to dash across the packed sand and frolic and fetch out in the gentle surf. Arroyo Burro is rockier than the downtown beaches, making it less pleasant for games and sunbathing. But the rocks and shells make for great beachcombing, and you might find it slightly less crowded on sunny weekend days. You'll find a snack bar, restrooms, outdoor showers, and a medium-size paid parking lot. At peak times, when the parking lot is full, there's nowhere else to park.

Recreation

With the year-round balmy weather, it's nearly impossible to resist the temptation to get outside and do something energetic and fun in Santa Barbara. From golf to sea kayaking, you've got plenty of options for recreation.

East Beach

Hiking

The 2-mile (3.2-km) hike up to **Inspiration Point** (4 mi/6.4 km round-trip, moderate-strenuous) gives you access to the best vistas of the city, the ocean, and the Channel Islands. The uphill hike starts out paved, then becomes a dirt road, and then a trail. To reach the trailhead from the Santa Barbara Mission, head up Mission Canyon Road. At the stop sign, take a right onto Foothill Road. Take a left at the next stop sign on Mission Canyon Road, and stay left at the fork onto Tunnel Road. Continue down Tunnel Road to the end, where there is a parking area.

Starting from the same spot, **Seven Falls** (3 mi/4.8 km round-trip, easy) begins as a hike but becomes a scramble up a creek bed to its namesake attraction, where bowls of rock hold pools of water. It's a good place to cool off on a hot day. Follow the paved road at the end of Tunnel Road; it's gated and locked against vehicle traffic but is accessible to hikers. After 0.75 mile (1.2 km), continue on the Tunnel Trail. When the trail dips down by the creek, head upstream. The hike requires some boulder-hopping and mild rock climbing.

Cycling

There are plenty of cycling opportunities in Santa Barbara, from flat leisurely pedals by the water to climbs up into the foothills. An option for Santa Barbara cycling information is **Traffic Solutions** (805/963-7283, www.trafficsolutions.info). Visit the website to obtain a copy of the free Santa Barbara County bike map.

If you'd rather be pedaling the dirt rather than the pavement, Santa Barbara's mountainous and hilly terrain makes for good mountain biking. **Velo Pro Cyclery** (15 Hitchcock Way, 805/963-7775, http://velopro.com, 10am-6pm Mon.-Sat., 11am-4pm Sun.) provides a fine introduction to the area's mountain biking resources. **Elings Park** (1298 Las Positas Rd., 805/569-5611, www.elingspark.org, 7am-sunset daily) has single-track trails for beginners and intermediates. Just a few minutes from downtown Santa Barbara, it's perfect for a quick, no-hassle ride.

Wheel Fun Rentals (24 E. Mason St., 805/966-2282, www.wheelfunrentals.com, 9am-sunset daily summer, 9am-sunset Fri.-Sun. and holidays winter, bike rentals $11-30 per hour) offers surrey bikes and beach cruisers for an easy ride along the coast, or rent a road bike to head up into the foothills.

Surfing

During the summer months, the Channel Islands block the south swells and keep them from reaching the Santa Barbara coastline. During fall and winter, the big north and northwest swells wrap around Point Conception, offering some of the best waves in the area and transforming places like Rincon in nearby Carpinteria into legendary surf breaks.

Beginners should head to **Leadbetter Point** (Shoreline Park, just north of the Santa Barbara Harbor), a slow, mushy wave that's also perfect for long-boarders. For a bit more of a challenge, paddle out to the barrels at **Sandspit** (Santa Barbara Harbor). The harbor's breakwater creates hollow right breaks for adventurous surfers only. Be careful, though: Sandspit's backwash has been known to toss surfers onto the breakwater.

Known as the "Queen of the Coast," **Rincon** (US-101 at Bates Rd., on the Ventura County-Santa Barbara County line) is considered California's best right point break, with long waves that hold up for as long as 300 yards (274 m). If it's firing, you'll also most likely be sharing Rincon with lots of other surfers. You might even see revered three-time world champion surfer Tom Curren in the lineup. Rincon truly comes alive during the winter months when the large winter swells roll into the area.

Looking for surfing lessons? Check out the **Santa Barbara Surf School** (805/708-9878, www.santabarbarasurfschool.com). The instructors have decades of surfing experience and pride themselves on getting beginners up and riding in a single lesson. **Surf Happens** (805/966-3613, http://surfhappens.com) has private and group lessons for beginning to advanced surfers.

Kayaking and Stand-Up Paddleboarding

You can see Santa Barbara Harbor and the bay under your own power by kayak or stand-up paddleboard. A number of rental and touring companies offer lessons, guided paddles, and good advice for exploring the region. **Channel Islands Outfitters** (117B Harbor Way, 805/899-4825, www.channelislandso.com, office 9am-5pm Mon.-Fri.) rents out kayaks and paddleboards and also offers kayak tours of Santa Barbara Harbor and stand-up paddleboard tours of Goleta Point.

Sailing

Hop aboard the ***Sunset Kidd*** (125 Harbor Way, 805/962-8222, www.sunsetkidd.com, from $50 adults) for a two-hour morning or afternoon cruise, or opt for the romantic sunset cocktail cruise.

Whale-Watching

With its proximity to the feeding grounds of blue and humpback whales, Santa Barbara is one of the best spots in the state to go whale-watching. **Condor Express** (301 W. Cabrillo Blvd., 805/882-0088, www.condorexpress.com, $50-99 adults, $30-50 children) offers cruises to the Channel Islands to see the big cetaceans feed (blue and humpback whales in summer; gray whales in winter).

Golf

It might not get the most press of the many golf destinations in California, but with its year-round mild weather and resort atmosphere, Santa Barbara is a great place to play a few holes. There's everything from a popular municipal course to championship courses with views of the ocean from the greens.

The **Sandpiper** (7925 Hollister Ave., 805/968-1541, www.sandpipergolf.com, $160-210, cart $25) boasts some of the most amazing views you'll find in Santa Barbara. The view of the Pacific Ocean is so great because it's right there, and on several holes your ball is in danger of falling into the world's largest water trap. And hey, there's a great championship-rated 74.5, par-72, 18-hole golf course out there on that picturesque beach too. Take advantage of the pro shop and the on-site restaurant.

Santa Barbara Golf Club (3500 McCaw Ave., 805/687-7087, www.playsantabarbara.com, sunrise-sunset daily, greens fees $55) is an 18-hole, par-70 course with views of the foothills and the sea.

Spas

Folks who can afford to live in Santa Barbara tend to be able to afford many

 Side Trip to Solvang

Founded in 1911 as a Danish retreat, Solvang makes a fun side trip. It's ripe with Scandinavian heritage as well as a theme-park atmosphere not lacking in kitsch. In the 1950s, far earlier than other themed communities, Solvang decided to promote itself via a focus on Danish architecture, food, and style, which still holds a certain charm over 60 years later. You'll still hear the muted strains of Danish spoken on occasion, and you'll notice storks displayed above many of the stores in town as a traditional symbol of good luck.

Solvang draws nearly two million visitors each year. During peak summer times and holidays, people clog the brick sidewalks. Try to visit during the off-season, when meandering the lovely shops can still be enjoyed. It's at its best in the fall and early spring when the hills are verdant green and the trees in town are beautiful.

The **Elverhøj Museum** (1624 Elverhoj Way, 805/686-1211, www.elverhoj.org, 11am-4pm Wed.-Sun., $5 suggested donation) features exhibits of traditional folk art from Denmark, including paper-cutting and lace-making, wood clogs, and the rustic tools used to create them. It also offers a comprehensive history of the area with nostalgic photos of the early settlers.

The small **Hans Christian Andersen Museum** (1680 Mission Dr., 805/688-2052, www.solvangca.com, 10am-5pm daily, free) chronicles his life, work, and impact on literature. Displays include first editions of his books from the 1830s in Danish and English.

Contact the **Solvang Visitor Information Center** (1639 Copenhagen Dr., 805/688-6144, www.solvangusa.com, 9am-5pm Mon.-Fri.) for more advice on a Solvang visit.

Getting There

If you're heading from Santa Barbara north to Solvang, you have two choices. You can drive the back route, **CA-154,** also known as the **San Marcos Pass Road,** and arrive in Solvang in about **30 minutes.** This is a two-lane road, with only a few places to pass slower drivers, but it has some stunning views of the coast as you climb into the hills. You pass **Cachuma Lake,** then turn west on **CA-246** to Solvang. The other option is to take **US-101,** which affords plenty of coastal driving before you head north into the **Gaviota Pass** to reach Solvang. This route takes longer, about **45 minutes.** Known as **Mission Drive** in town, CA-246 connects both to US-101 and CA-154, which connects to Santa Barbara in the south and US-101 farther north.

of the finer things in life, including massages, facials, and luxe skin treatments. You'll find a wide array of day spas and medical spas in town.

If you prefer a natural spa experience, book a treatment at **Le Reve** (21 W. Gutierrez St., 805/564-2977, www.lereve.com, 10am-7pm daily). Using biodynamic skin care products and pure essential oils, Le Reve makes good on its advertising that bills it as an "aromatherapy spa." Choose from an original array of body treatments, massage, hand and foot pampering, facials, and various aesthetic treatments.

Cielo Spa and Boutique (1725 State St., Ste. C, 805/687-8979, www.cielospasb.com, by appointment) prides itself on its warm, nurturing environment. Step inside and admire the scents, soft lighting, and the natural New Agey decor. Contemplate the colorful live orchids, feel soothed by the flickering candlelight, and get lost in the tranquil atmosphere.

Food

California Cuisine

Opal (1325 State St., 805/966-9676, http://opalrestaurantandbar.com, 11:30am-2:30pm and 5pm-10pm Mon.-Thurs., 11:30am-2:30pm and 5pm-11pm Fri.-Sat., 5pm-10pm Sun., $16-43) is a comfortable but lively local favorite. As a matter of fact, the menu points out local favorites, including the pesto-sautéed bay scallop salad and the chili-crusted filet mignon. In addition to its eclectic offerings, most with an Asian twist, the stylish eatery serves up gourmet pizzas from a wood-burning oven and fine cocktails from a small bar. A quieter side room with rotating art is ideal for a more romantic meal.

Seafood

It takes something special to make Santa Barbara residents take notice of a seafood restaurant, and **Brophy Brothers** (119 Harbor Way, 805/966-4418, www.brophybros.com, 11am-9pm Sun.-Thurs., 11am-10pm Fri.,-Sat., $10-22) has it. Look for a small list of fresh fish done up California style with upscale preparations. The delectable menu goes heavy on locally caught seafood. With a prime location looking out over the masts of the sailboats in the harbor, it's no surprise that Brophy Brothers gets crowded at both lunch and dinner, especially on weekends in the summer. There's also a location in Ventura Harbor.

Mexican

Looking for authentic Mexican food? ★ **La Super-Rica Taqueria** (622 N. Milpas St., 805/963-4940, 11am-9pm Sun.-Mon. and Thurs., 11am-9:30pm Fri.-Sat., $5) can hook you up. Just be prepared to stand in line with dozens of locals and even commuters from Los Angeles and the occasional Hollywood celeb. All agree that La Super-Rica has some of the best down-home Mexican cuisine in all of SoCal. This was Julia Child's favorite taco stand, and it has been reviewed by the *New York Times*. The corn tortillas are made fresh for every order, the meat is slow cooked and seasoned to perfection, and the house special is a grilled pork-stuffed pasilla chile pepper. Vegetarians can choose from a few delicious meat-free dishes, including the *rajas,* a standout with sautéed strips of pasilla peppers, sautéed onions, melted cheese, and herbs on a bed of two fresh corn tortillas. There's no need for ambience; the taqueria feels like a beach shack.

Spanish

Loquita (202 State St., 805/880-3380, www.loquitasb.com, 5pm-10pm Fri.-Sat., 5pm-9pm Sun.-Mon. and Thurs., $15-47) showcases the similarities between Spain and Santa Barbara: fresh seafood, wine, and abundant sunshine, particularly on the restaurant's outdoor patio. The menu highlights the greatest hits of Spanish cuisine—tapas, paella—and drinks include gin cocktails, sangria, and wine.

Italian

If you want a superb Italian meal and a sophisticated dining experience, ★ **Olio e Limone** (11 W. Victoria St., Ste. 17, 805/899-2699, www.olioelimone.com, 11:30am-2pm and 5pm-close Mon.-Sat., 5pm-close Sun., $18-37), care of Chef Alberto Morello who hails from Sicily, is the place to go in Santa Barbara. You'll be impressed by the artistic presentation of the dishes, which include homemade pasta. The duck ravioli with creamy porcini mushroom sauce is rave-worthy. The adjacent **Olio Pizzeria** (11 W. Victoria St., Ste. 21, 805/899-2699, 11:30am-10pm daily, $15-20) is a more casual affair, focusing on brick-oven pizzas. It also has a detailed menu of antipasti with salamis, cheeses, and breads.

Coffee

A long, narrow coffee shop right on State Street, **Dune Coffee Roaster** (1101 State St., 805/963-2721, www.dunecoffee.com, 6am-7pm Mon.-Fri., 7am-7pm Sat.-Sun.), formerly The French Press, is lined with hipsters and couples getting caffeinated and using the free Wi-Fi. The popular café serves drinks that'll leave your body buzzing, from a drip coffee to an iced tres leches. There's a small seating area out front and another out back on Figueroa Street, as well as a second location (528 Anacapa St.).

Markets

It's no surprise that Santa Barbara has two weekly farmers markets: **Saturday morning** (Santa Barbara and Cota St., 805/962-5354, www.sbfarmersmarket.org, 8:30am-1pm Sat.) and **Tuesday afternoon** (500-600 blocks of State St., 805/962-5354, www.sbfarmersmarket.org, 4pm-7pm Tues.).

Want to pick up some inventive Mexican, vegan, or Thai food? Or maybe grab a craft pint in a beer garden? If so, the **Santa Barbara Public Market** (38 W. Victoria St., 805/770-7702, http://sbpublicmarket.com, 7:30am-11pm Mon.-Fri., 8am-11pm Sat., 8am-10pm Sun.) is the place to go downtown. The multi-vendor facility is Santa Barbara's take on San Francisco's Ferry Building Marketplace and Napa's Oxbow Public Market.

Accommodations

If you want a plush beachside room in Santa Barbara, be prepared to pay for it. Almost all of Santa Barbara's hotels charge premium rates, but there are a few charming and reasonably priced accommodations near downtown and other attractions.

$150-250

Reasonably priced, **The Presidio** (1620 State St., 805/963-1355, www.presidiosb.com, $189-349) is close to the action. Its 16 guest rooms are clean and have been recently renovated. Second-floor guest rooms have vaulted ceilings, and every guest room has Wi-Fi and TVs with HBO. Other assets include the friendly staff, a sundeck, and a fleet of beach cruisers for motel guests.

The **Bath Street Inn** (1720 Bath St., 805/682-9680, www.bathstreetinn.com, $200-300) specializes in small-town charm and hospitality. It is large for a B&B, with eight guest rooms in the Queen Anne-style main house and another four in the more modern summer house. Each room has its own unique color scheme and style, some with traditional floral Victorian decor, others with elegant stripes. Some guest rooms have king beds, others have queens, and several have two-person whirlpool tubs. Despite the vintage trappings, you can expect a few modern amenities, including free Wi-Fi.

Over $250

Part of an international boutique hotel chain, ★ **Hotel Indigo Santa Barbara** (121 State St., 805/966-6586, www.indigosantabarbara.com, $149-340) is located just one block from the beach and two blocks from downtown, smack-dab in the Funk Zone, amid the neighborhood's boutique wine-tasting rooms, cafés, and art galleries. While the guest rooms are not spacious, they are artfully designed and have hardwood floors. The European-style collapsible glass shower wall is located right in front of the toilet. Some guest rooms also have small outdoor patios. The hotel's hallways are essentially art galleries, showcasing a rotating cast of regional and local artists. Note you can expect to hear the occasional train roll by as the hotel is near the train station.

The ★ **Canary Hotel** (31 W. Carrillo St., 805/884-0300, www.canarysantabarbara.com, $350-1,200) is stylish, playful, and right downtown. Worth splurging on, the elegant guest rooms have wooden floors, extremely comfortable canopied beds, and giant flat-screen TVs, along with unexpected amenities such as a pair of binoculars for sightseeing and bird-watching and a giant candle to set the mood for romantic evenings. While it may be difficult to leave such comforts, the hotel has a rooftop pool and a lounge on its 6th floor that offer stunning views of the Santa Ynez Mountains and the red-tiled roofs of the beautiful city.

The historic ★ **Simpson House Inn** (121 E. Arrellaga St., 805/963-7067, www.simpsonhouseinn.com, $329-599) is a wonderful place to spend an evening or two. The main house, constructed in 1874, is a historic landmark that withstood the 1925 earthquake. Stay inside one of the main building's six ornately decorated guest rooms or opt for one of the four guest rooms in the reconstructed carriage house. There are also four garden cottages. Whichever you choose, you will be treated to comfortable beds and a flat-screen TV with modern features that include Netflix, YouTube, and Pandora Radio access. The service is first-rate, and the staff is happy to help you get restaurant reservations or will deliver popcorn to your room if you opt to stay in with a movie. The grounds include English gardens with fragrant flowers, gurgling fountains, fruit trees, chairs, tables, and the oldest English oak tree in Southern California.

If you're willing to pay a premium rate for your room, the **Cheshire Cat Inn** (36 W. Valerio St., 805/569-1610, www.cheshirecat.com, $252-488) can provide you with true luxury accommodations. Each room has an *Alice in Wonderland* name, but the decor doesn't really match the theme: Instead of whimsical and childish, you'll find comfortable Victorian elegance. Guest rooms are spread through two Victorian homes, the coach house, and two private cottages. Some suites feel like well-appointed apartments complete with a dining room table, a soaking tub, and a bookshelf stocked with a few hardbacks. Relax in the evening in the spacious octagonal outdoor spa, or order a massage in the privacy of your own room.

For a taste of Santa Barbara's upscale side, stay at the **Inn of the Spanish Garden** (915 Garden St., 805/564-4700, www.spanishgardeninn.com, $369-700). This small boutique hotel gets it right from the first glimpse; the building has the whitewashed adobe exterior, red-tiled roof, arched doorways, and wooden balconies characteristic of its historic Presidio neighborhood. Courtyards seem filled with lush greenery and tiled fountains, while the swimming pool promises relief from the heat. The pleasing setup of this luxury hotel definitely has something to do with the two owners' urban planning backgrounds. Inside, guest rooms and suites whisper luxury with their white linens, earth-toned accents, and rich, dark wooden furniture. Enjoy the benefits of your own gas fireplace, sitting area, balcony or patio, fridge, and minibar.

Information and Services

The **Santa Barbara Conference and Visitors Bureau** (500 E. Montecito St., 805/966-9222, www.santabarbaraca.com, 8:30am-5pm Mon.-Fri.) maintains an informative website and visitors center. The **Outdoor Santa Barbara Visitors Center** (113 Harbor Way, 805/456-8752, http://outdoorsb.sbmm.org, 11am-5pm Sun.-Fri., 9am-3pm Sat.) provides information about Channel Islands National Park, the Channel Islands National Marine Sanctuary, the Los Padres National Forest, and the city of Santa Barbara.

Look for the ***Santa Barbara News Press*** (www.newspress.com) in shops, on newsstands, and in your hotel. It has information about entertainment, events, and attractions. The local free weekly, the ***Santa Barbara Independent*** (www.independent.com), has a comprehensive events calendar.

Santa Barbara Cottage Hospital (400 W. Pueblo St., 805/682-7111, www.cottagehealth.org) is the only hospital in town and has the only emergency room.

Getting Around

Santa Barbara has its own local transit authority. The **MTD Santa Barbara** (805/963-3364, http://sbmtd.gov, regular fare $1.75, waterfront service $0.50) runs the local buses, the Waterfront Shuttle, and the Downtown-Waterfront line. Have exact change to pay your fare when boarding the bus or shuttle; if you're going to change buses, ask the driver for a free transfer pass. Parking can be challenging, especially at the beach on sunny weekends. Expect to pay a premium for a good-to-mediocre parking spot, or to walk for several blocks. If possible, leave your car elsewhere and take the public shuttle from downtown to the beach. To get to the **Santa Ynez Valley** and other **local wine regions,** take **CA-154** east of Santa Barbara.

San Luis Obispo

Eleven miles (17.7 km) inland from the coast, San Luis Obispo (SLO) is a worthy home base to explore nearby Montaña de Oro State Park and Morro Bay. Founded in 1772 by Junípero Serra, SLO is one of California's oldest communities. Despite this, the presence of the nearby California Polytechnic State University (Cal Poly) gives the small city a youthful, vibrant feel.

Higuera Street is a one-way, three-lane street lined with restaurants, clothing stores, and bars. Half a block away, restaurant decks are perched over the small San Luis Obispo Creek, a critical habitat for migrating steelhead. A plaza, in front of the Mission San Luis Obispo de Tolosa, overlooks the creek with grassy lawn sections, plenty of benches, and a fountain with sculptures of bears, a fish, and one of the area's first human residents.

Getting There

San Luis Obispo is 95 miles (153 km) north of Santa Barbara via **US-101,** a drive that usually takes a little more than 90 minutes. Both CA-1 and US-101 run through San Luis Obispo, merging on the north side of town. From the south, take the CA-1/US-101-combined freeway into town.

Amtrak (800/872-7245, www.amtrak.com) has a San Luis Obispo station (1011 Railroad Ave.); the *Coast Starlight* train stops here once daily in each direction on its way between Seattle and Los Angeles, and SLO is also the northern terminus of the *Pacific Surfliner,* with several departures daily on its route to San Diego. There are scheduled flights from Los Angeles, San Francisco, Portland, Seattle, Dallas, Denver, Las Vegas, and Phoenix to the **San Luis Obispo County Regional Airport** (SBP, 975 Airport Dr., 805/781-5205, www.sloairport.com).

Greyhound (800/231-2222, www.greyhound.com) travels along US-101. The closest bus stop to San Luis Obispo is at the **Santa Maria Travel Center** (400 E. Boone St., Santa Maria), 31 miles (50 km) south. From there you'll need to connect with **San Luis Obispo Regional Transit Authority** (805/541-2228, www.slorta.org) buses to get to San Luis Obispo. There are various weekday and weekend routes.

Sights

Higuera Street

Similar to Santa Barbara's State Street, San Luis Obispo's **Higuera Street** is the heart of the city. For seven blocks, the one-way street is lined with restaurants, bars, gift shops, and lots of women's clothing stores. The clean sidewalks are perfect for a stroll under a canopy of ficus, carrot wood, and Victorian box trees.

★ Madonna Inn

The **Madonna Inn Resort & Spa** (100 Madonna Rd., 805/543-3000, www.madonnainn.com) is truly one of a kind. It's considered a pilgrimage site for lovers of kitsch, but it wasn't planned that way. When Alex and Phyllis Madonna

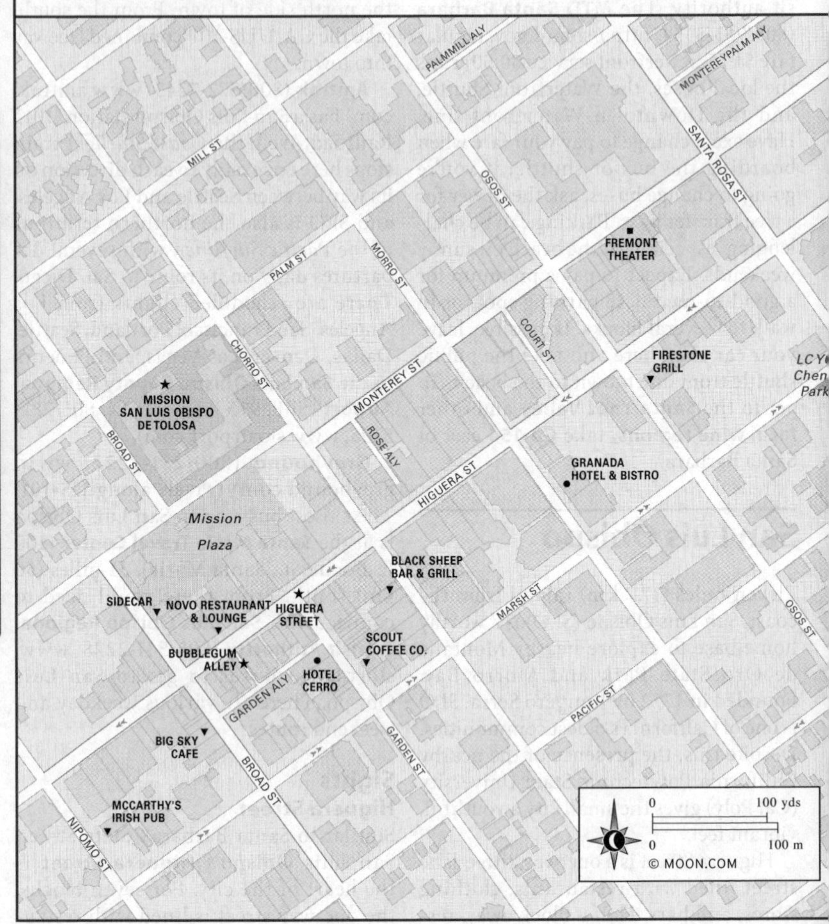

opened the inn in 1958, they wanted it to be different from a typical motel, and they made each guest room special. It started with 12 guest rooms; today, there are 110 unique guest rooms, each decorated wildly differently to suit the diverse tastes of the road-trippers who converge on the area. The creative names given to each over the years suggest what you will find inside: The Yahoo, Love Nest, Old Mill, Kona Rock, Irish Hills, Cloud Nine, Just Heaven, Hearts & Flowers, Rock Bottom, Austrian Suite, Caveman Room, Daisy Mae, Safari Room, Jungle Rock, and Bridal Falls. Then there is the famous men's restroom downstairs; the urinal is built out of rock and a waterfall flushes it. Men routinely stand guard so that their mothers, sisters, wives, and female friends can go in to gawk at the unusual feature.

Obviously, the rooms are for overnight guests, but there is still a lot to take in if you pull over for a peek. The **Copper Café**

& Pastry Shop has copper-plated tables and a copper-plated circular bar, while the **Gold Rush Steak House** is a garish explosion of giant fake flowers and rose-colored furniture. It might remind you of a room in your grandmother's home on steroids.

Bubblegum Alley

Bubblegum Alley (Higuera St. between Broad St. and Garden St.) is a 70-foot-long (21.3-m) alleyway whose walls are covered in pieces of already chewed gum. The newly chewed chunks are bright green, red, yellow, and so on, while the older pieces have turned a darker color. Some people have called this oddity an "eyesore," while others have touted it as one of the city's "special attractions." Regardless, Bubblegum Alley, which is rumored to have started as early as the late 1950s, is here to stay. Even after firefighters blasted the alleyway with water hoses in 1985, another layer of gum appeared a little later.

Entertainment

Bars and Clubs

As a college town, San Luis Obispo has plenty of bars in its downtown area. A refined option is **Sidecar** (1040 Broad St., 805/439-3563, www.sidecarcocktail.company, 4pm-close Wed.-Sat.), a multilevel mixology space. It has its own distillery, the staff is knowledgeable, food is served, and the ever-rotating cocktail list incorporates infused liquors, herbs, and syrups to create memorable drinks.

The **Black Sheep Bar & Grill** (1117 Chorro St., 805/544-7433, www.blacksheepslo.com, 11am-2am daily) has a cozy pub feel on uncrowded nights. This brick-walled, wood-floored tavern has a fireplace and a back patio. It also serves a burger basted in a Guinness beer reduction sauce, as well as a range of mac-and-cheese dishes, including versions with buffalo chicken, barbecued tri-tip, or carnitas.

Just a block off Higuera Street but a world away from the college bars there, **McCarthy's Irish Pub** (600 Marsh St., 805/544-0268, http://mccarthysirishtavern.us, noon-2am Sun.-Thurs., 2pm-3am Fri.-Sat.) is a dark, low-slung bar with loud music, friendly locals, and a shuffleboard table. Order up a draft Guinness, Smithwick's, or Magners Irish cider and get ready to make some new friends.

Live Music

SLO Brew Rock (855 Aerovista Pl., 805/543-1843, www.slobrew.com, ticket prices vary) is the concert venue of long-time local brewpub SLO Brew. Acts that have performed at SLO Brew include Jeff Bridges and Public Enemy.

Dating back to 1942, the **Fremont Theater** (1035 Monterey St., 805/329-5725, http://fremontslo.com, ticket prices vary) has hosted out of town touring acts including Collie Buddz, Courtney Barnett, and The Growlers.

Festivals and Events

The **San Luis Obispo Farmers Market** (Higuera St. between Osos St. and Nipomo St., http://slocountyfarmers.org, http://downtownslo.com, 6pm-9pm Thurs.) is a true phenomenon. One of the largest farmers markets in the state, this weekly gathering has the goods of 70 farmers and lots of live music.

The **San Luis Obispo International Film Festival** (805/546-3456, http://slofilmfest.org, Mar.) screens a range of films at the city's Palm Theatre (817 Palm St.) and Fremont Theatre (1035 Monterey St.) along with other venues around the county, including Paso Robles and Avila Beach. The five-day fest draws film folks like Josh Brolin, Alfred Molina, and Jeff Bridges.

Recreation

Hiking

Just north of San Luis Obispo, the 1,546-foot-high (471-m) **Bishop Peak**

(trailheads at the end of Highland Dr. and off Patricia Dr., 805/781-7300, www.slocity.org) is the city's natural treasure. A 4-mile (6.4-km) round-trip hike to the rocky crown of Bishop Peak offers commanding views of San Luis Obispo and the surrounding area. Named by Spanish missionaries who thought the mountain resembled a bishop's hat, Bishop Peak is the tallest of the *morros*, or "Nine Sisters," a chain of nine volcanic peaks stretching from San Luis Obispo up to Morro Bay. In addition to the fine views, Bishop Peak teems with wildlife, especially birds that float on the mountain's thermals. The hour-long hike passes through a forest, past Volkswagen Beetle-size boulders, and into a series of exposed switchbacks. Bring water!

Food

San Luis Obispo restaurants take advantage of their location near farms and wineries. The big college presence means that even the higher-end establishments keep things casual.

Contemporary

★ **Novo** (726 Higuera St., 805/543-3986, www.novorestaurant.com, 11am-9pm Sun.-Thurs., 11am-1am Fri.-Sat., $18-37) is often deemed SLO's best restaurant, for good reason. Its menu features wide-ranging fare, with items like perfectly done scallops over a bed of succotash studded with pancetta, Thai curries, and pappardelle pasta. Part of the Novo's appeal is that you can dine on a deck overlooking the San Luis Obispo Creek.

Celebrity chef Rachael Ray has approved **Big Sky Café** (1121 Broad St., 805/545-5401, www.bigskycafe.com, 7am-8pm Mon.-Thurs., 7am-9pm Fri. 8am-9pm Sat., 8am-8pm Sun., $15-26). It's known for healthy vegetarian entrées, but there are plenty of options for

From top to bottom: the tasty tri-tip sandwich at Firestone Grill; the mixology setup at Sidecar; fresh avocado-shrimp spring rolls at Novo.

carnivores, including a grass-fed beef burger and a Middle Eastern style lamb burger. While dining, check out the work of local artists on the walls.

Burgers and Steaks

The ★ **Firestone Grill** (1001 Higuera St., 805/783-1001, www.firestonegrill.com, 11am-10pm Sun.-Wed., 11am-11pm Thurs.-Sat., $5-22) creates a masterpiece of meat in its tender and tasty tri-tip sandwich. Locals swear by it. Brought to you by the same folks behind Cambria's Main Street Grill, the Firestone Grill also serves pork ribs, burgers, and salads. It also has a large outdoor patio.

A trip to the Madonna Inn is always worthwhile. Its over-the-top dining room, the **Gold Rush Steak House** (100 Madonna Rd., 805/543-3000, www.madonnainn.com, 4pm-10pm daily, $26-45), serves steaks of the filet mignon, ribeye, and prime rib varieties. If you are not feeling like red meat, seafood entrées are also available.

Coffee

Scout Coffee (1130 Garden St., 805/439-2175, http://scoutcoffeeco.com, 7:30am-2:30pm Sun.-Fri., 7:30am-4pm Sat., $5) is the place to get caffeinated in downtown SLO. It's a hip place with a young staff and exposed brick walls. The coffee is terrific, especially the flavorful Gibraltar, made with steamed milk and espresso, and the baked goods make worthy snacks.

Accommodations

$100-150

A superb value, the **Peach Tree Inn** (2001 Monterey St., 800/227-6396, http://peachtreeinn.com, $89-299) has nice guest rooms, friendly staff, and a complimentary breakfast. The finest guest rooms at the Peach Tree are the Creekside Rooms, each with its own brick patio. Next to the lobby is a large common room with a back deck and rocking chairs to enjoy San Luis Obispo's frequently pleasant weather. The Peach Tree is located on the Old SLO Trolley route and is an easy 1-mile (1.6-km) walk to San Luis Obispo's downtown.

$150-250

If you want to feel like you're spending the night in a cave, on safari, or on a showboat, stay at the ★ **Madonna Inn** (100 Madonna Rd., 805/543-3000, www.madonnainn.com, $209-489). An underhyped asset on Madonna Inn's 2,200 acres (890 ha) is its deck with a large heated pool, two hot tubs, a poolside bar, and a view of an artificial cascade tumbling down the hillside.

For a rejuvenating stay in a natural setting, head to ★ **Sycamore Mineral Springs Resort** (1215 Avila Beach Dr., 805/595-7302, www.sycamoresprings.com, $179-289), located in a tranquil canyon 9 miles (14.5 km) from San Luis Obispo. Amenities on the grounds include a yoga dome, a labyrinth, a wellness center, a restaurant, and sulfur mineral springs, which can be enjoyed in hillside hot tubs. The Bob Jones Trail offers a paved 2-mile (3.2-km) walkway that connects the resort to Avila Beach. Lodging options range from cozy guest rooms to a two-story guesthouse with three bedrooms and three baths. Up on stilts, the West Meadows Suites include a living room with a gas fireplace and a bedroom with a four-poster king bed. The back decks have large soaking tubs that can be filled with fresh mineral water.

The **Granada Hotel & Bistro** (1126 Morro St., 805/544-9100, www.granadahotelandbistro.com, $229-549) is a 17-room boutique hotel located just half a block off Higuera Street. The 1920s hotel has been renovated and modernized, with exposed brick walls, steel-frame windows, and hardwood floors. Most guest rooms also have fireplaces. On the 2nd floor is a comfortable indoor and outdoor lounge area.

Over $250

Stylish and modern, with nods to the past, ★ **Hotel Cerro** (1125 Garden St., 805/548-1000, www.hotelcerro.com, $285-1,000) brings SoCal luxury to the Central Coast. Occupying almost an entire city block in downtown San Luis Obispo, the Hotel Cerro complex includes 65 spacious rooms, a spa, a brasserie, a pie shop, a distillery, and an idyllic 2nd-floor garden. Guests have access to a rooftop pool deck with a shallow pool, private cabanas, chaise lounges, and panoramic views of town and the surrounding countryside.

Information and Services

Visitor information can be obtained at the **San Luis Obispo Chamber of Commerce Visitors Center** (895 Monterey St., 805/781-2670, www.slochamber.org, 9:30am-5pm Sun.-Wed., 9:30am-6pm Thurs.-Sat.). San Luis Obispo has its own daily newspaper, ***The Tribune*** (www.sanluisobispo.com), and its own free weekly newspaper, the ***New Times*** (www.newtimesslo.com).

There are two branches of the **post office** (893 Marsh St., 805/543-5353; 1655 Dalidio Dr., 805/543-2605).

San Luis Obispo is home to two hospitals: **Sierra Vista Regional Medical Center** (1010 Murray Ave., 805/546-7600, www.tenethealthcentralcoast.com) and **French Hospital Medical Center** (1911 Johnson Ave., 855/821-0827, www.dignityhealth.org).

Getting Around

The regional bus system, the **RTA** (805/541-2228, www.slorta.org), connects San Luis Obispo, Morro Bay, Cayucos, Cambria, and San Simeon. Fares range $1.75-3.25 for adults.

the rooftop pool deck at San Luis Obispo's Hotel Cerro

Morro Bay

The picturesque fishing village of Morro Bay is dominated by Morro Rock, a 576-foot-high (176-m) volcanic plug that looms over the harbor. In 1542, Juan Rodríguez Cabrillo, the first European explorer to navigate the California coast, named the landmark Morro Rock, because he thought it appeared to resemble a moor's turban.

With a view of the rock, the small city's Embarcadero is a string of tourist shops, restaurants, and hotels strung along Morro Bay, a large estuary that includes the harbor, the Morro Bay State Marine Recreational Management Area, and the Morro Bay State Marine Reserve. Uphill from the water, more restaurants, bars, and stores are located in Morro Bay's Olde Towne section.

With natural attractions that include the stunning Montaña de Oro State Park just miles from town and with a nice waterfront focus, Morro Bay is a worthy destination or detour for a weekend, and a lot of the area's lodgings fill up during high-season weekends.

Getting There

In San Luis Obispo, US-101 heads east over the mountains toward Paso Robles. San Luis Obispo's Santa Rosa Street becomes CA-1 North and continues along the coast. To get to Morro Bay, take **CA-1 North** for 13 miles (20.9 km) from San Luis Obispo. Take the **Morro Bay Boulevard** exit into town.

There is no direct bus service to Morro Bay, although **Greyhound** (805/238-1242, www.greyhound.com) travels along US-101 and stops at **Santa Maria Travel Center** (400 E. Boone St., Santa Maria), 46 miles (74 km) south. From there you'll need to connect with **San Luis Obispo Regional Transit Authority** (805/541-2228, www.slorta.org) buses to get to Morro Bay. There are various weekday and weekend routes.

Sights

★ Morro Rock

It would be difficult to come to the town of Morro Bay and not see **Morro Rock** (www.morro-bay.ca.us/383/Morro-Rock-Beach). The 576-foot-high (176-m) volcanic plug, which has been called the "Gibraltar of the Pacific," dominates the town's scenery, whether you are walking along the bayside Embarcadero or beachcombing on the sandy coastline just north of the prominent geologic feature. The rock was an island until the 1930s, when a road was built connecting it to the mainland. The area around the rock is accessible, but the rock itself is off-limits because it is home to a group of endangered peregrine falcons. Indeed, a multitude of birds always seems to be swirling around the rock they call home.

Montaña de Oro State Park

Montaña de Oro State Park (Pecho Rd., 7 mi/11.3 km south of Los Osos,

Morro Bay to Cambria

Nine Sisters

The ancient volcanic peaks known as the **Nine Sisters of the Morros** extend from the prominent 576-foot (176-m) **Morro Rock** of Morro Bay 14 miles (22.5 km) south to the 775-foot (236-m) **Islay Hill,** which is located in the city of San Luis Obispo. The Nine Sisters' highest peak is the 1,546-foot (471-m) **Bishop Peak.** The top portion is a part of the 360-acre (146-ha) Bishop Peak Natural Reserve and is a popular spot for hikers and rock climbers. The Nine Sisters also make for unique animal and plant habitats. Morro Rock is a nesting place for peregrine falcons, while **Hollister Peak** hosts a colony of black-shouldered kites.

805/772-6101, www.parks.ca.gov, 6am-10pm daily), is for those seeking a serious nature fix on the Central Coast. This sprawling 8,000-acre (3,237-ha) park with 7 miles (11.3 km) of coastline has coves, tide pools, sand dunes, and almost 50 miles (81 km) of hiking trails. A great way to get a feel for the park's immense size is to hike up the 2-mile (3.2-km) **Valencia Peak Trail** (4 mi/6.4 km round-trip). In springtime the sides of the trail are decorated with blooming wildflowers, and the 1,347-foot-high (411-m) summit offers commanding views of Montaña de Oro's pocked coastline and Morro Rock jutting out in the distance.

For a feel of the coast, park right in front of **Spooner's Cove** and walk out on its wide, coarse-grained beach. On the cove's north end, Islay Creek drains into the ocean. There's also a picturesque arch across the creek in the rock face on the north side. The **Spooner Ranch House Museum** informs visitors about early inhabitants of the park's land, the Spooner family. There are also displays about the area's plants, mountain lions, and raptors in the small facility.

Morro Bay State Park

Morro Bay State Park (Morro Bay State Park Rd., 805/772-6101, www.parks.ca.gov, 6am-10pm daily) is not a typical state park. It has hiking trails, a campground, and recreational opportunities, but this park also has its own natural history museum, a golf course, and a marina. Just south of town, it's situated on the shores of Morro Bay. One way to get a feel for the park is to hike the **Black Hill Trail** (3 mi/4.8 km round-trip).

The park's **Morro Bay Museum of Natural History** (Morro Bay State Park Rd., 805/772-2694, www.parks.ca.gov, 10am-5pm daily, $3 adults, children under 12 free) is small but informative, with displays that explain the habitats of the Central Coast and some interactive exhibits for kids. An observation deck hanging off the museum allows for a great view of Morro Bay. Beside the museum is a garden that shows how the area's original inhabitants, the Chumash people, utilized the region's plants.

Play a round of golf at the **Morro Bay State Park Golf Course** (201 State Park Rd., 805/772-1923, http://golfmorrobay.com, $45 Mon.-Fri., $54 Sat.-Sun.), or head out on the water in a kayak, a canoe, or a stand-up paddleboard rented from **A Kayak Shack** (10 State Park Rd., 805/772-8796, www.morrobaykayakrental.com, 9am-5pm daily summer, 9am-4pm Fri.-Sun. winter, kayaks $16-20 per hour, canoes $20 per hour, stand-up paddleboards $16 per hour).

Entertainment

Bars

Down on the Embarcadero, **The Libertine Pub** (801 Embarcadero, 805/772-0700, http://libertinebrewing.com, 11am-10pm Mon.-Thurs., 11am-11pm Fri.-Sat., 10am-10pm Sun.) is the place for the discerning beer drinker. It began as a craft beer bar before moving into brewing its own wild ales. The pub features more than 30 rotating craft beers on tap. One of the beers will always be a sour. Pub food, including seafood tacos, burgers, and gourmet tater tots, are available to accompany your suds. Live music typically happens Wednesday-Saturday nights.

Legends Bar (899 Main St., 805/772-2525, 10am-2am daily) has a red pool table and a giant moose head poking out from behind the bar. Grab a drink and look at the framed historical photos covering the walls.

Festivals and Events

Strong winds kick up on the Central Coast in the spring. The **Morro Bay Kite Festival** (805/305-0579, www.morrobaykitefestival.org, Apr.) takes advantage of these gales with pro kite fliers twirling and flipping their kites in the sky. The festival also offers kite-flying lessons.

For over 30 years, the **Morro Bay Harbor Festival** (805/772-1155, www.mbhf.com, Oct.) has showcased the best of the region, including wines, seafood, live music, and a clam chowder contest.

Recreation

Beaches

There are several beaches in and around Morro Bay. Popular with surfers and beachcombers, **Morro Rock Beach** (west end of Embarcadero, 805/772-6200, www.morro-bay.ca.us) lies within the city limits, just north of Morro Rock. Two lifeguard towers are staffed Memorial Day-Labor Day (10am-6pm daily).

Just north of town is **Morro Strand State Beach** (CA-1, 805/772-6101, www.parks.ca.gov). The 3-mile (4.8-km) strand of sand is popular with anglers, windsurfers, and kite fliers.

Surfing

Morro Rock Beach (west end of Embarcadero, 805/772-6200, www.morro-bay.ca.us) has a consistent beach break. It's a unique experience to be able

Morro Rock

to stare up at a giant rock while waiting for waves. **Wavelengths Surf Shop** (998 Embarcadero, 805/772-3904, 9:30am-6pm daily, board rental $20 per day, wetsuit $10 per day), on the Embarcadero on the way to the beach, rents out boards and wetsuits.

Kayaking and Stand-Up Paddleboarding

Paddling the protected scenic waters of Morro Bay, whether you're in a kayak or on a stand-up paddleboard (SUP), is a great way to see wildlife up close. You might see otters lazily backstroking in the estuary or clouds of birds gliding just above the surface of the water.

On the bay with a view of the rock, **Rock Kayak** (845 Embarcadero, 805/772-2906, http://rockkayak.com, 9:30am-5pm daily summer, 9:30am-3:30pm daily winter, kayaks $15-25 per hour, stand-up paddleboards $15 per hour) offers gear rentals for your aquatic adventure. In Morro Bay State Park, you can secure a canoe or kayak from **A Kayak Shack** (10 State Park Rd., 805/772-8796, www.morrobaykayakrental.com, 9am-5pm daily summer, 9am-4pm Fri.-Sun. winter, kayaks $16-20 per hour, canoes $20 per hour, stand-up paddleboards $16 per hour).

Boat Tours

Sub Sea Tours (699 Embarcadero, 805/772-9463, www.subseatours.com, $17 adults, $13 seniors and students, $8 children) is like snorkeling without getting wet. The yellow 27-foot (8.2-m) semi-submersible vessel has a cabin outfitted with windows below the water. The 45-minute tour takes you around the harbor in search of wildlife. Expect to see sea lions sunning on a floating dock and sea otters playing in the water. At a much-touted secret spot, fish congregate for feeding. You'll typically see smelt, appearing like silver splinters, but may also catch a glimpse of salmon, lingcod, perch, and sunfish. Kids will love it. Sub Sea Tours also schedules 2- to 3.5-hour **whale-watching excursions** ($50 adults, $45 seniors and students, $35 children under 12) to see California gray whales and humpback whales.

Hiking

Morro Bay State Park (Morro Bay State Park Rd., 805/772-6101, www.parks.ca.gov, 6am-10pm daily) has 13 miles (20.9 km) of hiking trails. One of the most popular is the **Black Hill Trail** (3 mi/4.8 km round-trip, moderate), which begins from the campground road. This climb gains 600 vertical feet (183 m) and passes through chaparral and eucalyptus on the way to the 640-foot-high (195-m) Black Hill, part of the same system of volcanic plugs that produced nearby Morro Rock.

Montaña de Oro State Park (Pecho Rd., 7 mi/11.3 km south of Los Osos, 805/772-6101, www.parks.ca.gov, 6am-10pm daily) has almost 50 miles (81 km) of hiking trails. Take in the park's coastline along the **Montaña de Oro Bluffs Trail** (4 mi/6.4 km round-trip, easy). The trailhead begins about 100 yards (91.4 m) south of the visitors center and campground entrance and runs along a marine terrace to the park's southern boundary. Starting at the parking area just south of the visitors center, **Valencia Peak Trail** (4 mi/6.4 km round-trip, moderate) leads to its namesake 1,347-foot-high (411-m) peak, which offers a nice view of the coastline spread out below. The **Hazard Peak Trail** (6 mi/9.7 km round-trip, moderate-strenuous) starts at Pecho Valley Road and climbs to the summit of 1,076-foot (328-m) Hazard Peak, with unobstructed 360-degree views. The **Islay Canyon Trail** (6 mi/9.7 km round-trip, moderate) takes you through the park's inland creek beds and canyons. Starting at the bottom of Islay Creek Canyon, this wide dirt path is popular with birders because of the 25-40 different bird species that frequent the area.

Bird-Watching

Morro Bay is one of California's great birding spots. **Morro Bay State Park** is home to a **heron rookery,** located just north of the Museum of Natural History. At **Morro Rock,** you'll see endangered peregrine falcons, ever-present gulls, and the occasional canyon wren. On the northwest end of **Morro Bay State Park Marina** (off State Park Dr.), birders can spot loons, grebes, brants, and ducks; you may also see American pipits and Nelson's sparrows. The cypress trees host roosting black-crowned night herons. The **Morro Coast Audubon Society** (805/772-1991, www.morrocoastaudubon.org) conducts birding field trips to local hot spots; check the website for information on upcoming field trips.

Food

Seafood

Seafood is the way to go when dining in the fishing village of Morro Bay. An unassuming fish house with views of the fishing boats and the bay, ★ **Tognazzini's Dockside Restaurant** (1245 Embarcadero, 805/772-8100, www.morrobaydockside.com, 11am-9pm daily, $18-27) has an extensive seafood menu as well as art depicting sultry mermaids hanging on the wall. Entrées include shrimp and scallop kebabs and wild salmon in a unique tequila marinade. Oyster lovers can't go wrong with Dockside's barbecued appetizer, which features the shellfish swimming in garlic butter studded with scallions. Behind the main restaurant is the **Dockside Too Fish Market** (10am-7pm Sun.-Thurs., 10am-8pm Fri.-Sat. summer, 10am-6pm Sun.-Thurs., 10am-8pm Fri.-Sat. winter), a local favorite with beer, seafood, and live music.

Located on a hill above the Embarcadero, **Dorn's Original Breakers Café** (801 Market Ave., 805/772-4415, www.dornscafe.com, 7am-9pm daily, $13-44) offers a great view of Morro Rock from its dining room. It has been family-owned and operated since 1942. Dinner begins with bread and a dish of garlic, olive oil, vinegar, and cheese. The large menu of seafood and steak includes fresh daily specials like snapper, petrale sole, salmon, and halibut from local waters.

Mexican

People worship the crab cake and fish tacos at ★ **Taco Temple** (2680 N. Main St., 805/772-4965, http://tacotemple.com, 11am-8pm Sun.-Thurs., 11am-8:30pm Fri.-Sat., $7-22). Housed in a big multicolored building east of CA-1, where colorful surfboards hang on the walls, this is not the standard taqueria. The California take on classic Mexican dishes includes sweet potato enchiladas and tacos filled with soft-shell crab or calamari. The tacos are served like salads, with the meat and greens piled on tortillas. The chips and salsa are terrific.

Breakfast and Brunch

★ **Frankie & Lola's** (1154 Front St., 805/771-9306, www.frankieandlolas.

com, 6:30am-2pm daily, $4-13) does breakfast right. Creative savory dishes include the fried green tomato Benedict topped with creole hollandaise sauce and tasty, colorful chilaquiles with red chorizo, avocado, and tomatillo salsa. Lunch focuses on salads and sandwiches, while dinner is a little heartier, with options like bacon-wrapped meatloaf or chorizo-stuffed chicken.

On the road toward Montaña de Oro State Park, **Celia's Garden Café** (1188 Los Osos Valley Rd., Los Osos, 805/528-5711, http://celiasgardencafe.com, 7:30am-2pm Mon.-Fri., 7:30am-2:30pm Sat.-Sun., $9-12) is an ideal place to fuel up for a day of hiking. Fill up on a pork chop and eggs or the chicken-fried steak. Other options include omelets, Benedicts, and hotcakes. Located in a plant nursery, the café has an indoor dining room and a dog-friendly outdoor patio.

Accommodations

Under $150

The ★ **Masterpiece Hotel** (1206 Main St., 805/772-5633, www.masterpiecehotel.com, $109-339) is a great place to stay for art enthusiasts and lovers of quirky motels. Each guest room is decorated with framed prints from master painters, and the hallways also have prints of paintings by Henri Matisse, Vincent Van Gogh, and Norman Rockwell. There's also a large indoor spa pool decorated like a Roman bathhouse that further differentiates this motel from other cookie-cutter lodging options.

The **Sundown Inn** (640 Main St., 805/772-3229 or 800/696-6928, http://sundowninn.com, $109-229) is a well-priced motel within walking distance of Morro Bay's downtown and waterfront areas. Guest rooms have fridges, microwaves, and—here's something different—coin-operated vibrating beds.

$150-250

Built in 1939, the bright ★ **Beach Bungalow Inn and Suites** (1050 Morro Ave., 805/772-9700, www.morrobaybeachbungalow.com, $129-309) has been extensively renovated. The 12 clean, spacious, and modern guest rooms have hardwood floors, local art on the walls, and flat-screen TVs. Eleven of the guest rooms have gas fireplaces. Family suites accommodate four people, while king deluxe suites have full kitchens. Two bicycles are available for cruising around town.

Over $250

The family-run **Anderson Inn** (897 Embarcadero, 866/950-3434 www.andersoninnmorrobay.com, $279-429) is an eight-room boutique hotel located right on Morro Bay's busy Embarcadero. Three of the guest rooms are perched right over the estuary with stunning views of the nearby rock. Those premium guest rooms also include fireplaces and jetted tubs.

Camping

Located a couple of miles outside downtown Morro Bay, the **Morro Bay State Park Campground** (Morro Bay State Park Rd., 800/444-7275, www.reservecalifornia.com, tents $35, RVs $50) has 140 campsites, many shaded by eucalyptus and pine trees; right across the street is the Morro Bay estuary. Six miles (9.7 km) southwest of Morro Bay, **Montaña de Oro State Park** (Pecho Rd., 7 mi/11.3 km south of Los Osos, 800/444-7275, www.reservecalifornia.com, $25) has more primitive camping facilities. There are walk-in environmental campsites and a primitive campground behind the Spooner Ranch House that has pit toilets.

Information and Services

The **Morro Bay Chamber Visitors Center** (695 Harbor St., 805/772-4467, www.morrochamber.org, 9am-5pm daily) has a vast array of printed material, including maps.

To access the **post office** (898 Napa

Ave., 805/772-0839, 9am-5pm Mon.-Fri., 9am-1pm Sat.), you'll need to leave the Embarcadero area and head uptown.

In an emergency, dial **911.** The local police are the **Morro Bay Police Department** (870 Morro Bay Blvd., 805/772-6225). **French Hospital Medical Center** (1911 Johnson Ave., San Luis Obispo, 855/821-0827, www.dignityhealth.org) is the closest hospital.

Getting Around

The **Morro Bay Trolley** (595 Harbor Way, 805/772-2744, 11am-5pm Mon., 11am-7pm Fri.-Sat., 11am-6pm Sun., Memorial Day-first Sun. in Oct., $1 per ride) operates three routes. The **Waterfront Route** runs the length of the Embarcadero, including out to Morro Rock. The **Downtown Route** runs through the downtown (as in uptown) area all the way out to Morro Bay State Park. The **North Morro Bay Route** runs from uptown through the northern part of Morro Bay, north of the rock, along CA-1. An all-day pass (not a bad idea if you plan on seeing a lot of sights) is $3.

Cambria

Cambria, originally known as Slabtown, retains nothing of its original if uninspired moniker. Divided into east and west villages, it is a charming area of low storefronts, easily walkable with moss-covered pine trees as a backdrop. When it comes to this area, there is only one true sight. Cambria owes much of its prosperity to the immense tourist trap on the hill in nearby San Simeon: Hearst Castle. Once you're through with the castle tours, a few attractions in the lower elevations beckon as well. Typically you'll see visitors meandering in and out of the local stores, browsing art galleries, or combing Moonstone Beach for souvenir moonstone rocks. The really great thing about Cambria is that, aside from the gas stations, you won't find any chain stores in town, and Cambrians, and most visitors, like it that way.

Getting There

Cambria is located 21 miles (34 km) north of Morro Bay, directly along **CA-1,** and is only accessible by this road, whether you're coming from the north or the south. Cambria is not accessible by public transit, so if you are planning to use the town as a base to explore the area, a car will be necessary.

Sights and Beaches

Nitt Witt Ridge

While William Randolph Hearst built one of the most expensive homes ever seen in California, local eccentric Arthur Harold Beal (a.k.a. Captain Nit Wit or Der Tinkerpaw) got busy building the cheapest "castle" he could. **Nitt Witt Ridge** (881 Hillcrest Dr., 805/927-2690, http://nit-wit-ridge.business.site, tours by appointment) is the result of five decades of scavenging trash and using it as building supplies to create a multistory home like no other on the coast. The rambling structure is made of abalone shells, used car rims, and toilet seats, among other found materials. It's weird, it's funky, it's fun. Make an appointment with owners Michael and Stacey O'Malley to tour the property.

Known for its namesake, a shimmering gemstone littering the shore, **Moonstone Beach** (Moonstone Beach Dr.) is a scenic pebbly slice of coastline with craggy rocks offshore. Huts constructed from driftwood can be found on some sections of the beach, and there is plenty more than just moonstones to find washed up on the shoreline. There is also a wooden boardwalk that runs along the top of the bluffs above the beach to take in the scenery and watch moonstone collectors with buckets wander below in the tideline. Access is at Leffingwell Landing, Moonstone Beach Drive, and Santa Rosa Creek.

Entertainment

If touring Hearst Castle leaves you thirsty for a beer, Cambria has a few different options. **Mozzi's Saloon** (2262 Main St., 805/927-4767, http://mozzissaloon.com, 1pm-midnight Mon.-Wed., 1pm-2am Thurs.-Fri., 11am-2am Sat., noon-midnight Sun.) is a classic old California saloon. Old artifacts like lanterns and farm equipment hang from the ceiling above the long redwood bar, jukebox, and pool tables in this historic watering hole. On Tuesday, well drinks and draft beers are just $2. Friday nights feature karaoke, while Mozzi's hosts live music on Saturday nights.

Cambria Pines Lodge Fireside Lounge (Cambria Pines Lodge, 2905 Burton Dr., 805/927-4200, www.cambriapineslodge.com, 2pm-midnight daily) has live music nightly, performed on a stage to the right of a big stone fireplace. Enjoy a cocktail, beer, or wine seated at one of the couches or small tables.

Food

The ★ **Main Street Grill** (603 Main St., 805/927-3194, www.firestonegrill.com, 11am-9pm daily June-Aug., 11am-8pm daily Sept.-May, $4-23), by the same people behind San Luis Obispo's Firestone Grill, is a popular eatery housed in a cavernous building located on the way into Cambria. The tri-tip steak sandwich (tri-tip drenched in barbecue sauce and placed on a French roll dipped in butter) is the favorite, even though the ABC burger (with avocado, bacon, and cheese topping the meat) puts most burger joints to shame.

If the smell of the salt air on Moonstone Beach leaves you longing for a seafood dinner, head for the ★ **Sea Chest Oyster Bar** (6216 Moonstone Beach Dr., 805/927-4514, 5:30pm-9pm Wed.-Mon., $20-30, cash only, ATM

From top to bottom: Montaña de Oro State Park; Moonstone Beach boardwalk; Sea Chest Oyster Bar.

on-site). No reservations are accepted, so expect a long line out the door at opening time, and prepare to get here early or wait for one of the window-side tables. But the wait is worth it. The restaurant is located in a wooden cottage with great ocean views. Framed photographs on the walls and books on bookshelves add to the homey feel of the place. Sit at the bar to watch the cooks prepare the impressive dishes like halibut, salmon, and cioppino, which is served in the pot it was cooked in. The menu of oyster and clam appetizers includes terrific calamari strips and the indulgent Devils on Horseback, a decadent dish of sautéed oysters drenched in wine, garlic, and butter and topped with crispy bacon on two slabs of toast. Yum!

The eclectic menu at **Robin's** (4095 Burton Dr., 805/927-5007, www.robinsrestaurant.com, 11am-9:30pm Sun.-Thurs., 11am-10pm Fri.-Sat., $20-34) has cuisine from around the world, including Thailand (tofu pad thai, green chicken), India (a selection of curries, tandoori chicken), the Mediterranean (meze plate), Mexico (lobster enchiladas), and the old U.S. of A. (flatiron steak, burgers). What makes it so impressive is that Robin's does it all so well. Start with the signature salmon bisque or the grilled naan pizzette of the day. The menu also has a number of vegetarian and gluten-free dishes. Expect fine service from a staff that's proud of its product.

Accommodations

A pebble's throw from Moonstone Beach, the ★ **Sand Pebbles Inn** (6252 Moonstone Beach Dr., 805/927-5600, www.cambriainns.com, $164-364) is a two-story gray building where most guest rooms have glimpses of the ocean through bay windows. The clean, tastefully decorated guest rooms have comfortable beds, mini fridges, and microwaves. The six guest rooms facing west have full ocean views, while the bottom three have patios. Expect amenities such as welcome cookies and a lending library of DVDs. Owned by the same family, the adults-only **Blue Dolphin Inn** (6470 Moonstone Beach Dr., 805/927-3300, www.cambriainns.com, $269-439) is more upscale than its neighbor. The six full ocean-view rooms come with fireplaces, Keurig coffeemakers, robes, and slippers. Breakfast is delivered to your room every morning.

Moonstone Landing (6240 Moonstone Beach Dr., 805/927-0012, www.moonstonelanding.com, $200-400) provides inexpensive partial-view guest rooms with the decor and amenities of a mid-tier chain motel as well as oceanfront luxury guest rooms featuring porches with ocean views, soaking tubs, and gas fireplaces.

Information and Services

The **Cambria Chamber of Commerce** (767 Main St., 805/927-3624, www.cambriachamber.org, 9am-5pm Mon.-Sat.) is probably the best resource for information on the area. It also provides a free annual publication that lists many of the stores, restaurants, and lodgings. Pick up a trail guide for additional hikes and walks.

Cambria is served by three medical facilities: **Twin Cities Hospital** (1100 Las Tablas Rd., Templeton, 805/434-3500, www.tenethealthcentralcoast.com), in Templeton, 25 miles (40 km) inland, and **Sierra Vista Regional Medical Center** (1010 Murray Ave., San Luis Obispo, 805/546-7600, www.tenethealthcentralcoast.com) and **French Hospital Medical Center** (1911 Johnson Ave., San Luis Obispo, 855/821-0827, www.dignityhealth.org), both in San Luis Obispo, 37 miles (60 km) south.

Getting Around

The regional bus system, the **RTA** (805/541-2228, www.slorta.org), connects San Luis Obispo, Morro Bay, Cayucos, Cambria, and San Simeon. Fares range $1.75-3.25.

San Simeon

From Cambria, San Simeon is 7 miles (11.3 km) north along **CA-1.** Its biggest attraction, Hearst Castle, quite frankly, *is* San Simeon. The town grew up around it to support the overwhelming needs and never-ending construction of its megalomaniacal owner.

Sights

★ Hearst Castle

There's nothing else in California quite like **Hearst Castle** (CA-1 and Hearst Castle Rd., 800/444-4445, www.hearstcastle.org, tours 9am-3:20pm daily). Newspaper magnate William Randolph Hearst conceived the idea of a grand mansion in the Mediterranean style on land his parents bought along the central California coast. He hired Julia Morgan, the first female civil engineering graduate from the University of California, Berkeley, to design and build the house for him. She did a brilliant job with every detail, despite the ever-changing wishes of her employer. By way of decoration, Hearst assisted in the relocation of hundreds of European medieval and Renaissance antiquities, from tiny tchotchkes to whole gilded ceilings. Hearst also adored exotic animals, and he created one of the largest private zoos in the nation on his thousands of Central Coast acres. Most of the zoo is gone now, but you still see the occasional zebra grazing peacefully along CA-1 south of the castle, heralding Hearst Castle ahead.

The visitors center is a lavish affair with a gift shop, restaurant, café, ticket booth, and movie theater. The film *Hearst Castle—Building the Dream* gives an overview of the construction and history of the marvelous edifice, as well as William Randolph Hearst's empire. After buying your ticket, board the shuttle that takes you up the hill to your tour. No private cars are allowed on the roads up to the castle. There are various tours to choose from, each focusing on different spaces and aspects of the castle.

Tours

Expect to walk for at least an hour on whichever tour you choose, and to climb up and down many stairs. Even the most jaded traveler can't help but be amazed by the beauty and opulence that drips from every room in the house. Lovers of European art and antiques will want to stay forever.

The **Grand Rooms Museum Tour** (1 hour, 159 stairs, 0.6 mi/1 km, $25 adults, $12 children under 12) is recommended for first-time visitors. It begins in the castle's assembly room, which is draped in Flemish tapestries, before heading into the dining room, billiard room, and impressive movie theater, where you'll watch a few old Hearst newsreels. The guide then lets you loose to take in the swimming pools: the indoor pool, decorated in gold and blue, and the stunning outdoor Neptune Pool.

For a further glimpse into Hearst's personal life, take the **Upstairs Suites Tour** (1 hour, 332 stairs, 0.75 mi/1.2 km, $25 adults, $12 children under 12). Among the highlights are a stop within Hearst's private suite and a visit to his library, which holds over 4,000 books and 150 ancient Greek vases. At the end of this tour, you can explore the grounds, including the Neptune Pool, on your own.

Epicureans should opt for the **Cottages & Kitchen Tour** (1 hour, 204 stairs, 0.75 mi/1.2 km, $25 adults, $12 children under 12). You visit the wine cellar first, where there are still bottles of wine, gin, rum, beer, and vermouth along the walls. Then take in the ornate guest cottages Casa Del Monte and Casa del Mar, where Hearst spent the final two years of his life. The tour concludes in the massive castle kitchen, before leaving you to explore the grounds on your own.

The seasonal **Evening Museum Tour** (1.75 hours, 303 stairs, 0.75 mi/1.2 km, $36 adults, $18 children under 12) is only given in spring and fall. Volunteers dress in 1930s fashions and welcome guests as if they are arriving at one of Hearst's legendary parties.

There are also specialty tours that lend insight into different subjects relating to Hearst and his castle. One year-round offering is **Designing the Dream** (1.25 hours, 320 stairs, 1.2 mi/1.9 km, $30 adults, $15 children under 12), good for architecture and interior design fans.

Fall-spring, the **Art of San Simeon** (2 hours, 750 stairs, $100 pp) canvases the castle's art collection, including paintings, tapestries, sculptures, and antiquities. Also available fall-spring is the **Julia Morgan Tour** (2 hours, 750 stairs, $100 pp), during which you'll learn more about the castle's famed architect, and **Hearst and Hollywood Tour** (2 hours, 750 stairs, $100 pp), which covers the castle's various celebrity visitors, like Charlie Chaplin, Cary Grant, and Greta Garbo. These tours don't have fixed routes and so mileages may vary.

Buy tour tickets at least a few days in advance, and even farther ahead for summer weekends. Wheelchair-accessible Grand Rooms and Evening Tours are available for visitors with limited mobility. Strollers are not permitted. Restrooms and food concessions are in the visitors center. No food, drink, or chewing gum is allowed on any tour.

Piedras Blancas Light Station

First illuminated in 1875, the **Piedras Blancas Light Station** (tours meet at the Piedras Blancas Motel, 1.5 mi/2.4 km north of the light station on CA-1, 805/927-7361, www.piedrasblancas.org, tours 9:45am-noon Mon.-Tues. and Thurs.-Sat., June 15-Aug. 31, 9:45am-noon Tues., Thurs., and Sat. Sept. 1-June 14, $10 adults, $5 children 6-17, children under 6 free) and its adjacent grounds can be accessed on a two-hour tour. The name Piedras Blancas means "white rocks" in Spanish. In 1948 a nearby earthquake caused a crack in the lighthouse tower and the removal of a first-order Fresnel lens, which was replaced with an automatic aero beacon.

Piedras Blancas Elephant Seal Rookery

Stopping at the **Piedras Blancas Elephant Seal Rookery** (CA-1, 7 mi/11.3 north of San Simeon, 805/924-1628, www.elephantseal.org, free) is like watching a nature documentary in real time. On this sliver of beach, up to 17,000 elephant seals rest, belch, breed, give birth, or fight one another to mate. The rookery is right along CA-1: Turn into the large gravel parking lot and follow the boardwalks north or south to viewing areas where informative plaques give background on the elephant seals; volunteer docents are available to answer questions (10am-4pm daily). The beaches themselves are off-limits to humans; they're covered in the large marine mammals.

William Randolph Hearst Memorial State Beach

Down the hill from Hearst Castle is **William Randolph Hearst Memorial State Beach** (750 Hearst Castle Rd., 805/927-2020, www.parks.ca.gov, dawn-dusk daily), with kelp-strewn sand along a protected cove. The 795-foot-long (242-m) pier is great for fishing and strolling, and the **Coastal Discovery Center** (805/927-2145, 11am-5pm Fri.-Sun., free), run by California State Parks and the Monterey Bay National Marine Sanctuary, warrants a stop. It focuses on local natural history and culture, with exhibits on shipwrecks, a display on elephant seals, and an interactive tide pool.

Food

An unassuming steak and seafood restaurant attached to San Simeon's Quality Inn, the family-owned **Manta Rey Restaurant** (9240 Castillo Dr., 805/924-1032, www.mantareyrestaurant.com, 5pm-9pm daily, $17-56) pleasantly surprises with its artfully done and tasty seafood dishes. Items like salmon, oysters, and sea bass come from nearby Morro Bay when in season. A good place to start is with Manta Rey's oysters Rockefeller appetizer, a rich mix of baked oyster, bacon, cheese, and spinach in an oyster shell. Try the perfectly breaded sand dabs in a creamy basil and sherry sauce, also often caught fresh in nearby Morro Bay.

The **Hearst Ranch Winery** (442 SLO San Simeon Rd., 805/927-4100, www.hearstranchwinery.com, 11am-4pm daily) offers a chance to sample wines from estate vineyards in nearby Paso Robles at its cliffside tasting room in San Simeon.

Accommodations

San Simeon has a small strip of hotels on either side of the highway south of Hearst Castle. There are more accommodations in Cambria, just 5 miles (8 km) away.

The **Cavalier Oceanfront Resort** (9415 Hearst Dr., 805/927-4688, www.cavalierresort.com, $240-439) occupies a prime piece of real estate in San Simeon on a bluff above the ocean just south of Pico Creek. The highest-priced rooms are oceanfront offerings with wood-burning fireplaces, soaking tubs, and private patios. The grounds include a pool, an exercise room, a day spa, and a restaurant.

One of San Simeon's best lodging options, **The Morgan at San Simeon Hotel** (9135 Hearst Dr., 800/451-9900, www.hotel-morgan.com, $149-299) is named for Hearst Castle architect Julia Morgan, paying tribute to her with reproductions of her architectural drawings in all the guest rooms. The rooms are clean and well appointed, and some have partial ocean views; eight rooms come with soaking tubs and gas fireplaces. The Morgan also has a wind-sheltered pool and deck.

Information and Services

Located in the Cavalier Plaza Shopping Center, the **San Simeon Chamber of Commerce** (250 San Simeon Ave., Ste. 3A, 805/927-3500, http://visitsansimeonca.com, 9am-5pm daily) has visitor information. Its website covers accommodations, restaurants, recreation, attractions, events, and the region's history.

San Simeon is served by three medical facilities that are each about 45 minutes away: **Twin Cities Hospital** (1100 Las Tablas Rd., Templeton, 805/434-3500, www.tenethealthcentralcoast.com), **Sierra Vista Regional Medical Center** (1010 Murray St., San Luis Obispo, 805/546-7600, www.tenethealthcentralcoast.com), and **French Hospital Medical Center** (1911 Johnson Ave., San Luis Obispo, 855/821-0827, www.dignityhealth.org).

Getting Around

The regional bus system, the **RTA** (805/541-2228, www.slorta.org), connects San Luis Obispo, Morro Bay, Cayucos, Cambria, and San Simeon. Fares range $1.75-3.25.

Big Sur

TOP EXPERIENCE

Big Sur welcomes many types of visitors. Nature-lovers come to camp and hike the pristine wilderness areas, to don thick wetsuits and surf often-deserted beaches, and even to hunt for jade in rocky coves. On the other hand, some of the wealthiest people from California and beyond visit to relax at unbelievably upscale hotels and spas with dazzling views of the ocean. Whether you prefer a low-cost camping trip or a luxury resort, Big Sur offers its beauty and charm to all. Part of that charm is Big Sur's determination to remain peacefully apart from the Information Age; this means that your cell phone may not work in many parts of Big Sur.

Getting There

Big Sur can only be reached via **CA-1.** The drive from San Simeon into Big Sur

Big Sur

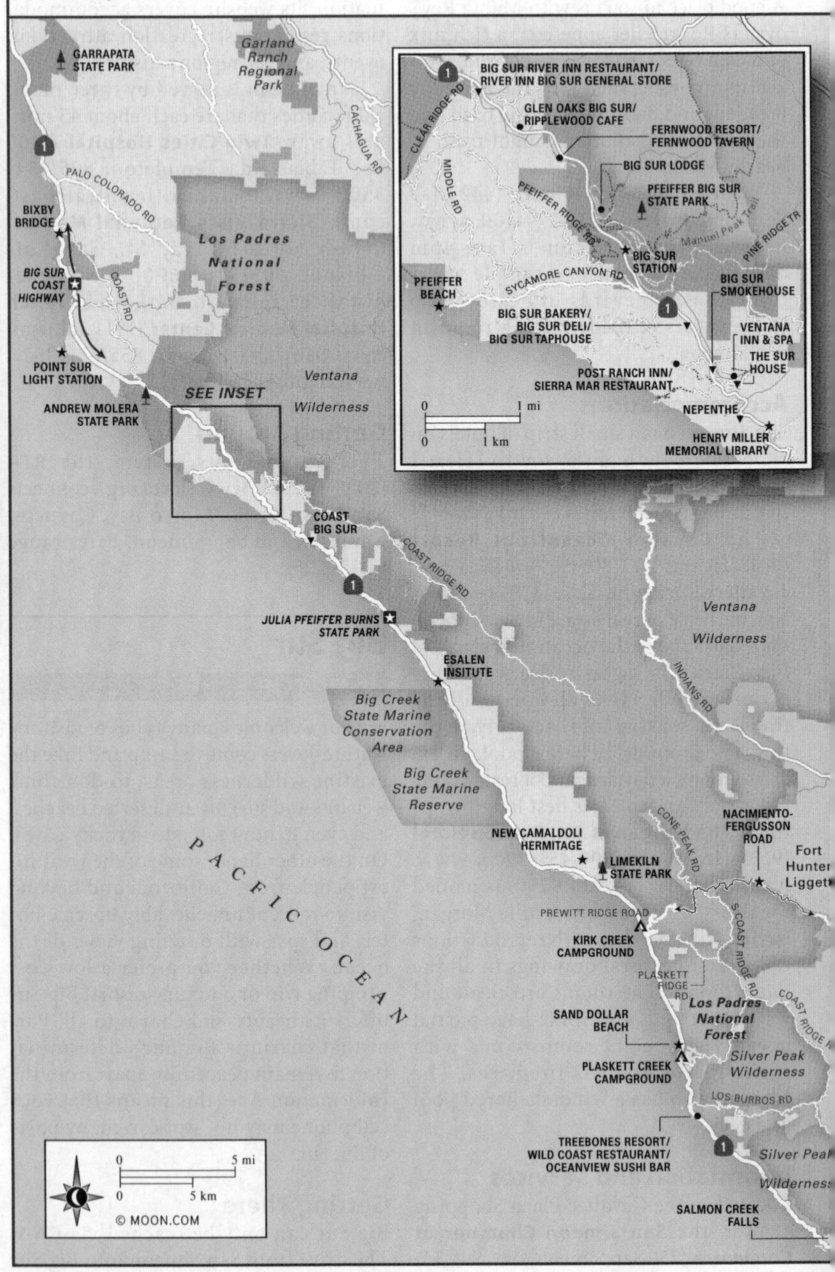

GARRAPATA STATE PARK
Garland Ranch Regional Park
CACHAGUA RD
1
PALO COLORADO RD
BIXBY BRIDGE
BIG SUR COAST HIGHWAY
COAST RD
Los Padres National Forest
POINT SUR LIGHT STATION
ANDREW MOLERA STATE PARK
SEE INSET
Ventana Wilderness
COAST BIG SUR
COAST RIDGE RD
JULIA PFEIFFER BURNS STATE PARK
ESALEN INSITUTE
Big Creek State Marine Conservation Area
Big Creek State Marine Reserve
PACIFIC OCEAN
NEW CAMALDOLI HERMITAGE
LIMEKILN STATE PARK
CONE PEAK RD
NACIMIENTO-FERGUSSON ROAD
Fort Hunter Liggett
PREWITT RIDGE ROAD
KIRK CREEK CAMPGROUND
S COAST RIDGE RD
PLASKETT RIDGE RD
COAST RIDGE RD
SAND DOLLAR BEACH
Los Padres National Forest
PLASKETT CREEK CAMPGROUND
Silver Peak Wilderness
LOS BURROS RD
TREEBONES RESORT/ WILD COAST RESTAURANT/ OCEANVIEW SUSHI BAR
SALMON CREEK FALLS
INDIANS RD
0 5 mi
0 5 km
© MOON.COM
BIG SUR RIVER INN RESTAURANT/ RIVER INN BIG SUR GENERAL STORE
CLEAR RIDGE RD
GLEN OAKS BIG SUR/ RIPPLEWOOD CAFE
FERNWOOD RESORT/ FERNWOOD TAVERN
MIDDLE RD
BIG SUR LODGE
PFEIFFER BIG SUR STATE PARK
PFEIFFER RIDGE RD
Manuel Peak Trail
PINE RIDGE TR
BIG SUR STATION
PFEIFFER BEACH
SYCAMORE CANYON RD
BIG SUR SMOKEHOUSE
BIG SUR BAKERY/ BIG SUR DELI/ BIG SUR TAPHOUSE
VENTANA INN & SPA
THE SUR HOUSE
POST RANCH INN/ SIERRA MAR RESTAURANT
NEPENTHE
HENRY MILLER MEMORIAL LIBRARY
0 1 mi
0 1 km

is where the Pacific Coast Highway gets really interesting, twisting and turning along with the coastline. Big Sur is not a town but rather the name for the lightly developed coastline stretching from San Simeon to Carmel. The largest concentration of businesses is located within the Big Sur Valley, 61 miles (98 km) north of San Simeon.

The drive from San Simeon to the Big Sur Valley usually takes around **1.5 hours,** but it can be slow going, especially if you are behind an RV. You may want to stop every few miles to snap a photo of the stunning coastline. If traffic is backing up behind you, pull into a turnout to let other cars pass; the local drivers can be impatient with tourist traffic.

CA-1 can have one or both lanes closed at times, especially in the winter months when rockslides occur. The 2016 winter made the highway through Big Sur impassable due to a bridge failure and a massive landslide. Check the **Caltrans** website (http://dot.ca.gov) or the ***Big Sur California Blog*** (www.thebigsurblog.com) for current road conditions. Also, the ***Big Sur Kate Blog*** (http://bigsurkate.blog) is run by a Big Sur local and is one of the best places to look for information when fires, storms, and road closures plague Big Sur.

Sights

★ Big Sur Coast Highway

The **Big Sur Coast Highway,** a 90-mile (145-km) stretch of CA-1, is quite simply one of the most picturesque roads in the country. A two-lane road, it twists and turns with Big Sur's jagged coastline, running along precipitous cliffs and rocky beaches, through dense redwood forest, over historic bridges, and past innumerable parks. In the winter, you might spot migrating whales offshore spouting fountains of air and water, while spring finds yucca plants feathering the hillsides and wildflowers coloring the landscape. Construction on this stretch of road was completed in the 1930s, connecting Cambria to Carmel. You can start out at either of these towns and spend a whole day making your way to the other end of the road. The road has plenty of wide turnouts set into picturesque cliffs to make it easy to stop to admire the glittering ocean and stunning wooded cliffs running right out to the water. There can be frequent highway delays due to road construction. Expect to take your time.

Salmon Creek Falls

One of the southern portion of Big Sur's best natural attractions is **Salmon Creek Falls** (8 mi/12.9 km south of Gorda or 3.5 mi/5.6 km north of Ragged Point on CA-1, 831/385-5434, www.fs.usda.gov). Flowing year-round, a pair of waterfalls pour down rocks over 100 feet (30.5 m) high, and their streams join halfway down. At the base of the falls is a deep green pool of water. To get a great perspective of the falls, take an easy 10-minute walk from the highway over a primitive trail littered with rocks. The unmarked parking area is a pullout in the middle of a hairpin turn on CA-1.

★ Julia Pfeiffer Burns State Park

Postcard-perfect views can be attained at **Julia Pfeiffer Burns State Park** (CA-1, 37 mi/60 km north of Ragged Point, 831/667-2315, www.parks.ca.gov, 8am-sunset daily, day use $10). Photo ops are available from the short **Overlook Trail,** which runs out to a stunning view of **McWay Falls,** the park's big draw. The 80-foot-high (24.4-m) waterfall cascades year-round off a cliff and onto the beach of a remote cove, where the water wets the sand and trickles out into the sea. The water of the cove gleams bright cerulean blue against the off-white sand of the beach; it looks more like the South Pacific than California. Anyone with an ounce of love for the ocean will want to build a hut right there beside the waterfall. But you can't. In fact, the reason you look down on a pristine and empty stretch of sand is that there's no way down to the cove that is even remotely safe. You can also catch views of McWay Falls from a highway pullout just north of the park entrance, near mile marker 36.2.

Also within the park are two superb hikes, one that heads to the coast and one that heads inland and up, accessed from an unmarked dirt pullout 2 miles (3.2 km) north of Julia Pfeiffer Burns State Park's main entrance. On the west side is the **Partington Cove Trail** (1 mi/1.6 km round-trip, easy), an underrated walk that heads to a striking, narrow coastal inlet via a tunnel blasted through rock. Heading inland and up, the **Tanbark Trail and Tin House Loop** (5.6 mi/9 km round-trip, strenuous) takes you through towering redwoods and offers sweeping coastal views on its 1,600-foot (488-m) climb to an oak forest and an abandoned building made out of the sidings of old gas station buildings.

Henry Miller Memorial Library

A number of authors have done time in Big Sur, soaking in the remote wilderness and sea air to gather inspiration for their work. Henry Miller lived and wrote in Big Sur for 18 years, and his 1957 novel *Big Sur and the Oranges of Hieronymus Bosch* describes his time here. Today, the **Henry Miller Memorial Library** (48603 CA-1, 831/667-2574, www.henrymiller.org, 11am-5pm Wed.-Sun.) celebrates the life and work of Miller and his brethren in this quirky community center, museum, coffee shop, and gathering place. What you won't find is a typical lending library or slicked-up museum. Instead, inside is a well-curated bookstore featuring the works of Miller as well as other authors like Jack Kerouac and Richard Brautigan, along with a crew of employees who are always worth striking up a conversation with. The library has also become an important arts and music center for the Central Coast. Check the website for upcoming events.

McWay Falls in Julia Pfeiffer Burns State Park

Big Sur Station

Big Sur Station (CA-1, 0.3 mi/0.5 km south of Pfeiffer Big Sur State Park, 831/667-2315, 9am-4pm daily) offers maps and brochures for all the major parks and trails of Big Sur, plus a minimal bookshop. This is also where the trailhead for the popular backcountry **Pine Ridge Trail** is located. You can get a **free backcountry fire permit** as well as pay for Pine Ridge Trailhead parking here.

Pfeiffer Big Sur State Park

The most developed park in Big Sur is **Pfeiffer Big Sur State Park** (CA-1, 0.25 mi/0.4 km north of Big Sur Station, 831/667-2315, www.parks.ca.gov, 8am-sunset daily, day use $10). It's got the Big Sur Lodge, a restaurant and café, a shop, an amphitheater, a somewhat incongruous softball field, plenty of hiking-only trails, and lovely redwood-shaded campsites. This park isn't situated by the beach; it's up in the coastal redwoods forest, with a network of roads that can be driven or biked up into the trees and along the Big Sur River.

Pfeiffer Big Sur hosts the tiny **Nature Center,** which features stuffed examples of local wildlife and an exhibit that allows you to see the Big Sur coastline from a California condor's viewpoint. It's open seasonally; call the park for days and hours. The historic **Homestead Cabin,** located off the Big Sur Gorge Trail, was once the home of part of the Pfeiffer family—the first European immigrants to settle in Big Sur.

No bikes or horses are allowed on trails in this park, which makes it quite peaceful for hikers. For a starter walk, take the **Nature Trail** (0.7 mi/1.1 km round-trip), an easy self-guided stroll that imparts information about local vegetation. A far more challenging option is the **Mount Manuel Trail** (8 mi/12.9 km round-trip).

Need to cool off after hiking? Scramble out to the undeveloped **Big Sur River Gorge,** where the river slows and creates pools that are great for swimming. Relax and enjoy the water, but don't try to dive here. The undeveloped trail to the gorge can be found at the eastern end of the campground.

Pfeiffer Beach

Big Sur has plenty of striking meetings of land and sea, but **Pfeiffer Beach** (end of Sycamore Canyon Rd., 831/385-5434, www.campone.com, 9am-8pm daily, $10) is one of the coastline's most picturesque spots. This frequently windswept beach has two looming rock formations right where the beach meets the surf, and both of these rocks have holes that look like doorways, allowing waves and sunlight to pass through.

For newcomers, getting to Pfeiffer Beach is a bit tricky. Heading south on CA-1 from Big Sur Station, take the second paved right turn. Motorists (no motor homes) must then travel down a narrow, windy road for 2 miles (3.2 km) before reaching the entrance booth and the beach's parking lot. It's part of the adventure. The road can get backed up during peak summer hours, so opt for an early morning or off-hour visit instead. Note that the beach can be incredibly windy at times.

Andrew Molera State Park

At 4,800 acres (1,942 ha), **Andrew Molera State Park** (CA-1, 4.5 mi/7.2 km north of Pfeiffer Big Sur State Park, 831/667-1112, www.parks.ca.gov, 8am-sunset daily, day use $10) is a great place to immerse yourself in Big Sur's coastal beauty and rugged history.

Today, the **Cooper Cabin,** which is off the Headlands Trail, is a remnant from the park's past. The redwood structure, built in 1861, is the oldest building standing on the Big Sur coast. The **Molera Ranch House Museum** (831/667-2956, www.bigsurhistory.org, 11am-3pm Sat. Feb.-Dec.) displays stories of the life and times of Big Sur's human pioneers and artists as well as the wildlife and plants of the region. Take the road toward the horse tours to get to the ranch house. Next to the ranch house is the **Ventana Wildlife Society's Big Sur Discovery Center** (831/620-0702, www.ventanaws.org, 10am-4pm Sat.-Sun. Memorial Day-Labor Day). This is the place to learn about the successful reintroduction of the California condor to the region.

The park has numerous hiking trails that run down to the beach and up into the forest along the river. Many trails are open to cycling as well. Most of the park trails lie to the west of the highway. The beach is a 1-mile (1.6-km) walk down the easy **Creamery Meadow Trail.** A seasonal footbridge crosses the Big Sur River connecting the parking area to the trail from mid-June to late October. Other times of the year, hikers can carefully wade across the river to reach the trail.

For a longer and more difficult trek up the mountains and down to the beach, take the 8-mile (12.8-km) **Ridge Trail and Panorama Trail Loop.** It offers a serious day hike and fine views of the coast by connecting the **Ridge Trail,** the **Panorama Trail,** and the **Bluffs Trails** to the park's **Creamery Meadow.**

Point Sur Light Station

Sitting lonely and isolated out on its cliff, the **Point Sur Light Station** (CA-1, 0.25 mi/0.4 km north of Point Sur Naval Facility, 831/625-4419, www.pointsur.org, 10am and 2pm Wed. and Sat., 10am Sun. Apr.-Sept., 1pm Wed., 10am Sat.-Sun., Oct.-Mar., $15 adults, $5 ages 6-17, children 5 and under free) crowns the 361-foot-high (110-m) volcanic rock Point Sur, keeping watch over ships navigating near the rocky waters of Big Sur. It's the only complete 19th-century light station in California that you can visit, and even here access is severely limited. First lit in 1889, this now fully automated light station still provides navigational aid to ships off the coast; families stopped living and working in the tiny stone-built compound in 1974. But is the lighthouse truly uninhabited? Take one of the moonlight tours (call for information) to learn about the haunted history of the light station buildings.

You can't make a reservation for a Point Sur tour, so you should just show up and park your car off CA-1 on the west side by the farm gate. A guide meets visitors there at designated tour times and leads them up the paved road 0.5 mile (0.8 km) to the light station. Once there, you'll climb the stairs up to the light, explore the restored keepers' homes and service buildings, and walk out to the cliff edge. Expect to see a great variety of flora and fauna, with brilliant wildflowers in the spring and gray whales in the winter, and flocks of pelicans flying in formation at any time of year. Dress in layers; it can be sunny and hot or foggy and cold, winter or summertime, and sometimes both on the same tour! Tours last three hours and require more than a mile of walking, with a bit of slope, and more than 100 stairs. If you need special

Best Big Sur Day Hikes

One of Big Sur's best day hikes is found within **Julia Pfeiffer Burns State Park.** You can access the trailhead from the unmarked dirt pullout 2 miles (3.2 km) north of the park's main entrance. The **Partington Cove Trail** (1 mi/1.6 km round-trip, easy) descends down a dirt road, heading west to the coast. It continues through a 60-foot (18.3-m) tunnel that was blasted through rock for John Partington, for whom the cove was named; he ran a business shipping the bark of tanbark oak trees harvested in the canyon above. After passing through the tunnel, you'll arrive at the cove, where you may spot more vestiges of his export business in the form of eye bolts embedded in the rocks.

For a long coastal hike, take the **Ridge Trail and Panorama Trail Loop** (8 mi/12.9 km round-trip, moderate-strenuous) at **Andrew Molera State Park.** You'll start at the parking lot on the Creamery Meadow Beach Trail, then make a left onto the long and fairly steep **Ridge Trail** to get a sense of the local ecosystem. Then turn right onto the **Panorama Trail,** which runs down to the coastal scrublands. From the **Panorama Trail,** you can take a short spur called the **Spring Trail** out to a secluded beach. The **Panorama Trail** turns into the **Bluffs Trail,** which takes you back to Creamery Meadow, on the last leg.

assistance for your tour or have questions about accessibility, call 831/649-2836 as far in advance as possible of your visit to make arrangements.

The docents at Point Sur Light Station also offer tours of the **Point Sur Naval Facility** ($10 adults, $5 ages 6-17, children 5 and under free), the cluster of buildings just south of Point Sur. The abandoned buildings and grounds are a relic from the Cold War when the U.S. Navy created a secret base in Big Sur, where they attempted to listen in on Soviet submarines offshore. Learn about this little-known history and tour buildings in varying states of decay.

Bixby Bridge

You'll probably recognize the **Bixby Bridge** (CA-1, 8.25 mi/13.3 km north of Andrew Molera State Park) when you come upon it on CA-1 in Big Sur. The picturesque cement, open-spandrel arched bridge is one of the most photographed bridges in the nation, and it has been used in countless car commercials over the years. It was also featured in the opening credits of the HBO series *Big Little Lies.* The bridge was built in the early 1930s as part of the massive government works project that completed CA-1 through the Big Sur area, connecting the road from the north end of California to the south. Today, you can pull out at the north of the bridge to take photos or just look out at the attractive span and Bixby Creek flowing into the Pacific far below. Get another great view of the bridge by driving a few hundred feet down the dirt Old Coast Road, which is located on the bridge's northeast side. Be careful here as there is no designated parking lot, and this section of the roadway frequently fills with drivers trying to snap a photo.

Recreation

Hiking

The main reason to come to Big Sur is to get out of your vehicle and hike its beaches and forests. There are lots of hiking opportunities, from short walks under a canopy of redwood trees to multiday backpacking trips into Big Sur's wilderness interior.

Bird-Watching

Many visitors come to Big Sur just to see the birds. The Big Sur coast is home to innumerable species, from the tiniest bushtits up to grand pelicans and

California Condors

With wings spanning 10 feet (3 m) from tip to tip, the California condors soaring over the Big Sur coastline are some of the area's most impressive natural treasures. But, in 1987, there was only one bird left in the wild, which was taken into captivity as part of a breeding program. The condors' population had plummeted due to its susceptibility to lead poisoning along with deaths caused by electric power lines, habitat loss, and being shot by indiscriminate humans.

The reintroduction of the high-flying California condor, the largest flying bird in North America, to Big Sur and the Central Coast is truly one of conservation's greatest success stories. In 1997, the Monterey County-based nonprofit Ventana Wildlife Society (VWS) began releasing the giant birds back into the wild. Currently, over 100 wild condors soar above Big Sur and central California.

The species' recovery in the Big Sur area means that you might be able to spot a California condor flying overhead while visiting the rugged coastal region. Look for a tracking tag on the condor's wing to determine that you are actually looking at a California condor and not just a big turkey vulture. Or take a tour with the **Ventana Wildlife Society,** which uses radio telemetry to track the released birds. You can also visit the **Ventana Wildlife Society's Big Sur Discovery Center** (Andrew Molera State Park, CA-1, 4.5 mi/7.2 km north of Pfeiffer Big Sur State Park), where there's an exhibit that details the near extinction of the condor and the attempts to restore the population.

beyond. The most famous avian residents of this area are no doubt the rare and endangered California condors. Once upon a time, condors were all but extinct, with only a few left alive in captivity and conservationists struggling to help them breed. Today, more than 100 birds soar above the trails and beaches of central California. You might even see one swooping down low over your car as you drive down CA-1!

The **Ventana Wildlife Society** (VWS, 831/455-9514, www.ventanaws.org) watches over many of the endangered and protected avian species in Big Sur. As part of its mission to raise awareness of the condors and many other birds, the VWS offers bird-watching expeditions. Increase your chances of spotting a condor by signing up for one of its two hour California Condor Viewing Tours (Sat. June-Nov., $75 pp).

Spas

Spa Alila (Ventana Big Sur, 48123 CA-1, 831/667-4222, www.ventanabigsur.com, massages $175-615) offers a large menu of spa treatments to hotel guests as well as visitors. Indulge in a soothing massage, purifying body treatment, or rejuvenating or beautifying facial. Take your spa experience a step further in true Big Sur fashion with an astrological reading, an essence portrait, a Javanese coffee scrub, or a jade stone massage. Hotel guests can choose to have a spa treatment in the comfort of their own room or out on a private deck.

Entertainment

Live Music

Big Sur has become an unexpected hotbed of concerts. More than just a place to down a beer and observe the local characters, **Fernwood Tavern** (Fernwood Resort, 47200 CA-1, 831/667-2422, www.fernwoodbigsur.com, 11am-11pm Sun.-Thurs., 11am-1am Fri.-Sat.) features live music. Most of the big-name acts (Mac DeMarco! Yo La Tengo! Ty Segall!) swing through in summer and fall, but a wide range of regional acts perform on Saturday night starting at 10pm. The tavern is also just a classic watering hole, with redwood timbers and a fireplace that warms the place in the chilly months. Indoors, it's a great place to watch a sporting event. Outdoors it features a large deck under the redwoods with heat lamps, fire tables, and a Ping-Pong table. The bar serves nine beers on tap along with a full bar featuring offerings like handmade Bloody Marys and margaritas. This is also the place to come for tacos, burgers, or pizzas. On any given summer evening, the Fernwood can include an intriguing mix ranging from longtime locals to international tourists. The bar also offers free Internet to customers—a prized commodity in Big Sur.

The **Henry Miller Memorial Library** (48603 CA-1, 831/667-2574, www.henrymiller.org) hosts big concerts, book readings, and film screenings throughout the year, but mostly concentrated in summer and fall.

Big Sur River Inn Restaurant (46480 CA-1, 831/667-2700, www.bigsurriverinn.com, noon-4pm Sun. late Apr.-early Oct.) holds Sunday afternoon concerts on its back deck during summer and fall. The live music tradition here began in the 1960s with famed local act Jake Stock and the Abalone Stompers. Now mostly local jazz bands play on the restaurant's sunny deck, while a barbecue is set up on the large green lawn.

Bars

The **Big Sur Taphouse** (47250 CA-1, 831/667-2197, www.bigsurtaphouse.com, noon-10pm daily) has 10 rotating beers on tap, with a heavy emphasis on West Coast microbrews. The cozy interior has wood tables, a gas fireplace, and board games. With two big-screen TVs, the Taphouse is also a good place to catch your favorite sports team in action. Out back is a large patio with picnic tables and plenty of sun. The bar serves better-than-average bar food, including tacos, wings, and sandwiches.

Festivals and Events

The **Big Sur Marathon** (831/625-6226, www.bigsurmarathon.org, Apr.), touted as one of the world's best, runs from Big Sur Station to Carmel. Participants enjoy the rare opportunity to experience the stunning Big Sur coastline without any traffic.

Each year, the Pacific Valley School hosts the three-day, fund-raising **Big Sur Jade Festival** (805/924-1725, http://bigsurjadefestival.com, Oct.). Come out to see the artists, craftspeople, jewelry makers, and rock hunters displaying their wares in the early fall. The school is located across CA-1 from Sand Dollar Beach. Munch snacks as your feet tap to the live music playing as part of the festival. Check the website for the exact dates and information about this year's festival.

Food

As you traverse the famed CA-1 through Big Sur, you'll quickly realize that a ready meal isn't something to take for granted. You'll see no In-N-Out Burgers, Starbucks, or Safeways lining the road here. While you can find groceries, they tend to appear in small markets attached to motels. Pick up staple supplies in Cambria or Carmel before you enter the area if you don't plan to leave again for a few days, to avoid paying premium prices at the mini-marts.

Casual Dining

One of Big Sur's most popular attractions is ★ **Nepenthe** (48510 CA-1, 831/667-2345, www.nepenthe.com, 11:30am-10pm daily, $19-53), a restaurant on the site where Rita Hayworth and Orson Welles owned a cabin until 1947. The deck offers views on par with those you might attain on one of Big Sur's great hikes. At sunset, order up a basket of fries with Nepenthe's signature Ambrosia dipping sauce and wash them down with a potent South Coast margarita. For dinner there is glazed duck and filet mignon,

but the best bet is the restaurant's most popular item: the Ambrosia burger, a ground steak burger drenched in that tasty Ambrosia sauce. If there's a line at Nepenthe, consider dining at its **Café Kevah** (9am-4pm daily mid-Feb.-Jan.1 weather permitting, $9-16), an outdoor deck below the main restaurant that serves brunch, salads, and paninis.

Located inside the Coast Gallery, **COAST** (49901 CA-1, 831/667-2301, http://coastbigsur.com, 11am-4pm Thurs.-Mon., $9-16) is a café that has a rotating menu featuring items like sourdough pizzas, salads, and sandwiches utilizing local ingredients. Eat on the ocean-view terrace or pack up for a picnic.

The **Big Sur Smokehouse** (48123 CA-1, 831/667-2419, www.bigsursmokehouse.com, noon-8pm Fri.-Sun. winter, 8am-8pm daily summer, $13-26) is located in the old Post family (of the Post Ranch Inn) homestead, a distinct red building right off CA-1 that dates to 1867. The casual barbecue joint serves the classics, including brisket, pulled pork, and smoked chicken, served as part of hearty platters or in sandwiches. The barbecue sandwiches are huge and one of the better values in Big Sur at $13. Make it even better with a cold draft beer or well-crafted margarita.

The **Big Sur Bakery** (47540 CA-1, 831/667-0520, www.bigsurbakery.com, 8am-3:30pm Mon.-Tues., 8am-9pm Wed.-Sun., $18-32) might sound like a casual, walk-up eating establishment, and the bakery part of it is. You can stop in from 8am every day to grab a fresh-baked scone, a homemade jelly donut, or a flaky croissant sandwich to save for lunch. But on the dining room side, an elegant surprise awaits. Make reservations or you might miss out on the creative wood-fired pizzas, wood-grilled meats, and seafood. For brunch, you can

From top to bottom: Big Sur coast; Big Sur Smokehouse's hearty tri-tip sandwich; a hiker at Julia Pfeiffer Burns State Park.

order a wood-fired bacon and three-egg breakfast pizza.

The unassuming **Ripplewood Café** (47047 CA-1, 831/667-2242, www.ripplewoodresort.com, 8am-2pm daily, $9-16) serves a breakfast menu including pancakes, chorizo and eggs, and omelets. The grilled potato gratin is a highlight. Ripplewood shifts to lunch at 11:30am, when it offers sandwiches, Mexican dishes, and salads. Dine at its classic breakfast counter or outside on the brick patio among flowering plants.

If it's a warm afternoon, get a table on the sunny back deck of the **Big Sur River Inn Restaurant** (46840 CA-1, 831/667-2700, www.bigsurriverinn.com, 8am-9pm daily, $15-40). If it's chilly out, eat in the wood-beamed main dining room. The restaurant serves sandwiches, burgers, and salads for lunch and a porterhouse steak, ribs, seafood, and the recommended Noelle's Favorite Salad for dinner. For dessert, order the famous apple pie that put the restaurant on the map in the 1930s. This is also a fine place to just grab a beer or cocktail—it's known for its spicy Bloody Marys. In the late afternoon and early evening, a fun, local crowd gathers in the intimate bar area. On summer weekends, order your drink in a plastic cup so you can take it out back to sip in one of a few giant chairs plopped right down in the middle of the Big Sur River.

Fine Dining

You don't need to be a guest at the gorgeous Ventana to enjoy a fine gourmet dinner at **The Sur House** (48123 CA-1, 800/628-6500, www.ventanabigsur.com, 7:30am-10:30am, 11:30am-4pm, and 6pm-9pm daily, à la carte entrées $30-85, four-course dinner tasting menu $95). The spacious dining room boasts a warm wood fire, an open kitchen, and comfortable banquettes with plenty of throw pillows to lounge against as you peruse the menu. Request a table outside to enjoy stunning views with your meal. The inside dining room has great views from the bay windows too, along with pristine white tablecloths and pretty wooden furniture. Even in such a setting, the real star at this restaurant is the cuisine, with entrées like a Skuna Bay salmon and New York strip loin.

The **Sierra Mar** (47900 CA-1, 831/667-2800, www.postranchinn.com, noon-2pm and 5:30pm-9pm daily, lunch $75, dinner $125 pp) restaurant at the Post Ranch Inn offers a decadent four-course prix fixe dinner menu every night. There's also a less formal three-course lunch every day. With floor-to-ceiling glass windows overlooking the plunging ridgeline and the Pacific below, it's a good idea to schedule dinner during sunset. The daily menu rotates, but courses have included farm-raised abalone in brown butter and a succulent short rib and beef tenderloin duo.

Markets

With no supermarkets or chain mini-marts in the entire Big Sur region, the local markets do a booming business. The best of these is the **Big Sur Deli** (47520 CA-1, 831/667-2225, www.bigsurdeli.com, 7am-8pm daily, $5-8), which offers basic goods. It is also the spot to grab a sandwich or burrito to bring on a picnic or take back to your campsite. Also good is the **River Inn Big Sur General Store** (46840 CA-1, 831/667-2700, 7am-8pm daily, $10), which has basic snacks as well as a burrito and fruit smoothie bar.

Accommodations

$150-250

Fernwood Resort (47200 CA-1, 831/667-2422, www.fernwoodbigsur.com, motel rooms $180-235, cabins $290-340) is a refreshing anomaly in Big Sur, with its range of moderately priced lodging options. Basic motel rooms flank the on-site bar, **Fernwood Tavern**—a gathering place for locals and a frequent host of live music—while higher-priced units have gas fireplaces and hot tubs. Down near the Big Sur River, the cabins have fully equipped kitchens and a refrigerator and are a good deal for groups of 2-6 people. Fernwood also has a campground, where coin-operated washer and dryer facilities are located.

Over $250

Filled with creative touches and thoughtful amenities, ★ **Glen Oaks Big Sur** (47080 CA-1, 831/667-2105, www.glenoaksbigsur.com, $350-860) offers the region's best lodging for the price. Its 16 units bring the motor lodge into the new millennium with heated stone bathroom floors, in-room yoga mats, spacious showers, and elegant gas fireplaces. Glen Oaks also has two cottages and eight cabins by the Big Sur River. Cabins have a modern but rustic feel and include kitchenettes and outdoor fire pits. Guests can also access to the property's two beaches, which are on scenic sections of the Big Sur River.

The best part about staying at the **Big Sur Lodge** (47225 CA-1, 800/424-4787, www.bigsurlodge.com, $250-430), inside Pfeiffer Big Sur State Park, is that you can leave your room and hit the trail. In the early 1900s, the park was a resort owned by the pioneering Pfeiffer family. The amenities have been updated somewhat (although the rooms could use a bit of a remodel), but the Big Sur Lodge still evokes the classic woodsy vacation cabin. Set on a sunny knoll, the lodge has 62 units, the majority of which are family- and group-friendly, with two-bedroom options. Some units also have kitchenettes. Every room has a front or back deck. There are no TVs here and connecting to the Internet costs extra, but all stays come with a pass that allows you entrance into all of Big Sur's state parks. Be sure to take advantage of the lodge's pool (Mar.-Oct.) during your stay and watch for the semi-wild turkeys that roam the property.

Ventana Inn & Spa (48123 CA-1, 800/628-6500, www.ventanabigsur.com, $900-2,550), Big Sur's other luxury resort, reopened in 2017 after a multimillion dollar renovation, though it retained its rustic design. Each of its 59 rooms comes with a private balcony or patio, but you'll also want to explore beyond your unit. Don your plush spa robe and rubber slippers and head for the Japanese bathhouses; choose from two, one at each end of the property. Both are clothing-optional and gender segregated, and the upper house has glass and open-air windows that let you look out to the ocean. The resort's swimming pools offer a cooler respite; the Mountain Pool is clothing-optional, and the Meadow Pool has a perch that offers enthralling views. A communal space, the Social House, has a stone fireplace, record player, pool table, and coffee lounge. Daily complimentary yoga classes are also yours for the asking.

Even though a night at **Post Ranch Inn** (47900 CA-1, 831/667-2200 or 888/524-4787, www.postranchinn.com, $925-2,585) can total more than some people's monthly paycheck, an evening staring at the smear of stars over the vast blue Pacific from one of the stainless steel hot soaking tubs on the deck of the Post Ranch's ocean-facing rooms can temporarily cause all of life's worries to ebb away. Set on a 1,200-foot-high (366-m) ridgeline, all the rooms at this luxury resort have striking views, whether it's of the ocean or the jagged peaks of the nearby Ventana Wilderness. The units also blend in well with the natural environment, including the seven tree houses, which are perched 10 feet (3 m) off the ground. Though it may be difficult to leave the resort's well-appointed units, it is a singular experience to soak in the Infinity Jade Pool, an ocean-facing warm pool made from chunks of the green ornamental stone.

Camping

Many visitors to Big Sur want to experience the unspoiled beauty of the landscape daily. To accommodate true outdoors lovers, many of the parks and lodges have overnight campgrounds. You'll find all types of camping, from full-service, RV-accessible areas to environmental tent campsites to wilderness backpacking. You can camp in a state park or out behind one of the small resort motels near a restaurant and a store and possibly the cool, refreshing Big Sur River. Pick the option that best suits you and your family's needs.

Note that camping on the Big Sur coast is wildly popular in summer, so if you haven't made reservations for a campsite months in advance (they typically book up six months prior), it's going to be difficult to find a place to pitch your tent. **Nacimiento Campground** (Nacimiento-Fergusson Rd., 11 mi/17.7 km east of CA-1, 831/385-5434, www.fs.usda.gov, $20) offers a possible place to stay nearby, just over 10 miles (16.1 km) inland, if you can't find a coastal spot. There are just eight first-come, first-served sites here, all located by the Nacimiento River.

Treebones Resort

For the ultimate high-end California green lodging-cum-camping experience, book a yurt (a circular structure made with a wood frame covered by cloth) at the **Treebones Resort** (71895 CA-1, 877/424-4787, www.treebonesresort.com). The yurts ($320-420) at Treebones tend to be spacious and charming, with polished wood floors, queen beds, seating areas, and outdoor decks for lounging. There are also five walk-in campsites ($98 for 2 people, breakfast and use of the facilities included). For a truly different experience, camp in the human nest ($188), a bundle of wood off the ground outfitted with a futon mattress, or the Twig Hut ($218). In the central lodge, you'll find hot showers and usually clean restroom facilities. There is also a heated pool with an ocean view and a hot tub on the grounds. Being away from any real town, Treebones has a couple of on-site dining options: the Wild Coast Restaurant and the Wild Coast Sushi Bar.

Plaskett Creek Campground

Plaskett Creek Campground (CA-1, 60 mi/97 km north of San Luis Obispo, 877/444-6777, www.recreation.gov, $35) is located right across the highway from Sand Dollar Beach. The sites are in a grassy area under Monterey pine and cypress trees. There are picnic tables and a campfire ring with a grill at every site along with a flush toilet and drinking water in the campground.

Kirk Creek Campground

A popular U.S. Forest Service campground on the south coast of Big Sur, **Kirk Creek Campground** (CA-1, 65 mi/105 km north of San Luis Obispo, 877/444-6777, www.recreation.gov, $35) has a great location on a bluff above the ocean. Right across the highway is the trailhead for the Vicente Flat Trail and the scenic mountain Nacimiento-Fergusson Road. The sites have picnic tables and campfire rings with grills, while the grounds have toilets and drinking water.

Pfeiffer Big Sur State Park

The biggest and most developed campground in Big Sur is at ★ **Pfeiffer Big Sur State Park** (CA-1, 0.25 mi/0.4 km north of Big Sur Station, 800/444-7275, www.parks.ca.gov, www.reservecalifornia.com, $35-50), with more than 150 sites, each of which can handle eight people and two vehicles or an RV (maximum 32 ft/9.8 m, trailers maximum 27 ft/8.2 m, dump station on-site). Some sites are shaded by redwoods, while others are situated along the Big Sur River. All of Pfeiffer's campsites provide access to the park's hiking trails and abundant natural resources. A grocery store and laundry facilities operate within the campground, and plenty of flush toilets and hot showers are scattered throughout. In the evenings, walk down to the Campfire Center for entertaining and educational programs. Pfeiffer Big Sur fills up fast in the summer, especially on weekends. Reservations are recommended.

Fernwood Resort

The **Fernwood Resort** (47200 CA-1, 831/667-2422, www.fernwoodbigsur.com, campsites $70-100, tent cabins $130-190, adventure tents $175-195) offers a range of camping options. There are 66 campsites located around the Big Sur River, some with electric hookups for RVs. Fernwood also has tent cabins, which are small canvas-constructed spaces with room for four in a double and two twins. You can pull your car right up to the back of your cabin. Bring your own linens or sleeping bags, pillows, and towels to make up the inside of your tent cabin. Splitting the difference between camping and a motel room are the rustic "Adventure Tents," canvas tents draped over a solid floor whose biggest comfort are the fully made queen beds and electricity courtesy of an extension cord run into the tent. All camping options have easy access to the river, where you can swim, inner tube, and hike. Hot showers and restrooms are a short walk away. Also, you will be stumbling distance from Big Sur's most popular watering hole, the **Fernwood Tavern.**

Information and Services

The **Big Sur Chamber of Commerce**'s website (www.bigsurcalifornia.org) includes up-to-date information about hikes as well as links to lodging and restaurants. The closest thing to a visitors center is the **Big Sur Station** (0.3 mi/0.5 km south of Pfeiffer Big Sur State Park, 831/667-2315, 9am-4pm daily), which has information on the backcountry. Pick up the ***Big Sur Guide,*** a publication of the Big Sur Chamber of Commerce with a map and guide to local businesses.

Your **cell phone** may not work anywhere in Big Sur, but especially out in the undeveloped reaches of forest and on CA-1 away from the valley. The **Big Sur Health Center** (46896 CA-1, Big Sur, www.bigsurhealthcenter.org, 831/667-2580, 10am-1pm and 2pm-5pm Mon.-Fri.) can take care of minor medical needs and provides an ambulance service and limited emergency care. The nearest full-service hospital is the **Community Hospital of the Monterey Peninsula** (23625 Holman Hwy., Monterey, 831/624-5311, www.chomp.org).

Getting Around

It is difficult to get around Big Sur without a car. However, on Saturday-Sunday from Memorial Day weekend to Labor Day, **Monterey-Salinas Transit** (888/678-2871, www.mst.org, $3.50) runs a bus route through Big Sur that stops at Nepenthe, the Big Sur River Inn, Pfeiffer Big Sur State Park, and Andrew Molera State Park as it heads to Carmel and Monterey. Check the website for times.

Carmel

Formerly a Bohemian enclave where local poets George Sterling and Robinson Jeffers hung out with literary heavyweights including Jack London and Mary Austin, Carmel is now a popular vacation spot for the well moneyed, the artistic, and the romantic. People come to enjoy the small coastal town's almost European charm: strolling its sidewalks and peering in the windows of upscale shops and art galleries, which showcase the work of sculptors, plein air painters, and photographers. Among the galleries are some of the region's most revered restaurants. The main thoroughfare, Ocean Avenue, slopes down to Carmel Beach, one of the finest on the Monterey Peninsula.

The old-world charms of Carmel can make it a little confusing for drivers. Because there are no addresses, locations are sometimes given via directions, for example: on 7th between San Carlos and Dolores, or the northwest corner of

Ocean Avenue. You get used to it. The town is compact, laid out on a plain grid system, so you're better off getting out of your car and walking anyway. Expect to share everything from Carmel's sidewalks to its restaurants with our furry canine friends; Carmel is very pro-pup.

Just north of Carmel is the gated community of **Pebble Beach,** famous for its scenic 17-Mile Drive and collection of high-end properties.

Getting There

From the Big Sur Valley to Carmel is just **32 miles (52 km),** but most likely you will spend **45 minutes** or more on the drive up **CA-1,** which still twists and turns with the coastline. From CA-1, take **Ocean Avenue** into downtown Carmel. A more expensive but also more scenic route is via Pebble Beach's **17-Mile Drive** from the north.

CA-1 can have one or both lanes closed at times, especially in the winter months when rockslides occur. Check the **Caltrans** website (www.dot.ca.gov).

Sights

★ Carmel Beach

Found at the end of Carmel's Ocean Avenue, **Carmel Beach** (Ocean Ave., 831/620-2000, http://ci.carmel.ca.us/carmel) is one of the Monterey Bay region's best beaches. Under a bluff dotted with twisted skeletal cypress trees, it's a long white sandy beach that borders a usually clear blue-green Pacific. In the distance to the south, Point Lobos juts out from the land like a pointing finger, while just north of the beach, the golf courses, green as billiard table felt, cloak the grounds of nearby Pebble Beach. A pathway lines the top of the bluffs above the beach, offering a scenic walk. For surfers, Carmel Beach is one of the Monterey area's most consistent breaks. And like most of Carmel, Carmel Beach is dog-friendly; on any given day, all sorts of canines fetch, sniff, and run on the white sand.

Carmel Mission

The rambling buildings and courtyard gardens show some wear at **San Carlos Borromeo de Carmelo Mission** (3080 Rio Rd., 831/624-1271, www.carmelmission.org, 9:30am-5pm daily, $10 adults, $7 seniors, $5 children, children 6 and under free), but enough restoration work has gone into the church and living quarters to make them attractive and eminently visitable. Notable features of the complex are the church with its gilded altar front and the shrine to the Virgin Mary. There's a small memorial museum in a building off the second courtyard, but this small and outdated space is far from the only historical display. In fact, the "museum" runs through many of the buildings, showing a small slice of the lives of 18th- and 19th-century friars.

Father Junípero Serra lived, worked, and eventually died here. His grave and an ancillary chapel dedicated to his memory are located here. In 2015, when Serra was canonized by Pope Francis, the mission was the site of protests by Native Americans voicing dissent over Serra's treatment of Indigenous peoples, many of whom were displaced or enslaved as a result of missionary work.

End your visit by walking out into the gardens to admire the flowers and fountains and to read the grave markers in the small cemetery. Look for the gravestone of Old Gabriel, a Native American who is believed to have lived to be 151 years old.

A working Catholic parish remains part of the complex, so be respectful when taking the self-guided tour.

Point Lobos State Natural Reserve

Said to be the inspiration behind the setting of Robert Louis Stevenson's *Treasure Island,* **Point Lobos State Natural Reserve** (CA-1, 3 mi/4.8 km south of Carmel, 831/624-4909, www.parks.ca.gov and www.pointlobos.org, 8am-7pm daily spring-fall, 8am-half hour after sunset daily winter, $10 per vehicle) is a wonderland of coves, hills, and jumbled rocks.

The reserve's Cypress Grove Trail winds through a forest of antler-like Monterey cypress trees that are cloaked in a striking red algae. Point Lobos also offers a lesson on the region's fishing history in the **Whaler's Cabin** (9am-5pm daily, staff permitting), a small wooden structure that was built by Chinese fishermen in the 1850s. Half of the reserve is underwater, open for scuba divers who want to explore the 70-foot-high (21.3-m) kelp forests located just offshore. The parking lots in Point Lobos tend to fill up on crowded weekends. In the near future, Point Lobos is going to be the first California state park to require day-use reservations but, until then, the reserve allows people to park on nearby CA-1 and walk in.

17-Mile Drive

Located between Carmel and Pacific Grove, the gated community of **Pebble Beach** (800/877-0597, www.pebblebeach.com) lays claim to some of the Monterey Peninsula's best coastal views—and highest-priced real estate, both represented in the collection of high-end resorts, restaurants, spas, and golf courses, along the **17-Mile Drive.** Because the stunning scenery is also a precious commodity, a toll ($10.25 per vehicle) is charged to use the road. The good news is that when you pay the fee at the gatehouse, you receive a map of the drive that describes the parks and sights that you will pass along the winding coastal road: the much-photographed Lone Cypress, the beaches of Spanish Bay, and Pebble Beach's golf course, resort, and housing complex. (You can also be reimbursed if you spend over $35 at one of Pebble Beach's restaurants.) You can get from one end of the 17-Mile Drive to the other in 20 minutes, but go slowly and stop often to enjoy the natural beauty of

From top to bottom: Carmel Beach; Point Lobos State Natural Reserve; a mansion along Pebble Beach's 17-Mile Drive.

the area (and get your money's worth). There are plenty of turnouts where you can stop to take photos of the iconic cypress trees and stunning coastline. Traveling the **17-Mile Drive** by bike means you don't have to pay the $10.25 vehicle admission fee. Expect fairly flat terrain with lots of twists and turns, and a ride that runs about 17 miles (27 km).

TOP EXPERIENCE

Wineries

The town of Carmel has nearly 20 wine-tasting rooms in its downtown area, even though the vineyards are in the nearby Carmel Valley or Santa Lucia Highlands. Visit the Carmel Chamber of Commerce website (www.carmelcalifornia.org) for a map of Carmel's tasting rooms.

In the sleek **Caraccioli Cellars Tasting Room** (Dolores St. between Ocean Ave. and 7th Ave., 831/622-7722, www.caracciolicellars.com, 2pm-7pm Mon.-Thurs., 11am-10pm Fri.-Sat., 11am-7pm Sun., tasting $25), taste wines made from pinot noir and chardonnay grapes. They also pour a brut and a brut rosé that you can enjoy on the wooden slab bar.

The family-owned **De Tierra Vineyards Tasting Room** (Mission St. and 5th Ave., 831/622-9704, www.detierra.com, 2pm-8pm Mon.-Thurs. and noon-8pm Fri.-Sun. summer, 2pm-6pm Mon.-Thurs. and noon-8pm Fri.-Sun. winter, tasting $10-15) has a range of wines including rosé, syrah, merlot, chardonnay, red blend, Riesling, and pinot noir. The chalkboard behind the counter has a cheese and chocolate plate menu.

Grammy award-winning composer Alan Silvestri has scored everything from the TV series *CHiPs* to *Forrest Gump* to the music in the new *Cosmos*. He also makes wines in Carmel Valley, which can be sampled in the **Silvestri Tasting Room** (7th Ave. between Dolores St. and San Carlos St., 831/625-0111, www.silvestrivineyards.com, noon-7pm daily, tasting $10-15).

Just a block away, **Scheid Vineyards Tasting Room** (San Carlos and 7th Ave., 831/626-9463, www.scheidvineyards.com, noon-6pm Sun.-Thurs., noon-7pm Fri.-Sat., tasting $10) pours 39 tasty varietals from the winery's Salinas Valley vineyards. It's worth a stop.

Entertainment

Live Music

Barmel (San Carlos St. between Ocean Ave. and 7th Ave., 831/626-2095, 2pm-midnight Sun.-Thurs., 2pm-1am Fri.-Sat.) is a Carmel-by-the-Sea hot spot. It's the only bar in town with a performance stage. The live music side of the equation happens 7pm-9pm Thursday-Saturday, while a DJ follows the band on Friday and Saturday.

The Arts

Despite its small size, Carmel has a handful of live theater groups. In a town that defines itself by its love of art, the theater arts don't get left out. The **Pacific Repertory Theater** (831/622-0100, www.pacrep.org) is the only professional theater company on the Monterey-Carmel Peninsula. Its shows go up all over the region, most often in the **Golden Bough Playhouse** (Monte Verde St. and 8th Ave.), the company's home theater. Other regular venues include the **Forest Theater** (Mountain View Ave. and Santa Rita St.) and the **Circle Theater** (Casanova St. between 8th Ave. and 9th Ave.) within the Golden Bough complex. The company puts on dramas, comedies, and musicals both new and classic. You might see a work of Shakespeare or a modern classic like *Mamma Mia!*

The **Sunset Center** (San Carlos St. at 9th Ave., 831/620-2048, www.sunsetcenter.org) is a state-of-the-art performing center with over 700 seats that hosts a true range of events and artistic endeavors, including rock shows, dance recitals, classical music concerts, and theater performances. Recent performers have included Dwight Yoakam, Shemeika Copeland, and Neil Sedaka.

Classical music aficionados will appreciate the dulcet tones of the musicians who perform for **Chamber Music Monterey Bay** (831/625-2212, www.chambermusicmontereybay.org). This society brings talented ensembles and soloists from around the world to perform on the lovely Central Coast in Carmel's **Sunset Center** (San Carlos St. at 9th Ave.). One night you might find a local string quartet, and another you'll get to see and hear a chamber ensemble. (String quartets definitely rule the small stage and intimate theater.) Far from banning young music fans, Chamber Music Monterey Bay reserves up-front seats at all its shows for children and their adult companions.

Festivals and Events

In a town famed for art galleries, one of the biggest events of the year is the **Carmel Art Festival** (Devendorf Park, Mission St., 831/626-4000, www.carmelartfestivalcalifornia.org, May). This four-day event celebrates visual arts in all media with shows by internationally acclaimed artists at galleries, parks, and other venues all across town. For a more classical experience, one of the most prestigious festivals in Northern California is the **Carmel Bach Festival** (831/624-1521, www.bachfestival.org, July). For 15 days, Carmel and its surrounding towns host dozens of classical concerts. Naturally the works of J. S. Bach are featured, but you can also hear renditions of Mozart, Vivaldi, Handel, and other heavyweights of Bach's era.

Pebble Beach hosts the annual **AT&T Pebble Beach Pro-Am** (831/649-1533, www.attpbgolf.com, Feb.), a charity golf tournament that pairs professional golfers with celebrities.

Shopping

One way to sample Carmel's art scene is to take part in its monthly **Carmel Art Walk** (www.carmelartwalk.com, 5pm-8pm second Sat. of the month), a self-guided tour of the town's artist-controlled galleries. Enjoy art, talk to the artists, sip wine, and listen to live music.

It is easy to spend an afternoon poking into galleries. The **Joaquin Turner Gallery** (Dolores St. between 5th Ave. and 6th Ave., 831/869-5564, www.joaquinturner.com, 11:30am-5pm Thurs.-Mon., Tues.-Wed. by appointment) has paintings that nod to the works of early 20th-century Monterey Peninsula artists, while **Steven Whyte Sculpture Gallery** (Dolores St. between 5th Ave. and 6th Ave., 831/620-1917, www.stevenwhytesculptor.com, 9am-5pm Mon. and Thurs., 9am-4:30pm Wed., 9am-6pm Fri., 10am-6pm Sat., 10am-4pm Sun.) is where you can watch the artist creating amazing life-sized sculptures in his open studio.

When your head starts spinning from all the art, head to **Carmel Plaza** (Ocean Ave. and Mission St., 831/624-0138, www.carmelplaza.com, 10am-6pm Mon.-Sat., 11am-5pm Sun.), which offers lots of ways to part with your money. This outdoor mall has luxury fashion shops like Tiffany & Co. as well as the hip clothing chain Anthropologie. But don't miss locally owned establishment **The Cheese Shop** (800/828-9463, www.thecheeseshopinc.com, 10am-6pm Mon.-Sat., 11am-5:30pm Sun.), which sells delicacies like cave-aged gruyère that you can pair with a local wine. You can taste before purchasing.

Recreation

Golf

There's no place for golfing quite like Pebble Beach, just north of Carmel. Golf has been a major pastime here since the late 19th century; today, avid golfers come from around the world to tee off inside the gated community. You can play courses trodden by the likes of Tiger Woods and Jack Nicholson, pause a moment before you putt to take in the sight of the stunning Pacific Ocean, and pay $300 or more for a single round of golf.

One of the Pebble Beach Resort courses, the 18-hole, par-72 **Spyglass Hill** (1700 17-Mile Dr., 800/877-0597, www.pebblebeach.com, $415) gets its name from the Robert Louis Stevenson novel *Treasure Island*. Don't be fooled—the holes on this beautiful course may be named for characters in an adventure novel, but that doesn't mean they're easy. Spyglass Hill boasts some of the most challenging play in this golf course-laden region. Expect a few bogeys, and tee off from the championship level at your own ego's risk.

One of three courses utilized during the popular AT&T Pebble Beach Pro-Am, **Pebble Beach Golf Links** (1700 17-Mile Dr., 800/877-0597, www.pebblebeach.com, $575) has been called the nation's best golf course by *Golf Digest*. Its high ranking might have something to do with the attractive fact that some of the fairways are perched above the Pacific Ocean.

Though it's not managed by the same company, the famed 18-hole, par-72 **Poppy Hills Golf Course** (3200 Lopez Rd., 831/622-8239, www.poppyhillsgolf.com, $250) shares amenities with Pebble Beach golf courses. Expect the same level of care and devotion to the maintenance of the course and your experience as a player.

Surfing

Carmel Beach has some of the area's most consistent beach breaks. Contact **Carmel Surf Lessons** (831/915-4065, www.carmelsurflessons.com, private lessons $200, group lessons $100 pp) if you want to try to learn to surf at Carmel Beach. To rent a board, head to Monterey's **On the Beach Surf Shop** (693 Lighthouse Ave., 831/646-9283, http://onthebeachsurfshop.com, 10am-6pm Mon.-Thurs., 10am-7pm Fri.-Sat., surfboard rentals $30-35 per day, wetsuits $20 per day).

Food

Fine Dining

Aubergine (Monte Verde St. at 7th Ave., 831/624-8578, www.auberginecarmel.com, 6pm-9:30pm daily, $205) has been racking up accolades, including coveted awards from the James Beard Foundation. Settle in for a lengthy chef's tasting menu (which may include the elusive abalone) and enjoy selections from the impressive 2,500-bottle wine cellar.

Mexican

Cultura Comida y Bebida (Dolores St. between 5th Ave. and 6th Ave., 831/250-7005, www.culturacarmel.com, 5pm-10pm Mon.-Thurs., 5pm-11pm Fri., 10:30am-11pm Sat., 10:30am-10pm Sun., $18-28) satisfies with superb upscale Mexican cuisine. Be adventurous and try the *chapulines* (toasted grasshoppers) appetizer. The restaurant's large Mezcal menu offers the smoky spirit in cocktails or one-ounce pours.

Sushi

★ **Akaoni** (Mission St. and 6th Ave., 831/620-1516, 5:30pm-8:30pm Mon.-Sat., $7-40) is a superb hole-in-the-wall sushi restaurant. Sit at the bar or one of the few tables if you can get in. The menu includes tempura-fried oysters, soft shell crab rolls, and a *unagi donburi* (eel bowl). The live Monterey spot prawn is the freshest seafood you'll ever eat, and the daily specials include items flown in from Japan.

Mediterranean

While **Dametra Café** (Ocean Ave. at Lincoln St., 831/622-7766, www.dametracafe.com, 11am-11pm daily, $11-27) has a wide-ranging international menu that includes everything from a cheeseburger to spaghetti alla bolognese, it's best to go with the lively restaurant's signature Mediterranean food. The Greek chicken kebab entrée is a revelation with two chicken-and-vegetable kebabs drizzled with a distinct aioli sauce over yellow rice and a Greek salad. The owner and his staff have been known to serenade evening diners.

Breakfast and Lunch

In the open section of an indoor mall, **Carmel Belle** (Doud Craft Studios, Ocean Ave. and San Carlos St., 831/624-1600, www.carmelbelle.com, 8am-5pm Mon.-Tues., 8am-8pm Wed.-Sun., $6-15) is a little eatery with a big attention to detail. Creative breakfast fare includes an open-face breakfast sandwich featuring a slab of toasted bread topped with a poached egg and wedges of fresh avocado. Meanwhile, its slow-cooked Berkshire pork sandwich with red onion-currant chutney is a perfect example of savory meets sweet.

Tucked into San Carlos Square, **Stationaery** (San Carlos St. and Mission St., 831/250-7183, www.thestationaery.com, 8am-2pm Mon.-Fri., 8am-3pm Sat.-Sun., $10-16) is worth seeking out. The intimate eatery—it has just 34 seats—serves a changing menu for breakfast and lunch. The coffee is great and the chilaquiles with chorizo are superb.

Accommodations

$150-250

Just two blocks from the beach, the **Lamp Lighter Inn** (Ocean Ave. and Camino Real, 831/624-7372 or 888/375-0770, www.carmellamplighter.com, $225-425) has 11 rooms in five cottages with comfortable, beachy decor. The cottages encircle a courtyard area with two fire pits. This is a pet-friendly property, and two of the units have fenced-in backyards.

Just south of downtown Carmel, **Mission Ranch** (26270 Dolores St., 831/624-6436, www.missionranchcarmel.com, $125-320) is a sprawling old ranch complex with views of sheep-filled pastures and Point Lobos in the distance. If you catch a glimpse of the Mission Ranch's owner, it might just make your day: It's none other than Hollywood icon and former Carmel-by-the-Sea mayor Clint Eastwood. On the grounds is a restaurant with a nightly sing-along piano bar.

Over $250

★ **La Playa Carmel** (Camino Real at 8th Ave., 831/293-6100 or 800/582-8900, www.laplayahotel.com, $599-899) began life in 1905 as a mansion, built for a member of the Ghirardellis—California's first family of chocolate. It retains many features from an earlier era, including a wood-walled bar, stained glass windows, and a tiled staircase. Half of the 75 rooms at La Playa look out onto nearby Carmel Beach, only two blocks away. Wander the grounds and stop by the library, heated outdoor pool, and courtyard featuring an oversize chessboard.

Touted by *Architectural Digest*, **Tradewinds Carmel** (Mission St. and 3rd Ave., 831/624-2776, www.tradewindscarmel.com, $255-575) brings a touch of the Far East to California. The 28 serene hotel rooms are decorated with Asian antiquities and live orchids. Outside, the grounds have a water fountain that passes through bamboo shoots and horsetails, along with a meditation garden where an oversize Buddha head overlooks a trio of cascading pools.

Information and Services

You'll find the **Carmel Visitor Center** (Carmel Plaza, 2nd Fl., Ocean Ave. between Junipero St. and Mission St., 831/624-2522, www.carmelchamber.org, 10am-5pm Mon.-Sat., 11am-4pm Sun.) right in the middle of downtown. For more information about the town and current events, pick up a copy of the weekly ***Carmel Pine Cone*** (www.pineconearchive.com), the local newspaper.

The nearest major medical center is the **Community Hospital of the Monterey Peninsula** (23625 Holman Hwy., Monterey, 831/624-5311, www.chomp.org).

Getting Around

As you read the addresses in Carmel and begin to explore the neighborhoods, you'll realize something interesting. There are **no street addresses.** Years ago, Carmel residents voted not to enact door-to-door mail delivery, thus there is no need for numeric addresses on buildings. You have to pay close attention to the **street names** and the **block** you're on. Just to make things even more fun, street signs can be difficult to see in the mature foliage, and a dearth of streetlights can make them nearly impossible to find at night. Luckily, there are GPS systems in our cars and phones these days.

Monterey

TOP EXPERIENCE

Monterey has a past as a fishing town. Native Americans were the first to fish the bay, and fishing became an industry with the arrival of European settlers in the 19th century. Author John Steinbeck immortalized this unglamorous industry in his novel *Cannery Row.* Its blue-collar past is still evident in its architecture, even though the cannery workers have been replaced by tourists.

Monterey is the "big city" on the well-populated southern tip of the wide-mouthed Monterey Bay. There are two main sections of Monterey: the old downtown area and "New Monterey," which includes Cannery Row and the Monterey Bay Aquarium. The old downtown is situated around Alvarado Street and includes the historic adobes that make up Monterey State Historic Park. New Monterey bustles with tourists during the summer. The canneries are long gone, and today the Row is packed with businesses, including the must-see Monterey Bay Aquarium, seafood restaurants, shops, galleries, and wine-tasting rooms. The aquarium is constantly packed with visitors, especially on summer weekends. One way to get from one section to the other is to walk the Monterey Bay Coastal Recreation Trail, a paved path that runs right along a stretch of coastline.

Just northwest of Monterey is the quiet town of **Pacific Grove,** worth a visit to stroll its colorful turn-of-the-century Victorian homes on Lighthouse Avenue and striking strand of coastline.

Getting There

Monterey can be reached from Carmel by driving 4.5 miles (7.2 km) north on **CA-1.** Take Exit 399B for **Munras Avenue,** which leads to downtown Monterey. Both **Greyhound** (3 Station Pl., Salinas, 831/424-4418, www.greyhound.com, 5am-11:30pm daily) and the **Amtrak *Pacific Surfliner*** (800/872-7245, www.amtrak.com) stop in nearby Salinas. From there, you can rely on **Monterey-Salinas Transit** (MSRT, 888/678-2871, www.mst.org, $1.50-2.50) to reach Monterey.

Sights

Cannery Row

Cannery Row (www.canneryrow.com) did once look and feel as John Steinbeck described it in his famed novel of the same name. In the 1930s and 1940s, fishing boats offloaded their catches straight into the huge warehouse-like cannery buildings. Low-wage workers processed the fish and put it into cans, ready to ship across the country and around the world. But overfishing took its toll, and by the late 1950s, Cannery Row was deserted; some buildings even fell into the ocean.

A slow renaissance began in the 1960s, driven by new interest in preserving the historical integrity of the area, as well as a few savvy entrepreneurs who understood the value of beachfront property. Today, what was once a workingman's wharf is now an enclave of boutique hotels, big seafood restaurants, and souvenir stores selling T-shirts adorned with sea otters. Cannery Row is anchored at one end by the aquarium and runs for several blocks

Monterey Bay

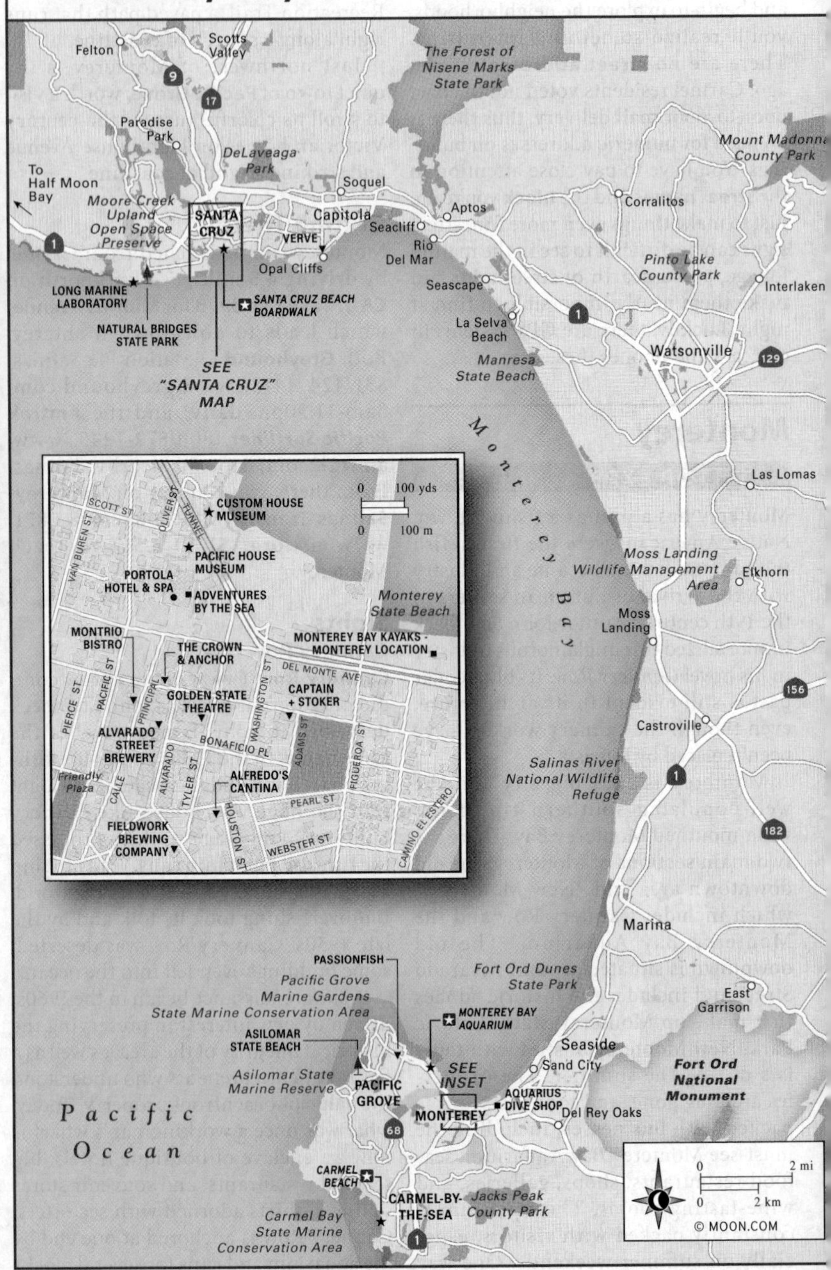

Steinbeck

John Ernst Steinbeck was born and grew up in Salinas, then a tiny, isolated agricultural community, in 1902. He somehow managed to escape life as a farmer, a sardine fisherman, or a fish canner and ended up living the glamorous life of a writer for his too-short 66 years.

Steinbeck's experiences in the Salinas Valley farming community and in the fishing town of Monterey informed many of his novels. The best known of these is *Cannery Row*, but *Tortilla Flat* is also set in working-class Monterey (though no one knows exactly where the fictional Tortilla Flat neighborhood was supposed to be). The Pulitzer Prize-winning novel *The Grapes of Wrath* takes more of its inspiration from the Salinas Valley. Steinbeck used the valley as a model for farming in the Dust Bowl—the wretched, impoverished time during the Great Depression.

Steinbeck was fascinated by the plight of working men and women; his novels and stories depict ordinary folks going through tough and terrible times. Steinbeck lived and worked through the Great Depression, and thus it's not surprising that many of his stories don't feature Hollywood happy endings. Steinbeck was a realist in almost all of his novels, portraying the good, the bad, and the ugly of human life and society. His work gained almost immediate respect: In addition to his Pulitzer Prize, Steinbeck also won the Nobel Prize for Literature in 1962. Almost every U.S. high school student from the 1950s onward has read at least one of Steinbeck's novels or short stories; his body of work forms part of the country's literary canon.

As the birthplace of California's most illustrious literary son, Salinas became famous for inspiring his work. You'll find a variety of Steinbeck maps online (www.mtycounty.com) that offer self-guided tours of the regions made famous by his various novels. Steinbeck's name is taken in vain all over now-commercial Cannery Row—even the cheesy Wax Museum tries to draw customers in by claiming kinship with the legendary author. More serious Steinbeck fans prefer the **National Steinbeck Center** (1 Main St., Salinas, 831/796-3833, www.steinbeck.org, 10am-5pm daily, $15 adults, $12 seniors and students, $7 children 6-17, children under 6 free) in the still-agricultural town of Salinas. Plan to be in Monterey County in early August for the annual **Steinbeck Festival** (www.steinbeck.org), a big shindig put on by the Steinbeck Center to celebrate the great man's life and works in fine style.

that include a beach; it then leads to the Monterey Harbor area.

Thankfully, a few remnants of Cannery Row's past remain in the shadows of the area's touristy shops. The most important is a battered little shack located between the Monterey Bay Aquarium and the shiny new InterContinental luxury hotel. The **Pacific Biological Laboratories** (800 Cannery Row, 831/646-5640, www.monterey.org) was the workplace and home of famed marine biologist Ed Ricketts, a good friend of Steinbeck's who inspired the character of Doc in *Cannery Row.* Now owned by the city, the lab is open for free tours one day a month and for group tours by reservation.

★ Monterey Bay Aquarium

The first aquarium of its kind in the country, the **Monterey Bay Aquarium** (886 Cannery Row, 831/648-4800, www.montereybayaquarium.org, 10am-5pm daily, $50 adults, $40 seniors and students, $30 children) is still unique in many ways. From the beginning, the aquarium's mission has been conservation, and they're not shy about it. Many of the animals in the aquarium's tanks were rescued, and those that survive may eventually be returned to the wild. All the exhibits you'll see in this mammoth complex contain only local sea life.

The aquarium displays a dazzling array of species. When you come to visit,

a good first step is to look up the feeding schedules for the tanks you're most interested in. The critters always put on the best show at feeding time, and it's smart to show up several minutes in advance to get a good spot near the glass. Check the website for current feeding times.

The living, breathing **Kelp Forest** is just like the kelp beds outside in the bay, except this one is 28 feet (8.5 m) tall. Between the swaying strands of kelp, leopard sharks glide over the aquarium floor, and warty sea cucumbers and starfish adorn rocks. Try to time your visit for the feeding times here, too, when the fish in the tank put on quite a show.

The deep-water tank in the **Open Sea** exhibit area always draws a crowd. Inside its depths, hammerhead sharks and an enormous odd-looking sunfish coexist. The aquarium has even had one of the ocean's most notorious predators in this tank: the great white shark. The aquarium has great whites infrequently, but if one is on display, it's definitely worth looking at this sleek and amazing fish up close.

The **Sea Otters** exhibit gives visitors a personal view of rescued otters. The adorable, furry marine mammals come right up to the glass to interact with curious children and enchanted adults.

Another of the aquarium's most popular exhibits is its **Jellies** display, which illuminates delicate crystal jellies and the comet-like lion's mane jellyfish.

The aquarium is a wildly popular weekend destination. Especially in the summer, the crowds can be forbidding. Weekdays can be less crushing (though you'll run into school groups during much of the year), and the off-season is almost always a better time to visit. The aquarium has facilities for wheelchair access to almost all exhibits.

From top to bottom: Monterey Bay Aquarium; the Custom House in Monterey State Historic Park; Asilomar State Beach in Pacific Grove.

Monterey State Historic Park

Monterey State Historic Park (park office 20 Custom House Plaza, 831/649-2907, www.parks.ca.gov, 9am-5pm daily May-Sept., 10am-4pm daily Oct.-Apr., free) pays homage to the long and colorful history of the city of Monterey. This busy port town acted as the capital of California when it was under Spanish and Mexican rule. Today, the park is a collection of old buildings scattered about Old Monterey, and provides a peek into the city as it was in the mid-19th century.

Built in 1827, the **Custom House** (east of Fisherman's Wharf, 10am-4pm daily) is the oldest government building still standing in the state. Wander the adobe building and check out the artifacts on display, meant to resemble the goods one might find in the building when it was under Mexican rule. Also on the plaza is the **Pacific House Museum** (hours vary seasonally). The 1st floor shows a range of Monterey's history from the Native Californians to the American Period, while the 2nd floor has a plethora of Native American artifacts.

The other buildings comprising the park were built mostly with adobe and/or brick between 1834 and 1847. These include the **Casa del Oro** (210 Oliver St., 831/649-3364, check website for hours); the **Larkin House** (464 Calle Principal, 831/649-7172, private tours $75 for up to 12 people); the **Sherman Quarters** (on the grounds of the Larkin House, closed to the public); the **Old Whaling Station** (391 Decatur St., 831/375-5356, 10am-2pm Tues.-Fri.); the **First Brick House** (next to the Old Whaling Station, 10am-4pm daily); and the **Stevenson House** (530 Houston St., hours vary seasonally), once a temporary residence of Robert Louis Stevenson.

For an introduction to the park and its history, take a one-hour **guided walking tour** (hours vary seasonally, $10); it starts at the Custom House. A self-guided **cell phone tour** (831/998-9458, free) offers a two-minute rundown of each building.

Asilomar State Beach

Popular **Asilomar State Beach** (Exit 68 West from CA-1, turn left on Sunset Dr., Pacific Grove, 831/646-6440, www.parks.ca.gov, 8am-8pm daily) draws beachgoers, walkers, and surfers. Located in nearby Pacific Grove, the beach itself is a narrow 1-mile (1.6-km) strip of coastline with a boardwalk trail on the dunes behind it. You can keep walking on the trail into nearby Pebble Beach, an easy, cost-free way to get a taste of that exclusive community.

Adjacent to the state beach is the **Asilomar Conference Grounds** (888/635-5310, www.visitasilomar.com), a cluster of meeting rooms and accommodations designed by Hearst Castle architect Julia Morgan. Take one of four self-guided tours of the grounds that focus on the living dunes, the coast trail, the forest, and Julia Morgan's architecture. Or opt for one of the free tours given by state park staff; check with the front desk for tour information.

Entertainment

Bars and Clubs

Descending into **The Crown & Anchor** (150 W. Franklin St., 831/649-6496, www.crownandanchor.net, 11am-1:30am daily) feels a bit like entering a ship's hold. Along with the maritime theme, The Crown & Anchor serves up 20 international beers on tap. It also has good pub fare, including cottage pies and curry fries, a local favorite.

Craft beer fans should head to **Alvarado Street Brewery & Grill** (426 Alvarado St., 831/655-2337, www.alvaradostreetbrewery.com, 11:30am-10pm Sun.-Thurs., 11:30am-11pm Fri.-Sat.). The popular brewery has made downtown Monterey a hot spot. It has a big, boisterous, modern space and serves more than 20 beers on tap, including its own sours, ales, and Mai Tai PA, a Great American Beer Festival gold-medal winner. Enjoy a tasty brew out front on the sidewalk patio or in the beer garden in back.

Fieldwork (560 Munras Ave., 831/324-0658, http://fieldworkbrewing.com, noon-11pm daily) is a Berkeley-based craft brewery with a satellite taproom in Monterey. This is a stripped-down operation with the taps and bathrooms in shipping containers, and the beer garden-style seating outdoors. People come here for creative brews like the Churro Cream Ale, inspired by the Mexican dessert, and Galaxy Juice, a hazy IPA.

A distinct stone building just a couple of blocks off Alvarado Street, **Alfredo's Cantina** (266 Pearl St., 831/375-0655, 10am-midnight Sun.-Thurs., 10am-2am Fri.-Sat., cash only) is a cozy, comfortable dive bar with dim lighting, a gas fireplace, cheap drinks, and a good jukebox.

The Arts

Downtown Monterey's historic **Golden State Theatre** (417 Alvarado St., 831/649-1070, www.goldenstatetheatre.com) hosts live music, speaker series, and other arts events. The theater dates back to 1926 and was designed to look like a Moorish castle. Performers in its ornate main room have included music legends like Patti Smith and Arlo Guthrie and newer acts like the Fleet Foxes.

Festivals and Events

The Monterey region hosts numerous festivals and special events each year. Whether your pleasure is fine food or funky music, you'll probably be able to plan a trip around some sort of multiday festival with dozens of events and performances scheduled during Monterey's busy year.

One of the biggest music festivals in California is the **Monterey Jazz Festival** (Monterey County Fairgrounds, 2004 Fairground Rd., tickets 888/248-6499, office 831/373-3366, www.montereyjazzfestival.org, Sept.). As the site of the longest-running jazz festival on earth, Monterey attracts 500 artists from around the world to play on its eight stages. Held each September at the Monterey County Fairgrounds, this long weekend of amazing music can leave you happy for the whole year. Recent acts to grace the Monterey Jazz Festival's stages include Herbie Hancock, Booker T. Jones, and The Roots.

One way to get into the holiday spirit while exploring Monterey's historic buildings is to secure a ticket to **Christmas in the Adobes** (www.mshpa.org, Dec.). This popular event allows ticketholders to explore Monterey's oldest buildings, including those comprising Monterey State Historic Park as well as other private adobes that are only open to the public for this event. Inside the buildings, you'll find people in period dress, dancers, and music performances.

Recreation

Monterey Bay is the premier Northern California locale for a number of water sports, especially scuba diving.

Scuba Diving

Any native Northern Californian knows that there's only one really great place in the region to get certified in scuba diving—Monterey Bay. Even if you go to a dive school up in the Bay Area, they'll take you down to Monterey for your open-water dive. Accordingly, dozens of dive schools cluster in and around the town of Monterey.

A local's favorite, **Bamboo Reef** (614 Lighthouse Ave., 831/372-1685, www.bambooreef.com, 9am-6pm Mon.-Fri., 7am-6pm Sat.-Sun.) offers scuba lessons and rents equipment just a few blocks from popular dive spots, including Breakwater Cove.

The **Aquarius Dive Shop** (2040 Del Monte Ave., 831/375-1933, http://aquariusdivers.com, 9am-6pm Mon.-Thurs., 9am-7pm Fri., 7am-7pm Sat., 7am-6pm Sun.) offers everything you need to go diving out in Monterey Bay, including air and nitrox fills, equipment rental, certification courses, and help booking a trip on a local dive boat.

Sea Sanctuary

Monterey Bay is in a federally protected marine area known as **Monterey Bay National Marine Sanctuary** (MBNMS, http://montereybay.noaa.gov). Designated a sanctuary in 1992, the protected waters stretch far past the confines of Monterey Bay to a northern boundary 7 miles (11.3 km) north of the Golden Gate Bridge and a southern boundary at Cambria in San Luis Obispo County.

MBNMS holds many marine treasures, including the Monterey Bay Submarine Canyon, right offshore of the fishing village of Moss Landing. The canyon is similar in size to the Grand Canyon and has a rim-to-floor depth of 5,577 feet (1,700 m). In 2009, MBNMS expanded to include another fascinating underwater geographical feature: the Davidson Seamount. Located 80 miles (129 km) southwest of Monterey, the undersea mountain rises an impressive 7,480 feet (2,280 m), yet its summit is still 4,101 feet (1,250 m) below the ocean's surface.

The sanctuary was created for resource protection, education, public use, and research. The MBNMS is the reason so many marine research facilities, including the Long Marine Laboratory, the Monterey Bay Marine Laboratory, and the Moss Landing Marine Laboratories, dot the Monterey Bay's shoreline.

Aquarius works with five boats to create great trips for divers of all interests and ability levels. Call or check the website for current local dive conditions as well.

Kayaking and Stand-Up Paddleboarding

Relatively protected Monterey Bay is one of the best places on the California coast to head offshore in a kayak or stand-up paddleboard. The Monterey Peninsula protects paddlers from some ocean swells, and you can frequently see sea otters, harbor seals, and other marine life.

Adventures by the Sea (831/372-1807, www.adventuresbythesea.com, 9am-sunset daily, 2.5-hour kayak tours $60 pp, kayak rentals $30-60 per day, SUP rentals $50 per day) has a whopping four locations in Monterey (299 Cannery Row, 685 Cannery Row, 32 Cannery Row, 210 Alvarado St.), plus one in Pacific Grove (624 Ocean View Blvd.). Come by to rent kayaks or stand-up paddleboards, or join a kayaking tour of the area.

Right on Monterey Beach, **Monterey Bay Kayaks** (693 Del Monte Ave., 831/373-5357, www.montereybaykayaks.com, 9am-7pm daily summer, 9am-6pm daily fall, 9am-5pm daily winter, tours $55-150 pp, kayak rentals $30-50 per day, SUP rentals $75 per day) specializes in tours of central Monterey; it also rents a range of kayaks and SUPs. There's also a branch up in Moss Landing on the Elkhorn Slough.

Whale-Watching

Whales pass quite near the shores of Monterey year-round. While you can sometimes even see them from the beaches, any number of boats can take you out for a closer look at the great beasts as they travel along their own special routes north and south. The area hosts many humpbacks, blue whales, and gray whales, plus the occasional killer whale, minke whale, fin whale, and pod of dolphins. Most tours last 2-3 hours and leave from Fisherman's Wharf, which is easy to get to and has ample parking.

Monterey Bay Whale Watch (84 Fisherman's Wharf, 831/375-4658, www.montereybaywhalewatch.com) leaves right from an easy-to-find red building on Fisherman's Wharf and runs tours in every season (call or check the website for schedules). You must make a reservation in advance, even for regularly scheduled tours. Afternoon tours are available. **Princess Monterey Whale Watching** (96 Fisherman's Wharf, 831/372-2203, www.

montereywhalewatching.com) prides itself on its knowledgeable marine biologist guides and its comfortable, spacious cruising vessels.

Hiking

If you want to explore Monterey's coastline without the possibility of getting wet, head out on the **Monterey Bay Coastal Recreation Trail** (www.monterey.org). The 18-mile (29-km) paved path stretches from Pacific Grove to the south all the way to the northern Monterey County town of Castroville. The best section is from Monterey Harbor down to Pacific Grove's Lovers Point Park.

Food

The organic and sustainable food movements have caught hold on the Central Coast. The **Monterey Bay Seafood Watch program** (www.seafoodwatch.org) is the definitive resource for sustainable seafood, while inland, the Salinas Valley hosts a number of organic farms.

Seafood

For a South Pacific spin on seafood, head to ★ **Hula's Island Grill** (622 Lighthouse Ave., 831/655-4852, www.hulastiki.com, 4pm-9:30pm Sun.-Mon., 11:30am-9:30pm Tues.-Thurs., 11:30am-10pm Fri.-Sat., $13-25). With surfing movies playing on the TVs and tasty tiki drinks, it's a fun place to hang out. In addition to fresh fish and a range of tacos, the menu has land-based fare like Jamaican jerk chicken. Hula's also has one of Monterey's best **happy hours** (4pm-6pm Sun.-Mon., 2pm-9:30pm Tues., 2pm-6pm Wed.-Sat.), with superb cocktails and not-the-usual-suspects appetizers (ceviche, edamame).

Located in nearby Pacific Grove, ★ **Passionfish** (701 Lighthouse Ave., Pacific Grove, 831/655-3311, www.passionfish.net, 5pm-9pm daily, $18-34) is one of the region's most highly regarded seafood restaurants. It sources its ingredients from sustainable farms and fisheries, and its delectable menu—featuring dishes like sea scallops in a tomato-truffle butter and black cod in a red curry vinaigrette—changes daily.

The **Sandbar & Grill** (Municipal Wharf II, 831/373-2818, 11am-9pm Mon.-Sat., 10:30am-9pm Sun., $18-33) has the best calamari around—the strips are pounded thin and golden fried. The restaurant's also known for its fresh sand dabs and Dungeness crab sandwich with bacon. The restaurant hangs off the Municipal Wharf over Monterey Harbor.

Contemporary

Inside an old brick firehouse, ★ **Montrio** (414 Calle Principal, 831/648-8880, www.montrio.com, 4:30pm-close daily, $20-42) is a long-running leader in elegantly casual Monterey dining. The menu boasts a wide range of small bites and appetizers alongside heartier meat and seafood entrées and inspired cocktails.

Coffee

Lines form in the morning outside the converted garage that houses **Captain + Stoker** (398 E. Franklin St., 831/901-3776, www.captainandstoker.com, 6:30am-4pm Mon.-Fri., 7:30am-4pm Sat.-Sun.). Its espresso and coffee drinks are made with coffee beans roasted in house. The hip shop's name refers to the two positions on a tandem bicycle, and the vibrant space is decorated with all sorts of bikes. A few light eats are available, including avocado toast and some snack-worthy peanut butter balls that are $3 a pop.

Markets

The primary farmers market in the county, the **Monterey Farmers Market** (Alvarado St. between Del Monte Ave. and Pearl St., www.oldmonterey.org, 4pm-8pm Tues. summer, 4pm-7pm Tues. winter) takes over downtown Monterey with fresh produce vendors, restaurant stalls, jewelry booths, and live music every Tuesday late afternoon.

Accommodations

$150-250

The ★ **Portola Hotel & Spa** (2 Portola Plaza, 888/222-5851 or 831/649-4511, www.portolahotel.com, $229-600) occupies a prime piece of real estate between the western end of Alvarado Street and Monterey State Historic Park's Custom House. Connected to the Monterey Conference Center, the large hotel complex has 379 rooms and numerous amenities. The comfortable rooms have a red-and-blue motif, and many have balconies or patios so you can take in views of downtown and the harbor. The hotel's larger-than-average fitness center, pool, hot tub, spa, on-site brewery Peter B's, and on-site restaurant Jack's, might make it difficult to leave the complex even though you're located in walking distance of many of Monterey's attractions.

Jabberwock Inn (598 Laine St., 831/372-4777, www.jabberwockinn.com, $209-599) takes its name from Lewis Carroll's nonsense poem in *Through the Looking-Glass.* But, despite its name, the amenities at this comfortable former convent are no-nonsense. The bed-and-breakfast has eight rooms as well as common areas, including a covered wraparound sun porch with views of Monterey Bay. Perks include free parking, afternoon wine and appetizers, and evening milk and cookies. There are no TVs or telephones. The B&B is just a short walk to Cannery Row and the aquarium.

Over $250

The ★ **Spindrift Inn** (652 Cannery Row, 831/646-8900, www.spindriftinn.com, $309-689) towers above the golden sands and green waters of scenic McAbee Beach. This 45-room boutique establishment has been called the country's most romantic hotel. Most of the hardwood-floored rooms have wood-burning fireplaces and full or half canopy beds. The friendly staff delivers a complimentary continental breakfast and offers a wine and cheese reception (4:30pm-6pm daily).

Located between San Carlos Beach and Cannery Row, the **Monterey Bay Inn** (242 Cannery Row, 831/373-6242 or 800/424-6242, www.montereybayinn.com, $309-600) has oceanfront rooms with private balconies that overlook Monterey Bay, plus in-room binoculars for spotting wildlife. The hotel's rooftop hot tub offers another vantage point. Enjoy a continental breakfast delivered to your room in the morning and cookies in the evening.

Camping

The campground at the 50-acre (20-ha) **Veterans Memorial Park** (Via Del Rey and Veterans Dr., 831/646-3865, www.monterey.org, $30) is a little-known secret. A mile up a hill from downtown Monterey are 40 first-come, first-served campsites with bay views.

Information and Services

In Monterey, the **El Estero Visitors Center** (401 Camino El Estero, 888/221-1010, www.seemonterey.com, 10am-6pm daily) is the local outlet of the Monterey County Convention and Visitors Bureau. A few miles from downtown, the **Monterey Peninsula Chamber of Commerce** (243 El Dorado St., Ste. 200, 831/648-5350, www.montereychamber.com, 9am-5pm Mon.-Fri.) can also provide helpful information.

The local daily newspaper is the ***Monterey County Herald*** (www.montereyherald.com). The free weekly ***Monterey County Weekly*** (www.montereycountyweekly.com) has a comprehensive listing of the area's arts and entertainment events.

The **Monterey Post Office** (565 Hartnell St., 831/372-4063, www.usps.com, 8:30am-5pm Mon.-Fri., 10am-2pm Sat.) is a couple of blocks from downtown. The **Community Hospital of the Monterey Peninsula** (23625 Holman

Hwy., 831/624-5311, www.chomp.org) provides emergency services.

Getting Around

Once in Monterey, take advantage of the free **Monterey Trolley** (Waterfront Area Visitor Express, 831/899-2555, www.monterey.org, daily Memorial Day-Labor Day, Sat.-Sun. Labor Day-Memorial Day) that loops between downtown Monterey and the aquarium. When in operation, the trolley typically runs 10am-7pm—until 8pm on summer Saturdays—with departures every 10-15 minutes. Also, **Monterey-Salinas Transit** (888/678-2871, www.mst.org, $1.50-2.50) has routes through Monterey.

Santa Cruz

TOP EXPERIENCE

There's no place like Santa Cruz. Even in the left-leaning Bay Area, you won't find another town that has embraced cultural experimentation, radical philosophies, and progressive politics quite like this little beach city, which has made out-there ideas into a kind of municipal cultural statement. Everyone does their own thing: Surfers ride the waves, nudists laze on the beaches, tree-huggers wander the redwood forests, tattooed and pierced punks wander the main drag, and families walk their dogs along West Cliff Drive.

Most visitors come to Santa Cruz to hit the Boardwalk and the beaches. Locals and UC Santa Cruz students tend to hang downtown on Pacific Avenue and stroll on West Cliff. The east side of town has fewer attractions for visitors but offers a vibrant surf scene situated around Pleasure Point.

Getting There

In light traffic, Santa Cruz is **45 minutes** north of Monterey on **CA-1.** The problem is that the highway goes from four lanes to two lanes a few miles south of Moss Landing, which causes traffic to slow. North of Monterey 28 miles (45 km), CA-1 has a section called **"the fishhook,"** where **accidents** regularly occur. Consider taking the **Soquel Avenue** or **Morrissey Boulevard** exits to miss this mess.

Sights

★ Santa Cruz Beach Boardwalk

The **Santa Cruz Beach Boardwalk** (400 Beach St., 831/423-5590, www.beachboardwalk.com, daily Memorial Day-Labor Day, Sat.-Sun. and holidays Labor Day-Nov. and Dec. 26-Memorial Day, check website for hours, individual rides $4-7, all-day pass $40-50, parking $10-30), or just "the Boardwalk" as it's called by the locals, has a rare appeal that beckons to young children, too-cool teenagers, and adults of all ages.

The amusement park rambles along each side of the south end of the Boardwalk; entry is free, but you must buy either per-ride tickets or an unlimited ride wristband. The Giant Dipper is an old-school wooden roller coaster that opened back in 1924 and is still giving riders a thrill after all this time. The Double Shot shoots riders up a 125-foot (38.1-m) tower with great views of the bay or inland Santa Cruz before freefalling straight down. In summertime, a log ride cools down guests hot from hours of tromping around. The Boardwalk also offers several toddler and little-kid rides.

At the other end of the Boardwalk, avid gamesters choose between the lure of prizes from the traditional midway games and the large arcade. Throw baseballs at things, try your arm at Skee-Ball, or take a pass at a classic or newer video game. The traditional carousel even has a brass ring you (or your children) can try to grab.

During the summer, the Boardwalk puts on free Friday-night concerts on the beach featuring retro acts like hair metal band Great White and 1980s New Wave

Santa Cruz

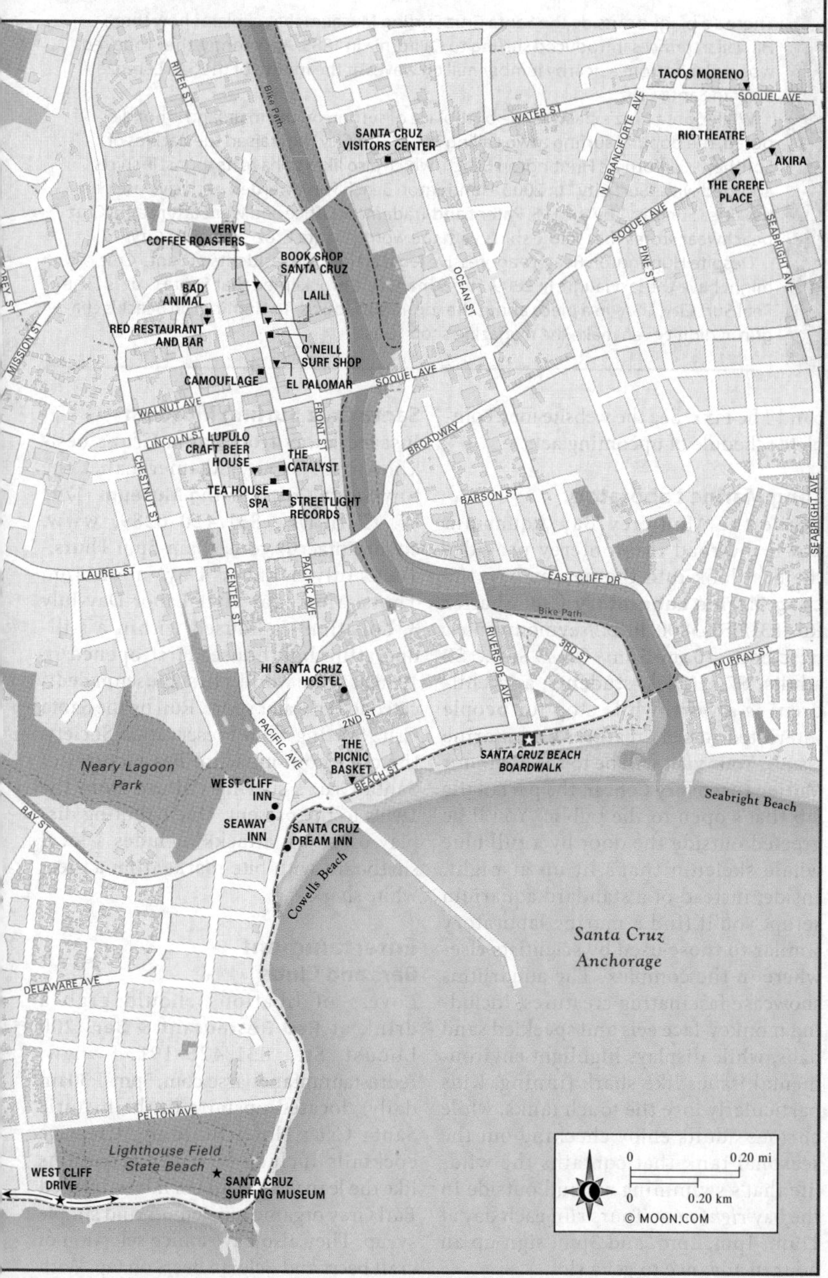
TACOS MORENO
SOQUEL AVE
WATER ST
N BRANCIFORTE AVE
SANTA CRUZ VISITORS CENTER
RIO THEATRE
AKIRA
THE CREPE PLACE
RIVER ST
Bike Path
VERVE COFFEE ROASTERS
BOOK SHOP SANTA CRUZ
BAD ANIMAL
LAILI
RED RESTAURANT AND BAR
O'NEILL SURF SHOP
CAMOUFLAGE
EL PALOMAR
MISSION ST
WALNUT AVE
LINCOLN ST
LUPULO CRAFT BEER HOUSE
THE CATALYST
TEA HOUSE SPA
STREETLIGHT RECORDS
CHESTNUT ST
FRONT ST
OCEAN ST
PINE ST
SEABRIGHT AVE
BROADWAY
BARSON ST
LAUREL ST
CENTER ST
PACIFIC AVE
EAST CLIFF DR
RIVERSIDE AVE
3RD ST
MURRAY ST
HI SANTA CRUZ HOSTEL
2ND ST
THE PICNIC BASKET
BEACH ST
SANTA CRUZ BEACH BOARDWALK
Neary Lagoon Park
WEST CLIFF INN
SEAWAY INN
SANTA CRUZ DREAM INN
BAY ST
Seabright Beach
Cowells Beach
Santa Cruz Anchorage
DELAWARE AVE
PELTON AVE
Lighthouse Field State Beach
WEST CLIFF DRIVE
SANTA CRUZ SURFING MUSEUM
0
0.20 mi
0
0.20 km
© MOON.COM

Surf City

There's a plaque outside the Santa Cruz Surfing Museum that explains how three Hawaiian princes introduced surfing to California in 1885. Apparently, they rode redwood planks from a nearby lumber mill on waves at the mouth of the San Lorenzo River in Santa Cruz.

While Santa Cruz's claim as the birthplace of surfing on the mainland is not disputed, the popular surfing town calling itself "Surf City" has raised the hackles of Southern California's Huntington Beach, which also likes to have its tourist T-shirts adorned with "Surf City." In 2006, Huntington Beach was awarded exclusive use of the title "Surf City" by the U.S. Patent and Trademark Office and went after Santa Cruz beachwear stores that sold T-shirts with the words "Santa Cruz" and "Surf City."

Despite Huntington Beach's aggressive legal action, the residents of Santa Cruz might have the last laugh. In 2009, *Surfer* magazine proclaimed that Santa Cruz is "The Real Surf City, USA" in a piece about the top 10 surf towns. To Huntington Beach's chagrin, it didn't even make the magazine's top 10 list.

band The Fixx. See the website for a complete schedule of upcoming acts.

Long Marine Laboratory

While the Monterey Bay Aquarium down the road in Monterey provides the best look into the nearby bay, the **Long Marine Laboratory** (100 Shaffer Rd., 831/459-3800, http://seymourcenter.ucsc.edu, 10am-5pm Tues.-Sun., $9 adults, $7 seniors, students, and children) is a worthwhile stop for people interested in sea creatures and marine issues. Your visit will be to the **Seymour Marine Discovery Center,** the part of the lab that's open to the public. You'll be greeted outside the door by a full blue whale skeleton that's lit up at night. Inside, instead of a standard aquarium setup, you'll find a marine laboratory similar to those used by scientists elsewhere in the complex. The aquariums showcase fascinating creatures, including monkey-face eels and speckled sand dabs, while displays highlight environmental issues like shark finning. Kids particularly love the touch tanks, while curious adults enjoy checking out the seasonal tank that contains the wildlife that's swimming around outside in the bay *right now.* Tours run each day at 11am, 1pm, 2pm, and 3pm; sign up an hour in advance to get a slot.

Santa Cruz Surfing Museum

Just feet away from Santa Cruz's best-known surf spot, Steamer Lane, the tiny **Santa Cruz Surfing Museum** (1701 W. Cliff Dr., 831/420-6289, www.cityofsantacruz.com, 10am-5pm Thurs.-Tues. July 4-Labor Day, noon-4pm Thurs.-Mon., day after Labor Day-July 3, donation) is housed within a still-operating lighthouse. First opened in 1986, it is the world's first museum dedicated to the water sport. Run by the Santa Cruz Surfing Club Preservation Society, the one-room museum has pictures of Santa Cruz's surfing culture from the 1930s to the present. One haunting display on shark attacks includes a local surfboard with bite marks from a great white shark.

Entertainment

Bars and Clubs

Lovers of libations should grab a drink at **Red Restaurant & Bar** (200 Locust St., 831/425-1913, www.redrestaurantandbarsc.com, 5pm-1:30am daily), located upstairs in the historic Santa Cruz Hotel Building. Creative cocktails include signature creations like the Jean Grey, a mix of house-infused Earl Grey organic gin, lemon, and simple syrup. They also have a nice selection of craft beers and Belgian beers on tap. With its dark wood paneling and burgundy bar stools, Red feels like an old speakeasy. It also serves a comprehensive late-night menu until 1am for those who need some food to soak up their alcohol.

The Crepe Place (1134 Soquel Ave., 831/429-6994, http://thecrepeplace.com, 11am-midnight Mon.-Thurs., 11am-1am Fri., 9am-midnight Sat.-Sun.) has recently emerged as a hangout for the hipster crowd, who are drawn in by the high-profile indie rock acts and popular Bay Area bands that perform in its intimate front room. They also have outdoor seating and a comprehensive menu of creative crepes.

Hopheads and other beer fans should make their way to the **Lupulo Craft Beer House** (233 Cathcart St., 831/454-8306, www.lupulosc.com, 11:30am-10pm Mon.-Thurs., 11:30am-11:30pm Fri., 11am-11:30pm Sat., 11am-10pm Sun.). A small spot with a hip industrial feel, Lupulo has 16 rotating craft beers on tap and over 100 types of bottled beer, which can also be taken to go. A small-bites menu features tacos, salads, and sandwiches. This husband-and-wife-owned business also conducts brewing demos, tastings, and other events.

Live Music

The Catalyst (1011 Pacific Ave., 831/429-4135, www.catalystclub.com), right downtown on Pacific Avenue, hosts a variety of reggae, rap, and punk acts from Snoop Dogg to FIDLAR. The main concert hall is a standing-room-only space, while the balconies offer seating. Meanwhile, the remodeled Atrium is now an attached mid-size venue that attracts indie rock and punk acts.

A former 1940s movie house, the **Rio Theatre** (1205 Soquel Ave., 831/423-8209, www.riotheatre.com) has been hosting everything from film festivals

From top to bottom: Pleasure Point; Giant Dipper roller coaster on the Santa Cruz Beach Boardwalk; a slice at Pleasure Pizza.

to performances by national touring acts from Judy Collins to Built to Spill. Check the theater's website for a full list of upcoming events.

Theater

The nonprofit **Santa Cruz Shakespeare** (831/640-6399, www.santacruzshakespeare.org) was formed so residents could get their Elizabethan theater fix. Productions are staged at the Audrey Stanley Grove in **DeLaveaga Park** (501 Upper Park Rd.).

Shopping

For a small city, Santa Cruz has a bustling downtown, centered on Pacific Avenue. The quirky performance artists on the sidewalk might make you think you're in Berkeley or San Francisco. It's a good idea to park in one of the structures a block or two off Pacific Avenue and walk from there. Among the worthy downtown shops are **Book Shop Santa Cruz** (1520 Pacific Ave., 831/423-0900, www.bookshopsantacruz.com, 9am-10pm Sun.-Thurs., 9am-11pm Fri.-Sat.); **Bad Animal** (1011 Cedar St., 831/900-5031, www.badanimalbooks.com, 10am-10pm Thurs.-Sun.), a bookstore/wine bar/café; **O'Neill Surf Shop** (110 Cooper St., 831/469-4377, www.oneill.com, 10am-9pm Sun.-Thurs., 10am-10pm Fri.-Sat.); **Camouflage** (1329 Pacific Ave., 831/423-7613, www.shopcamouflage.com, 10am-9pm Mon.-Thurs., 11:30am-11:30pm Fri., 11am-11:30pm Sat., 11am-10pm Sun.), which is an independent, family-owned, and women-friendly adult store; and **Streetlight Records** (939 Pacific Ave., 831/421-9200, www.streetlightrecords.com, noon-8pm Sun.-Mon., 11am-9pm Tues.-Thurs., 11am-10pm Fri.-Sat.).

Recreation

Beaches

At the tip of the West Side, **Natural Bridges State Beach** (2531 W. Cliff Dr., 831/423-4609, www.parks.ca.gov, 8am-sunset daily, $10) used to have three coastal arches right offshore. Even though there is only one arch remaining, this picturesque state park has a beach that doesn't stretch wide, but falls back deep, crossed by a creek that feeds out into the sea. Hardy sun-worshippers brave the breezes, bringing out their beach blankets, umbrellas, and sunscreen on rare sunny days (usually in late spring and fall). Back from the beach, a wooded picnic area has tables and grills for small and larger parties. Even farther back, the park has a monarch butterfly preserve, where the migrating insects take over the eucalyptus grove during the fall and winter months.

At **Cowell's Beach** (350 W. Cliff Dr.), lots of beginning surfers have ridden their first waves. This West Side beach sits right at a crook in the coastline that joins with underwater features to create a reliable small break that lures new surfers by the dozens.

At the south end of Santa Cruz, down by the harbor, beachgoers flock to **Seabright Beach** (E. Cliff Dr. at Seabright Ave., 831/427-4868, www.santacruzstateparks.org, 6am-10pm daily, free) all summer long. This miles-long stretch of sand, protected by the cliffs from the worst of the winds, is a favorite retreat for sunbathers and loungers. While there's little in the way of snack bars, permanent volleyball courts, or facilities, you can still have a great time at Seabright.

Surfing

The coastline of Santa Cruz has more than its share of great surf breaks. The water is cold, demanding full wetsuits year-round, and the shoreline is rough and rocky. But that doesn't deter the hordes of locals who ply the waves every day they can.

The best place for beginners is **Cowell's** (stairs at W. Cliff Dr. and Cowell's Beach). The waves rarely get huge here, so they provide long, mellow rides, perfect for surfers just getting their balance. Because the Cowell's break is acknowledged as the newbie spot, the often-sizable crowd tends to be polite to newcomers and visitors.

Visitors who know their surfing lore will want to surf the more famous spots along the Santa Cruz shore. **Pleasure Point** (between 32nd Ave. and 41st Ave.) encompasses a number of different breaks. You may have heard of The Hook (steps at 41st Ave.), a well-known experienced long-boarder's paradise. But don't mistake The Hook for a beginner's break; the locals feel protective of the waves here and aren't always friendly toward inexperienced newcomers.

The most famous break in all of Santa Cruz can also be the most hostile to newcomers. **Steamer Lane** (W. Cliff Dr. between Cowell's and the Lighthouse) has a fiercely protective crew of locals. But if you're experienced and there's a swell coming in, Steamer Lane can have some of the best waves on the California coast.

Yes, you can learn to surf in Santa Cruz despite the distinct local flavor at some of the breaks. Check out either **Club Ed** (831/464-0177, http://club-ed.com, beginner group lesson $100 pp) or the **Richard Schmidt School Inc.** (849 Almar Ave., 831/423-0928, www.richardschmidt.com, 2-hour class $100 pp) to sign up for lessons. Who knows, maybe one day the locals will mistake you for one of their own.

Stand-Up Paddleboarding

The latest water-sports craze has definitely hit Santa Cruz. Stand-up paddleboarders vie for waves with surfers at Pleasure Point and can also be found in the Santa Cruz waters with less wave action. **Covewater Paddle Surf** (726 Water St., 831/600-7230, www.covewatersup.com, 2-hour lesson $200) conducts beginner stand-up paddleboarding (SUP) classes in the relatively calm waters of the Santa Cruz Harbor. They also rent SUPs for $35-60 a day.

Hiking and Bicycling

To walk or cycle where the locals do, just head out to **West Cliff Drive.** This winding street with a full-fledged sidewalk trail running its length on the ocean side is the town's favorite walking, dog-walking, jogging, skating, scootering, and biking route. You can start at Natural Bridges (the west end of W. Cliff Dr.) and go for miles. The *To Honor Surfing* statue is several miles down the road, along with plenty of fabulous views.

Spas

It's hard to beat a soak in some hot water after a day of surfing Santa Cruz's breaks or walking the city's vibrant downtown area. The **Tea House Spa** (112 Elm St., 831/426-9700, www.teahousespa.com, 11am-midnight daily, $22-60 per hour pp) is half a block off Pacific Avenue and offers private hot tubs with a view of a bamboo garden. It's not a fancy facility, but the tubs will warm you up and mellow you out.

Food

Mexican

Santa Cruz has some great taquerias, but **Tacos Moreno** (1053 Water St., 831/429-6095, 11am-8pm daily, $6-11) may be the best. Around lunch, locals line up outside the nondescript eatery. Tacos Moreno serves just the basics: burritos, tacos, quesadillas, and beverages to wash them down. The standout item is the al pastor burrito supreme with crispy barbecued pork, cheese, sour cream, and guacamole, among other savory ingredients.

El Palomar (1336 Pacific Ave., 831/425-7575, http://elpalomarsantacruz.com, 11am-9:30pm Mon.-Wed., 11am-10pm Thurs., 11am-10:30pm Fri., 10am-10:30pm Sat., 10am-9:30pm Sun., $13-27) is located in the dining room of an old luxury hotel. Enjoy shrimp enchiladas or chicken mole while mariachi bands rove around and play to diners. The informal taco bar is great for a quick bite and drink. It also has a happy hour (5pm-8pm Sun.-Thurs.).

Japanese

South of downtown, ★ **Akira** (1222 Soquel Ave., 831/600-7093, www.akirasantacruz.com, 11am-11pm daily, special rolls $10-17) is a modern sushi bar with some interesting creations. Some of the rolls employ unconventional ingredients like skirt steak, Sriracha sauce, and spicy truffled shoestring yams. There are also more traditional rolls, all served up at the sushi bar or your table. This being Santa Cruz, skateboard art decorates the restaurant. Stop by happy hour (4pm-6pm and 9:30pm-10:30pm daily) to snack on appetizers and enjoy beer, sake, or wine.

Pizza

An untold number of surfers have stopped into ★ **Pleasure Pizza** (4000 Portola Dr., 831/475-4002, http://pleasurepizzasc.com, 11am-9pm daily, slices $3-6) for a slice after catching waves at nearby Pleasure Point or The Hook. The unassuming slice shack is just a couple of blocks from the beach. The large, tasty slices are served on paper plates in a somewhat dingy building decorated with old surf memorabilia. Legend Jay Moriarity once worked here, as immortalized in the 2012 film *Chasing Mavericks*. On Tuesday, slices of cheese pizza go for just $2. There is also a **downtown location** (1415 Pacific Ave., 831/600-7859, 11am-10pm Sun.-Wed., 11am-12:30am Thurs.-Sat.).

Afghan

Laili (101 B Cooper St., 831/423-4545, http://lailirestaurant.com, 11:30am-2:30pm and 5pm-close Tues.-Sun., $10-28) is in a sleek, modern building with an open kitchen and marbled bar that oozes style. This Afghan restaurant's cuisine complements the space with artfully prepared dishes, from a cilantro Caesar salad to bolani, a vegan flatbread. Meals begin with a serving of naan bread the size of a plate and some dipping sauce. From there, the filet mignon kebab, which is three tender pieces of meat with dipping sauces, is exceptional.

Casual Eats

Just feet from the corndog-slinging Santa Cruz Boardwalk is a causal eatery that prides itself on its simple menu that utilizes locally sourced, tasty goodness: **The Picnic Basket** (125 Beach St., 831/427-9946, http://thepicnicbasketsc.com, 7am-9pm daily, $3-9). Its attention to detail shines through, even if it is on a deceptively simple turkey, cheese, and avocado sandwich. Other options include breakfast items, salads, mac-and-cheese, and even local beer and wine. Dine inside or out front, where you can take in the sounds of the bustling boardwalk.

Coffee

Verve Coffee Roasters (1540 Pacific Ave., 831/216-4448, www.vervecoffee.com, 6:30am-9pm daily) offers a hip, open space with lots of windows at the eastern edge of Pacific Avenue. Verve roasts its own beans in the nearby Seabright neighborhood. After ordering your coffee drink at the counter, look for a seat in this frequently crowded coffee shop.

Accommodations

Under $150

The ★ **Seaway Inn** (176 W. Cliff Dr., 831/471-9004, www.seawayinn.com, $107-274) offers a night's stay in a great location across from Cowell's Beach. The rooms are clean but not fancy, and the bathrooms are small. All have a shared patio or deck with chairs. The 18 units in the main building boast of TVs with DVD players along with microwaves and mini fridges. Family suites can accommodate up to five adults. Add in a friendly staff, and you have a good place to stay without breaking the bank. The inn also operates a nearby building with five studio apartments, each with a full kitchen. Pets are welcome in all units with a $15 fee.

Staying at a hostel in Santa Cruz just feels right. And the **Santa Cruz Hostel** (321 Main St., 831/423-8304, www.hi-santacruz.org, dorm beds $36-40, private rooms $79-189) offers the area's only real budget lodging. These historic renovated cottages are just two blocks from the Santa Cruz Boardwalk. It's clean, cheap, friendly, and also close to Cowell's Beach. The big, homey kitchen is open for guest use and might even hide extra free food in its cupboards. Expect all the usual hostel amenities, a garden out back, an outdoor deck, free linens, laundry facilities, and a free Internet kiosk. The private rooms are a real deal due to their size and cleanliness.

$150-250

The ★ **West Cliff Inn** (174 W. Cliff Dr., 831/457-2200, www.westcliffinn.com, $209-429) is a gleaming white mansion topping the hill above Cowell's Beach and the Boardwalk. This three-story historic landmark was constructed back in 1877, the first of the "Millionaires' Row" residences. Since that time, it's been a nurses' headquarters and auto court before becoming the elegant inn it is now. The nine rooms in the main house have stunning white-marble bathrooms, and some have oversized soaking tubs. The more moderately priced and pet-friendly "Little Beach Bungalow" is behind the main house. The inn's veranda and 2nd-floor balcony provide wonderful views.

Over $250

The ★ **Santa Cruz Dream Inn** (175 W. Cliff Dr., 831/426-4330, www.dreaminnsantacruz.com, $259-629) is in a location that cannot be beat. Perched over Cowell's Beach and the Santa Cruz Wharf, the Dream Inn has 165 rooms, all with striking ocean views and either a private balcony or a shared common patio. The rooms have a retro-chic feel that matches perfectly with the vibrant colors of the nearby Santa Cruz Boardwalk. On a sunny day, it would be difficult to ever leave the Dream Inn's sundeck, which is located right on Cowell's Beach. You can take in the action of surfers, stand-up paddleboarders, and volleyball players from the comforts of the deck's heated swimming pool or large multi-person hot tub. Or you could just relax on a couch or reclining chair while sipping a cocktail from the poolside bar.

Information and Services

While it can be fun to explore Santa Cruz just by using your innate sense of direction and the bizarre, those who want a bit more structure to their travels can hit the **Santa Cruz County Visitors Center** (303 Water St., Ste. 100, 800/833-3494, www.santacruz.org, 9am-noon and 1pm-4pm Mon.-Fri., 11am-3pm Sat.-Sun.) for maps, advice, and information.

The daily ***Santa Cruz Sentinel*** (www.santacruzsentinel.com) offers local news plus up-to-date entertainment information. The free weekly newspaper ***Good Times*** (http://goodtimes.sc) is also filled with upcoming events.

You can get your mail on at the **post office** (850 Front St., 831/426-0144, www.usps.com, 9am-5pm Mon.-Fri.) in downtown Santa Cruz. Medical treatment is available at **Dominican Hospital** (1555 Soquel Ave., 855/399-8824, www.dignityhealth.org).

Getting Around

Visitors planning to drive or bike around Santa Cruz should get a good map, either before they arrive or at the visitors center in town. Navigating the winding, occasionally broken-up streets of this oddly shaped town isn't for the faint of heart. **CA-1,** which becomes **Mission Street** on the West Side, acts as the main artery through Santa Cruz and down to **Capitola, Soquel, Aptos,** and coastal points farther south. You'll find that CA-1 at the interchange to **CA-17,** and sometimes several miles to the south, is a parking lot most of the time. No, you probably haven't come upon a major accident or a special event; it's just like that a lot of the time.

In town, the buses are run by the **Santa Cruz METRO** (831/425-8600 www.scmtd.com, $2 per ride adults, passes available). With routes running all around Santa Cruz County, you can probably find a way to get nearly anywhere you'd want to go on the METRO.

Half Moon Bay

To this day, the coastal city of Half Moon Bay retains its character as an "ag" (agricultural) town. The locals all know each other, even though the majority of residents commute "over the hill" to more lucrative peninsula and Silicon Valley jobs. For those who farm in the area, strawberries, artichokes, and Brussels sprouts are the biggest crops, along with flowers, pumpkins, and Christmas trees, making the coast the place to come for holiday festivities. Half Moon Bay enjoys a beautiful natural setting and earns significant income from tourism, especially during the world-famous Pumpkin Festival each October.

Some people know Half Moon Bay for Maverick's, a monster wave that can rise to 80 feet (24.4 m) off nearby Pillar Point during the winter months. Maverick's is one of the world's most renowned surf spots and has been chronicled in the 2004 surf documentary *Riding Giants* and the 2012 feature film *Chasing Mavericks.*

Getting There

It takes about **one hour** to make the **49-mile (79-km)** drive from Santa Cruz to Half Moon Bay on **CA-1.** You may want to stop at a beach or a produce stand in the tiny town of **Pescadero;** Half Moon Bay is **18 miles (29 km)** north of it.

Beaches

The beaches of Half Moon Bay draw visitors from over the hill and farther afield all year long. As with most of the North Pacific region, summer can be a chilly, foggy time on the beaches. For the best beach weather, plan your Half Moon Bay trip for September-October. **Half Moon Bay State Beach** (650/726-8819, www.parks.ca.gov, 8am-sunset daily, parking $10 per day) encompasses three discrete beaches stretching 4 miles (6.4 km) down the coast, each with its own access point and parking lot. **Francis Beach** (95 Kelly Ave.) has the most developed amenities, including a good-size campground (800/444-7275, www.reservecalifornia.com, $35) with grassy areas to pitch tents and enjoy picnics, a visitors center, and indoor hot showers. **Venice Beach** (Venice Blvd., off CA-1) offers outdoor showers and flush toilets. **Dunes Beach** (Young Ave., off CA-1) is the southernmost major beach in the chain and the least developed.

At the end of West Point Avenue in Princeton, a long stretch of beach wraps around the edge of the Pillar Point Marsh. This is the launch pad for surfers paddling out to tackle the famous **Mavericks Break** (Pillar Point Marsh parking lot, past Pillar Point Harbor). Formed by unique underwater topography, the waves at Mavericks are some of the biggest rideable waves in the continental United States.

Entertainment

The biggest annual event in this small agricultural town is the **Half Moon Bay Art & Pumpkin Festival** (www.miramarevents.com). Every October, nearly 250,000 people trek to Half Moon Bay to pay homage to the big orange squash. The festival includes live music, food, artists' booths, contests, activities for kids, an adults lounge area, and a parade. Perhaps the best-publicized event is the pumpkin weigh-off, which takes place before the festivities begin.

Half Moon Bay boasts one of the best jazz venues in the Bay Area. Since it opened in 1964, the **Bach Dancing and Dynamite Society** (311 Mirada Rd., 650/726-4143, www.bachddsoc.org) has been a hangout for bohemians and jazz aficionados, hosting the biggest names in jazz, including Bill Evans, Dizzy Gillespie, Etta James, and Duke Ellington. Not only is the music fantastic, but the venue, the Douglas Beach House, can't be beat.

Shopping

Strolling Main Street is another reason folks come to Half Moon Bay. A holdover from the town's agricultural roots is **Half Moon Bay Feed and Fuel** (331 Main St., 650/726-4814, http://hmbfeedandfuel.com, 8:30am-6pm Mon.-Fri., 9am-5pm Sat., 10am-4pm Sun.). In addition to animal feed, the store sells home goods, gardening supplies, plants, clothing, and gifts.

To see what Half Moon Bay does best, drop by the **Coastside Farmer's Market** (225 Cabrillo Hwy., 650/726-4895, www.coastsidefarmersmarket.org, 9am-1pm Sat. May-Dec.). There is plenty of local meat, bread, produce, pottery, art, and even wool skeins, spun and dyed by hand. Local bands are always at the market, and there is plenty of street food.

Recreation

Hiking

There are plenty of great trails around Half Moon Bay. A local favorite is **Purisima Creek Redwoods** (4.4 mi/7.1 km up Higgins Canyon Rd., 650/619-1200, www.openspace.org, dawn-half hour after sunset daily). There are a multitude of trails in this 4,711-acre (1,906-ha) preserve, and many ascend to Skyline Boulevard for an elevation gain of 1,700 feet (518 m). You can take a leisurely stroll through the redwoods, complete with dripping ferns, flowering dogwood, and wood sorrel, along Purisima Creek Trail (3.9 mi/6.3 km, easy to strenuous), until it turns steep and eventually takes you to its literally breathtaking Skyline terminus. If you don't want to crest the ridge of the Santa Cruz Mountains, choose the Harkins Ridge Trail (6 mi/9.7 km, moderate), which rises out of the canyon shortly past the trailhead. You'll hike through redwoods, then oaks and chaparral, and back again into firs, pines, and redwoods as you gain 800 feet (244 m) in elevation over 2.5 miles (4 km). To make a loop, cut down Craig Britton Trail, which meets Purisima Creek Trail.

The most popular trail in Half Moon Bay is the **Coastside Trail** (www.parks.ca.gov). Extending 5 miles (8 km) from Miramar Beach to Poplar Beach, this flat, paved trail follows the coast and is filled with joggers, dog walkers, and bikes. There are a multitude of beach-access points along the way, and if you want to go downtown, jump off at Kelly Avenue and take it across CA-1 to the heart of Half Moon Bay.

Fishing

For a sedate ocean adventure, take a winter whale-watching cruise or a shallow-water rockfish fishing trip on board the ***Queen of Hearts*** (Pillar Point Harbor, 510/581-2628, www.fishingboat.com, reservations recommended, $85-99). Whale-watching trips (Jan.-Apr.) cost a bit less than fishing trips on the *Queen of Hearts*. Deep-sea fishing for albacore and salmon (if the season isn't canceled) makes for a more energetic day out on the Pacific, although motion-sickness medication is recommended.

Kayaking and Stand-Up Paddleboarding

One of the coolest ways to see the coast is from the deck of a sea kayak or stand-up paddleboard. Many tours with the **Half Moon Bay Kayaking Company** (Pillar Point Harbor, 650/773-6101, www.hmbkayak.com, 9am-5pm daily Memorial Day-Labor Day, 9am-5pm Wed.-Mon. Labor Day-Memorial Day, kayak rental $75-150 per day, SUP rental $75 per day, tours $75-150) require no previous kayaking experience. For an easy first paddle, try the Pillar Point tour, the full-moon tour, or the sunset paddle.

Food

Twenty miles (32 km) south of Half Moon Bay in the blink-and-you-missed-it town of Pescadero, ★ **Duarte's Tavern** (202 Stage Rd., Pescadero, 650/879-0464, www.duartestavern.com, 7am-8pm Wed.-Mon., $13-25) has been honored by the James Beard Foundation as "An American Classic." Once you walk through the doors, you'll see why. The rambling building features sloping floors and age-darkened wooden walls. The food is good, the service friendly, and the coffee plentiful. And while almost everybody comes to Duarte's for a bowl of artichoke soup or a slice of olallieberry pie, it's really the atmosphere that's the biggest draw. Locals of all stripes, including farmers, farmhands, ranchers, and park rangers, sit shoulder to shoulder with travelers sharing conversation and a bite to eat, particularly in the dimly lit bar but also in the dining room or at the old-fashioned lunch counter.

The quality of food in Half Moon Bay itself also is superb. For seafood, go to ★ **Sam's Chowder House** (4210 N. Cabrillo Hwy., 650/712-0245, www.samschowderhouse.com, 11:30am-9pm Mon.-Thurs., 11:30am-9:30pm Fri., 11am-9:30pm Sat., 11am-9pm Sun., $12-35), a fusion of an East Coast chowder and lobster shack with West Coast sensibilities and views of the Pacific from both inside and outside on its large oceanfront patio. The lobster clambake for two is a splurge, but it's an excellent introduction to Sam's seafood-heavy menu. Armed with a lobster cracker, bib, and wet nap, attempt to finish the starting bowl of clam chowder followed by a tasty mound that includes a whole lobster, clams, mussels, potatoes, and a spicy andouille sausage. Many other diners opt for the buttery lobster roll.

Good bread is the secret weapon of great sandwiches at the **Garden Deli Café** (356 Main St., 650/726-9507, www.sanbenitohouse.com, 10am-5pm daily, $8.50), located in the historic San Benito House. Basic sandwiches like turkey, roast beef, and ham taste better lying between slabs of tasty homemade bread. Get your sandwich to go or eat in the adjacent courtyard.

Accommodations

Twenty miles (32 km) south of Half Moon Bay near the tiny town of Pescadero, the **Pigeon Point Lighthouse Hostel** (210 Pigeon Point Rd., at CA-1, 650/879-0633, www.hiusa.org, dorm beds $38, private rooms $96, family rooms $228) has simple but comfortable accommodations, both private and dorm-style. Amenities include three kitchens, free Wi-Fi, a fire pit, and beach access. But the best amenity of all is the cliff-top hot tub ($8 per half hour). Note if you're not already a Hostelling International USA member, you'll need to purchase a $4 membership.

The ★ **Beach House at Half Moon Bay** (4100 N. Cabrillo Hwy., 650/712-0220 or 800/315-9366, www.beach-house.com, $245-385) is situated in an ideal location a few feet from Pillar Point Harbor and the popular Coastside Trail. All the rooms, which are multilevel lofts, have a private patio or balcony to take in the bobbing sailboats and the groaning foghorn. On fog-shrouded days, the Beach House has in-room real wood-burning fireplaces and an outdoor hot tub and heated pool on the pool deck to warm up with.

The stunning **Ritz-Carlton Half Moon Bay** (1 Miramontes Point Rd., 650/712-7000, www.ritzcarlton.com, $750-4,000) resembles a Scottish castle transported to the California coast. Surrounding the luxury hotel are two emerald-green golf courses perched above the Pacific. The sprawling grounds are dotted with always-lit fire pits and chairs to take in the marvelous ocean views. Right out front is Half Moon Bay Coastside Trail, where you can hike for up to 7 miles (11.3 km). The hotel also has a spa, restaurant, two fitness rooms, a pool, tennis courts, and a basketball court. Inside, guests enjoy the finest of modern amenities. Baths have marble floors and marble countertops, while many of the upscale guest rooms overlook the sea. The superb staff seems to be as excited to be here as you are.

Information and Services

Visitor information, including maps, brochures, and a schedule of events, can be found at the **Half Moon Bay Chamber of Commerce** (235 Main St., 650/726-8380, www.visithalfmoonbay.org, 9am-noon and 1pm-5pm Mon.-Fri., 10am-3pm Sat.-Sun.), located in the red house just after you turn on Main Street from CA-92.

The ***Half Moon Bay Review*** (www.hmbreview.com) is published weekly and provides the best information about live local entertainment.

The **post office** (500 Stone Pine Rd., 650/726-4015, www.usps.com, 9:30am-5pm Mon.-Fri., 9:30am-noon Sat.) is off Main Street before the bridge heading south. **Cell phones** work fine in the town of Half Moon Bay, but coverage can be spotty up in the hills above town and out on the undeveloped coastline and beaches along CA-1.

There is a 24-hour emergency room at the **Seton Coastside Hospital** (600 Marine Blvd., Moss Beach, 650/563-7100, http://setoncoastside.verity.org). For non-urgent care, the **Coastside Clinic** (Shoreline Station, Ste. 100A, 225 S. CA-1, Half Moon Bay, 650/573-3941, www.smchealth.org) is just north of the intersection of Kelly Avenue and CA-1.

Getting Around

Parking in downtown Half Moon Bay is an easy proposition except during the **Pumpkin Festival in October,** when it becomes a nightmare of epic proportions. Your best bet is to stay in town with your car safely stowed in a hotel parking lot before the festival.

7N
FREE
SHUTTLE
STOP

Essentials

Getting There

Getting to San Francisco

By Air

San Francisco's major airport is **San Francisco International Airport** (SFO, US-101, 650/821-8211 or 800/435-9736, www.flysfo.com), located approximately 13 miles (20.9 km) south of the city center, near the town of Millbrae. Plan to arrive at the airport up to three hours before your flight leaves. Airport lines, especially on weekends and holidays, are notoriously long, and planes can be grounded due to fog.

To avoid the SFO crowds, consider booking a flight into one of the Bay Area's less crowded airports. **Oakland International Airport** (OAK, 1 Airport Dr., Oakland, 510/563-3300, www.oaklandairport.com) serves the East Bay with access to San Francisco via the Bay Bridge and commuter trains. **San José International Airport** (SJC, 1701 Airport Blvd., San Jose, 408/392-3600, www.flysanjose.com) is 45 miles (72 km) south of San Francisco. These airports are quite a bit smaller than SFO, but service is frequent from many U.S. destinations.

Several public and private transportation options can get you into San Francisco. **Bay Area Rapid Transit** (BART, 415/989-2278, www.bart.gov, one-way ticket to any downtown station $8.95) connects directly with SFO's international terminal, providing a simple and relatively fast (under one hour) trip to downtown San Francisco. The BART station is an easy walk or a free shuttle ride from any point in the airport. BART trains also connect Oakland Airport to the city of San Francisco. Both BART and **Caltrain** (800/660-4287, www.caltrain.com, tickets $3.75-13.75) connect San José International Airport to San Francisco. To access Caltrain from the airport, you must first take BART to the Millbrae stop, where the two lines meet. This station is designed for folks jumping from one line to the other. Caltrain tickets vary in price depending on your destination.

Shuttle vans are another cost-effective option for door-to-door service, although these make several stops along the way. From the airport to downtown San Francisco, the average one-way fare is $17-25 per person. Shuttle vans congregate on the second level of SFO above the baggage claim area for domestic flights, and on the third level for international flights. Advance reservations guarantee a seat, but these aren't required and don't necessarily speed the process. Some companies to try include **Quake City Shuttle** (415/255-4899, www.quakecityshuttle.com) and **SuperShuttle** (800/258-3826, www.supershuttle.com).

For **taxis,** the average fare to downtown San Francisco is around $40. Use your cell phone to access ride-sharing services **Lyft** (www.lyft.com) or **Uber** (www.uber.com), which charge $29-85 for a ride from the airport to downtown.

By Train

Several long-distance **Amtrak** (800/872-7245, www.amtrak.com) trains rumble through California daily. There are eight train routes that serve the region: The ***California Zephyr*** runs from Chicago and Denver to Emeryville; the ***Coast Starlight*** travels down the West Coast from Seattle and Portland as far as Los Angeles; the ***Pacific Surfliner*** will get you to the Central Coast. There is no train depot in San Francisco; the closest station is in Emeryville (5885 Horton St.) in the East Bay. Fortunately, comfortable coach buses ferry travelers to and from the Emeryville Amtrak station with many stops in downtown San Francisco.

By Bus

An affordable way to get around California is on **Greyhound** (800/231-2222, www.greyhound.com). The San Francisco Station (425 Mission St., 415/495-1569, 5:15am-10:30pm daily) is a hub for Greyhound bus lines. They also have stations all along the coast from Crescent City down to San Diego. Greyhound routes generally follow the major highways, traveling US-101. Most counties and municipalities have bus service with routes to outlying areas. Another option is **Megabus** (http://us.megabus.com), which has stops in San Francisco and San Jose.

How about going to sleep in San Francisco and waking up in Los Angeles? That's the idea behind **Cabin** (www.ridecabin.com), a charter bus with sleeping pods that leaves from San Francisco's Bayside Lot (1 Bryant St.) at 11pm and arrives at 7am at Santa Monica's Palisades Park (Palisades Park at Ocean Ave. and Arizona Ave.).

Getting to Los Angeles

By Air

The greater Los Angeles area is thick with airports. **Los Angeles International Airport** (LAX, 1 World Way, 855/463-5252, www.flylax.com) serves the region and is located about 10 miles (16.1 km) south of the city of Santa Monica. If you're coming in from another country or from across the continent, you're likely to find your flight coming into this endlessly crowded hub. If you're flying home from LAX, plan plenty of time to get through security and the check-in lines, up to three hours for a domestic flight on a holiday weekend.

To miss the major crowds, consider flying into one of the many suburban airports. Just 20 miles (32 km) north of downtown Los Angeles is **Hollywood Burbank Airport** (BUR, 2627 N. Hollywood Way, Burbank, 818/840-8840, http://hollywoodburbankairport.com) in Burbank. **John Wayne Airport** (SNA, 18601 Airport Way, Santa Ana, 949/252-5200, www.ocair.com) serves Disneyland perfectly, and **Long Beach Airport** (LGB, 4100 Donald Douglas Dr., Long Beach, 562/570-2600, www.longbeach.gov/lgb) is convenient to the beaches. **Ontario Airport** (ONT, 2500-2900 E. Airport Dr., Ontario, 909/544-5300, www.flyontario.com) is farther out but a good option for travelers planning to divide their time between Los Angeles, Palm Springs, and the deserts.

From LAX, free shuttle buses provide service to **Metro Rail** (323/466-3876, www.metro.net, $1.75), accessible at the Green Line Aviation Station. Metro Rail trains connect Long Beach, Hollywood, North Hollywood, downtown Los Angeles, and Pasadena. Passengers should wait under the blue "LAX Shuttle Airline Connection" signs outside the lower-level terminals and board the "G" shuttle. Passengers may also take the "C" shuttle to the **Metro Bus Center** (323/466-3876, www.metro.net), which connects to city buses that serve the entire L.A. area. Information about bus service is provided via telephones on the Information Display Board inside each terminal.

Shuttle services are also available if you want to share a ride. **Prime Time Shuttle** (800/733-8267, www.primetimeshuttle.com) and **SuperShuttle** (800/258-3826, www.supershuttle.com) are authorized to serve the entire Los Angeles area from LAX. These vans can be found on the lower arrivals deck in front of each terminal, under the orange "Shared Ride Vans" signs. Average fares for two people are about $32 to downtown Los Angeles, $34 to West Hollywood, and $30 to Santa Monica.

Taxis can be found on the lower arrivals level islands in front of each terminal, below the yellow "Taxi" signs. Only licensed taxis are allowed into the airport; they have standard rates of about $40 to downtown and $30 to West Los Angeles. Use your cell phone to access ride-sharing services **Lyft** (www.lyft.com) or **Uber** (www.uber.com), which charge $27-99 for a ride from LAX to downtown.

By Train

Amtrak (800/872-7245, www.amtrak.com) travels to Los Angeles. The main stop is **Union Station** (800 N. Alameda St., www.unionstationla.com, 4am-1am daily), though there are other stops in **Glendale** (400 W. Cerritos Ave.), **Anaheim** (2626 E. Katella Ave.), and **Santa Ana** (1000 E. Santa Ana Blvd.). Both of the train's classic *Coast Starlight* (Seattle to Los Angeles) and *Pacific Surfliner* (San Luis Obispo to San Diego) routes stop in Los Angeles. In addition, the *Sunset Limited* (New Orleans to Los Angeles) and *Southwest Chief* (Chicago to Los Angeles) bring out-of-state visitors to the city.

By Bus

Greyhound (800/231-2222, www.greyhound.com) provides cheap transportation to Los Angeles and many of the surrounding communities. There's the **Los Angeles Station** (1716 E. 7th St., 213/629-8401) along with other stations including **Long Beach** (1498 Long Beach Blvd., 562/218-3011), **North Hollywood** (11239 Magnolia Blvd., 818/761-5119), and **Anaheim** (2626 E. Katella Ave., 714/999-1256). **Megabus** (http://us.megabus.com) provides another inexpensive bus seat to Los Angeles.

Cabin (www.ridecabin.com) allows you to sleep on a charter bus with sleeping pods that leaves Santa Monica's Palisades Park (Palisades Park at Ocean Ave. and Arizona Ave.) at 11pm and arrives at 7am in San Francisco's Bayside Lot (1 Bryant St.).

Getting to Las Vegas

By Air

McCarran International Airport (LAS, 5757 Wayne Newton Blvd., 702/261-5211, www.mccarran.com) is the airport for Las Vegas. Southwest Airlines is the largest carrier serving the city. Other big airlines (Delta, American Airlines, United) fly into Las Vegas, but many smaller airlines (Allegiant, Spirit, Volaris) sometimes offer better deals. Vision Airlines flies into the significantly less crowded **North Las Vegas Airport** (VGT, 2730 Airport Dr., 702/261-3801, www.vgt.aero).

The Las Vegas Strip and its hotels are just 3 miles (4.8 km) from the airport. Numerous taxicab companies pick up from the airport, including the **Desert Cab Company** (702/386-9102, www.desertcabinc.com). The ride will cost around $15. Shuttles are also an option. **SuperShuttle** (800/258-3826, www.supershuttle.com) picks up at the airport. Ride-sharing services **Lyft** (www.lyft.com) and **Uber** (www.uber.com) can pick you up at McCarran International Airport, but only from the parking garage, not the terminals.

By Train

Believe it or not, there is no **Amtrak** (800/872-7245, www.amtrak.com) train stop in Las Vegas. But passengers who take the train to Kingman, Arizona, can catch an Amtrak shuttle bus to the **Las Vegas Curbside Bus Stop** (6675 Gilespie St.). In addition, Amtrak reserves a number of seats on Greyhound buses from Los Angeles to Las Vegas, which can be booked through Amtrak.

By Bus

Greyhound (800/231-2222, www.greyhound.com) and **Megabus** (http://us.megabus.com) both have buses traveling to Las Vegas. Like the casinos, the **Greyhound Bus Station** (200 S. Main St., 702/384-9561) is open 24-7.

Road Rules

In California, scenic coastal routes such as CA-1 and US-101 are often destinations in themselves. **CA-1,** also known as the Pacific Coast Highway, follows the North Coast from Leggett to San Luis Obispo on the Central Coast and points south. Running parallel and intertwining with CA-1 for much of its length, **US-101** stretches north-south from Crescent City on the North Coast through the Central Coast, meeting CA-1 in San Luis Obispo.

CA-120 from San Francisco to Yosemite National Park starts off going through nondescript Central Valley towns, but the road really becomes scenic as it climbs up into the foothills of the Sierra Nevada. From the town of Groveland to the entrance to the park, it is a nice drive with occasional mountain vistas and worthwhile stops like Rainbow Pool on the Tuolumne River. If it's summer or fall, you can take CA-120 across the park and over Tioga Pass. It is one of California's best mountain drives.

Uncrowded **US-395,** on the route between Yosemite and Las Vegas, skirts the dramatic eastern Sierra. Desert highways **I-95** and **I-40** connect California with neighboring states Nevada and Arizona, respectively.

Car and RV Rental

Most car-rental companies are located at each of the major California airports. To reserve a car in advance, contact **Budget Rent A Car** (U.S. 800/218-7992, outside U.S. 800/472-3325, www.budget.com), **Dollar Rent A Car** (800/800-5252, www.dollar.com), **Enterprise** (855/266-9289, www.enterprise.com), or **Hertz** (U.S. and Canada 800/654-3131, international 800/654-3001, www.hertz.com).

To rent a car, drivers in California must be at least 21 years of age and have a valid driver's license. California law also requires that all vehicles carry liability insurance. You can purchase insurance with your rental car, but it generally costs an additional $10 per day, which can add up quickly. Most private auto insurance will also cover rental cars. Before buying rental insurance, check your car insurance policy to see if rental-car coverage is included.

The **average cost** of a rental car is $50 per day or $210 per week; however, rates vary greatly based on the time of year and distance traveled. Weekend and summer rentals cost significantly more. Generally, it is more expensive to rent from car rental agencies at an airport. To avoid excessive rates, first plan travel to areas where a car is not required, then rent a car from an agency branch in town to further explore more rural areas. Rental agencies occasionally allow vehicle drop-off at a different location from where it was picked up for an additional fee.

Another option is to rent an **RV.** You won't have to worry about camping or lodging options, and many facilities, particularly farther north, accommodate RVs. However, RVs are difficult to maneuver and park, limiting your access to metropolitan areas. They are also expensive, both in terms of gas and the rental rates. Rates during the summer average $1,300 per week and $570 for three days, the standard minimal rental. **Cruise America** (800/671-8042, www.cruiseamerica.com) has branches in San Mateo (just south of San Francisco), San Jose, San Luis Obispo, Los Angeles, Burbank, and Costa Mesa. **El Monte RV** (888/337-2214, www.elmonterv.com) operates out of San Francisco, Santa Cruz, Los Angeles, and Newport Beach.

Jucy Rentals (U.S. 800/650-4180, U.K. 0808 234 7261, Canada 1844 261 0376, Germany 0800 181 7169, www.jucyrentals.com) rents minivans with pop-up tops. These colorful vehicles are smaller and easier to manage than large RVs, but still come equipped with a fridge, a gas cooker, a sink, a DVD player, and two double beds. Rental locations are in San Francisco, Los Angeles, and Las Vegas.

Road Conditions

Road closures are not uncommon in winter. CA-1 along the coast can shut down due to flooding or landslides. I-5 through the Central Valley can close or be subject to hazardous driving conditions resulting from tule fog, which can reduce visibility to only a few feet.

Traffic jams, accidents, mudslides, fires, and snow can affect interstates and local highways at any time. Before heading out on your adventure, check road conditions online with the state highways department, **Caltrans** (www.dot.ca.gov).

Roadside Assistance

In an emergency, **dial 911** from any phone. The American Automobile Association, better known as **AAA** (800/222-4357, www.aaa.com), offers roadside assistance—free to members; others pay a fee.

Be aware of your car's maintenance needs while on the road. The most frequent maintenance needs result from **summer heat.** If the car gets hot or overheats, stop for a while to cool it off. Never open the radiator cap if the engine is steaming. After the engine cools, squeeze the top radiator hose to see if there's any pressure in it; if there isn't, it's safe to open. Never pour water into a hot radiator because it could crack the engine block. If you start to smell rubber, your tires are overheating, and that's a good way to have a blowout. Stop and let them cool off. During **winter** in the high country around Yosemite, a can of silicone lubricant such as WD-40 will unfreeze door locks, dry off humid wiring, and keep your hinges in shape.

Parking

Parking is at a premium in big cities. Most hotels within San Francisco, Los Angeles, and Las Vegas will charge guests $50 or more per night for parking. Remove any valuables from your vehicle for the evening, because some hotel valets just park your car in an adjacent public parking deck. Many attractions charge visitors an admission fee *and* a parking fee. For instance, Disneyland charges a $20 parking fee.

Parking is strictly regulated at the national parks. At Yosemite and the Grand Canyon, **park entrance fees** include entry and parking for up to seven days. Visitors are encouraged to park their cars at the outer edges of the parks and use the extensive network of **free shuttles** to get around the parks.

International Drivers Licenses

If you are visiting the United States from another country, you need to secure an International Driving Permit from your home country before coming to the United States. It can't be obtained once you're here. You must also bring your government-issued driving permit.

Visitors from outside the United States should check the driving rules of the states they will visit at www.usa.gov/motor-vehicle-services. Among the most important rules is that traffic runs on the right side of the road in the United States. Note that both California and Nevada have bans on using handheld cell phones while driving. If you get caught, expect to pay a hefty fine.

Maps and Visitor information

When visiting **California,** rely on **local, regional,** and **national park visitors centers,** which are usually staffed by rangers or volunteers who feel passion and pride for their locale. The **Golden State Welcome Centers** (www.visitcalifornia.com) scattered throughout the state are less useful, but can be a good place to pick up maps and brochures. The state's **California Travel and Tourism Commission** (916/444-4429, www.visitcalifornia.com) also provides helpful and free tips, information, and downloadable maps and guides.

The website **Travel Nevada** (www.travelnevada.com) has downloadable visitor guides, including the US-95 Adventure. The **Arizona Office of Tourism** (www.visitarizona.com) also offers a free downloadable state map online.

The American Automobile Association, better known as **AAA** (www.aaa.com), offers free maps to its members. The **Thomas Guide Road Atlas** (866/896-6277, www.mapbooks4u.com) is a reliable and detailed map and road guide and a great insurance policy against getting lost. Almost all gas stations and drugstores sell maps.

California and Nevada are in the Pacific time zone (PST and PDT) and observe daylight saving time March-November. Arizona is in the Mountain time zone (MST), and only the Navajo Nation observes daylight saving time.

Visas and Officialdom

Passports and Visas

Visiting from another country, you must have a **valid passport** and a **visa** to enter the United States. If you hold a current passport from one of the following countries, you may qualify for the **Visa Waiver Program:** Andorra, Australia, Austria, Belgium, Brunei, Chile, Czech Republic, Denmark, Estonia, Finland, France, Germany, Greece, Hungary, Iceland, Ireland, Italy, Japan, Latvia, Liechtenstein, Lithuania, Luxembourg, Malta, Monaco, the Netherlands, New Zealand, Norway, Poland, Portugal, San Marino, Singapore, Slovakia, Slovenia, South Korea, Spain, Sweden, Switzerland, Taiwan, and the United Kingdom. To qualify, you must apply online with the Electronic System for Travel Authorization at www.cbp.gov and hold a **return plane or cruise ticket** to your country of origin dated less than **90 days** from your date of entry. Holders of Canadian passports don't need visas or visa waivers.

In most other countries, the local U.S. embassy should be able to provide a **tourist visa.** The application fee for a visa is US$160, although you will have to pay an issuance fee as well. While a visa may be processed in as little as 24 hours on request, plan for at least a couple of weeks, as there can be unexpected delays, particularly during the busy summer season (June-Aug.). For information, visit http://travel.state.gov.

Consulates

San Francisco and Los Angeles are home to consulates from many countries around the globe. If you should lose your passport or find yourself in some other trouble while visiting California, contact your country's offices for assistance. The website of the **U.S. State Department** (www.state.gov) lists the websites for all foreign embassies and consulates in the United States. A representative will be able to direct you to the nearest embassy or consulate.

The **British Consulate** (www.gov.uk) has California offices in **San Francisco** (1 Sansome St., Ste. 850, 415/617-1300) and **Los Angeles** (2029 Century Park E., Ste. 1350, 310/789-0031). The Los Angeles office also represents Nevada and Arizona.

The **Australian Consulate** has offices in **Los Angeles** (2029 Century Park E., 310/229-2300, www.losangeles.consulate.gov.au) and **San Francisco** (575 Market St., Ste. 1800, 415/644-3260, www.usa.embassy.gov.au).

The **Consulate General of Canada** has an office in **San Francisco** (580 California St., 14th Fl., 415/834-3180) and **Los Angeles** (550 S. Hope St., 9th Fl., 213/346-2700).

Customs

Before you enter the United States from another country by sea or by air, you'll be required to fill out a customs form. Check with the U.S. embassy in your country or the **Customs and Border Protection** website (www.cbp.gov) for an updated list of items you must declare.

If you require medication administered by injection, you must pack your syringes in a checked bag; syringes are not permitted in carry-ons coming into the United States. Also, pack documentation describing your need for any narcotic medications you've brought with you. Failure to produce documentation for narcotics on request can result in severe penalties in the United States.

If you're driving into California along I-5 or another major highway, prepare to stop at **Agricultural Inspection Stations** a few miles inside the state line. You don't need to present a passport, a visa, or even a driver's license; instead, you must be prepared to present all your fruits and vegetables. California's largest economic sector is agriculture, and a number of the major crops grown here are sensitive to pests and diseases. In an effort to prevent known pests from entering the state and endangering crops, travelers are asked to identify all produce they're carrying in from other states or from Mexico. If you've got produce, especially homegrown or from a farm stand, it could be infected by a known problem pest or disease. Expect it to be confiscated on the spot.

You'll also be asked about fruits and veggies on your U.S. Customs form, which you'll be asked to fill out on the airplane or ship before you reach the United States.

Travel Tips

Conduct and Customs

The legal **drinking age** everywhere in the United States is 21. Expect to have your ID checked if you look under age 30, especially in bars and clubs, but also in restaurants and wineries. California bars and clubs that serve alcohol close at 2am; you'll find the occasional after-hours nightspot in San Francisco.

Smoking is banned in many places throughout California. Don't expect to find a smoking section in any restaurant or an ashtray in any bar. Smoking is illegal in all bars and clubs, but your new favorite watering hole might have an outdoor patio where smokers can huddle. Many hotels, motels, and inns throughout California are also strictly nonsmoking, and you'll be subject to fees of hundreds of dollars if your room smells of smoke when you leave. There's no smoking in any public building, and even some parks don't allow cigarettes. There's often good reason for this; the fire danger is extreme in the summer, and one carelessly thrown butt can cause a catastrophe.

The states of California and Nevada have officially legalized **recreational cannabis** for adults 21 years old and over. However, note that it is still illegal to consume marijuana in public. And although legal in certain states, marijuana is still illegal under federal law, which means possession when crossing state lines or on national park lands is still illegal. Visit http://potguide.com, which lists regulations for each state and offers tools such as a dispensary directory.

Money

California, Nevada, and Arizona use the **U.S. dollar ($)**. Most businesses also accept the **major credit cards** Visa, MasterCard, Discover, and American Express. ATM and debit cards work at many stores and restaurants, and ATMs are available throughout the region.

You can **change currency** at any international airport in California and at McCarran International Airport in Las Vegas. Currency exchange points also crop up in downtown San Francisco and at some of the major business hotels in urban areas.

ATMs

As with anywhere, traveling with a huge amount of cash is not recommended, which may make frequent trips to the bank necessary. Fortunately, most destinations have at least one major bank. Bank of America and Wells Fargo have a large presence throughout California. **Banking hours** tend to be 8am-5pm Monday-Friday, 9am-noon Saturday. Never count on a bank being open on Sunday or on federal holidays. If you need cash when the banks are closed, there is generally a **24-hour ATM** available. Furthermore, many cash-only businesses have an ATM on-site for those who don't have enough cash ready in their wallets. The unfortunate downside to this convenience is a fee of $2-4 per transaction. This also applies to ATMs at banks at which you don't have an account.

Tax

California sales tax varies by city and county, but the base rate is 7.25 percent. All goods are taxable with the exception of food not eaten on the premises. For example, your bill at a restaurant will include tax, but your bill at a grocery store will not. The hotel tax is another unexpected added expense to traveling in California. Most cities have enacted a **hotel room tax** largely to make up for budget shortfalls. As you would expect, these taxes are higher in areas more popular with visitors.

Nevada sales tax is 4.6 percent and can reach up to 8.1 percent, depending where you are. **Arizona sales tax** is 5.6 percent but can reach as high as 10.7 percent, depending on the municipality.

Tipping

Tipping is expected and appreciated, and a **15 percent tip** for **restaurants** is the norm. When ordering in bars, tip the bartender or waitstaff $1 per drink. Cafés and coffee shops often have tip jars out. There is no consensus on what is appropriate when purchasing a $3 beverage. Often $0.50 is enough, depending on the quality and service. For **taxis,** plan to tip **15-20 percent** of the fare, or simply round up the cost to the nearest dollar.

Traveling Without Reservations

During the busy summer months, accommodations can be hard to come by. If you find yourself without reservations in one of the cities, many online travel services, including www.hotels.com, can set you up with a last-minute room. Download the superb **HotelTonight** (www.hoteltonight.com) app on your smartphone for great last-minute deals on hotel stays.

It's also typical for national park lodgings and campgrounds to be full during high season. It may be possible to find a last-minute campsite at one of the nearby national forests. The **Stanislaus National Forest** (www.fs.usda.gov/stanislaus) and the **Sierra National Forest** (www.fs.usda.gov/sierra) surround Yosemite, while the **Kaibab National Forest** (www.fs.usda.gov/kaibab) is near the Grand Canyon.

Discount hotel chain **Super 8** (800/454-3213, www.wyndhamhotels.com/super-8) has locations in Los Angeles, San Francisco, Las Vegas, and Williams, Arizona, gateway to the Grand Canyon. Slightly more upscale, **La Quinta** (800/753-3757, www.wyndhamhotels.com/laquinta) has hotels in California and Las Vegas.

Communications and Media

Cell phone reception is good except in places far from any large town. Likewise, you can find **Internet access** just about anywhere. The bigger cities are well wired, but even in small towns you can log on either at a library or in a café with a computer in the back. Be prepared to pay a per-minute usage fee or purchase a drink. The desert regions of Arizona and Nevada have limited or nonexistent cell phone reception, but Las Vegas is a good place to retrieve voicemails if you've missed incoming calls.

The main newspapers in California are the ***San Francisco Chronicle*** (www.sfchronicle.com) and the ***Los Angeles Times*** (www.latimes.com). The big daily paper in Las Vegas is the ***Las Vegas Sun*** (www.lasvegassun.com). Each major city also has a free weekly newspaper that has comprehensive arts and events coverage. Of course, there are other regional papers that may offer some international news in addition to the local color. As for radio, there are some news stations on the FM dial, and in most regions you can count on finding a **National Public Radio** (NPR, www.npr.org) affiliate. While they will all offer some NPR news coverage, some will be more geared toward music and local concerns.

Because of the area's size both geographically and in terms of population, you will have to contend with multiple **telephone area codes.** The 800 or 866 area codes are **toll-free numbers.** Any time you are dialing out of the area, you must dial a 1 plus the area code followed by the seven-digit number.

To **mail** a letter, find a blue post office box, which are found on the main streets of any town. Postage rates vary by destination. You can purchase stamps at the local post office, where you can also mail packages. Stamps can also be bought at some ATMs and online at www.usps.com, which can also give you the location and hours of the nearest post office. Post offices are generally open Monday-Friday, with limited hours on Saturday. They are always closed on Sunday and federal holidays.

Access for Travelers with Disabilities

Most California attractions, hotels, and restaurants are accessible for **travelers with disabilities.** State law requires that public transportation must accommodate travelers with disabilities. Public spaces and businesses must have adequate facilities with equal access. This includes national parks and historic structures, many of which have been refitted with ramps and wider doors. Many hiking trails are also accessible to wheelchairs, and most campgrounds designate specific campsites that meet the Americans with Disabilities Act standards. The state of California also provides a free telephone TDD-to-voice relay service; just dial 711.

If you are traveling with a disability, there are many resources to help you plan your trip. **Access Northern California** (http://accessnca.org) is a nonprofit organization that offers general travel tips, including recommendations on accommodations, parks and trails, transportation, and travel equipment. **Gimp-on-the-Go** (www.gimponthego.com) is another travel resource. The message board on the **American Foundation for the Blind** (www.afb.org) website is a good forum to discuss travel strategies for the visually impaired. For a comprehensive guide to wheelchair-accessible beaches, rivers, and shorelines from Santa Cruz to Marin County, including the East Bay and Wine Country, contact the **California Coastal Conservancy** (510/286-1015, www.scc.ca.gov), which publishes a free and downloadable guide. **Wheelchair Getaways** (866/224-1750, www.wheelchairgetaways.com) in San Francisco (800/638-1912), Los Angeles (800/638-1912), and Las Vegas (888/824-7413) rent wheelchair-accessible vans and offer pickup and drop-off service from airports ($100-300).

The **Las Vegas Convention and Visitor's Authority** (www.lasvegas.com) provides for information on the assistance available in Las Vegas. **Grand Canyon National Park** operates wheelchair-accessible park shuttles and the park's website (www.nps.gov/grca) has a downloadable accessibility guide.

Traveling with Children

Many spots in California are ideal destinations for families with children of all ages. Amusement parks, interactive museums, zoos, parks, beaches, and playgrounds all make for family-friendly fun. On the other hand, there are a few spots in the Golden State that beckon more to adults than to children. Frankly, there aren't many family activities in Wine Country. This adult playground is all about alcoholic beverages and high-end dining. In fact, before you book a room at a B&B that you expect to share with your kids, check to be sure that the inn can accommodate extra people in the guest rooms and whether they allow guests under age 16.

Senior Travelers

Senior discounts are available nearly every place you go, including restaurants, golf courses, major attractions, and even some hotels. The minimum age ranges 50-65. Ask about discounts and be prepared to produce ID if you look younger than your years. You can often get additional discounts on rental cars, hotels, and tour packages as a member of **AARP** (888/687-2277, www.aarp.org). If you're not a member, its website can also offer helpful travel tips and advice. **Elderhostel** (800/454-5768, www.roadscholar.org) is another great resource for senior travelers. Dedicated to providing educational opportunities for older travelers, Elderhostel provides package trips to beautiful and interesting destinations. Called "Educational Adventures," these trips are generally 3-9 days long and emphasize nature, history, art, and music.

LGBTQ Travelers

The Golden State is a golden place for LGBTQ travelers. As with much of the country, the farther you venture into rural and agricultural regions, the less likely you are to experience liberal attitudes and acceptance. The **International Gay and Lesbian Travel Association** (www.iglta.org) has a directory of gay- and lesbian-friendly tour operators, accommodations, and destinations.

San Francisco has the biggest and arguably best **Gay Pride Festival** (www.sfpride.org) in the nation, usually held on the last weekend in June. Year-round, the **Castro** neighborhood offers fun of all kinds, from theater to clubs to shopping, mostly targeted at gay men but with a few places sprinkled in for lesbians. South of San Francisco on the Pacific Coast, **Santa Cruz** is known for its lesbian-friendly culture. In **Los Angeles, West Hollywood** has its own upscale gay culture, where clubs are havens of the see-and-be-seen crowd.

Gay and lesbian travelers may find Arizona less welcoming, but **Las Vegas** has some gay-friendly fixtures, whether it's the glamorous entertainers on stage or the **Fruit Loop,** a cluster of gay bars along Paradise Road, north of the airport.

Health and Safety

Medical Services

For an emergency anywhere in California, Nevada, or Arizona, **dial 911.** Inside hotels and resorts, check your emergency number as soon as you get to your guest room. In urban and suburban areas, full-service hospitals and medical centers abound, but in more remote regions, help can be more than an hour away.

Wilderness Safety

If you're planning a **backcountry expedition,** follow all rules and guidelines for obtaining **wilderness permits** and for self-registration at trailheads. These are for your safety, letting the rangers know roughly where you plan to be and when to expect you back. National park and state park visitors centers can advise in more detail on any health or wilderness alerts in the area. It is also advisable to let someone outside your party know your route and expected date of return.

Being out in the elements can present its own set of challenges. Despite

Coronavirus in California

At the time of writing in fall 2020, the coronavirus pandemic had significantly impacted the United States, including California and the other areas covered in this guide. Most, if not all, destinations required that face masks be worn in enclosed spaces, but the situation was constantly evolving.

Now more than ever, Moon encourages its readers to be courteous and ethical in their travel. We ask travelers to be respectful to residents and mindful of the evolving situation in their chosen destination when planning their trip.

Before You Go

- Check regional websites (see page right) for local restrictions and the overall health status of the destination and your point of origin. If you're traveling to or from an area that is currently a COVID-19 hotspot, you may want to reconsider your trip.
- If possible, take a coronavirus test with enough time to receive your results before your departure. Some destinations may require a negative test result before arrival, along with other tests and potentially a self-quarantine period once you've arrived. Check local requirements and factor these into your plans.
- If you plan to fly, check with your airline and the destination's health authority for updated travel requirements. Some airlines may be taking more steps than others to help you travel safely, such as limited occupancy; check their websites for more information before buying your ticket, and consider a very early or very late flight, to limit exposure. Flights may be more infrequent, with increased cancellations.
- Check the website of any sights, parks, and other venues you wish to patronize to confirm that they're open, if their hours have been adjusted, and to learn about any specific visitation requirements, such as mandatory reservations or limited occupancy.
- Pack hand sanitizer, a thermometer, and plenty of face masks. Consider packing snacks, bottled water, a cooler, or anything else you might need to limit the number of stops along your route, and to be prepared for possible closures and reduced services over the course of your travels.
- Assess the risk of entering crowded spaces, joining tours, and taking public transit.
- Expect general disruptions. Events may be postponed or cancelled, and some venues and tours may require reservations, enforce limits on the number of guests, be operating during different hours than the ones listed or offering reduced services, or be closed entirely.

California's relatively mild climate, **heat exhaustion** and **heatstroke** can affect anyone during the hot summer months, particularly during a long strenuous hike in the sun. Common symptoms include nausea, lightheadedness, headache, or muscle cramps. **Dehydration** and loss of electrolytes are the common causes of heat exhaustion. The risks are even higher in the desert regions of Arizona and Nevada. If you or anyone in your group develops any of these symptoms, get out of the sun immediately, stop all physical activity, and drink plenty of water. Heat exhaustion can be severe, and if untreated can lead to heatstroke,

Resources

- ♦ Centers for Disease Control and Prevention (www.cdc.gov)

CALIFORNIA

- ♦ Official California State Government Website (http://covid19.ca.gov)
- ♦ California Department of Public Health (www.cdph.ca.gov)
- ♦ San Francisco Department of Public Health (www.sfdph.org)
- ♦ Yosemite National Park (www.nps.gov/yose)
- ♦ County of Los Angeles Public Health (http://publichealth.lacounty.gov)
- ♦ Local culture websites (including information on what's open and closed due to the coronavirus): 7x7 (www.7x7.com), Funcheap SF (http://sf.funcheap.com), Eater Los Angeles (http://la.eater.com)

LAS VEGAS, NEVADA

- ♦ Southern Nevada Health District (www.southernnevadahealthdistrict.org/coronavirus)
- ♦ Nevada Health Response (http://nvhealthresponse.nv.gov)

GRAND CANYON, ARIZONA

- ♦ Grand Canyon National Park (www.nps.gov/grca)
- ♦ Arizona Department of Health Services (www.azdhs.gov)
- ♦ Native American Nations: Havasupai (http://theofficialhavasupaitribe.com), Hopi (www.hopi-nsn.gov), Hualapai (http://hualapai-nsn.gov), Navajo (www.navajo-nsn.gov

in which the body's core temperature reaches 105°F (41°C). Fainting, seizures, confusion, and rapid heartbeat and breathing can indicate the situation has moved beyond heat exhaustion. If you suspect this, call 911 immediately.

Similar precautions hold true for **hypothermia,** which is caused by prolonged exposure to cold water or weather. For many in California, this can happen on a hike or backpacking trip without sufficient rain gear, or by staying too long in the ocean or another cold body of water without a wetsuit. Symptoms include shivering, weak pulse, drowsiness, confusion, slurred speech, or stumbling. To treat hypothermia, immediately remove wet clothing, cover the person with blankets, and feed him or her hot liquids. If symptoms don't improve, call 911.

Ticks live in many of the forests and grasslands throughout California, except at higher elevations. Tick season generally runs late fall-early summer. If you are hiking through brushy areas, wear pants and long-sleeve shirts. Ticks like to crawl to warm moist places (armpits are a favorite) on their host. If a tick is engorged, it can be difficult to remove. There are two main types of ticks found in California: dog ticks and deer ticks. Dog ticks are larger, brown, and have a gold spot on their backs, while deer ticks are small, tear-shaped, and black. Deer ticks are known to carry Lyme disease. While Lyme disease is relatively rare in California, it is very serious. If you get bitten by a deer tick and the bite leaves a red ring, seek medical attention. Lyme disease can be successfully treated with early rounds of antibiotics.

There is only one major variety of plant in California that can cause an adverse reaction in humans if you touch the leaves or stems: **poison oak,** a common shrub that inhabits forests throughout the state. Poison oak has a characteristic three-leaf configuration, with scalloped leaves that are shiny green in the spring and then turn yellow, orange, and red in late summer-fall. In fall, the leaves drop, leaving a cluster of innocuous-looking branches. The oil in poison oak is present year-round in both the leaves and branches. Your best protection is to wear long sleeves and long pants when hiking, no matter how hot it is. A product called Tecnu is available at most California drugstores; slather it on before you go hiking to protect yourself from poison oak. If your skin comes into contact with poison oak, expect a nasty rash known for its itchiness and irritation. Poison oak is also extremely transferable, so avoid touching your eyes, face, or other parts of your body to prevent spreading the rash. Calamine lotion can help, and in extreme cases a doctor can administer cortisone to help decrease the inflammation.

Wildlife

Many places are still wild in California, making it important to use precautions with regard to wildlife. While California no longer has any grizzly bears, **black bears** thrive and are often seen in the mountains foraging for food in the spring, summer, and fall. Black bears certainly don't have the size or reputation of grizzlies, but there is good reason to exercise caution. Never get between a bear and her cub, and if a bear sees you, identify yourself as human by waving your hands above your head, speaking in a calm voice, and backing away slowly. If a bear charges, do not run. One of the best precautions against an unwanted bear encounter is to keep a clean camp; store all food in airtight, bear-proof containers, and strictly follow any guidelines given by the park or rangers.

Even more common than bears are **mountain lions,** which can be found in the Coast Range as well as in grasslands and forests. Because of their solitary nature, it is unlikely you will see one, even on long trips in the backcountry. Still, there are a couple things to remember. If you come across a kill, probably a large partly eaten deer, leave immediately. And if you see a mountain lion and it sees you, identify yourself as human, making your body appear as big as possible, just as with a bear. And remember: Never run. As with any cat, large or small, running triggers its hunting instincts. If a mountain lion should attack, fight back; cats don't like to get hurt.

The other treacherous critter in the backcountry is the **rattlesnake.** They can be found in summer in generally hot and dry areas from the coast to the Sierra Nevada. When hiking in this type of terrain (many parks will indicate if rattlesnakes are a problem in the area), keep your eyes on the ground and an ear out for the telltale rattle. Snakes like to warn you to keep away. The only time this is not the case is with baby rattlesnakes that have not yet developed their rattles. Unfortunately, they have developed their fangs and venom, which is particularly potent. Should you get bitten, get immediate medical help.

While mountain lions and rattlesnakes also exist in the Grand Canyon area, it is wild deer, elk, and, believe it or not, rock squirrels that have caused visitors to the park the most harm. Squirrel bites are actually the most common wildlife- inflicted injury in the area.

Crime

In both rural and urban areas, **theft** can be a problem. Don't leave any valuables in the car. If you must, place them out of sight, either in a locked glove box or in the trunk. Don't leave your wallet, camera, or other expensive items accessible to others, for example, in a backpack or purse. Keep them on your person at all times if possible.

Take some **basic precautions** and pay attention to your surroundings, just as you would in any unfamiliar place. Carry your car keys in your hand when walking out to your car. Don't sit in your parked car in a lonely parking lot at night; just get in, turn on the engine, and drive away. When you're walking down a city street, be alert and keep an eye on your surroundings and on anyone who might be following you. Certain **city neighborhoods** are best avoided at night. If you find yourself in these areas after dark, call a taxi to avoid walking blocks and blocks to get to your car or waiting for public transportation. In case of a theft or any other emergency, **call 911.**

Internet Resources

Spend some time on the Internet before your trip to find out about current conditions in the areas you are visiting. You also may be able to find out about some places to visit that you never knew existed.

Transportation

Caltrans (California Department of Transportation)
www.dot.ca.gov
Check Caltrans for state map and highway information before planning a coastal road trip.

Nevada Department of Transportation
www.nevadadot.com
Nevada Department of Transportation's website has a map detailing current road conditions.

Arizona Department of Transportation
http://azdot.gov
For information about the conditions of Arizona's roadways, visit this site.

California

Visit California
www.visitcalifornia.com
Before your visit, visit the official tourism site of the state of California.

California State Parks
www.parks.ca.gov
The official website lists hours, accessibility, activities, camping areas, fees, and more information for all parks in the state system.

San Francisco

SFGate
www.sfgate.com
This website affiliated with the *San Francisco Chronicle* offers information on activities, festivals, and events in the city by the bay.

SF Weekly
www.sfweekly.com
This website for one of the city's weekly alternative papers has a strong arts and entertainment emphasis.

Los Angeles

Los Angeles Convention and Visitors Bureau
www.discoverlosangeles.com
It's the official website of the Los Angeles Convention and Visitors Bureau.

LATourist
www.latourist.com
This informative tourism website is dedicated to the City of Angels.

LA Weekly
www.laweekly.com
One of the best alternative weeklies out there, the *LA Weekly* has superb arts, music, and food coverage.

Disneyland
http://disneyland.disney.go.com
Find information on all things Disney.

National Parks

Yosemite National Park
www.nps.gov/yose
The park's website has lots of great information for trip planning, including an overview of park features, a write-up on trails, and the latest road conditions.

Grand Canyon National Park
www.nps.gov/grca
The park's website has lots of great information for trip planning including an overview of park features, a write-up on trails, and the latest road conditions.

Las Vegas

Las Vegas
www.lasvegas.com
"The only official website of Las Vegas" has hotel deals, show deals, and a downloadable visitors guide.

INDEX

A

B

D

E

F

G

H

I

INDEX

N

O

P

QR

S

T

U

V

W

XYZ

LIST OF MAPS

Front Map

Discover the California Road Trip

San Francisco

Yosemite

Las Vegas

The Grand Canyon

Los Angeles

Pacific Coast Highway

PHOTO CREDITS

Title page photo: Andrelix | Dreamstime.com;
All interior photos © Stuart Thornton, except: page 4 © Tom956 | Dreamstime.com; page 7 © (top) StockPhotoAstur | Dreamstime.com; (bottom) Prochasson Frederic | Dreamstime.com; pages 8-9 © Dell | Dreamstime.com; page 10 © Sburel | Dreamstime.com; page 11 © (top) Lorcel | Dreamstime.com; (bottom) State Bird Provisions; pages 12-13 © (top) Sean Pavone | Dreamstime; (bottom) Korzeniewski | Dreamstime.com; page 14 © (top) Americanspirit | Dreamstime.com; (middle) Meinzahn | Dreamstime.com; (bottom) Photoquest | Dreamstime.com; page 15 © Michaelurmann | Dreamstime.com; page 22 © (bottom) Ghirardelli Square; page 28 © (top left) Universal Studios Hollywood; (top right) Zhukovsky | Dreamstime.com; (bottom) trekandshoot | Dreamstime.com; pages 30-31 © Somchai Jongmeesuk/123rf.com; page 34 © minnystock | Dreamstime.com; page 39 © Rosanascapinello | Dreamstime.com; page 42 © (middle) Evgeshag | Dreamstime.com; page 46 © (top) Maksershov | Dreamstime.com; (middle) Ghirardelli Square; page 56 © Lukich | Dreamstime.com; page 65 © City Lights Bookstore; page 67 © (top) Remix71 | Dreamstime.com; (middle) Lucidwaters | Dreamstime.com; (bottom) Bennnn | Dreamstime.com; page 68 © Nito100 | Dreamstime.com; page 70 © Emilycrone | Dreamstime.com; page 73 © (bottom) State Bird Provisions; page 84 © Hotel Zetta; page 86 © (top) Fairmont SF; page 89 © Jack Yaco | Dreamstime; pages 92-93 © kateleigh/123rf.com; page 135 © Bjoernalberts | Dreamstime.com; page 143 © Nikolasjkd | Dreamstime.com; pages 144-145 © Rambleon | Dreamstime.com; page 147 © Ritu Jethani/123RF; page 159 © (top) Solarisys13 | Dreamstime.com; (bottom) Kobby_dagan | Dreamstime.com; page 165 © (top) Kobby_dagan | Dreamstime.com; (middle) Songquan Deng | Dreamstime.com; (bottom) Vacclav | Dreamstime.com; page 169 © Jason P Ross | Dreamstime.com; page 172 © Nicknickko | Dreamstime.com; page 174 © Oliver7perez | Dreamstime.com; page 178 © Paul Maguire | Dreamstime.com; page 184 © (top) Diego Grandi | Dreamstime.com; (middle) Kobby Dagan | Dreamstime.com; (bottom) Kobby Dagan | Dreamstime.com; page 193 © Veeterzy | Dreamstime.com; page 196 © Meinzahn | Dreamstime.com; page 208 © Sergii Figurnyi | Dreamstime.com; pages 212-213 © Wildradphoto | Dreamstime.com; page 216 © Tim Hull; page 220 © Tim Hull; page 226 © Tim Hull; page 234 © Peresanz | Dreamstime.com; page 238 © Tim Hull; page 243 © Tim Hull; page 246 © Tim Hull; page 258 © Tim Hull; page 262 © Tim Hull; page 265 © Tim Hull; page 268 © Tim Hull; page 273 © (bottom) Pancaketom | Dreamstime.com; page 278 © Skiserge1 | Dreamstime.com; page 282 © Robert Wilson/123rf.com; pages 284-285 © Nata_rass | Dreamstime.com; page 287 © Mirko Vitali | Dreamstime.com; page 299 © (top) courtesy of Union Station; (bottom) Kitleong | Dreamstime.com; page 302 © Remusgruber | Dreamstime.com; page 307 © (top) Universal Studios Hollywood; (middle) Balbuenaraul | Dreamstime.com; (bottom) Alkan2011 | Dreamstime.com; page 308 © Mauricio Hoyos Photography; page 312 © (top) bonandbon | Dreamstime.com; (middle) Jul3s83 | Dreamstime.com; page 320 © 4kclips | Dreamstime.com; page 323 © (bottom) Jerome G. Favre; page 326 © (top) Eddie Mullins; page 331 © Courtesy of Palisociety; page 344 © Idpeacev | Dreamstime.com; page 350 © (top) Richard Billingham | Dreamstime; (middle) The Inn at Laguna Beach; page 356 © Jon Bilous | Dreamstime.com; page 372 © (middle) Scukrov | Dreamstime.com; page 374 © Tupungato | Dreamstime.com; page 384 © (middle) Mark C. Anderson; page 390 © Adeliepenguin | Dreamstime.com; page 402 © Valevenezia | Dreamstime.com; page 422 © (top) Monterey Bay Aquarium; (bottom) LE; page 431 © (middle) Andreistanescu | Dreamstime.com

MOON
ACADIA
NATIONAL PARK

MOON
ARCHES &
CANYONLANDS
NATIONAL PARKS

BANFF
NATIONAL
PARK
HIKE CAMP
SEE WILDLIFE

MOON
DEATH VALLEY
NATIONAL PARK

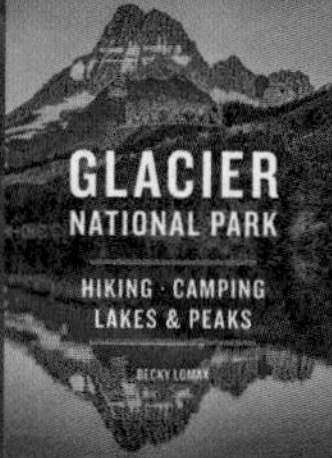
GLACIER
NATIONAL PARK
HIKING · CAMPING
LAKES & PEAKS

GRAND
CANYON
HIKE CAMP
RAFT THE
COLORADO RIVER

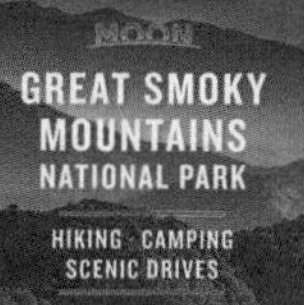
GREAT SMOKY
MOUNTAINS
NATIONAL PARK
HIKING · CAMPING
SCENIC DRIVES

MOON
MOUNT RUSHMORE
& THE BLACK HILLS

SEQUOIA &
KINGS CANYON
HIKING CAMPING
WATERFALLS & BIG TREES

MOON
ZION &
BRYCE

MAP SYMBOLS

- Expressway
- Primary Road
- Secondary Road
- Unpaved Road
- Trail
- Ferry
- Railroad
- Pedestrian Walkway
- Stairs

- City/Town
- State Capital
- National Capital
- Highlight
- Point of Interest
- Accommodation
- Restaurant/Bar
- Other Location

- Information Center
- Parking Area
- Church
- Winery/Vineyard
- Trailhead
- Train Station
- Airport
- Airfield

- Park
- Golf Course
- Unique Feature
- Waterfall
- Camping
- Mountain
- Ski Area
- Glacier

CONVERSION TABLES

°C = (°F - 32) / 1.8
°F = (°C x 1.8) + 32
1 inch = 2.54 centimeters (cm)
1 foot = 0.304 meters (m)
1 yard = 0.914 meters
1 mile = 1.6093 kilometers (km)
1 km = 0.6214 miles
1 fathom = 1.8288 m
1 chain = 20.1168 m
1 furlong = 201.168 m
1 acre = 0.4047 hectares
1 sq km = 100 hectares
1 sq mile = 2.59 square km
1 ounce = 28.35 grams
1 pound = 0.4536 kilograms
1 short ton = 0.90718 metric ton
1 short ton = 2,000 pounds
1 long ton = 1.016 metric tons
1 long ton = 2,240 pounds
1 metric ton = 1,000 kilograms
1 quart = 0.94635 liters
1 US gallon = 3.7854 liters
1 Imperial gallon = 4.5459 liters
1 nautical mile = 1.852 km

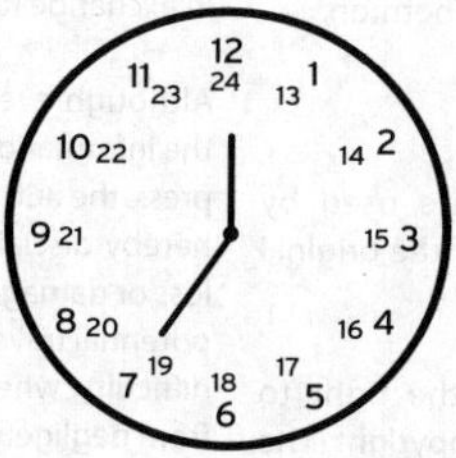

12 24 · 1 13 · 2 14 · 3 15 · 4 16 · 5 17 · 6 18 · 7 19 · 8 20 · 9 21 · 10 22 · 11 23

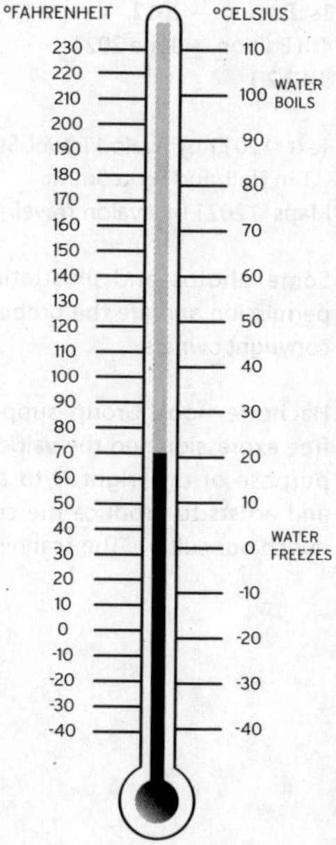

°FAHRENHEIT: 230, 220, 210, 200, 190, 180, 170, 160, 150, 140, 130, 120, 110, 100, 90, 80, 70, 60, 50, 40, 30, 20, 10, 0, -10, -20, -30, -40

°CELSIUS: 110, 100 WATER BOILS, 90, 80, 70, 60, 50, 40, 30, 20, 10, 0 WATER FREEZES, -10, -20, -30, -40

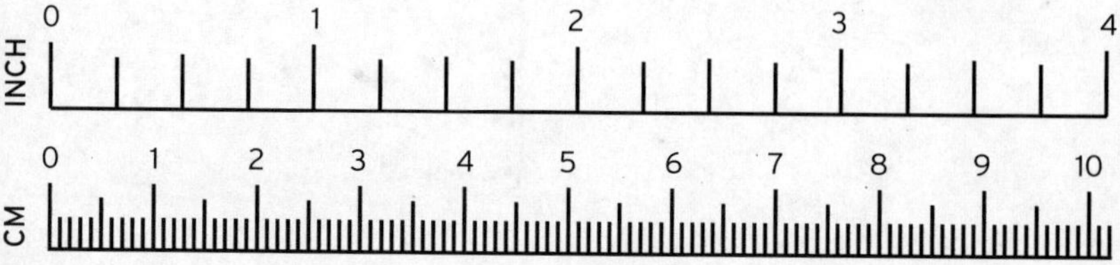

INCH: 0, 1, 2, 3, 4

CM: 0, 1, 2, 3, 4, 5, 6, 7, 8, 9, 10

MOON CALIFORNIA ROAD TRIP

Avalon Travel
Hachette Book Group
1700 Fourth Street
Berkeley, CA 94710, USA
www.moon.com

Editor: Kristi Mitsuda
Graphics and Production Coordinator:
Lucie Ericksen
Cover Design: Erin Seaward-Hiatt
Interior Design: Darren Alessi
Moon Logo: Tim McGrath
Map Editor: Albert Angulo
Cartographer: John Culp
Indexer: Greg Jewett

ISBN-13: 978-1-64049-434-3
Printing History
1st Edition — 2012
4th Edition — June 2021
5 4 3 2 1

Front cover photo: sunset over Santa Monica Pier © Az Jackson/GettyImages

Printed in Thailand by RRD